Sketch by Ken Carlson

BOONE AND CROCKETT CLUB'S

24th Big Game Awards
1998-2000

▼ ▼ ▼ ▼ ▼ ▼ ▼

Boone and Crockett Club's 24th Big Game Awards, 1998-2000
Edited by George A. Bettas, C. Randall Byers, and Jack Reneau

Library of Congress Catalog Card Number: 2001087630
ISBN: 0-940864-37-1
Published September 2001

Published in the United States of America
by the
Boone and Crockett Club
250 Station Drive
Missoula, Montana 59801
Phone (406) 542-1888
Fax (406) 542-0784
Toll-Free (888) 840-4868 (book or merchandise orders only)
www.boone-crockett.org

BOONE AND CROCKETT CLUB'S

24th Big Game Awards
1998-2000

▼   ▼   ▼   ▼   ▼   ▼   ▼

A Book of the Boone and Crockett Club
Containing Tabulations of Outstanding North American
Big Game Trophies Accepted During the
24th Awards Entry Period of 1998-2000

Edited by
George A. Bettas
C. Randall Byers
Jack Reneau

2001

The Boone and Crockett Club

Missoula, Montana

Photographs courtesy of Alvin M. Wallen and © NYZS/The Wildlife Conservation Society

CLOCKWISE FROM THE TOP: The 24th Awards book is the first records book to list a new category for tule elk, a species that was not hunted in modern times until 1989. Pictured is Alvin M. Wallen with his award-winning tule bull. ▪ In 1983, the Club began publishing the three year Awards books, beginning with the 18th Big Game Awards book. ▪ The purpose of the National Collection of Heads and Horns (photo circa 1910) was to preserve examples of big game for future generations as species became extinct. Examples such as the new tule elk category demonstrate how far we've come since the early 1900s.

iv   BOONE AND CROCKETT CLUB

FOREWORD

▼ ▼ ▼ ▼ ▼ ▼ ▼ ▼

EARL E. MORGENROTH
President of the Boone and Crockett Club

The Boone and Crockett Club is sincerely pleased to bring you the Boone and Crockett Club's 24th Big Game Awards book at the start of a new century. It is the seventh in a series that started with publication of the Boone and Crockett Club's 18th Big Game Awards book in 1983.

The 24th Awards Program records book is the culmination of three years (1998-2000) of trophy data collection and recording. It lists data on 3,955 specimens of native North American big game animals, representing 35 of the 36 categories presently recognized by the Club. These statistics represent the greatest number of trophies ever recorded by the Club during a single triennial Awards Program. There are 444 more trophies listed in this book than in the 23rd Awards Program records book that was released just three years ago. The 18th Awards Program records book, which was published less than 20 years ago in 1983, listed only 910 trophies in 29 categories of North American big game.

The Boone and Crockett Club's 24th Big Game Awards book provides us with a means of recognizing hunters who have accomplished something that most of us can only dream about — the taking of a truly trophy-class animal. It is also a simple barometer of the successes of wildlife managers in restoring our herds of native North American big game during the last century. Healthy big game herds produce a greater number of trophy-size animals being taken in a wider array of areas. The greater the number of trophy-size animals available, the more likely it is that these trophies will be entered into the Club's records books.

The 24th Awards book is a treasure trove of valuable information we can glean to plan our own hunts. By perusing the trophy data listed herein, we can determine where the big ones are currently being taken and use it to plan our own hunts.

The hunting stories of the trophies that were recognized with Boone and Crockett Club medals and/or certificates at the 24th Awards Program Banquet, Bass Pro Shops, Springfield, Missouri, in June 2001, provide us with countless hours of entertaining and informative reading. If carefully read, we can learn hunting techniques and skills used by those who successfully bagged truly exceptional animals. In a matter of minutes we can accompany M.R. James, the editor of *Bowhunter* magazine, on his hunt in the Arctic for his near World's Record muskox, or we can travel to the deserts of Mexico and hunt desert sheep with George Harms.

The numerous photographs illustrate trophy qualities. They give us an idea of what it takes to "make the book" and what to look for before we decide to pull the trigger.

As we enter a new century, it is a good time to pause and reflect on where we have been, where we are, and where we are going. The Boone and Crockett Club, which was founded in 1887 by Theodore Roosevelt, is the oldest conservation organization in North America today. The Club was founded before anyone knew what conservation was and before the word and practice of "conservation" was even coined and defined to mean "wise use" of our natural resources. Needless to say, the future for native North American big game at the time the Club was founded must have looked extremely bleak to those early hunter-conservationists.

The future for wildlife looked so bad, in fact, that the Club was instrumental in establishing the National Collection of Heads and Horns at the Bronx Zoo in 1906, which was dedicated to, "The memory of the vanishing big game of the world." In 1932 the Club published its first records book under the auspices of the National Collection of Heads and Horns.

The initial intent of the National Collection was to preserve examples of big game for future generations as species became extinct. The first records book was an effort to scientifically record those specimens for future generations. Again, the future of wildlife must have really looked bleak to those early conservationists even into the 1930s and 1940s.

I am very pleased to note that the Boone and Crockett Club and its Members played an extensive role in preserving and enhancing our native North American big game populations. As we now know, big game populations did not become extinct, and are flourishing in areas where they were absent, or nearly so, at the start of the last century. In fact, the 24th Awards book is the first records book to list a new and separate category for tule elk, a species that was not hunted in modern times until 1989. This book also lists two Atlantic walrus, representing the first two such trophies ever taken by modern day hunters. The other nine specimens listed in the Atlantic walrus category in the all-time records book, *Records of North American Big Game*, are only museum specimens.

The Club was founded at a time in our nation's history when big game populations were at their lowest. Its founders, who had visited the West and observed the vast herds of big game animals became alarmed at the rate big game animals were being extirpated from North America by the end of the 19th century.

It was Club Members who stepped forward and did what they could to reverse the trend. I am sure that it was a lonely, frustrating, tiring, and thankless struggle at times. But, I am also sure they would agree, if they were here today, that it was well worth it. The accomplishments of those early conservationists are for our benefit more than it was for their benefit. We are reaping the harvest of their labors.

What does the future hold for us? While much has been accomplished, there is still a lot of work necessary to conserve and more importantly enhance our accomplishments. We must be ever vigilant.

What can you do as an individual to preserve the legacy of hunting? You may be surprised at just how much you can do. The first thing you should do is get involved at national, state, and local levels. You can start by becoming a Boone and Crockett Club Associate if you have not already done so. As an Associate you will not only receive a subscription to Boone and Crockett Club's highly informative and entertaining *Fair Chase* magazine and numerous other benefits, but you will be aligning yourself with a venerable conservation organization with a significant track record in the conservation arena. You will also be making a statement about yourself and your ethics when you become a B&C Associate. Remember, there is strength in numbers. I can assure you that the anti-hunters realize the impact numbers can have with their anti-hunting agenda.

You can also have an impact on the future of hunting by, first of all, supporting and voting on issues that have a positive impact on hunting and wildlife. At the same time, be sure to vote against those issues that would have a negative impact.

In the last decade hunters have lost the spring bear hunting season in Colorado and cougar hunting in California, and the use of hounds for hunting cougar and bear in Washington and Idaho, to mention only a few. If you don't hunt these animals you may think that such decisions will not impact you. Well, I can assure you they can and will. For example, unmanaged cougar populations will have an impact on the big game populations as well as domestic live-stock, and there will be increased human contact with the resulting consequences.

Other hunting opportunities and seasons, such as trapping and dove seasons, are being challenged each year. Rather than discouraging anti-hunters, wins that favor their agenda in the political arena, no matter how small or seemingly insignificant, only serve to encourage them to go after other hunting opportunities. They will not rest until all hunting is banned.

Even if you don't hunt bears, cougars, doves, etc., in your state, don't just stand back and let the anti-hunters take away the rights of other hunters. Get out and vote. Support the hunters who do hunt those species. Sooner or later anti-hunters will be going after your favor-ite animal.

Secondly, you should get involved with the hunter safety program in your state and local community. By doing so you will be passing the hunting legacy on to future generations. There really is a lot you can do to support and promote hunting. Perhaps your efforts will insure that hunting will be around at the start of the next century.

In the meantime, good luck on all your hunting trips. May you connect with a trophy for the records book on your upcoming hunts. Once you have read and analyzed the data in this book, I would have to say that your odds of taking one for "The Book" should be much better. ▲▲▲

Earl Morgenroth is the former President and Chairman of the Board of Western Communications, Inc., an International Broadcast Company. Morgenroth was associated with W.C.I. for 25 years until its sale to the Scott-Forsman Publishing Company. Morgenroth is the Principal of Western Investments, a private investment company located in Reno, Nevada. He is also Chairman of the Board of Western Financial Inc., J-Mar Music, Inc; Montana Band Instruments, Inc.; and Times Square, Inc.

Morgenroth is President of the Boone and Crockett Club. He also served as an officer and director of numerous public service organizations, including President of the University of Montana Century Club, President of the Missoula, Montana Chamber of Commerce, and President of the Rocky Mountain Broadcasting Association. He was a six-year member of the Craighead Wildlife Wildlands Foundation and nine years as a member of the Board of the University of Montana Foundation. He works with several wildlife and conservation organizations.

Earl and his wife, Noella, make their home in Reno, Nevada. They have three children, Dolores and Denise, who live in California, and David, who lives in Montana. They have two grandsons, Landon and Dakota, who live in California.

RECORDS OF NORTH AMERICAN BIG GAME COMMITTEE

TABLE OF CONTENTS

24TH NORTH AMERICAN BIG GAME AWARDS

PANEL OF JUDGES
SPRINGFIELD, MISSOURI
2001

Frederick J. King, Chair
Bozeman, Montana

Roger W. Atwood
Rexburg, Idaho

Mark O. Bara
Georgetown, South Carolina

Robert A. Black
Whitewater, Colorado

L. Victor Clark
Verdi, Nevada

Albert C. England
Lloydminster, Alberta

Robert H. Hanson
Wapiti, Wyoming

Dale H. Ream
Unionville, Missouri

Ronald L. Sherer
Atlanta, Idaho

John L. Stein
San Antonio, Texas

Larry Streiff
Rochester, Minnesota

Paul D. Webster
Wayzata, Minnesota

CONSULTANTS

C. Randall Byers
Moscow, Idaho

Jack Graham
Edmonton, Alberta

Glenn E. Hisey
Chatfield, Minnesota

ILLUSTRATIONS

24th Awards Field Photographs continued...

The stories included in this edition reflect significant diversity among the big game species featured, the hunts, and the hunters themselves. The stories about Anthony J. Berardi's cougar and Mary Isbell's Wyoming moose demonstrate the importance of family and friends in teaching hunting traditions to our youth.

INTRODUCTION

▼ ▼ ▼ ▼ ▼ ▼ ▼ ▼ ▼

GEORGE A. BETTAS, ED.D.
Executive Director, Boone and Crockett Club

The Boone and Crockett Club's 24th Awards Program's public display of invited trophies was held at Bass Pro Shops National Headquarters in Springfield, Missouri, during May and June of 2001 to recognize the top trophies accepted during the three year period beginning January 1, 1998, and concluding on December 31, 2000. Estimates indicate that approximately 130,000 people viewed the trophy exhibit. Seven of the 86 trophies displayed at the museum were declared new World's Records in the following categories: Rocky Mountain goat, Roosevelt's elk, barren ground caribou, grizzly bear, non-typical Coues' whitetail deer, and tule elk. The Club's highest honor for trophy awards, the Sagamore Hill Award, was awarded for the 16th time in the 53 year history of the award.

Boone and Crockett's 24th Big Game Awards, 1998 - 2000, features the big game animals and the hunting stories about these animals written by the sportsmen and sportswomen who took the top 86 award winning big game trophies from 3,955 total trophies accepted during the 24th Awards Period. Included also are the listings and rankings of all of the trophies accepted during the 24th Awards Entry Period. The 24th Awards book complements the previous big game awards books that started with the *Boone and Crockett Club's 18th Big Game Awards* covering the 1980-82 Awards Program and published in 1983. The awards books are different from the "all-time" records books in that they feature trophies that received awards and certificates at the close of each Awards Program. The lower minimum scores for listing in the Awards books, compared to the all-time standards, provide recognition for hundreds of additional outstanding trophies. The Club also publishes the all-time records books, ranking entries within each of the various big game categories. The most recent all-time records book, the 11th edition of *Records of North American Big Game*, was published in 1999.

The stories included in this edition reflect significant diversity among the big game species featured, the hunts, and the hunters themselves. Mary Isbell's story about hunting with her family and the role family tradition played in everything from the selection of a rifle to use on the hunt to her learning to hunt and shoot illustrated the importance of families in the introduction of hunting to our youth. Family and friends worked together to help Mary and her sister, Becky, be successful in their efforts to find their moose. Anthony Berardi's story about his record book cougar similarly reflected the importance of family and friends in teaching hunting traditions to our youth. Anthony's "porcupine" in the tree turned out to truly be "the best memory a person could have, especially a 12-year-old boy."

Roy LePage's story about his cougar hunt with his wife Louise illustrates the special relation of husband and wife in sharing the hunting experience together. April Preston's Wyoming moose hunt also involved her husband in a teaching, supporting role as well as the participation of her children as they camped, scouted, and prepared for her hunt. April's opportunity of a lifetime turned into a hunt of a lifetime for her and her family. Another husband-wife team of Tara and Eli Lucas provided the opportunity for Eli to take a record book Sitka blacktail. In this case the wife provided the catalyst for her husband to shoot a trophy buck. The antlers displayed in their cabin in Alaska provide the special feeling they get when they revisit the smells, companionship and thrill of the hunt. Both of them are ready to go there again.

David Malzac's story about his world record grizzly hunt reflected a wonderful Alaskan adventure conducted in traditional Alaskan style. Long-time Alaskans who had hunted together for years literally pioneered their way into the bush over a nearly impassable road to access their hunting area. The extreme difficulty of this trip and the tremendous team effort required from each member of the team made this a very special adventure. Was it worth the effort? In David's words the answer was "undeniably, YES!" These men were "adventurers, gatherers and above all hunters!" After eight difficult days afield, literally in the middle of Alaska 50 miles from the nearest road, David and his friend Robert took a World's Record grizzly. Even without the World's Record bear, this trip would have been a great success because of the adventure and camaraderie associated with the trek.

Another Alaskan, James Baichtal, had a similar experience in his hunt for his Sitka blacktail. James' hunt involved a great deal of planning and two years of failed attempts due to weather. In the end, good planning and eight hours of grueling climbing through Sitka alder, devil's club, salmon berry and currant put James and his hunting partner in an area which enabled him to take his Sitka blacktail with his .54 caliber muzzleloader.

Keith Brossard is a deer hunter. Keith had no idea that he would take Wisconsin's top scoring whitetail in nearly a century when he began his hunt near his home in 1999. Hunting from a tree where he had taken many nice bucks over many years Keith had the opportunity of a lifetime when this buck presented itself. Keith's whitetail is the biggest typical whitetail in Wisconsin for 85 years and is second only to the Jordan buck. It illustrates the unpredictability of when a truly outstanding whitetail will show up! W. Eugene Zieglowsky's whitetail is another example of a tremendous whitetail surprising a hunter

M.R. James' muskox was special for many reasons, including the fact that he harvested the bull with archery gear. In some respects, muskox do not appear to be a difficult animal to harvest, but when one considers the extreme conditions under which they are hunted the special aspects of this hunt become apparent. Although the hunt was frustrating, M.R. and his hunting partner did this hunt their way — a very special way. Darcy Hernblad's muskox hunt was different. First, Darcy drew a resident permit for the hunt in the Northwest Territories. Unlike most muskox hunters who need a guide, he was able to do a self-guided hunt. Second, instead of getting bounced around in a sled being towed across the ice by a snow machine, Darcy got bounced around every bit as much in his pickup truck driving from Yellowknife to Norman Wells! In the end Darcy beat the odds and took an outstanding bull in an area where only one muskox had ever been taken.

James R. Coe shot his non-typical American elk in 1932, a year before he died. The bull has been displayed at the Squeeze Inn on Chinook Pass in Washington state for the past 68 years. What makes this story special is the tremendous pride which motivated Jim's grandson, James Walter, and his family to ride the greyhound bus across the country from Yakima, Washington to Springfield, Missouri to attend the 24th Awards and accept the certificate of merit awarded for his grandfather's trophy American elk.

Thomas Farmer's hunt which produced his record Canada moose reminds one of the hunts in the Canadian Rockies in the era of Jack O'Connor. Horseback treks across the country hunting many different species of game are somewhat uncommon these days. Farmer's success in his hunt for goat, sheep, grizzly and moose was classic. His perseverance and willingness to hunt hard and be patient paid off in a wonderful Canada moose. On the other end of the spectrum is William Nelson's Alaska-Yukon moose. Nelson, hunting for meat in an area where he had hunted moose 40 years earlier as a boy, had no idea he might have the opportunity for a record moose. Hunting in a snowstorm looking for a bull, any legal bull, he took the bull of a lifetime.

THE SAGAMORE HILL MEDAL

Fifty-three years ago, the Roosevelt family, in memory of Theodore Roosevelt, the founder of the Boone and Crockett Club, established the Sagamore Hill Award Medal. This prestigious award was to be given to an outstanding trophy worthy of great distinction, which was hunted in a way that upholds the true ideals and traditions of Theodore Roosevelt. The Sagamore Hill Award was named after Teddy's home in Long Island that he built at the turn of the century for his wife and family.

The Sagamore Hill Award is the highest award the Boone and Crockett Club can bestow on a hunter and an animal. It has only been presented fifteen times during the 53 years it has been in existence. For award consideration, it takes two rare ingredients—a new or near World's record and an incredibly challenging hunt.

The previous World's Record for this particular trophy category has been in the Book since 1949, when E.C. Haase took a magnificent Rocky Mountain goat in the Babine Mountains of British Columbia. Fifty years later, a new World's Record Rocky Mountain goat was taken near Bella Coola, British Columbia. During the Club's 24th Big Awards ceremony the Club presented the prestigious Sagamore Hill Award to Gernot Wober.

Rocky Mountain goats can be the toughest hunt of all the North American trophies. And this hunt was extraordinarily difficult, both physically and mentally. Gernot and his hunting partner, Lawrence Michalchuk, carried 60 pound backpacks into a remote area of the Canadian Rockies. They spent almost a week stalking billies, without success, braving sheer vertical cliffs, rain, fog, and very demanding hunting conditions looking for a great trophy. When they finally spotted a very promising billy, he was in the lower reaches of a deep, narrow valley with sheer cliffs for walls making a stalk from above impossible.

Instead of a looking for an easier animal to harvest closer to camp—and there were several — Gernot and Lawrence decided to try to close the distance on this particular billy in spite of its almost inaccessible location. This meant backpacking out of the area they were in, driving to another trailhead, and bushwacking up an isolated valley through miles of treacherous and exhausting terrain. At least twice Gernot and Lawrence wanted to give up and turn around, but they kept talking each other into pressing ahead, through devil's club that tore their clothes and alder so thick that they had to crawl on top of it.

Their extensive knowledge of Rocky Mountain goat behavior and the habitat the big billies prefer, coupled with their determination and supreme physical effort, enabled them to again locate this massive billy. The Boone and Crockett Club and the participants at the 24th Awards ceremony where pleased that Gernot persisted and was able to take this new World's Record goat. Gernot's outstanding trophy is worthy of great distinction and was hunted in a way that upholds the true ideals and traditions of Theodore Roosevelt.

Photographs by Sandy Poston

The outstanding trophy taken in the Bella Coola Valley of British Columbia by Gernot Wober and his hunting partner, Lawrence Michalchuk, is worthy of great distinction and was hunted in a way that upholds the true ideals and traditions of Theodore Roosevelt.

PREVIOUS WINNERS OF THE SAGAMORE HILL MEDAL INCLUDE:

1948 - ROBERT C. REEVE - Alaska brown bear
1949 - E.C. HAASE - Rocky Mountain goat
1950 - R.C. BENTZEN - typical American elk
1951 - GEORGE H. LESSER - woodland caribou
1953 - EDISON A. PILLMORE - typical mule deer
1957 - FRANK COOK - Dall's sheep
1959 - FRED C. MERCER - typical wapiti
1961 - HARRY L. SWANK, JR. - Dall's sheep
1963 - NORMAN BLANK - Stone's sheep
1965 - MELVIN J. JOHNSON - typical whitetail
1973 - DOUG BURRIS, JR. - typical mule deer
1976 - GARRY BEAUBIEN - mountain caribou
1986 - MICHAEL J. O'HACO, JR. - pronghorn
1989 - GENE C. ALFORD - cougar
1992 - CHARLES E. ERICKSON, JR. - non-typical Coues' whitetail

THE BOONE AND CROCKETT CLUB'S RECORDS KEEPING PROGRAM

The Boone and Crockett Club maintains the records of native North American Big Game as a vital conservation record in assessing the success of wildlife management programs. In response to public interest generated by the Club's National Collection of Heads and Horns in the 1920s, and increased interest in hunting by the general public, the Club called on Member Prentiss N. Gray to help establish an official measurement and scoring system for trophy animals. The Collection of Heads and Horns and the measurement system were initially conceived to record species of North American big game thought to be "vanishing." Club Members and others in the scientific community soon recognized that the system was an effective means of tracking the success of new conservation policies.

The Boone and Crockett Club's current records program dates back to the establishment of a committee in 1949 charged with the task of devising an objective measuring system for scoring and ranking native North American big game trophies. Members of the committee included Samuel B. Webb who served as Chair, Grancel Fitz, James L. Clark, Milford J. Baker, Harold E. Anthony, and Frederick K. Barbour. Through the diligent efforts of these gentlemen, the Boone and Crockett Club's scoring system was adopted and copyrighted in 1950. Originally there were 15 score charts for scoring 30 categories (species and subspecies) of native North American big game recognized by the Club. With the recent addition of the non-typical American elk, Roosevelt's elk, and tule elk categories the total number of the Club's copyrighted score charts and categories is 17 and 36, respectively. The fact that the Boone and Crockett scoring system has gained wide public acceptance and has remained virtually unchanged since it was developed by Samuel B. Webb's committee stands as a testimonial to the overall quality of the work of these individuals.

The Club uses the Records of North American Big Game Awards Program to communicate the basics of conservation and fair chase to the general hunting public. Since first published, the Club's *Records of North American Big Game* emphasized that a thorough and keen understanding of species biology and proper habitat management is necessary to ensure the future of all species. Population data show that conservation practices have had a dramatic, positive effect on the abundance of wildlife in our country. The growing populations of big game and associated wildlife stand as testament to the foresight of Club Members.

The Club has gathered and maintained statistics on trophies that meet the stated requirements of fair chase, minimum score, and other documentation since 1932. The Club's first five Competitions were held at yearly intervals from 1947 to 1951. The next eight were conducted at two-year intervals, and since the 14th Awards Program held in 1971 they have been conducted at three-year intervals. They have been described as "Awards" programs since the 15th rather than "Competitions" in order to better state the purpose of awarding recognition to fine trophies, current conservation practices, and excellent hunting opportunities.

Following the close of each three-year period of trophy entry, the finest few trophies are invited to the Final Awards Judging and Display. On these occasions select teams of official measurers re-measure and certify trophies for Boone and Crockett Club Big Game Medals and/or Certificates. The trophies, which were on display at 24th North American Big Game Awards, represent the finest of their respective categories entered during 1998 to 2000 (over 3,955 entries total).

The official 17 score charts used to measure the 36 North American big game categories are reproduced in this book using the exact measurements of some of the largest trophies entered and accepted into the 24th Awards Entry Period. You may wish to use these score charts to compare your trophies with those listed in this book.

FAIR CHASE

FAIR CHASE, as defined by the Boone and Crockett Club, is the ethical, sportsmanlike and lawful pursuit and taking of any free-ranging wild, native North American big game animal in a manner that does not give the hunter an improper advantage over such animals.

HUNTER ETHICS

Fundamental to all hunting is the concept of conservation of natural resources. Hunting in today's world involves the regulated harvest of individual animals in a manner that conserves, protects, and perpetuates the hunted population. The hunter engages in a one-to-one relationship with the quarry and his or her hunting should be guided by a hierarchy of ethics related to hunting, which includes the following tenets:

1. Obey all applicable laws and regulations.
2. Respect the customs of the locale where the hunting occurs.
3. Exercise a personal code of behavior that reflects favorably on your abilities and sensibilities as a hunter.
4. Attain and maintain the skills necessary to make the kill as certain and quick as possible.
5. Behave in a way that will bring no dishonor to either the hunter, the hunted, or the environment.
6. Recognize that these tenets are intended to enhance the hunter's experience of the relationship between predator and prey, which is one of the most fundamental relationships of humans and their environment.

GEOGRAPHIC BOUNDARIES

Geographic boundaries for trophy entries are important in official record keeping. The Boone and Crockett Club's records cover only native North American big game animals. For record keeping purposes, the southern geographic boundary is the southern border of Mexico. The northern boundary is the northern limit of the continent and associated waters held by the United States, Canada, and Greenland. Continental limits and held waters define east and west boundaries for all categories.

There are species-specific boundaries within the borders of the United States, Canada, and Mexico that distinguish smaller subspecies of American big game from larger subspecies. For example, the Roosevelt's elk boundary in Washington and Oregon is Interstate Highway 5, (I-5). Trophy elk taken west of I-5 in these two states are classified as Roosevelt's elk. Trophies taken east of I-5 are classified as American elk. Roosevelt's elk also include trophy elk taken on Vancouver Island, B.C.; Afognak and Raspberry Islands of Alaska; and in Del Norte, Humboldt, and Trinity Counties, California, as well as that portion of Siskiyou County west of I-5 in northern California. Elk taken in other areas in North America are classified as American elk.

While Roosevelt's elk have larger bodies than American elk, they carry smaller antlers. The boundary thus prevents the inclusion of the larger antlered American elk in the Roosevelt's elk category, and enables the Club to set a lower minimum score for the Roosevelt's elk. Similar boundaries separate other subspecies of native North American big game from their larger cousins. Complete boundary descriptions are given in *Measuring and Scoring North American Big Game Trophies*, 2nd edition, which was published by the Club in 1997 and revised in 2000.

BOONE AND CROCKETT: 100 HUNTERS WHO HAVE WORKED FOR CONSERVATION FOR MORE THAN A CENTURY

Over a century ago, a group of concerned individuals banded together to save wildlife and a place known as Yellowstone. The story that follows from the efforts of those visionaries is cherished as one of our nation's greatest accomplishments.

The history of the Boone and Crockett Club is a tale of over 100 years of measured and thoughtful commitment to conservation. It is a commitment that balances human needs with wildlife needs; a commitment that sees deep value in preserving the hunting tradition, as well as in conserving wildlands and wildlife; a commitment that grows out of a powerful love of wildlife, but that is also shaped by a common-sense, business-like approach to managing natural resources.

By the turn of the century, unrestricted killing of wildlife for markets, pioneer settlement of the West, and Native American/government conflict had taken their toll on most North American big game populations, and on many species of bird and fish. At that time, a national conscience that opposed the destruction of America's wildlife and natural resources was in its infancy.

Theodore Roosevelt was a firsthand witness to the near decimation of one of our nation's most valuable resources — its wildlife. When he committed himself to restoring America's wildlands he did so with characteristic zeal. Founding the Boone and Crockett Club was one of his first steps. Working with Club Members George Bird Grinnell, General William Tecumseh

Sherman, Gifford Pinchot, and 20 other visionaries comprised of outdoor sport enthusiasts, scientists, military and political leaders, explorers, artists, writers and industrialists, the foundation for the world's greatest conservation system was laid.

Over the next several decades, Theodore Roosevelt, along with Members such as Aldo Leopold and J.N. "Ding" Darling, championed the passage of laws, the establishment of institutions, and the designation of wildlands which today make up our nation's conservation system. The National Forests, the National Parks, and the National Wildlife Refuge Systems exist today in large part because of the extensive efforts of the Club and its dedicated membership.

As a vital element of the foundation supporting our nation's conservation system, the Club began publishing and championing a "fair chase" hunting ethic in the late 1800s. The original constitution of the Club addresses hunting ethics. The Club's fair chase statement and philosophies later became the foundation for hunting and game laws in this country.

In addition to sponsoring numerous research programs and countless symposia, the Club has supported continuing growth of America's conservation system. One of the more enduring examples of Club-supported research is the timber wolf/moose study on Isle Royale National Park conducted by Drs. Durward L. Allen and Rolf Peterson. Sponsored from the beginning by the Club, this on-going study is recognized as the definitive work on predator-prey relationships for these two species. Exemplifying the Club's long-term investment in the future of America's natural resources, this research helped to remove the eastern timberwolf from endangered status and helped to change public perception of the wolf. Knowledge gained from research of this caliber helps Boone and Crockett to develop outstanding, ongoing programs for sustaining wildlife populations.

In recognition of the Club's centennial, Members committed to "Blazing New Trails for Conservation" by expanding the Club's role in education, research, and demonstration. As part of this commitment, the Boone and Crockett Club purchased the Theodore Roosevelt Memorial Ranch (TRM) in 1986. Located on the Rocky Mountain Front, the TRM Ranch adjoins the Bob Marshall Wilderness, the Blackfeet Wildlife Management Area, and prime wildlife wintering grounds on privately owned ranches. Here, the Club conducts habitat research and demonstrates innovative land management practices, as well as conservation education programs. These activities are linked to a program of graduate scholarships directed by the Boone and Crockett Professor's Chair at The University of Montana. Dr. Hal Salwasser was hired as the first Professor to develop and lead the Club's Wildlife Conservation Program. Dr. Dan Pletscher was the second person to hold this position. Dan was followed by Dr. Jack Ward Thomas, the current Boone and Crockett Professor of Wildlife Conservation.

Dynamic and evolving, the conservation program continues to test convention and look for new solutions to ever-changing challenges. The most recent initiative of the Boone and Crockett Club is the Club's K-12 Conservation Education Program. The future of our world depends on the choices people make. Education is a key factor in what those choices are. The Boone and Crockett Conservation Education Program strives to offer perspectives that will foster shared use of natural resources, conservation, sustainable development, and stewardship of the land to build a common ground for sustaining healthy ecosystems.

The Conservation Education Program began in 1994 as a research project titled "Conservation Education Curricula for Montana Schools." The project, conducted by Lisa Flowers for the completion of her Master of Science for Teachers of Biological Sciences at The University

Photograph by Sandy Poston

The Elmer E. Rasmuson Wildlife Conservation Center, located on the Theodore Roosevelt Memorial Ranch, is an education and research facility that serves as a hub for the Boone and Crockett Club's Wildlife Conservation programs.

of Montana, was funded by the Boone and Crockett Club with Dr. Hal Salwasser as the principal investigator. The project focused on developing multi-day teaching units for public schools along the Rocky Mountain Front and used the Theodore Roosevelt Memorial Ranch as an outdoor classroom. The original project was successful in developing a foundation for the Boone and Crockett Club's Education Program at the TRM Ranch.

Today, the education program is constructed around a theme of appropriate, and shared, use of natural resources. It specifically integrates agriculture and wildlife conservation and has an actual model—a working cattle ranch—to base or illustrate the disseminated information. Our efforts differ from others in that we are teaching about the components of the landscape in such a way that people are kept in the picture. The information participants take away will help them better understand the interconnections between the various strands that make up the landscape tapestry. We hope, and believe, that people who take part in our education program come with questions and leave with answers, new questions, and information that helps them discover new ways that can help sustain the land upon which we all depend.

We have developed a strong working relationship with organizations such as Montana Department of Fish, Wildlife and Parks, U.S. Forest Service (Region 1), Project WILD, Agriculture in Montana Schools, Browning Public Schools, Rocky Mountain Elk Foundation, Montana Natural History Center, Glacier Institute, Montana Association of Conservation Districts, and Project WET Montana. We have also been instrumental in organizing and building the Crown of the Continent Ecosystem Education Consortium which has a membership of over 15 federal, state, and non-governmental organizations. The consortium is committed to education around the Ecosystem which extends from Waterton Provincial Park in Alberta, Canada, south to the Missoula Valley, east to the Rocky Mountain Front region, and west to the Flathead Valley.

The education program is conducted in various classrooms, but the very best classroom is the TRM Ranch and the Elmer E. Rasmuson Wildlife Conservation Education Center. The Ranch has an inherent magic that provides a setting for the evolution and discussion of ideas and realism behind multiple-use, sustainable-use, and shared-use issues. The magic comes alive when individuals visit the ranch to participate in an educational function conducted by the program managers. The magic results from the dynamic combination of many influences—the individuals, the activities, and the physical location of the ranch.

The Elmer E. Rasmuson Wildlife Conservation Center is an education and research facility that serves as a hub for the Boone and Crockett Club's Wildlife Conservation programs. Elementary and secondary school students and teachers, university students and faculty, natural resource managers, local community groups, and others use this facility in the pursuit of the Boone and Crockett Club's conservation research, education and demonstration mission. This mission seeks to increase humanities' awareness and understanding of wildlife and the ecosystems we share and our influences on the natural and cultural resources of these ecosystems. The goal of the program is to apply the results of wildlife related research and demonstration techniques that strive to increase wildlife and land use compatibility.

The personal discovery of our surroundings leads each of us to life-long learning and helps to build self-confidence. The more we know about the environment we live in, we build a better idea of who we are and where we fit into the grand scheme of things.

LOOKING INTO THE NEW MILLENNIUM

The essential character of the Boone and Crockett Club has changed little in its century of existence. In the Club's 1910 history, founding member George Bird Grinnell stated, "It has not been the Club's practice to announce its purposes, nor to glory in what it has accomplished, but rather to move steadfastly forward, striving constantly to do whatever fell within its province which would tend to promote the country's welfare ... a small body of individuals, scattered all over the country, working individually and constantly on behalf of things once laughed at or unknown, but now as familiar to the public mind as household words. The results accomplished by the Boone and Crockett Club bear testimony to the alertness and energy of its members, and to the success of the methods which they have pursued." His words accurately reflect the Club today

Since 1887, the Boone and Crockett Club has worked to create, support and enhance what is the world's finest system of natural resource conservation. Today, Club Members are committed to ensuring abundant natural resources through a second century and into a third. Success requires the active partnership of conservation organizations, corporations, foundations, and private citizens who recognize the vital nature of our mission. Today people come from all over the world to marvel at, study, and learn from our country's conservation system. Future generations depend on the support of responsible management of our natural resources today.

OVER A CENTURY OF BUILDING SUCCESS . . . PARTNERSHIPS[1]

The Club has been forging partnerships since 1887, when the challenge was to save Yellowstone. Club Members have been responsible for, or involved in, the formation of many other conservation groups. The early successes of Boone and Crockett Club Members and the citizen-sportsmen of the turn-of-the-century offer insight into the value of unity. Back then, wildlife was visibly depleted and their habitats-like pine forests in the Northeast-had been cut and burned. There was a common need to protect wildlife and restore lost habitat. Again in the 1930s, drought and low waterfowl numbers presented a rallying point for hunters and other conservationists to take action. In each case, people interested in wildlife could see some uncomplicated, visible threats they could combat directly. Formation of the Forest Reserves and their evolution into the National Forests, development of treaties to conserve migratory birds, passage of the Pittman/Robertson Act, and other movements came to fruition because people of like-minds, with specific objectives, worked together.

Our hunting traditions are being pulled in multiple directions by diverse factors, including demographic change, urbanization, broad concepts like ecosystem management and biological diversity, mass turnover in professional staffs of state and federal wildlife agencies, the smaller segment of our population that hunts or fishes, anti-management philosophies and values, and the crowded, fast paced lives of everyday Americans. It should not come as a surprise to realize that, in spite of great successes in restoration of wildlife over the past 100 years, the changing structure of our society makes it necessary for wildlife managers and hunter/conservationists to work together more effectively to build on the successes achieved in the past. Further, the decade of 1995-2005 is recognized as critical for wildlife as the die is being cast for its future. Against this backdrop of challenge, hunter/conservationists are arrayed in literally hundreds of organizations potentially diluting their effectiveness. The Wildlife Conservation Partners Summit (WCPS) was simply a gathering of wildlife leaders to unify their collective strength and apply it to common challenges and opportunities to protect wildlife, habitat, hunting, and the way of life it represents.

In the heat and smoke of a major fire season in August 2000, 35 wildlife organizations representing 4.3 million hunter/conservationists gathered in Missoula at the Wildlife Conservation Partners Summit as guests of the Boone and Crockett Club for a meeting about the future of wildlife in America. At Club headquarters over two days of meetings, representatives of this diverse group worked hard to answer four focus questions:

1. Should our organizations build unity and increase collective effectiveness; if so, what are some of the specific ways to do it?
2. Should our organizations develop a vision for wildlife; if so, what should it contain?
3. Should our organizations collectively address some key issues; if so, what is the "short list" of issues and how should resolution be accomplished?
4. Should our organizations develop a wildlife conservation agenda for the next Administration and Congress; if so, what should it contain?

During the meeting, the nearly 60 participants said yes to the four questions and made significant progress in putting together the who, what, why, and how.

As a result of the August 2000 Summit, the Wildlife Conservation Partners (see *Fair Chase* Winter 2000 issue) has prioritized a set of recommendations to take to the new Adminis-

[1] Written by Rollin D. Sparrowe, Professional Member, Boone and Crockett Club and President of the Wildlife Management Institute

tration addressing a wide array of land, wildlife, and people issues that need attention under this Administration. They are:

RECOMMENDATIONS

▲ Establish federal budget priorities that will restore wildlife funding to the 1980 level.

▲ Maintain and restore forest and rangeland habitats in the West through proactive public land management.

▲ Maintain and restore forest habitats in the East through proactive national forest management.

▲ Emphasize cooperative national forest decision making.

▲ Re-establish effective federal natural resource leadership.

▲ Support wildlife conservation provisions in the 2002 Farm Bill.

▲ Reaffirm state authority and responsibility for wildlife management-legal issues.

▲ Reinforce state authority and responsibility for wildlife management-funding issues.

▲ Increase funding to provide for hunter retention, recruitment, and education.

▲ Remove disincentives for private land wildlife conservation.

▲ Initiate an assessment of federal land laws to identity legal and regulatory problems.

These are broad issue statements that encompass a complex array of needs. This requires an adjustment of federal agency procedures, different approaches to managing public lands, stronger incentives for conservation on private land, more conservation provisions in farm legislation, and more funding for wildlife to better balance federal and state influence over wildlife. Perhaps most important would be swinging the pendulum of cultural change and attitudes about wildlife and public lands to include people in the equation. Most of this cannot be accomplished in one or even two presidential terms. The Boone and Crockett Club and those who choose to work through the Wildlife Conservation Partnership have to take on these issues in a variety of ways, and for the long term. They are that important!

The time is right for wildlife management advocates to be a larger voice in how government and the Congress deal with wildlife and public access to it in America. And we submit that now after the Summit, we are ready as never before!

ACKNOWLEDGMENTS

One of the unique aspects of the Boone and Crockett Club is that a very significant portion of the Club's work is performed by Club Members and volunteers including official measurers and others who are interested in the Club's work. The preparation for and accomplishment of a successful Awards Program is a significant task involving many different individuals. The Club's official measurers are the starting point for the trophy entry process. The initial good work of the official measurers begins the process. The headquarters staff in Missoula is to be commended for the great work they do on processing and tabulating the entries, as well as the behind-the-scenes work it takes to conduct a memorable event like the 24th North American Big Game Awards Program that took place at Bass Pros Shops in Springfield, Missouri, during May 1 through June 16, 2001. Jack Reneau's leadership as Director of Big Game Records, is essential in the processing and acceptance of the entries in each Awards Program. The Club's Big Game Records Commit-

WILDLIFE
FOR THE 21ST CENTURY

RECOMMENDATIONS TO PRESIDENT GEORGE W. BUSH

WILDLIFE CONSERVATION PARTNERS

Mule deer photograph by Milo Burcham

As a result of the August 2000 Summit, the Wildlife Conservation Partners has prioritized a set of recommendations to take to the Bush Administration addressing a wide array of land, wildlife, and people issues that need attention under this Administration.

Photograph by Jack Reneau

Bass Pro Shops in Springfield, Missouri, hosted the 24th Awards Judges Panel, Trophy Display, Welcoming Reception and Buffet, as well as the Club's Wildlife Workshop and scoring clinics. It's estimated that over 130,000 people viewed the Club's 24th Awards trophy display in May and June while on display at Bass Pro Shops Outdoor World.

tee, with Randy Byers as chair, provides general oversight for the entire process and insures that the Club's ethical standards are upheld.

The actual 24th Awards Program Banquet, seminars, and related activities involves the work of other Club Members and volunteers. Club Member Tommy L. Caruthers was instrumental in making the arrangements with the hotel and other logistic arrangements. Bass Pro Shops, owned by John L. Morris, was the perfect host and setting for the 24th Awards Program activities. Bass Pro Shops' staff provided invaluable and unreserved support from day one when trophies began arriving at their Outdoor World store in Springfield, Missouri. Over 130,000 people viewed the 24th Awards Program Trophy Exhibit at Bass Pro Shops. The Missouri Show-Me Big Bucks Club, under the leadership of Dale H. Ream, provided invaluable assistance with unpacking, packing, and transporting the trophies for the museum display, and the trophy display at the 24th Awards Program Banquet.

The 24th Awards Program Judges Panel comprised the select teams of official measurers who re-measured and certified the trophies honored at the 24th Awards Program Banquet. The 24th Awards Program Panel of Judges included: Frederick J. King, Bozeman, Montana, Chair; Roger W. Atwood, Rexberg, Idaho; Mark O. Bara, Georgetown, South Carolina; Robert A. Black, Whitewater, Colorado;   L. Victor Clark, Verdi, Nevada;   Albert C. England, Loydminister, Alberta; Robert H. Hanson, Wapiti, Wyoming; Dale H. Ream, Unionville, Missouri; Ronald H. Sherer, Atlanta, Idaho; John L. Stein, San Antonio, Texas; Larry Streiff, Rochester, Minnesota; and Paul D. Webster, Wayzata, Minnesota. Consultants for the Panel of Judges included: C. Randall Byers, Moscow, Idaho; Jack Graham, Edmonton, Alberta; and Glenn E. Hisey, Chatfield, Minnesota.

George A. Bettas, Ed.D., Missoula, Montana, is the Boone and Crockett Club's Executive Director and the editor of Fair Chase magazine. He became a Member of the Boone and Crockett Club in 1989. He has served as the Club's Vice President of Administration and Vice President of Communications.   He has been an official measurer since 1990 and was chairman of the Associates Committee.

BOONE AND CROCKETT CLUB'S

24th Big Game Awards
1998-2000

▼ ▼ ▼ ▼ ▼ ▼ ▼

Photograph © Neal and MJ Mishler

The highly precise nature of the Boone and Crockett Club's quantifiable scoring system, and its international recognition as "the" standard for measurement of antlers, horns, and skulls, allows biologists not only to compare individuals, but to compare herds as well.

Chapter One
THE BOONE AND CROCKETT SCORING SYSTEM
A Reliable Benchmark for Evaluating Research and Management

▼ ▼ ▼ ▼ ▼ ▼ ▼ ▼ ▼

FRED C. BRYANT
B&C Professional Member

AND

ROBERT D. BROWN
B&C Professional Member

THE SCORING SYSTEM AS A TOOL

The Boone and Crockett system of scoring is more than just a means of quantifying the size of one animal's antlers over another's for the purpose of awards or bragging rights. The system is a useful tool for wildlife researchers and managers. The highly precise nature of this quantifiable system, and its international recognition as "the" standard for measurement of antlers, allows biologists not only to compare individuals, but to compare herds as well. And, if one can quantify the antler sizes of herds or groups of animals, then we can examine the effects of different management regimes on antler growth.

In the following paragraphs we will give examples of how the Boone and Crockett scoring system has been used to compare the effect of harvest strategies, such as manipulating buck/doe ratios, age class structure or population size on antler development. Other examples include studies of the impact on antler size of supplemental feeding, specific nutrient supplementation, genetics, weather, parasite loads, and the interaction between deer or elk and cattle on different grazing systems. But to be honest, the reports of most of these studies often end with "and more research is needed." The reason is that there are so many factors that impact antler growth that it is difficult, no matter how well designed the study, to separate out one factor from another.

THE NATURE OF ANTLER GROWTH

Antlers are a secondary sex characteristic of male cervids, like the red breast of a male robin or the cock's comb of a rooster. And, like with so many of the laws of nature, there are exceptions to every rule. Some cervids, like the Chinese water buck or the musk deer, have no antlers at all — they have tusks instead. And, of course in caribou and reindeer — both males and females grow antlers. Unlike horns, antlers are deciduous, that is, antlers are grown and then dropped each year. That gives the cervid the opportunity to grow antlers of different size and configuration each year — thus the interest in using antlers as a means of judging the effect of management on the "quality" of the resulting deer.

Unfortunately from the managers' and researchers' standpoint, the physiology of antler growth is highly complex. Hundreds of scientific papers and not a few books have been written on the subject, with experiments going back to the days of Aristotle. Early on it was discovered that if male fawns were castrated, they would not grow antlers at all, but if adult deer were castrated, they would grow antlers in the velvet that would never harden (rub out) or be dropped (casting). Thus it was determined that the testes, and the testosterone they produce, were needed for antler growth and hardening. In more recent times, it was found that injections of testosterone given to castrated deer could simulate normal antler growth and rub out. About 30 years ago it became possible to actually measure testosterone levels in deer, and it was found that the levels in the blood fluctuated with the antler cycle. But what causes that? The endocrine system, the system that controls hormones, is also highly complex, with one hormone controlling another. Over the years, scientists have studied the possible effects of a number of hormones on antler growth, including thyroxine, estrogen, cortisol, growth hormone, the pituitary hormones LGH and FSH, prolactin, and even insulin-like hormones. All seem to have some effect on antler size or cycles, though the effects are not always clear. Thus anything that affects hormone levels in a cervid may impact antler growth.

FACTORS IMPACTING ANTLER GROWTH OR CYCLES
Light cycles
And what affects hormone levels? Well, day length for instance. Naturalists have long known that deer living in northern latitudes have more distinct antler cycles. That is, all of the deer grow and shed their antlers within a couple for weeks of each other. The cycles become less distinct as we move towards the equator. Deer actually on the equator have no synchrony at all—with individual deer coming in and out of antler growth annually, but on no particular schedule. Scientists have manipulated lighting for deer and have gotten them to grow two and even three sets of antlers a year, or to grow antlers every other year. Other weather factors, such as temperature, do not seem to have a similar effect, although severe early freezes can freeze off the tips of velvet antlers.

The connection between light cycles and antler cycles is through the endocrine system. The length of day (or night) determines the amount of the hormone melatonin that is produced by the pineal glad—a pea-sized organ at the base of the brain. Melatonin then determines the levels of the pituitary hormones produced, and they determine how much and when testosterone is produced. Interactions of melatonin with other hormones are not as clear, but the day length/antler cycle experiments have been duplicated with constant day length but varying doses of melatonin. It is not certain if overcast or cloudy conditions might modify melatonin production —and thus antler cycles.

Nutrition
Although weather besides day length may not affect antler growth directly, clearly weather affects plant growth, and nutrition impacts antler growth. We know that during hard times, the deer's body needs take precedence over antler growth, so that a shortage of groceries will

cause stunted antlers. Interestingly, short rations in whitetail deer cause them to drop their antlers early, whereas undernutrition in red deer cause them to hold their hard antlers longer. Biologists have long looked for a "silver bullet" of nutrition that is the key to superior antler growth. Antlers are made of first of protein as they grow (like cartilage), then that matrix is replaced by bone. We know protein, energy, calcium, phosphorus, sodium, and selenium at least are required for antler growth, but we don't know whether there are needs of a host of other micro-minerals, much less things like fatty acids or vitamins. Much like in human nutrition, a lot of nutrients are probably required, and a serious deficiency of one or more might detract from bone growth, but such deficiencies are rare. Taking more of a nutrient than is needed, or mega-dosing, is not generally helpful—a deer can only grow the antlers it is genetically programmed for, regardless of its nutrition.

Genetics

Not long ago we held a symposium on deer genetics in Texas. There is a wealth of anecdotal information that suggests the size and configuration of antlers can be inherited ("Hey—that buck's antlers sure look like his daddy's."). In addition, there have been some sizeable and long-term studies of the genetics of antler growth. Unfortunately, the results of the studies are often conflicting. Few topics raise as much controversy among deer biologists, and for good reason. The issue as to whether spike bucks are inferior and should be culled, or if they are not inferior and should be protected, has led to the varying spike buck harvest regulations among states. In some states, Texas being the foremost example, breeding bucks from other states and even artificial insemination of does has become a big business. Antler size and characteristics are no doubt inherited, but the percent heritability, and how much it varies from one animal to the next, is still a question. Further complicating the matter is that we assume 50% of the antler gene comes from the doe. In fact, physiologists know that if you remove the ovaries of a doe and give it injections of testosterone—it will grow antlers, so the gene has to be there. An even more disturbing fact, at least for those investing in breeding bucks, is the recent discovery in Texas that whitetail twins and triplets can have multiple sires. And, which bucks are doing the breeding?

Health

So genetics, hormones, day length, weather, and nutrition are the normal factors affecting antler growth. Anything else? Sure. An animal has to be healthy to grow a good set of antlers. Old deer, for instance, wear their teeth down to the point that they don't chew or digest well, despite being on a good diet. We know that in most species of cervids, after a certain age, the annual set of antlers actually gets smaller, not larger. Stress can also impact antler growth. Many years ago there was an adult tule elk in a California zoo that had grown no antlers one year. Testicular biopsies showed that the animal was normal. The elk had small antler nubs that were polished. The reason was that the elk had been put in with its herd just as antler growth was to begin. We suspect that the social stress of that situation caused the elk's adrenal glands to produce cortisol, a steroid much like testosterone, which in high level caused the developing nubs to rub out immediately. Likewise, we once had a castrated whitetail in Texas that had maintained a large set of velvet antlers for many years. It took ill from unknown causes, and as it did, it rubbed out, then shed its antlers. Again, cortisol production was the body's response to stress.

Photograph © Neal and MJ Mishler

At Vermejo Park Ranch in eastern New Mexico, Dr. Gary Wolfe launched a 3-year (1978-80) study on 482 harvested elk and used the B&C scoring system to correlate with age of bull elk. What he learned was that we must let bull elk live at least to the age of 7.5 years before they can express their genetic potential.

Injuries

Finally, there are few stresses on the body that have the impact of a physical injury. Deer fight, and they run into things, like fences and trees when trying to escape predators. Fighting can cause broken tines and even broken main beams. More interesting, however, is the phenomenon of antlers broken in the velvet. The velvet antler is rigid, but somewhat spongy, and heavy with arteries, veins and nerves. A small injury to the velvet antler, such as a puncture, might heal completely, so that it won't even be seen in the hardened antler. Slightly more severe injuries in the velvet might mean the antlers are misshaped this year, but normal next year when a new set are grown. But serious injuries in the velvet, especially if the pedicel that attaches the antler to the skull is involved, will be "remembered." That is, not only will this year's antlers be misshapen, but apparently the antler nerves have been damaged, and every set of antlers that deer grows from now on will be misshaped. No one knows how or why that happens, but it is one of the many factors that impact the Boone and Crockett score of a set of antlers, and therefore one of the many factors that have to be considered when using the system as a means of measuring the value of a harvest or habitat management strategy.

CURRENT USES OF THE B&C SCORING SYSTEM
Monitoring ungulates in long-term studies

Significant questions arise as we try to understand how best to manage ungulate populations. For example, it is important to know at what age ungulates reach maturity in terms of antler development. Once this is known, we can safely harvest ungulates without diminishing a male's potential to reach optimum antler development.

Two case studies have demonstrated this by correlating B&C scores with age of animals using the tooth wear and replacement method to estimate age. In both of these studies, data were collected over at least a 10-year period from harvested animals.

At Vermejo Park Ranch in eastern New Mexico, Dr. Gary Wolfe launched a 3-year (1978-80) study on 482 harvested elk and used the B&C scoring system to correlate with age of bull elk. Although antler mass increased each year to age 10.5, average B&C score peaked at 9.5 years. What he learned was that we must let bull elk live at least to the age of 7.5 years before they can express their genetic potential. His overall conclusion was that the best trophy elk in New Mexico are produced at ages 7.5 to 9.5.

On the Faith Ranch in South Texas, Dr. Charles DeYoung and landowner Stuart Stedman conducted a study for 14 years correlating the antler development with a buck's age in a free-ranging herd. They also were able to look at how timing of rainfall affects antler development, as well as what the reasonable expectations are for a certain percentage of bucks to exceed certain antler size. In all three instances, the B&C scoring system was used as the primary factor in judging antler growth and development. They measured over 500 bucks captured or harvested over this period. They found that of the whitetail bucks in South Texas reach antler maturity at 5-6 years of age, and that March-April rainfall is key to producing the best antler growth in any given year. Last, Mr. Stedman was able to show that, on a free-ranging ranch, it is unlikely for large (160-170 raw B&C scores) whitetail bucks in this region to ever make up more than 7% of the buck herd, even in a good year. For bucks exceeding 170 raw B&C scores, one can expect less than 3% of a buck herd to have such great specimens. These results were for a herd that was also not provided with nutritional supplements.

Short-term research

Several short-term studies in South Texas used the B&C scoring system to evaluate numerous factors that potentially affect antler growth and development in whitetail deer.

In caribou, researchers noticed that animals with lower parasite loads had more symmetrical antlers. They found that adding medication to feed improved antler symmetry. In South Texas, Dr. Tim Ginnett explored this phenomenon in whitetail deer, but could find no relationship between antler symmetry and parasite loads.

Supplemental feeding and food plots are used as management tools to enhance female reproduction and male antler growth in many states. It is also used to improve harvest efficiency and accuracy (harvesting the right deer in culling programs) and to reduce total populations below the threshold that the habitat will support. Several studies have used the B&C scoring system to evaluate this effect of added nutrition. Some have even evaluated the influence of micro-nutrients as feed additives to enhance antler growth and development.

Harvest strategies and culling programs beg for a technique to help researchers and managers evaluate their programs. For example, the theory has been proposed that yearling bucks that start out slow (smaller antlers) may never catch up to their same-age counterparts that start out with better antlers. This was demonstrated by Donnie Harmel and Bill Armstrong at the Kerr Wildlife Management Area of Texas Parks and Wildlife Department. At Mississippi State University, this theory was called into question by penned studies conducted by Harry Jacobson, who found that he could not predict the size of an adult deer's antlers from its antlers as a yearling. In each case, the researchers used the B&C scoring system to monitor deer later in life relative to their antler development at a young age.

The B&C scoring system has been used to evaluate the paternal contribution to antler development at both the Kerr Wildlife Management Area and at Mississippi State University. In addition, the question of how heritable antler traits are has been studied at both places.

Using a 140 and 160 B&C bucks as benchmarks, Dr. Fred Bryant, David Synatske and their colleagues in Texas were able to show the effects of wet years versus dry years, supplementation and harvest strategy in terms of the rate of harvest (number of acres per 140 B&C buck harvested).

Future research needs

Despite these many examples, clearly "more research is still needed." Regulations on the harvest of yearling deer still vary from state to state because we do not yet fully understand the causes or impact of the spike buck phenomenon. We believe that antler growth is heritable, but we still do not know the percent heritability of antler size and conformation, or how much the doe contributes to the genetics of antler growth. We know generally that good nutrition is needed, but we do not know if there are any specific nutrients that could be limiting antler growth. We believe antler size determines social status among males, but we question if social status before antler growth might impact later antler size. Big bucks may do the fighting, but maybe it's the little bucks that do the breeding—or some of it, leading to multiple sires. We know stress can impact antler growth negatively, but might small amounts of stress have a positive impact? What might be the effects of buck/doe ratios, population density, early weaning, and date of birth on social stress, and thus antler size? And what are the impacts of management schemes, such as selective culling, on antler size? And although all of these questions are interesting to researchers and important to managers, we could not address them at all with out a quantifiable and widely accepted means of measuring and comparing antlers. The Boone and Crockett system of scoring has provided that, and in doing so, has provided the world with an important wildlife research and management tool. ▲▲▲

Fred Bryant received his B.S in Wildlife Management from Texas Tech University, his M.S. in Wildlife Ecology from Utah State Univ, and his Ph.D. in Range Science from Texas A&M Univ. He was at Texas Tech University for 19 years as a teacher and researcher and is currently the Director of the Caesar Kleberg Wildlife Research Institute at Texas A&M University - Kingsville. His research interests are in big game ecology and habitat management. He has co-authored over 50 journal articles, two book chapters and one book. Besides serving as a professional member in the Boone and Crockett Club, he serves on the Board of Directors for the Rocky Mountain Elk Foundation.

Dr. Robert Brown received his B.S. in animal nutrition from Colorado State University and his Ph.D. in animal nutrition with a minor in physiology from Pennsylvania State University. He then joined the faculty of Texas A&I University in Kingsville as an assistant professor of animal nutrition. He was promoted to associate professor in 1979. From 1981 to 1987 he served as a research scientist with the Caesar Kleberg Wildlife Research Institute at Texas A&I University.
In 1987 he assumed the position as head of the Department of Wildlife and Fisheries at Mississippi State University. Dr. Brown was appointed professor and head of the Department of Wildlife and Fisheries Sciences at Texas A&M University in 1993, and Director of the Institute for Renewable Natural Resources in 1995. Dr. Brown's research expertise is directed toward comparative wildlife nutrition and physiology. He has edited three books and is the author or co-author for over 100 scientific and popular publications and 100 scientific presentations.

CLOCKWISE FROM TOP LEFT: Tools of the trade for members of the 24th Awards Program Judges Panel include the scoring manual, cables, rulers, tape, pencils, pens, and a laptop computer. ▪ Fred King, chair of the Judges Panel, and Randy Byers, chair of the B&C Club's Records Committee, review the scoring procedure of the New World's Record Roosevelt's elk. ▪ 24TH AWARDS PROGRAM JUDGES PANEL: Standing (l. to r.): Glenn E. Hisey (MN), John L. Stein (TX), Paul D. Webster (MN), Robert H. Hanson (WY), Roger W. Atwood (ID), L. Victor Clark (NV), Robert A. Black (CO), Frederick J. King (MT), Ronald L. Sherer (ID), and Dale H. Ream (MO). Kneeling (l. to r.): Albert C. England (AB), Larry Streiff (MN), Mark O. Bara (SC), C. Randall Byers (ID), Jack Graham (AB), and Jack Reneau (MT).

Chapter Two
REVIEW OF THE 24TH
AWARDS PROGRAM

▼ ▼ ▼ ▼ ▼ ▼ ▼ ▼ ▼

C. RANDALL BYERS
Chair, Records of North American Big Game Committee

AND

JACK RENEAU
Director, Big Game Records

The panel judges arrived, the panel judges left, and when the dust settled the final scores for seven New World's Records were official. This is the highest number of World's Record trophies since the 13th Competition (prior to the 15th Awards in 1974, the Awards Programs were referred to as Competitions) back in 1968. The new World's Records occurred in Roosevelt's elk, tule elk, non-typical Coues' whitetail deer, barren ground caribou, mountain caribou, Rocky Mountain goat, and grizzly bear categories.

Certainly the highlight of the 24th Awards Program Banquet was the presentation of the Sagamore Hill Award to the Rocky Mountain goat taken by Gernot Wober in 1999. The Sagamore Hill Award is the greatest honor the Boone and Crockett Club can bestow upon a trophy and a hunter. The Judges Panel selects the award recipient. The recognition of this trophy marked the 16th time the Award has been presented to a hunter and his trophy. Mr. Wober's hunt and this exceptional animal epitomize the standards under which the Sagamore Hill Award is given. When you read Mr. Wober's account of his hunt in this edition, you will sense the fair chase aspects of his pursuit of this magnificent goat that, in part, lead to this selection. Chair of the Sagamore Hill Committee and past President of the Boone and Crockett Club, Paul Webster, made the presentation.

The availability of trophy-class animals is at all-time highs. Along with the seven new World's Records, a record number of 3,955 entries mark the completion of the 24th Awards Program. The 3,955 trophies exceed the previous high of 3,511 in the 23rd Awards Program by 13%! This growth is the second straight time the rate has exceeded 13% and the near 4000 trophies in this recording period are almost 28% more than we had just a few short years ago at the close of the 22nd Awards Program. Figure 1 on the next page illustrates the growth in entries since publication of the first Awards Program book at the close of the 18th Awards Program.

Unlike some of the conditions that lead to recent declines in the stock market, there are no signs that would indicate that we should not expect this growth to continue well into the 21st century. Selective hunting for quality animals coupled with effective game management practices both on private and public lands may well make these early years of the 21st century the true golden era of hunting. It is hoped the conservation efforts, habitat programs, and wildlife management practices of today will provide the basis so that the person writing these pages at the beginning of the 22nd century too can claim to live in the golden era of hunting.

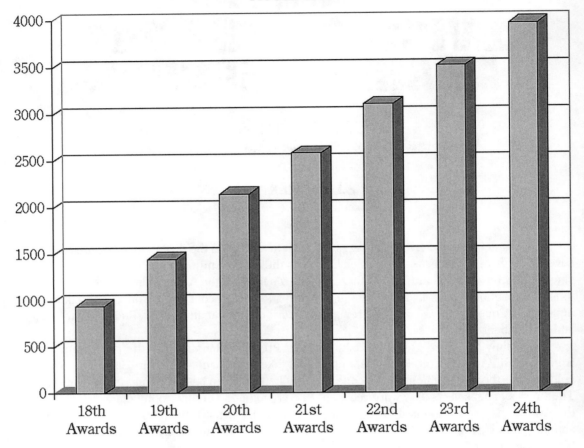

Comparison of the total number of trophy entries since the 18th Awards in 1983.

One other set of general comparisons can be made, and one that is less obvious than those noted above relates to trends in number of entries meeting the all-time records book minimums as a percentage of those in a given Awards Program. Overall some 66% of the entries in the 24th Awards Program qualified for the all-time records book as compared to over 69% in the 23rd. For whitetail deer, the percentage in the 23rd Awards Program qualifying for the all-time records book was over 63% while in the 24th it dropped to 61%. Dall's sheep is the category where the percentage is the lowest; 24% in the 24th and 31% in 23rd. Obviously, in some categories, ALL trophies qualify for the Awards and all-time books since the minimums are the same for both (e.g. muskox and polar bear).

Most categories exhibit the same pattern as whitetails—that being a slight decrease in the percentage of entries qualifying for all-time records. Some might say this points to some overall decline in trophy quality; more likely it is due to a greater acceptance of the Awards minimums. In either case, the Awards books provide a very interesting snapshot of current hunting conditions today.

So what is "hot" and what is not? Once again, typical whitetail deer topped the entries with 881 being accepted in the 24th Awards Program and listed in this book. Of those, 542 met the 170-point minimum for listing in the all-time records. Non-typical whitetail deer were second with 467 entries. Whitetail deer, in total, accounted for over 34% of the total entries in this Awards Program consistent with the percentage of whitetail deer in the 23rd Awards Program. Again black bear are third (318 entries). Pronghorn antelope (279) and typical mule deer (260) round out the list as the most common big game trophies recognized in this edition. A table that accompanies the review for each group of species provides a category-by-category comparison of the last three Awards Programs.

Certainly this was the Awards Program for both elk and caribou with two new World's Records in each grouping along with a number of other fine trophies. Both the caribou and elk displays at Bass Pro Shops were excellent as a large number of exceptional trophies were present in both groups. Other noteworthy mentions are highlighted below in the discussions of selected category groupings.

During every panel judging session a few problems are encountered. This time proved to be no exception. Two trophies were rejected. One was a black bear for which the skull was not properly cleaned. In order to be eligible for scoring, skulls must be display clean and this one clearly was not. Once again an antelope was rejected because basal circumferences had been altered by the use of a bonding substance to attach the horns to the horn sheath.

Two other magnificent trophies, both potential World's Records were not shipped in sufficient time to arrive in Springfield for panel judging. The first of these was Bryce Evans' tule elk with an entry score of 365 points; the other was a muskox taken by Vincente S. Sanchez-Valdepenas with a score of 127-2/8. Both of these fine trophies appear with an asterisk in this edition. As potential World's Records, these two trophies underwent a special panel judging procedure reserved for Potential World's Records this past August.

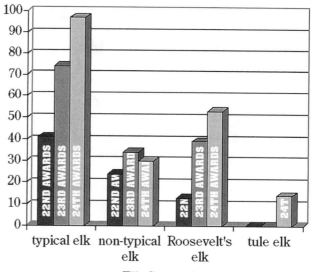

Elk Categories

ELK

It is very appropriate that a painting of a magnificent bull elk grace the cover of the 24th Awards book. During the last two Awards Programs all four elk categories have seen new World's Records. In the 23rd Awards Program, Alonzo Winters' typical American bull became the new World's Record with a score of 442-5/8 points. The other bull to become a new World's Record in the 23rd Awards Program was a picked up set of non-typical American elk antlers owned by British Columbia Environment scoring 465-2/8. Who would have imagined that World's Records would be established in the other two elk categories this time?

For sure, lots of hunters would have predicted one new World's Record as the 24th Awards Program marked the first Entry Period in which tule elk were accepted in a separate category. In all, 14 tule elk entries were accepted in the 24th Awards Program. Since this is a new category, 10 of the top 11 heads were invited to panel. The head with the highest entry score in this Awards Program unfortunately can never be verified. This bull, picked-up in 1995 on Grizzly Island, Cali-

Photograph by Jack Reneau

The 24th Awards elk display at Bass Pro Shops was truly impressive and featured two new World's Record elk -- Quentin Hughes' tule elk and Karl Minor's Roosevelt's elk.

fornia, and scoring 403 points, was being transported for display when it fell from the back of the truck in which it was being transported and was promptly destroyed by a semi-truck. As noted previously, Evans' tule elk was one of the two trophies that did not arrive in time for panel judging. The final score of Evans' bull was verified by a Special Judges Panel that convened in Missoula, Montana, August 2001. His trophy will appear in its rightful place in future record books. The scores of both of these fine bulls appear in this edition with an asterisk.

Of the 10 tule elk requested, seven were sent and measured by the Judges Panel. The first World's Record tule elk was taken in 1990 by Quentin Hughes from the Grizzly Island herd in Solano County, California, and is currently owned by his widow Florence Sparks. This magnificent bull became the first World's Record in this category with a score of 351 points. This fine trophy is on loan to the Boone and Crockett Club's National Collection of Heads and Horns in Cody, Wyoming. Another notable tule elk is the Christian Weise bull that scores 346-6/8. It is currently owned by Harry Weise. This bull, taken in 1851, has remained in the family for 150 years and is the oldest entry in Boone and Crockett Club's record books!

Once near extinction, the tule elk truly is one of several great success stories in wildlife management during the last century. A separate chapter in the 11th edition of *Records of North American Big Game* was devoted to the telling of this story. With seven big California tule elk on display in Springfield, nearly 150,000 people had an opportunity to view fine representatives of this new category.

The top ranking Roosevelt's elk also was certified as a new World's Record. This bull, taken in 1997 and scoring 396-5/8 points, broke the existing record by 8-4/8 points. Mr. Karl Minor, Sr., harvested this fine bull while hunting on the Campbell River in British Columbia. The previous World's Record, taken by Wayne Coe, was also a British Columbia elk.

California also had another distinction in the 24th Awards Program. Mr. Brad Peters took the second place non-typical American elk, scoring 420-4/8 points, in the fall of 2000 in Kern County, California. This fine bull is the first American elk, typical or non-typical, from California to qualify for entry into the Boone and Crockett Club's all-time records book.

CARIBOU

Like elk, entries in the caribou categories also contained two new World's Records. Daniel L. Dobbs was hunting in the Iliamna Lake area of Alaska in the fall of 1999 when he was fortunate to take a monstrous barren ground caribou scoring 477 points. Mr. Dobbs' record bull surpassed Roger Hedgecock's previous World's Record by 11-7/8 points. Mr. Dobbs' bull, with its double shovels, long antler beams, and exceptional top points, is a classic representative of the barren ground caribou category.

A year earlier, C. Candler Hunt took an exceptional mountain caribou while hunting Prospector Mountain, Yukon Territory. Mr. Hunt's bull finished with a score of 453 points. At this score, this bull surpassed the former World's Record taken by Garry Beaubien in 1976 by one point. The Beaubien caribou is regarded by many as one of the finest trophies in "The Book," to some only surpassed by the Chadwick Stone's sheep as the exceptional representative of North American big game. The Beaubien bull received a Sagamore Hill Award at the completion of the 16th Awards Program in 1977.

While these two exceptional trophies mark this caribou grouping, the woodland caribou entries as a whole are worth noting. Clearly the woodland caribou hunts are among those in the "what's hot" right now. Sixty-three woodland caribou entries were received in the 24th recording period; 48 of these qualified for the all-time records. The number of woodland entries exceeds the number of barren ground caribou, mountain caribou, and Quebec-Labrador caribou entries. In recent, past Awards Programs the woodland caribou category typically had the lowest number of entries among the five caribou categories. While none of the entries in this category approached the score of 419-5/8 held by the current World's Record taken in 1910, several excellent trophies were submitted this time. The list was topped by a picked-up head owned by Gerard Beaulieu scoring 359-2/8, ranking fifth in the all-time records. Mr. Beaulieu served as a Panel Judge for the 22nd and 23rd Awards Programs. This bull and another that also qualifies for the records book were a set of locked antlers that Mr. Beaulieu donated to the Boone and Crockett Club's National Collection of Heads and Horns.

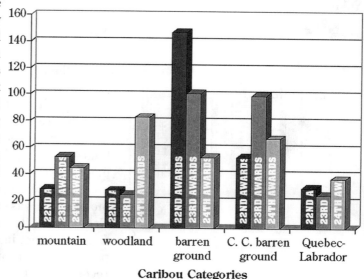

Caribou Categories

Photograph by Jack Reneau

Mr. Dobbs' record bull with its double shovels, long antler beams, and exceptional top points, make it a classic representative of the barren ground caribou category. Mr. Dobbs is pictured here with his wife Julie Dobbs after the 24th Awards Banquet.

MOOSE

There were a number of noteworthy moose accepted in all three categories of moose recognized by the Club during the 24th Awards Program. The most notable is an Alaska-Yukon bull taken by William Nelson in 1997 along the Beluga River in Alaska. At its entry score it was a potential World's Record by nearly two inches for the Alaska-Yukon moose category. The 24th Awards Program Judges Panel, however, adjusted the final score primarily because a projection off a normal point was initially scored as a normal point. Such points, which are sometimes difficult to identify, are always abnormal points. As a result of the necessary adjustments, Nelson's massive bull holds the second place honor in the Alaska-Yukon moose category.

Another exceptional bull is the Wyoming moose that was taken by Mary Isbell on the Tex Creek Wildlife Management Area in Bonneville County, Idaho, in 2000. Mary's bull scores 185-5/8 points and ranks in the top 15 Wyoming moose ever recorded. It received the First Place Award during

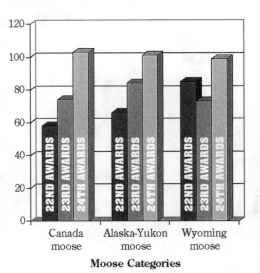

Moose Categories

the 24th Awards Program Banquet at Bass Pro Shops, Springfield, Missouri, during June 2001. What makes this trophy exciting is the fact that Mary took this spectacular bull on her very first hunt when she was only 12 years old. Most of us only ever dream of taking such a fine trophy. There are younger youth hunters with trophies in the records book, but none with such an impressive Wyoming moose. Hats off to Mary's dad and other parents who introduce their children to shooting and hunting at such a young age.

THE HORNED SPECIES

As noted earlier, the Sagamore Hill Award was presented to a Rocky Mountain goat taken by Gernot Wober in 1999. The judges measured this goat at a score of 56-6/8 points. That score ties the score of the Haase goat taken in 1949. The Haase goat is one of the longest standing World's Records in the book having been first recognized as the World's Record in the 3rd edition of *Records of North American Big Game*. The 3rd edition was the first of the Club's record books to use the current Boone and Crockett measuring system. Mr. Haase was recognized for his accomplishment in 1949 with the presentation of the Sagamore Hill Award for his fine goat. Fittingly, some 52 years later Mr. Wober received the same recognition.

As in the 23rd Awards Program, a number of potentially high-ranking muskox trophies were requested for panel judging - ten in all. Five of the bulls were submitted for panel measurement. When the judging was over, we had a new number two, a tie for number six and a new number ten. The other two bulls submitted for panel judging now rank at number 12 and 13. In the last two Awards Programs the top 15 trophies in the muskox category have nearly been rewritten in their entirety with the fine trophies coming from the Coppermine region and other areas in Northwest Territories.

One other muskox, a potential World's Record, taken by Vincente S. Sanchez-Valdepenas of Zamora, Spain, was shipped to panel for measuring, but it unfortunately arrived too late to be considered at this Awards Program. Mr. Sanchez-Valdepenas and his wife traveled from Spain to attend the 24th Awards Program Banquet and related activities in

Horned Categories

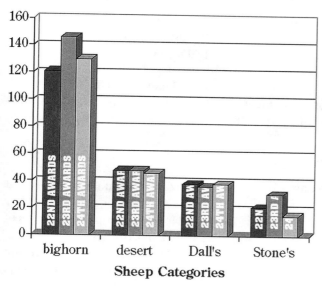

Sheep Categories

Photograph by Jack Reneau

Mr. Malzac shot the new World's Record grizzly bear while on a moose hunt in his home state of Alaska in 1998. This new record exceeds the previous World's Record skulls (three-way tie) by 3/16ths of an inch.

Springfield, Missouri, and were very gracious about the logistical problems associated with this trophy. The final score of Mr. Sanchez-Valdepenas' muskox was also verified at the Special Judges panel in Missoula, Montana, in August 2001. The asterisk will be removed and his trophy will take its rightful place in future records books.

The top pronghorn at 92-6/8 was taken by Mr. Sam Barry in Harney County, Oregon, in August 2000. This buck ties for third in the all-time records and is the top pronghorn ever entered from Oregon, and it is the only entry in the top five pronghorn not from Arizona.

One disappointment in the trophy display for the 24th Awards Program had to be the sheep display. Only one ram, a desert sheep taken by bowhunter George Harms, scoring 178-6/8 points, was the only ram submitted for panel measuring despite requests being sent to 20 trophy sheep owners. The Club plans to follow up with those owners to see if we can isolate causes for this low rate of participation.

BEARS AND COUGAR

The highlight of this grouping is the new World's Record grizzly bear taken on the Toklat River (a fitting place for a big grizzly) in Alaska. Mr. David Malzac shot this bear in September 1998. Its score of 27-5/16 exceeds the old three-way tie for first place by a whopping 3/16ths of an inch, which, for skulls, is a tremendous leap in a World's Record score.

What by now should not be a surprise is that again Pennsylvania continues to be the place for BIG black bears. The 1st and 2nd Awards this time both went to Pennsylvania

18   BOONE AND CROCKETT CLUB

bears - Joseph Mindick's 22-13/16 and Elwood Maurer's 22-8/16. Mr. Mindick's bear ranks as number six all-time and, with his entry, Pennsylvania now claims five of the top ten black bear entries. It well may be that the next World's Record black bear comes from Pennsylvania.

The 1st Award in the cougar category was received by a tom harvested by Roy LePage near Hinton, Alberta, scoring 15-15/16 points. This cougar ties for 5th place in the all-time records. A number of very large cougars have been taken in Alberta in recent years. Another cougar with an entry score of 16 points was entered from Alberta. It, however, was not submitted for panel judging and appears with an asterisk in this book.

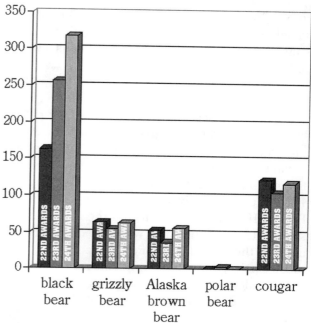

Skull Categories

WALRUS

The Boone and Crockett Club has recognized two walrus categories, Atlantic and Pacific, since it began records-keeping activities with the publication of the 1st edition of the records book, *Records of North American Big Game*, in 1932. However, hunting opportunities for either category have been somewhat limited over the years. Pacific walrus hunting was curtailed in the late 1970s with implementation of the Marine Mammals Act. The only Pacific walrus accepted in the Awards Programs since the 1970s are those hunter-taken trophies harvested before the Act took effect, or those specimens picked up on Alaskan beaches and legally possessed under the Marine Mammals Act.

So far as Atlantic walrus are concerned, only nine specimens have been listed in the records books published since 1932. It is not known if any were taken by sport hunters, but all nine are in major museum collections.

During the 24th Awards Program the Boone and Crockett Club accepted the first two hunter-taken Atlantic walrus ever entered in the Club's records books. Both of these animals were taken

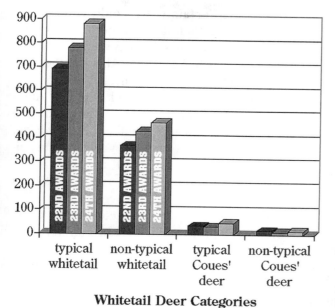

Whitetail Deer Categories

in Northwest Territories in Canada. They were invited to the 24th Awards Program Judges Panel in Springfield, Missouri, but neither was sent for final judging because Atlantic walrus cannot be imported into the United States, even temporarily for exhibition purposes, because of federal laws.

DEER

In the deer categories the overall top entry was a non-typical Coues' deer taken in 1941 by Peter Chase in Hildalgo County, New Mexico. This buck scores 186-1/8 points, surpassing the previous World's Record, a picked-up head, owned by the Boone and Crockett Club's National Collection by 27-5/8 points. This amounts to more than just beating the prior World's Record; it amounts to smashing it. Interestingly, a picked-up, non-typical Coues' buck scoring 151-3/8 points received a Certificate of Merit at this awards banquet. That buck, owned by Patrick H. Taylor, ranks fifth in the all-time records. It was joined by another typical head scoring 126-6/8 points that was picked up and is currently owned by Joshua Epperson. It ranks ninth in the typical category. It appears that maybe the best way to obtain a book entry for these elusive, diminutive whitetails is to wander around in the desert looking for their antlers.

Mule deer entries were up slightly again during the 24th Awards Program. Some of that increase is due to a large number of older mule deer trophies being recently entered into the Records. A similar statement can be made for Columbia blacktail deer entries. Sitka blacktail deer entries dropped, partially due to severe winterkill on Kodiak Island in recent years. The top Sitka blacktail in this recording period was taken on Prince of Wales Island by James Baichtal with a muzzleloader. His 121-6/8 buck is a new number nine.

As noted in the beginning of this chapter, whitetails continue to show dramatic increases in numbers entered into the Club's Awards Programs. I am sure that many wonder why, with 881 entries, you and I cannot seem to even see a book whitetail. Maybe, just maybe, this year!

Certainly, we could continue to discuss a number of other fine trophies shown in this 24th Awards Program records book such as Alan Hamberlin's non-typical American elk with its 450-6/8 (yes 450!) score placing it at number two in its category. But if you are like us, you will, and likely already have, turned to the pages of your favorite animal to see what is "hot" and what is not. Once again, the 24th Awards Program was the most productive three-year Entry Period ever conducted by the Club, both in terms of overall numbers and quality of trophies accepted. The Club's Awards Programs continue to serve as an excellent barometer of the effectiveness of wildlife management practices

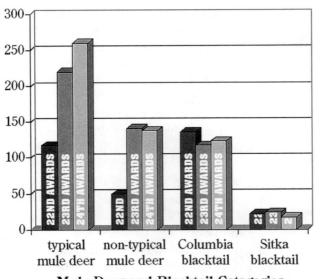

Mule Deer and Blacktail Categories

Photograph by Arlene Hanson

These outstanding whitetail deer were included in the 24th Awards Program Trophy Exhibit at Bass Pro Shops, Springfield, Missouri, during May through June 2001. Approximately 130,000 people viewed the exhibit making it an excellent tool to educate the public on the contributions of hunters to conservation.

initiated in North America at the end of the last century by Theodore Roosevelt and other early Boone and Crockett Club Members. Let us hope we can make a similar statement at the close of the 25th Awards Program that ends December 31, 2003. Good hunting and "shoot straight." ▲▲▲

C. Randall Byers has served as the Chair of the Boone and Crockett Club's Records of North American Big Game Committee since 1995. He is a Professor of Statistics and Information Systems in the Department of Business at the University of Idaho. Dr. Byers is also a Senior Member of the Pope and Young Club and is currently First Vice President of that organization.

Jack Reneau is a certified wildlife biologist who has been Director of Big Game Records for the Boone and Crockett Club since January of 1983. He was responsible for the day-to-day paperwork of the Boone and Crockett Club's records-keeping activities from 1976 to 1979 as an information specialist for the Hunter Services Division of the National Rifle Association (NRA) when NRA and Boone and Crockett Club cosponsored the B&C Awards Programs. Jack earned a M.S. in Wildlife Management from Eastern Kentucky University and a B.S. in Wildlife Management from Colorado State University.

AWARD WINNING TROPHY STORIES

Photograph courtesy of Joseph E. Mindick

Joseph E. Mindick with his First Award black bear scoring 22-13/16 points.

TROPHY STATS

▼ ▼ ▼ ▼ ▼

Category
black bear

Score
$22^{13}/_{16}$

Location
Luzerne County, Pennsylvania - 1998

Hunter
Joseph E. Mindick

Length of Skull
14

Width of Skull
$8^{13}/_{16}$

Photograph by Jack Reneau

Joseph E. Mindick accepting his plaque and medal from Randy Byers, Chair of the Big Game Records Committee.

BLACK BEAR
First Award - 22¹³/₁₆

▼ ▼ ▼ ▼ ▼ ▼ ▼ ▼ ▼

JOSEPH E. MINDICK

The weather was warmer than usual for this late in November. Hopefully, it would continue for the next few days. Even so, at this early hour of the morning, I could feel a little chill setting in. I was on stand at the edge of a Luzerne County swamp as the sun was rising on the opening day of the 1998 Pennsylvania bear season. This was my third year hunting with the Four Seasons Sportsmen's Association.

The hunting plan was as usual. Some of the club members would use their opening day buck stand to start off the bear season. This year we only had 13 members on our bear roster for opening day. Later that morning as we were set-ting up our first drive, I commented to the group "We will be the Lucky 13." At present, I was not feeling very lucky. I don't hunt deer in Luzerne County, so I was using an old stand not used anymore. The stand was facing directly into the rising sun. Fifty yards in front of my stand there was a dense growth of pine trees. All things combined made for poor shooting conditions.

Four Seasons Bear

On the bright side, I knew by 9:00 a.m. we would leave our stands and meet at the woodpile on Sullivan's Trail. Just then, a bear came out of the pine trees. I put the rifle up only to have the sun right in the scope. I dropped to iron sights below, but too late. He was a blur, then gone off to my left, and I could not get off a shot. When we all met at the woodpile, the sun was getting quite warm, and everyone was talking about what they had seen. I was the only hunter who actually saw a bear.

This is where the bear hunting really begins. We have two swamps on our hunting prop-erty, and there are almost always bear in one, or both. Our hunting plan is simple — some drive, some stand. The drivers normally use hip boots, a necessity because the water can be even higher than hip boots in some areas of the swamps. We set up our standers and drivers, and alternately drive both swamps. Our hunt master, Rob Davis, decided to drive the big swamp first, because this was close to where I saw my bear. Both swamps are bordered on one side by the same road, so we always start at the road edge and drive through the swamp toward the hardwoods at the end.

We had barely started our first drive when a shot was fired. Chris Paolone had taken the first bear. We finished the drive and all went to see Chris's bear. At this point, I realized this was not the bear I had seen on my stand in the early morning. By now the day was warming up, so we decided to take a break and eat lunch. Many of us wanted to put on lighter clothing for the afternoon drives. The two swamps are separated by a few hundred yards of high ground and often driven bear will double back over from one to the other. Knowing this, we decided to drive the small swamp after our break.

Back at the woodpile we were getting set up for the next drive. We knew there was at least one more bear in the area and it was possible he had been pushed into the small swamp. I was getting ready to drive when Rob suggested I stand. For the last two seasons, I had been mostly driving, so I said I would like to stand this time.

From my position above the small swamp, I could hear the drivers getting closer. Just then a bear came into view, and to my surprise, he was coming straight up the small hill toward me. He approached at a fast walk and I thought to myself at this angle he would be close enough for a handgun shot. At that same moment, two things happened to change my mind. First, I realized how large this animal was and using a handgun, even my .44 magnum, could be risking a wounded animal. Second, the bear had cleared the swamp, but was still about 50-60 yards away when he became aware of my presence and made an abrupt left turn. I shouldered my Model 70 Winchester and squeezed the trigger. At the recoil, I saw the bear drop to the ground. I chambered another round and watched as the bear slowly regained his footing. I did not want him to get back into the swamp, so I fired again and he dropped to the ground. For a few seconds everything was still. I slowly walked down to him and arrived about the same time as the drivers and other standers.

The next thing I knew, I was shaking hands with all the guys and Walt was offering to field-dress him for me. I needed a little time to settle down, so I told Walt to go ahead. My Model 70 is a 7mm Remington Magnum firing 160-grain Sierra Spitzer boat-tail hand-loads with 61 grains of Dupont IMR 4350, in a Winchester case. As the bear was being field-dressed, I found out either shot would have been fatal.

Now it was time to move the bear and get to a check station. Bill Kratz was able to get his 4 wheel drive truck about 70 yards above us. With the help of all the guys, we built a pole-type carrier from dead fall and some rope. Then, six at a time, we carried him up to the truck. At the truck, we took pictures and a break before going back to camp, and then on to a Pennsylvania Game Commission Check Station. At the Check Station, they pulled some teeth and weighed him in at 448 pounds dressed, and estimated his live weight at 528 pounds. I later found out my bear was seventeen years, ten months old. The day ended with a good meal and some celebrating, but not too much, because we would do more driving and hunting the next day before all heading home.

Several days later, I was at Stranix Taxidermy in Doylestown, Pennsylvania, making arrangements for a bear rug with the owner, Mark Stranix. He suggested to me that I could have a trophy class black bear and should have the skull properly cleaned and officially measured. On August 13, 1999, I had the skull measured by Doug Killough at the Regional Office of the Pennsylvania Game Commission. He measured the skull at 22-13/16 points. Later, I was advised this could be a new Pennsylvania record for legally harvested black bear.

Preparation, hard work, and patience are essential for successful hunting, but I think teamwork by my hunting partners and a little luck were the main contributors to my success. I will always be thankful to them for my Four Seasons Bear. ▲▲▲

Special thanks to:

Karl Bauz	Frank Paolone	Jim Davis	Glenn McGrath
Rob Davis	Chris Paolone	Bill Kratz	Dave Smyth
Butch McMillan	Walt Smakulski, Jr.	John Thompson	Mike McMillan

Award Winning Moments...

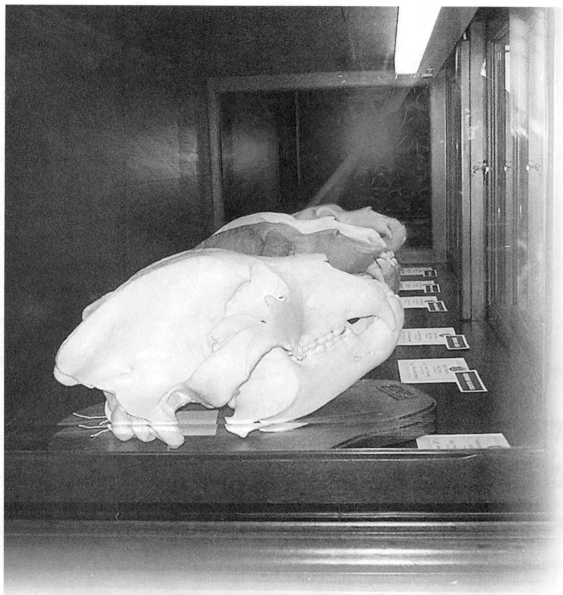

Photograph by Julie T. Houk

The Alaska brown bear display at the 24th Awards Program was one of the finest exhibits ever assembled for this category. All six of the six trophies that were invited were sent in for final judging, including Michael Ward's bruin from the Aliulik Peninsula, Alaska, that scores 30-3/16 points. Mike's trophy, which ranks in the top 15 for its category, took First Award.

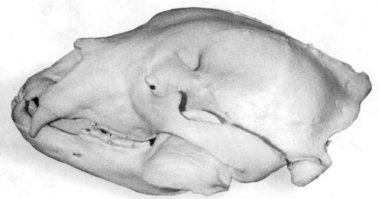

Photograph courtesy of Elwood W. Maurer

TROPHY STATS

▼ ▼ ▼ ▼ ▼

Category
black bear

Score
$22^8/_{16}$

Location
Schuylkill County, Pennsylvania - 1997

Hunter
Elwood W. Maurer

Length of Skull
$13^{11}/_{16}$

Width of Skull
$8^{13}/_{16}$

Photograph by Jack Reneau

Elwood W. Maurer accepting his plaque and medal from Randy Byers, Chair of the Big Game Records Committee.

BLACK BEAR
Second Award - 22⁸/₁₆

$$22^{8}/_{16}$$

▼ ▼ ▼ ▼ ▼ ▼ ▼ ▼ ▼

ELWOOD W. MAURER

The first time I saw the bear I was watching the end of a cornfield on the first morning of archery season. He came out of the field and entered the open area between the field and the woods. Two weeks later on a misty, rainy day, the wind was just right for a stalk through the cornfield. I was hoping to find a nice buck bedded down for the day; instead, I came across the big guy one more time. He was sitting down facing into the wind about 15 yards away pulling as many cornstalks to him as he could reach. As he finished eating what he had, he would slide down the row on his butt to a place where he could reach more.

From the first day of the archery season until the bear season opened, I saw him a total of four times, but I was able to keep weekly tabs on him by checking the end of the field. He made this easy for me because he would spend all day in the field and would come out only to help fertilize the weeds. I never found any bear scat in the field; it appeared he didn't want to contaminate his feeding area.

The field was located on the crest of a steep hill surrounded by hardwoods on three sides. At the bottom of the hill on one side is a native trout stream. The bear had all the requirements of life without traveling more than a quarter mile.

I was lucky to harvest a nice whitetail buck and a fall turkey in the woods adjacent to the field, both with the bow. Could this be my year to take the triple trophy? With the bow?

As the bear season approached I developed my plan. I would sit at the end of the field from first light with my .35 Whalen to see if he would come out or maybe catch him coming back from his nightly jaunt. If I didn't see him until mid-morning, I would take my bow and work through the field looking for him. The day before the season opened, my 9 year-old grandson Josh and I climbed the hill. I wanted to scout the area one more time and give Josh the experience of bear hunting. The next morning about an hour before daylight I parked my truck and began to get my rifle and bow ready for the hike. I was holding both weapons in my hand and looking up the hill; I decided to leave my bow in the truck. MISTAKE. The first light had brought the first snowfall of the season, just a

Photograph courtesy of Elwood W. Maurer

The author's daughters, Kim and Jackie, helped him get the downed bear from the cornfield to the truck.

The author and his nine-year-old grandson Josh with the big boar in the cornfield. The skull measured 22-8/16 inches and earned a Second Award at the 24th Big Game Awards in Springfield, Missouri.

dusting, but enough to keep the wildlife from moving. I soon came to the conclusion that if I wanted this bear, I would need to go in to the field after him.

It was about 8 a.m. when I entered the field. I hadn't gone 60 yards when I looked up a row and there he was about 40 yards away. My Whalen only has iron sights and I couldn't distinguish a vital target. Now what do I do? I decided to slowly approach him. If I got close enough, or if he decided to move, I would be able to tell where to aim. When I got within 20 yards of him I wished I'd brought the bow. He started to raise his head and he was facing away from me into the wind. The bullet took him in the back of the neck and exited through his nose. He traveled only 15 yards and fell about five rows short of exiting the field.

I tagged him and went home to try to get some help to get him off the hill. The only help available was my two daughters, Kim and Jackie. Josh had asked me to get him out of school if I was successful. So the four of us — two girls, a nine year-old and one excited hunter — climbed back up the hill, took some pictures, and started to roll the bear downhill to the closest place I could get my truck. After an hour and a half we had traveled the 75 yards to the truck. Some carpenters working on a roof nearby came over to help load the big guy on the truck. It took six of us to get the job done. ▲▲▲

Photograph courtesy of Dan B. Pence

Outfitter Duke LeCroix, the author, and guide Chris Dumbleton with Scarnose. This bear made Duke the winner of the 1999 Alberta Professional Outfitters Society black bear trophy.

TROPHY STATS

▼ ▼ ▼ ▼ ▼

Category
black bear

Score
22⁷/₁₆

Location
Owl River, Alberta - 1999

Hunter
Dan B. Pence

Length of Skull
13¹⁴/₁₆

Width of Skull
8⁹/₁₆

Photograph by Jack Reneau

Dan B. Pence accepting his plaque and medal from Randy Byers, Chair of the Big Game Records Committee.

BLACK BEAR
Third Award - 22⁷/₁₆

▼ ▼ ▼ ▼ ▼ ▼ ▼ ▼ ▼

DAN B. PENCE

"Before this week's over you'll see more bear than you've ever seen before. Why, a few days ago we even had a bear climb up to the tree stand the hunter was in - he had to boot it in the nose to get it to leave." These were some of the introductory comments of outfitter Duke LaCroix of Raven Outfitters, Ltd. as he talked with his last group of hunters for the 1999 spring bear season. We were at the Cedar Park Inn in Edmonton, Alberta. It was Sunday, the last week in May, 1999. Then looking right at me, Duke commented, "This guy looks like he doesn't believe a word of anything I've said!" "Look, I'm from Texas where everything is bigger and better. Besides, I'm just a natural skeptic anyway. So we'll see," was my retort.

An End to Skepticism

Duke muttered something about Texans under his breath and continued his discourse about the past exploits of this season's bear hunters. I must admit that I did have my doubts that the forthcoming hunt was going to be as good as it was being touted. This was to be my first hunt for baited bear in Alberta, but I had spot-and-stalk hunted there several years previously. I knew the Province's reputation for having a large bear population, several areas with bears of extraordinary size, and a high proportion of color phase bears. I was hoping for a large trophy-class bruin from this trip.

Next morning we left Edmonton and made the three-hour trip north to the hunting area near Lac La Biche. Our camp was located at the edge of the bush on the shore of a small lake. It was a tent camp, but the tents were large and comfortable. There were spacious cooking and eating tents and even an outside hot shower that really worked. The outfitter provided boats with outboard motors from which we could fish for northern pike in the mornings. Bear hunting was an afternoon affair. With over 100 maintained bait sites, there were plenty of opportunities for the guides to place their hunters on frequently visited sites or on sites that are visited by particularly big bears. The baiting strategy was simple, but highly effective — use a variety of bait and lots of it as at as many baiting sites as possible. With only two hunters per guide, there was plenty of personal attention for each hunter. I was assigned to Chris Dumbleton, an experienced guide who had worked several seasons for Duke.

For years I have hunted with nothing but break-action single or double rifles. On this trip I was carrying one of my favorite side-by-side double rifles, a Chapuis Utility Grade Express in .30-06 caliber. A Steiner 1.5-5x30 variable scope equipped with a #4 heavy duplex reticle was mounted on the rifle with a factory installed detachable mount. The barrels had been regulated by J.J. Perodeau. Shooting Federal High Energy cartridges with 180-grain Trophy-Bonded Bearclaw bullets I could achieve about 1-inch groups at 100 yards. This is about as good as it gets with a double rifle!

The second afternoon of the hunt, Chris and I made our way into the bush to a bait stand that was located several hundred yards off the road. Until very recently, this bait had been hit only at two or three day intervals, an indication that a really large boar might be visiting it. The bait site

Photograph courtesy of Dan B. Pence

The bear's hide measured exactly nine feet from nose to tail and is the third largest bear ever recorded in Alberta.

was at the end of a small creek that was at the head of a large swamp that extended for miles back into the bush. After crossing the creek bed Chris froze abruptly and whispered "There's a bear at the bait barrel and he's colored!" I eased forward just in time to see a massive light brown bear about 40 yards in front of me. He stood up on his hind legs and smelled the tree trunk to which the 55-gallon bait barrel was attached. The bear was enormous and the light reflecting through his fur gave him a silver-tipped appearance. I hesitated for a moment, thinking this might be a grizzly. Grizzlies are rare, but not unheard of in this area.

As he dropped to all four feet and began to sniff the ground and area around the bait barrel, I could tell that this was a black bear. Clearly, he was checking the area for signs of estrus females rather than showing a lot of interest in the bait. Unlike so many large bears, even his ears were large in proportion to his head. There was the characteristic massive crease in the crown of his head and he had a shoulder hump usually seen only in the large boars. Fortunately, we were downwind from the bait site as a gentle breeze kicked up. "Take him. He's a b-i-g bear," Chris prodded. I stepped forward to a small tree just in front of me and rested the double .30-06 so the crosshairs of the scope were on his front shoulder as the bear turned partly broadside to me. I squeezed the rear trigger and could see him lunge forward as the rifle's report broke an otherwise silent forest. In two or three bounds we watched the bear disappear down the side of the creek bank in front of us.

"I think you hit him good. I saw him lurch forward when you shot," Chris commented as we searched the area around the bait bucket for signs of blood. None were found. Two trails diverged a few yards from the single trail that led out of the creek to the bait site. We checked the upper trail first as we both thought this was the route taken by the fleeing bear. Wrong! We found no blood anywhere on this trail after following it for about 15 minutes. We backtracked and checked all the trees in the projected path of the bullet to make sure that it had not been deflected by a branch or had grazed a tree trunk. Nothing! I then began following the lower trail that led along the bottom of the creek bed. It was overgrown in places, but in other spots it was covered with thick moss. It was then I saw that the huge tracks that sunk several inches into the moss and were spaced over three feet apart. I also noticed the enormous piles of droppings containing the oats that had been used as bait earlier that season. The droppings were over four inches in diameter. We were indeed dealing with a large bear!

As I slowly made my way a few more yards down the creek bottom, I was startled by a deep guttural growl just ahead in the thick undergrowth. At this point the creek bottom had opened up to about 20 yards wide and the banks were six to eight feet high on each side — not a good place to be with a wounded bear of any size, much less this monster. Chris was somewhere on the bank to my right and behind me. "We've got a wounded bear somewhere ahead," I yelled to Chris. "Just stay where you are and I'll come to you," was his reply. A few moments later I was joined by Chris and we made our way very slowly up and over

BLACK BEAR
Third Award - 22⁷/16

▼ ▼ ▼ ▼ ▼

DAN B. PENCE

the bank of the creek that turned in a horseshoe bend directly in front of us. We topped the bank and peered over the opposite side. There in the creek bottom lay the largest black bear either of us had ever dreamed of. I had heard the bear's death groan. He had traveled no more than 50 yards from the bait site. I looked at Chris and he looked at me in disbelief as we both simply sat down beside each other in silence on the creek bank for a full minute as we tried to comprehend the magnitude of the event. Then, we both began an uncontrollable bout of laughter, hand shaking, and backslapping. We both remained speechless for another several minutes.

It was only when we walked the few yards down to the bear that we fully comprehended its immense size. Then we noticed that there was an old healed scar on its left nostril. Something had thoroughly ripped through its nose during some past battle, probably over a sow. The downed bear was henceforth known as "Scarnose." Shortly, another guide showed up, having seen Chris's pickup and heard our laughter in the bush. Tony's comments on seeing the bear was quiet matter-of-fact. "You know, I used to guide for grizzlies in Alberta's Swan Hills where they got really big. I haven't seen too many of them that reached this size. Why, this bear must weight 550 or 600 pounds. Can you imagine what he would weigh in the fall?" Chris, with his husky 5 foot 10 inch stature could hardly link hands around the bear's huge neck.

A call by cell phone was made to Duke for additional help plus an ATV to transport the bruin out to the pickup. Duke's only comment on the cell phone was to ask Chris how much "ground swell" there was following his initial comments on the bear's size. He asked to speak with Tony whose reply to the same question was "None." That is when Duke rounded up everyone he could find in camp and came to get the bear. On first seeing the bear, Duke looked at me and said, "This is an outfitter's dream! You know you got a grizzly for the price of a black bear, don't you?" "Well, I guess this does end my skepticism about hunting with Raven Outfitters," was my retort. "Touché," was Duke's only comment. ▲ ▲ ▲

New World's Record

Photograph courtesy of David F. Malzac

What started out as a moose hunt, ended with a new World's Record grizzly bear for David. F. Malzac.

TROPHY STATS

▼ ▼ ▼ ▼ ▼

Category
grizzly bear

Score
$27^5/_{16}$

Location
Toklat River, Alaska - 1998

Hunter
David F. Malzac

Length of Skull
$16^{11}/_{16}$

Width of Skull
$10^{10}/_{16}$

Photograph by Jack Reneau

David F. Malzac accepting his plaque and medal from Randy Byers, Chair of the Big Game Records Committee.

GRIZZLY BEAR
First Award - 27⁵/₁₆

▼ ▼ ▼ ▼ ▼ ▼ ▼ ▼

DAVID F. MALZAC

I wish I could say that this started out to be a bear hunt, but it didn't. My friends and hunting partners, Robert Caywood and Harold Bryant, long time Alaskans who live, breathe, and sleep to hunt, my father, Gerald Malzac, and I started out on what was supposed to be the moose hunt of a lifetime!

After our 1997 fall moose hunt we decided it was time to find a different place to hunt where there was more game and fewer hunters. The winters in Alaska are long, so this gave us plenty of time to study maps and make plans for the following year's hunt. After spending several evenings together looking at area and topographic maps, Robert and I had decided to check out the Bearpaw Trail. The Bearpaw Trail is 75 miles north of the majestic Denali (or Mt. McKinley as outsiders call it) and southwest of Nenana, Alaska. This trail was the original route to the northern Denali gold fields, built at the turn of the century, and was accessed by steam ships from the Nenana River and the town of Nenana. The Bearpaw Trail and its roadhouses were consequently abandoned in the 1930s when the Stampede Trail was built 30 miles to the south. When the current road into the park was built about 20 years later, the Stampede Trail was abandoned. Since then a few trappers have used the Bearpaw Trail, keeping it cleared mainly for snowmobiles and dogsleds.

Hard-fought Alaskan Grizzly

I contacted Alaska Fish and Game and spoke to the area biologists as well as several air taxi operators, some whom mentioned seeing quite a few large bulls in the area. During the summer Robert and I flew over the area to scout the trail and terrain. From the air the trail looked spotty in places, but seemed to be accessible. But, you cannot trust what you see from an airplane! Overall, the area, which was 90 to 100 miles from the Parks Highway, looked promising. Our minds were made up; the Kantishna River and eastern hills that form the headwaters of the Kuskokwim River would be our destination!

Robert and I talked with Harold and he was game. Then I called my father in Arizona to see if he would like to join us. He was ready to go before I hung up the phone!

I had met Harold and Robert years ago through a very good friend and expert hunter, Bill Newman. Bill is renowned throughout the state for his design, development, and construction of the finest all-around hunting buggy anywhere. These buggies are vehicles built on old army M-17, 1 1/4-ton jeep frames with 4-foot tires. They stand roughly 9 feet high, 8 feet wide, and can be as much as 24 feet long. With gin poles that will hoist any moose off the ground, it makes for fast, efficient, and clean butchering. Each buggy is hand-crafted to meet the individual needs of each owner. Their basic design is what makes them work so well in the Alaskan terrain. Large tractor tread implement tires give the buggies one quarter the ground pressure of a man walking. Small V-8 and 6-cylinder engines, and a low gear ratio in the drive train, produce high torque and a top speed of 15 miles per hour. These buggies have been referred to as an Alaskan grocery cart!

Robert's buggy is one of Bill's original buggies. Bill has since left us for the great hunting grounds in the sky, so Harold built his own buggy using Robert's as a model and following Bill's basic guidelines. With these buggies, we could take in a luxurious camp 120 miles from the nearest road, get to areas that even air guides would like to hunt, and still haul back a couple of moose, one or two caribou or bear! This is essential because it is not uncommon for our hunts to last from 20 to 25 days, much to the dismay of our wives and girlfriends. As more and more land is being gobbled up by special interest groups, these rigs are a necessity for those of us who live and work in Alaska, depend on it's natural resources to feed our families, and want to have a true wilderness experience by getting away from the crowds.

On September 1st and 2nd the equipment was packed into the buggies. I had my 8-mm video and 35 mm still camera packed also, hopefully for some unforgettable footage.

By the 4th we were on the trail! The first 20 miles were fantastic, taking us about 5 hours — easy trail and beautiful country! A large 60 to 65-inch bull moose crossed the trail in front of us and stood watching us pass. We didn't want to take any game yet since it was hot and meat would spoil if not hung and cared for properly.

Our first night was spent on the Teklanika River, at a calm 50 degrees, with a nice campfire, good food and conversation, an absolutely beautiful sunset as the backdrop, and the distant roar of the river. There was no problem with sleep that night!

We awoke to an overcast morning. After a good breakfast, we hit the trail and in the next few days would find the next 30 miles to be a living hell! Most of the trail was no more than a moose path, which had been overgrown for the last 60 years. The only way we were able to find some of the trail was to use our Global Positioning System (GPS) and topographic maps. The GPS was new to us. We knew better than to rely on this new fangled contraption completely, because it is a machine and machines break down! Besides, Murphy (of Murphy's Law) usually rode shotgun! The second day was spent clearing trees and brush for 14 hours only to make two miles. Camp that night was hastily set up in pouring rain.

Day three was mostly easy going. There were two streams and a gully, which we needed to build makeshift log bridges to cross, because the original bridges had either washed out or collapsed over the years. We traveled until dark and were so close to the Toklat, but the trail was swamped. A trail through or around needed to be found and that would require daylight. A campsite was set up, again in a moderate rain.

Up and going by seven o'clock, we found a trail through the swamp. After two chain saw chains, seemingly endless brush clearing, getting lost twice and stuck a few times, and four 13-15 hour days, we finally made the Toklat River. We had traveled only fifty miles of the planned one hundred. I think we were all beginning to question our sanity! Do we really want to hunt this bad? Would this be a great outdoor experience? Was a moose or bear worth all this? Undeniably, YES! We were adventurers, gatherers and, above all, hunters!

We arrived at the Toklat River around noon on the 8th, the sixth day of the hunting trip. After walking the trail west of the river for a couple of miles, it was decided that we would not go on to the Kantishna River, which was another twenty-five miles away! The trail was getting worse and we'd had all the bushwhacking we could handle. A campsite was selected on a high, dry gravel bar. We spent the rest of the day setting up camp, which consisted of two 10 x 12 wall tents with carpet, a covered kitchen between the two tents, barrel stoves, tables, chairs, cots and of course meat poles. It was a very comfortable camp. After a large meal, we relaxed, reminisced about the trip in, and planned our hunt for the next day.

After a hearty breakfast of eggs, chorizo, tortillas and pancakes, we scouted a couple of square miles around camp and found very little moose sign. There were plenty of bear tracks, some wolf tracks, but none of the swampy areas moose prefer. The next five days were spent taking the buggies to different areas and hunting

GRIZZLY BEAR
First Award - 27⁵/₁₆

▼ ▼ ▼ ▼ ▼

DAVID F. MALZAC

the small ridges, sloughs and clearings. Many hours were spent still-hunting the heavy forested areas, and then everyone met back at the buggies at dark to go back to camp. With no luck close to camp, we would travel five to ten miles away, putting us into areas that had more moose sign. All the tracks we saw were from mature moose — none from calves or yearlings. The bears and wolves were clearly taking a large toll on the younger population. Why can't those animal lovers understand this? Everyday there would be fresh bear tracks in our foot or buggy tracks. It would be nice to get a bear or two even if we couldn't find any moose. The area biologist had told me a few months earlier that the bears and wolves were decimating the moose calves in this unit. It was apparently true. Wolves and bears are protected in Denali Park, which was just eight miles to the south. These predators are rapidly migrating outside of the park because of higher concentrations and a dwindling food source.

On the fifth day of the hunt, after no game sightings, my father had to leave. I had arranged for a bush plane to fly in and take him out to Fairbanks. I was quite heartbroken because this was his first trip to Alaska and he still hadn't seen a moose or bear. He later told me that on the flight out he did see a cow and calf moose, a large bull and a grizzly bear, so I felt better. He said he would not have traded the experience for a million bucks! That's the sign of a true sportsman!

September 13 — another long and frustrating day, just as the last eight days before it had been. We had been in the area for six days, and still hadn't seen a single moose. This was unbelievable. Here we were, literally in the middle of Alaska, 50 miles from the nearest road, and NO MOOSE! We were beginning to test our friendship and were hardly talking, as all of us had different ideas about what we should do next. After calling, rattling and everything else we could think of to root these creatures out of the dense brush, we were desperate. But desperate times call for desperate measures! Our legs were burning and plum worn out from high stepping through the brush and bogs!

It had been raining lightly all day, and we had been sitting here on a bend in the river for a while glassing, just hoping a moose would cross somewhere so we could put on a stalk and hopefully take one. It was cloudy, a mist was in the air, and heavier rain was eminent, plus it was starting to get dark. We didn't have much time left, maybe an hour or so. I was anxious to get back before dark because camp was so hard to find in this flat country, with no hills or landmarks anywhere. We had to rely on our sense of direction, gut feelings and to a small degree, the GPS.

"There is another bear," Robert said flatly. We had already seen five bears, three grizzlies and two blackies. Every morning there would be fresh tracks around camp. There were some exceptionally large tracks that we had seen in the riverbed close to camp. It would be nice to see and take the maker of those prints we thought to ourselves.

"Too many bears. This place needs thinning out really bad," Robert remarked a few minutes later. When there are more sightings of bear than moose, this indicates something is wrong! I turned my glasses to where Robert was looking.

Photograph courtesy of David F. Malzac

The hunters used this Alaskan hunting buggy to get to camp. These custom-made buggies top out at 15 miles per hour and are commonly called Alaskan grocery carts!

"Yeah", I said. It looks big, but at this distance and in flat light they all look big. Since I have worked in the Alaskan bush as a heavy equipment mechanic for the past 10 years, I've been fortunate enough to have seen lots of bear, so I am able to judge size fairly well.

"What do you think?" Robert asked. "Well, lets get a little closer and see," I replied. "I don't want anything puny," I answered. I have always refrained from killing a bear just to take one. I wanted a big one.

The bear was a long way off, about a half mile, and in the middle of a 300-yard wide river. So, heading straight up the center of the river and using what little cover there was, we quickly made our way toward the bear, knowing that if he headed for the brush there may not be any chance of a shot. When we were within two hundred yards I brought my binoculars up, and my heart skipped a beat. I was amazed at how large its shoulders were, plus seeing its huge block-head and small looking ears, I knew he was a monster! His shoulders and back glowed in silver. This was a bear worth taking!

"Well, do you want him?" whispered Robert. I answered, "You bet." The bear was down over a bank so only the top of his back was showing. He was occupied with something in the water with his head down most of the time. There was one more minor problem; he was in the middle of the river leaving very little cover for us! We would stick out like sore thumbs! So do I wait and hope he makes his way to me? He could stay out there for a while. Or do we try to get closer? Either way I would have to shoot him far enough out in the river to ensure at least three more shots. I wanted him down for good before he could get to the thick brush and trees, or to us if he charged. Tracking a wounded grizzly into the brush in the dark was not high on my priority list! Either way, quick and accurate action on my part would be essential. I was glad I had Robert as my backup. He's a crack shot and this is absolutely necessary, especially when on a potentially dangerous hunt like this!

Man, I thought to myself. If he gets a whiff of us, he'll go straight away and I'll never get a good shot. As we approached, his body came into view, and I knew I wanted this bear! We could see him next to some small bushes and watched him feeding on something. Then I realized that the clump of brush was actually across the channel on the other side of him. In the flat riverbed with the light fading fast, the colors of the bear, brush and gravel blended together. I hoped we hadn't made a mistake. All we could do is keep closing the distance.

At 150 yards, the brute suddenly lifted his huge head and began to quickly look around. He winded us and we froze in our tracks! He jumped up on the bank nearest us! Still looking around, he wasn't sure what he winded, but he knew he didn't want to hang around. He was HUGE! He turned and started to slowly bound to my left and slightly toward us, still looking around. I clicked the safety off and brought the sights to his shoulder. He wasn't really spooked, just more anxious to know what that smell was. He was headed toward the trees at the river's edge, and then he stopped for a moment.

The crosshairs of my Leupold 1.5 X 5 were right on his shoulders as I let the hammer down on my Winchester .375 H&H. I jacked another shell into the chamber as I looked over the top of the gun. I heard the unmistakable thud of a solid hit. He stumbled, but didn't go down! He was loping again toward the edge of the river and thick trees. I fired again! Bang! He went down on his haunches and turned so his chest was facing us. I fired once more! Through my scope I saw a large spray of water come from his massive chest. I jammed another shell into the chamber! He was swatting and snapping his teeth at his chest and letting out some horrific growls like he was being stung by an angry swarm of hornets. I stood still, my rifle trained on his chest. Then, he just sat there for what seemed like a full minute. I watched the life draining from this wonderful bruin's body. Then he just turned and fell forward onto his chest. He didn't want to fight anymore. It was as if he just gave up, accepted the fact that he had lived a long life, and it was now his time to go. As we approached him, I felt sadness come over me, as it always does when I kill any animal. Another life gone. At 20 yards we waited about ten minutes. It was just about dark as the bear took a long breath and exhaled the last of the air from his lungs. His eyes clouded. He was dead.

Robert went back for the buggy. We decided to take the whole animal back to camp since it was dark and started to rain again. Using a come-along, we hoisted the mammoth body into the bed of the buggy. I took a few minutes of video, and then slowly we made our way back to camp.

The next day after breakfast, we took a few pictures and marveled at the size of the bear. I knew he was a larger-than-average bruin! His body was small for a fall bear but his head was huge! We knew he was old just by the condition of his teeth. They were worn down so far that nerve endings were showing. He had one broken canine tooth and another front tooth was broken off, just hanging by the gum — this was not a happy bear!

When we started the task of skinning, it was apparent this guy would not have survived another winter. He barely had a half-inch of fat on his rump, and because of the condition of his teeth, he probably was not able to provide enough for himself to survive another long Alaskan winter. He wasn't fit to eat. We just skinned him and cleaned the skull. We spent the next two days cleaning the skull and fleshing and salting the hide. After these chores we decided to leave the area for lack of moose, and to hunt another open unit for an extra five days.

The trip out was uneventful and took only 19 hours. We used the GPS to find the trail, making it easy to get to previously marked coordinates. It took a couple of days to get into the other area to hunt, and all three of us came back with our moose. Harold and I took a couple of small bulls while Robert got a nice 69 inch bull!

Robert called me a couple of weeks later and asked what measurement Fish and Game had taken from the skull. I didn't know, so we did our own measurements and were surprised to get a green score of 27-5/16 points! It could be a new Worlds Record! Because I didn't have any luck finding a beetle colony in Alaska to clean the skull I made the mistake of boiling it myself. I was sure this shrunk the skull. The 24th Big Game Awards Judges' Panel officially declared my grizzly the new World's Record with a final score of 27-5/16 points.

It was the finest hunt I can remember! ▲▲▲

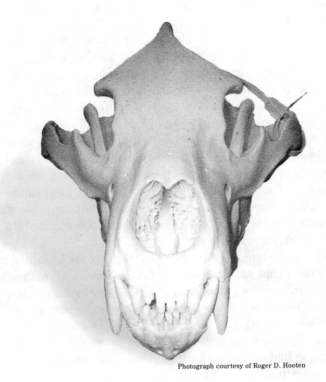

Photograph courtesy of Roger D. Hooten

TROPHY STATS

▼ ▼ ▼ ▼ ▼

Category
   grizzly bear

Score
   $26^{10}/_{16}$

Location
   Kaltag, Alaska - 1999

Hunter
   Roger D. Hooten

Length of Skull
   $16^{14}/_{16}$

Width of Skull
   $9^{12}/_{16}$

Photograph by Jack Reneau

Roger D. Hooten accepting his plaque and medal from Randy Byers, Chair of the Big Game Records Committee.

GRIZZLY BEAR
Second Award - 26¹⁰/₁₆

▼ ▼ ▼ ▼ ▼ ▼ ▼ ▼ ▼

ROGER D. HOOTEN

The end of tax season, April 15, 1999, was the beginning of my departure to fly to Alaska to begin my grizzly hunt. After spending the night in Anchorage I started my last leg of the journey to Kaltag. The weather-delayed trip took me to two other stops along the Yukon River before reaching Kaltag. The Ford Family along with my guide Earl Esmailka met my plane. I knew John, Ken and Kyra Ford before they moved to Alaska. John had been my daughter's volleyball coach the previous fall and they had moved to Kaltag in the winter to teach there. It was good to see them again and I really started to get excited when we loaded my gear onto their snowmobiles and rode to the Ford's house. The only modes of transportation were snowmobiles or snowshoes. I had never in my life seen so much snow. It was a snow covered white paradise.

The next day we rode our snowmobiles. This was my first experience on one and it was exhilarating and challenging. We followed the frozen river to the next town. The trail up the river is part of the Iditarod race course that had been run earlier in the year. Once in town we were told that a bear had been feeding on a moose kill nearby. We picked up the bear's tracks and followed on snow shoes for a time, but realized that the tracks indicated that this was a bear not worth pursuing. I was looking for a really large bear and was willing to keep up the search. The next morning, outside of Kaltag, bear tracks were spotted on a mountainside. When we arrived at the tracks the bear had traveled from a low draw covered with trees, and had continued over the top of a mountain into another valley. I thought my first experience riding a snowmobile was exhilarating and challenging. Now, trying to keep up with my guide, who had run in the Ironman race before the Iditarod, was even more challenging. After seeing the tracks head over the mountain where we could not follow, we headed back and went to other mountains in search of a big bear. On the way we saw a beautiful lynx out on his own hunt.

The next few days were spent riding out on snowmobiles to different vantage points hoping to find a set of tracks that would indicate the size of bear we were determined to find. Upon arriving at these different spots I discovered it was the most beautiful, scenic mountain range I had ever seen. Then, on the morning of the 20th, we went to a mountain that led down into the next valley. We knew that if we took this route we would have to go all the way to the Yukon River, and then down the river back to Kaltag. It was Nine-Mile Creek and there would be no turning back.

This was exactly the kind of place where a old dominant grizzly would make his home. An old male grizzly will not tolerate another bear, unless it is breeding season and a female enters his home turf. At this time I had no idea what was in store for us. If you have never ridden a snowmobile in virgin territory it is unbelievable how easy you can get stuck in the snow. Every time you stop and get off your machine you are up to your waist in snow. I learned the hard way you cannot leave your snowmobile without snowshoes!

Once we went over the top it was mostly downhill following a creek bed. All of a sudden, there they were — the largest bear tracks I had ever seen. Of course, I said something out loud about the size of the tracks and was immediately told to keep quiet. The snowmobile motors do not bother the bears, but the human voice will send them running. With great anticipation we went down the creek. We noticed the bear was going from beaver den to beaver den looking for something to eat. Apparently he had not eaten since he had come out of his winter hibernation.

To my surprise, all of a sudden, there he was. The size of his head and body was unbelievable. As the late Jack O'Connor always said, "When they are really big you know it the instant that you look at them." I knew he was what I had traveled this long trip, and ridden in this cold rough terrain for. He ran for maybe 25 yards and then stopped to have a look back at what had disturbed his nap. The .300 Winchester Gale McMillian had made for me with a 3.5x10 Leupold was instantly at my shoulder. A slight squeeze later he was down, and then a follow up shot just to make sure. He was far too magnificent an animal to let him suffer or risk getting away. I was pleased with the performance of my handload — 165-grain Nosler Partition bullet pushed by a maximum load of IMR 4350.

Earl was astounded at the size of the bear. After a frozen-finger skinning job we loaded the skull that was wrapped up in the hide onto my snowmobile for the journey back to Kaltag. The trip down to the Yukon River with the additional weight was a lot tougher than I had imagined. Earl stated that the trip was so tough that he would never take another hunter down Nine-Mile Creek. The effort we made was well rewarded and I am glad we made the decision to go for it. After we slid down the final embankment we were on the mighty Yukon River and on our way back to Kaltag.

It was not until the next day when the final skinning was done that the skull was roughly measured and the reality of its size was realized. This bear was destined for the record book and I was extremely grateful he was mine!

His skull was huge and he squared just over nine feet. His pelt is a beautiful dark brown with no rubs and extremely long thick coarse hair. He is now mounted life-size in my Great Hall trophy room. He was not the first, but he will certainly be the last grizzly I will ever hunt! ▲▲▲

Award Winning Moments...

Photograph by Jack Reneau

Visitors to the 24th Awards Trophy Exhibit at Bass Pro Shops admire grizzly bear skulls, including the new World's Record grizzly taken by David F. Malzac. There were sixteen award-winning skulls from three species of bears and cougar on display for the public at Bass Pro Shops from May through June 2001.

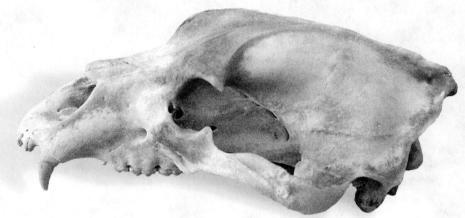

Photograph courtesy of Thomas M. Sharko

TROPHY STATS

▼ ▼ ▼ ▼ ▼

Category
grizzly bear

Score
26⁹/₁₆

Location
Anvik River, Alaska - 1999

Hunter
Thomas M. Sharko

Length of Skull
16⁶/₁₆

Width of Skull
10³/₁₆

GRIZZLY BEAR
Third Award - 26⁹/₁₆

▼ ▼ ▼ ▼ ▼ ▼ ▼ ▼

THOMAS M. SHARKO

Tom Sharko's grizzly hunt took place in late August 1999 in the region between St. Michael and Unalakeet, Alaska. After 14 days of hiking and glassing the area near the headwaters of the Golsolvia River with guides Duane Halverson and Jerry Austin the trio located what appeared to be a trophy boar on the morning of September 4th. Tom's .338 Winchester magnum loaded with 250-grain Speer Nitrex Glam Slam bullets dropped the bear at 125 yards.

After the 60-day drying period his bear was officially scored by Boone and Crockett measurer David Pawlicki in Cheyenne, Wyoming. The skull measured 16-6/16 inches long and 10-3/16 inches wide for a score of 26-9/16 inches.

Photograph courtesy of Jon D. Seifert

Both the lower canines were broken off and three of the upper incisors were hanging by a shred on this old grizzly taken by Jon D. Seifert. The boar was estimated to be 20 to 25 years old.

TROPHY STATS

▼ ▼ ▼ ▼ ▼

Category
grizzly bear

Score
$26^{7}/_{16}$

Location
Lone Mountain, Alaska - 2000

Hunter
Jon D. Seifert

Length of Skull
$16^{7}/_{16}$

Width of Skull
10

Photograph by Jack Reneau

Jon D. Seifert accepting his plaque and medal from Randy Byers, Chair of the Big Game Records Committee.

GRIZZLY BEAR
Fourth Award - 26⁷/₁₆

▼ ▼ ▼ ▼ ▼ ▼ ▼ ▼

JON D. SEIFERT

All hunting trips are special. Some for the quality, or quantity of game taken. Some for the grandeur of the scenery or the camaraderie; friendships made or strengthened. Still others for the hardships encountered and endured. Most often, hunts are a mixture of these elements. Experienced hunters don't expect perfection. The pieces of the puzzle are too numerous and the opportunity for poor weather, mishap or just plain bad luck too great. So it is the rarest of times when everything falls neatly into place culminating in the "perfect hunt." I was fortunate enough to have such an experience — the result of which was the harvest of one of the largest grizzly bears ever taken.

For 15 years my friends and hunting companions, Tim Crombie, Troy Auth and I had dreamed about hunting Alaska. Troy's first cousin, Rod Schuh, is one of the proprietors of R&R Guide Service operating out of Anchorage. Rod had encouraged Troy to bring his buddies up for a hunt for years, but school, work and family had always won out. Finally in the fall of 1998 the three of us decided the time was right and we booked a hunt for September 2000. We would be hunting bear and moose. The months passed slowly as we read books about the game we would be hunting. We watched videos, reviewed gear lists, and spent long hours at the range. Unfortunately, a few months before the trip, one of Troy's sons was diagnosed with a medical condition that required his attention. Troy's hunt would have to wait a season or two. My wife Tracey and daughter Rachel escorted me from our home in Pepin, Wisconsin, to the airport in Minneapolis. Tim and I boarded a flight bound for Anchorage on September 9, 2000.

I've always considered myself to be pretty lucky. Whether it's hunting whitetails, bear or turkeys back home in Wisconsin or meeting my lovely wife, things always seem to work out. But the next few days would be more than even a lucky man could expect. Skies were clear and at 30,000 feet we had a panoramic view of the Rockies from British Columbia over the Yukon and into Alaska. Once on the ground, Tim remembered that an old friend of his had moved to Anchorage ten years earlier — the last time Tim had seen him. His friend's name is John Hanson and Tim decided that, since we had a day before leaving for base camp, he'd give his friend a call. Turns out that John lived two blocks from our hotel. Better yet, he had the next day off and wanted nothing more than to give us a guided tour of the city. We video taped moose in the woods along the airport, and saw salmon and huge rainbow trout running in Ship Creek in downtown Anchorage. We picked up last minute supplies and made mental notes of all the hot spots to tour upon our return. John even invited us to his cabin north of Anchorage for a float-fishing trip if we had time after the hunt. So far so good; things would only get better.

The next morning the hotel shuttle dropped us off at R&R's hangar. The weather was poor — low ceiling, overcast and raining. Rob Jones, the other "R" in R&R Guide Service, was flying in from base camp this morning to pick us up. By mid-morning Rob had fought his way through the clouds and made it to Anchorage. Before the whine of the 206's engine had died, Rob leapt from the Cessna and greeted Tim and me. He was a man on a mission. There was no time for pleasantries or long conversation about our trip. The weather was bad. We had supplies to round up, a plane to load, and clouds to beat before they shut down the passes. Time is always precious to men who make their living during the short months of hunting season, but there was another reason for urgency. The day before, a moose-hunting client had spotted a big grizzly guarding a wolf-killed cow moose. If we could get through the Alaska Range (you don't go "over" the Alaska Range in a 206 Cessna) in time he might still be on the kill. Part of Rob's rush — I would be the only hunter in camp booked for grizzly.

We headed for Rainy Pass, which seemed appropriate as a steady drizzle streaked the windshield. Between mouthfuls of cold pop-tart that substituted for breakfast and dinner, Rob continually checked with other pilots in the area to determine if we would make the pass in time. We didn't. When we were close enough to see the V formed by the mountains guarding Rainy it looked like someone had opened the door to a giant steam-bath on a cold day — no chance. We had to backtrack. Rob figured Merrill Pass might be worth a try. It would mean flying the hour and a half back to Anchorage then swinging North. As we flew up the pass the slot narrowed around us. Rob kept easing the 206 closer and closer to the rock faces to the East while peering at the tiny triangle formed by the upper reaches of the pass and the clouds squeezing down against them. Finally I had to ask, "Aren't you getting a little close over here?" "Got to," Rob yelled over the drone of the engine. "If the clouds close the pass before we get to it, I'll need all the room I can get to turn this thing around. Look down there. Those are the guys who waited too long to make up their minds." Looking out the window we could see the mangled wreckage of at least a dozen light aircraft scattered along the upper end of the Pass. I had been intermittently taping the scenery, but since my wife was certain to see the video I choose not to add the wreckage to my little documentary. I might want to come back some day! We slipped through. For a few minutes the sun shone brightly on the backside of the Alaska Range illuminating the Big River Drainage, home to R&R Guide Service.

Once the plane hit the strip things didn't slow down. Half a dozen guides and packers converged on the Cessna like an Indy pit crew. Gear out; fuel in. First to welcome us to base camp was Scott Christian, "Chris." Once again this outfit proved to be all business. Chris instructed me to get my gear stowed in the comfortable two-man guest cabin set aside for Tim and me, pack my backpack, grab a bite to eat at the cook shack, and meet him back at the strip. The pilots would be flying Chris and me out to spike camp before dark. If we could get in on the Middle Fork of the Kuskokwim River northeast of Lone Mountain before dark, the big grizzly might still be on the kill the next morning.

Rob had traded the workhorse 206 for a nifty little 150 Super Cub on tundra tires. He and Billy Ray Vollendorf in his black 150 Cub, the "Dirty Bird," dropped Chris and me in on a gravel bar about two miles upstream from the moose kill. The "runway" was strewn with rocks the size of basketballs and other assorted river trash. Fortunately the pilots operate the Cubs like flying go-carts and we landed without incident. I helped Chris make camp, a comfortable four-man "bomb shelter" tent on the gravel bar. Chris has 25 years of guiding experience, 10 with R&R. If the "griz" was still there he assured me, we'd get him.

That night we cooked over a mountain climber's stove and Chris told me bear stories.

The air turned crisp as the sun went down and the cool breeze in the golden aspen harmonized with the flowing river. The anticipation, as I sat there cross-legged in the tent door under the glow of the Coleman was like a thousand opening mornings on my deer stand or in my duck blind. Somewhere out there in the fading light was a big boar grizzly guarding a kill, and in the morning we were going looking for him.

GRIZZLY BEAR
Fourth Award - 26⁷/₁₆

▼ ▼ ▼ ▼ ▼

JON D. SEIFERT

Before turning in, Chris lay a loaded Smith & Wesson Model 29 .44 Magnum on the gear box between his head and mine. "If you hear anything wake me up," he said. "Oh, you don't sleep walk or anything do you?" "No," I replied. "You have to be able to sleep before you can sleep walk!" I must have slept some but I was up two hours before the sun, ready to head out.

Chris was up too, making coffee and frying pop-tarts. "How far are we going to go before it gets light?" I eagerly inquired. The .44 was already in the breakfast chefs' shoulder holster. He smiled and said, "We don't go anywhere in grizzly country in the dark." After only a moment's reflection, that made perfect sense. We set out at first light.

The Middle Fork is a braided stream this time of year as glacial melt slackens. We made good time the first mile or so crossing and recrossing the thigh deep rivulets. We weren't certain where the bear was. We knew he was on the West bank just below a jack pine snag that jutted out ninety degrees over the river. The moose hunter and his guide had told us the kill was right on the bank and the bear had hauled up a big pile of sand and mud to bury his prize. They had walked to within one hundred yards before they spotted him lying ominously atop his cache. They didn't stick around; there's a lot of good moose country in Alaska. After the first mile or so we slipped into the brush on the East bank. We made half-moon loops out to the edge to glass as far down the opposite side as we could.

The brush was thick and it was tough going. We had all day though, and we were moving cautiously. As we passed two and a half hours into the stalk, it hit nine thirty. The sun was high and I figured the bear would feed at first light then lie-up until afternoon. Our strategy was to find the kill and set up an ambush from our side of the river. If that didn't work we'd look for him in the thick brush near the kill. I'm sure you understand why that was plan B. At about 10 a.m. and after a half dozen half-moons, Chris eased out to the edge of the river. He scanned up, down — then stopped. By this time I was certain that we were just looking for the kill, not the bear. All Chris said was, "He's on it." Boom! Instant adrenalin rush. I was light-headed as we maneuvered to the thin brush on top of a cut-bank. There he was, one hundred and fifty yards distant, diagonally across the river. He was standing on the kill, angled away from me. I was using a Ruger No. 1 Tropical in .375 H&H Magnum. I knew I would have to place my single shot perfectly and in part, that's why I opted for this rifle. I'd practiced hard and had the bruised shoulder to prove it. As I slid into a half kneeling position I found a stout sapling with a convenient fork. The bear looked huge through the Swarovski 30 mm tube. As the crosshairs settled behind his right shoulder I knew the angle should take the 300-grain Failsafe straight through the joint on the far side; lungs and a broken shoulder. It was classic "Field & Stream," the kind of mental image that rivals the covers of outdoor magazines. There stood a mammoth boar grizzly over a moose at just the right angle 150 yards away across a beautiful Alaskan river. The crosshairs had stopped moving. I squeezed the trigger. The recoil of a .375 H&H Magnum does not allow you to watch for bullet impact. When I reacquired the bear, he had spun back toward us and was favoring his left leg. He lunged up the bank on three legs and disappeared before I could reload. Chris called the shot. "Looked good, broke the offside shoulder." We waited. Chris had a smoke and I a chew. I dug out my video camera and did a bit for the folks back home. After a half-hour we crossed the river, and as we neared the place where we had last seen the bear, Chris provided one of the most memorable moments of my hunting life.

I had met Chris only 18 hours earlier. He didn't know me. I didn't know him. But standing on that gravel bar, for better or for worse, we were going to become a team engaged in some potentially very tricky business. "I'll go first," Chris said. I thought, so far I like this plan. "You follow 10 yards behind, move when I move, stop when I stop. I'll be looking for sign, you'll be looking for the bear. Look ahead of me 45 degrees on both sides then behind us. It's awful thick in there and he might try to backtrack on us." The thought of a wounded grizzly sneaking up behind me dissipated the enthusiasm I had first felt for the scheme. "If you see the bear," Chris continued, "don't yell, don't point, just shoot." As he gave these directions Chris was staring me straight in the eye as a man does when he wants to emphasize his point. "Don't yell, don't point, just shoot. I'll hit the ground at the shot and locate the bear. Got it?" I nodded and hoped the old bear was dead. We moved slowly up the bank. Chris was looking down for blood. My little prayer had been answered. The bear lay stone dead ten yards in.

He was a tough customer in bad shape. His spine was clearly visible, like someone had draped a bearskin rug over a sawhorse. His hipbones stuck out six inches. His hump was exaggerated and made his long frame look out of proportion. After the backslapping and hand shaking we looked him over more closely. His teeth were all but gone. Both lower canines were broken off and three of the upper incisors were hanging by a shred of gum. We later learned that he had an abscessed molar in his upper jaw. The infection had eaten a quarter-sized hole through his palate and into his sinuses. This torment must have been with him for several years. As if that wasn't enough he was missing a toe and a testicle. The Fish and Game biologist in Anchorage estimated his age to be between 20 and 25.

His hide measured nine feet from front paw to front paw and was eight-feet two-inches long making him close to a nine-foot square interior grizzly. We taped the skull at 10 inches wide and 17 inches long, bottom jaw included. The official score was 26-7/16 points; tied for 13th all-time as of the 23rd edition of the Boone and Crockett records book.

We made the long hike back to camp and settled in with a few "Swift River screwdrivers," vodka and Tang. The first day of my hunt was over, but not the trip by a long shot. I also took a decent moose and a nice black bear.

Like I said, all hunts are special. I've hunted harder and not seen game. I've had opportunities and missed. I've spent days in the back of a truck snowed-in in the Bighorn Mountains of Wyoming. They are all good memories in their own way. This time everything came together. The timing of the hunt, the weather, the skill of the pilots and the guide, the wind, the quarry, and the shot. I'll remember these things as my "Perfect Hunt." ▲▲▲

Award Winning Moments...

Photograph by Jack Reneau

Jon Seifert with his grizzly skull (Fourth Award) at the 24th Awards Trophy Exhibit. The skull measured 16-7/16 inches long by 10 inches wide for a final score of 26-7/16.

Michael L. Ward and his hunting partner, George Pappas, located this bear near the end of their hunt on Aliulik Peninsula. The skull score 30-3/16 inches.

TROPHY STATS

▼ ▼ ▼ ▼ ▼

Category
Alaska brown bear

Score
$30^3/_{16}$

Location
Aliulik Peninsula, Alaska - 1999

Hunter
Michael L. Ward

Length of Skull
$18^5/_{16}$

Width of Skull
$11^{14}/_{16}$

ALASKA BROWN BEAR
First Award - 30³/₁₆

▼ ▼ ▼ ▼ ▼ ▼ ▼ ▼ ▼

MICHAEL L. WARD

I could not believe my eyes. I double-checked and it really was my name, and the address was correct. I was reading an Anchorage newspaper listing results of the recent drawing for Alaska permit hunts. I had just won a highly coveted Kodiak brown bear permit in the best area for trophy bears, the southern end of Kodiak Island. This was July of 1998 and the hunt was for the following spring, over nine months away. I felt like a kid again waiting for the opening day of duck season.

Another fortunate event occurred shortly thereafter when Dr. George Pappas from Denver called me. His son, a former co-worker with me as a biologist with the Alaska Department of Fish and Game in Dutch Harbor, told him about my bear permit. George loves bear hunting, particularly Kodiak Island. He asked me about my plans and who would accompany me. I told him my plans were not set but if he was interested in going, he was welcome to come along. Having hunted the same area six years previously, he was a wealth of information. He killed a huge bear with a 29-inch skull. His hunting story was published in the Boone and Crockett Club's *22nd Big Game Awards* book. Additionally, his picture is included in the eleventh edition of *Records of North American Big Game*. Yes, George was interested in accompanying me. Over the months we made many phone calls formulating our plans. My permit allowed 15 continuous days of hunting between April 1 and May 15. We would arrive in Kodiak on Sunday evening April 25, then check in with Fish and Game and fly out to camp on Monday morning.

This was not going to be a backpack hunt. George and I planned to stay at least 17 days; consequently, we wanted a comfortable camp. Instead of my usual Super Cub flight, I chartered Peninsula Airlines Grumman Goose to fly us to camp. This is a large amphibious plane that can carry nearly a ton of gear. We would be fully loaded when we took off.

After an interminable wait, April 24 arrived. I left my homestead near Tok, Alaska, early for the five-hour drive to Anchorage where I would pick up George at the airport. We visited some friends and did some packing in preparation for our flight to Kodiak the next evening.

Winter ran late on Kodiak in 1999. Lakes remained frozen with lots of snow on the ground, not typical for late April. Advice to leave snowshoes behind proved a big mistake. I was unable to borrow a pair but did manage to purchase emergency shoes that pilots carry as part of their survival gear.

Monday morning dawned clear and calm. At 8 a.m. we checked into Fish and Game and then proceeded to the airport for our flight to camp. At 11:00 we took off on the hour flight south to a small bay. The day was gorgeous. Clear blue skies with snowy mountains of Kodiak Island and the Alaska Peninsula to the north and west, and calm blue waters of the North Pacific Ocean to the south and east. Rugged Kodiak Island was spectacular! There is nowhere as pretty as coastal Alaska on a clear day. We unloaded our gear and the plane was off. The rest of the day was spent setting up camp. Kodiak winds are notorious for shredding tents. We used George's eight-man dome tent, double or triple guying each of the numerous tie-off points.

Toward evening we spotted two people walking along the beach. As they neared our camp we

Photograph courtesy of Michael L. Ward

View of the ocean from the hunters camp on the beach. The wind blew for days and only let up after the author took his bear.

greeted them. It was the guide who operates out of that area and a client. They were packing a bear hide taken the previous day. It was a large well-furred male that green scored just short of the Boone and Crockett minimum. They had hunted hard for 13 days seeing few bear.

Sleep came hard to me that night; I was too excited. Red foxes were breeding and their screams could be heard throughout the night. Toward dawn the wind came up and by 8 a.m. it was blowing a gale. It was to be our constant companion for the rest of the hunt. Southern Kodiak Island is wide open, with treeless wind-swept rolling hills and a spine of mountains. We ate a good breakfast and were out early. A long day of hunting produced a sighting of one bear at long range. The wind was fierce, at least 70 knots. We hid from it most of the day, spending long hours glassing.

The second day was pretty much a repeat of the first, very strong winds making hunting difficult. A sow and two cubs were spotted at long range. The snow line was at about 900 feet and very few tracks were visible. It appeared few bears were out of their dens yet. This would correspond to what the previous hunters had seen.

We decided to change tactics the next day. We would hunt up in the mountains in the area George had taken his bear. The wind had switched directions and was now out of the west, again at a fierce 70 knots. We followed an old bear trail used for many years and by noon we arrived at a good vantage point just below snow line to glass for the rest of the day. We hid behind car size boulders daring to stick our head up into the raging wind to glass as long as we could stand it. I cannot over-state how fierce the winds were. After about three hours George looked up, and on the mountain right above us about 1,000 feet was a bear digging roots. We sized him up and decided he was very large and un-rubbed with long hair blowing in the wind. I decided to circle back downwind and climb up to him. A large boulder was my goal. It would shelter me from his view during the half hour stalk and allow me a good rest for a shot at about 100 yards. The harsh wind was now my ally; it remained constantly in my face.

The bear was intent on digging out something and he was not looking around. Climbing the steep mountain was fatiguing. As I closed to within ten feet of the boulder I felt the wind on the back of my neck for just an instant. I ran to the boulder, peeked around, and was horrified to see the bear, with his nose up, moving away. After over three hours of constant wind I had been betrayed. He was speeding up as I chambered a round and I quickly threw a shot at him as he disappeared around the mountain. It was a foolish off hand shot. I was tired and unsteady. After over an hour of searching his tracks in the snow I was relieved to find no blood. A fortunate miss, as a wounded bear traveling long distance would have been the most likely result if I hit him with a bad shot. I was also very sad. It was a very large bear with a beautiful hide. I was afraid it would be my only chance at a great bear.

We glassed a few more hours before returning to camp. A delicious lamb chop dinner livened my spirits. Hunting conditions may be harsh, but at least we were eating well — no freeze-dried food on this trip.

The next morning we arose early and headed north to hunt a large valley that looked like good bear habitat. The valley was ringed by steep snow covered mountains that would provide good denning areas. Very few bear trails could be seen in the snow, however. A creek meandered through the valley floor, terminating in an estuary at salt water. This would provide good early season food in the form of grass and roots. Winter-killed deer could be found on the flats. We glassed from a knob most of the day. The west wind was still howling. I literally threw myself to the ground to keep from being blown down the hill. A young bear that spent about an hour roaming the flats was spotted early. It was fun to watch, and encouraged us. Spring bear hunting on Kodiak Island involves long hours of patient glassing. This is the breeding season. Large males roam widely in their search for a mate. Winter snow has knocked down the luxuriant summer vegetation allowing excellent glassing over expansive terrain. We did spot another medium-sized bear before returning to camp for dinner, after which I climbed into the hills behind camp and glassed the flats to the south. The hills trailed off to the ocean about two miles away. A few deer, survivors of the hard winter, and a fox kept me entertained until dark.

We were on the same knob enduring the same raging west wind on the fifth day. George quickly spotted two bears, one chasing another, far to the south near the ocean. This is the area where the previous hunter took his bear. These bears appeared to be a large male chasing a female. They soon moved out of sight heading up into the foothills. Shortly I spotted another bear, nose down like a bird dog, following their trail. This bear also quickly moved out of sight. This was very encouraging. Bear were becoming more abundant as the hunt progressed. After a few more hours of glassing we returned to camp for lunch. I decided to hunt up in the hills where the bears headed while George remained to work around camp. Toward evening I spotted two bears, presumably the same courting couple, near where we had last seen them. The third bear was not seen. Possibly there was a fight and one was run off. They were moving slowly, allowing me to approach to about 500 yards. The larger bear appeared to be a medium-size male that was rubbed. They slowly moved out of sight over about an hour while I enjoyed watching them. The smaller, presumably female, bear would not allow the larger bear to get close to her. Returning to camp at dark I was again treated to one of George's lamb dinners. We discussed the next day's hunt and decided on the area where the previous hunter made his kill.

There was a diminishment in the wind that evening, still a gale from the west but only about 40 knots. We hiked south about two miles to a small range of hills where we spent much of the day glassing from the highest point. Remains of the previous kill could be seen. Eagles and a fox took turns feeding on the meager remnants of what a week previously must have been close to half a ton of brown bear carcass. The gray whale migration was now in full swing around Kodiak Island. From our vantage point we would see three or four whales an hour swimming past on their way north to summer in the Bering Sea and Arctic Ocean. I was getting drowsy in the mid-day sun when all of a sudden George said, "There's a bear." About 400 yards away stood an enormous bear. He was absolutely huge, with a belly to match. He was pestering a female that would not let him get near her. She was much more aggressive toward him than the female I observed the previous day. He cornered her at the edge of a 100-foot cliff with jagged rocks below where she whirled on him, snapping at his face, and then agilely eluded him. He stood over twice her height and was also completely rubbed; no trophy here, except for the potential World's Record skull. I decided not to take him. This hurt George.

He really wanted me to get this bear. The two quickly moved off. We attempted to follow, but never did see them again.

We returned to camp for an early dinner and then hunted behind camp until dark. No more bears were seen that day. We discussed the next day's hunt and decided to climb into the mountains again.

The next day the wind conditions kept us from going to the mountains we planned to hunt and ended up not seeing a bear the entire day. We were starting to feel a little discouraged.

A big break came during the night when the wind switched around to a west wind. This allowed us to hunt the area we considered most productive, the mountain where George killed his bear and I missed a bear. A big breakfast of bacon and eggs started our day. We were then off on the three-hour climb into the mountains. A comparatively calm 50-knot wind blew into our faces. We posted ourselves on a rock affording the best visibility and settled in for a long day of glassing. In early afternoon George spotted a good-sized bear below us, probably about a nine-footer, moving along slowly at 300 yards. George strongly recommended I quickly go down and kill it. I looked it over. He was obviously rubbed. George reminded me we were running out of time and not seeing many bears. "I'd rather go home without a bear than kill one I would not be proud of," was my reply. "That may well be the case," was his.

The next morning we rode out a biting sleet storm and stayed in camp to set up another dome tent. We did hunt close to camp in the afternoon, but no bears were spotted.

The wind gradually switched around to a north wind during the night. We decided another try in the mountains was in order. We took our customary promontory to glass from throughout the day. In early afternoon I decided to take a hike and look over some country to the south. After a couple hours I returned and continued to glass with George. All of a sudden he spotted a bear. It was on the mountain across a narrow pass from us. I looked up in time to see it stand, stretch, yawn, and then lay back down. I got a good look at the hair on its back and side blowing in the wind. He was not rubbed, and a good-sized bear. He was lying on a bench high up on a steep mountainside above us about 250 yards away. It seemed tired and we felt it had just emerged from its den. We wanted to get closer but to do so meant dropping down off our mountain into the pass. My only shot was to shoot from where we were. He was lying lengthwise to us with only his head and shoulder tops visible. He looked small through my scope. The wind was also roaring out of the north crosswise to us at about 50 knots, a very difficult shot. I set up a padded rest and waited, planning to shoot when he stood.

After about 45 minutes I was getting cold. Temperatures were in the high 30s and I was exposed to the wind. I was afraid I would start shivering and miss my shot. About every five minutes the wind would stop for 5 or 10 seconds. I told George my predicament and that I planned to shoot during the next lull. We got ready. Sure enough the wind stopped a couple of minutes later, at which point I said, "Here we go, George" and fired. It was a hit. Just when I thought he was finished he arose and staggered off behind a rock, apparently dying. I now had the formidable task of climbing up a snow chute and skinning out the bear. This would obviously be an individual effort as I would not ask George to attempt the climb. I was crossing the pass to assess the situation when all of a sudden the bear appeared, staggering through the snow, obviously hit hard. He was crossing in front of me at about 50 yards as I fired twice more at his lungs. Down he went for the final time. As I approached I had the feeling that he looked rather small. I poked his rump repeatedly with the muzzle of my rifle, then in the eye. There was no movement. Still, I was afraid to touch him. He wasn't small anymore, but I finally mustered up the courage to touch him. His hide was the most luxurious I had ever seen.

His claws were white and his head was massive. He was flawless, a perfect bear. I said a prayer of thanks to God for allowing me to kill such a magnificent animal.

ALASKA BROWN BEAR
First Award - 30³/₁₆

▼ ▼ ▼ ▼ ▼

Michael L. Ward

George waded across the thigh deep snow and after a few minutes of joyous backslapping and admiring the bear we decided pictures were in order. It was now 6 o'clock, not enough time for us to skin out the bear and return to camp. We rolled it onto its back. I worried the thick hide and huge body would insulate it from the snow and keep it from cooling down. I decided to skin open the belly and down the sides to allow it to cool as best it could. I left some stinky socks near the bear and relieved myself around it in the hope of discouraging any scavengers.

I awoke the next morning to beautiful, calm blue skies. It is as if killing the bear also killed the wind. For the first time in 12 days it was pleasant to be out. I left camp with my pack and skinning gear. George loaned me his .44 magnum revolver to carry in place of my rifle. The farther I walked into the hills the more I regretted that decision. I felt nervous walking those hills in the presence of large bears without a rifle, especially as I neared the kill, which a bear may have been claiming.

Once I finally had the hide off I was then even more in awe of the bear. What a physical specimen. Not fat as you think of a large bear. It was all massive muscle. There were some puncture wounds in one leg that were festering, probably from a fight the previous fall. The neck was nearly three feet in circumference. It took me seven hours to finish the skinning chores and I was tuckered out. I tried to load the hide and head back to camp, but kept bogged down in the deep snow. I would have to return the next day with more cord and my snowshoes. I returned to camp with only the head. George was amazed when he saw it. His bear scored high in the Boone and Crockett book and he said this one was bigger. We did a very rough measurement without calipers of about 12 inches by 19 inches or 31 inches, which was larger than the current number one bear. I was excited but worried as I still had an unprotected bear hide in the hills to pack out. I gathered up my snowshoes and the cord I needed to attach it to my pack the next day.

After a long struggle I finally got the hide back to camp. The stretched measurement was 11 feet claw to claw and 9 feet nose-to-tail for a squared size of 10 feet. I added 50 pounds of salt to the hide, and covered it with a tarp to keep off the light rain while we waited the last two days for our trip back to Anchorage.

After our plane ride back we checked into a hotel and cleaned up before heading to Fish and Game for the mandatory check out. When John Crye at Fish and Game saw my bear he said, "This may be the one we've been looking for." A few years previously, a very large bear was tranquilized, sampled, measured, and a number tattooed in its lips. A very rough measurement of the skull with, of course, the hide still attached indicated that it was larger than the current number one bear. John proceeded to measure my bear. While not the big one, it still was the fifth largest bear sealed by Fish and Game at 30.188 inches, since they started record keeping in 1954. John also discovered that my bear had also been sampled, as he found a number tattooed in the lips. A year latter I received a letter from him telling me that the premolar tooth he extracted was sectioned and found to be 12 years old.

I will always wonder if the huge bear we saw was the big one, a new World's Record. Body wise, he was substantially bigger than my bear. Still, I would not trade my bear with its flawless hide for the World's Record skull. ▲▲▲

Photograph courtesy of John E. Schuchart

The author took this boar from 150 yards across a deep ravine after waiting several hours for the bear to wake up and retreat to a safe distance away from the edge.

TROPHY STATS

▼ ▼ ▼ ▼ ▼

Category
Alaska brown bear

Score
$29^{14}/_{16}$

Location
Uyak Bay, Alaska - 1998

Hunter
John E. Schuchart

Length of Skull
$18^6/_{16}$

Width of Skull
$11^8/_{16}$

Photograph by Jack Reneau

John E. Schuchart accepting his plaque and medal from Randy Byers, Chair of the Big Game Records Committee.

BOONE AND CROCKETT CLUB'

ALASKA BROWN BEAR
Second Award - 29¹⁴/₁₆

▼ ▼ ▼ ▼ ▼ ▼ ▼ ▼

John E. Schuchart

The first thing I saw upon arrival at the airport in Anchorage was a beautiful mounted 10-foot plus brown bear, encased in glass, along with a record book Sitka blacktail deer. It was truly a sight to behold. Little did I know that I'd soon see another bear of similar stature, but this one would have a pulse. I had planned this hunt for nearly three years, and the time had finally come. My weeks of training spent backpacking with bricks and target practicing were about to be put to the test. Kodiak Island was just a short plane hop away from Anchorage. The date was April 15, 1998. I had chosen the early hunt of the spring season because larger bear tend to leave their dens first, and hide quality is better with minimal rubbing. The outfitter I selected, Alaskan Trophy Safaris, has a long history of successful bear hunting on Kodiak, and this

The Sleeping Giant

island has more bears in Boone and Crockett's top 100 than any other area.

Once on the island, I was introduced to my guide, Kreg, and packer, Billy. Billy had just completed guide school and this was his first taste of brown bear hunting. Kreg, on the other hand, had over a dozen years under his belt. Looking back, both did an outstanding job in all areas. I shared base camp on Uyak Bay with another hunter from my home state of Wisconsin, Tim Neitzel, along with his guide, also named Billy.

The scenery was spectacular, and wildlife abundant. Seals swam in a nearby cove, while deer and fox cruised the shoreline. We wasted no time glassing the far away hills in search of small brown dots moving in the snow. On our second day it began to rain, and rain it did for five straight days. We stayed close to base camp and continued to glass. On the third day I spotted a large group of mountain goats and would see many more as the hunt progressed. The turbulent weather seemed to keep the bears inactive as only a few small bears were sighted.

Finally, on the fifth day, the weather cleared and the wind shifted. Kreg, Billy, and I were now able to make our way to spike camp several miles inland from the bay. Midway on our long hike upstream, we came upon an eight-foot brownie making his way up an embankment. I had my heart set on a nine-foot plus bear, but even the immense size of this juvenile had my adrenaline flowing. Once at camp, we set up the tent and had dinner. Later that evening, I videotaped a deer as it made its way to within a few yards of us.

The next morning, on our sixth day, Kreg decided to take us to high ground to do some spotting. He had luck in the past with this valley that now surrounded us. As anyone who has hunted Kodiak will tell you, the terrain can be one of your biggest adversaries — second only to the unpredictable weather. Hip boots are worn almost exclusively, due to constant stream crossings, and deep, wet spring snow. Although a necessity, they also make for difficult walking up and down hills through thick walls of tag elders. Once at the top, Kreg immediately set up his sporting scope while Billy and I scanned the surroundings with our binoculars.

Not more than 30 minutes had passed before Kreg announced he had spotted movement far

Photograph courtesy of John E. Schuchart

The author's packer, Billy was fresh out of guide school and was working on his first Alaska brown bear hunt. Here he glasses for bears across a small glacier lake.

below. Another half-hour later, he confirmed that a very nice boar was in his sights, and a lone female was sunbathing nearby. The wind was in our favor, so we decided to waste no time. Between our quarry and us lay over a mile of snow, gulches and super-thick brush. The snow was so deep that snowshoes were required. To date, my experience with these oversized shoes was nonexistent, and it was obvious by my struggles. Several hours were spent trudging clumsily along, taking them off, then putting them on, going up and down ravines — all the while praying my bear would stay put. As it turned out he would do just that and then some.

As we drew closer the terrain began to open up. The wind was still in our favor, but I feared being spotted. At one point we were less than 150 yards from the female, in plain view, as she lay snoozing on her back. But we had no choice, as there was no other way to approach. Onward we went until finally, exhausted and sweating, we reached a knoll overlooking the bear. He, too, was taking his afternoon nap. The distance was 80 yards. I figured my time had come and my heart began to race. Kreg quickly put a damper on my intentions by pointing out that our bear was bedded down at the edge of a cliff, and a deep ravine separated him from us. Evan a lethal shot could leave our trophy with enough adrenaline to crawl to the bottom of this very deep crevice. Rappelling back up with 160 pounds of cape and skull would be out of the question.

So we decided to play the waiting game. The first hour passed without event, then the second. As the sun made its way to the west, the temperature began to drop. I asked Kreg if a headshot should be considered. He declined my offer, and I later found out why. After over three hours of waiting, the bear got up only twice — just long enough for a quick stretch. Meanwhile, the female had decided to stroll out of sight.

With darkness rapidly approaching, we had to make some decisions. Should we quietly return to camp, with hopes that he'll be there tomorrow? Or, should we give the bear a wake-up call, and hope that he retreats up the glacier,

ALASKA BROWN BEAR
Second Award - 29¹⁴/₁₆

▼ ▼ ▼ ▼ ▼

JOHN E. SCHUCHART

offering a safe shot, and not into the ravine? It was obvious we were looking at a very large bear. It didn't take long for us to decide that we were not about to let this big bruin out of sight. So, as Billy operated the video camera, Kreg and I began to scream and wave our arms as though we were castaways on a life raft.

This was not the scene I had envisioned during my three-year wait for this hunt! Here we were actually hoping that this Kodiak brown bear would see us and begin its retreat! For the first 30 seconds there was no reaction. The wind was strong, carrying both our voices and our scent directly away from the bear. We then increased our volume, which eventually drew his attention. Slowly he stood up, took a good look at us, and began to walk uphill, just as we had hoped. Meanwhile, I propped my backpack into the snow, preparing a gun rest. As the monster made his huge strides, I began to appreciate his immense size. The crosshairs of my scope had no trouble locating his mammoth shoulder. At 150 yards he stopped to take a final look at those three noisy figures above. Kreg decided that the bear was far enough away to avoid ending up in the crevice, and gave me the go ahead to shoot. My .340 Weatherby roared, and the bear instinctively turned to bite the point of impact — his right front shoulder. As he did, he lost his balance and he broke into a roll, stopping just a few yards from the cliff's edge. I fired another round as he rolled and in a matter of seconds, it was all over.

It would be the next morning before we would make it over to our trophy. Once there, I was amazed by its immense size. Kreg confessed that he knew yesterday it was an extraordinary animal, but he didn't want to get me excited! This also explained why he didn't want me taking a headshot. A damaged skull cannot be scored properly. After pictures and caping, we headed for spike camp where we spent the night. I could hardly sleep knowing that we had successfully hunted one of the most spectacular and majestic species in North America — a lifelong dream had come true.

The next day we headed back to Uyak Bay. We took turns packing out the oversized cape, which cracked the backpack frame. Once at main camp, Kreg squared the hide at a whopping 10 feet 6 inches. Alaska Fish and Game estimated the bear to be 16 years old. He was no doubt the dominant bear in the area, and there's no doubt another giant has since taken over his domain. In the words of Dennis Harms, master guide and owner of Alaskan Trophy Safaris, "One of the classics of all hunts is a brown bear hunt on Kodiak Island." I've done a fair share of big game hunting and must admit he's right on the money. This hunt ranks among the best in my book, and I feel blessed to have been fortunate enough to have encountered such a spectacular representative of this great beast. ▲▲▲

Photograph courtesy of Larry G. Collinson

After crossing countless rivers and sloshing through mud fields, Larry was finally within shooting distance of this big boar.

TROPHY STATS

▼ ▼ ▼ ▼ ▼

Category
Alaska brown bear

Score
$29^5/_{16}$

Location
Seal Islands, Alaska - 1999

Hunter
Larry G. Collinson

Length of Skull
$18^6/_{16}$

Width of Skull
$10^{15}/_{16}$

ALASKA BROWN BEAR
Third Award - 29⁵/₁₆

▼ ▼ ▼ ▼ ▼ ▼ ▼ ▼ ▼

LARRY G. COLLINSON

I decided to go on an Alaska brown bear hunt with my long-time friend and hunting buddy Dan Montgomery with Alaska Trophy Adventures from Wasilla, Alaska. Dan personally guided me on a Dall's sheep hunt back in 1997. The sheep hunt was an eight-day, hard and treacherous trip up and down the mountains until I got my 40-1/2 inch ram. After that great experience I knew what to expect for my Alaska brown bear hunt with Dan and his guides. I had to be in excellent physical shape. The hunt was booked for October 1999. The closer to October the greater my anticipation of hunting the ultimate big bear became.

Dan sent me a list of hunting clothing and gear to bring on the hunt, which was somewhat different gear than on previous hunts. The list included items like neoprene chest waders with Army swamp boots (two sizes over my normal size), along with a pair of hip waders. He said the hunt was going to be in muskeg and lots of water. He also told me that walking in these conditions gets old very quickly. After that statement I knew I'd better be in even better physical shape.

I left Phoenix the morning of September 27th for Anchorage, and as I sat in my seat on the plane, I started thinking about the hunt. I was getting more and more excited as each hour passed. Finally, I arrived in Anchorage, and after spending the night I was off to Port Heiden on the Alaska Peninsula. This is where I meet Dan along with three other hunters. All of us started waiting for Dan to haul us into base camp with his Super Cub. The Super Cub could only carry one hunter and his gear at a time. We all collected our luggage and piled it up outside one of the terminal buildings and waited for our ride to base camp.

By the time Dan finished hauling drinking water and fuel for the plane it was about dinner time when we all had made the trip to camp. The flight in was exciting as Dan showed me some of the country between Port Heiden and base camp. From the air we did see one good sized bear and a few head of caribou. As we arrived at camp we landed right on the beach, "pure black sand" with the Bearing Sea to our north and camp a few hundred yards off the beach behind a huge berm. Dan and I tied the plane down for the night and then he took me into the cook tent to introduce me to all the other hunters and guides. Two of the hunters, Dan Lilja and Dick Jacob, I knew from my previous sheep hunt. Dan and Dick both had successful hunts with Dan and after all the introductions and a big camp supper, we all turned in for the night.

The next day was the 29th of September; we all hung around camp and got to know each other. Dan was already flying hunters and guides into their fly camps while a few of us decided to check our guns, making sure they were still sighted in properly.

As we returned back to camp from shooting, Dan decided it was time to finish pairing everyone with their guides. There were to be two hunters with one guide in each fly camp. Dan teamed me up with Dan Lilja since we already knew each other from our previous sheep hunt.

Our guide was Shawn Andres. Dan and I already knew Shawn as he was our taxidermist from Missoula, Montana.

Shawn was the first to fly into our hunt location the next day with the camp gear and tents to setup, while Dan flew Dan Lilja and me into camp. Shawn was glad to finally see us because when he landed in camp there was a good size bear just a few hundred yards away, which we all saw later that evening as we were glassing over the country. Finally, we were in our fly camp, all set up and waiting for opening day the following morning. Our camp consisted of two tents, one bomb shelter type for sleeping and the other a smaller tent for stowing our gear. There was a six-foot high berm to our west separating us from the lake where we would fly out using Dan's other Super Cub with floats.

The night before opening day Dan Lilja and I flipped a coin to see who would be the shooter the first day. My partner won the toss and would get the first shot opportunity.

Opening morning we were all up in the dark having hot oatmeal and coffee. We were glassing from the berm before it was light enough to see — that's how excited and anxious we were. Just as it was getting light Shawn found a big bear fishing for salmon in the river about one mile to the southwest of our camp. It was a good size bear and we were getting ready to leave and go after him. We were doing a final glassing of the whole area when we saw Dan Montgomery already heading for the bear from his camp, which was about the same distance to the bear as our camp, only they were coming at him from the east. Since Dan and Dick were already after this bear we decided to let them try and get him. Shawn said it was still early and we should keep glassing for another bear. I can remember hearing Dick's first shot and watching his bear turn, spin and splash in the water so hard I could see the water flying in the air. There were more shots, and the first bear in Montgomery's camp was down.

The next day it was my turn to shoot. We did the same thing, got up on the berm and glassed and glassed. We did see a couple of bears, either too small or a long ways off going away from us.

After seeing bear traveling along the river to the east and going away from us we decided to leave camp and walk to the river and hunt those areas. We were getting tired after a couple of days of walking in several inches of water and around lakes. We never did reach the big river Shawn wanted to get to, but we did make it to a smaller river with lots of fresh bear tracks along its banks.

It was four days into the hunt when we spotted a bear that looked better than eight feet working his way down a small river about one mile from camp. Dan Lilja said he would take him, so Shawn and Dan left camp to go after the bear. I stayed back to keep glassing the bear and give them hand signals if he changed his direction.

I was glassing the bear watching him feeding along the small river bank and I could tell that Dan was going to intercept the bear just perfectly. I was standing there watching them in the scope and I could hear sounds like geese taking off the water. I didn't look or pay too much attention to the sound. Then I started thinking it's sure taking those geese a long time to get airborne. I looked in the direction of the sound to see that what I was hearing was a sow and two cubs running straight toward me in the water. I saw the bears and said to myself, "I have my gun in the tent about 15 feet away." I ran and got my gun out of the tent then ran back to the berm; just as I got to the top of the berm the sow spotted my movements. She stopped, stood on her hind legs and looked huge. She sniffed the air, picked up my scent, turned and never stopped running until she and her two cubs reached a small alder patch about one mile away. I couldn't believe that they could run that fast for such a long time. My heart finally stopped pounding in my chest and I started to glass again for Dan

ALASKA BROWN BEAR
Third Award - 29⁵/₁₆

▼ ▼ ▼ ▼ ▼

LARRY G. COLLINSON

and his bear. I watched him get into position just in time for the bear to come into the desired area in which he wanted the bear. I heard one shot and Dan had his bear.

The next morning we were admiring Dan's trophy and glassing for a bear for me when I saw some movement off to my left. I put up my glasses to see two wolves chasing a bull caribou. The caribou ran into a lake a few hundred yards from us and swam down the center of the lake and onto the shore on the other side. The wolves started around the lake on our side and got within 120 yards of us. They finally spotted us, turned and never looked back. We didn't have wolf tags, or there would have been a couple of tagged wolves in camp.

Later that day Dan came in with the plane to check on us and took Dan Lilja back out to base camp. Before leaving Dan asked me if I wanted to stay in this camp or if I wanted to move. I said we are seeing bears everyday, so I would stay a couple more days. We didn't have any luck the next couple of days, and Dan flew back to check-up on us. He said that I was the last hunter still to get his bear, and told me to pack my gear. I was moving back to base camp. That night Dan said that he knew of an area to hunt right out of base camp and the next morning he would take me out himself. He wanted Shawn to work on all the bear hides the next day since Shawn is the expert in that department. Dan and I left camp after breakfast about 7:30 a.m. We walked down the coast for the better part of an hour, then we cut inland toward a river.

We stopped to glass when we got to a high point of land before the terrain started to drop back off to the river. Dan spotted a bear about two miles away and pointed it out to me. He said it looks like a big bear with a black coat, which meant he was probably a boar. I found him in my glasses and thought he was huge considering how far away he was. It was raining as Dan studied how to get closer to the bear. He said we had to head for the river and get across before the tide got too high. We were about a mile from the river and I heard some noise in the distance. Dan and I stopped to find a couple of native guides and their hunters on ATVs coming over to us. Dan said he knew the native guides. One of the guides said with his native accent, "I guess we're all after the same bear?" Dan said, "Yep!" The native replied, "Well, I guess that's hunting," as he looked at Dan's backpack with the rubber raft in it. He also had an inflatable raft strapped to his ATV.

We separated, the ATVs heading up the river, Dan and I heading straight for the river. When we got there Dan just started wading into the water. The crossing was about 50 yards wide as I remember, and when we reached the half-way point the water was only inches away from the top of our neoprene chest waders. I was hoping the bottom didn't drop off anymore or I would be in trouble. Then I could see Dan was starting to show some distance between the top of his waders and the water. After reaching the opposite bank we had about 200 yards of silty, muddy river bottom to cross. Every step of the way the mud would stick to the bottom of our over-sized swamp boots. It was raining, but that wasn't the reason I was soaking wet. After all the hiking in chest waders I had worked up a pretty good sweat by the time I made it across the mud field.

When I caught up with Dan I asked him, "What do you think about all that?" He said "About what?" I said, "The native guides and their hunters." Dan looked at me and said, "I don't mind being in a race, but I don't like coming in second place!" He then said, "Let's go," as he turned and started walking very briskly toward the area where we last saw the bear. The rain now had turned into large, wet snowflakes. We kept hiking toward a high spot in the terrain where we last saw the bear, stopping to glass as often as the terrain would allow. About this time Dan spotted a different bear — a big sow, we thought, by her silver-blond color. We detoured around the sow and got back on track. When we finally got to where we thought the big bear was we started glassing for him again. We found him about a mile away and he was still on the move heading in our general direction. Dan said we'd better get a move on if we're going to have a chance for him. At about 11 a.m. we saw the bear again at 800 yards. The wind was in our favor; sort of a cross-wind from the bear to our left. Now the bear was getting closer and still coming toward us. All of a sudden we came across another small river and we had to drop down out of sight to find a place to cross the river. It only took a few minutes to find a place to cross and the water wasn't as high as our previous crossing. We climbed up on the other side to the height of the land and started looking for the bear. We glassed and glassed until Dan found another bear about two miles away. I said, "That couldn't be our bear. He couldn't travel that far in the time it took us to cross the river." Dan replied, "You never know." A couple of minutes passed and while I was glassing the tall grass I thought I saw something dark. I kept glassing and finally the dark object moved. I tapped Dan on his shoulder and said, "There he is." You could hardly see him laying in the tall grass feeding on the small white bulbs in the roots of the grass.

Dan checked with the rangefinder and said we were 200 yards from him and we should get a little closer. We started creeping very slowly toward him as he lay there feeding. When we got to within 120 yards Dan said, "This is close enough." We stood there for a while. The snow had stopped and there was a slight crosswind. After a half-hour Dan noted that bear could stay there feeding all afternoon so he said, "I will bark like a dog and the bear should get up." I got ready with my gun as Dan started his barks. The bear lifted his head a little and sniffed the air. Dan was glassing and I was ready to shoot. When he saw the bear's head he whispered to me, "Larry you want to shoot this bear," with an inflection meaning he is really big. Since the bear didn't smell or see anything, he lowered his head back down. After waiting a few minutes Dan said, "I'm going to bark again a little louder, this time the bear should get up." He told me to get ready and when the bear gets up, don't stop shooting until he stays down.

Dan barked much louder and this time the bear lifted his head, raised his right front shoulder and then he raised his hind end. It was like a house coming up out of the ground. Dan said, "Let him turn broadside and start shooting." Then the bear turned and stopped; I fired four times, but he still wasn't down. I reloaded as we ran toward the big bruin. He ran about 20 yards and jumped into a lake, probably to cool his wounds. We got to within 30 yards from him and started yelling and banging our rifle barrels together. The noise chased him out of the water and I finished him with one last shot. When we walked up to the bear I couldn't believe how big he was. I was so excited; I couldn't believe what just happened. It seemed to happen so quickly.

We shook hands, hugged each other and we were smiling from ear to ear. What a trip. I'll never forget it!

I'd like to thank Dan Montgomery, Shawn Andre, and all of Dan's personnel who helped to make my hunt an experience of a lifetime. What a wonderful hunt and what a prize — an official score of 29-5/16 points. ▲▲▲

Moments in Measuring...

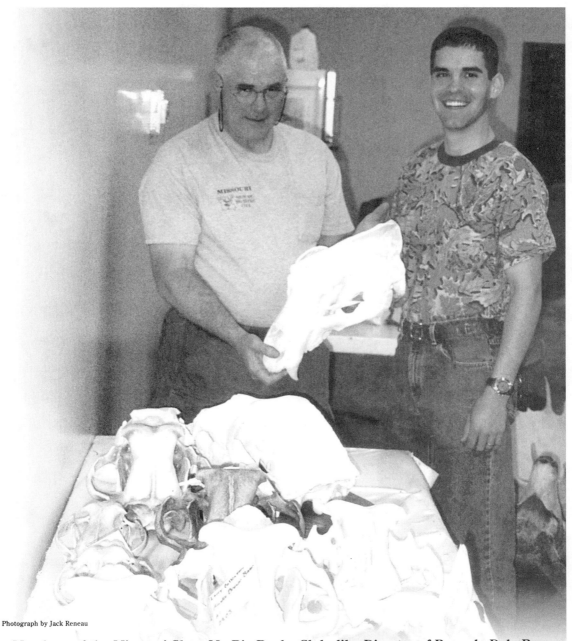

Photograph by Jack Reneau

Members of the Missouri Show-Me Big Bucks Club, like Director of Records Dale Ream and his son Brad pictured above, volunteered countless hours of their time for the 24th Big Game Awards Banquet in Springfield, Missouri.

Photograph courtesy of Peter K. Berga

Peter K. Berga connected with big bruin on the tenth day of his hunt on the Alaska Peninsula.

TROPHY STATS

▼ ▼ ▼ ▼ ▼

Category
　　Alaska brown bear

Score
　　$29^4/_{16}$

Location
　　Alaska Peninsula, Alaska - 2000

Hunter
　　Peter K. Berga

Length of Skull
　　$18^8/_{16}$

Width of Skull
　　$10^{12}/_{16}$

　　　　　　　　　　　　　　　　　　　　BOONE AND CROCKETT CLUB'

ALASKA BROWN BEAR
Fourth Award - 29⁴/₁₆

▼ ▼ ▼ ▼ ▼ ▼ ▼ ▼ ▼

PETER K. BERGA

My lungs were burning, my heart pounding, and my legs ached as I tried to get to the top of the knoll as fast as I could. Murch and I had been running through rough terrain for an hour trying to cut off the biggest brown bear I had ever seen. The knoll was the last high spot before the bear would cross a creek and possibly my last chance at getting a shot. Murch reached the top first, and I stopped fifteen feet below hoping to rest and catch my breath while we waited for the bear. Just as I was turning to face the anticipated crossing point Murch said, "There he is." The bear turned his head to look at us just as I looked at him. He had already crossed the creek and was heading for thick cover. Automatically I raised my Remington .338 Magnum and fired at the huge target 200 yards away.

My friend, David Oryall, and I started planning a brown bear hunt in late 1999 for the fall of 2001. The Alaska Peninsula alternates between fall hunts in the odd numbered years and spring hunts during even numbered years. By April 2000 we had decided on an unguided hunt out of King Salmon, Alaska. We picked an outfitter to fly us out; however, my plans changed almost overnight. My friend Mike Taylor called me in April and asked if I wanted to go brown bear hunting on May 9. I really needed a break from the long hours I was putting in at work so I decided to go. After all, I had the fall 2001 hunt to fall back on if I didn't have any success on this hunt.

Mike Taylor was living in Kenai, Alaska, at the time so he flew to Anchorage on May 9 where we both caught a Penn Air flight to King Salmon. We boarded a second Penn Air flight to the village of Pilot Point where we met up with our guide, Mike "Murch" Mroczynski of Wild Alaskan Guides, his partner and guide Marty Myre, and our pilot Doug Brewer of Alaska West Air. Marty was guiding a client from California on a separate hunt. Murch and Marty had already set up both camps and had spent several days scouting. After making sure our licenses and tags were in order, we spent the next several hours ferrying everyone to the camps. After arriving at camp Mike and I took a scouting trip while Murch fixed the evening meal. Hunting season didn't open until the next day (May 10th) but we thought we'd use the time to check out the territory. The weather was sunny with the temperature in the mid 40s all day and we hoped for more of the same. That evening over dinner we discussed what the general plan for the next ten days would be. We would get up at 6 a.m., eat, and be at our stand by 7 a.m. We planned to glass all day, or as long as weather permitted. Our hunting territory between the mountains was generally flat with knolls scattered around that rose ten to 25 feet in elevation. These offered good vantage points to glass the creek bottom and mountainsides. As we prepared for bed that first night, snow began to fall.

The wind picked up during the night and even though our tents were pitched in a low area, somewhat protected from the wind, the shaking of the tent woke me many times during the night. We awoke to fresh snow and high winds.

May 10 — We spent the first day about a half-mile from camp glassing and watching it snow sideways. Needless to say we hoped the weather wouldn't be this bad for the next ten days. I don't

On the fifth day of the hunt, the group was visited by Fish and Game personnel. They informed the hunters the area had experienced the worst winter in the last 20 years and felt the bears may still be denned up.

think we saw another living creature that day. A hot meal and warm sleeping bag helped me forget a miserable day one.

May 11 — The weather on our second day was much better. We sat in the same spot as the day before and we saw our first few bear, which looked to be seven-footers.

May 12 — We sat and glassed for several hours, then Mike and I decided to go down to the creek and look around while Murch stayed at the knoll to continue glassing. Even though the terrain was generally flat in the valley the elevation change to the creek bottom was probably 100 feet in places. Mike crossed the creek and headed for higher ground. I walked along the creek looking for bear sign. Pumice Creek is a creek in name only. Most of the creek is wide, deep and fast. It wasn't long before Mike shouted at me from across the creek and thirty feet above me. He had spotted a large (over eight-foot) bear upstream a half a mile or so that was heading down into the creek bottom. The problem was, he couldn't see if he headed upstream away from us or downstream toward us. After 30 minutes of waiting we knew he had headed upstream. Mike threw me his otter socks (small, packable waders that weigh less than a pound) and I waded the creek and met up with him. We climbed up to where we had seen the two seven-footers the day before and sure enough there were two sets of seven-inch wide tracks, which confirmed our seven-foot estimate. We went back and met up with Murch for lunch and finished out the day glassing without spotting any more bear.

May 13 — I started thinking that a trend was developing. We were seeing all of the bear before noon, and with the exception of the one bear in the creek bottom, they were generally six-to seven-and-a-half feet in size. Up until today we had been going to the same spot a half a mile west of camp. We spent this day about 1 mile east of camp with Mike and I watching the creek bottom and Murch glassing the mountain sides to our east and south.

ALASKA BROWN BEAR
Fourth Award - 29⁴/₁₆
▼   ▼   ▼   ▼   ▼
PETER K. BERGA

Also to the south, at the foot of the mountains was a large meadow that was very wet this time of year. It was about one mile by two-and-one-half miles in size and caribou were usually there every day. After lunch Mike had just dozed off when I noticed movement along a brush line about 250 yards away. It was a wolverine. He was working the brush line looking for eggs and getting closer. I watched him for 30 minutes, and at one time he was within 50 yards of me. The rest of the day fit the pattern — no bear in the afternoon.

May 14 — Sitting for 12 hours each day glassing wasn't bothering Murch nor I, but Mike was getting antsy. He needed to do some hiking and burn off some energy. We decided to hike toward the back of the valley. We took our time, stopping a lot to glass. We had only traveled about a mile from camp when I heard what appeared to be the faint sound of a helicopter. It didn't take us long to spot the mini-helicopter which circled us and landed. It was Fish and Game. We talked with the officer as he checked our licenses and tags and found out that the area had the worst winter in the last 20 years and he felt that a lot of the bears were still denned up. We thanked him for the information and continued on. We covered the six miles to the back of the valley by about 10 a.m. and climbed to about the 500 foot level to glass for the rest of the day. We saw the usual moose and caribou, but no bear. We stayed until 4 p.m. and then hiked back to camp.

May 15 — It poured down rain. There were no animals moving. We cut our hunting short that day.

May 16 — We went to our spot one mile east of camp. The morning was uneventful, but right after lunch Murch came and got Mike and me. He had spotted a bear. All three of us went back to Murch's vantage point. The bear had come down from the mountains to the south and came out of the brush between the mountains and the meadow. The body of the bear was all blond, but from the knees down on all four legs was dark brown. It looked to be seven and one half feet. It started chasing the caribou and it appeared the bear was stirring up the herd to see if there were any calves for taking. The speed at which the bear was running was phenomenal and I thought that after a few hundred yards it would have to stop and rest; not so. It proceeded to chase the caribou about a mile across the meadow and then a mile back before it gave up and started to walk back up the mountain. I think it was the most impressive thing I'd ever seen in the wild. Later that afternoon I did get a glimpse of what appeared to be a large bear in the brush on the side of the mountain about two miles to the south. I lost him in the thick brush and couldn't find him again. Those were the only two bears we saw after noon on the entire hunt.

May 17 — We saw a couple of small bears before lunch.

May 18 — Mike was in need of another hike so we spent the day hiking across the swampy meadow and up to the 2,000 foot level on the mountains to the south of camp. We didn't encounter any bears, but we did see numerous foxes and three more wolverines.

May 19 — We didn't see any bears on this day, and at dinner that night we talked about our plans for the next day. We decided we'd hunt until 9 a.m. and then start breaking camp. Our pilot was supposed to pick us up around noon. When we hit the sleeping bags Mike said he might just sleep in while Murch and I hunted. It sounded pretty tempting to me too.

May 20 — It turned out to be a pretty morning and I was glad I decided to hunt the last few hours. We decided to go to our spot a half mile west of camp. Murch was glassing the meadow and the mountains to the south while I scanned the creek bottom and beyond. I had just put down my binoculars when out of the corner of my eye I thought I saw a bear. I turned to look at the area where I thought the bear was and saw nothing. It was about a mile away and on the other side of the creek. Then, walking up out of a low spot about a mile away was the bear. He looked big with the naked eye and he walked big! As I brought up my binoculars I said to Murch, "Looks like we got one over eight feet." Murch swung around and took a quick look with his glasses. All he said was "Let's go!" The chase was on. It was 8 a.m. The bear was headed into the creek bottom so we immediately started angling toward him. We automatically assumed he would head upstream based on the direction he was traveling as he headed into the bottom. Murch was setting a fast pace. The ground we had to cover was rough as we started down toward the bottom through 5 to 10-foot tall brush. We realized we would have to change our angle of attack and headed back up through the brush. We tried being as quiet as possible, but also realized that speed was more important if we were going to catch him. We came out of the brush into a swampy area that made traveling very difficult, slow, and tiring. At times the water went above my knees, but Murch kept pushing us. We came to a clearing that gave us a shooting lane about 70 yards to the creek and we decided to wait a few minutes to see if he would cross the lane. After a few minutes we walked to the creek bank. We looked downstream — nothing. I turned and looked upstream and saw his massive rear end about 300 yards upstream, so we decided to circle around and try to cut him off. If he followed every curve of the creek it would give us enough time to do it. We headed for the only high spot left. It overlooked the creek where it turned 90 degrees to the south and where the bear would more than likely have to cross. As we ran this last mile I thought I was going to die before I got the chance to get off a shot. Somehow I made it to within 15 feet of the top of the knoll where Murch was when I heard him say, "There he is." I turned and saw that the bear had already crossed the creek. Without thinking I raised my rifle, aimed and fired. I heard the smack of the bullet hitting the bear. The bear's legs buckled but he didn't go down. I hit him two more times before he disappeared into the brush. Murch and I both stood and watched for any movement in the brush but saw nothing. It was 9 a.m. Murch decided to go back to camp to get Mike, our packs and skinning knives. I waited and watched. Ten minutes after Murch left I heard the bear let out his death groan. It was ten o'clock by the time Murch and Mike got back. It took us another hour to cross the creek and find my bear during which time he had already stiffened up pretty good. We took another hour to cut an opening in the brush big enough to be able to shoot some pictures.

After shooting a few rolls of film we started skinning. My first shot hit the bear in the right front shoulder and the 225-grain Swift A Frame bullet exited his left shoulder. While we were skinning the bear our pilot flew over and we contacted him by radio. Doug said he would bring Marty and his client back to Pilot Point first and then come back for us. We finished skinning the bear about 4 p.m., at which time the weather changed from sunny and 45 degrees to freezing, blowing and snowing. It took us two hours to pack everything back to camp. As it turned out we were all back to Pilot Point by 8 p.m. that night where we rechecked our measurements of the bear. The hide was nine feet ten inches from tail to nose. I had thought about sleeping in that morning and I hadn't even planned to go on the hunt in the first place. Someone once said that sometimes it's better to be lucky than good. ▲▲▲

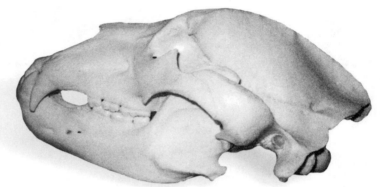

Photograph courtesy of R. Dale Ziegler

TROPHY STATS

▼ ▼ ▼ ▼ ▼

Category
  Alaska brown bear

Score
  $28^{13}/_{16}$

Location
  Uganik Bay, Alaska - 1998

Hunter
  R. Dale Ziegler

Length of Skull
  $17^{8}/_{16}$

Width of Skull
  $11^{5}/_{16}$

Photograph by Jack Reneau

R. Dale Ziegler accepting his plaque and
medal from Randy Byers, Chair of the Big
Game Records Committee.

ALASKA BROWN BEAR
Fifth Award - 28¹³/₁₆

▼ ▼ ▼ ▼ ▼ ▼ ▼ ▼

R. DALE ZIEGLER

After listening to different hunters talk about their trips to Kodiak Island, Alaska, I decided to take a trip of my own. I had been talking with Dick Rohrer of Rohrer's Bear Camp for a few years, and made arrangements for a Spring 1998 hunt. The 12-day hunt would be scheduled for May 2 through May 12 and we would be hunting Uganik Bay on Kodiak Island. I was thrilled to find that fellow hunters Dale Gaugler and Gene Bell would also be in camp with me. After filing all the forms and borrowing fellow hunter Jim Nyce's .338, all I could do was wait until the day of my departure.

Prepared for the hunt of a lifetime, we flew into the bay camp by floatplane where I met my guide, Alan Huling. Alan told me that while Gene and Dale would be hunting out of the base camp, he and I would hunt from a spike camp and do some backpacking.

We spotted the big bruin the first afternoon of the hunt, but darkness and wind prevented a decent stalk. The rain and fog fought us for four days. On the fifth day we spotted a nice nine-footer; however, the stalk ended in a missed opportunity. At this point my spirits were very low — two decent opportunities, but no bear.

It rained off and on for the remainder of the hunt, and my prospects looked very dim. I was hoping for a nine-footer or better, but time was running out. Dale had bagged a beautiful nine-footer already and Gene was seeing numerous bears.

I had made previous commitments before the hunt began that would prevent me from hunting the final day of the hunt, so I was determined to hunt the eleventh day. When the rain let up in the afternoon, Alan and I decided to climb the mountain one last time. Before we got set up, the skies let lose again.

We were completely soaked when a boar came into view at 600 yards. We waited until he bedded down about a half mile away and at 6:00 p.m. we began our stalk. At just under 200 yards, the bear spotted us. Alan had me use his rifle as a rest as I squeezed off the first shot. I heard the first bullet hit, but I heard Alan saying "Keep shooting." The boar finally stopped about 400 yards, just shy of some thick alders.

It wasn't until we got up to him that I saw just how big he really was. Suddenly the rain wasn't so cold. Before the stalk Alan judged him at around ten foot, but seeing him up close took my breath away. At camp he squared out at a solid ten plus.

I would recommend Rohrer's Bear Camp to any hunter who wants an excellent brown bear hunt. Camp facilities, equipment, and food were top notch. My guide never gave up on finding a big bear for me. I won't soon forget Kodiak Island or the monster bruin I brought home. ▲▲▲

Photograph courtesy of Robert B. Johnson

TROPHY STATS

▼ ▼ ▼ ▼ ▼

Category
Alaska brown bear

Score
$28^8/_{16}$

Location
Cold Bay, Alaska - 2000

Hunter
Robert B. Johnson

Length of Skull
$18^1/_{16}$

Width of Skull
$10^7/_{16}$

ALASKA BROWN BEAR
Honorable Mention - 28⁸/₁₆

▼ ▼ ▼ ▼ ▼ ▼ ▼ ▼ ▼

ROBERT B. JOHNSON

This was my third try for an Alaska brown bear. The first was in 1978, on a multi-species hunt in the Wrangell Mountains with master guide and outfitter Dennis Harms. We spent most of the hunt climbing glaciers. I shot a Dall's ram and a goat, but I had to do with little food and shelter for six days and endured other miseries. After the Wrangells, we flew to the Alaska Peninsula, first to King Salmon and then on to Pilot Point near Ugashik, where I shot a moose and a caribou. We saw bear, but they were not in season on the Peninsula.

My second bear hunt was in May of 1994 on a 72-foot "yacht" with guide Jim Rosenbruch. Accommodations aboard the boat were cramped, but at least you could get a hot meal and a shower after a day's hunting. We saw a few bears, and I shot at and solidly hit a three-legged brown bear on Admiralty Island; the bear immediately turned and disappeared into the impenetrable fir rain forest. Two guides and I tried to track him, but he couldn't be found in that jungle. I have been in mourning ever since, because to lose a wounded animal is very hard for me to accept.

In 1999, still determined to get a bear, I felt I needed a fresh start in a new area. When I ran into Dick Gunlogson at his booth at the FNAWS convention in Reno, it took only a few minutes of conversation before I handed him a deposit check for a bear hunt in the spring of 2000 on the Alaska Peninsula. Later, I joined Dick and his guides at the FNAWS banquet, at which Dick got the "Frank Golota Award" for being an outstanding outfitter. When I got back home, I told my hunting partner Chuck about my plans, and he spent the next six months talking Dick into taking him, too.

We landed in a dense fog at a village on an island offshore of Trio Peninsula, on the Gulf of Alaska side. On arrival, we soon realized we were weathered out of camp and that we'd be staying in Sand Point overnight. We found a B&B and a "restaurant," but not much else. At the B&B, we ran into another outfitter, Larry Rivers, who also outfits and guides on the Kamchatka Peninsula in Russia. I asked him about the rumor of giant bears in Russia, and he told us that it's just a myth — a "giant" Russian bear is a nine-footer. The biggest bears in the world, he said, are found on the Alaska Peninsula, where we were headed.

Dick Gunlogson picked us up the next day in his Cessna 206, and flew us to his David River base camp, about a half-hour flight across the Peninsula. His David River Camp is on the Bering Sea side of the Alaska Peninsula about 40-miles from where the Peninsula ends and the Aleutian Islands begin. The camp is a collection of sturdy plywood cabins (formerly wall tents), including comfortable bunk houses and a cook house. Upon our arrival Chuck and I trimmed our loads of gear, and were then ferried by Super Cub to separate spike camps in and around the Cathedral Valley — 15 to 20 miles south of David River.

My hunt took place out of one of Dick's camps called Pavlov, because it was located on the lower slopes of a 6,500-foot volcano of that name, and several miles away from the beach on the Gulf of Alaska side of the peninsula. The ground was wet, rolling tundra. Another hunter before me had shot a small bear at the camp, and was flown out as I arrived. The camp consisted of two small tents.

The author took this giant Alaska brown bear scoring 28-8/16 points just a few hundred yards from spike camp. It was the first time his guide Todd had successfully guided one of his hunters to a really big bear.

I was reasonably uncomfortable, because I couldn't stand up in the tent. My guide was Todd Lee, a good companion, and we found lots to talk about.

Our hunting for the first few days consisted of hours of glassing in the vicinity of the camp. We saw a wolverine, which approached within 30 yards, but only a couple of bears, at some distance. A smaller bear, which I assume was a sow, approached us and came within 100 yards of camp. After five days, Dick flew in with the Super Cub and said that Chuck had taken a bear in another camp to which I was being moved after Chuck had vacated. Chuck's bear was a beautifully haired bear with a hide squaring slightly under nine feet.

Chuck's former spike camp, "Scuddy," was luxurious by comparison to Pavlov. It was still full of choice food, which had been brought into camp by the hunter immediately prior to Chuck. It consisted of one large tent in which I could stand up.

Todd let me know that, to his regret, he had never guided a hunter to a really big bear, and that it troubled him. "Now we'll have to get you a ten-footer," I replied. The next day would be Sunday, May 21, which was my late sister's birthday. I told him I'd love to shoot a big bear to commemorate the day.

Sunday was our first day of hunting at the new location. We discovered that you could glass the whole valley from camp. The rain had stopped, but the wind direction was blowing from us right up the valley — not favorable for bears approaching us. Todd told me that he didn't expect much. We saw several large bear on the skyline, but they were moving away. About 2:00 p.m., I suggested we hike up the valley, although Todd told me that he was not optimistic because of the wind. It was tough going.

ALASKA BROWN BEAR
Honorable Mention - 28⁸/₁₆

▼ ▼ ▼ ▼ ▼

ROBERT B. JOHNSON

After a mile we looked back and saw a large bear descending into the valley behind us; of course, the wind was now perfect for stalking him. We walked as fast as we could, Todd remarking that it was a "big bear." We watched it explore a recent bear den on the hillside, and it kept descending on an angle while we were almost running to keep up with it.

We lost sight of the bear when it reached the bottom of the valley, and we hurried across a small patch of snow so that we would not be silhouetted against its brightness. Suddenly, the bear got up on its hind feet only 200 yards in front of us. Then he dropped to all fours and started to run away. I dropped to the kneeling position to shoot and touched off one round. The big bear disappeared at the shot. In an instant he was up and running again, but more slowly — I knew I'd hit him solidly. I remember shooting all of the seven .340 Weatherby rounds that were in my rifle and in my pocket. Todd joined in, and the bear was down. I found another round, approached and gave it the coup de grace. It was a giant boar!

It took us several hours and two trips to camp to skin the carcass and haul the hide and skull even though the camp was only a few hundred yards away across the creek.

Dick flew in later that afternoon to check on us, saw the bear, and took his measuring tape to its rear paw. "Ten and three quarter inches on the pad — a very big bear!" he said. The only hide measurement we had time to make was 12 feet across the front paws. When Todd was ferried into camp later with the hide, he told Dick that he'd measured the hide without stretching it, and that it had squared ten feet eight inches.

When we returned to Dick's David River Camp the giant bear was quite a sensation. It was, by far, the biggest bear of the season in that camp, and my preliminary measurement of the skull indicated that it would go almost 29 inches. The skull officially scored 28-8/16 points.

We had a jolly, liquid evening in camp, and our Aleut neighbors from Nelson Lagoon (all of whom are old friends of Dick's) joined us for a farewell party at sundown (at 10:30 p.m.!). The next day, Dick flew us and another hunter directly to Anchorage in his 206, saving us a long wait for a commercial flight from Cold Bay. The scenery was spectacular, and it was a fitting finale to a memorable hunt. ▲▲▲

Photograph courtesy of Roy LePage

TROPHY STATS
▼ ▼ ▼ ▼ ▼

Category
cougar

Score
$15^{15}/_{16}$

Location
Hinton, Alberta - 1999

Hunter
Roy LePage

Length of Skull
$9^{5}/_{16}$

Width of Skull
$6^{10}/_{16}$

COUGAR
First Award - 15¹⁵/₁₆

▼ ▼ ▼ ▼ ▼ ▼ ▼ ▼ ▼

Roy LePage

My name is Roy LePage and my wife's name is Louise. We both hunt and have hunted together every year for the last 14 big game hunting seasons. We enjoy hunting trophy whitetails in November, also mule deer, elk, and black bear. I had been talking about wanting to go on a cougar hunt for about five years, ever since I talked to an acquaintance of mine. He went on a cougar hunt and had a great time; also shot a very large cat for a reasonable price.

In November 1999 I brought up the idea about going on a cougar hunt to Louise and she was all for me going. I started calling guides in Alberta to find out about their prices, their techniques, how they operate, and how close they were to where I live in Grande Prairie, in case the first hunt was not successful.

I'm not sure about other provinces of Canada or the United States, but all the Alberta guides have guaranteed hunts, even if it takes several trips, due to changing weather conditions or other circumstances. I talked with one guide named George Kelly from George Kelly Outfitters. He lives in Hinton and guides out of that area. I liked his guarantee; he did not want any money up front, whereas the other guides wanted half up front and the other half when the hunt was finished. He was also only three hours traveling time away from Grande Prairie, so if he was on a hot trail of a cat I could be there in a few hours. He also told me that the further you travel north, the larger the cats tend to be, which also piqued my interest in his hunts. He also said that he only wanted to be paid when I was content or happy with a cat on the ground. I asked him how long I should expect to stay with him to take my cat and he told me that his hunts usually do not take more than a day, unless there are unusual circumstances. Other guides I spoke with told me I should plan to stay a week and hopefully go home with a cat. George explained that he first locates a track, assesses whether it is large enough to pursue, then notifies the hunter. He then tracks the animal until the hunter arrives, trying to pinpoint its location so as not to disturb it until the hunt starts. I liked the sound of everything George told me so I decided to book a hunt with him.

It was late November and I was anxious to go hunting before the end of 1999. The cougar season started in December and I had already used up my holidays. I was also planning to attend a trade college for two months in January and February 2000, and the only days I had off were four days at the Christmas break and four days at the New Year's break. I explained my time situation to George and he said he might be able to accommodate me because most people do not want to hunt around or through the holidays. So it was set. If he found tracks of a good cat in that time period he would call me. Things were not looking good for this year, however, because there was not much snow on the ground and it had been a very warm winter making for tough cat hunting.

On December 21, I decided to call George to see if he had any news on a cougar or if there was a possibility of my hunt coming up around the 25th. I reached his son Kipp who told me that George was in Edmonton, but that he had been out following a set of good tracks. I asked him if I would be the hunter to come and hunt the cat if it turned out to be a good one. He told me that his Dad would get in touch with me the next day. I then received a call from George and he said I should come. I told him

Photograph courtesy of Roy LePage

Nannette Kelly, Roy LePage, and his wife Louise with Roy's cougar scoring 15-15/16.

my wife would like to be in on the hunt too, but he was a little skeptical because there could be a lot of climbing involved and running up and down hills or mountains for several miles. I insisted that Louise was in fine shape and up for the challenge, so he agreed to take her too.

On December 22, Louise and I arranged to leave work early. It was an especially beautiful night for our drive to Hinton. We had a full moon and a clear sky so you could see through the trees off on each side of the road farther than you could see with your headlights. We arrived in Hinton at about ten o'clock at night and found a room at a local motel. I called George and his wife, Nanette. It was too late to meet them that night so we agreed to meet at 6 a.m. at a Denny's restaurant for breakfast.

The next morning we met George and Nanette at the restaurant. Since I knew little about cougar, their habits, and how they are hunted effectively, I had many questions to ask George. He was very knowledgeable about cougar since he was raised in the Hinton area and had hunted and trapped there for more than 40 years. He also knows how the cougar travel through the area, right down to what trails they like to use and what ledges they use as travel routes.

George told me that the cougar we were hunting was coming toward Hinton from the mountains and was moving approximately 15 miles a day. This was a lot for a cougar because they are a short-winded animal and do not usually travel more than a mile or two in a day unless they are in the mating mood, which apparently this one was. We followed George in our vehicle and left Hinton going south.

We were no further than ten miles out of town when George stopped his truck, got out, looked on the side of the road and there was my first sight of the cat's tracks. They were much larger than I had expected and more like a black bear track in size.

From there we turned around and drove back down the highway toward Hinton and took a turn on another road looking for where the cat might have crossed. We didn't find where the cat had crossed so we drove back to George's house, leashed up four of his dogs, and loaded two snow machines. We also rounded up Kipp and his assistant, Frank Lloyd, and drove back out to the area. George and Kipp unloaded the machines and started driving up and down the cutlines closest to where the cat's tracks were last sighted. George told me that they were trying to pinpoint the cat into a one or two-mile radius. At this point, when everyone was ready, he would let the dogs go on the freshest track if it was not too late in the day. Hopefully the dogs would tree the cat within a mile or two. He didn't want to let the dogs go too late in the afternoon for fear of losing them over night to the cat or wolves.

George, Kipp, and I searched the cutlines, and after two hours of searching on the snow machines we discovered that we had missed the cat's tracks as he crossed the road because they were mixed in with the tracks from a herd of elk. Back on the track, George put Frank and a dog on the cat's trail while we climbed a hill to see where they crossed on a timber cut; this would give George an idea of what trail or direction the cat was heading. Unfortunately, this plan didn't work. It only flushed the herd of elk out in front of us, but the cat was going in a different direction.

COUGAR
First Award - 15 15/16
▼ ▼ ▼ ▼ ▼
ROY LEPAGE

George had a different idea at this point as to the cat's whereabouts and line of travel. So we traveled up a large hill and stopped on top. George unloaded the snow machine and drove down an old mining trail. In the next hour the winds picked up considerably while we were waiting for George's return. When he made it back to the top of the hill he told me he had found very fresh tracks about a mile down the mining trail. This was when the excitement started.

George first took me down to the cat's tracks, then picked up Louise, Nanette, and Kipp. By this time George had instructed Louise and me to climb the ridge because that's where the hounds would be released.

We all met on the ridge where the dogs were released. The tracking was very tough because the snow on the ridge had all melted, and the wind was very noisy making it hard to hear the hounds barking. While George, Kipp and I were tracking the dogs and the cat, Louise and Nanette heard the hounds barking feverishly in the distance. Because of the noise and pitch the hounds were making, George could tell his dogs had the cat treed and the chase was on! It was every man for himself as everybody ran toward the sound of the dogs. It turned out to be about a 600-yard chase to where the cat was treed.

When I reached the tree I could tell the cat was a very large tom and there was no question whether to shoot. He was only about 15 yards up in the tree and with one shot from my 7mm he jumped from the tree to the ground, took one large swoop at the dogs with his front paw and was dead. By the size of it George thought it might be a Record Book cat. He was glad to get it out of his area because big tomcats like this one are very territorial and will kill other male adolescent cats. You could tell he had been in many fights by the scars visible on his butt, forearms, neck, and ears. There was a fresh scar on the back of his neck about the size of a Canadian dollar coin that had not yet healed.

George tied up the dogs and went to get a snow machine. I was not looking forward to dragging this cat out of the woods since we were at least a couple miles from any road and the cat weighed in the area of 225 pounds. To my amazement I could hear the snow machine getting closer and closer until George pulled right up to the cat.

When we made it back to Hinton I registered my cat and we all stopped for a well-deserved cup of coffee before our trip home with my once-in-a-lifetime trophy. It was another beautiful moonlit night for our trip home. From the time we left our house to the time we arrived home, 23 hours had passed. It was what I call a perfect day.

The next day we took the cat to the taxidermist and found his overall length was 91 inches. Even more impressive was that his skull, after cleaning, measured 16 inches even as a green score. The 24th Awards Judges' Panel ended up with an official score of 15-15/16 points.

Also, we learned from George Kelly that in 1976 another book cat was taken only 400 yards from where our cat was taken, by a man named John T. Shillingburg. His cat scored 15-5/16 points. I found that quite interesting, so I asked George about how many book cats he feels his clients have taken over the years. He knew of four for sure and perhaps three others that might not have been entered into the records book. ▲▲▲

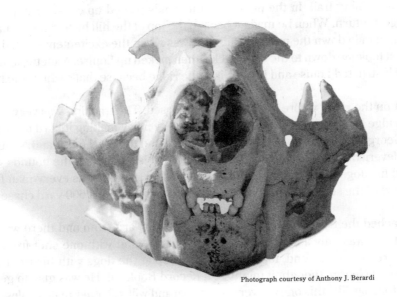

Photograph courtesy of Anthony J. Berardi

TROPHY STATS

▼ ▼ ▼ ▼ ▼

Category
  cougar

Score
  15^{13}/$_{16}$

Location
  Carbon County, Utah - 1999

Hunter
  Anthony J. Berardi

Length of Skull
  9^4/$_{16}$

Width of Skull
  6^9/$_{16}$

COUGAR
Second Award - 15¹³/₁₆

▼ ▼ ▼ ▼ ▼ ▼ ▼ ▼

ANTHONY J. BERARDI

I was 12 years old and had just passed my hunter's safety course. I put in for a lion tag because I wanted to get a lion like my dad. I was excited when I found out that I drew a tag.

The first day of the hunt I was ready to go with my dad and our friend, houndsman Roger Cyfers. We rode around in the truck looking for tracks for awhile. Later we took the snowmobiles out and rode up Castle Valley Ridge, where we stopped and watched a herd of about 400 elk running and jumping into each other. It was funny. We never saw a lion track so we headed back to the truck. I was wet, cold, and tired.

We were waiting for snow to fall before we went out again. It finally snowed on December 21 so we decided to go early the next morning.

It was clear and cold in Corner Canyon in Carbon **The Fab Five** County, Utah, when Roger showed us the track left by the lion. It was huge! I was so excited. We let the dogs out, and away they went barking and singing. So we got our fanny packs and I got my gun and off we went.

We walked for about an hour, but couldn't hear the dogs anymore. We kept walking and the snow was getting deeper and it was cold as we topped the ridge. We could now hear the dogs. Dad and Roger said they were barking treed. I got excited again, when Roger said, "It sounds like they treed on a porcupine." I was mad and I thought I would die, but of course they were joking with me; they thought it was funny. I did not.

We finally got to the tree about two hours later and there were the dogs with the cat in a big dead tree. We called them, "The Fab Five," Daisy, Brandy, Pistol, Zeke, and Annie. Dad, Roger, and I talked about where I should sit and what I should do while they took some pictures.

My dad took me over to where I was to shoot. He also told me that I should not look the cat right in the eye, because he might feel like I was challenging him. I sat down. Man, I was shaking so bad I thought I would miss, but I took my time, took a deep breath, and shot. Then the cat turned on the limb and I got scared. Roger and Dad said, "Shoot him again." So I shot again and the cat came out of the tree, ran a little ways, and went down. I was still shaking.

As we walked up to the lion to skin him I noticed that in all the excitement I had walked right out of my gators. After about eight hours we finally made it home and Dad took that lion and put it right on my Mom's kitchen floor. Then we called all my family, friends, and neighbors. My next door neighbors came over and we took pictures. It was great. I was a little embarrassed in the days to come because my parents had my picture put in the newspaper, and since we lived in a small town everyone knew who I was and what I had done. When we took the lion over to the DWR for them to tag they measured him and took a tooth. I shook so many hands I thought my hand would fall off.

Later Roger went back up the mountain to weigh the carcass — it weighed 200 pounds.

Photograph courtesy of Anthony J. Berardi

After completing his hunter safety course, the author put in and successfully drew for a cougar tag. With the help of his father and several friends including "The Fab Five" hounds, he took this award-winning cougar. The skull scores 15-13/16 points.

The cougar was eight feet two inches long. We took the skull to Kenny Leo to be measured after the sixty-day drying period and it scored 15-12/16 points. The 24th Awards Judges' Panel declared the final score to be 15-13/16 points. I think this is just about the best memory a person could have, especially a 12 year-old boy.

I want to extend a special thank you to a good friend, Roger Cyfers, to "The Fab Five," my dad Brian Berardi, and to Kenny Leo. ▲▲▲

Moments in Measuring...

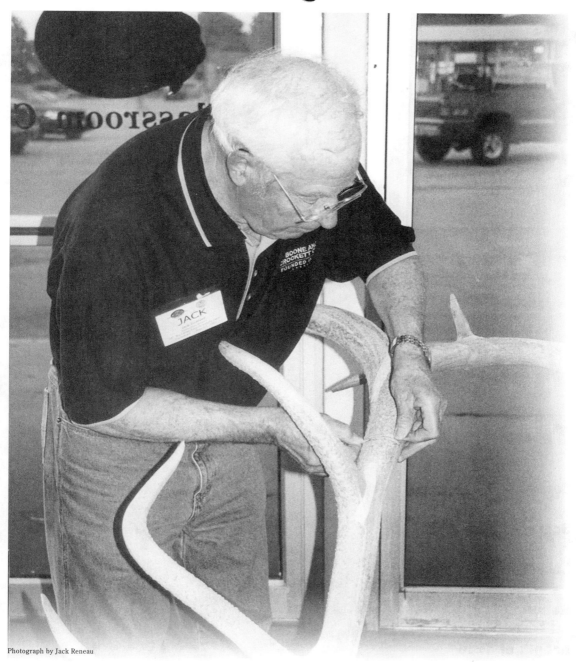

Photograph by Jack Reneau

Consultant for the 24th Awards Program Judges' Panel, Jack Graham of Edmonton, Alberta, verifies the H-3 circumference measurement on James Walter's non-typical American elk. The bull, taken by Jim R. Coe in 1932 has a final score of 419-4/8 points.

Photograph courtesy of Dave Hiatt

TROPHY STATS

▼ ▼ ▼ ▼ ▼

Category
   cougar

Score
   15^{12}/$_{16}$

Location
   Idaho County, Idaho - 1994

Hunter
   Dave Hiatt

Length of Skull
   9^{3}/$_{16}$

Width of Skull
   6^{9}/$_{16}$

COUGAR
Third Award - 15^{12}/$_{16}$

▼ ▼ ▼ ▼ ▼ ▼ ▼ ▼ ▼

DAVE HIATT

The winter of 1994 I was hunting on the upper Selway River with friends Cal Ruark, Mike Skroch, and their dogs. Our camp was about 45 miles from the end of the plowed road, accessible only by snow machine at that time of year. Cal and Mike would come and go as work and conditions allowed.

The hunting had been generally good throughout the winter, seeing several cougar and a few bobcats, taking pictures of most. I had been saving my tag for one cat in particular. The winter before I found a goat he'd killed, but I was a couple of weeks behind him. He left the biggest track and longest stride I'd ever seen, even to this day.

The morning of February 3rd, the weather was clear and cool. The wind really blew the night before, leaving an inch or two of fresh snow in some places. My good friend Mike Richie showed up just after daylight. Mike was guiding hunters out of his camp 12 miles down river and was in between hunts at the time. He sat down and poured a cup of coffee, warming his hands by the fire, and said a cougar had crossed about four or five miles down river. It didn't take long and I had the dogs loaded and we were on our way. We had five dogs with us this day: Hammer, Ike, Rocky, Sis, and Sam, all Hammer-bred Blueticks.

The track was made late in the day before and was blown shut in a lot of places. We found an ice bridge across the river and got the dogs started. They started slow and sure, pecking on the trail here and there. Before long they outdistanced us and were out of hearing range.

We were on the trail a couple of hours before we could start seeing the track more clearly. It was now evident it was a good tom. The snow depth varied from bare ground on some south slopes to three and a half feet on the north slopes and we had to use snowshoes when needed. A couple more drainages and five hours later we could finally hear dogs barking treed.

Once at the tree we praised the dogs and took some pictures. I told Mike it wasn't the cat I had been looking for and that he ought to take it. He said, "No, you go ahead." So we argued like this for awhile and finally rounded up the dogs and started out. We had taken a few steps when I looked back over my shoulder again and stopped. That's when I decided it was too good a tom to pass up.

Before long we had the hide off and the shoulders, hams, and backstraps loaded on our packs and were on our way back down to the river. We made camp that night at a little after dark. The dogs were tired and so were we, but content and happy after a good hunt. For me it's the love of the outdoors and being able to hunt my dogs in country like the Selway that keeps me coming back and always will. The kill is just a bonus. ▲▲▲

Photograph by Cliff White

TROPHY STATS
▼ ▼ ▼ ▼ ▼

Category
American elk - typical antlers

Score
425³/₈

Locality
Nye County, Nevada - 1999

Hunter
Jerry McKoen

Length of Main Beam
Right: 56⁷/₈ Left: 60²/₈

Circumference Between 1st and 2nd Points
Right: 10³/₈ Left: 10⁷/₈

Number of Points
Right: 6 Left: 7

Inside Spread
54⁶/₈

Photograph by Jack Reneau

Jerry McKoen accepting his plaque and medal from Randy Byers, Chair of the Big Game Records Committee.

BOONE AND CROCKETT CLUB

AMERICAN ELK TYPICAL ANTLERS
First Award - 425³/₈

▼ ▼ ▼ ▼ ▼ ▼ ▼ ▼

JERRY McKOEN

I started bow hunting the Oregon desert in 1969 as a teenager. Archery hunting for trophy mule deer in Oregon and Nevada's high desert became a big passion of mine. I'd pretty much hung the rifle up in my early 20s except for wintertime coyote calling.

The hunt took place in the Monitor Range, central Nevada, a place where I had never been. Preparing for the hunt, I had talked with people who had hunted and were acquainted with

Switcherrroo

the Monitors. The stories from those conversations included: "there's probably a 400 bull in the unit, but it's a big unit," "don't shoot a 300 bull, hold out, they are there," (meaning bigger bulls) and "there's never been a bull taken in the Monitors that makes the Boone and Crockett records book." The hunt was an any-weapons hunt and from those conversations my intent was to try for a nice bull with the bow.

In two mid-summer scouting trips, I had seen a lot of elk and a lot of bulls, but nothing over 300. A majority of the elk live in the Table Mountain Wilderness. This area consists of a plateau, rising from a 6,000-foot valley floor, through a thick pinon pine belt about half way up, then to a mix of sagebrush and mahogany, to over 9,500 feet with quaking aspen and sagebrush draws on top. Oregon's archery elk season was the same time as this hunt, mid September, and my other hunting partners were hunting Oregon. Thus, I was going to hunt alone. As departure time for the hunt neared, there was still a big question on my gear for the hunt. Should I bring the rifle or not? Some of my hunting buddies told me I'd be silly not to, so I packed it.

Arriving in the Monitors four days before the opener, I located more elk and more bulls but still no huge bulls. On Friday afternoon, the day before the opening, I spotted a large herd with some pretty good bulls but they were a mile and half away. It started to thundershower, so I decided to stay where I was. The rain ended about midnight. The next morning I made my way to a good vantage point. The herd was still there, but three horses and two men were heading straight for them and busted the elk in all directions. I sat and watched from a high point until about 11 o'clock that morning. I saw lots of elk, probably over 150 head, but there was only one problem — I saw almost as many packhorses as elk. I had to move.

Sunday's move became very eventful. I was among elk all day, calling one small six-point to within 45 yards. Late that afternoon while glassing, I spotted a huge bull. The bull was in scattered mahogany in a herd of about 30 cows and other bulls. He was massive! With other rifle hunters in the unit I decided right then I'd switch to the rifle for the rest of the hunt.

I made my way out of the wilderness a little after dark that night so I could change weapons. I got an early start the next morning — couldn't sleep anyway. The morning's wind direction changed my plans of the night before. Trying to get the wind in my favor, I had to travel up an open country

Photograph courtesy of Jerry McKoen

The antlers from the author's elk dwarf the pack horse on the trip out. The bull scored an impressive 425-3/8 points.

ravine. Traveling up the ravine, I could glass elk on the mountainside but couldn't see most of the country I'd seen the elk in the day before. Getting close with only two-foot sagebrush as cover, I eased out of the ravine to find cow elk strung out all over. I spotted the huge bull, but he was too far to shoot and I couldn't get any closer. While watching from this vantage point I got trapped by the cows and couldn't move. A bull came from the ridge to my left and stole a cow and calf from the herd. Two bulls to my right were bugling back and forth, mingling with other quiet bulls. The big bull was straight in front of me and all I could do was watch. The wind hadn't changed and the elk had me pinned down for almost an hour before they finally wandered off in three different directions. During all that time the big bull bugled only twice and never really seemed bothered by all the other commotion.

With most of the elk bedded by now, I backtracked down the ravine, studying it from a distance. I felt my best chance now was to circle the ridge and try to get above them. It took almost two hours to circle the ridge. I was pushing it pretty hard because all this time I was on the backside of the ridge and couldn't see the elk. Finally, breaking out on top, I saw the elk. They were up heading toward the top and I was still over a 1,000 yards away. I knew if they reached the top of the ridge, I might not be able to shoot. Dropping below the ridge and almost running trying to beat the elk, I came over the top again, this time 350 to 400 yards away. The big bull was presenting a shot, and wasting no time I lay down, got a pretty good rest, and quickly judged the distance. I thought if I aimed at his backbone I'd be all right. My first shot missed high over his shoulder. The bull jumped, but didn't run, so I compensated by aiming lower and touched off another round. The second shot connected, but the big bull still didn't go down. My third shot dropped him for good. As the other elk took off, I counted 13 bulls and estimated about 25 cows in the herd.

Approaching the bull, I saw he was magnificent, extremely massive in body and antler. Now the fun was over and the work began. That's a story of SWITCHERROO. ▲▲▲

Photograph by Cliff White

TROPHY STATS
▼ ▼ ▼ ▼ ▼

Category
American elk - typical antlers

Score
396^4/$_8$

Locality
Gila County, Arizona - 1997

Hunter
Dan J. Agnew

Length of Main Beam
Right: 53^3/$_8$ Left: 53^2/$_8$

Circumference Between 1st and 2nd Points
Right: 9^2/$_8$ Left: 9^1/$_8$

Number of Points
Right: 6 Left: 7

Inside Spread
37^4/$_8$

AMERICAN ELK TYPICAL ANTLERS
Second Award - 396⁴/₈

▼ ▼ ▼ ▼ ▼ ▼ ▼ ▼ ▼

DAN J. AGNEW

I acquired a tag for the Dry Lake unit on the San Carlos Reservation at the 1997 Safari Club Convention. The hunt was scheduled from September 1 through 15, 1997. I arrived on September 3rd and was accompanied by guide/companion John McClendon and a friend, Gary Smith. My tribal guides for the hunt were Donovan Case and Billy Joe.

When I arrived at camp, the weather was unusually hot — hovering near 80 degrees during the day. I knew we could only hunt the early morning hours (daylight until about 9:00 a.m.) and the late afternoon hours (about 4:00 p.m. until sunset) as the elk would bed down in the heat of the day. We also chose not to take any action that would possibly spook them out of their bedding areas.

We hunted all day on September 3rd and 4th , spotting and calling in several nice bulls. My friend Gary had never experienced calling in a monster bull to within 10 yards while having to lay prone. We called in several bulls in the 360 to 370 class — good bulls, but not what we had hoped to tag. On September 5th, we awoke several hours before daylight and drove to an area Case and Joe had scouted several days prior to my arrival, but where no one had hunted for about four days. After we parked our pickup, we heard no less than 12 to 15 different bulls — we were literally surrounded by bugling bulls. We had to make some choices. Gary and Billy Joe decided to go one direction while Donovan, John and I went another. In listening to the bugles, John and Donovan tried to figure out which bugle sounded the "biggest" and follow it. I've certainly learned that sometimes when following a big deep, throaty bugle you can end up calling in a bull that sounds a lot bigger than he really is.

We made our choice and set out to track "the" bull we'd chosen and see if we could get a look. As we got closer, we couldn't see the bull (who was bugling constantly), but we could tell he had a group of cows with him. Not wanting to risk jumping a wary cow, John said, "You wait here; I'll see if I can sneak in a little closer by myself." Donovan and I waited for some time knowing the elk were moving away from us. Finally, John returned and said, "I think I've found your bull — he's a beauty." I said, "Let's go get him." John replied, "No, we'd better wait. He's bedded down with his cows in some deep brush and we've got no chance to get him now. Let's come back this afternoon." So, heeding his advice, we decided to head back to camp to wait.

That afternoon we went back to the area where John had "bedded" the bull and waited for him to start bugling and to come out to feed. After several hours of waiting, we realized we were alone — the bull and his harem had gotten up and left. We didn't hear his bugle that afternoon and we were all puzzled. I was disappointed and wondered where in the heck he'd gone.

We were up early the next morning and went back into the same area. As we anxiously waited for daylight, John was certain he heard the same bull bugle again, so off we went. The wind was perfect and this time our cover was good. As we got closer, I was nervous with anticipation; finally, a chance to get a 400-class B&C bull. Again, the bull got into some deep cover and John wanted to get a better look at him before we tried to set up for a shot. John said "You've waited for a long time for a bull like this. I want to be sure the bull is as big as I think he is." Donovan and I again waited patiently for John to return and when he did he said the bull had "bedded" again and he could only get a few brief glimpses of his antlers. He said, "I think that's your bull, but I still want to be sure."

We went back to camp with a plan to return again that afternoon, but this time, several hours earlier so the bull couldn't sneak off like he'd done the day before. When we went back that afternoon, as luck would have it, a warm September wind came up and was blowing from the absolute wrong direction for the stalk we'd have to make. We decided to sit and wait, hoping either the wind would change or the bull would walk right out in front of us. Unfortunately, neither happened and although we could hear the bull bugling, we simply couldn't get in closer without running the risk of being either seen or winded. I'd been waiting a long time for a bull like this, so I decided to be patient and wait some more. I still had another eight days of hunting left and I was prepared to spend it all if I had to.

The next morning we drove back into the area where we'd left the bull the day before. We arrived an hour before daylight and as soon as we stepped out of our pickup, we all jumped as the bull bugled less than a 100 yards from where we stopped the truck. It was almost scary. We could all now recognize the bull's bugle and he was closer than he'd ever been. But with no light, we could not see or do anything.

As we crouched by the pickup in silence, afraid to even whisper to one another, the bull miraculously kept bugling and stayed close for about 45 minutes. While I was trying ever so quietly to get my gun out of its stainless steel case, it seemed like every sound I made was magnified ten times. I just knew the bull was going to bolt! As daylight approached, the bull began moving and the bugles were getting farther away. John said, "He's on the move, let's go!"

John, Donovan, and I began our stalk by following and tracking the bull. It was 6:45 a.m. on September 7th, the fifth day of my hunt. We couldn't see the bull because it was brushy and still getting light, but his bugles let us know where he was — it was like he was saying, "Here I am, follow me." While we couldn't hear or see any cows with him, he'd had a harem every other time we'd seen him or heard him, so we decided to follow at a pretty safe distance for fear of spooking a wary cow. After following him for about 45 minutes, John and Donovan finally saw him. He was alone and feeding across an old burn area that was waist deep in summer grass and virtually "wide open." I was sweating from the uphill climb and when I finally saw the bull, I said, "John, he's big!" As I lay out on the rocky ground getting ready for a shot and extended the bi-pod on my .340 Weatherby magnum, I asked John, "How far do you think he is?" He replied, "You've got about a 400-yard shot, uphill." When I finally settled and looked through my Swarovski 3-12x50 scope, the bull looked huge. I tried to relax and remember the many hours I'd spent that summer practicing shots at various distances. I knew if I missed, it wasn't going to be the gun's fault. I'd have nobody to blame but myself. As I set up for my shot, the bull was walking away from me and feeding with his head down. John said, "I'll cow call him and when he lifts his head, be ready to shoot." I said, "Okay, I'm as ready as I'll ever be." As John cow-called, the bull lifted his head and bugled while turning to the left and looking down the hill right at us. It was probably the last thing he saw. I squeezed the trigger and the one shot from my .340 Weatherby's 180-grain factory load hit home. The bull staggered a couple of feet forward and fell in his tracks. He was a monster 6x7 with a small non-typical kicker on one side, otherwise he'd have been a straight 6x6. We field scored him at 416. The bull officially scored 396-4/8 points. I'd been waiting a long time for a bull like this — and boy was it worth the wait. ▲▲▲

AMERICAN ELK TYPICAL ANTLERS
Second Award - 396⁴/₈

▼ ▼ ▼ ▼ ▼

DAN J. AGNEW

Photograph by Cliff White

TROPHY STATS

▼ ▼ ▼ ▼ ▼

Category
American elk - non-typical antlers

Score
450^6/8

Locality
Apache County, Arizona - 1998

Hunter
Alan D. Hamberlin

Length of Main Beam
Right: 59 Left: 52^6/8

**Circumference Between
1st and 2nd Points**
Right: 9^1/8 Left: 9^3/8

Number of Points
Right: 8 Left: 8

Inside Spread
39^4/8

BOONE AND CROCKETT CLUB

AMERICAN ELK NON-TYPICAL ANTLERS
First Award - 450⁶/₈

▼ ▼ ▼ ▼ ▼ ▼ ▼ ▼ ▼

ALAN D. HAMBERLIN

By Lary Nicholds as told by Dave Martin

When I finished talking with Alan Hamberlin I felt like the luckiest guy in the world. Alan had asked me to be his guest this year as he hunted for a monster elk on the White Mountain Apache Indian Reservation. The Reservation is famous for huge bulls, and there was no way I was going to pass up this opportunity. I have been fortunate enough to go on some really great elk hunts in the last ten years, but none of them had the potential this offered. One thing was for sure: I was not prepared for what I was about to experience.

Our hunt started on a Saturday, and when we arrived in camp our guide Ralph Thomas said that he had a few book bulls spotted for us. A book bull to the Apaches is any bull that will net 375 B&C points or better; a rarity in most parts of the world. Hearing this brought some excitement to the hunt, but Alan hadn't come here to hunt just any book bull. His goal was to kill an elk that would net over 400 points.

The first day of the hunt we saw quite a few bulls, including one that would go about 360. None of these interested Alan so we kept hunting. We were hunting high in the pines and covering a lot of ground — the more we moved the more elk we saw. At the end of the first day we had seen a lot of great bulls, but not the right one.

Early in the second day we saw a bull in the 420 range, and Alan quickly said, "The hunt is over; it's that bull or nothing." I knew at that moment that if we didn't see that bull, or a better one, he would go home empty handed, choosing to hold out for an animal that met his standards, as opposed to shooting a "good" animal.

For the next three days we looked at more bulls than we could count. We hunted high and low and found good elk everywhere we went, but still not our bull. On the evening of the fifth day we found a monster, one we all felt would score 390-400. We had this bull at 100 yards for a long time and could have harvested him, but Alan passed. After we let this one go I asked Alan, "If you aren't going to kill that bull, why are we hunting here? Let's go back and hunt the big one."

On Thursday evening we were working an area that another guide had told us about. He said he had seen a couple of 400-class bulls there, but his client couldn't physically get around well enough to hunt them. That was all we needed to hear and we were off. We found a series of ridges and started hunting the area. When we got set up and started looking, the place just came alive. There were bulls everywhere, calling, screaming, fighting, raking trees, and causing genuine chaos. You could hear antlers crashing as bulls fought everywhere around us. It was the most awesome sound I had ever heard. There was no doubt in any of our minds that we were in the right spot.

I heard one bull bugle nearby and we took off to see what kind of bull he was. When we

Alan Hamberlin's non-typical elk is one of only two bulls in the records book scoring over 450 points. It was taken on the White Mountain Apache Indian Reservation in Arizona in the fall of 1998.

finally did get a look at him he was a nice bull, but not a shooter. While we were looking him over I heard another bugle and saw a different bull. I called Alan and Ralph over to look at him and to see what they thought. They both said that he was not a good bull. I told them that they were looking in the wrong location; the bull I was talking about had gone down the hill. We moved and quickly found the elk again, but he was in the pines and it was hard to get a good look at him. Ralph was looking at his rack and kept saying, "There's something wrong with his antlers." He was seeing the triple forks on his sword point, and from his angle his rack looked weird. Alan was not about to waste his tag on a bull that he couldn't completely evaluate. When the elk finally moved into the open we knew at once this was the bull Alan wanted. Alan said. "He's a shooter. I'm taking him!" He got into position and hit him with the first shot. The second shot hit him in the shoulder and the bull spun and ran straight at us. Alan's third shot hit the big bull square in the chest. The third shot started what looked like a train wreck, with the bull tumbling forward and coming to a halt. We were absolutely amazed that it took three shots from a .338 Winchester magnum with 225-grain bullets to put this elk down.

When we got up to the bull we couldn't believe what lay before our eyes. Here was the biggest elk any of us had ever seen. One of his tines was buried in the ground and we had to pull it out to get a better look. This monster suffered no ground shrinkage; in fact, he seemed to be growing before our eyes. We took out a tape, made a few quick measurements and guessed the bull would score in the 440 point range, even bigger than we had first thought. We were excited, particularly Alan, for he had finally achieved his goal of taking an elk that would score over 400 Boone and Crockett points. Once we got

AMERICAN ELK
NON-TYPICAL ANTLERS
First Award - 450⁶/₈
▼   ▼   ▼   ▼   ▼

ALAN D. HAMBERLIN

back to camp we taped him again and just about fainted! We came up with a green score over 450 points. The 24th Awards Judges' Panel measured the bull in Springfield, Missouri, with a final score of 450-6/8 points. The pictures don't do this bull justice; you have to see him to believe it! I have seen some big elk in my years of hunting, but nothing compares to him.

This was truly the greatest place on earth I have ever seen for elk. I had the notion going into this hunt that a guy just had to pay the money and he would kill a monster bull. That is not true at all. Yes, you could kill a great bull by sitting on one of the meadows waiting for a bull to come by, but to take a monster you have to work at it. We were up at 3:00 a.m. every morning and in the field by 3:30. We hunted hard all day long and got back to camp well after dark. According to our GPS units we walked over 80 miles in our quest for this monster. While this hunt is no cake walk, one thing is true — if you hunt hard you will kill the bull of a lifetime. Alan sure did! ▲▲▲

Photograph by Cliff White

TROPHY STATS

▼ ▼ ▼ ▼ ▼

Category
American elk - non-typical antlers

Score
420⁴/₈

Locality
Kern County, California - 2000

Hunter
Brad Peters

Length of Main Beam
Right: 52 Left: 55⁵/₈

**Circumference Between
1st and 2nd Points**
Right: 10⁴/₈ Left: 10⁴/₈

Number of Points
Right: 8 Left: 9

Inside Spread
36²/₈

Photograph by Jack Reneau

**Brad Peters accepting his plaque and medal
from Randy Byers, Chair of the Big Game
Records Committee.**

AMERICAN ELK NON-TYPICAL ANTLERS
Second Award - 420⁴/₈

▼ ▼ ▼ ▼ ▼ ▼ ▼ ▼ ▼

BRAD PETERS

Who would believe this tremendous bull was taken only two hours from downtown Los Angeles from an unfenced population of wild elk on a quarter-million acre ranch?

We did everything wrong on this hunt. I missed my first opportunity at the bull and we miscommunicated the next morning, which had us going up the hill into hunting country way behind schedule. Fortunately, it all worked out, and I took this tremendous 8x9 non-typical American elk bull on Southern California's 250,000-acre Tejon Ranch. With elk hunting you normally have to work like a dog, and are lucky to get anything, but everything that happened on this hunt was pure luck. Well, maybe not everything.

I've done a lot of elk hunting in New Mexico, Colorado, Idaho, and here in my home state of California, taking ten bulls over the years. I make at least three or four hunts each fall for big game and have learned there is a tremendous amount of planning that goes into a successful hunt, by both the hunter and his guides. Yes, the reality is I was the lucky guy in the right place at the right time for this bull. Don Geivet, the Game Manager of the Tejon Ranch, is managing for quality animals. That is very important to the fact that we got a good bull, maybe the most important thing.

Elk were first released on this sprawling ranch in southern Kern County in the early 1960s. The population stayed between 25 and 60 animals for years, but during the 1980s, the herd began to grow rapidly. Geivet conservatively estimates the population today to be over 400, and some elk are actually dispersing off the ranch onto public lands to the north as the herd continues to grow.

I honestly believe that the Tejon Ranch has the best elk hunting opportunity in the United States. The biggest problem is staying off the trigger. There are so many good bulls, it's hard not to get excited and hold out for a really good bull. Most hunters settle for 330 or 340 bulls, and don't get me wrong, that's a good animal, but you really need self-control and a little luck to see the really nice bulls. Another major factor is the kind of dedication and service they have at The Tejon. There are four guys doing nothing but catering to you. You're the only guy on the ranch hunting these bulls, and they don't consider the hunt over until you fill your tag.

The first time I went up there, I hunted 21 days before I shot a bull that scored 372 points. Conservatively, I looked at 40 or more bulls. After that hunt, I applied for five more tags. By the time my turn came up again, I had heard of a 400-point class bull that had been passed up, and I knew that was the bull I wanted to hunt.

Geivet said they'd had a report of a big bull that was seen by one of the ranch's cowboys in an area they normally don't hunt, and he asked me if I wanted to go have a look. So on the first day of our hunt we headed for the west side of the ranch. Since the ranch is only an hour

The author with his non-typical American elk taken on the Tejon Ranch in Kern County, California. The bull is the highest ranking elk ever taken from California scoring 420-4/8 points, earning a Second Award at the 24th Awards Banquet.

from my home in Bakersfield, I had my youngest son Joe and a neighbor, Curt Carter with me to help spot. That morning the three of us, along with Geivet and guide Darrell Francis were out getting the lay of the land in this new area.

Toward evening we stopped on a flat plateau and my son and Don went out to the point to glass. I just happened to turn and look behind us and spotted a cow crossing the road 250 yards away. She was joining a second cow, but I also saw legs in the brush that I knew from their size didn't belong to another cow. As they moved back through the brush I could see they would come out into an opening. As soon as the bull stepped into the opening, I knew he was a huge animal and told everyone our searching was over.

We tried to make a quick stalk, but the cows saw us moving for position and the game was up. The elk moved over two ridges into another canyon. Don said that we could meet the next morning and take a road he hadn't been on in a couple of years on the opposite side of the basin which would take us above where he figured the elk might bed down.

That night I slept in my own bed. Actually, I only tried to sleep. Mostly I tossed and turned. Sleeping was impossible. I was up and at our meeting place early. Don wasn't there yet, so I leaned back in the truck to rest my eyes for a few minutes. It was 4:45 a.m. I dozed, but at 5:15 I saw truck headlights coming from the wrong direction. I thought to myself, "What's up with this?" I then decided to go to the house where the guides were staying and knocked on the door. I knew they were awake because I could hear them practicing bugling. Larry Johnson opened the door and wanted to know

AMERICAN ELK NON-TYPICAL ANTLERS
Second Award - 420⁴/₈

▼ ▼ ▼ ▼ ▼

BRAD PETERS

where the heck I'd been. The plans had changed after I'd left the previous evening, and the rendezvous point was on the other side of the ranch. So we burned the rubber off the tires flying to where we were supposed to meet Don with Darrell and guide Cody Plank 10 minutes behind.

It was already getting light as we headed up the hill, and Don proved that he hadn't been on the road in a while by taking a wrong turn, backtracking, and then easing up the right fork in the road. It was legal shooting time by now and we were all thinking that we should have been here half an hour earlier. As we moved up the south side of the ridge to a vantage point where we could see into the basin, Larry said he could see a cow, then another cow, and then Mr. Big came into view.

It was THE bull and he was bedded down facing us. We scrambled to get a good shooting position, and Don said, "If you're gonna shoot that bull, you'd better shoot him right now!" The cows were getting nervous, so I got into a steady position and dropped the bull with a single shot from my custom 7mm/.300 Weatherby.

If we had been on time and drove up that road in the dark, we certainly would have spooked the bull and his harem. Sometimes things go wrong and make for things going right.

With the elk on the ground, all of us knew it was a good bull, but none of us really knew how good. So we started a pool, each of us guessing scores. They ranged from the 380s up to my 397 guess. Don told me later that as he followed the truck carrying the bull back down the road he kept thinking that it was better than he'd originally thought. You always hear about ground shrinkage, but this bull seemed bigger each time you looked at him. He was deceiving. By the time we got down the hill, Don decided that he wanted to have the bull scored right now. So we called taxidermist Matt Johnson to do a preliminary score.

Matt came out to the ranch and started working with his tape and jotting down numbers. He came out of the house where he was adding up the score with a funny look on his face. "What's wrong?" I asked. "I'm not adding this up right. I've got 442. That can't be right," he continued as he went back in to re-tape the bull and add up his numbers again. The next time he came out, he smiled. "I was wrong," he said. "It's 436."

After the 60-day drying period, the bull officially scored 420-4/8 points. I can't help thinking about the possible 400-point bull that had been turned down the previous year. If everyone thought this bull would score 400 points, I wonder how big he might actually be. They only thought my bull was around 390, missing the score by 45 points. Could there be a new World's record on the Tejon Ranch? It wouldn't surprise me. ▲▲▲

Photograph by Cliff White

TROPHY STATS

▼ ▼ ▼ ▼ ▼

Category
American elk - non-typical antlers

Score
409³/₈

Locality
Coconino County, Arizona - 2000

Hunter
Brent V. Trumbo

Length of Main Beam
Right: 52⁶/₈ Left: 53

Circumference Between 1st and 2nd Points
Right: 9³/₈ Left: 9⁴/₈

Number of Points
Right: 7 Left: 8

Inside Spread
42²/₈

Photograph by Jack Reneau

Brent V. Trumbo accepting his plaque and medal from Randy Byers, Chair of the Big Game Records Committee.

BOONE AND CROCKETT CLUB'

AMERICAN ELK NON-TYPICAL ANTLERS
Third Award - 409³/₈

▼ ▼ ▼ ▼ ▼ ▼ ▼ ▼

BRENT V. TRUMBO

Ever since my first Idaho elk hunt in 1985, I have dreamed of killing a huge bull. Big bulls are regal and majestic creatures, and they inhabit some of the most beautiful and pristine country on the planet. I especially enjoy hunting elk during late September. The fall colors are at their peak, the temperatures are very pleasant, and the bulls are bugling. The excitement level of calling and stalking screaming bulls in timber is unparalleled.

Quest for a Monster Bull

During an elk hunt in 1996, another hunter told me about the trophy bulls coming off the Hualapai Indian reservation. After researching their hunts, I booked a spot for the second hunt in 1999. The Hualapai reservation encompasses over one million acres and is located one hundred miles east of Las Vegas. Their northern border is the Colorado River and includes the southwestern portion of the Grand Canyon. It is comprised of pinion juniper forest with a mosaic of old burns that create great feed and ideal elk habitat.

After waiting three years and preparing all summer, I was really pumped up by the time I finally got to the Hualapai. Loren Bravo was my guide. It was the last week of September and the bulls were on fire. To be honest, I wasn't really sure what to expect. Outfitters and guides tell lots of stories about Arizona's infamous bulls, but as is typically the case, it's difficult to separate fact from fiction.

Our strategy was to locate bugling bulls in the morning before daylight and try to intercept them before they made it to the trees. This primarily involved glassing and stalking hunting techniques. The evenings were spent sitting in blinds at water holes (or tanks).

The first morning of the hunt seemed like a dream. Ten minutes into the hunt I had already seen a beautiful 355 gross 6x6 bull in the edge of the timber 100 yards distant, and two hours later I was in the forest with a screaming 8x7 at 40 yards. As the bull stepped out from behind a tree to follow a cow, I could see that it had good top points with lots of mass, but I couldn't see his lower points. I elected not to shoot unless I got a better look. This turned out to be a good decision. Another hunter shot the bull the next evening. Although my first impression in the timber was that the bull might go over 380 gross, it had short front points, a broken ten inch crown point. That evening I sat at a nearby tank and video taped the same 6x6 I saw early that morning.

The following evening we went to Oak tank. Oak tank is in a very remote area near the Grand Canyon. Historically, it has produced some of the best bulls from the Hualapai. At 4:00 p.m. a herd of elk walked up the draw below the tank, but winded us before they reached the dam. We quickly moved to the other side of the tank and constructed a blind from tree branches. At 5:30 p.m. bulls converged on the water hole from all directions. One very large bull walked below the dam, but reentered the timber after only a few seconds in the open. Fifteen minutes later, the same bull emerged from the forest above the tank and timidly approached the water. I immediately asked Loren's brother Morris to video the bull. During the ten minutes of filming this great bull, Loren and Morris were urging me to shoot. While bulls were screaming all around us in the timber, this bull never bugled and was very cautious. The bull was perfectly symmetrical and had a beautiful shape. His royals were 24 inches, the fifths were 14, and the inside spread was 40 inches. I like bulls with big top points, but this bull had average mass and did not appear to be fully mature. I estimated that the bull would score 355 points. Loren and Morris estimated the bull would go over 370 points. Although this bull really impressed me, I was convinced we could do better. After all, this was only the second day of the hunt and I was having the hunt of my life. I thought that since the elk were in an apparent pattern, surely this bull would reappear at this tank during the next four days. This would allow me to hunt for an even bigger bull during the mornings.

During the last several years I have enjoyed video taping my hunts. This has helped me to pass on marginal animals. In the event that I don't succeed, the video becomes my "trophy." However, in this case it was a curse. After watching the film, hunters and guides in camp confirmed that the bull was indeed a 370-class bull and that I had made a judgment error. I take my hunting far too seriously, and for the next four nights I slept less than two hours.

Over the next four days I saw lots of 330 to 350 class bulls, but the big boy never came back to Oak tank. Another hunter killed an absolute monster on the fourth day. The bull's first three points all measured between 20 and 26 inches and had an amazing 64 inches of mass. It scored 388 points and was the most incredible elk I had ever seen.

As the sun was setting on Oak tank during the last day of hunting, I asked Loren if we had enough time to get to Prospect Canyon before dark. We made a mad dash and arrived with ten minutes of shooting light left. Shortly after moving up the canyon, I saw a lone 6x6 bull walking in the edge of a large sage flat. Closer inspection with binoculars revealed that the bull had huge tops and was very wide. My Leica Geovid rangefinder read the distance at 368 yards, and I decided to take the shot. I was shooting a custom barreled Model 70 .300 Winchester magnum with Nosler 180-grain handloads at 3,110 fps. After the shot, the bull ran 50 yards and stopped. Before I could shoot again, he fell over dead. It was a gorgeous bull with 55-inch beams, 21-inch royals, 17-inch fifths, huge whale tails, and a 45-inch inside spread. The bull scored around 370 points. What tremendous luck for a last minute elk!

After the exciting hunt in 1999, I had to re-book for 2000. However, the drought and forest fires during the summer had me concerned about trophy quality. I decided to look on the Internet for rainfall records from the area during the last six years. I wanted to compare January through June precipitation to the average B&C scores from the Hualapai for the same period. Not surprisingly, there was a perfect correlation with 1995 as their wettest year with 12.6 inches of precipitation and an average B&C score of 373, and 1996 their driest with 2.2 inches and a 309 average. Their six-year average is 348. This winter and spring was their driest on record, and my expectations were minimal.

Two days prior to leaving for my hunt, I received a call from a hunter that I met at the Hualapai the previous year. He was on the first hunt this year and stated that the hunting was their worst ever, with the best bull scoring in the 350s out of 12 hunters. His advice was to forfeit my deposit and stay home.

After two sleepless nights, I elected to go ahead with my hunt. Upon arrival in camp, several hunters remaining from the first hunt said the hunting was going to be tough, but that the rut was still not occurring. My first day of hunting confirmed that there were few elk, very little bugling, and poor antler development. Half of the tanks were dry, and many of those that remained were mud puddles. Temperatures were fifteen degrees above normal and the best bull I saw the first day was a 330 class 6x7.

AMERICAN ELK NON-TYPICAL ANTLERS
Third Award - 409³/₈

▼   ▼   ▼   ▼   ▼

BRENT V. TRUMBO

The second morning we went to a rock cliff overlooking the upper part of Prospect Canyon. Using my spotting scope, I found two bulls in the edge of a small meadow two miles away. The largest bull was tearing a small tree to pieces. Closer inspection revealed that it was a wide, heavy, well-balanced 6x6 that I thought would score around 35 points, although Loren thought he was bigger. He also stated that this was the best bull he had seen all season, and that we should go after him. It was a beautiful bull, but it wasn't what I came to Arizona to shoot, so we watched it feed for over an hour before disappearing into the timber. Part of trophy hunting is maximizing your time afield in good areas, and I was willing to go home with an unused tag in my pocket.

Over the next three days, we didn't see any bulls over 300 points, and many of the bulls had weak tops or antler deformities. Even though it was the first week of October, some bulls were still in velvet. Most mature bulls were not bugling or with cows. The best bull killed by another hunter scored just over 338 points and was killed at Oak tank on the third evening.

We knew that the big bull I passed in 1999 had not been killed last year or this year because of its antler size, symmetry, and shape. Oak tank had a high concentration of bulls this year and had received constant hunting pressure for several weeks. However, nobody hunted this tank the day after the 300-class bull was killed, so we decided to get there early on the fifth evening. The early morning hours of October fourth began with a severe thunderstorm. When we got up at 4:30, the rain had almost stopped and the temperature had dropped 20 degrees. This was the break we needed, and I predicted that the bulls would be much more vocal and active.

At 5:15 p.m., I saw a very large bull walk through a small opening in the forest 200 yards above the tank. Morris got the video camera ready while I began to cow call softly. At 5:30, a bull began bugling below the dam and was closing the distance quickly. The bull had broken antlers and was following a lone cow. Without hesitation, they walked over the dam and began splashing in the water. Beyond the tank we could barely make out the shape of what looked like a big bull. Because of the hunting pressure, I believe that this bull was staging above the tank to check the thermals and search for danger. The wind was in our favor, and with the other bull splashing and bugling, the big bull assumed all was clear and came on in. My first head-on glance at this bull left no doubt that it was a monster. It was a huge 7x7 with a small cheater on the left G1. My .300 Winchester was rested on the side of an oak tree, but the bull faced me as it walked to the water. The distance to the elk was about 80 yards, and I contemplated shooting it between the antlers and through the back as it drank, or directly into the front center of the chest as it raised it's head to look around. My preference was for a broadside pass-through shot, so I waited. If the bull suddenly spooked, I knew I would have to get a shot off quickly while the bull was turning to leave. The bull was very cautious, and several times raised its head and looked directly at us, sensing that something wasn't right. After several minutes the bull finally turned to leave, and while he was still in motion the .300 broke the silence. The enormous bull ran about 30 yards and collapsed on the bank.

Photograph courtesy of Brent V. Trumbo

The author with his Arizona bull scoring 409-3/8 points. The G-1s measure 21-6/8 inches and 22-1/8 inches and are the bulls most outstanding features.

After the backslapping and photography, we loaded the bull and took it back to camp. I was very surprised when we scored the elk. The bull's body was so huge that I severely underestimated the size of its antlers. With the exception of the 21-6/8 inch and 22-1/8 inch G-1s, the bull has no outstanding features. However, the bull also had no weaknesses. Arizona elk frequently have weak third points, but this bull was even strong on these points at 21 inches and 18-6/8 inches. The symmetry of this elk was amazing. After the 60-day drying period, the bull scored 417-7/8 points. The 24th Awards Judges' Panel officially declared the score at 409-3/8 points.

Matson's Laboratory in Milltown, Montana, performed cementum analysis, which aged my bull at 8-1/2 years. Elk typically don't produce their maximum antler mass until 10-1/2 years old, so this bull could have grown even larger. Given that this was one of the driest years ever recorded in that area, one can only wonder what this bull might have been in a normal antler growth year.

Interestingly, the bull we video taped at Oak tank in 1999 has not been seen since our encounter. It is possible that it is the same bull that I killed in 2000. The antler conformation is different, but the main beam shape and the color, behavior, and age of the bull would be consistent with the 2000 bull. Whether an elk could add 45 inches of antler in a drought year is also questionable, but what are the odds of there being two enormous and symmetrical bulls at one water hole?

I am convinced that finding a monster bull is eighty percent luck. You have to be at the right place at the right time. I feel extremely fortunate to have had the opportunity to harvest this magnificent bull. ▲▲▲

BOONE AND CROCKETT CLUB'

Moments in Measuring...

Photograph by Jack Reneau

24th Awards Judges' Panel Consultant Glenn E. Hisey explains how to locate the proper place to start the measurement for length of the main beams on an elk to Bass Pro Shops staff members Eric Volmer (Promotions Manager) and Kent Phillips (Director of Stores).

Photograph by Cliff White

TROPHY STATS

▼ ▼ ▼ ▼ ▼

Category
American elk - non-typical antlers

Score
419⁴/₈

Locality
Yakima County, Washington - 1932

Hunter
Jim R. Coe

Owner
James Walter

Length of Main Beam
Right: 55⁵/₈ Left: 56

Circumference Between 1st and 2nd Points
Right: 9⁶/₈ Left: 9¹/₈

Number of Points
Right: 8 Left: 8

Inside Spread
38⁷/₈

Photograph by Jack Reneau

James Walter accepting his plaque from Randy Byers, Chair of the Big Game Records Committee.

AMERICAN ELK
NON-TYPICAL ANTLERS
Certificate of Merit - 419⁴/₈

▼ ▼ ▼ ▼ ▼ ▼ ▼ ▼ ▼

Jim R. Coe - Hunter
James Walter - Owner

For most of his 43 years living in the state of Washington, James Richard Coe (born February 8, 1890, died August 12, 1933) hunted in the Cascade Mountains. The whole story of his hunt of "Jim Bull" was never passed down in the family because of Jim's early death and a shooting accident in the family that left a 12 year-old friend of the family dead.

Jim Coe was a tall man, strongly built, congenial, and somewhat assertive. He had a passion for life, the type of restless adventurer that belonged in the mountains. His scrappy, high-spirited ways were more suited to the Chinook Pass wilderness. Hunting on horseback from early morning until dusk was common, and sitting around night campfires by the Naches River retelling stories with hunting friends was just part of it.

In 1932 a three-acre section of the Anderson Homestead on the Naches River, 35-miles northwest of the little town of Yakima, was up for sale. Jim pitched camp here on weekends and later built a hunter's cabin between a Douglas fir and Ponderosa pine and named it "Squeeze Inn."

Early one autumn morning on a hunt, he encountered "Jim Bull," and for one brief moment their eyes met. Then, in a clap of thunder that echoed off Edgar Rock and Gold Creek Ridge, the bull was brought down. Eventually the rack from this special animal was hung over the entrance to Squeeze Inn, where it has remained for the past 68 years. ▲▲▲

New World's Record

Photograph by Cliff White

TROPHY STATS

▼ ▼ ▼ ▼ ▼

Category
Roosevelt's elk

Score
396⁵/₈

Locality
Campbell River, British Columbia - 1997

Hunter
Karl W. Minor, Sr.

Length of Main Beam
Right: 46³/₈ Left: 46⁷/₈

**Circumference Between
1st and 2nd Points**
Right: 8⁷/₈ Left: 9⁵/₈

Number of Points
Right: 10 Left: 9

Inside Spread
32³/₈

Photograph by Jack Reneau

Karl W. Minor, Sr. accepting his plaque and medal from Randy Byers, Chair of the Big Game Records Committee.

BOONE AND CROCKETT CLUB'

ROOSEVELT'S ELK
First Award - 396⁵/₈

▼ ▼ ▼ ▼ ▼ ▼ ▼ ▼ ▼

KARL W. MINOR, SR.

Having been successful on previous hunts with Trophy West Outfitters, taking trophies that made the Records Book, I looked forward to hunting with them again. This time I requested a combination hunt for coastal grizzly and Roosevelt's elk. My request was accepted and plans were made for what turned out to be one "helluva" great hunt.

I hunted grizzly first at Knights Inlet on British Columbia's mainland — God's Country. It was an exciting, very wet, and successful hunt — but a story for another day. This adventure concerns a huge Roosevelt's elk.

"No time to relax after the grizzly hunt; elk season starts tomorrow over on Vancouver Island," I thought to myself. I was on a roll. My last three hunts had produced record trophies. This hunt should have been easy. Wrong!

Opening day we saw several bulls, but not the quality that my guide Bruce or I were looking for and not the ones he had seen in earlier scouting. It was the same story second, third, and fourth days out. Uh, oh! Maybe my luck has changed…

Bruce decided we should move approximately 40 miles to an area he had not yet scouted. I must admit I had second thoughts, but I trust Bruce, and I know the quality of elk on this island. By mid-afternoon we were in a new area and seeing elk. At first a few cows, then after a while, many more. Bruce commented, "There has to be a good bull in with all these cows." Day's are short in mid-October on Vancouver Island and we didn't have too much time left before sunset.

Finally we spotted a bull coming out of the timber. Immediately we both knew it was a giant bull. I worked at staying calm until the bull presented a good shot. After a short wait behind the rifle scope he presented the shot for a clean kill and down he went. As we got closer to my bull he kept looking better and better. Wow! No ground shrinkage on this one! One look at this bull up close and I knew he had to be a really good one. Bruce, who is usually laid back, was very excited.

We calmed down just enough to count the points. I couldn't believe it. An incredible 9x10 with exceptional mass. It was getting dark so Bruce went back to the truck to call for help packing him out. I still couldn't believe it — none of the guides or friends had seen this bull prior to opening day. We all agreed he would have to score high in the records book. The 24th Awards Judges' Panel measured the elk with a score of 396-5/8 points making it a new World's Record.

Great time, great guide, great hunt — and a great trophy. ▲▲▲

Photograph by Cliff White

TROPHY STATS
▼ ▼ ▼ ▼ ▼

Category
Roosevelt's elk

Score
372^1/$_8$

Locality
Del Norte County, California - 2000

Hunter
Robert H. Gaynor

Length of Main Beam
Right: 53^4/$_8$ Left: 55^4/$_8$

Circumference Between 1st and 2nd Points
Right: 8^6/$_8$ Left: 8^1/$_8$

Number of Points
Right: 8 Left: 8

Inside Spread
37^3/$_8$

BOONE AND CROCKETT CLUB

ROOSEVELT'S ELK
Second Award - 372¹/₈

▼ ▼ ▼ ▼ ▼ ▼ ▼ ▼

ROBERT H. GAYNOR

I arrived in Crescent City, California, three days early and planned on doing some serious scouting. That was before I lost my wallet. So, much of my pre-hunt time was spent reestablishing my identity and refilling a new wallet. I've only known a few guardian angels, but for this hunt they appeared in the form of KOA campground owners Patty and Eric Lund. Like family, they helped me get through local red tape. My saving grace was in not carrying my hunting license and limited entry Roosevelt's elk tag in my wallet. I just couldn't bear to sit on them, so they had adorned my dashboard.

The day before my hunt there was a required orientation at the local Rowdy Creek Gun Club. I showed up along with nine other bull tag and five cow tag holders. The hunt, in its ninth year, had just increased bull tags from five to ten. Two landowners were providing this premium hunt opportunity: The Simpson Timber Company and the Stimpson Redwood Company. Of course, the hunt was overseen by the California Department of Fish and Game; however, the Simpson Lumber Company and the local gun club had each provided several individuals to act as facilitators. They put in 18-hour days to ensure safety, adherence to fair chase principals, and proper handling of downed game. The rules were few and simple: Sign in and out, no camping in the hunt area, no shooting from vehicles, and no horses or ATVs. The vast hunting area extended from the Smith River to the Oregon border.

Early in the hunt, several days were hampered by ocean fog at all but the highest elevations. Very early and late was best spent glassing clearcuts and the less vegetated benches, which gave way to hazy, dark-forested drainages. Most mid-afternoons, temperatures reached the high 70s, making scouting from ridge vantage points a sweat-drenching, heart-thumping proposition. Glassing clearing edges in the sun's lee seemed to be most productive when looking for the telltale light buff coloring of bulls as opposed to the much darker cows. A true Pacific Northwest rain forest, the density of secondary growth made glassing in those locations fruitless. Hemlock and fir grew at higher elevations. Redwood trees and aspen-lined creeks held sway below a thousand feet where there seemed to be a greater amount of fresh sign.

The 2000 hunt was held a week earlier than previous hunts. This was the reason most offered to explain the scarcity of bulging. The second week the bulls were a bit more vocal but not much more. On the first day of the hunt a fireman from Davis, California, took a 7x7 that later would score 340 points B&C. That really got everyone psyched up. On the fourth day of my hunt, late in the afternoon, a hunter from Redding, California, downed an animal in an overgrown clearcut. It was a beautiful large-bodied ivory-tipped 7x7, with very dark pelage and antlers. I pitched in to help with field dressing chores, mostly accomplished under cover of darkness. It was 2 a.m. and pouring buckets, as we quit the hillside — wobbly kneed, with one working light. I slept until noon the next day.

On the fifth day of the ten-day hunt, two unfilled bull tag holders went home. This is a bitter pill to local hunters who often glimpse these beautiful creatures, but have never had the

The author with his Roosevelt's elk scoring 372-1/8 points. The Simpson Timber Company and the Stimpson Redwood Company, along with the California Department of Fish and Game have provided premium hunting opportunities for Roosevelt's elk each year since 1992.

luck-of-the-draw. The remaining hunters filled their tags by the end of the fifth day.

First light of the eighth day there was a moderately heavy fog layer at the lower elevations. I was eager and full of anticipation even though I was the sole remaining bull tag holder. I was determined, if necessary, to hunt to the last minute of the final day. Hunting at a few hundred feet of elevation, I entered a sharp bend in a logging road. On the far side of the bend, not 30 yards away, a cow and calf were just slipping over the edge of the road. After sprinting to the edge, perhaps 25 yards below in an overgrown clearcut, I spotted a massive bull with six cows that seemed to be waiting for stragglers. The cows scattered and the bull headed straightaway downslope at a clip. The only decent shot that appeared to present itself was the old Texas heart shot. With the animal's hindquarters anchored, a neck shot presented itself at about 100 yards. Mr. Whelen and a 250-grain Core-lokt had the final say.

As large in death as in life, the magnificent creature had come to rest against a large redwood stump, the only obstacle remaining above a very deep and steep, brush choked ravine. Occasionally, I would lift my head from the chores at hand and gaze out at a shimmering Pacific Ocean. At that moment, I knew contentment and gratitude beyond measure. ▲▲▲

Photograph by Cliff White

TROPHY STATS

▼ ▼ ▼ ▼ ▼

Category
Roosevelt's elk

Score
372

Locality
Humboldt County, California - 2000

Hunter
Scot A. Christiansen

Length of Main Beam
Right: $47^4/8$ Left: $49^5/8$

**Circumference Between
1st and 2nd Points**
Right: $8^6/8$ Left: $8^4/8$

Number of Points
Right: 8 Left: 8

Inside Spread
$34^5/8$

Photograph by Jack Reneau

**Scot A. Christiansen accepting his plaque
and medal from Randy Byers, Chair of the
Big Game Records Committee.**

ROOSEVELT'S ELK
Third Award - 372

▼ ▼ ▼ ▼ ▼ ▼ ▼ ▼ ▼

Scot A. Christiansen

I need to start by telling you that I am 42 years old and have been hunting with my dad all my life. We live in California where you can't buy elk tags; you have to pay to enter special drawings for Roosevelt's elk, and very few hunters are drawn each year for very limited hunts. I have been entering the draw, whenever, and wherever; it was available since I was 18 years old.

We have many beautiful Roosevelt's elk in Humboldt County, but my last elk hunt had been 11 years earlier. In 2000, only 25 hunters were drawn for Humboldt County. I was lucky enough to be one of them.

The hunt was to be in an exceptionally beautiful area called Big Lagoon, which is located within an area of approximately 76,000 acres. The hunt was on property owned by Simpson Timber Company who was kind enough to open up their land for the hunt. It was behind locked gates, and although I have been a resident of Humboldt County, and a hunter all of my life, I had never seen this area from inside. It was an honor to be allowed inside. You were allowed to take two people with you, and believe me I had many offers from fellow hunters who would have gladly accompanied me. I chose my dad, Eugene Christiansen, because we have hunted together forever and we usually know what the other is thinking. I also chose a close family friend, Larry Ward, because he is also an experienced hunter and the best elk caller I know. Although I was allowed to take two friends, hunters were only allowed to bring one gun, so I chose my Remington Model 700 .30-06.

On Tuesday, August 29, 2000, we had a mandatory orientation for all hunters and their companions. We were given maps of the area and were shown the boundaries of Simpson Timber property. We were told how to take care of downed animals and told that all kills had to be removed the same day due to the large population of black bear. There were to be guards at the gates to check your vehicle license number and the number of people in your party to ensure everyone's safety. You could only enter the gate at 5:00 a.m., and had to check out by 9:00 p.m. There was no camping on the property, which was fine with us since we only had a 40-minute drive home!

The hunt was to begin on Wednesday, August 30th and end no later than Saturday, September 9th. It was legal to take either one bull, or one cow, per hunter. I had taken the time off from work and was determined that I would kill a large bull because I knew there were several trophies to be had. On the last day I would have taken a cow, had that been my only option.

On the first day of the hunt my dad, Larry, and I arrived at 5:30 a.m. while it was still dark. We drove around all day looking for areas we thought had potential, and orienting ourselves with the lay of the land. We saw a couple of fellow hunters that day, but never saw one elk! We saw a few blacktail deer, and although it was archery season for blacktail, we were forced to pass them up! On the way out that night at around 6:00 p.m., we asked at the gate and were told that several bulls and one cow had been taken that first day. We thought those hunters were the luckiest guys in the world and wondered how long we'd be out there "looking around."

The second day of the hunt we arrived at about 6:00 a.m. It was just about daylight, Dad was driving, Larry was in the middle, and I was on the right-hand side of the truck. Off to my right I was sure I saw the silhouette of a bull elk, just a few yards off the road. We were on a paved road and traveling at a pretty good speed when I told them that I saw a nice bull. These guys are great spotters, but they saw nothing and didn't believe me. And besides, after yesterday, it seemed too soon and too easy! When we got to the next spot in the road wide enough to turn around we headed back so I could show them what they thought I didn't see. There it was! We all agreed it was a big bull and one that we were interested in, but it was not on Simpson Timber property, which made the bull illegal to hunt.

We drove out of sight and parked the truck. Larry and I got out and walked quietly to get as close as we could, so that we could call the bull over to us, and get him to cross over into our hunting area. Larry sat about 20 yards behind me, and I sat in a bush, creating a blind. Larry started the cow call and it worked! The bull came within 30 feet of me, I would later find out, but I could not see it. I could only hear him snort. Something spooked the animal and it retreated. Staying in the same spots, Larry began calling again and this time, 80 yards in front of me, a cow walked out from behind a big bush. I had no idea there were any cows in the area. One by one, I watched through my rifle scope, as 19 cows passed in front of me. My heart was pounding as I waited for the bull and wondered if it would ever come my way! After what seemed like an eternity, the bull stepped out from behind the same bush. I took a deep breath, aimed, and shot. It fell, but got right back up and ran off. I knew I hit it hard but didn't know where it went. The three of us went to track it when Dad spotted the tips of its antlers in the tulies. I snuck closer to the bull, when it jumped up and ran, again! I wasn't able to get another shot off because the tulies were higher than my head. I kept trailing my bull and finally, it went into an open area and turned to face me. At only 20 yards the bull snorted and I was sure it was going to charge. I took aim and fired again. It seemed like slow motion. I was sure I had hit the bull, but it just stood there, and slowly fell to the ground. When it didn't move I walked over to it and went back to Dad and Larry and told them, "We got a good bull!" It was a very nice 8x8.

It turned out my bull was only 500 yards from the road and we drove the truck as close as we could. I wanted to have the head mounted so we wrapped the whole bull in a tarp, and drug it back to the road with the truck. At the road, Tom McDonald, a Simpson Timber employee who was also in charge of the hunt, was waiting for us. He drove back to the mill ,which was only a half mile away, and returned with a 966 log loader. Luckily for us he was able to pick up the bull and loaded it into the back of our truck.

We drove the 40-minute trip back to Eureka, with a lot of stares from everyone we passed and went straight to the California Department of Fish and Game office to have my bull validated. Everyone there was impressed with the size of the bull.

By the time I drove home, half the town had heard about my bull. After I was home for a few minutes several friends showed up and convinced me that this one should be scored for the Boone and Crockett Club's records book.

After the 60-day drying time, I contacted Guy Hooper, an official measurer for Boone and Crockett. He scored the bull at 369-4/8 and assured me it would be well up in the book. After Boone and Crockett invited me to the 24th Big Game Awards Banquet, I had the antlers shipped to them. I received a letter from the Club stating they had panel scored the bull and gave it a score of 372 points. ▲▲▲

Award Winning Moments...

Photograph by Jack Reneau

Bass Pro Shops staff member, Jim Millikin, marvels at the new World's Record tule elk on display at 24th Awards Trophy Exhibit. This is the first Awards Program to include entries in the new tule elk category.

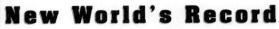

Photograph by Cliff White

TROPHY STATS

▼ ▼ ▼ ▼ ▼

Category
tule elk

Score
351

Location
Solano County, California - 1990

Hunter
Quentin Hughes

Owner
Loaned to B&C National Collection

Length of Main Beam
Right: 48⁶/8 Left: 47⁴/8

**Circumference Between
1st and 2nd Points**
Right: 7¹/8 Left: 6⁴/8

Number of Points
Right: 9 Left: 9

Inside Spread
51³/8

TULE ELK
First Award - 351

▼ ▼ ▼ ▼ ▼ ▼ ▼ ▼

QUENTIN HUGHES - HUNTER

LOANED TO B&C NATIONAL COLLECTION BY FLO SPARKS - OWNER

On the way home one Friday afternoon, my husband and a friend from work decided to purchase a couple of lottery tickets. Quentin said they should put in for the Grizzly Island elk drawing since they were in a lottery mood. Several days later, both applications were placed in the same envelope and mailed.

The notification of the drawing was mailed in mid-June and both had been selected for the third hunt for a branch antlered bull. This was the first time in 18 years that tule elk could be hunted, and excitement was high.

On August 24, 1990, Quentin arrived at Grizzly Island, attended the required orientation for hunters, and scouted for a big bull until dark. His hunting partner insisted that Quentin was to take the first bull the following morning.

As dawn was breaking across the marsh, the two hunters headed to the area where the large bulls were seen the night before. After some time, a large antler top was seen above the tules. They checked the wind and planned a route to get within 150 yards of the bull. Just after 9 a.m., the feeding bull stepped out of the tall grass and continued to feed on the lower salt grass. The crosshairs on Quentin's 7mm Magnum settled behind the shoulder area and the shot was made. The bull crumpled.

Within a short time, the giant bull was in the back of a truck and headed for the hunting camp area. Quentin's partner deposited the bull and set off on his own quest. The temperature began to rise and the bull had to be caped and skinned.

Quentin didn't know how to cape the bull, but there was a person in the camp who did, and it was done quickly as the thermometer read 85 degrees at 11 a.m. Various measurements were taken and tallied. It was said at the time that it was the largest hunter-killed tule elk known. At the end of October, J.J. McBride came to Park Merced and officially measured the elk and praised it. Since it was one of the best specimens known, he had a request.

On June 21, 1991, the Boone and Crockett Club celebrated the opening of the National Collection of Heads and Horns at the Buffalo Bill Historical Center in Cody, Wyoming. It was one of the proudest days in Quentin's life to see his tule elk hanging among some of the greatest trophies ever taken in North America. Quentin loaned his trophy to the National Collection to share it with other sportsmen, and it still resides there today. ▲▲▲

Photograph by Cliff White

TROPHY STATS

▼ ▼ ▼ ▼ ▼

Category
  tule elk

Score
  341⁴/₈

Location
  Solano County, California - 1990

Hunter
  Alvin M. Wallen

Length of Main Beam
  Right: 49⁵/₈ Left: 52²/₈

Circumference Between 1st and 2nd Points
  Right: 7⁶/₈ Left: 7⁵/₈

Number of Points
  Right: 8 Left: 7

Inside Spread
  48³/₈

Photograph by Jack Reneau

Alvin M. Wallen accepting his plaque and medal from Randy Byers, Chair of the Big Game Records Committee.

TULE ELK
Second Award - 341⁴/₈

▼ ▼ ▼ ▼ ▼ ▼ ▼ ▼ ▼

ALVIN M. WALLEN

When checking my mail one-day in early July 1990, I received a letter from the California Department of Fish and Game. This letter would lead me to my greatest hunting experience to date. In the letter was a coveted tag for the first ever hunt on the Grizzly Island Wildlife area for the rare tule elk. I had applied some months earlier with little confidence of drawing one of the eight tags assigned for bull elk. The hunt would be held over four weeks with two hunters allowed per week.

My hunt was the first period, August 11th through August 14th 1990. Grizzly Island Wildlife area is located near Fairfield, in California's Delta region, an area broken with waterways and carpeted with grass and tall tules. My son Dan Wallen volunteered to assist me in the hunt and I quickly took him up on the offer. Over the next four weeks leading up to my hunt I scouted the hunt area extensively. The rut was near, but the bulls were not active, and most of the older ones were still in the foothills out of the hunt area.

Photograph courtesy of Alvin M. Wallen

There was an orientation with Department of Fish and Game personnel prior to the hunt, and I got to meet several of the men and women involved in the tule elk management – a fine, dedicated group. On August 10th I arrived at the hunt area with my small camping trailer in tow, prepared for my hunt starting the next morning.

It had been more than 100 years since the bugle of a wild tule elk had been commonplace in California's Delta region, but that was the first sound my son Dan and I heard as we stepped out of our trailer the next morning. We could hear calls coming from several directions and I was aware of the fact that we were experiencing a

Alvin M. Wallen, center, goes over the details of the orientation meeting with CA Fish and Game Department personnel, Brian Hunter and Doug Updike.

rare occurrence. I was hearing a creature that had been considered almost extinct since the early 1870s, but had been brought back to huntable populations by the efforts of the dedicated personnel of the California Department of Fish and Game.

I scouted the marshy islands and was able to observe several of the larger bulls that had moved down out of the hills. It was obvious that the rut was in full swing. After many hours of glassing and stalking we located what appeared to be a very large bull. The bull was about 500 yards away so we hid in some tall tules, with Dan setting up 30 yards behind me to call. The bull

Alvin M. Wallen with his tule elk bull scoring 341-4/8 points which received a Second Award at the 24th Big Game Awards Banquet in Springfield, Missouri.

responded immediately. After some minutes of back and forth calling, the bull started moving in our direction and Dan switched to a cow call. We could not see the bull, but he kept bugling and coming in our direction. Dan gave one last plaintive cow call.

Less than 50 feet away a huge bull elk stepped out of the tules, stopped and bugled in our direction. The bullet from my .300 Winchester Magnum hit the bull behind a shoulder dropping him. Both Dan and I were awed as we approached the magnificent animal. The quartered weight with cape and horns was over 750 pounds. He scored 341-4/8 points, making him one of the highest scoring tule elk in the world. My thanks go to the dedicated California Department of Fish and Game personnel that made this hunting experience possible. ▲▲▲

Photograph by Cliff White

TROPHY STATS

▼ ▼ ▼ ▼ ▼

Category
tule elk

Score
330¹/₈

Location
Solano County, California - 1999

Hunter
Tod L. Reichert

Length of Main Beam
Right: 52³/₈ Left: 52⁴/₈

**Circumference Between
1st and 2nd Points**
Right: 7⁶/₈ Left: 7²/₈

Number of Points
Right: 9 Left: 7

Inside Spread
38⁴/₈

BOONE AND CROCKETT CLUB

TULE ELK
Third Award - 330¹/₈

▼ ▼ ▼ ▼ ▼ ▼ ▼ ▼

TOD L. REICHERT

I always wanted a tule elk to put on my wall and the only way I knew of doing that was to buy a Governor's tag for California, where you hunt on Grizzly Island Wildlife Refuge. I acquired the tag in April of 1999.

I had three other Governor's tags for Alberta and did not get a good bull on any of my hunts, so I knew there was no guarantee of taking a good bull even with a Governor's tag.

My Pressure Elk Hunt

A friend of mine, Jim Cook, had taken a nice tule elk a few years earlier with a guide named Richard Cox. So I started talking to Richard about his hunts and the possibility of taking a really good bull. The fun part about this hunt was that prior to the hunt, Richard would take pictures of different bulls while he was scouting. He would send me photos of bulls he had seen once a month, which really got me excited about hunting tule elk. When it got down to the last month before our hunt he sent me some more pictures with his guess as to each bull's possible score. We had it narrowed down to three or four bulls. I really liked the one that they called "Louie I."

The only thing that made me nervous was that they wanted to video my hunt. Jim Zumbo, Editor-at-Large for *Outdoor Life* magazine, was writing a story on tule elk and he wanted to tag along. That's more people looking over my shoulder than I was used to, but I finally agreed.

This hunt started on August 10th with the elk already starting to rut. My wife and I drove from Washington to California. I took my pickup with a freezer and small generator in the back so I could bring my meat back home with me. The Central Coast Chapter of the Mule Deer Foundation was kind enough to have a motor home for us to stay in. A lot of other Foundation members were there with their motor homes and the hunt was looking like a big camp out.

We got there early Friday and I met with Richard and Ed Fisher, with California Fish & Game. We also met Ron Jolly, a videographer who was doing the video, and Jim Zumbo.

We went scouting that evening and we found "Louie I" not too far from camp. He looked bigger in real life than in any of the pictures I had seen of him. We also found a non-typical elk, which really caught my eye. He had more antler mass than "Louie I," but would not score as well. I told Richard if we cannot find "Louie I" in the morning I would take the non-typical. After that first evening we all went back to camp and had a nice cookout.

I did not get much sleep that night as I was really nervous about the hunt in the morning — more about all the people who were going to be following along, two camera men, Jim, and my guide Richard. All I could think about was what if I missed or wounded the elk with all these guys looking on, and to have it on film.

The next morning came and we left in the dark. When it finally got light enough to see we couldn't find "Louie I." We hiked around for an hour or so with no luck. There were lots of tule weed patches tall and thick enough to hide a bull forever. Finally we got a quick look at "Louie I" who

Tod Reichert with his award-winning Roosevelt's elk scoring 330-1/8 points taken with a Governor's Tag on a Grizzly Island hunt in California.

showed up back over by our elk camp. We quickly hustled back to our rig while Richard reassured me he knew where the bull was headed. He obviously knew the area, and the elk's patterns well.

As we drove around by camp, some of the people left there said they saw the bull almost come right through camp. We found the spot Richard had in mind, got out, and started hiking down an old road with the tule weeds eight feet tall on both sides. I sure hoped he was not hiding in the weeds. Richard stopped and bugled; he got a quick response from just ahead. We eased forward and came to a big opening to our left and immediately hit the ground. There were about ten plus head of elk in the opening with my bull doing battle with a nice 7X7.

"Louie I" must have taken a night off and returned to his girls that morning. It took me a good half hour to get the shot I wanted. To get a solid rest I had to shoot off Richard's back as he lay on the ground. Boy, was I nervous. I don't think I have ever had more pressure than in that 30-minute time frame. I was not going to pull the trigger unless I was sure of the right hit. He was fighting with the other bull most of the time, and then a cow or spike would be in the way of a shot. I wanted to make sure I had a good, clear shot. The camera crew even had to change batteries, as it took so long for the bull to be clear. After a grueling wait behind the scope I got the shot I wanted at approximately 250 yards. He stopped on a little rise and I let fly. I could tell it was a hit and wasted no time getting another shot off before he went down. After a number of pictures and video we all continued to admire this tremendous bull. This will be a hunt I will never forget.

I would like to thank the California Department of Fish & Game for the fine job they are doing at Grizzly Island the Mule Deer Foundation, Central Coast Chapter, and my guide Richard Cox. I never in my life have met so many nice people in one group and the food was also great. Thanks again for their help in making this a great hunt. ▲▲▲

Photograph by Cliff White

TROPHY STATS

▼ ▼ ▼ ▼ ▼

Category
tule elk

Score
319²/₈

Location
Solano County, California - 1992

Hunter
H. James Tonkin, Jr.

Length of Main Beam
Right: 47⁶/₈ Left: 43

**Circumference Between
1st and 2nd Points**
Right: 6⁶/₈ Left: 7⁴/₈

Number of Points
Right: 8 Left: 7

Inside Spread
44⁷/₈

TULE ELK
Fourth Award - 319²/₈

▼ ▼ ▼ ▼ ▼ ▼ ▼ ▼

H. James Tonkin, Jr.

While crawling on an old overgrown ditch, beads of sweat trickled down my forehead. It had to be close to 85 degrees. Another 50 yards of crawling should put me where there might be a chance at the big tule elk bull. After scrambling up the bank and parting the high grass, there before me were 27 bulls sunning themselves on a dry pond bed. Right in the middle of the group was the bull on which I wanted to put my tag.

There was no chance for a shot as the bullet could easily pass through the elk and into one of his sleeping brethren. Under the scorching sun I lay there waiting for the bull to move and present a clear, safe shot.

The sight of bugling bulls sparring and carrying on in the marsh was a sight that intrigued me. Prior to my hunt I attended a Boone and Crockett Club scorer's workshop. As part of the workshop the instructor arranged for a field trip to see the rarest of all elk. While viewing these amazing animals I decided I had to have one for my trophy room.

In the 1830s there were an estimated 500,000 tule elk in the valleys and coastal foothills of California. The high demand for meat by the population explosion of gold miners and new cities caused extreme pressure on the elk by market hunters. In 1870, four tule elk stepped out of some willows near Bakersfield, California, and they were all that separated the species from extinction. They were taken to the nearby Miller-Lux ranch for protection and to propagate. After 150 years and these four animals we now have a population of approximately 3,600 in 23 different herds.

Since restoration and management programs are expensive operations, in 1990 the state authorized two governor's tags, with all the proceeds going to benefit the elk. At a Sacramento Safari Club dinner in February, I purchased one of these tags and the Total Elk Dream Hunt.

The day to leave on the hunt finally arrived and I took all the gear I might need to my office. Soon, the special 38-foot truck Limousine used to transport the governor's tag holders to the hunting grounds, arrived and my wife Sherry and I were on our way. "Camp" consisted of the large tent (for meals), cooks, guides, well wishers, video personnel, and Fish and Game personnel.

A makeshift rifle range was set up near the headquarters and it showed that both of the pistols I brought were well within one inch at the 100-yard mark. They were a .375 JDJ on a Thompson Contender frame firing 270-grain. Hornady slugs, and a .375/.284 JDJ on a Remington XP 100 with 250-grain Sierra bullets.

For the previous month, a teacher friend of mine from Glen Ellen had scouted the bulls of Grizzly Island. He knew them all and had videos of them as well as telephoto shots of the biggest bull on the island — my dream bull. He was easily identifiable due to a lone tine on the end of his left antler, and no other bull looked anything like him.

The camp was "home" for both of the governor's tag holders, and prior to dinner, Brian Hunter presented both hunters with their special tags. The meal was a sit down barbecue steak dinner for 35 and there was not a want that was overlooked. About 9 p.m., it was time to get some rest, so my wife

Photograph courtesy of H. James Tonkin, Jr.

B&C Official Measurer, H. James Tonkin used a .375 JDJ firing 270-grain Hornaday slugs at 170 yards to take this Grizzly Island bull scoring 319-2/8 points. He had studied hours of video and numerous still shots of the bulls in the area taken by a friend on a scouting trip and had his eye out for this bull throughout the hunt.

and I retired to a 25-foot trailer provided as part of the hunt. Sleep did not come easy knowing that tomorrow was "the" day.

Well before first light, the coffee was brewed and the aroma of bacon and eggs swirled around the grove. Outside, the vehicles were readied and hunters gathered their gear. As the faint traces of red began to appear in the early dawn, the hunters were off on their quest as the main camp slept.

Grizzly Island is a 14,400-acre wildlife area operated by California Fish & Game. It is located in the 84,000-acre Suisun Marsh, which is the largest tidal marsh in the U.S. and borders the Sacramento River Channel. The elk were first brought to this jungle of tule, pickleweed, and salt grass in 1977. You may only hunt them on the state property and they freely roam the numerous private duck clubs in total protection.

Shadows of big bulls moved about the field and tule, near Montezuma Slough. My teacher/guide began to search for the special bull and soon located him with streamers of freshly stripped velvet fluttering in the breeze as hundreds of ducks took to the air at the intrusion of the elk. A group of six of the older bulls, including my white horn dream, began to move out of the area at a slow grazing pace.

Dave McLean, with his video camera, followed behind as J.J. and I worked toward a hopeful intercept point ahead. A group of river otters scampered along the slough bank and dove in the water as we made our way through the tule grass. Out in a wide field of salt grass and pickleweed, 200 yards distant, the bulls were grazing. We had to narrow the distance so an accurate shot could be made.

Seventy-five yards away was a grassy mount in the field and we decided that was our best bet for a sure shot. We bent over and walked closely together to try to appear elk-like and walked diagonally to the mound. I flopped down and began to set the rest up, and readied the pistol as the elk looked at us nervously. They began to mill about and there was no clear shot at my bull as we waited. After several minutes, the crosshairs rested behind the bull's shoulder and he was clear as I heard, "Take him" from over my shoulder. The squeeze on the trigger started and was followed by the most dreaded sound ever heard. PPFffftttt! A misfire due to improper ignition of my hand load as the bullet hit the ground harmlessly 80 yards away. The bulls heard the odd sound and it was all they needed to break into a steady trot, right into the slough, and swim over to Van Sickle Island and safety.

We returned to camp and hoped the elk would return during the night. Only the hunter and guides were allowed to leave the camp area so no hunt would be disturbed. Late in the afternoon the Fish & Game radio crackled and called for the "mule" to Field 10. Camp came alive as several trucks were started and bodies piled aboard to follow a 4-wheeler towing a small tilt trailer into the sea of grass. Jim Hatcher of Oregon had found his lone bull coming upwind to the large herd of cows with rutting intentions that would not be fulfilled. The camp crew gleefully admired the bull, took photos of the event and loaded the carcass on the trailer for transport and processing in the camp area.

The celebration began before dinner and carried on well after. Thoughts of where and what my bull was doing danced through my head as sleep came slowly. In the darkness a voice came from the trailer door saying, "It's time Jim, let's go!" Hot coffee drove the drowsiness from my system as my wife and I headed out.

The scanning of endless fields showed the main group of bulls were having an early breakfast, but my bull was not among them. About two miles away a flash of antler was spotted in a heavy tule patch. It turned out to be the group of six bulls from the day before and they had indeed returned to the island in the dark. They seemed to be moving toward the main herd and in the direction of a dry pond bed. The sun began its journey across the sky as the bulls joined the main herd and then headed for their sunbath in the dry pond.

Having an idea of exactly where they were, my guide made several decisions. I was dropped off at the spot and told to go out about 200 yards and get into a five-foot deep ditch on the right. Then I was to go about 500 yards down the ditch and then carefully look over the top. A large stand of tule jutted away from the ditch and concealed the dry pond for most of the stalk. My wife and guide went to a spot about a mile away to watch and await the outcome.

I prepared my pack as a rest and set the pistol in the ready position as the sun beat down. For 90 minutes the resting elk shielded my bull. Then one moved from behind him and my bull was going to stand up 170 yards away. He stood and shook the fine peat dust from his coat. His long, identifier tine still had a shred of velvet hanging off, dangling in the wind. The report from my pistol caused the main herd to mill about in confusion as their monarch faltered in a vain attempt to move. When I stood up, the main herd of bulls hastily departed, leaving their comrade behind. Although we started before sunrise, my watch read 3:15 p.m.

After several minutes, the area was bustling with people. The "mule" and trucks were coming from one direction and my wife was skipping through the pickleweed, along with my smiling guide. Cameras recorded the moment and the bull taken the with my .375 JDJ, but, his final moment was a private one between him and me.

As the sun was dropping behind the hills overlooking San Francisco Bay, the white truck limousine was headed home. Piled on top of our gear was a large tule elk rack and memories of what a Total Tule Elk Dream Hunt was like. From the brink of extinction to over 3,600 huntable elk in 150 years — this is truly the comeback story of the 20th Century. ▲▲▲

TROPHY STATS

▼ ▼ ▼ ▼ ▼

Category
   tule elk

Score
   317³/₈

Location
   Solano County, California - 1996

Hunter
   Donald L. Potter

Length of Main Beam
   Right: 51⁵/₈ Left: 49⁶/₈

**Circumference Between
1st and 2nd Points**
   Right: 7⁴/₈ Left: 7⁴/₈

Number of Points
   Right: 9 Left: 8

Inside Spread
   39⁴/₈

TULE ELK
Fifth Award - 317³/₈

▼ ▼ ▼ ▼ ▼ ▼ ▼ ▼ ▼

DONALD L. POTTER

In 1996 I was fortunate to win a tule elk bull permit for Grizzly Island Wildlife Area, which is located near Fairfax City in Solano County, California, east of San Francisco Bay. That year 10 bull elk tags, six of which were for spike bulls, and 9 anterless elk tags were allocated. The season runs from the second Saturday in August straight through the first week in September. In order to generate funds for elk management and research, three bull elk tags are auctioned to the highest bidder. These tags netted the Department of Fish and Game $36,000 in 1996. Rifles using centerfire cartridges with expanding softnose bullets, and archery gear are allowed. All hunts are fair chase with vehicles only allowed on designated access roads to the hunting areas. There is a campsite available at the "elk pen," which is also an animal processing area. The "elk pen" area is for successful hunters to hang, skin, and/or butcher their elk. The Fish and Game requires the ungutted elk be weighed and biological samples taken at this area.

I scouted the island for three days about three weeks before the hunting season. The results were very disappointing as I did not see one elk. The Fish and Game people on site were also surprised, but thought that the herd had crossed the sloughs onto the adjacent private cattle ranches. I realized I needed a lot of help to hunt this area. The island consists of sloughs of fresh to brackish water with upland grasslands, scattered tule weed groupings, and a few bunches of trees. The stalking would require experience I did not have. I was fortunate to be put in contact with a guide who had hunted this island for many years, Richard Cox. Richard assured me that he would show me some elk and I would have an opportunity to take one.

We began scouting a couple days just prior to my scheduled hunt. On the second day we were moving along a levee road when Richard's eyes focused intently to our left and he practically exhaled "Its Spot." About 100 yards away, standing with his front legs on top of a levee and his hind legs on the lower side was the most heart pounding sight I have ever experienced and will never forget. The bull's antlers and body were huge and amplified by his position on the levee. He stared at us with his head cocked hard to the left. That was the clue that allowed Richard to quickly identify the bull as a legend on the island with the Fish and Game people. Years before this bull had been gored so badly that he had a foot and a half black scar on his left shoulder and lost his left eye. They almost put him down because of the seriousness of his condition, but decided to monitor him. He was known to be spoiling for a fight most of the time, probably due to pain. After a minute he turned to his left and walked to the levee bottom and totally disappeared.

When the hunt began I recalled Richard's prior promise about showing me some elk, and that was no exaggeration. We found a few good bulls over the next few days, but stalking was difficult due to the lack of cover. We moved from one tule patch to another in order to maneuver into a range and position to take a shot. I had one opportunity for a shot as a bull and a herd of cows slowly moved toward us as we knelt between two tule patches. They passed us at about 50 yards at full gallop, and the window of available sighting was so brief and unexpected I declined to shoot. I

The author with his tule elk scoring 317-3/8 points taken in the Grizzly Island Wildlife Area east of San Francisco.

am glad now that I passed on that opportunity.

On the last day of the scheduled hunt we drove along a levee to a parking area where we planned to start hunting. Shortly after leaving the parking lot, Richard's hand quickly shot out toward my right, and there stood a bull at about 150 yards. He was behind some brush, grazing, head down and quartering away. Quietly we crept out to where our view was not obstructed by bushes. All this time the bull kept grazing without paying us any notice. The first shot hit him in the left shoulder completely disabling his front left leg. I could not believe that he did not go down, but instead took off at a gallop. The second shot dropped him. This shot entered his left side, through a rib, the lung and heart cavity, then through a rib on the right side lodging in the skin. My initial excitement that he was really down was exceeded by disbelief as we walked up to him. That's when I began to fully realize his body bulk and antler reach. Once on him we discovered the large black scar on his left shoulder and the missing left eye. I had just taken the Fish and Game's prize bull elk, legend and all. It was obvious then why he seemed so calm before I shot the first time - we were on his side with the missing eye.

We called in the camp personnel and they came out with an ATV pulling a flat bed trailer. It took five of us to roll his carcass up onto the flat bed. When we got back to the "elk pen" we added up the score — 878 pounds, 9x8 antler count, 323-1/8 green score, and anticipation of a full freezer of venison. Boned and butchered he was 452 pounds.

In closing, I would like to say a sincere "thank you" to my guide Richard Cox, Jon Fischer and Dennis Becker with the Fish and Game at GIWA. I would also like to acknowledge Larry Bangs of Kountry Meats in Elk Grove, Chuck Means, Imperial Taxidermy in Sacramento, and Richard Brown of the Rocky Mountain Elk Foundation. ▲ ▲ ▲

Award Winning Moments...

Photograph by Jack Reneau

Seventeen-year-old Clint Ream, receives a congratulatory handshake from Boone and Crockett Executive Director, George Bettas, for winning the Ruger Red Label 12-gauge shotgun in a raffle at the 24th Awards Banquet. Sturm, Ruger and Company, along with Bass Pro Shops, Leupold & Stevens, Mossy Oak Brand Camo, Remington, Bushnell, and Walker's Game Ear were all sponsors of the events surrounding the 24th Awards Program.

Photograph by Cliff White

TROPHY STATS
▼ ▼ ▼ ▼ ▼

Category
  tule elk

Score
  346⁶/₈

Location
  Sonoma County, California - 1851

Hunter
  Christian Weise

Owner
  Harry Weise

Length of Main Beam
  Right: 48 Left: 49⁴/₈

**Circumference Between
1st and 2nd Points**
  Right: 7⁵/₈ Left: 6⁷/₈

Number of Points
  Right: 8 Left: 8

Inside Spread
  37⁴/₈

Photograph by Jack Reneau

Harry Weise accepting his plaque from
Randy Byers, Chair of the Big Game
Records Committee.

TULE ELK
Certificate of Merit - 346⁶/₈

▼ ▼ ▼ ▼ ▼ ▼ ▼ ▼ ▼

CHRISTIAN WEISE - HUNTER
HARRY WEISE - OWNER

Northern California in 1849 meant Gold Rush fever; however, not all of the 49ers who arrived in San Francisco sought to make their fortune in gold. Christian Weise, an immigrant from Germany, made his modest income by hunting game and selling it to the markets. In or around 1851 Christian Weise, a market hunter, killed this magnificent tule elk.

On the northern tip of San Francisco Bay, in a foggy marsh-like area close to what is now the town of Petaluma, hunting camps provided a home for some of the market hunters. It was from one of these hunting camps that my great grandfather, Christian Weise, made his way out into the tidal land, small valleys and rolling hills of southern Sonoma County in search of the prized tule elk. As with most market hunters this was not a "horn" hunt. "Prized" in 1849 meant $40 for each hindquarter. He was unaware that 150 years later the land near Tolay Creek where he was hunting would be a wildlife preserve and that results of his hunt would be recognized as one of the best scoring tule elk ever recorded.

Christian died in 1898. Although the antlers from his elk have remained in our family, we cannot precisely establish the exact date, the mode of transportation, the gun utilized, or the weather conditions for the hunt. I can state with certainty that no motor-powered vehicle was used, and that the gun was probably a muzzleloader of some type.

In the 1850s, market hunting served to provide food to those who did not hunt and to provide profits to those who did. There were no laws, no licenses, and unfortunately, no conservation efforts governing hunting. I am proud that hunting has remained a tradition in my family for five generations and grateful that with each generation an increased understanding and commitment to conservation emerges. ▲▲▲

Photograph by Cliff White

TROPHY STATS

▼ ▼ ▼ ▼ ▼

Category
tule elk

Score
315^4/$_8$

Location
Solano County, California - 1994

Hunter
David G. Paullin

Length of Main Beam
Right: 46^4/$_8$ Left: 48^7/$_8$

Circumference Between 1st and 2nd Points
Right: 7^6/$_8$ Left: 7^2/$_8$

Number of Points
Right: 7 Left: 7

Inside Spread
39^7/$_8$

Photograph by Jack Reneau

David G. Paullin accepting his plaque from Randy Byers, Chair of the Big Game Records Committee.

146

TULE ELK
Honorable Mention - 315⁴/₈

▼ ▼ ▼ ▼ ▼ ▼ ▼ ▼ ▼ ▼

DAVID G. PAULLIN

Growing up in Sacramento, I first became aware of tule elk in 1967 in a rather unusual and surprising way. In the fall of that year a construction crew had uncovered a rich Nisenan-Maidu Indian campsite within the city limits. Construction was halted to allow the local university to do a full scale archeological dig. When the site was opened for public tours, Dad and I drove over for a look. The site had the usual carefully excavated trenches exposing skeletal remains of native Americans, stone implements, and much to my surprise, a six-point antler from the indigenous California tule Elk. The heavy, well preserved antler was buried horizontally just a few inches below the surface and it looked strangely out of place just a few feet from one of Sacramento's busy boulevards. It was hard to comprehend that at one time the lush Central Valley of California harbored thousands of these wetland-loving animals.

Twenty-seven years later I would cross paths again with the tule elk. In 1994, I was drawn for a highly coveted elk tag for the Grizzly Island Wildlife Area managed by the California Department of Fish and Game. The good news was that I had beaten odds of 1,089 to 1 to draw the tag. The bad news was that of the five branch-antlered bull tags issued that year (three lottery draw and two auction tags) my four-day hunt in early September would be the last hunt. While I was excited at the prospect of harvesting this rarest of North American elk, I was concerned that the four hunters ahead of me would harvest the biggest and best bulls before I had a chance.

My pre-hunt research turned up a name that would have a lasting impact on my hunting career — J.J. McBride. Besides being an avid hunter, one of his hobbies is video taping tule elk. When it comes to field scoring big game J.J. knows his stuff. He is well known in the Boone and Crockett Club and was instrumental in putting together the National Collection of Heads and Horns in Cody, Wyoming (see *Records of North American Big Game,* 10th Edition, 1993, page 35). After several phone calls I was convinced J.J. knew Grizzly Island, knew tule Elk, and knew how to size them up on the hoof. We agreed to meet on Grizzly Island the morning before opening day.

The shrieking of bugling bulls in full rut shattered the pre-dawn darkness. At first light the spectacle before my eyes was something I will never forget. Spread across a broad plain of grasslands and wetlands were herd bulls engaged in combat — flinging mud, hair, and vegetation high into the air. While this drama unfolded, smaller satellite bulls were trying to sneak in and steal harems of cows and calves. Before the morning was over, I counted 27 bulls that were five points or better and several bulls had seven, eight, and even nine points on a side. As far as I was concerned I would be glad to take any of them, but then J.J. arrived and he gave me my first real lesson on sizing up elk in the field. One by one he pointed out why certain bulls would score well and why I should pass on others. It was hard to imagine I was listening to a perfect stranger telling me why I should not shoot a 7x8 bull elk! I was beginning to think this guy was nuts when suddenly a set of antlers appeared in the tall "tulies" (Spanish word for bulrush). The tulies were so tall, all we could see were antlers. Once we put the spotting scope on them there was no doubt this high, wide, 7x7

Photograph courtesy of David G. Paullin

The author thought he might end up empty-handed as he watched several six-pointers and a couple of non-typical bulls pass in front of him and move on to private land while he waited for this big 7x7. Fortunately the bull was found over two miles away. After hours of stalking he ended up with a 325 yard shot for the bull, which scored 315-4/8 points.

rack was superior to anything we had seen. Without hesitation J.J. said, "That's the one you want to shoot tomorrow." When I asked what it would score he quickly replied, "317." The bull emerged from the tulies and sauntered, stiff-legged and grunting, into the middle of a huge battle between two large herd bulls that were fighting over a dozen cows. Little did I know that by sunrise the next morning, this bull would whip the other two and the harem would be his. I memorized his rack, hoping I would see it again the following morning when my hunt began.

That night my brother-in-law, Mark Dobson, joined me in camp for his first elk hunt. He was more excited than I was. Well before daylight Mark and I were in position. At dawn, we watched as another hunter who had a spike bull tag shoot his animal. At the sound of the shot all the elk headed north for private land that was off limits for hunting. Fortunately for us we had positioned ourselves between the elk and the private land. They would pass in front of us at distances varying from 250 to 400 yards. After passing up several six-pointers and a couple non-typicals, all the elk had vanished to the safe haven of the adjacent private land. Mark couldn't believe his eyes. I had passed on several trophy bulls looking for the big 7x7 and now there were no elk to be seen anywhere. It was now mid-morning, and sitting there empty-handed I began to question the wisdom of my strategy when suddenly I caught a glimpse of elk over two miles away.

BOONE AND CROCKETT CLUB'

Mark and I closed the gap and through the spotting scope we could tell it was the big 7x7. He now had a harem of 12 cows stolen during the night from another bull. The elk were bedded down in a large expansive shortgrass prairie and getting within rifle range would be

TULE ELK
Honorable Mention - 315⁴/₈

▼ ▼ ▼ ▼ ▼

DAVID G. PAULLIN

very difficult. For over two hours we attempted stalking the bull from several different angles but each time we failed as the distance was too far for a shot and there was no suitable cover to get closer. Finally, I proposed a long and circuitous stalk that would require an extensive belly crawl through sparse marsh vegetation. If successful, it would put us within rifle range.

Half an hour later Mark and I crawled up on a small hummock of land hidden by a handful of grassy tussocks. This was as close as we could get. I estimated the distance at 300 yards. Cows surrounded the bull, and there was no way I could safely shoot without endangering the cows. I waited 20 minutes and finally the bull stepped away from his harem. I was calm, relaxed, and confident as I held the crosshairs behind his front shoulder and squeezed the trigger. What happened next left me dumbfounded. My bullet kicked up dust in front of the bull's brisket. For the past two hours I had been so intent on stalking this bull I failed to realize that the late morning delta breezes had turned into very strong mid-afternoon winds. I had not taken the 20-30 mph crosswinds into consideration and they blew my bullet completely off target. The wind was blowing so hard the bull did not run at the sound of the shot or the small dust cloud that kicked up near him. I quickly compensated for the wind by holding on the leading edge of his left hindquarter, and my second shot went right through his heart. The distance was 325 yards. He was a magnificent trophy with numerous battle scars on his flanks, neck, and face where other bulls had raked him with their antlers.

Fish and Game personnel were notified and they collected their data. On the hoof he weighed 720 pounds, which was a little light for a five year-old bull. When they pulled a tooth to age him we discovered one possible reason why he might be a little light. Embedded in his jawbone were the remains of a large caliber bullet. The jaw was not broken but the wound was abscessed. It was difficult to determine when the wound happened or whether it was a deliberate attempt at poaching or poor marksmanship from a previous hunter.

A week later J.J. green scored the bull at 318-2/8 points (officially scoring 315-4/8 points) and I gave him a bad time for being off his original estimate. Even though I had the very last branch-antlered bull tag, as it turned out, my bull was the biggest tule elk shot on Grizzly Island in 1994. I attribute that to a little luck, some skill, and excellent coaching by J.J. McBride. ▲▲▲

Photograph by Cliff White

TROPHY STATS

▼ ▼ ▼ ▼

Category
mule deer - typical antlers

Score
$212^7/_8$

Locality
Garfield County, Colorado - 1971

Hunter
Errol R. Raley

Length of Main Beam
Right: $27^1/_8$ Left: $26^6/_8$

Circumference Between burr and 1st Point
Right: $4^5/_8$ Left: $4^6/_8$

Number of Points
Right: 5 Left: 5

Inside Spread
$28^4/_8$

Photograph by Jack Reneau

Errol R. Raley accepting his plaque and medal from Randy Byers, Chair of the Big Game Records Committee.

MULE DEER
TYPICAL ANTLERS
First Award - 212⁷/₈

▼　▼　▼　▼　▼　▼　▼　▼　▼

ERROL R. RALEY

Errol started hunting when he was 11 years old with his father, cousin, and uncle. He received his first guide's license when he was 18 years old and worked as a guide and outfitter for the next 18 years. Since he spent the majority of the hunting seasons guiding, he rarely had the opportunity to trophy hunt for himself, saving the truly big bucks for paying clients. In 1971 Errol harvested this B&C buck. He had it roughly scored in 1977. At that time he figured the buck was about eighth largest in the world, based upon the Boone and Crockett Club's 7th Edition of its all-time records book.

The hunt took place on the third or fourth day of the deer-hunting season when Errol and a friend, Rick Lyons, set off for a late afternoon hike into a draw running into Alkali Creeks. This area was on Bureau of Land Management land that they both knew fairly well from previous hunting trips. They had previously sighted the buck several times and felt confident they knew where the buck might be before they entered the draw. Both men were hoping for a non-typical muley, but as soon as Errol saw his typical buck he knew he wanted it. Rick decided to pass on the buck, so without hesitation, Errol settled in for a shot. Raising his .270 Springfield Express from a distance of about 200 yards, he fired a single shot. The 130-grain bronze point bullet dropped the buck in its tracks.

For years after Errol took the buck he was satisfied with the unofficial score. In 1997 an official measurer from the Boone and Crockett Club, Bob Black, asked him if he could officially measure the buck. He was especially impressed at the care Bob took to measure and re-measure the rack before completing the official score sheet. The buck's final score after the 24th Awards Judges' Panel was 212-7/8 points. Errol then decided that the wooden plaque he had the antlers mounted wasn't good enough for such a buck. He took the rack to Darryl Powell of Darryl's Taxidermy in Grand Junction to have the antlers mounted in full shoulder position. ▲▲▲

Photograph by Cliff White

TROPHY STATS

▼ ▼ ▼ ▼ ▼

Category
mule deer - typical antlers

Score
$206^{6}/_{8}$

Locality
Sonora, Mexico - 1998

Hunter
Jack Gurley

Length of Main Beam
Right: $28^{1}/_{8}$ Left: $27^{4}/_{8}$

Circumference Between burr and 1st Point
Right: $6^{1}/_{8}$ Left: $6^{2}/_{8}$

Number of Points
Right: 7 Left: 7

Inside Spread
26

Photograph by Jack Reneau

Jack Gurley accepting his plaque and medal from Randy Byers, Chair of the Big Game Records Committee.

152

MULE DEER TYPICAL ANTLERS
Second Award - 206⁶/₈

▼ ▼ ▼ ▼ ▼ ▼ ▼ ▼ ▼

JACK GURLEY

How could the Sonora desert produce trophy mule deer? What food was available? Where did they get water? Surely the harsh environment of the desert would stunt their growth and limit the size of their antlers. The brochure we had, however, showed photographs of world-class deer and promised the opportunity of a mule deer rack exceeding 30 inches. As we planned our trip, my hunting companion Larry Wagoner and I discussed the method of field judging a trophy rack. Neither of us planned on returning with anything less than a 30-inch buck.

We flew into Hermosilla, in western Mexico, in mid December 1998. Rick West, Larry, and I were to be the first three hunters that season on the 60,000 acre Rancho El Bamury. A four-hour truck ride later put us at the Hacienda. The road from the highway to the Ranch would have been better traveled on horseback. The rocks, ruts, and washouts only allowed a 15-20 mile per hour pace. A concrete block building with four rooms and concrete floor stood within 200 yards of a collapsing adobe building I assumed to be the old ranch house. Rogelio Lizarrage ran this ranch his family has owned since 1887. No one spoke English, but Rogelio hired Omar, the local English teacher, as a translator during our stay. Because we arrived late at night it was impossible to get an idea of the terrain we would hunt the next day. Through Omar, Rogelio explained we would set up on the nearby wheat field before sunup and shoot the first big buck that came our way. What could be easier? One day of hunting and six days of relaxing.

Wrong-amundo!!!

Before we left I had sighted my rifle for a 200-yard dead on shot. The Redfield 3x9 tracker scope and my Remington Model 700 .30-06 bolt action are rugged, reliable, and accurate. Four hours from the nearest small town in Mexico is no place for gun problems. I stepped up from the 150-grain bullet I normally used for Texas whitetail to a 165-grain Hornady. If the deer were as big as promised I wanted a little extra punch. The gun, the range, and the load all proved, in my opinion, to be crucial to a successful hunt.

On the entire ranch one area collects and holds enough of the sparse rain to allow a wheat crop. Guess where the deer show up? The next morning we were up at 4:30 a.m. It's cold in the desert in the morning and I wished I would have brought a pair of gloves. Omar introduced us to our guides. Chico and Ramone, two brothers who worked the ranch, would guide for me. After a breakfast cooked on the wood burning stove, we headed out. We approached the wheat field in darkness. A dirt road led us from the open west side of the field around the north edge to a treeline cover on the field's eastern border. Moving slowly through the cactus and mesquite, we stopped 20 yards from the field's edge and waited for daybreak. Low light and haze made details sketchy, but we could see movement 400-500 yards away. At full light the deer began to move out of the field.

Only having hunted in Texas and Colorado, I found it difficult to tell a "big rack" from a trophy. A line of deer walked single file 50 yards in front, moving south to north. The last deer was a ten point that I judged to have no more than a 28-inch spread. After they passed we moved south along the treeline to the southeast corner of the field. Another group of deer were leaving the field. One large buck stopped and looked our direction. With the sun behind him all I saw in my scope was a black silhouette. He was a ten-pointer and it was certainly the biggest rack I had ever seen through a rifle scope. From a kneeling position the 40 yard shot would be easy. I felt Chico move beside me and whisper, "Shoot. Shoot, muy grande." I clicked off the safety. One more "shoot" from Chico and I decided there was no way I was going to "shoot" the first 30 minutes of a seven day hunt, no matter how "muy grande" the deer. I had already seen enough big bucks to let me know this was going to be easy. No need to rush. Chico and Ramone were laughing and talking as we walked the mile back to the hacienda and planned the rest of the day's hunt. I later learned they thought the audible click of my safety had been a misfire. They refused to believe I had passed on such a trophy. We would drive the ranch roads in a truck with an elevated seat hoping to spot a buck moving through the cactus or crossing the road. We left and drove and drove until Chico banged on the truck roof for the driver to stop. From there on we would walk. The rest of the day was spent climbing the unlimited number of low hills that cover that part of Mexico. The next five days became a blur of hills, valleys, and more hills. At any moment I expected to see a sign that read Phoenix - 5 Miles. Each day we would go to the wheat field, yet, never get close enough for a shot. We would then hike the desert until dark, following trails and droppings hoping to stir something from the underbrush. After six days of hunting, I was desperate.

Tomorrow was the last day. I had never hunted harder in my life. I was tired, sore, and wishing I had pulled the trigger that first morning. We planned an ambush for the final morning and would set up along the road at the east side of the wheat field. At daybreak the ranch hands would move through the wheat field from the west hoping to drive a suitable buck across the clearing to the east. A running shot would be better than no shot at all. Shortly after first light does began to move through the treeline and across our field of fire. We could tell they were starting the push. Suddenly, a buck appeared, but it was only a four, then another, then another. Larry and I saw a ten-point at the same time. The buck went right instead of left and crossed about 60 yards in front of Larry at a full run. Just as he cleared the road Larry dropped him with one clean shot. I knew after that shot the hunt was over. I was going home empty-handed. It was 7:30 a.m. Ten minutes later Rogelio and Omar slid up in a cloud of dust. Excitedly Omar blurted, "There's a big one leaving the field to the north; if you hurry you might catch him." While everyone else was examining Larry's 28-inch ten point, Chico, Ramone, and I jumped in the truck and headed to the north side of the field. We slowed after rounding the corner to see where the deer had crossed the road. Four hundred yards from the corner we found their trail. Several deer had crossed the tracks Rogelio had made on his way in. We stopped the truck and headed north into the desert. We moved at a slow trot to cover the half mile to the first low hill to the north. Perhaps we could catch a glimpse of them as they crossed the valley floor. Chico and I started up the hill as Ramone circled to the left at the foot of the hill. As we crested the ridge my heart sank — nothing moved between the next ridge and us. We stood there straining and hoping for any sign of movement. Suddenly, off to the right, I saw them. A small heard of mulies ambling due north across the desert floor. I whispered a prayer, "Please, please let there be a buck in that bunch." I motioned to Chico, who had seen them by now, and looked for a place to take a shot. I was slightly down from the crown of the hill and the best I could do was a prone position over a coral-like outcropping of rocks. My head pointed downhill. In the scope I saw a half dozen does and a buck — a small four-point. An instant later "Muy Grande" stepped

MULE DEER TYPICAL ANTLERS
Second Award - 206⁶/₈

▼ ▼ ▼ ▼ ▼

JACK GURLEY

into view. He trailed the others and I knew he was the best of the bunch. This was my last chance. I judged the distance to be 230-240 yards as he stood quartered toward me. I held dead on just in front of his left shoulder and squeezed. I can still remember the crack of the rifle as it echoed back and forth across the hills. In an instant it was over and he was gone. I looked at Chico in puzzlement, had I missed? Chico waved his arm and we headed back up the hill and down the other side. We met Ramone half way down. He held his arms wide in excitement and spoke in Spanish to Chico. Ramone then flopped his limp right arm back and forth indicating I had broken one of the buck's front legs. My heart raced. I had not missed after all. Chico's pace quickened and we headed northwest, deeper into the desert.

Chico and Ramone fell into a rhythm of experience. Chico tracked and Ramone followed There was no blood trail; where were we going? When I asked, "Why no blood," Chico would point to a scuff mark in the dirt and flop his right arm. Another 30 minutes passed. We had traveled close to a mile and both guides seemed convinced of the direction we were heading. With no evidence I was less sure. We moved through dry sandy creekbeds, across gravel strewn flats, and up rocky hills. We entered a small clearing covered with tracks. Chico stopped and spoke to Ramone. Chico stood still while Ramone fanned out in a widening half circle behind us. Chico had lost the trail! A minute later Ramone shouted from a short distance away and we headed in a new direction. An hour and a half after my shot I saw a red flick on a pebble. I picked it up — it was blood. We had covered more than two miles across desert pavement and we were right on his trail. These guys knew what they were doing. I believe they could track a Wall Street banker across New York City. At 10:00 a.m., two hours after my first shot, Chico froze. As I moved closer Chico slowly waved his hand at his side for me to stop. A flash of motion, a momentary glimpse, and he was gone again. No chance for a shot. The buck had been resting in a shaded clump of trees. We took a short break then headed out again. It would be another hour before we saw him again. He moved decidedly slower this time. I was leery of a quick shot through underbrush. If I missed he might not stop again. Another hour of tracking and Chico froze for the second time and I moved to his right for a clear shot. The deer loped right to left 75 yards away dragging his right foreleg. An off hand shot right behind the shoulder took him down.

It had taken four hours of the best tracking I had ever seen. We had covered more than seven miles across rugged desert terrain. My first shot had been on line, but slightly left. I had clipped his esophagus and taken out his right shoulder. The 14-point rack measured 31 inches. It would take another three hours for Ramone to walk back to camp to have a truck pick us up.

When Rogelio arrived he brought the entire camp. Ramone had already told and re-told the story. This was the largest deer ever taken from the Rancho El Bamury. The group picture of Rogelio and me still hangs in the Hacienda next to the photograph he took of the 42-inch monster that is still out there. ▲▲▲

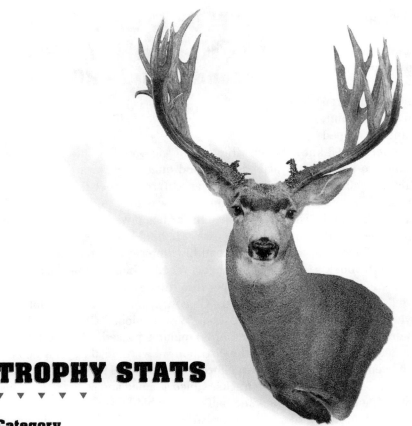

Photograph by Cliff White

TROPHY STATS

▼ ▼ ▼ ▼ ▼

Category
   mule deer - non-typical antlers

Score
   269^6/$_8$

Location
   Sherman County, Oregon - 1998

Hunter
   James G. Petersen

Length of Main Beam
   Right: 27^6/$_8$ Left: 26^7/$_8$

**Circumference Between
   burr and 1st Point**
   Right: 4^7/$_8$ Left: 5

Number of Points
   Right: 17 Left: 12

Inside Spread
   22^5/$_8$

Photograph by Jack Reneau

**James G. Petersen accepting his plaque and
medal from Randy Byers, Chair of the Big
Game Records Committee.**

MULE DEER NON-TYPICAL ANTLERS
First Award - 269⁶/₈

▼ ▼ ▼ ▼ ▼ ▼ ▼ ▼

JAMES G. PETERSEN

The year 1997 had been a good year for my son Scott and me. The portion of a ranch we had hunted selectively for four years was producing some nice bucks. In July I had spotted seven nice bucks together and kept track of them most of the summer. Two were exceptionally nice. In late August after I returned from British Columbia with a 40-inch Stone's ram scoring 170-4/8, points. I told my wife Peggy that I wanted Scott to get a chance at this one nice buck. Scouting as much as I could, I just could not find him again. I was kind of despondent, but opening morning we found him while stalking another buck, and Scott made a great shot. The buck scored 189-6/8 points, but there was a bigger one with this buck that we did not see until after the shot. Unfortunately though, in April of 1998 that portion of the ranch sold, and we were not permitted to hunt. Applications were due in May so we really scrambled to find a place to hunt.

One of my patient's parents had a ranch and we made an agreement for Scott and me to hunt there that fall. During the summer I scouted extensively, seeing several bucks, but only one that interested me. Unfortunately, it was in an area of the ranch we were not permitted to hunt. On opening day Scott returned from college to hunt. We spotted several bucks, but the flat terrain made stalking difficult and shots long. So after two days without spotting a good buck, I returned to work and called Ron Mobley to tell him of our progress. Ron told me that he would take Scott and me to the place I had seen the good buck on Saturday after Scott returned from a week at school. With renewed hopes I looked forward to Saturday and hunting with Scott again.

Photograph courtesy of James G. Petersen

James and his late father Gale "Pete" with James' non-typical mule deer scoring 269-6/8 points.

On Friday I returned to the ranch for a short morning hunt by myself and went to an area where I had spotted five bucks together earlier in the season. Arriving after daylight, I was kicking myself for not getting an earlier start, but I was looking forward to Saturday's hunt. I spotted three bucks together — two four-points and a 4X3, all nice, and one was about 27 to 28 inches wide with nice forks and mass. After putting up the spotting scope I planned and executed a stalk that put me about 175 yards from the bucks. I looked at the buck for a long time as he fed, and I talked myself in and out of shooting several times. Finally I told myself that I had taken larger bucks than this one, and if I did shoot this one, even if he was the best I had seen thus far, my hunt is over and my son was coming tomorrow. Wishing I could hunt my old spot, I got up and walked away. Leaving the bucks to feed, I hoped Scott and I could find a nice buck the next day.

Along my retreat, I hiked to a small vantage point and started glassing. Almost immediately I spotted "Mr. Big." My mouth must have dropped and all I could say was, "Oh, my God!!!" There were two bucks — a large non-typical and the smallest forked horn I have ever seen, feeding together. I planned a stalk. The terrain was flat and the forked horn was all over the place, while the large buck fed in a very small area. I was able to get within 800 yards, but then ran out of cover and had to re-evaluate the stalk. I needed to crawl about 600 yards to get to a small hump that would disguise my outline and allow me to get my rifle above the low vegetation.

As I crawled along on my belly, I kept saying to myself, "God, do not let me mess this up. I will never get another chance like this one." As I crawled, I tried to talk myself into shooting from where I was, but I kept saying, "Stick to your plan. Do not mess this up!" Crawling 600 yards was painfully tiring, and I don't know how long it took, but I finally made it to my destination. When I made it to the hump the big buck was still there, but the forked horn was in the way. I waited, and when he cleared I fired, and the big buck dropped. I was instantly elated, until he regained his feet. One more shot put him down for good. I knew he was big, but it wasn't until I reached him that I realized how big! What a buck. I thanked the appropriate authorities for my privileges.

As soon as I could, I phoned my wife Peg, my son, and my parents so they could join in my wonderful experience! ▲ ▲ ▲

Moments in Measuring...

Photograph by Jack Reneau

Dale Ream and Paul D. Webster of the 24th Awards Judges' Panel verify the H-1 and H-2 circumference measurements on Errol R. Raley's typical mule deer. The First Award winning buck's final score is 212-7/8 points.

TROPHY STATS

▼ ▼ ▼ ▼ ▼

Category
mule deer - non-typical antlers

Score
265^2/8

Location
Wheeler County, Nebraska - 1959

Hunter
Leo Dwyer

Length of Main Beam
Right: 25^5/8 Left: 24^5/8

**Circumference Between
burr and 1st Point**
Right: 6^2/8 Left: 5^6/8

Number of Points
Right: 14 Left: 13

Inside Spread
24^5/8

MULE DEER
NON-TYPICAL ANTLERS
Second Award - 265²/₈

▼ ▼ ▼ ▼ ▼ ▼ ▼ ▼ ▼

LEO DWYER

In the fall of 1959 I was living on the ranch that was homesteaded by my father and grandfather on the eastern edge of the Nebraska sandhills. I had hunted whitetail deer in the "Bear Lodge" of Wyoming, but never in the sandhills. Having bought a Nebraska license, my ten-year-old son Pat and I drove to a neighbor's land about six miles away to hunt. I thought this was better "deer country."

After eating lunch at the neighbors, four of us started our drive through his sandhill pasture. When we came over a "knob" and looked in a small grove of scrub cottonwood trees, there were seven or eight big mule deer about 250 yards away. I fired at the one I thought had the largest rack. I saw him "hunch" and quickly let it be known to my companions I had hit the biggest buck, and not to shoot at him again even though he was on the move.

The buck traveled about 200 yards before he went down. The big deer "hog dressed" at 265 pounds. If I had realized at the time what a prize trophy I had just shot, I would have certainly had it mounted. ▲▲▲

Photograph by Cliff White

TROPHY STATS

▼ ▼ ▼ ▼ ▼

Category
mule deer - non-typical antlers

Score
256²/8

Location
Oneida County, Idaho - 1998

Hunter
S. Tracey Davis

Length of Main Beam
Right: 24⁶/8 Left: 24¹/8

Circumference Between burr and lst Point
Right: 4⁵/8 Left: 4⁴/8

Number of Points
Right: 12 Left: 11

Inside Spread
21⁶/8

Photograph by Jack Reneau

S. Tracey Davis accepting his plaque and medal from Randy Byers, Chair of the Big Game Records Committee.

MULE DEER NON-TYPICAL ANTLERS
Third Award - 256²/₈

▼ ▼ ▼ ▼ ▼ ▼ ▼ ▼ ▼

S. TRACEY DAVIS

It finally happened! We drew for a trophy mule deer hunt in Idaho. Jerry Thomas, Tod Daniels, my brother Terry, and I all drew tags. We had been applying for this area for several years and finally got lucky.

We did a lot of scouting and looking for our trophy bucks before the hunt started. We didn't see much — a lot of does and some 24-inch to 26-inch bucks. We really needed some weather to get the deer moving. Things began looking better and a storm was brewing. By opening day we had six inches of new snow.

The first day of the hunt, my friend Jerry killed a nice 4-point with a 28-inch spread. On the second day, late in the afternoon, we found another nice buck. We all saw him and agreed he was worth chasing. Two days later, my brother Terry shot him. He was an eight-point on one side and a six-point on the other side with a 32-inch spread. Since it was getting late in the day by the time we got Terry's buck out we headed for home.

The next morning we started back out and hunted almost all day without seeing anything of size, so we decided to return to the drainage where Terry killed his buck. We were on a high ridge glassing the area and spotted about 15 does, which spotted us about the same time. There was a buck with the does, but as soon as he saw us he immediately walked over and stuck his head into a bush. Because of the way the head was hidden, we couldn't see how big the buck was. It seemed as if this buck had a lot of experience hiding from hunters, and we figured we needed to get a closer look.

We planned to stalk the buck and started sneaking down the drainage toward him. Terry stayed on top of the ridge where he could watch the buck in case he spooked, and he could signal to us if the buck moved. I decided to go over a ridge to the west of the buck and try to sneak down to where I could get a shot. As we made our way down the canyon, the does started to get nervous and wanted to go out the bottom of the canyon. Each time they began to move down the canyon, the buck would head them off and push them back up the hill toward us. He had about fifteen does in the harem and was determined to keep them bunched up and close. There was no question the rut was in full swing. I took one last look at the buck before I headed down the canyon.

As I made my way down I found a small cedar tree and used it for a landmark. When I reached the tree, I headed back to the east over a hog's-back ridge. I could only hope that the buck was still there. As I crested the ridge, I was breathing so hard from the hike and the excitement that I stopped for a minute to catch my breath and to calm down. I knew that when I went over the ridge, I had to make a very quick field judgment on his size. If he was the one, I had to be able to make the shot equally as fast. As I went over the ridge, there was no time wasted judging his size; I was only 40 yards away, and all I could see was antlers. I still wonder where the first shot went, but the

Photograph courtesy of S. Tracey Davis

The author took this magnificent non-typical mule deer after years of applying for an Idaho mule deer tag. The buck scores 256-2/8 points.

second one connected solidly. When the buck fell, his antlers landed right in a bush and I still couldn't see how big he was. When I got to the buck and pulled him out of the bush, I couldn't believe my eyes. He was huge! I quickly counted the points; he had 11 points on one side and 12 points on the other. On the side with 11 points, he had broken one large point off or he would have been a perfect 12-point buck. I just happened to have a small tape measure in my pocket from measuring Terry's buck the day before. This buck had a 38-inch spread!

After my buddies heard the shots, they came running. We all gathered around to admire the buck. By the time we got the buck taken care of and off the mountain, it was about three hours after dark.

When we reached home, we took some photos and again admired the buck. After looking him over, we noticed that he had been fighting with another buck and was very bruised with many puncture wounds around his neck and back. Since Terry's buck and my buck were killed only one draw apart, we figured that the two bucks had been fighting over the does and my buck lost. However, when Terry took his buck out, that left the does free for the taking and that was when my buck showed up. If he had only let the does go, he would probably have escaped.

This is one hunt that I will never forget, and we can only hope to see offspring from these two great bucks in the future. ▲▲▲

Award Winning Moments...

Photograph by Jack Reneau

Visitors to the 24th Awards Trophy Exhibit at Bass Pro Shops were greeted by an impressive display of typical and non-typical mule deer.

TROPHY STATS

▼ ▼ ▼ ▼ ▼

Category
   Columbia blacktail

Score
   167

Location
   Jackson County, Oregon - 1958

Hunter
   Riley F. Bean

Length of Main Beam
   Right: 23 Left: 23

**Circumference Between
burr and 1st Point**
   Right: $4^2/8$ Left: $4^3/8$

Number of Points
   Right: 5 Left: 5

Inside Spread
   20

COLUMBIA BLACKTAIL
First Award - 167

▼ ▼ ▼ ▼ ▼ ▼ ▼ ▼ ▼

RILEY F. BEAN

This Columbia blacktail was a buck that I killed in 1958 when I was home on leave from the Navy. Joining me on this hunt were my dad, Fred Bean, and my uncle, Rob Bean. We had decided to hunt a big canyon under the lookout on Anderson Peak just a few miles from Talent, Oregon.

It was an early October morning when the three of us took Dad's old 1949 Chevy pickup to the lookout. We parked there, split up, and started hunting down the big canyon just under the lookout. We had picked this particular canyon because it had a lot of thick brush — great blacktail habitat. We hunted all the way down to the bottom of the canyon without seeing a deer. When I reached a big opening where I could see back to the top of the canyon, I saw a big buck sneaking out from the rimrock. The buck was about 300 yards away. I was shooting a 200-grain bullet out of a .348 Model 71 Winchester that I had just bought before the hunt. I knelt down on one knee, steadied and fired one shot. The old buck dropped like a stone — that's when I first fell in love with my .348.

After the shot the three of us hiked back up to the top where the buck was and when we got there we all agreed he was one heck of a big blacktail buck. We field dressed him and dragged him back to the pickup. We figured he weighed about 200 pounds. Fortunately, we weren't that far from the rig. ▲▲▲

Photograph by Cliff White

TROPHY STATS

▼ ▼ ▼ ▼ ▼

Category
Columbia blacktail

Score
$162^2/_8$

Location
Jackson County, Oregon - 1979

Hunter
Norman J. Shanklin

Length of Main Beam
Right: 25 Left: 24

Circumference Between burr and 1st Point
Right: $4^4/_8$ Left: $4^6/_8$

Number of Points
Right: 6 Left: 5

Inside Spread
$19^1/_8$

COLUMBIA BLACKTAIL
Second Award - 162²/₈

▼ ▼ ▼ ▼ ▼ ▼ ▼ ▼ ▼

NORMAN J. SHANKLIN

Dad and I had first seen a glimpse of Ol' Blackie in the early morning just before day-break. We were doing our early hike into a spot that we knew had nice blacktail bucks. Dad and I had felled timber in that area a time or two and had seen some really super bucks. On this morning in the early gray we had seen a big blacktail with tall, heavy antlers.

Dad Calls Him, "Ol' Blackie"

You know, sometimes in that kind of light you don't always see what you thought you saw, if you know what I mean. Dad asked if I could tell what it was. "Yes," I said, "It was big!" We both knew that, and he gave me that look that said, "Snap out of it!" So I replied quickly that he was at least a four- or five-pointer. Dad nodded and we moved off in the direction "Ol' Blackie" had vanished. He seemed to be headed right for a big patch of brush.

It was getting light fast and by the time we had covered a hundred yards it was light enough to shoot. We stopped just long enough to put together a plan that just might produce a good shot for one of us. The patch was extra-thick bitterbrush with an occasional scrub oak. We decided that dad would go down, then work his way across the bottom of the brush patch. I would zigzag like a coyote down through the middle. We thought that I could possibly jump one out to dad or get a good shot myself.

I waited as Dad made his way down the slope to the bottom of the brush patch, when all of a sudden I noticed he made a couple of quick moves. Whenever Dad moved like that I knew some-thing was up. The very next second I watched as he released an arrow. I cautiously headed down to him. When I reached Dad, he said something below had spooked the buck out! He told me that he was just starting into the brush when he noticed movement out of the corner of his eye.

Suddenly, there was the huge blacktail buck coming across in front of him at high speed! Dad doesn't normally shoot at running deer, but he had practiced on the running deer target all summer and had gotten quite good. That, coupled with the fact that it was such a dandy buck, made it impossible to resist taking the shot.

Praise God the arrow found its mark. Dad had made an excellent shot with the kind of blood trail that lets you know what kind of hit you made. After trailing this buck about a 100 yards or so we came to a place where the big blacktail had previously laid down. The buck had found a powdered out fir tree windfall and wallowed in it to stop the bleeding. It worked. From the tracks, we could see the direction he went, but the heavy blood trail had all but dried up. We managed to stay on the trail, finding only a small drop of blood here and there, and then we lost the tracks and any sign of the big deer.

Dad and I both knew what we had to do. Now was the time to split up and get down on the ground and start circling to see if we could pick up his trail. We talked back and forth until we were far enough apart that we couldn't hear one another any longer. I picked up the big deer's trail again and followed him for an hour on not much more than the kind of scuff marks and tracks that only hint he had passed this way.

In the next half hour I caught up with the big buck, but now he had five does traveling with him. I was thinking to myself that I needed to get in front of them and let them come to me if I was going to get a good shot. I moved fast to cut them off. It seemed like an hour went by, but really just a few minutes had passed when the does came out one by one. Another long minute later, and out stepped "Ol' Blackie." He was moving slow.

I waited for a shot, came to full draw, picked a spot, concentrated, and released. The arrow fell short and hit the ground just in front of the big blacktail. Taking a quick left turn, the buck started back down the hill in the direction he had come, and toward Dad. He could hear and see him coming, and was ready when the buck came into range. He said watching this trophy blacktail deer coming to him was an awesome sight he'll never forget! He knew also that, God-willing, he was getting ready to harvest the biggest blacktail buck that he had ever taken with a bow. "Ol Blackie" was about ten yards away when he stopped to check a noise that caught his attention. It was Dad at full draw. The rest is history as they say and "Ol' Blackie" set a score hard to match: a Boone and Crockett score of 162-2/8 points. Good hunting and may God Bless! ▲ ▲ ▲

Moments in Measuring...

Photograph by Jack Reneau

24th Awards Judges' Panel Member Robert H. Hanson and Consultant Paul D. Webster double check the measurements on Jack Gurley's typical mule deer (206-6/8 points). The entry score for each trophy is verified by two sets of Judges.

Photograph by Cliff White

TROPHY STATS
▼ ▼ ▼ ▼ ▼

Category
Columbia blacktail

Score
178⁴/₈

Location
Jackson County, Oregon - Picked up prior to 1950

Owner
Mervyn R. Thomson

Length of Main Beam
Right: 23 Left: 23⁶/₈

Circumference Between burr and 1st Point
Right: 4⁵/₈ Left: 4⁷/₈

Number of Points
Right: 5 Left: 5

Inside Spread
23²/₈

COLUMBIA BLACKTAIL
Certificate of Merit - 178⁴/₈

▼ ▼ ▼ ▼ ▼ ▼ ▼ ▼ ▼

MERVYN R. THOMSON - OWNER

The year 1940 was the Golden Age of the Silver Screen and a wonderful year for 29 year-old movie star, Ginger Rogers. Ginger won her Oscar for "Kitty Foyle" and she also bought the 4R Ranch, a vacation place for her and her mother, Lela. It was far away from the pressures of Hollywood — 1,200 acres along Oregon's beautiful Rogue River.

In the Fall of 1940 while Ginger was riding her horse, three rifle shots rang out and one whizzed right past her. She rode to the edge of the trees near the river were she saw two men rowing across toward her and to where a large buck lay dying. Ginger took off on a dead-run back to the house and had her mother call the Jackson County Sheriff's office. Within 20 minutes two officers arrived. The police arrested the trespassers as they were dragging the gutted deer to their boat. The hunters were placed in the squad car and an officer said he would send a game warden to get the deer. Lela (little, but very persuasive), told the sheriffs that she hadn't had venison since she was a little girl. She asked whom she needed to talk to in order to keep the deer and was eventually given the tagged deer.

Ginger, Lela, and the ranch foreman skinned, cut up and wrapped the deer. They had venison for the ranch and took frozen venison in an ice box back to California with them — they loved it. Ginger had the tall graceful horns mounted and they hung on her Oregon ranch house walls for over 50 years. Clark Gable tossed his fishing hat on the horns. Lucille Ball scared her poodle half to death introducing it to the 4-point. David Niven used it as a rack for his fly rod. This deer was the official greeter to many famous people.

After the close call with the hunters, Ginger decided to purchase the property on the west side of the Rogue. No hunters, photographers, or anyone else could gain access to her ranch from across the river. Her ranch now totaled 1,800 acres. Ginger owned the property across the river from her ranch until 1970, when the Government wanted it for a State Park. She fought them until they threatened to "condemn" the land. This piece of land is now known as Takelma Park on Rogue River Drive, directly across from her Shady Cove ranch that still has her signature red roofs.

Ginger sold her Rogers Rogue River Ranch in 1991. She asked my husband, Mert, if he would like to have her cherished mount. He was grateful, if she was sure it wouldn't fit in her new pioneer home.

Several years later, our local newspaper wanted to write a story about a huge black bear our son Chris took. It had been lurking around our ranch and tearing up our beehives. We took our bear and Ginger's deer to the Northwest Big Game Show in January 1998. The 7 foot 3 inch black bear weighed over 600 pounds and scored roughly 19-10/16 points. To our amazement, Ginger's Columbia blacktail 5-point buck scored 178-4/8 points and is presently number 1 in Oregon.

The battered 60 year-old cape was replaced by Brad Stallsworth Taxidermy of Grants Pass, Oregon, and has been on exhibit with Northwest Big Game. I would like to thank Glenn Abbott, a real gentleman, who did the measuring. As Ginger's secretary, I am happy the name of this great lady and sportswoman will be listed in the prestigious records of Boone and Crockett. ▲▲▲

Photograph by Cliff White

TROPHY STATS

▼ ▼ ▼ ▼ ▼

Category
Sitka blacktail

Score
$121^{6}/_{8}$

Location
Dall Island, Alaska - 1998

Hunter
James F. Baichtal

Length of Main Beam
Right: $18^{1}/_{8}$ Left: $18^{5}/_{8}$

Circumference Between burr and 1st Point
Right: $4^{4}/_{8}$ Left: 5

Number of Points
Right: 5 Left: 5

Inside Spread
16

Photograph by Jack Reneau

James F. Baichtal accepting his plaque and medal from Randy Byers, Chair of the Big Game Records Committee.

BOONE AND CROCKETT CLUB'

SITKA BLACKTAIL
First Award - 121⁶/₈

▼ ▼ ▼ ▼ ▼ ▼ ▼ ▼ ▼

JAMES F. BAICHTAL

Dennis Landwehr and I worked our way toward the three point he had just shot. We used the topography to keep as concealed as possible because we suspected that other deer were around. As we rounded one of the rock ledges we spotted a group of five bucks feeding at about 600 yards. Several other deer were feeding on the adjacent ridges so we sat down and slowly glassed the landscape.

One of the five bucks was a dandy — a large three-point with eyeguards and good mass. We were discussing how I might get close enough with my custom Hawken muzzleloader for a shot when in the periphery of my binoculars I saw a movement. I shifted and refocused on the movement near one of the small trees in the alpine meadow. What I saw shook me to the bone. Rising above a rock ridge some 300 yards in front of us was a set of antlers, each side supporting four long points. In eight years of hunting Sitka blacktail in Southeast Alaska I had never seen such a rack. The height, symmetry, and mass of the velvet-covered antlers were incredible.

We were hidden from the buck's vision by the rock outcropping. Dennis' earlier shot had not alerted the buck, however a doe just above him stared at us intently. I had to move fast. Dennis and I moved behind the rock ledge. I took off my pack as I described to Dennis how I thought I might get close enough for a shot.

I backtracked into the draw we had just climbed. The wind was perfect — a light steady breeze from the buck to me. I moved forward keeping the rock outcropping between us. I tried not to think about the massive antlers I had seen through the binoculars. I tried to focus on the spot I had last seen the buck and on what I needed to do to make the shot. It took me about 15 minutes to get within range and still out of sight of the buck and doe. I checked the powder under my nipple.

The last 80 yards were the toughest. I crawled slowly to another rock outcropping only 30 yards from the bedded buck. I calmed myself once more and crept forward. I could see the doe, standing alert at only 40 yards. As I crept forward the buck was suddenly in full view, still in his bed at 30 yards.

The hunt had started seven years before. In my work as a geologist with the U.S. Forest Service I had flown by helicopter to this remote site in 1991, leaving an inventory crew in the alpine for a week. Upon returning they had videos of huge blacktails crossing the alpine meadows in the rain. I again visited the area in 1993 and 1995, this time photographing large deer myself. In 1995, I tried a solo hunt to the area. I borrowed a skiff and motored the 50 miles to the beach below the alpine ridge. After securing the boat I began the climb from salt water to the ridge above. The weather front that had threatened had come early and clouds obscured the ridge by mid-afternoon. After many hours of pushing through the thick undergrowth and surviving a fall, I decided it best to return to the beach, spend the night on the skiff, and return home in the morning. The weather and the terrain had beaten me. When I reached the beach at 10:00 p.m. I found the tide out. It took me until midnight to water the boat. I weathered the night's storm anchored in the bay and worked

Photograph courtesy of James F. Baichtal

B&C Lifetime Associate, James F. Baichtal with his award-winning Sitka blacktail buck scoring 121-6/8 points. The weather had hampered his hunting plans the previous three years before this successful hunt in 1998.

my way home the next morning. Weather hampered attempts to reach the ridge in 1996 and 1997.

Dennis and I had planned this year's trip well in advance, and when it looked like the weather would cooperate we were ready. We chartered a ride to the beach and began our ascent in the morning hours of a crystal clear day. The first three hours of the climb were not bad through the dense rainforest of Southeast Alaska, but the last five were grueling. The only route to the top was through a Sitka alder-choked chute. The alder was entwined with devil's club, salmon berry, and currant. For five hours we pushed against the wall of vegetation. We made camp that evening just below the alpine level, gathered water, and went to bed early. On the morning of August 1, 1998, we climbed the last hour to the ridge crest and began our hunt. Within moments of reaching the alpine we spotted a nice three-point in its bed. We discussed whether to take the buck or not, and Dennis decided not to let the opportunity pass. As I previously described, I now found myself 30 yards from the buck of my dreams.

I had expected the massive four-point to rise and give me the shot I needed. The other deer we had spotted stood on the surrounding ridges seemingly unconcerned. The massive animal rocketed from his bed, running quartering away. I rose to one knee and held on his shoulders, swinging with him. I did not want to make a running shot, but within 90 yards the buck would be into the next draw. Not believing that he would stop, I set the rear trigger and took careful aim. At about 60 yards he suddenly turned broadside and attempted to leap between two rock ledges. He faltered, missing his footing on the upper ledge. I swung the sights of the .54 caliber muzzleloader deep into the buck's heavy chest and fired. At that same time he bent forward on his forelegs, preparing

SITKA BLACKTAIL
First Award - 121⁶/₈

▼ ▼ ▼ ▼ ▼

JAMES F. BAICHTAL

to leap onto the rock ledge above. The roundball smashed through his spine and the buck slumped to the base of the outcropping. He lay motionless. I slowly reloaded and Dennis appeared from where I had left him with both of our packs. Dennis quickly worked his way over toward me, announcing that he wanted a chance at the largest of the five bucks still watching from the meadow above. Suddenly my buck began to thrash, coming to rest on his front legs. I sat down and took careful aim on this throat and fired.

Dennis came to my side and stacked our packs on the rocks where we stood. He laid down and took careful aim on the massive three-point that was still watching with curiosity. Dennis' .30-06 roared and a third buck was added to the morning's hunt.

We had no concept of just how big my buck was. I did know that we had three deer on the ground, which meant we would be boning and packing a lot of meat. Dennis and I gathered our gear and moved toward my buck, which was the closest.

The closer we got the larger the animal became. Not only were his antlers unbelievable, his body was nearly twice the size of the average buck. We paid our respects to the magnificent buck and stood by it for a long time both in admiration and awe. It was only then that I realized that I had shattered the existing record for a Sitka blacktail taken with black powder.

We photographed and cleaned all three deer and then began the boning process. We rested that evening in camp under clear, starlit skies. We radioed our ride that we needed an early pickup the next morning. We then began what would be a 12-hour climb down off of the mountain to our camp on the beach. Our ride arrived promptly at 6 o'clock the next morning. The long ride home gave us plenty of time to reflect on the spectacular hunt that we had both experienced. After the mandatory 60-day drying period the buck scored 121-6/8 points. ▲▲▲

Photograph by Cliff White

TROPHY STATS
▼ ▼ ▼ ▼ ▼

Category
 Sitka blacktail

Score
 115^{1}/$_{8}$

Location
 Thomas Bay, Alaska - 1997

Hunter
 Eli Lucas

Length of Main Beam
 Right: 17^{5}/$_{8}$ Left: 16^{6}/$_{8}$

Circumference Between burr and 1st Point
 Right: 4^{2}/$_{8}$ Left: 4^{6}/$_{8}$

Number of Points
 Right: 5 Left: 5

Inside Spread
 14^{7}/$_{8}$

SITKA BLACKTAIL
Second Award - 115¹/₈

▼ ▼ ▼ ▼ ▼ ▼ ▼ ▼

ELI LUCAS

Our fishing boat "Grebe" lay quiet — its anchor sucked firm in a mud bottom. It was December 6, 1997, on southeast Alaska's mainland; only a few hour's boat run from Petersburg.

My wife Tara and I were hunting in the hopes she would get her first buck. I had spent the rut guiding hunters, so we were left to the challenge of still-hunting in the dense timber. The winter woods were sun dappled and snowless. Dense waves of alder and blueberry brush were bare of leaves. While shades of blood red and mellow greens unrolled, open muskegs, towering spruce, western hemlock, and stunted spindly pines overshadowed us. The lowland trails showed that the moose and deer were in abundance, even without a heavy snow to push them down.

We eased along these trails dressed in our woolens. Tara held an ancient .250 Savage that old Earl had given her. The stock was rough. Earl said he had used a hatchet in much of its making. I carried my battered boat rifle, a .270 Winchester. Our guns were clean and accurate.

The past two days we had eased up to several moose and a few blacktail does. This was our last day afield and we decided to hunt an hour or two and then pull anchor to head home to our little cabin on Kupreanof Island.

Winter browsed brush was only knee-high in many places, and made for exceptional visibility for these typically dense forests. It felt like a "deery" afternoon. Tara would often glance at me from a few yards to my right, and we would give each other a nod and a raised eyebrow. While easing a bit forward of my partner I saw a foreleg and broad chest 75 yards ahead.

I raised my fingers above my head to indicate I thought I saw a buck, and pointed to where I was looking. Tara moved quietly to a tree, and raised for the shot at a one-antlered three-point. His head was high and watching. Crack! At the shot he whirled and jumped, then stood with head swiveling and ears rotating. At the commotion, another deer made a bound from the dense brush to land 20 feet to the left of "one horn."

This new deer's frame was massive and his horns heavy and wide. He also faced us, head high. With no hesitation, I knelt down taking a wrap of my sling around my forearm, and took aim at the large buck. At the shot he collapsed immediately, one antler becoming buried to the base in muskeg. Breathing heavy with excitement, Tara missed her deer clean on her second shot.

Seeing that all was not safe, he began a full blown escape, bounding away. Tara draped herself over a moss-covered log and took aim. As it paused at a rise 120 yards off, Tara's shot was made good. We dressed both deer, wiped the cavities clean with Spaghnum moss, and made Indian packs. Then we lifted our loads and made tracks toward the beach in the fading light.

With deer on the back deck, the radar making its constant sweep, we put the diesel engine in gear and headed homeward. Mugs of hot tea in our laps, we retold the story laughing in the moonlight.

When we arrived at home, we cleaned the skulls. The big one hangs in our loft bedroom now. Often, I feast my eyes on the curve of his forked tines and revisit the smells, companionship and thrill of the hunt. I am ready to go there again. ▲▲▲

Photograph by Cliff White

TROPHY STATS

▼ ▼ ▼ ▼ ▼

Category
  whitetail deer - typical antlers

Score
  197$^6/8$

Location
  Kenosha County, Wisconsin - 1999

Hunter
  Keith S. Brossard

Length of Main Beam
  Right: 30 Left: 26$^7/8$

**Circumference Between
burr and 1st Point**
  Right: 5$^7/8$ Left: 6

Number of Points
  Right: 7 Left: 10

Inside Spread
  18$^7/8$

Photograph by Jack Reneau

**Keith S. Brossard accepting his plaque and
medal from Randy Byers, Chair of the Big
Game Records Committee.**

WHITETAIL DEER TYPICAL ANTLERS
First Award - 197⁶/₈

▼ ▼ ▼ ▼ ▼ ▼ ▼ ▼

KEITH S. BROSSARD

Wisconsin has long held a reputation as a top trophy whitetail state, with big bucks being taken from the southern farmlands to the northern forests. There are a handful of counties, though, that do not have a reputation for producing good numbers of trophy bucks.

Kenosha County, located in the extreme southeast corner of the state, is among those counties. In fact, of all 72 counties, Kenosha County has one of the lowest numbers of entries in the Wisconsin Buck & Bear Club's state records book. So, it's easy to see why, when Kenosha County hunter Keith Brossard climbed into his treestand November 20, 1999, he had no clue he was about to take Wisconsin's top-scoring typical in nearly a century!

The day before the nine-day gun season opened, Keith headed out to hang his stand in the spot he'd hunted for the past six years. Known to Keith and his brothers as "the slot," it's a typical funnel — a narrow strip of woods connecting two larger pieces of cover.

Several factors make "the slot" a great place to hunt. Keith's stand is located on one end of the funnel, where deer typically exit on their way into bigger woods. Because the funnel is only 150 yards wide, the woods are fairly open and Keith's stand hangs 38 feet above the ground, almost any deer traveling through the cover is within shotgun range.

Going into the 1999 season, Keith had shot many nice deer from this tree, including a 12-point scoring 147-4/8 points on opening day 1995, and a nine-pointer on Thanksgiving 1997 that scored 144-3/8 points. These two trophies, along with several other bucks and does, all ended up traveling within 20 yards of the hunter's tree.

Despite all of this success, Keith actually considered going to another spot for the '99 opener. His alternative was a spot his brother Dave had bowhunted earlier in the fall. Located 600 yards from Keith's usual opening day stand in "the slot," Dave's stand hung in a large piece of cover on the opposite end of the funnel. The stand was on the edge of a large tract of hardwoods where several trails coming out of good bedding cover merged.

Dave had a big buck within bow range there, and Keith knew it was an outstanding spot. The problem was that the tree stood only 30 yards from a property line and a frequently hunted stand on the other side of the line. Still, the evening before the opener, Keith announced that he planned to hunt there the next morning, rather than in the stand he'd just hung. "You're not going to hunt the stand that's produced two trophy bucks for you since 1995, not to mention several other nice deer?" Dave asked.

Deep inside, Keith knew his brother was right. Why hunt the other stand — especially at the risk of finding another hunter sitting just over the fence? So Keith decided to hunt his familiar stand in "the slot" the next morning.

Opening day dawned cloudy with calm to light winds and temperatures in the lower 40s.

After warmer temperatures in the lower 60s the previous two days, the coolness was welcome. Hunting alone, Keith got into his stand at 5:50 a.m., a half hour before legal shooting time.

Other than a handful of shots ringing out in the distance, the day began quietly; in fact several hours passed without Keith seeing a deer, but he was prepared to sit all day if necessary.

At 10:30, Keith finally spotted some movement — a flash of brown about 100 yards behind his stand. Sensing the deer was alone, Keith thought there was a good chance it was a buck, and as the hunter turned to get a better look, his suspicion was confirmed. In fact, walking straight toward Keith was the biggest buck he'd ever seen!

The deer kept making his way closer, walking slowly and stopping often. Such casual behavior seemed unusual for a trophy buck on opening morning of gun season, but Keith wasn't complaining. Remaining seated, Keith got his 12-gauge shotgun into position for a shot. By now, the buck was 75 yards away and still coming. Looking at this rack would give any hunter a serious case of buck fever, and Keith was no different. As he held his sights on the approaching monster, he grew increasingly nervous.

The deer presented numerous shot opportunities, but Keith kept waiting patiently. Based on the buck's direction of travel and calm demeanor, he was confident the animal would pass within close shotgun range, and he felt no reason to rush.

His shaking increased, and his breathing grew heavier as the buck neared. Two to three long minutes after first coming into view, the brute was only 18 yards away. Suddenly, the buck sensed something was wrong. "I was breathing really hard, and with almost no wind and the cool temperatures, I know he heard me," Keith says.

The buck stopped behind some overhanging limbs and vines, well within range, but too hidden for a good shot. If the buck took two steps, he'd be in the clear, but for three nervous minutes he stood surveying the scene with extreme caution. Sensing danger, the monster buck was constantly bobbing his head and peeking over and through the brush.

By now, Keith had been holding his sights on the buck for about five or six minutes, and the shotgun's barrel was swaying back and forth. Several times he had to lift his head a take a deep breath to try to relax before looking back down the open sights of his gun. The buck was looking in his general direction the entire time, but never looked up directly at him.

After a few tense moments, the buck took two steps forward, and as soon as he cleared the cover, Keith shot. The buck arched his back slightly and before he had much chance to react, Keith shot a again. The buck toppled over on the spot. The monster typical was down for good.

Keith anxiously descended his stand and walked over to the downed buck. He knew the deer was big, but he couldn't believe the sheer amount of antler he was holding in his hands. After admiring his prize, Keith headed to his truck. Several other hunters stopped by to see how he'd done, and after he told them the story, they headed out to get the deer. Fortunately, Keith could pull his truck to within ten yards of the animal.

This whitetail's rack is truly world class. It has 17 scorable points on a basic 12-point frame. The antlers received a score of 197-6/8 points by the 24th Awards Judges' Panel in Springfield, Missouri. The rack sports numerous long tines, with G-2's, G-3's, and G-4's on both sides ranging between 10-1/8 and 12 inches. Long G-5's of 7-7/8 and 9-2/8 really help the buck's score. The mass on the Brossard buck is amazing, with all H-1 through H-4 measurements ranging between 5 and 6 inches.

WHITETAIL DEER TYPICAL ANTLERS
First Award - 197⁶/₈

▼ ▼ ▼ ▼ ▼

KEITH S. BROSSARD

Keith's brothers Brian and Dave say they recognized the buck as one they'd seen during bow season. Dave had spotted him in October in a field bordering the north edge of the funnel. Brian had seen him just 100 yards from Keith's treestand a week earlier on the last Saturday of early bow season. But no one recalls seeing the buck prior to 1999; either he'd stayed out of sight, or he'd grown a lot his final year.

State Wildlife Biologist Tom Howard aged the buck at 4-1/2 to 5-1/2 years old. The animal wasn't weighed, but most people who saw him estimated his dressed weight at no more than 170 pounds. Keith notes that the buck had unusually small hooves, no larger than those of an average doe.

Keith joins an elite group of five other hunters who've shot Wisconsin typicals scoring 190 or higher. The only bigger typical in Wisconsin history is James Jordan's famous former World's Record, which scores 206-1/8 points and was shot in 1914 in far-northern Burnett County.

At 216-3/8 points, the gross typical score of Keith's buck actually is 7 inches higher than that of the state record. But the Jordan buck hangs onto this title due to amazing symmetry (just 3-2/8 inches of total deductions, versus 18-2/8 inches for the challenger.)

The biggest typical in Wisconsin in 85 years — and second only to the Jordan buck? Not bad for Kenosha County's first-ever B&C whitetail! ▲▲▲

Photograph by Cliff White

TROPHY STATS
▼ ▼ ▼ ▼ ▼

Category
  whitetail - typical antlers

Score
  195^5/$_8$

Location
  Rock Island County, Illinois - 1999

Hunter
  Kent E. Anderson

Length of Main Beam
  Right: 29^4/$_8$ Left: 27^5/$_8$

**Circumference Between
burr and 1st Point**
  Right: 4^6/$_8$ Left: 4^7/$_8$

Number of Points
  Right: 9 Left: 8

Inside Spread
  18^7/$_8$

Photograph by Jack Reneau

**Kent E. Anderson accepting his plaque and
medal from Randy Byers, Chair of the Big
Game Records Committee.**

WHITETAIL DEER TYPICAL ANTLERS
Second Award - 195⁵/₈

▼ ▼ ▼ ▼ ▼ ▼ ▼ ▼ ▼

KENT E. ANDERSON

On November 6, 1999, I was in my tree stand well before sunrise on the family farm in Rock Island County, south of Moline, Illinois. It was a dead-calm morning and the heavy frost looked like snow covering the valleys when the sun came up. There were no signs of deer tracks so I knew I hadn't spooked any deer on the way to my stand.

Shortly after the sun was up past the horizon, a doe and a button buck came down the hill-side, following the treeline along the creek that runs through the farm. I watched them for several minutes before the buck started prancing around and darted into the field. I figured the chilly morning had the little buck feeling frisky. He kept looking toward the timber and I suspected there was another deer that had not yet stepped into view. After a while the doe and buck wandered into the alfalfa field to feed, then disappeared into the timber.

A few minutes later I spotted movement, suspecting it was the two deer I had been watching making their way back. In the sunlight I could see antlers glistening a 100 or more yards away. As the large figure came into view I realized it was not the two deer I had been watching, but a monster buck. The buck jumped the fence, and to my dismay started angling away from me and heading into the wooded area where I knew bucks preferred to bed.

The large deer, and my opportunity, was slipping away. I made a loud grunt in a last attempt to turn the buck back in my direction. The "big guy," to my surprise, stopped in his tracks and I could see him scan the hillside for what he considered an intruder. He didn't seem very interested, so I made three soft grunts and the brute stopped, turned and started walking in my direction. The large buck started to circle around behind my stand, obviously trying to pick up the scent of the other buck he heard. When he had closed the distance by half, I stood up with arrow nocked and mentally prepared for the shot.

The buck walked behind a couple of trees where I lost sight of him. I repositioned myself facing toward an opening, hoping he would step out. Time seemed to stand still. Finally the buck strutted into the open, but was moving much faster. My stand was on the opposite side of the creek, on the hillside between him and the thicket where I suspected he had been holding up all year. I had not seen the maker of the large tracks I saw during scouting trips, until this moment. I was certain it was not the same buck I had seen two years earlier. I was not about to miss the opportunity of a lifetime.

As the buck crossed the creek, I brought my Martin Phantom to a full draw. The buck closed the gap to a mere 20 yards when he stopped in my shooting lane, looking in the opposite direction. The 100-grain Wasp mechanical broadhead penetrated the massive buck's chest. He bolted a short distance before he stopped. He seemed confused and headed back toward where I had taken the shot. Taking a few more steps, the huge deer buckled and went down.

This whole experience took about five adrenalin-filled minutes. I did have time to gather my

Photograph courtesy of Kent E. Anderson

The author took this massive typical whitetail deer on his family farm in Rock Island County, Illinois in 1999. The buck scores 195-5/8 points and earned a Second Award.

thoughts and calm myself before taking the shot. When I saw the massive buck lying on the ground, my knees got weak and my hands were shaking. An unforgettable rush!

It did not occur to me how large this buck was until I was standing over him. The first thing I did was start counting his points — 14 typical and three stickers. I started shaking all over again and my breathing became irregular when I realized that I had just put down a real trophy. When I called my mom to have my brother help me get the buck out, she asked me, what was the matter, had I been running? I told her, "No, I just forgot to breathe for ten minutes."

My brother and son came down with my son's four-wheel drive truck and we were able to drive right up to where the deer lay. We tagged him, field dressed and then took it to the bait shop to check in. After caping the deer we hung it in the corn crib. I knew this one had to be mounted.

Later, when I took it to the taxidermist, I began to realize what a trophy I really had. The taxidermist told me that this buck would score in the top 10 and possibly around number five. I took him to the Deer Classic 2000 to have it officially scored. To my surprise he scored 195-2/8 points with a 18-7/8 inch inside spread (The 24th Awards Judges' Panel found the score to be a bit higher at 195-5/8 points.). At the time he was the new number two buck for Illinois. The mount took first place in its category and Best of Show. In 2001 he took first place in the historical division. My trophy and I were featured in *Illinois Game and Fish*, October 2000 issue, *Bow and Arrow*, January 2001 issue and also appeared in the local papers, *The Republic* and *The Argus/Dispatch*.

November 6, 1999, will always be a memorable day in my life. The countless hours of pre-season and post-season scouting and deer management on the 160-acre farm preceding this hunt paid off in a trophy of a lifetime. I thank my wife, Martha, and my children for their patience and understanding of my passion for bowhunting and hunting in general. ▲▲▲

186   **BOONE AND CROCKETT CLUB**

Moments in Measuring...

Photograph by Jack Reneau

Randy Byers, Chair of the Boone and Crockett Club's Records Program, works with Judges' Panel Consultant Glenn E. Hisey to verify the scoring procedure on Kent E. Anderson's typical whitetail deer that scores 195-5/8 points.

Photograph by Cliff White

TROPHY STATS

▼ ▼ ▼ ▼ ▼

Category
    whitetail - typical antlers

Score
    193$^7/_8$

Location
    Van Buren County, Iowa - 1997

Hunter
    W. Eugene Zieglowsky

Length of Main Beam
    Right: 25$^2/_8$ Left: 25$^2/_8$

**Circumference Between
    burr and 1st Point**
    Right: 4$^7/_8$ Left: 4$^7/_8$

Number of Points
    Right: 7 Left: 6

Inside Spread
    21$^5/_8$

BOONE AND CROCKETT CLUB

WHITETAIL DEER TYPICAL ANTLERS
Third Award - 193⁷/₈

▼ ▼ ▼ ▼ ▼ ▼ ▼ ▼ ▼

W. Eugene Zieglowsky

The day was December 13, 1997. It was a bright sunshiny day, with a nice covering of snow on the ground. Some of my fellow hunters of 22 years and I were enjoying our first day of the 1997 shotgun deer hunting season. We were hunting in Van Buren County, Iowa, which has been our favorite deer hunting spot for many years. We were beginning another drive through the area. As a stander for this drive, I was next to a fence row, holding my Browning A-5 12-gauge shotgun that has been my trusty hunting companion since 1953. I saw the drivers getting lined up to make a drive through a small thicket patch where we had a buck get away from us the previous three hunting seasons. I do not know if this was the same buck or not, but more than likely it was, as each year the rack on the deer got larger. The men were all lined up on the road when I saw the buck coming out of a deep gully quartering to the fence line that I was standing on. I had to wait for him to jump the fence because of the location of the drivers. As he jumped the fence he was quartering sidewise to me across an open pasture running full out when I began to shoot. I fired not once, but five times. I couldn't believe it. I felt I had hit him, but I never saw him falter or drop. After the third shot, I saw his tail drop, which usually indicates that a deer has been wounded. I couldn't believe, after all the hunting I have done, I shot at a deer five times and still didn't know if I had killed him or not.

Photograph courtesy of W. Eugene Zieglowsky

The author with his typical whitetail deer scoring 193-7/8 points.

The drivers proceeded to make the drive and my son Jim was coming down the fence row. I asked Jim when he got closer to check and see if he saw any blood. He replied, "Yes, I see some blood, but I also see a deer hanging on the fence." He said, "It looks like a nice one Dad." The deer's antlers had caught in the fence. Jim and a fellow hunter, Fritz Engle, went down to where the buck came to rest and dragged him up to where I was standing. It was then that I knew he was an above average buck. I knew it was a nice deer, but I never figured that it was as big as it turned out to be. The rest of the hunting party was as excited as I was.

Upon closer examination, I had hit the deer with four of the five shots but only one was in a vital kill area. I feel very strongly that it was the third shot that killed the deer. I have hunted deer since 1963 and only once have seen what I believed to have been a larger antlered deer in the wild. After all my years of hunting, it is wonderful to have the experience of a lifetime, taking a truly trophy buck. ▲▲▲

TROPHY STATS

▼ ▼ ▼ ▼ ▼

Category
   whitetail - non-typical antlers

Score
   $266^1/_8$

Location
   Pike County, Missouri - 2000

Hunter
   Randy J. Simonitch

Length of Main Beam
   Right: $26^6/_8$ Left: 27

Circumference Between burr and 1st Point
   Right: $6^4/_8$ Left: $7^1/_8$

Number of Points
   Right: 17 Left: 16

Inside Spread
   $20^4/_8$

Randy J. Simonitch accepting his plaque and medal from Randy Byers, Chair of the Big Game Records Committee.

BOONE AND CROCKETT CLUB

WHITETAIL DEER
Non-typical ANTLERS
First Award - 266 1/8

▼ ▼ ▼ ▼ ▼ ▼ ▼ ▼ ▼

RANDY J. SIMONITCH

My story is one of agonizing patience. It all began in the mid-morning hours of a miserably hot July day. I was driving out of my driveway, when I looked into the soybean field below the house and noticed six big bucks. They were running around the field by a pond. One buck stood out from the rest; he had a rack with numerous points, still in the velvet. I watched for a few minutes until the group disappeared into a wall of trees. I observed this buck again in August behind my house along with a few other bucks. After these two sightings I couldn't wait until September when the real fun would begin.

My neighbor, Mary Dempsey called late in the afternoon on September 21. She said she had something to show me. With a video camera in hand, she arrived at my house in a rush and produced a videotape. She had captured footage of antlers sticking out of her bean field. She walked toward the antlers with her camera rolling and came very close to a monster buck, when it swiftly jumped to its feet and vanished. After studying the video, we still could not ascertain exactly how many points it had; however, we felt sure it was a remarkable animal and I knew it was the same buck I had seen previously.

One week later Mary called again — the buck was back and I rushed over to her land to see. Mary, her son Randy and his two sons were there. Standing outside her house at the bottom of a hill, we were able to watch the deer for some time. The buck was incredible! All I could think of from that day on was imagining it hanging on my wall.

Bow season finally arrived and the enormous buck I had seen several times was always in the back of my mind as I hunted. On Tuesday, October 3rd, I hunted until about 9 a.m. I was at my house when Mary called once again. When I got there, the buck was nowhere to be seen. Mary had put a boot on a fence post to mark approximately where she had spotted the buck jump the fence. We looked for what seemed an eternity, then the antlers popped up a good 20 yards from where Mary had last seen them. We talked about going after it and after mulling it over for a while I decided to try for the super buck — what did I have to lose?

With my grunt call around my neck and bow in tow I started out into the field toward the trophy buck. I slowly and painfully took it one step at a time — never taking my eyes off the prize. After a few more steps the antlers disappeared into the beans. I stopped and after waiting a few minutes, his rack reappeared. The antlers were moving all around and all I could see was the very top of his rack. I anxiously moved closer and closer, when again the antlers vanished. This time I waited a good ten or 15 minutes. The antlers came up again, but still I didn't move. I just watched, then advanced slowly. The deer still didn't know I was there.

When I was about 25 yards away, I grunted twice on the call to no avail. I grunted again and this time the deer started to come out of the beans rear-end first. When he moved back

The author spotted this deer in the summer and was able to harvest it with a bow once the season began. The buck scores 266-1/8 points and received a First Award.

enough for a clear shot, I released my arrow.

The arrow entered behind his rib cage and he immediately bolted through the field and across the road. He bounded through the field where I first spotted him and then disappeared into the woods. My heart dropped! It looked like a good shot.

I trudged back to Mary's house to wait. I didn't want to chase him right away. After an hour Mary and I headed back out to the last spot I had seen him.

Combing the strip of woods along the dried creek bed, I found a little blood. On the other side of the woods was a cornfield. I walked along the edge, looking for blood or tracks — anything! Moving up the hill through the woods I came to the fence that bordered my land. As I looked across the fence I spotted him piled up, propped up against the fence.

I could not believe the size of this buck! He looked absolutely massive laying against the fence. I quickly pulled him through the fence. Although he was probably 250 pounds, I can't remember him being heavy. Mary was as excited as I was to see such an animal. She took pictures and another video of me with the trophy.

It was approximately 85° that day so I raced to get my buck to Wild Creations Taxidermy in Frankford, but was unable to find their shop. I didn't want to keep driving around so I purchased ice to pack the deer for the night, and headed home. In the middle of the night I became worried and couldn't sleep, so I got up and caped the deer.

The next day I found Wild Creations and that's when Jamie Graham, the owner, filled me in on the buck's true size. Although the deer could be judged many different ways, my 33-point buck will always be one of the ultimate pinnacles in my hunting career. ▲ ▲ ▲

Award Winning Moments...

Photograph by Jack Reneau

Four whitetail deer on display at the 24th Awards Program Trophy Exhibit were a sight to behold. Whitetail deer, both typical and non-typical, are by far the biggest categories represented in this book with 1,337 listings combined.

Photograph by Cliff White

TROPHY STATS

▼ ▼ ▼ ▼ ▼

Category
Coues' whitetail - typical antlers

Score
$124^6/8$

Location
Gila County, Arizona - 1998

Hunter
Tommy T. Zienka

Length of Main Beam
Right: $16^7/8$ Left: $17^1/8$

Circumference Between burr and 1st Point
Right: $3^7/8$ Left: $4^1/8$

Number of Points
Right: 7 Left: 6

Inside Spread
$15^1/8$

Photograph by Jack Reneau

Tommy T. Zienka accepting his plaque and medal from Randy Byers, Chair of the Big Game Records Committee.

COUES' WHITETAIL DEER TYPICAL ANTLERS
First Award - 124$^6/_8$

▼ ▼ ▼ ▼ ▼ ▼ ▼ ▼ ▼ ▼

TOMMY T. ZIENKA

After a successful fall archery bull elk hunt, December finally rolled around as I anxiously awaited deer season. I had drawn a late rifle Coues' whitetail deer tag in unit 23 near Young, Arizona. I was extremely excited because I had wanted to hunt in this unit for many years.

After scouting the unit with my friend and hunting partner Brandon Perkins, opening day finally came. After a few days of hunting we had seen quite a few deer and a couple of nice bucks. Having a good feeling about the area and plenty of time left to hunt, we decided to pass them up hoping for a monster buck. The weekend came to an end and we returned home since we had to work on Monday. The Christmas holiday was approaching and we planned to head back early the day after Christmas.

After a long week, Christmas day finally came and went. The next morning we headed out early so we could get to our hunting area at first light. The weather was chilly, but nice for December. We decided to try another area that we had found earlier when scouting. Most of the morning passed as we carefully glassed the hillsides. Not seeing much, we moved on. Late in the afternoon things started to pick up, seeing some deer on a distant hillside. We moved in closer to get a better look, being careful not to spook them. As we got closer we noticed a very nice buck. It looked big enough to be a mule deer. As we moved within shooting range they disappeared like gray ghosts. Determined not to give up, we headed back to our vantage point and tried locating them again. After carefully glassing the hillsides for a long while, realizing they were long gone and nowhere in sight, we headed back to the truck discouraged.

The sun was starting to dip behind the hillsides when out of nowhere appeared a very large buck ahead of us. Without hesitation I pulled my .270 to my shoulder, released the safety, and pulled the trigger. The buck dropped. We slowly headed toward the buck and as we approached him, I could not believe my eyes. He was just what I had been waiting for after many years of hunting Coues' deer. After taking some photos we packed up and headed for the truck. By now it was dark. I headed home happy with a typical 6x7 Coues' whitetail buck that scores 124-6/8 points. It was the best Christmas present ever! ▲▲▲

Photograph by Cliff White

TROPHY STATS

▼ ▼ ▼ ▼ ▼

Category
Coues' whitetail - typical antlers

Score
124

Location
Sonora, Mexico - 1998

Hunter
Joseph P. Kalt

Length of Main Beam
Right: $18^7/_8$ Left: $18^6/_8$

Circumference Between burr and 1st Point
Right: $3^4/_8$ Left: $3^4/_8$

Number of Points
Right: 6 Left: 5

Inside Spread
15

COUES' WHITETAIL DEER TYPICAL ANTLERS
Second Award - 124

▼ ▼ ▼ ▼ ▼ ▼ ▼ ▼

JOSEPH P. KALT

Boone and Crockett Club member Joe Kalt hunted Rancho Chirababi County in northern Sonora, Mexico, where he harvested his typical Coues' buck on the last day of December in 1998. Hunting with guide Michael Miller, on a ranch east of Magdalena, Joe dropped this buck at 11 a.m. with a 400 yard shot from his Remington Model 700 7mm Magnum. This 6x5 Coues' deer scores 124 points with an inside spread of 15 inches.

Photograph courtesy of Joseph P. Kalt

Photograph by Cliff White

TROPHY STATS

▼ ▼ ▼ ▼ ▼

Category
   Coues' whitetail - typical antlers

Score
   122⁵/₈

Location
   Chihuahua, Mexico - 1997

Hunter
   Kirk Kelso

Length of Main Beam
   Right: 20⁵/₈ Left: 20⁶/₈

**Circumference Between
burr and 1st Point**
   Right: 4⁴/₈ Left: 4⁴/₈

Number of Points
   Right: 5 Left: 4

Inside Spread
   15

Photograph by Jack Reneau

**Kirk Kelso accepting his plaque and medal
from Randy Byers, Chair of the Big Game
Records Committee.**

COUES' WHITETAIL DEER TYPICAL ANTLERS
Third Award - 122⁵/₈

▼ ▼ ▼ ▼ ▼ ▼ ▼ ▼ ▼

KIRK KELSO

As I sat glassing the faraway canyon behind my Docter 30x80 binoculars, my mind kept drifting back and forth from the job at hand, to the world I would soon be returning to. This was the last day of my five-day hunt in Chihuahua, Mexico, with Alex Ortiz and his American partner Wayne Curtis of Rough Country Outfitters.

I had come to Chihuahua with my good friend, mentor, and Coues' deer fanatic, David Miller, in the quest for a records book Coues'. David had been there twice before and had great results. He had taken a magnificent double main beamed non-typical and a great 110-5/8 point Boone and Crockett typical in his first two trips. As an outfitter myself for Coues' deer in Arizona and Sonora, Mexico, I am often unable to hunt due to client obligations. So, needless to say, I was very excited when David invited me to join him for this hunt. David even offered me the use of his backup rifle, since the deadline for getting my own gun permit had passed.

Chihuahua Coues'

On December 26th, 1997, David and I loaded up my truck and left Tucson with high expectations. We drove to the Texas border town of El Paso, where we met up with Wayne Curtis. We crossed the border there, and headed south toward the town of Nuevo Casas Grande, where we met Wayne's Mexican partner, Alex. I was amazed by the difference between the Mexican States of Chihuahua and Sonora. The terrain was the same, but the towns were much like any you would pass through in the midwest United States.

Our camp was a very comfortable tent camp on a remote ranch, located southeast of town. They had just endured a terrific storm prior to our arrival, and the ground was covered with about six inches of new snow, with the possibility of more snow coming. To most deer hunters, snow is good fortune, but to the Coues' hunter it can be a curse. Coues' deer are a fair weather deer, and will simply vanish when bad weather moves in.

The first four days of the hunt were very uneventful. The skies were overcast and the deer were not moving. We glassed several canyons with no luck. The deer were holding to heavy cover, and were extremely hard to find. We could see tracks in the snow, but no deer. Finally, late in the afternoon on the fourth day the sun broke through the clouds and gave us new hope for our last day. We knew that if the sun was up in the morning a new world would await us.

The following morning Alex, David, and I worked our way up a long ridge to a high point to glass a huge canyon where Alex had previously seen a tremendous Coues' buck. We were in position before daylight, and when it was light enough to see, we began picking apart the country-side. David and I were glassing with our 30x80s and Alex with his 15x60s, when I noticed a doe standing in the open, soaking up the sun's first morning rays. The rut was in full swing so I

B&C Official Measurer, Kirk Kelso with his award-winning typical Coues' whitetail scoring 122-5/8 points. He was on a five-day hunt in Chihuahua, Mexico, with good friend and hunting partner David A. Miller.

immediately concentrated on the surrounding area for a buck. As I moved the big tripod mounted 30s to the next frame to the right, I saw what I had dreamed of seeing in over 15 years of hard-core trophy Coues' deer hunting. A buck so huge he didn't look real. Needless to say, all hell broke loose on our side of the canyon. He was over 800 yards away, so we bailed off the point and worked our way down the ridge to close the distance. We couldn't close the gap by much; the canyon bluffed up on both sides and he was standing almost directly on top of the other ridge. If we dropped down too far we would lose sight of him. We worked our way to a low secondary point that would offer me the closest shot possible. Luckily, the buck had not moved. He was still standing in the same place soaking up the long awaited rays of sunlight, and totally oblivious to our presence. At 637 yards, measured with my Leica rangefinder, I had a choice: make the shot or let the buck of a lifetime walk away. I was using David's rifle, a custom David Miller Company Marksman, chambered in .300 Weatherby Magnum, firing 168-grain Sierra Match King bullets and topped with a special Leupold 6.5x20 scope. The scope has additional stadia wires added for aiming points out to 700 yards. This was a carbon copy to my own personal rifle, which I have used on numerous occasions to take animals cleanly out to 660 yards.

While I built a rest out of rocks, daypacks, and jackets, David and Alex set up their binoculars to call the shot. David and I conferred over the shot, and decided that since there was not a breath of wind, and a steep uphill angle, that I should hold the 600-yard stadia right on the buck's backline. At the shot both Alex and David confirmed a solid hit! The bullet had broken both shoulders, and after three unsteady steps he piled up!

COUES' WHITETAIL TYPICAL ANTLERS
Third Award - 122⁵/₈

▼ ▼ ▼ ▼ ▼

KIRK KELSO

After almost two hours of sidehilling and steep climbing, I reached down and pulled the great buck's rack up out of the snow. What a buck! He was beyond my wildest dreams. His typical eight-point frame, with 21-inch main beams and 11-inch back tines was greater than any buck I had ever seen.

A lot of thanks go to Alex and Wayne. They put on a great hunt and are extremely concerned with the quality of the experience. Very special thanks go to David Miller. David has spent most of his life successfully pursuing trophy Coues' deer, and has unselfishly taught me much more about hunting them and the art of marksmanship, than I can put on paper. He was just as happy to see me shoot this great buck as he would have been shooting it himself. I look forward to many more Coues' deer hunts with him, and I hope the next time we glass up a buck of this caliber that it's his turn to shoot. ▲▲▲

TROPHY STATS

▼   ▼   ▼   ▼   ▼

Category
Coues' whitetail - typical antlers

Score
126⁶/₈

Location
Yavapai County, Arizona - Picked up in 1999

Owner
Joshua E. Epperson

Length of Main Beam
Right: 20 Left: 18⁷/₈

**Circumference Between
burr and 1st Point**
Right: 4⁷/₈ Left: 5¹/₈

Number of Points
Right: 5 Left: 5

Inside Spread
17⁶/₈

COUES' WHITETAIL DEER TYPICAL ANTLERS
Certificate of Merit - 126⁶/₈

▼ ▼ ▼ ▼ ▼ ▼ ▼ ▼ ▼

JOSHUA E. EPPERSON - OWNER

Living in Arizona and being an avid shed hunter for the past 12 years, I had always known that it was only going to be a matter of time before I found something truly awesome. I had found some really nice Coues' whitetail deer and elk sheds over the years, with a few of them from Boone and Crockett class animals.

One particular spring day in April of 1999, my good friend Chris Dunn and I set out to look for a set of antlers off a bull elk that I had seen while archery deer hunting. As we entered the woods I realized that I had left my two-way radio at home. When shed antler hunting with a friend it's always nice to be in contact with the other person in case one of us happens to find one antler and needs help locating the match.

We had been walking near each other for several hours when we decided to split up. Chris was very familiar with the area and told me that if I had time, to hike up on a specific bench that he had been on previously. He mentioned that the area looked like the perfect place for a huge buck or bull to live.

When I reached the bottom of the canyon I stopped at the creek to drink and to wet my hat. I sat there for several minutes enjoying the beauty of the creek and all the massive elk rubs that were everywhere along the banks. Some of them reached over eight feet off the ground. I couldn't decide whether to go up or down the canyon when I remembered what Chris had said about the bench above me.

I had only gone about 300 yards and was approaching the edge of the bench when I spotted a deer skull with the nose pointed towards the sky. I knew that it had to have antlers to be lying in that position. Upon my approach I realized that the antlers were sort of non-typical. It was a small rack, unlike any I had ever seen before. The eyeguards were normal but both beams drooped slightly and then grew back around in a normal fashion. I was very excited to come across such a rack and considered it a truly unique find. Being quite content with my success, I continued searching. I couldn't believe there weren't any more sheds to be found so I made a couple of large loops around the area. Just as Chris had mentioned, it sure looked like an area that a monster buck should and could live without ever being seen by a human. Keeping all this in the back of my mind, I continued my search.

As occasionally happens when I'm not having any luck shed hunting, my mind starts to drift and I kind of forget why I'm out there. Just when I wasn't expecting it, I happened to glance behind me over my left shoulder and spotted a leg bone on the ground. I walked back toward it and around a little bush when I saw the biggest Coues' rack I had ever seen. I started shaking not only because of the size of the rack, but I realized had I taken two more steps I never would have found it. I quickly figured this typical rack would measure close to 130 points. After many pictures and video

Photograph courtesy of Joshua E. Epperson

Josh Epperson, right, and his good friend and fellow shed antler hunter, Chris Dunn, with their day's findings. The two had set out to find a set of antlers from a bull elk and ended up with much more. The typical Coues' whitetail that Josh is holding scores 126-6/8 points.

taping I started hiking back to the bottom of the canyon to find Chris. I waited for a while, but realized I had a long two-hour hike back to the truck.

I waited at the truck for about a half-hour when I heard Chris holler from the ridge above me. I looked up and saw that he was holding up a large six-point elk antler off the bull we were searching for. He said that had I brought my radio with me I could have helped him look for the match. I told him that had I brought my radio I wouldn't have found what I did. First, I showed him the small non-typical rack. When he asked if I had found anything else I told him to look under my flannel shirt, which was hanging on a barbed wire fence. I had the video camera going when he pulled back the shirt to record his reaction. Needless to say he freaked out just as I had, and sat there in amazement holding the rack. When I told him where I found it he said, "I knew it! I told you there had to be something like that there!"

That night we put a tape to the rack and scored it at 127 points. The 24th Awards Judges' Panel scored the buck at 126-6/8 points. Although I'm sure that I will never find a bigger rack, it won't keep me from trying. There are many miles to cover and many antlers still waiting to be discovered, some, which I am sure, I have probably already walked right past. ▲▲▲

204   **BOONE AND CROCKETT CLUB'**

Photograph by Cliff White

TROPHY STATS

▼　▼　▼　▼　▼

Category
Coues' whitetail - non-typical antlers

Score
148⁴/₈

Location
Sonora, Mexico - 2000

Hunter
Bruce K. Kidman

Length of Main Beam
Right: 20³/₈ Left: 20⁴/₈

**Circumference Between
burr and 1st Point**
Right: 4⁶/₈ Left: 4⁶/₈

Number of Points
Right: 6 Left: 6

Inside Spread
17³/₈

Photograph by Jack Reneau

Bruce K. Kidman accepting his plaque and medal from Randy Byers, Chair of the Big Game Records Committee.

BOONE AND CROCKETT CLUB

COUES' WHITETAIL DEER NON-TYPICAL ANTLERS
First Award - 148⁴/₈

▼ ▼ ▼ ▼ ▼ ▼ ▼ ▼ ▼

BRUCE K. KIDMAN

January 2, 2000 — "Cold and windy, a great day for taking a monster buck," my diary read as I prepared for the day's hunt. Little did I know what that day would bring.

I had been hunting for mule deer on the Great Sonora Desert in Mexico since December 27 with my good friend and outfitter, Arturo Malo of Baja Hunting. This was my third year, and having taken a great buck the previous year scoring 201-1/8 points, I had passed up a lot of good bucks looking for another "muy-grande buck," as my guide and tracker Antonio would say. The plan was to hunt the giant mule deer first, and after being successful, go after the elusive Coues' deer. The mule deer inhabit the great desert valleys and the Coues' deer are found in the mountains surrounding these valleys. The area we hunt has great genetics for producing extremely heavy and large antlers on both the mule deer and Coues' deer. During 1999 12 of 17 hunters took deer over 30 inches. The largest was a 38-inch 4x4 with extremely heavy mass. Both typical and non-typical bucks inhabit over 200,000 acres of adjacent leases. In my opinion, no where else in the world can you go to hunt where your chance of taking a deer over 30 inches is good. The quality of antler growth is as good as it gets in this area of Sonora, Mexico. If you are planning a Mexico hunt be careful and ask for references from the previous years' hunters as a lot of outfitters will lease a property, book as many hunters as possible, completely hunt it out, and then move on; it's just the Mexican way. Arturo limits the number of bucks taken from each lease each year to maintain and ensure the quantity and quality of the deer he hunts.

We had been hunting one lease for several days and had seen some good bucks, but not the one I wanted, so I went to another lease to see if my luck would change. We had hunted all day, and just before dark we came across a very large track. I lay my 7mm Magnum cartridge in the track, which was one cartridge wide and one cartridge long. The right front foot was either broken on one side or deformed leaving a very unique and distinguishable track to follow. Thinking of what great monster buck could leave this size track was making my imagination run wild. We tracked him to the road where we met my hunting partner, Dan Heyne, and his guide, Freddy. We all agreed it was the biggest track we had ever seen. As darkness fell upon us, Antonio looked at me and pointed to the track and said, "Manyana."

We were on the track before it was light enough for me to see it, but Antonio was anxious to get going to make up for the many hours the buck was ahead of us. The deer walked with a side-to-side movement rather than an in-line movement like normal. Antonio would make this side-to-side moving gesture with his body telling me it was an extremely large deer walking with this swaying motion. My mind ran wild again while following the track and watching for him to appear around the next cactus or bush. We had walked for three hours and the deer had led us back to the foothills where we lost his tracks on the almost solid rock covered ground. We walked a quarter of a mile to

Photograph courtesy of Bruce Kidman

The author thought he had taken a small mule deer buck when his guide pointed out it was in fact a monster non-typical Coues' whitetail. The buck scores 148-4/8 points and received a First Award at the 24th Awards Banquet.

the mountain and climbed up high enough to glass the desert below us in hopes of spotting him, but after half an hour Antonio motioned, "Lets go back." So back to the desert floor we went. We traveled north of where we lost the track and had only walked for a short time before we were on his track again. The disappointment I had felt after losing the track left and excitement took over again. Unlike other deer we had been tracking that would pretty much walk in a general direction and walk around any brush, this deer was all over the place. He was going every which way like he was lost, and he was walking right through the brush. He was extremely hard to follow and I was amazed how Antonio stayed on the track. When we were getting close, the deer became aware of us and did a lot of doubling back and walking in washes and rocky ground.

We had walked now for five hours and many miles, when we approached a wash. While Antonio was following the tracks through the brush, I walked around it to be able to see anything on the other side when I heard him go, "Psst, psst." I turned and he motioned for me to come over. He was pointing to the brush to the side of him, but I could see nothing. He motioned for me to look with my binoculars. I looked through my 10x40 Leica binoculars into the brush, and at 30 feet I could only see a face and antlers staring back at me. At 10 power he filled my whole field of view and his antlers looked as round as a baseball bat and extremely wide. I thought "40-inch buck," as my mind had already been programmed for many hours since first seeing the track the night before.

Antonio said, "Shoot, shoot." I dropped my binoculars, grabbed my rifle from my shoulder, looked through my Swarovski scope, centered the crosshairs on the neck and shot. He bolted from the brush and was gone. I chambered another round while running around the brush with Antonio close behind in hopes of getting an-

COUES' WHITETAIL NON-TYPICAL ANTLERS
First Award - 148⁴/₈

▼ ▼ ▼ ▼ ▼

BRUCE K. KIDMAN

other shot, but after clearing the brush there was no deer. Antonio thought I had missed. He went back to where the deer was standing and could find no blood or any sign that it was hit. I felt there was no way I could have missed at that distance. We started in pursuit of him, but still no blood. After going about 75 yards Antonio turned around and excitedly pointed out in front of him and started to slap my back. I finally saw the buck laying on his side 25 yards away. As I approached him the antlers weren't 40 inches wide as I had envisioned, but still very heavy and somewhat unique. I checked his feet and sure enough the right front foot was deformed and also one half of his toe was broken off on one side matching the print exactly. This was indeed the same buck we had been tracking. I took my tape from my pack and measured his hoof at five inches long.

Knowing the great quality of the bucks here and seeing so many bucks over the 30-40 inch mark, I thought, "I'll come back next year for my monster buck." After a couple of pictures we dragged him over to the wash and hung it up in a palo verde tree where Antonio gutted him. We called Dan and Freddy on the radio, who were five miles away back on the mountain hunting Coues' deer, and told them to bring the truck. Antonio broke a branch from the tree to drag on the ground so we could make our way back to the deer. By the time we got back to the road Dan and Freddy were waiting for us. I described the events to Dan and told him how I really screwed up and shot a deer less than I wanted, something I haven't done in many years. With Antonio leading the way we were able to get the truck to the deer. Freddy jumped out and walked fast over to the deer with Antonio and started to yell, "Cola blanca, cola blanca," as he grabbed the deer's tail and held it out. He and Antonio were ecstatic as they talked in Spanish and showed their excitement. I looked at Dan and said, "What's the matter?" (I thought I might have shot something illegal.) Dan looked at me and said, "Bruce, you don't know what you've shot. That's a freaking Coues' deer. If that's not a World's Record, it's got to be close." I had no idea. Only then did I realize what all the excitement was about. I had taken a trophy Coues' deer that was unbelievable. We actually had been tracking a monster buck after all and I had taken a trophy of a lifetime. After many pictures from four cameras and just admiring this magnificent deer we returned to camp where, with the other hunters and guides, the celebration began again.

After the 60-day drying period my good friend and longtime hunting partner, John Israelsen, along with Victor Clark, who are Boone and Crockett measurers, scored my buck at 152-2/8 points. The 24th Awards Judges Panel officially scored the buck at 148-4/8 points. This is truly a monster buck. ▲▲▲

Photograph by Cliff White

TROPHY STATS

▼ ▼ ▼ ▼ ▼

Category
  Coues' whitetail - non-typical antlers

Score
  147

Location
  Pima County, Arizona - 1991

Hunter
  James A. Reynolds

Length of Main Beam
  Right: 18⁶/₈ Left: 19⁶/₈

Circumference Between burr and 1st Point
  Right: 5 Left: 4⁵/₈

Number of Points
  Right: 10 Left: 7

Inside Spread
  16⁶/₈

Photograph by Jack Reneau

James A. Reynolds accepting his plaque and medal from Randy Byers, Chair of the Big Game Records Committee.

COUES' WHITETAIL DEER NON-TYPICAL ANTLERS
Second Award - 147

▼ ▼ ▼ ▼ ▼ ▼ ▼ ▼

JAMES A. REYNOLDS

My first encounter with this great Coues' deer was on March 31, 1990. This day found me scouting a series of low ridges that had the look of an area that could hold a big buck. As I was taking a short break, I noticed movement below me on the opposite side of the canyon. The buck was violently shaking his head as he moved through the brush, and if not for this, I may not have known he was there. As I watched him, he entered a small patch of brush and disappeared. To my amazement, as he reentered my field of view, he was missing an antler! I closely watched him, hoping he would shed the other antler, but he managed to move down the canyon and out of sight, still carrying half of his incredible rack.

Persistence Pays Off

Despite all my efforts, during the months following my first encounter, I could not locate the other antler, nor did I see the buck again. I was beginning to think that he may not be alive. In hopes that I was wrong, I spent eight days hunting him during the November 1990 season. I saw several nice bucks, but I couldn't bring myself to pull the trigger on any of them. My heart was set on the great buck, and I was willing to pass on all others.

On January 14, 1991, while scouting for any sign that he might still be alive, I found him again! The rut was in full swing, and he was tending does in the same series of small ridges, where I had seen him almost a year earlier! I now knew that this area had to be the buck's home, so I spent every spare minute trying to pattern his habits and movements. By the middle of August, I had seen him numerous times from the same vantage point — a small rocky point overlooking a large dry wash at the base of the mountains.

My confidence was flying high when I received a permit in the mail for the unit he lived in. What made it all the more interesting was that the opening day of the hunt, November 8th, was also my birthday. A good omen!

For seven long days, I sat on my favorite vantage point, meticulously scanning the buck's home area, with my tripod-mounted, 15-power Zeiss binoculars. He was nowhere to be found. It was as if he knew that this was the week he needed to stay low. On the eighth day, I awoke to a very overcast sky, with the threat of rain in the air. It started drizzling moments after I reached my glassing spot, and I spent the morning glassing with my binoculars under a plastic bag. By this time discouragement was setting in, and thoughts of calling it quits were running through my head.

Around 2:00 p.m., the storm started to break and intermittent sunshine was once again returning to the desert. I was glassing with my handheld 10x binoculars when I spotted three deer moving through the mesquite. The first two were does, and since the rut was better

Photograph courtesy of James A. Reynolds

After picking up five sets of shed antlers from this buck over the years, the author was finally able to connect with this non-typical Coues' whitetail scoring 147 points.

than a month and a half away, I felt sure that the third deer was also. To my amazement, a buck appeared out of nowhere — my buck! I quickly gathered my gear, stuffed it in my pack, and made my move. I backed over and down the ridge I was on in order to get into a position that would put me directly across the canyon from him. Settling into position, I benched my .300 Weatherby in a small rock outcropping and waited.

The buck was approximately 300 yards from me, feeding in and out of the mesquite where I first relocated him. I was so overwhelmed with excitement when he offered me my first opportunity for a shot that I didn't shoot! I tried the best I could to calm myself and waited for him to step clear again. This time I felt good, and squeezed the trigger. At the rifle's report he collapsed!

After 20 long months of scouting for this one deer, and picking up his five previous sets of shed antlers, I was finally able to see him up close. His ten scorable points on one side and seven on the other, were everything I had dreamed he could posses, and then some! He is one of the greatest non-typical Coues' deer ever taken and quite possibly, the crowning achievement of my hunting career. ▲ ▲ ▲

212

BOONE AND CROCKETT CLUB

Awards Winning Moments...

Photograph by Jack Reneau

Coues' whitetail deer hunters, Kirk Kelso, Tommy T. Zienka, and James A. Reynolds pose in front of their trophies at the 24th Awards Program Trophy Exhibit at Bass Pro Shops. Coues' whitetail deer were well represented at the program with four typical and four non-typical trophies, including a new World's Record non-typical scoring 186-1/8 points.

Photograph by Cliff White

TROPHY STATS
▼ ▼ ▼ ▼ ▼

Category
Coues' whitetail - non-typical antlers

Score
186$^{1}/_{8}$

Location
Hidalgo County, New Mexico - 1941

Hunter
Peter M. Chase

Owner
W.B. Darnell

Length of Main Beam
Right: 17$^{6}/_{8}$ Left: 16$^{5}/_{8}$

Circumference Between burr and 1st Point
Right: 4$^{5}/_{8}$ Left: 4$^{6}/_{8}$

Number of Points
Right: 8 Left: 8

Inside Spread
18$^{2}/_{8}$

COUES' WHITETAIL DEER
Non-typical ANTLERS
Certificate of Merit - 186¹/₈

▼ ▼ ▼ ▼ ▼ ▼ ▼ ▼ ▼

PETER M. CHASE - HUNTER
W.B. DARNELL - OWNER

Peter M. Chase, a local druggist and businessman of Lordsburg, New Mexico, was invited to go on a deer hunt in November of 1941 with two friends. He really didn't want to go since he was not a deer hunter and had never had an inclination to shoot a deer, but he decided to go just to be with the boys. His friends Marshall Fuller and Benny Cochran, were delighted to have him along.

Hunting in Hidalgo County, New Mexico, Peter, with a borrowed a .30-30 Savage and four cartridges, followed his two friends into the mountains. He said he never even got a sweat up enough to remove his tie when the hunters split up and each went his own way.

The Drugstore Buck

He remembered spotting a deer with large antlers, but didn't shoot because he thought he had seen movement in the direct line of fire between him and the deer. Seconds later the deer moved into a series of juniper draws. Shortly after, the deer reappeared and walked toward him. At about 60 yards the buck stopped and looked right at Peter. He quickly pulled his rifle up and fired one shot, hitting the deer. The buck went a short distance, fell and had expired before he reached him.

Peter was very excited, but discovered that he didn't have a knife. Benny had come toward the shot to see what the shooting was about and to help Peter if he had a deer down. After field dressing the buck they packed the head and antlers back to the truck, where they met up with Marshall. Then the three returned with pack boards to recover the remainder of the meat.

All three friends were very elated and amazed because of the number of long points on the buck's rack. The rack wasn't overly wide, but was very unusual.

Peter remembered the deer had a red tint to his hair on his front shoulders, turning more gray on his ribs and hips, with a gray and white tail. He saved the hide and had a pair of gloves made, which he kept for over 35 years. He also kept a shed antler found in the area.

Mr. Chase had the deer mounted in a short neck mount and the head hung in his local Drug Store in Lordsburg, New Mexico, for many years. This is where I first noticed the unusual deer in 1957. This buck is the only deer Mr. Chase has ever taken.

I grew up on a cattle ranch near the Chiricahua Mountains on the Arizona/New Mexico border in Rodeo, New Mexico, 47 miles from Lordsburg. About twice a month my parents would shop in Lordsburg at Mr. Chase's drug store which had an old-time malt and ice cream shop. I always enjoyed going there, not just for the ice cream, but I could also look at the deer heads he had in his store.

At 13 years of age and reared on a ranch, hunting was part of my family's life. We hunted mule deer, Coues' deer, cougar and javelina. Having taken both species of deer I began to get more interested in big bucks and deer hunting. This is when I really became fascinated with Mr. Chase's buck.

He had related the previous story to me in 1957. I didn't take any notes, but remembered everything he told me.

In 1962 I started guiding hunters for Coues' and mule deer in southeast Arizona and southwest New Mexico. I eventually developed an outfitting business called Del Pitic Desert Hunting. Today we offer hunts in Hermosillo, Sonora, and Mexico.

In 1976 I went to work for the Hidalgo Sheriff Department as a Deputy Sheriff. I continued to guide hunters and occasionally visit with Mr. Chase about his unusual deer head. He told me his interesting story again that year.

Mr. Chase had retired from the pharmacy business and was living in Lordsburg. The cape on the Chase head had deteriorated away and the antlers had been put on a board and eventually stored under a workbench. When he showed them to me again they had paint spilled on them from overturned paint cans.

After visiting with Mr. Chase over the years he knew I was a serious hunter. We talked about his buck many times. I often mentioned that his deer should be preserved and recognized since I felt his buck was one in a million. To keep it tucked away or be lost would be an injustice. I explained to him that interviews and affidavits would have to be done, along with notarization of documents to submit the buck to the Boone and Crockett Club. Mr. Chase was not too interested in all the fan fare, but agreed to tell his story and sign the affidavits. He told me that he would give the antlers to me because of my great admiration for the species. This was in 1985.

By this time I had become sheriff, and in a small New Mexico county my work obligations put the buck on the back burner.

In 1987 I decided it was time to contact the Boone and Crockett Club. The Club's office staff put me in touch with one of their measurers, Tim Kelly of Albuquerque, New Mexico. Tim measured the head and sent me the necessary forms. On September 27, 1989, Mr. Chase signed the Fair Chase statement and other required forms. We then sent all the notarized forms to Tim.

I had Rex Jenson of Virden, New Mexico, do a competition mount on the Chase buck. I also had the buck scored by Jake Jacobson and John O. "Buzzi" Cook.

Days turned into months, months into years; then, in December 2000 I talked with Jack Reneau of the Boone and Crockett Club in reference to the Chase buck. I sent him the forms he requested, an entry fee, and some photos. He also directed me to contact Tim Kelly in Albuquerque to get the original scoring sheet. When I talked to Tim I learned the original forms had apparently been misplaced.

Mr. Reneau sent me new forms for Tim to sign. I also met with Jack in Albuquerque on February 22, 2001, to have him verify a couple of measurements on the rack. He then told me that if this was a legitimate head of the Coues' species it would be a new World's Record non-typical. I felt good at the possibility Mr. Chase's buck was finally headed for its rightful place in history.

One other amazing fact about this deer — the Chase buck has never been "out" of Hidalgo County, New Mexico, except for display in the 24th Awards Program Trophy Exhibit. The Chase buck speaks for itself; it is what it is. ▲▲▲

Moments in Measuring...

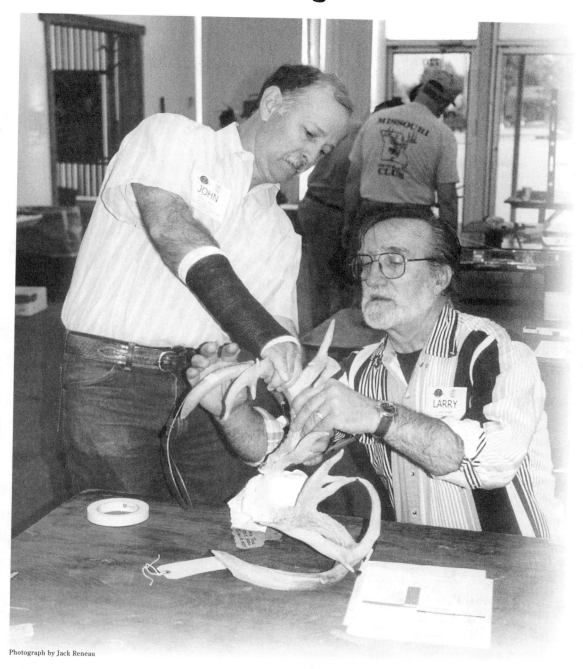

Photograph by Jack Reneau

24th Awards Judges' Panel Members John Stein and Larry Streiff draw a point base line with a measuring cable on the main beam of Patrick H. Taylor's non-typical Coues' whitetail. The buck was picked up in Pima County, Arizona, in 1997, and scores 151-3/8 points.

Photograph by Cliff White

TROPHY STATS

▼ ▼ ▼ ▼

Category
Coues' whitetail - non-typical antlers

Score
151³/₈

Location
Pima County, Arizona - Picked up in 1997

Owner
Patrick H. Taylor

Length of Main Beam
Right: 19⁶/₈ Left: 19⁷/₈

**Circumference Between
burr and 1st Point**
Right: 4³/₈ Left: 4⁴/₈

Number of Points
Right: 7 Left: 8

Inside Spread
15³/₈

Photograph by Jack Reneau

Patrick H. Taylor accepting his plaque and medal from Randy Byers, Chair of the Big Game Records Committee.

COUES' WHITETAIL DEER NON-TYPICAL ANTLERS
Certificate of Merit - 151³/₈

▼ ▼ ▼ ▼ ▼ ▼ ▼ ▼ ▼

PATRICK H. TAYLOR - OWNER

It was pure luck that I even noticed the remains of a deer lying among the ocotillo cactus as I slowly made my way up the foothills near Las Quijas Mountain in southern Arizona. Even though I couldn't allow myself time to stop to get a closer look, I do remember being amazed at what good shape the antlers seemed to be in. If rodents had been gnawing on them it wasn't noticeable. An automatic mental note was filed away in my head, reminding me to come back this way and pick them up if, and only if, I didn't get a buck out of the herd of mule deer I had been following. At that moment, I was committed to continuing my "sneak attack," hoping against hope that there would be a buck among the does. I had seen a total of two bucks in the last five days. The first buck I saw was at first light on opening morning with a woman who looked a lot like my wife, Joyce, attaching her deer tag to it. The second deer was a nice, three-point my dad shot an hour later. I was getting pretty good at packing other people's deer back to camp without excessive grumbling.

So here I was, next to the last day of my hunt, less than an hour's worth of daylight left and I was beginning to sweat. Not just because I was feeling the pressure of "odd man out," but also because November in southern Arizona was not supposed to be this hot. The mule deer population was moving from the flats and foothills to higher ground, crossing over into the whitetail territory. In turn, the whitetail had been spotted at lower elevations. The Coues' whitetail species in southern Arizona and western New Mexico are small and delicate appearing and paler in color than our northern whitetail. Their antlers are also much smaller, but no less beautiful. Through the years, stories of sightings of "Super" Coues' bucks had been told around the campfires. They were said to have had a much larger set of antlers. As a matter of fact, Joyce and I had caught a glimpse of what looked to have been a "Super" Coues' while we were on a scouting trip. We had unexpectedly startled him out of his bed. Daylight was limited and all we got was a quick glance, but we have never forgotten how grand he looked silhouetted against the glow of morning's false dawn.

On that special late afternoon in November 1997, everything seemed to come together at the right time and in the right sequence. No bucks were in the herd I had been following, which enabled me to return to the bones I had spotted earlier. Standing there staring at the bleached and somewhat scattered remains, I realized that this deer was as grand in death as he had to have been in life. The antlers were still attached to the skull and when I picked them up I noticed that they were whitetail.

Hurrying back to the truck where Joyce was waiting, I smiled at the thought of how excited she would be. My wife dearly loves to hunt and collecting antlers runs a close second. After handing the rack to her, she just stood there saying nothing! Her lips were moving, but no words were coming out, at least anything decipherable. All I was able to hear were the little mewing sounds she kept making, and as I looked into her eyes, I could tell they were glazed over. When her verbal skills finally returned, all she kept saying was how lucky I was and that she was sure that I had just found one of the largest sets of antlers in the state. Never having hunted Coues' deer, I had no idea what a record set of antlers looked like.

While at work a few days later, I was walking back to my truck when a friend of mine stopped me. He was an avid whitetail archery hunter and said that he had heard a rumor about a 'decent' set of antlers that I had found on my hunt. They were lying in the back of my truck so I just pointed at them. His knees almost buckled. When he told me that I should get them out of my truck bed and find someone who was certified to score for Boone and Crockett, I knew then that I had better take his advice.

Several weeks went by when my wife suddenly asked me if I thought I could find my way back to the spot where the rest of the buck's remains were. It seemed that she had been having dreams of a ghost deer coming to her trying to make her understand something. She felt that we needed to return and honor him in the Native American way by leaving offerings of tobacco and sage. The taxidermist that we had left the skull with had mentioned that he would have liked to have been able to examine the bottom jaw as he was curious at the age of the deer. Joyce and I returned to retrieve the lower teeth and also to leave our offerings, thanking the spirit of the deer for allowing us to find him.

No one will ever know for sure what caused the death of this deer. We did, however, find what appears to be puncture marks at the base of the skull. A mountain lion may have very well taken him down as we later found several more partial deer skulls and broken jawbones nearby.

My wife is a cowboy poet and in honor of the deer in her dreams, she wrote the following short story.

DEATH in the DESERT

The morning is soundless and still as the false dawn approaches, morning birds not yet awake. The chill of daybreak finds me sitting under an old mesquite hoping to find the exact patch of ground where the first rays of sunlight will warm me.

Being as quiet as possible, I clear an area free of small rocks and twigs and eventually lean up against the tree's cool bark. Finding a comfortable position my fidgeting halts the moment my eyes detect movement down hill, and up wind, from my location. The silhouette of a deer comes into view, tentatively working its way through the ocotillo flats. Adjusting my binoculars, the image of a huge buck comes into focus: a whitetail of the Coues' clan, sporting a magnificent rack.

Excitedly I breathe in…watching. Cautiously he breathes out…testing…pausing.

He surveys the four corners of his immediate domain, ears continually twitching. His gaze eventually fixes on a nearby clump of trees that are lightly scattered above the rim of a narrow arroyo that separates us, one from the other. With reasons known only to him, he selects a place to bed down for the day, finishing a long night's journey into sleep.

With the grace of his many years, he nimbly kneels on front legs, allowing the back to follow. Watching…my heart races. Resting…his heart slows.

What a wise soul he must be to have eluded so many hunters for all these years. I begin to wonder if there might be other bucks nearby so I reluctantly begin to scan the near-distant hills when suddenly the tranquility of the morning ceases.

DEATH has arrived! It is sweeping in on the back of a mountain lion. The cougar must have used the arroyo as cover until it was close enough to initiate an ambush, becoming a blur as it reaches its destination.

For a brief moment my eyes opened wide…in surprise. The deer's eyes close tight…in resignation.

COUES' WHITETAIL
NON-TYPICAL ANTLERS
Certificate of Merit - 151³/₈

▼ ▼ ▼ ▼ ▼

PATRICK H. TAYLOR - OWNER

It will never be known if this big buck realized for sure that his life was about to end. I am of the opinion that he did know for I saw his regal head come up at the last second as he felt…heard…smelled?…DEATH coming.

I turn away as a sob escapes from the confines of my throat, reminding me just how tenuous life is and how tenacious nature can be.

Today I leave this place and he will stay, to forever travel these hills.

Perhaps he will wander through the minds of those who may have caught a glimpse of him during the prime years of his life, to be mentioned in stories told around campfires late at night. Perhaps his antlers will be found one day by someone who will take them home…

To be forever remembered.

To be forever grand.

Perhaps.

This story is written for my husband, Patrick H. Taylor who found a trophy Coues' rack while hunting mule deer in 1997, dedicated to the spirit of this deer and to the lion that may have taken it. ▲▲▲

Photograph by Cliff White

TROPHY STATS

▼   ▼   ▼   ▼   ▼

Category
Canada moose

Score
219^6/$_8$

Location
Kinaskan Lake, British Columbia - 1998

Hunter
Thomas E. Farmer

Greatest Spread
61^2/$_8$

Length of Palm
Right: 46^6/$_8$ Left: 45

Width of Palm
Right: 15^7/$_8$ Left: 16

Number of Normal Points
Right: 13 Left: 11

Photograph by Jack Reneau

Thomas E. Farmer accepting his plaque and medal from Randy Byers, Chair of the Big Game Records Committee.

CANADA MOOSE
First Award - 219⁶/₈

▼ ▼ ▼ ▼ ▼ ▼ ▼ ▼ ▼

Thomas E. Farmer

It was cold and clear as Chris and Jerry Creyke guided me through the northern British Columbian wilderness in hopes of finding a really respectable Canada moose. As our five horses picked along a ghost of a trail that had not been traveled in several years, the three of us sensed something extraordinary was about to occur. It had been an extraordinary week. On my first day of hunting, I had taken a fantastic mountain goat with heavy horns almost ten inches long and an "October cape" so full and beautiful, it made me wonder why any hunter would prefer to hunt them earlier in the season. Two days later I took my first mountain sheep, a full curl and beautifully flared Stone's ram, off the top of a tall snow covered butte. The ram slid all the way to the bottom without so much as scratching his horns or burning his fantastic cape. He would make another beautiful trophy. I was on a roll. Three days later, I bagged an old grizzly with a gorgeous pelt. Then we moved back to the Creyke's base camp at Kinaskan Lake, with the intention of re-provisioning and heading 25 miles north to another area the Creyke's knew would be full of rutting bull moose.

The Bulls of Forgotten Valley

My Talbtan Indian guides were proving they knew their stuff and they were confident that taking a big bull was nearly a certainty.

As I think back on it now, I don't remember who suggested that we might also consider hunting near an old campsite used long ago by the Creyke's uncle. If we chose the abandoned hunting area, the trail would be hard to follow and the old campsite would be worthless, if we could find it at all. We'd have to bring everything we needed and be prepared to live like coyotes. Since no one had been back in that region for years, the Creyke's could only hope that moose would be using the area. Call it a gut feeling, intuition, a hunch, or blind faith, I wanted to go there!

At about 10:00 a.m. the following day, we were packed and ready to go. I think Jerry and Chris were as anxious as I was to be going back into an area they had not hunted in a long time. The October air seemed a bit colder and darker each day as fall rapidly advanced on the Northern Canadian Rockies. The forest breathed a deathly quiet winter's warning as we hacked our way along this almost forgotten Indian trail. There were no birds! I presumed they must have moved south leaving this vast and completely untamed wilderness to avoid the brutal chill that would be unrelenting for several months to come. I've never felt farther from my warm Texas home on Galveston Island.

As we broke out of lower country thickets into gorgeous alpine meadows nestled among snow-capped peaks, we began to follow a long flowing creek. Each new vista was a postcard in the raw.

We had been riding about three or four hours, when Chris pulled up the reins and pointed far up the valley. Two bull moose and three cows could clearly be seen against the straw colored valley more than a mile away. The bulls looked huge.

We quickly tied the two pack horses and the three of us rode along the edge of the timber to close the gap as quickly as possible. We tied our horses and climbed a bluff that would put us above the moose. As we eased over the crest, the scene below needed no explanation. One bull was leaving the cows and was heading generally toward our position. The other was almost 500 yards further up the valley and moving away with the prized cows. He was the obvious victor of the battle we had just missed.

I quickly studied both bulls with my Leica 10x42s and decided the best antlers resided with the departing conqueror. Jerry was focused on the closest bull that was now only 200 years away, a chip shot for my .300 Weatherby. Jerry encouraged me to shoot him quickly because he was certainly a Book bull. I put the cross hairs of my Schmidt & Bender on the bull, but never considered taking the safety off! He was tremendous, but the other bull was even better, having massive fronts, great mass throughout, wide palms, and lots of points. I wanted the one that was busy herding his girlfriends as far away from the competition as possible. Chris agreed. Jerry thought I was crazy to pass a slam-dunk record candidate and was quick to tell me so!

We debated our stalking options and the Creyke's figured we should move down to the creek and hot foot it straight toward the departing bull. We dropped down to the creek and began moving along the moose's path, but soon discovered that we couldn't travel nearly as fast as the moose in the boggy tundra-like marsh flanking the creek. We almost caught up with them just before dark, but a reasonable shot never materialized. We retreated quietly to retrieve the horses and moved back down the valley to make camp.

In the cold and dark skies of an October night, Chris taught me how to make a spruce bow bed, while Jerry took the horses down to the valley below to feed. We were so tired when all the work was done that we simply unrolled our sleeping bags and crashed under the gray night sky.

We woke with a light skiff of snow on our sleeping bags overlooking a horseless valley. Chris and Jerry set out to find them on foot. I agreed to finish setting up our camp and then hunt for my bull in the area close to camp. By early afternoon I had seen two bulls and two cows. About 2:00 p.m. Jerry and Chris returned with the wayward horses and soon thereafter we were saddled and moving on up the valley, stopping often to glass the hillsides and meadows for the only bull I wanted. We continued our trek for a couple of hours and then tied our horses at the base of a tall hill. The three of us climbed to the top and each began to glass in a different direction. I quickly found a 50" class bull with a cow about a mile from my perch. I kept the vigil. When we had been there about 20 or 30 minutes, Chris trotted up from his venue and exclaimed, "I've spotted him!" We all moved to Chris's lookout and glassed the big bull with his cows. The same smaller bull was lurking about 200 yards behind; a proper distance considering the whipping he must have taken the day before.

The bull was at least one mile away and it was going to be a push to get to him before dark. After a brief tactical discussion, we scampered down the hill and began a hard fast ride through timber and brush.

Jerry took the lead and after an exhilarating ride, he pulled up and tied his horse to a tree. "We'll go on foot from here," he proclaimed. We hadn't gone far at all when Jerry said he heard the moose. Chris decided to go back to keep the horses quiet. Jerry and I continued to stalk toward the sounds of the grunting moose. We eased into a relatively clear area in the timber that was covered with six-foot tall brush. In the fading light, you could just see glimpses of the great bull's rack as he moved about. Jerry mouth called a long mournful challenge that stimulated an immediate response from the bull. The massive rack seemed to glide silently toward our position. Intermittently, low coughing grunts punctuated his determined approach. The massive antlers drifted to the right and began to swivel left and right as he searched for his challenger.

CANADA MOOSE
First Award - 219⁶/₈

▼ ▼ ▼ ▼ ▼

THOMAS E. FARMER

At about 80 yards, the large rack moved back to our left and disappeared behind a tree. Moments passed in complete silence as we waited for the bull to appear in the evening's gloom. I remember thinking that if I were rattling whitetails back home in Texas, this would be the moment to "burp" a challenge grunt or click the antlers slightly. I whispered to Jerry, "Call softly." Jerry moaned a low guttural challenge and the bull stepped from behind the tree turning straight toward us and stopped at about 70 yards. "Shoot him in the shoulder!" Jerry hissed. I already had the rifle up, safety off. The 3x12 Schmidt and Bender scope was on 3X as I focused on the enormous bull. With the tall brush and the angle of approach, the bull's shoulder was not presenting the proper shot. It would be totally dark within 30 minutes or so - no time to be trailing a wounded animal. I put the crosshairs between and slightly below the eyes. I'll never forget the sight picture, as the crosshairs were amazingly steady for the off hand shot. Boom! The massive bull sank straight downward in the brush. Jerry began to shout directions as we quickly approached the fallen giant. "Be ready to shoot if he tries to get up! They often get up! This bull can still kill you! Get Ready! Shoot him if he moves at all!"

I said, "I'm ready, but he's not getting up with no brains. I shot him between the eyes!"

Jerry said, "You did what?" As we reached the lifeless bull, we found it bleeding from a small pencil hole dead center between his eyes. The 180-grain Nosler Partition had gone completely through the massive head without breaking his skull plate.

Chris had maneuvered to be able to see the whole show from above. When he rode up, he exclaimed, "Never have I seen a moose die like that! Not even a twitch!"

I marveled at the size of the animal. It was bigger than our horses! Jerry and Chris said it was the biggest moose they had ever seen. We snapped photo's in the remaining light and began to skin my trophy.

After the necessary chores were completed we left the bull to cool overnight, hoping that the bears wouldn't find him before our return in the morning. I left a bit of my sweaty clothing draped over a nearby bush hoping to discourage the bruins.

After sleeping like rocks, we awoke to a beautiful clear British Columbia sky. Jerry and Chris rode out to pack in my bull and I stayed behind to pack up our campsite. We left the area as pristine as we had found it. My first hunt in the North woods was now complete. By any standards it had been an incredible success. As we rode away I looked back up the valley and recalled the first sight of the great bull with his cows and his magnificent competitor. I think of that scene often as I remember the "Bulls of Forgotten Valley" and the wonderful guides who shared the experience with me. ▲▲▲

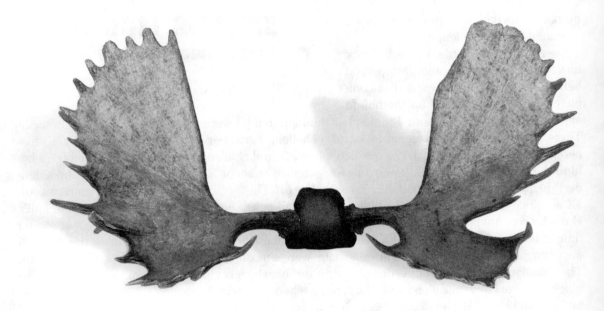

TROPHY STATS

▼ ▼ ▼ ▼ ▼

Photograph by Cliff White

Category
Canada moose

Score
211

Location
Red Earth Creek, Alberta - 2000

Hunter
M. Nathan Sabo

Greatest Spread
63^2/$_8$

Length of Palm
Right: 41^1/$_8$ Left: 42^2/$_8$

Width of Palm
Right: 18^5/$_8$ Left: 15^6/$_8$

Number of Normal Points
Right: 16 Left: 10

CANADA MOOSE
Honorable Mention - 211

▼ ▼ ▼ ▼ ▼ ▼ ▼ ▼ ▼

M. Nathan Sabo

"Nath," my dad's voice cut the tension, "you better put the camera down and get ready to shoot. You can video him all you want once he's on the ground." My father was beginning to express his concern that the bull would get away, when BOOM, the shot from my Ruger .300 Winchester echoed through the wilderness. At that moment the first four days of the hunt didn't matter anymore.

Our annual moose hunting trip was planned for September 28, 2000. My hunting partners Lou Gajdos, Don Sabo, Fred Bullegas, my father Moses and I planned to spend ten days calling moose in the area near Red Earth, Alberta. Due to unfortunate circumstances beyond our control the trip was not starting out very good. With flat tires on the trailer and mechanical breakdowns with the ATVs, we were beginning to wonder why anyone would spend so much time and money to be so frustrated.

In the Land of Giants

On the morning of October 3rd, we were finally ready to put in our first full day of hunting. We awoke to a frozen, windy morning. Our spirits were a little down because of the howling winds, but we were happy just to be able to finally hunt. Lou and Don wanted to spend the day at a lake where Don had shot a young bull the previous afternoon, while Fred, my dad, and I decided to try a lake about three hours south of camp.

We arrived at the lake by mid-afternoon and started to call. While I was calling I noticed something black on the other side of the lake through a clearing and into the willows. I didn't know if it was a bull or a cow, but I knew its body was big. Between wind gusts and sardine sandwiches I continued calling when I faintly heard a grunt. I then noticed something that resembled a sheet of plywood on the far side of the lake. Through my 10x42 binoculars I realized that the sheet of plywood was actually the antlers of a massive bull looking over the willows in our direction. As I continued to call, the bull sauntered toward the ice-covered lake. With the strong crosswind blowing, I gave out another cow call and the bull was hooked. He stood on the shoreline and seemed to be debating which was the quickest route to the love-sick cow. The direction he chose was the closest, but a frozen creek about 40 feet wide lay in his path. Failing to find a way across the creek, he decided to try and cross on the ice. Putting his front legs on the ice, he broke through causing him to make a hasty retreat. I let out a grunt hoping to persuade him to try and cross again. This got the big bull's juices flowing, making him mad. He started thrashing his head from side to side and ended the life of the closest willow bush. He then forged back into the creek. Using his front legs he began to break through the ice. We watched in awe as he disappeared and reemerged with his legs coming up on the ice in front of him, busting his way through. About half way through the creek, our hearts sank as we watched the bull turn around and head back to the bank he came from. We were starting

Photograph courtesy of M. Nathan Sabo

The author successfully coaxed this massive Canada moose across a frozen creek to within shooting distance. The bull scores 211 points.

to doubt he would be able to cross at all. I figured I had nothing to lose so I let out the loudest bull grunt I could possibly conjure up. Without hesitating he turned around and plunged back into the ice-covered creek, sending an array of water and ice into the air. Occasionally we would catch a glimpse of his antlers as he lunged forward through the ice. It seemed like an eternity as we waited for him to appear on the other side. Finally, out of the creek he emerged, looking for stable ground as he stumbled from exhaustion. Finding his footing, the bull stood and shook his coat violently, ridding himself of the freezing water. I gave a cow call to set his bearings straight and get him moving.

We decided to cut the distance between us, so we quickly made our way to a position around the lake, which gave us the best view. After getting to within 340 yards of the beast, I decided to video this exciting event. It seemed like seconds later the wind shifted, putting our scent directly in line with the bull. That's when my dad gave me a friendly reminder to drop the camera and pick up my rifle. One shot dropped the massive bull in its tracks. We quickly grabbed our gear and made our way to where the fallen giant lay. We were shocked beyond belief to discover just how big this bull was. With palms measuring nearly 20 inches wide and a spread of over 63 inches, this boy surely was a king of his domain. ▲▲▲

Award Winning Moments...

Photograph by Jack Reneau

Visitors to the 24th Big Game Awards Trophy Exhibit saw some extraordinary taxidermy work. Shown here is the pedestal mount of Dawson H. Colby, Jr.'s, Alaska-Yukon moose scoring 241 points (Third Award).

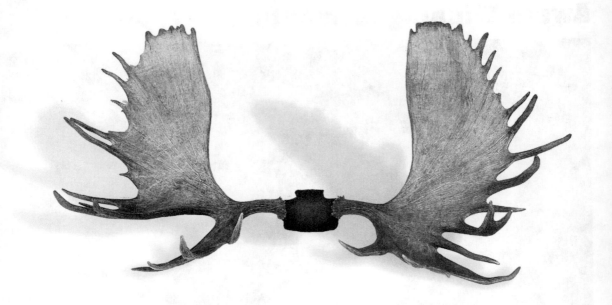

Photograph by Cliff White

TROPHY STATS

▼ ▼ ▼ ▼ ▼

Category
Alaska-Yukon moose

Score
256⁶/₈

Location
Beluga River, Alaska - 1997

Hunter
William G. Nelson

Greatest Spread
78²/₈

Length of Palm
Right: 49⁶/₈ Left: 50⁵/₈

Width of Palm
Right: 17³/₈ Left: 18²/₈

Number of Normal Points
Right: 16 Left: 15

ALASKA-YUKON MOOSE
First Award - 256⁶/₈

▼ ▼ ▼ ▼ ▼ ▼ ▼ ▼ ▼

WILLIAM G. NELSON

As we set up our tent next to the little swamp lake, we laughed at our situation. It was the 15th of November 1997, and I was still looking for a moose. I was with my son Brian and long time friend and hunting partner Dean. We had hunted through the fall season with no luck, and were into the beginning of the winter season. Between us we had 80 years of moose hunting experience and three empty freezers.

That was hunting, though, and our luck could change at any time. My winter tag was good for any bull and I would take the first bull that I could.

We were hunting the Beluga River drainage, 30 miles west of Anchorage, Alaska. I killed my first moose there 40 years earlier as a boy, and we had taken many more out of that area since. It was a good area, certainly, but the conditions for this hunt looked anything but promising. The win-

Any Bull Will Do

ter had been mild to that point and there was only a foot and a half of snow. It was about 25 degrees and windy, and the weather forecast was calling for snow showers. The ice was not very thick on the lakes, and there was overflow between the snow and ice. It was snowing by the time we got our tent up. We did not see any moose when we came in, but the visibility had been pretty poor. Hopefully, there were moose around and we just had not seen them.

That night was spent in our sleeping bags listening to the wind blow. In and around the tent was our usual collection of winter camping equipment. We had a lantern, stove, frying pan, coffee pot, cold weather sleeping bags, polypropylene long johns, fleece, and wool clothing, gloves, mittens, balaclavas, hats, bunny boots, and snowshoes. In the coolers (used to keep food from freezing) were moose hot-dogs and sausage, sandwiches, bread, eggs, instant oatmeal, powdered milk, coffee, chocolate bars, and cookies. Our hunting gear included our daypacks, binoculars, rifles, shells, and headlamps. Our other gear included knives, game bags, a saw, and plastic sled for dressing the animal and hauling it out if we were fortunate enough to find one.

The next morning we got up while it was still dark, dressed and dug the food and hunting gear out of the newly fallen snow. After breakfast, we packed our hunting gear and some spare clothes and waited for daylight. It was snowing hard, with a stiff wind blowing out of the north. Almost a foot of snow had fallen during the night.

We left camp at first light, snowshoeing into the wind. Every few minutes we would stop and glass, but there was not much to see. The falling, blowing snow and low light limited the usefulness of the binoculars. We snowshoed across one small swamp after another, weaving through stands of scrub spruce and skirting patches of alder. We meandered over a couple of birch-covered hills and back down to the swamps. Nothing moved around us. In the flat light all we could see were snow and trees. We worked into the wind for two hours as the snow

Photograph courtesy of William G. Nelson

The author had committed to shooting the next bull moose he saw and it turned out to be this award-winning bull scoring 256-6/8 points.

continued to fall, the wind kept blowing, and the visibility remained terrible.

At the top of a little ridge, we broke out of an alder patch into a small clearing. The spot offered a view across a ravine and into a series of swamps and patches of brush. With the wind driving the snow into our faces, and the flat light conditions, it was difficult to see. This was as far as we would go. We decided to glass the swamps and head back to camp, since there was no sense pushing the limited daylight in such marginal conditions. The three of us looked across the ravine and out into the swamps for several minutes. It looked like more of the same - snow and trees.

Suddenly I saw a movement out of the corner of my eye. Dean saw it too. Less than three hundred yards away, there were antlers moving through the brush. The three of us watched from the ridge as a big bull emerged from the alders. He stopped at the edge of the alder patch, still partially obscured by shoulder-high brush. Through the snow, we could just see a vague silhouette of the body and antlers as he started to browse.

The palms of his antlers were full of snow. As he fed, his rack moved slowly from side to side. He was upwind, facing slightly away, and had no idea we were there. His antlers were covering most of the front shoulder and rib cage. Nothing was close by to use as a rest, so I watched, waiting for a shot as my scope filled with snow, rendering it useless. I brought the rifle down and cleaned the objective with my finger and brought it back up. I was 250 yards from a massive bull, but I could barely see him. His right antler was still covering the side facing me. I brought the rifle up and then back down several times, to wipe the snow off the scope. Finally, I brought the rifle up just as he tilted his head down. With the rack forward and out of the way, and with a relatively clear scope, I could see his rib cage and front shoulder. I put the cross hairs on the middle of his rib cage and squeezed off a shot. All three of us heard a good solid thump after the shot. He turned, facing directly away, and stood motionless in the brush. I chambered another shell, but could not see through the scope. I cleaned the scope again, watching as the moose stood there. Without the side profile, we could barely see his body in the brush. I waited for another opportunity to shoot, but lost sight of him through the scope. As I cleaned it again, he laid down in the brush, disappearing from sight. I kept looking at the last spot that we had seen him, trying to keep my scope clear in case he stood up again. After a couple of minutes, with all of us straining to watch the spot where we had last seen the moose, Dean headed down the hill on his snowshoes. Brian and I stayed on the ridge and watched as Dean crossed the ravine and worked his way around toward the moose. We lost sight of Dean in the brush, 100 yards from the moose.

After another minute or so, Dean appeared off to the right of the moose, crossed a small clearing, and went into the brush. I kept my scope clean and Brian and I kept watching and waiting. Dean came back out into the clearing and waved for us to come down. We crossed the ravine and followed his snowshoe tracks into the clearing. When we got to Dean, his grin said it all.

ALASKA-YUKON MOOSE
First Award - 256⁶/₈

▼ ▼ ▼ ▼ ▼

WILLIAM G. NELSON

He led us into the alders. Brian and I first saw the rack and then the body of the motionless bull. Dean had already walked around the moose. The old bull had laid down and died with a lung shot that entered the right side of the rib cage and lodged in the left front shoulder.

The three of us stood there in the snow staring at the rack for some time. Moose are always impressive, but this was staggering. Brian stepped up to the rack and tried to reach across it, but was well short. Then Dean lay down in the snow lengthwise between the antlers. We looked at each other in disbelief. This was a huge moose!

Brian, Dean, and I have been hunting together for a long time now, and have killed a lot of moose. But this moose was an incredible exception to the 40, 50, and 60 inch bulls that have fed our families for so many years. As always, we enjoyed the meat from this moose, and we continue to marvel at the size of its rack. A 78-inch wide bull scoring 256-6/8 points is hard to believe. We were hunting in a snowstorm that day, looking for a bull — any bull. Unbelievable. ▲▲▲

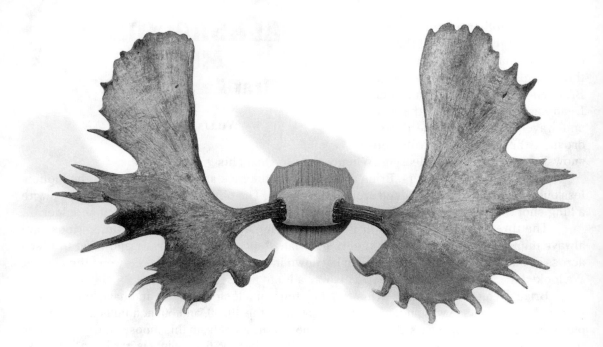

TROPHY STATS
▼ ▼ ▼ ▼ ▼

Category
Alaska-Yukon moose

Score
245²/8

Location
Ruby Creek, Alaska - 1997

Hunter
James W. Gelhaus

Greatest Spread
70⁴/8

Length of Palm
Right: 46⁴/8 Left: 44⁴/8

Width of Palm
Right: 22²/8 Left: 19

Number of Normal Points
Right: 16 Left: 16

Photograph by Jack Reneau

James W. Gelhaus accepting his plaque and medal from Randy Byers, Chair of the Big Game Records Committee.

ALASKA-YUKON MOOSE
Second Award - 245²/₈

▼ ▼ ▼ ▼ ▼ ▼ ▼ ▼ ▼

JAMES W. GELHAUS

On September 8, 1997, I arrived at Anchorage airport on my first trip to Alaska to hunt moose, caribou, and black or grizzly bear. I had booked the hunt through a booking agent in Wyoming who had given me the phone number of Mike (Buck) Bowden at Hidden Alaska Guides and Outfitters, Inc. I talked to Mike at length about the hunting conditions and the camp he had in mind. He recommended his Ruby Creek camp, as until that year no one had hunted there. Sure, I thought, I've heard that one before, and then once you arrive at the camp there is evidence everywhere that other hunters had been there. However, I was to find out first hand that Mike was telling the truth; we would be the first. So I booked the hunt for September 10 through 19.

I arrived at Anchorage to find reasonable weather. I was booked into a motel near the floatplane base and watched the planes landing and taking off the rest of the day. The aerial show only added to my excitement for my turn to fly to camp.

Runway Moose - Alaska Style

That night I awoke several times to the sound of the rain on the parking lot below. The next morning I was awake and up at 5 a.m., 30 minutes before my alarm was set to go off. I met Mike's wife, Sharon, at 8 a.m. to purchase my license and tags. By the time she arrived, it was raining hard. She informed me that no one was flying due to the weather and I could "take it easy" for the day and check in for messages to see if the weather had cleared enough for flying. Take it easy! I was pumped and ready to hunt moose, not to take it easy. So, to pass the time I went souvenir shopping in downtown Anchorage. At noon I anxiously flagged down a taxi and headed back to the motel. There was a message waiting from my guide, Ron Michael, that read we wouldn't fly out until the next morning. At 4:30 p.m. Ron called again with an update. Floatplanes were flying out of Anchorage; however, our plan was to drive to Willow, 140 miles northeast of Anchorage, to meet our floatplane.

Ron met me at the motel room for our drive to Willow. He was a very friendly and fun person to be with. Once in camp I was to be the only hunter with Ron as my guide and Ron's eldest son, Trevor, as the guide's assistant and packer. After loading up supplies, we headed to the floatplane base at Willow.

When we arrived in Willow, it was more waiting. With the weather shutting down the flights the past two days, the floatplanes were backed up with hunters being hauled in and out of camp. Finally, it was our turn. We loaded the gear for us and also for another hunter who was being flown into a separate camp. The pilot announced that we may be a little bit over-loaded but he would give it a try anyway. Oh, that makes one feel good! The plane was sitting on a small lake surrounded by trees. The pilot taxied the plane down the lake and then made circle eights around the lake. I found this a little un-nerving but later discovered this was to add chop to the water, which made it easier to lift the floats off the water. Now, on the west end of the lake we made our try. We headed across that lake bouncing, but didn't seem to gain much elevation. He lifted one float and suddenly the shoreline and trees were coming up fast, too fast. Just short of the trees he shut the engine down and announced he couldn't make it and would have to reduce the load. Someone would have to get off. There were a lot of volunteers; however, they chose to unload the other hunter and his gear.

On our second try the plane was up and cleared the trees with no problem. Thank goodness we were on our way. We flew to the Rainy Pass Lake where we were to meet a Super Cub for the final leg into the camp. At Rainy Pass Lake we unloaded the plane and portaged the supplies to a makeshift runway about 300 yards from the shore. We waited for the Super Cub for several hours before it finally landed. The pilot informed us that because of the number of trips it would take to get us into camp, and the lateness of the day, we would have to wait until tomorrow morning. So we would have to camp on the runway for that night.

As it turned out, it took five trips with the Super Cub to haul everything into the camp. While loading, Ron, the pilot, informed us that he flew over the airstrip at camp and noted that is was too short. While we were there we would have to extend the runway 150 feet and smooth out the bumps from washouts. The runway was long enough to take us in, but not long enough to get us out due to the weight. So, as each of us was flown in we set to work, first leveling out the washouts on the runway. After the last load was hauled in, the pilot bid us good hunting and was off. We were on our own for the next eight days.

We decided to set up camp adjacent to the runway, as the clearing gave us a good view of the hillsides and was not far from the creek for water. We set up two tents; the larger was an umbrella tent, in which Trevor and I were to sleep. Ron would sleep in a smaller, A-frame style tent with the canned and boxed food. The fresh food we stored some distance away in the creek.

Our camp was in the Ruby Creek drainage off the Kichatna River southeast of Denali National Preserve in the Alaska Range, which was about 2,000 feet above sea level. The small drainage was surrounded by mountains on both sides rising up to 4,500 feet. The sides of the mountains had small clearings separated by thick groves of alders about nine feet tall. The alders were so thick that it was virtually impossible to walk through them. The only option left was to spot game in the clearings and hope to make a good stalk. The Ruby Creek drainage was small, allowing hunting only three miles upstream of camp and two miles downstream. However, this was five miles of alder tangle and creek boulders, making the trek that far a major undertaking.

The next morning I was up and ready to go. Ron informed me that because of the threat of grizzly bears it was best not to start hiking until it was daylight. Sounded like good advice to me. As we were getting loaded for our first hike I spotted a large bull moose on the first hill to the southeast of camp. The moose was about three-quarters of a mile away and looking at us. I was excited but it was hard to get everyone in gear. The moose walked slowly over the hill as we made our way closer. We climbed and slowly stalked, watching for the bull. Nothing! He simply disappeared, which is not hard in those tall alders. Red Hill (as we named it after the red colored blueberry bushes covering it) provided a good vantage point to watch the valley below. So we decided to sit and watch. We watched, ate blue berries, and soaked up the warm sun. We could see black bears high up on the mountainsides gorging themselves on the berries. The bears looked huge; however, they were way too high for us to stalk, considering the alder groves between them and us.

The weather had really warmed up and any walking or work easily broke us into a sweat. Each day we would pick a high vantage point to watch for game

ALASKA-YUKON MOOSE
Second Award - 245²/₈

▼ ▼ ▼ ▼

James W. Gelhaus

in the morning and evening. During the mid-day we would work on the runway cutting brush and shoveling gravel in washouts. The only game we saw for five days were the black bears high on the mountainsides and one lonely cow moose standing in the middle of a beaver dam. The weather was just too warm and the moose were not showing any signs of rutting activity. The bugs, white socks as Ron called them, were also bad. By now my optimism was dropping and I was getting pretty worried that I was not even going to get a chance at any bull, let alone the big one I dreamed of. Finally, after falling in the creek during one of our long hikes, I informed Ron that I would shoot the first legal moose that stepped out. Ron tried to encourage me that we would still get a good moose, it would just take time. However, time was running out. I had only three days left.

That night the weather changed and we awoke to a cold rain and low clouds. Ron said we had better get going because this would be good. We headed for Red Hill. About halfway up the hill Ron grabbed me and pointed down in the alders. Standing some 400 yards away in the middle of the alders was a big bull moose. He looked so big it reminded me of a radar dish. Then a second bull stood up. Ron laid down and put the spotting scope on them. He said the larger bull was a good one with at least six brow tines on each side. The smaller bull laid back down and the other bull started walking through the alders heading for the creek. I said I better get down to the creek and try to head him off, as the creek was the only clearing to shoot through. Ron said he would stay on the hill and watch the bull through the spotting scope. That way he could direct me which way to go.

I took off down the hill at a trot and had to cross the creek several times. I got to about where I figured the moose should be and, nothing. He was gone! I looked back at Ron and all I could see was fog and rain. I threw up my arms in frustration and slowly walked upstream hoping to catch a glimpse of the bull. Suddenly about 200 yards upstream the bull stepped out of the brush on the other side of the creek. He had already crossed the creek and was now coming back out. He was heading away from me going up the creek. I sat down and tried to steady my nerves. I put the crosshairs on him and fired. The bull just stopped and turned his head toward me and looked. He acted like a bug had bitten him. He lowered his head and started to walk. I hurried a second shot and later found out that second shot hit the top of his antler. I tried to calm myself and squeezed off another shot. This time the big bull dropped. I hurried up to him. He was lying with his head up. From the side I finished him off with one more shot and slowly approached him. I had never seen any animal that big in my life. He was huge!

Ron came walking up the creek looking for me. He had not seen any of the action due to the fog and rain but heard the shooting and headed my way. We admired the massive bull and shot a lot of rainy pictures. We cut a willow branch the width of the antlers for a measurement

**On his first trip to Alaska, James W. Gelhaus took this award-winning
Alaska-Yukon moose scoring 245-2/8 points.**

and I held the branch up to me. I stand 6 foot 1 inch and the branch was about an inch shorter than I was. That made it about 72 inches! The antlers later officially measured 70-4/8 inches wide. Both antlers had 16 points.

Ron returned to camp to get Trevor and the pack frames. Ron walked around the first bush and announced that camp was right here. The bull was lying just across the creek from the runway. If I had waited five minutes he would have been in camp. Because of the rain on the tent Trevor hadn't heard the shooting. Ron brought him to the site and we took more pictures, then set to butchering. We set up a system. Ron deboned and strapped the meat on the pack frames. Trevor carried a load across the creek and handed it to me. I then carried the load to camp and unstrapped it. After four hours we were finished and the entire moose was in camp.

We continued to watch the moose carcass for the next two days hoping that a bear — black or grizzly — would visit it. However, the rain had not stopped and we decided the scent was being washed out. It was still raining the day we were to fly out. Snow was starting to show up on the mountaintops and was slowly advancing down the sides. It did not look good for getting out of camp. We had not even started breaking camp because of the weather, when out of the fog came the yellow Super Cub. That was quite a sight! We ran around camp as fast as we could throwing things in bags getting ready to abandon camp.

Prior to the Supercub coming we had discussed the runway and none of us were overly optimistic on the test flight of the first load out. We came to the conclusion that we would send a load of moose meat out with the pilot on the first trip. Now that the pilot was here, he informed us that on the first flight, because of the weather worsening, he would take one of us and I was chosen as the first load. That announcement came with mixed feelings. Ron and Trevor held the tail while the pilot revved up the engine and then let 'er loose and we were off. The plane cleared the trees with little effort and we headed down the drainage. As the plane climbed through the fog, the pilot looked off where he planned to fly out and there was no way he could make that direction. So he followed the Kichatna River until he reached a large gravel bar where he landed and dropped me off. He informed me he would be back shortly with Trevor and would radio for a floatplane to pick us up. About an hour later the Super Cub came with Trevor, and after six trips the camp was hauled out. The floatplane showed up mid-afternoon and we loaded up all the gear then headed for Willow. The moose hunt had come to an end and I was glad to be headed home. ▲▲▲

Photograph by Cliff White

TROPHY STATS

▼ ▼ ▼ ▼ ▼

Category
Alaska-Yukon moose

Score
241

Location
Anvil Range, Yukon Territory - 2000

Hunter
Dawson H. Colby, Jr.

Greatest Spread
$74^2/_8$

Length of Palm
Right: $42^7/_8$ Left: $47^3/_8$

Width of Palm
Right: 18 Left: 20

Number of Normal Points
Right: 15 Left: 16

Photograph by Jack Reneau

Dawson H. Colby, Jr., accepting his plaque
and medal from Randy Byers, Chair of the
Big Game Records Committee.

BOONE AND CROCKETT CLUB'

ALASKA-YUKON MOOSE
Third Award - 241

▼ ▼ ▼ ▼ ▼ ▼ ▼ ▼ ▼

Dawson H. Colby, Jr.

My buddy Jim McDowell and I had traveled from Michigan to Whitehorse, Yukon, to hunt moose with MacMillian River Outfitters Ltd., owned and operated by Dave Coleman. All my luggage didn't arrive at the same time we did, so I later had to borrow a rifle for my hunt. We flew 200 miles north of Whitehorse to Dave's hunting area and landed at Two Pete Camp — Dave's base camp. After a day and a half at base camp, our guides, Blair Chisholm and A. J. Cochrane, arrived from Tay River Camp on horseback and we all rode back together nine hours to Tay River Camp. The next day we rode another nine hours in the rain and set up a spike camp on Gillis Mountain. The following day we stayed in our tents all day because we couldn't see 20 yards (rain and snow).

Day 6, August 27th — we had great weather and finally went hunting. At about 10 a.m. we were glassing from a high point when we spotted two bull moose. Jim and A. J. stalked them for two hours and Jim shot the largest of the two, a 50-inch plus bruiser, at more than 350 yards with his .340 Weatherby. The rest of the day was spent taking care of Jim's moose and bringing it by pack horses back to our spike camp.

On the seventh day it was my turn as Blair and I spent most of the day glassing, and finally at

Photography courtesy of Dawson H. Colby, Jr.

about 5:00 p.m. we spotted the bull we were hoping to find. After tethering our two saddle horses and one packhorse, we stalked within 50 yards of where the moose first appeared. Blair gave me the go-ahead and with one off hand shot the enormous bull collapsed. The 180-grain Winchester Silvertip from my Ruger .308 did its job. Before us lay a bulldozer that looked like a moose. After congratulations and picture taking the work began. It started getting dark, so we loaded the horses with what they could handle and headed back to spike camp two miles away.

The next day we finished my moose chore and then broke camp to head back to Tay River Camp. We could only make it to one of Dave's remote cabins on Goodfish Creek in the rain and darkness. The next morning we headed out for Tay River with ten horses, one mule, and our two trophies. Five hours of riding had passed when Radar, our mule, broke his leg in a creek bog and had to be put down. After another hour of riding we had a very nasty and treacherous crossing of the Tay River as the water was high because of rain and snow run-off in the mountains. We made it to Tay River Camp, spent the night, and continued for base camp the next morning.

After nine hours or more and cutting several trees with a chainsaw so my moose antlers could make it through the woods, we finally got to Two Pete Camp. The next day we flew back to Whitehorse, thus ending a fabulous hunt and a great time with Blair and A.J. ▲▲▲

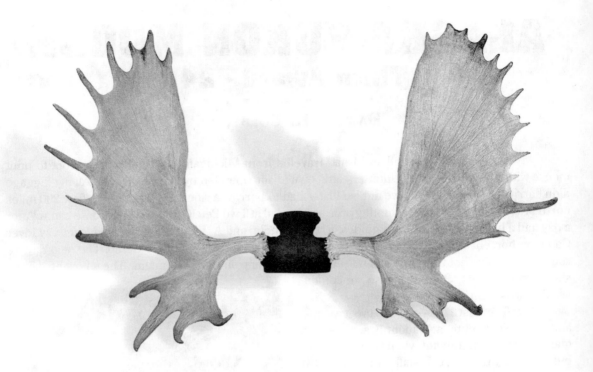

TROPHY STATS

▼ ▼ ▼ ▼ ▼

Category
Wyoming moose

Score
185$^5/_8$

Location
Bonneville County, Idaho - 2000

Hunter
Mary A. Isbell

Greatest Spread
48$^5/_8$

Length of Palm
Right: 35$^4/_8$ Left: 36$^3/_8$

Width of Palm
Right: 13$^6/_8$ Left: 14$^7/_8$

Number of Normal Points
Right: 13 Left: 14

BOONE AND CROCKETT CLUB'

WYOMING MOOSE
First Award - 185⁵/₈

▼ ▼ ▼ ▼ ▼ ▼ ▼ ▼ ▼

Mary A. Isbell

Hunting has always been a very important activity for our family. My grandpa Isbell taught my dad how to hunt and the tradition has continued through the generations. Our family consists of my mom, dad, and four daughters. I'm the youngest of the girls. Dad started each of us shooting when we were about five years old with .22s and used various firearms working up to a bolt action, scoped .22 Long Rifle. We've all spent countless hours practicing shooting. Once we reached ten years of age, we started with hunting rifles. We all started with the same .243 and then progressed on to our .270s and .30-06 rifles. Shooting isn't all; we just love the outdoors and the wildlife. We ride our horses, hike, study animals, and then when we're home, we pour over books and videos.

The hunt for my moose took place when I was 12 years old. Even though this was the first trip I was the hunter, I'd been going for years when my sisters and dad were hunting. I've hiked with them over some of the most difficult country in southeastern Idaho that you could imagine. My dad loves the steepest, roughest, and rockiest mountains he can find. My sisters and I have given them names like "Death Mountain," "Heart attack hill," or "Heart-stroke Mountain." I actually shouldn't complain, though, because we've been very successful in finding our game.

In Idaho each hunter can apply for special controlled permits for hunting. If you apply for moose, sheep, or goat then you can't apply for special deer, antelope, or elk permits. Each year seems to be a ritual in deciding what each of us wants to apply for. My quest for moose actually began in late summer 1999. On a late August morning, my dad and one of my sisters had gone on an early morning hike while the rest of us stayed at our cabin. When they returned, my dad was almost speechless. He claimed that he had seen a moose bedded about a mile away that appeared to be a top end B&C class animal. They had hiked down reasonably close to the animal and studied it through the binoculars. As I listened to the excitement in their voices, I could tell that this one must be very special. Dad's very objective and knowledgeable about evaluating trophy game and doesn't usually get as easily excited as he was this time. Right then and there it was decided that all of us would apply for moose, hoping that someone could draw a permit while this special animal was still alive. None of us had drawn in 1999, but one of our close friends did. She took a gorgeous bull, but it wasn't the one that Dad had seen.

As the year 2000 approached, we did the traditional application scheme. We'd check on the Internet each evening until the results were posted. When the results were out, we couldn't believe it. Even though drawing odds are low, my older sister Becky and I, along with our close friend Craig Heiner, had drawn! The quest for the giant moose began.

It was traditional in our family that I would use my grandpa Isbell's .30-06 for the hunt. It is a Model 70 Winchester that he bought in 1945. My dad had a custom stock made for it in 1982 and had developed some handloads with 165-grain Nosler Partition bullets. It shoots very well and my older sisters had taken great game with it including trophy Wyoming moose. Dad had me practice all summer with the rifle in anticipation of the hunt. My sister, Becky, would also use the rifle since

Photograph courtesy of Mary A. Isbell

The author with her First Award Wyoming moose scoring 185-58 points. Mary and her older sister Becky both drew Idaho moose permits in 2000.

it wouldn't be likely to have us both see two great bulls together at the same time.

Summer is a hard time to find trophy bull moose. They are in the thick timber bedded during most of the day and we didn't see very many large bulls on our scouting trips. We did spend a lot of time scouting by hiking, by horseback, and by riding in the pickup. About two weeks before the hunt, our close friend, Bob Hudman called. He could hardly speak. When he started telling us about the moose, I could tell it was the one we had hoped to find again. I could get a good impression of the size of the animal by listening to my dad and his friends. When they seem uncontrollably nervous, then I know it's special. As he described this great animal and its location, we decided that we'd all try to keep an eye on him until opening day in August 2000. We tried to keep track of the animal, but he seemed to disappear a few days before the hunt. We were afraid that something had happened to him or that he'd just left the country. Even though we hadn't seen the moose for four or five days, opening day was a must. After some discussion, it was decided that I'd have the opportunity on opening day and my parents arranged for me to miss school. I must thank our dear friend Craig Heiner. He was present and helped on the hunt, and didn't even bring his rifle so that it would be my day.

We all met at Hudman's cabin near the Tex Creek Wildlife Management Area on opening morning. Our group included my mom and dad, Bob, Sandy, and Charity Hudman, and Craig and

Debbie Heiner. This was one big moose expedition. We traveled by ATVs to a place where we could glass. It wasn't 30 minutes until the monster was spotted. He was back in the exact spot where Bob had seen him two weeks earlier. We immediately

WYOMING MOOSE
First Award - 185⁵/₈

▼ ▼ ▼ ▼ ▼

MARY A. ISBELL

maneuvered in front of him, but couldn't get a shot. We watched him through binoculars as he went into the next canyon and into an aspen stand. Then we crept over the ridge above him and I prepared for the shot. The wind was howling, blowing a light drizzle of rain and the range was about 250 yards. All in all, it was a perfect moose day. My dad got me set up on a large rock. Bob and Craig were using separate video cameras so we'd be sure to record the event. The rifle seemed to jump around uncontrollably with the wind and the pounding of my heart. It seemed like a long time, but my dad told me to wait until there was a break in the wind and then take the shot. When the wind slowed, I carefully pulled the trigger. Immediately after the shot, Bob exclaimed, "You got him! You don't realize how big of a moose you just shot! He's going high in the records book!"

This really got me shaking. All of a sudden the moose stood up again, Dad and Bob both told me to hit him again. As I squeezed the trigger for the second shot the bull went down for good just as the shot went off. The next few minutes were pure chaos. My dad, Bob, Craig, and Sandy were all acting almost crazy with the excitement of this great animal. They hiked down to the moose first, leaving Dad and me on the ridge in case the moose got up.

As my dad and I hiked down to him, I can still hear Craig almost screaming what a monster he was. He was everything we'd imagined and more. Bob and Sandy went to get the remainder of the crowd. Dad, Craig, and I simply marveled at the size of the animal. Not only were his antlers huge, but his body was immense. We all discussed this, and later when the carcass was weighed at the meat processor, they confirmed how big he was. The photo session went on for a long time. There was video with both cameras and several rolls of film from three different 35mm cameras. After the photo session, I really learned how big a large moose is. With all eight of us helping, it was a real chore to take care of and pack out a large animal like that. When we checked my moose in at Fish and Game the excitement rose again. It was a continuous emotional high.

Our moose hunting didn't end that day. For the next two months we hunted every Saturday, several weekdays and after school for my sister Becky's and Craig's moose. We spent those days hiking, riding, and checking out several trophy bull moose. There are many unique stories about those two other great bulls like the day my sister got hypothermia, but that's another story. They both did get their trophy animals near the end of the season.

After getting this bull, we took him to one of the premier taxidermists in the west, Jay Ogden, in Richfield, Utah. Even though he's mounted some amazing trophy animals, he was excited about the opportunity to mount this magnificent specimen and will create a mount that compliments my trophy. We have already chosen a spot in our home for him.

I'll probably never take another animal as large for its species as my first bull moose. This day will be with me forever; the memory of the hunt, the family and friends, and the privilege to be in the great outdoors hunting. ▲▲▲

TROPHY STATS
▼ ▼ ▼ ▼ ▼

Category
Wyoming moose

Score
$177^2/_8$

Location
Shoshone County, Idaho - 1999

Hunter
April H. Preston

Greatest Spread
$54^2/_8$

Length of Palm
Right: $35^6/_8$ Left: $37^7/_8$

Width of Palm
Right: 12 Left: $11^3/_8$

Number of Normal Points
Right: 8 Left: 8

BOONE AND CROCKETT CLUB

WYOMING MOOSE
Second Award - 177²/₈

▼ ▼ ▼ ▼ ▼ ▼ ▼ ▼

APRIL H. PRESTON

Both of us stood staring in disbelief at the 1999 Idaho Moose permit with my name on it. "This is a once-in-a-lifetime opportunity," my husband said, "you better make the most of it." Once-in-a-lifetime opportunity was meant literally! If a person beats the remote odds of getting drawn for a moose permit in Idaho, it is the only one you get. It was early June when the permit arrived in the mail, so we had about three months to prepare.

I began hunting with my husband, Ken, a few years earlier. He started me out shooting grouse while I accompanied him on preseason scouting trips for deer and elk. My husband had once been a professional guide, and had a knack for putting me in the right spot at the right time. I was able to take whitetail deer and elk, despite being a relative newcomer to the wonderful sport of hunting. My permit area for moose was located approximately 50 miles northeast of where we live. Ken knew the area, and suggested that I also purchase a bear tag because he had seen a considerable amount of bear sign in that region. His suggestion would later prove prophetic.

To prepare for this special hunt, Ken, our son Zack age 7, our daughter Hillary age 11, and I, spent every weekend in my permit area. We camped, scouted for sign, and target practiced as a family. Normally, I use a Remington Model 7 in .260 caliber for deer. However, the .260 was too light for me to use responsibly on an animal the size of a moose. So Ken took a Ruger M77UL Ultra-light in .30/06 caliber to a local gunsmith where the stock was cut to fit my length of pull exactly, and a delightfully cushy recoil pad was installed. Ken then put a Nikon Monarch 4X power scope on a .22 magnum, bolt action rifle, which was to serve as practice simulation. The Nikon scope was identical to the one on the Ruger I was to use for moose, and the rifles were nearly identical in weight. This provided me an opportunity to target practice with hundreds of more rounds using identical optics and virtually matching rifle weights. Had I used the .30/06 exclusively, my shoulder would have become bruised and sore even with the special recoil pad. Each day of practice I would use the .22 magnum to shoot 50-100 rounds from a bench rest, another 50-100 rounds off hand, and finally, finish my practice session using the .30/06 until soreness began to set in.

Weeks went by, and despite all of our scouting, we hadn't sighted a single moose! Ken kept saying, "This spot looks good," or, "we'll be back at this spot once the season opens!" I voiced my concern about not seeing any moose, but Ken reassured me they would be there by the time the season arrived. The first part of the season was unusually warm, and Ken advised against getting an animal as big as a moose down in those temperatures. So, I agonized with anticipation, waiting for a cool spell that would allow us the time necessary to pack out and properly care for an animal of such size. At last, the weather forecast was for the first frosts of the season, and we made plans to head into the mountainous region of my permit area.

On our first day out, we set up on the edge of a tree line where we could watch a brushy cut-over area. We nestled behind a blow down which provided good cover and a perfect bench rest. Ken had called moose many times before, and had a particular sequence of grunts and bawls, which he liked to

Photograph courtesy of April H. Preston

The author made good on her once-in-a-lifetime moose permit in Idaho by taking this award-winning bull scoring 177-2/8 points

use. He had barely finished his first sequence, when to our left, a magnificent bull elk stepped out of the timber to investigate the sounds. I got to look at him for nearly two minutes before he jogged away. I had an elk tag, but the season wasn't yet open for them. Nevertheless, the experience was a breathtaking moment I'll never forget! Interestingly, Ken had two more smaller elk come to the moose calls on different occasions. It was their rutting season and they seemed to want to check out the sounds.

A couple of weekends had passed, and the only moose we had seen were one cow and her calf. Ken had seen a small bull while scouting alone one day, but overall, sightings were few and far between. The next weekend we were just getting ready to set up overlooking a steep, brushy draw. Ken was getting things out of the pack, and I was glassing the steep terrain below. As if by Mother Nature's sleight-of-hand, a handsome bear suddenly materialized on the slope below us. He climbed up onto a log jam and stood broadside. His coat looked like wet coal in the early morning sun. His head bobbed gently as he tested the air. I nudged Ken and whispered, "Bear!" Ken said the bear was about 150 yards away, urged me to stay calm, pick a spot on the bear, and shoot just like during target practice. When I fired, the bear flipped end over end down into the brushy ravine. All that happened next is a story in and of itself for another time. I'll just say that what transpired in that brush-choked ravine was an exhilarating encounter that neither I, nor my husband, shall ever forget! Fortunately, neither of us were seriously hurt, and I finally got to finish the bear. He's now a beautiful rug on our wall, and one of our most cherished hunting memories!

The following weekend, we were back to the task of trying to find a big bull moose. On the way to our hunting spot, we stopped the truck and looked at some fresh moose tracks, which had crossed the logging road sometime during the night. Ken asked if I was ready to go get my moose. I told him that after the bear incident of the previous week, I was ready for almost anything! We parked the truck at the head of an old gated logging road. The plan was to hike the trail for about 1.5 miles as it twisted down to a ravine choked with mountain maples and alders. At a spot where we had seen moose sign earlier in the season, we would set up and Ken would try calling in a bull.

The old logging trail was covered with knee-deep grasses and some small trees. The morning sun had melted the night's heavy frost, and our legs were soaked quickly, almost as if we had waded a stream. Barely 200 yards from our truck, we came upon some very fresh moose droppings. We pondered whether or not to call from that location and finally agreed there wasn't a good place to set up, and we should continue farther down the trail. We hadn't gone more than 50 yards when my "guide" grabbed my arm and whispered in my ear, "There's your moose!" All I could see were the huge palmated antlers sliding across the brush about 80 yards away. The moose stopped just before entering the grassy trail. I could see his head and massive rack, but none of his vital shoulder area. My heart was hammering the inside of my rib cage like an angry blacksmith as I waited in the kneeling position with the rifle ready. Ken was crouched just behind me and whisper-

WYOMING MOOSE
Second Award - 177²/₈

▼ ▼ ▼ ▼ ▼

Aᴘʀɪʟ H. Pʀᴇsᴛᴏɴ

ing in my left ear to "relax." I was breathing as heavily as if I had just run a mile! Ken said, "Calm down! You sound like an obscene phone call! Just relax, and when his shoulder comes into view, take him."

The huge animal stood there twisting his big rack from side to side against some maples. He nudged out a bit further and I whispered to Ken, "He's a big one, right?" "He's exceptional," Ken whis-pered back. I don't know if it was Ken's whispering in my ear, or the cold, wet grasses I was kneeling in, or just the sight of that moose's huge rack, but chills were racing across my whole body like capillary lightning. After what seemed like waiting for geologic time to pass, the massive bull stepped forward, and his shoulder was now squarely centered in my 3-foot wide shooting lane. I was concerned about flinching because I was so overwhelmingly nervous. I squeezed and squeezed on the trigger. I thought the gun would never go off! Finally, the gun fired and the barrel leapt upwards; the stock jumped back against my shoulder as if it were as startled as I was by the gun's report.

I was amazed at the speed and agility with which the moose swapped ends and bulldozed uphill through the tangled brush. Ken said he thought I had made a solid hit, and I, too, believed the shot was good. We gave the big fella some time to himself before trailing after him, (the harrowing experience with the bear the week before was still fresh in our minds).

Remarkably, the bull had run nearly 160 yards despite having the back of both lungs perforated by a .30-06 bullet. He had fallen barely 200 feet from the logging road we had driven in on before parking at the gated road. This proved fortuitous, as it enabled us to winch the big bull up onto a cleared, level log landing, where working on him was much easier than on the steep, heavily brushed hillside where he had dropped.

We took the antlers to Kirk Miller of Kirk's Taxidermy in Moscow, Idaho, to be mounted on a plaque. Kirk immediately called local Boone and Crockett scorer, Randy Byers, and told him there was a moose rack in his shop that Randy would definitely want to see. When Randy walked into the taxi-dermy shop, he took one quick glance at the rack and stated, "Yep, that one makes the book!"

What began as an "opportunity of a lifetime" in early June of 1999, had ended as the "hunt of a lifetime" on October 17, 1999. What makes this moose so special to me though, is much more than just his final score and ranking. It's all the memories that surround him that matter most to me. I'll always remember the family outings to target practice and scouting for moose sign, the huge bull elk that came to investigate the moose calls, the pulse-pounding thrill of tracking a wounded bear in thick brush, the fun of having a great guide (who just happens to be my husband), and the ultimate culmination to it all — a Boone and Crockett Wyoming moose.

In closing, I would like to say thank you to the following folks: first, to everyone associated with Boone and Crockett, they've all been so friendly, thoughtful, and helpful; second, to the Idaho Fish and Game Department for their guardianship and stewardship of our wildlife resources; third, thank you to the logging companies who so graciously allowed us access to their landholdings; and finally, thank you to my guide and husband, Ken, for sharing the sport of hunting with me. ▲▲▲

TROPHY STATS

▼ ▼ ▼ ▼ ▼

Category
  Wyoming moose

Score
  177

Location
  Teton County, Wyoming - 2000

Hunter
  James E. Jones

Greatest Spread
  54²/₈

Length of Palm
  Right: 36⁴/₈ Left: 37⁷/₈

Width of Palm
  Right: 10⁷/₈ Left: 11⁷/₈

Number of Normal Points
  Right: 8 Left: 7

Photograph by Jack Reneau

James E. Jones accepting his plaque and medal from Randy Byers, Chair of the Big Game Records Committee.

BOONE AND CROCKETT CLUB

WYOMING MOOSE
Third Award - 177

▼ ▼ ▼ ▼ ▼ ▼ ▼ ▼ ▼

JAMES E. JONES

After applying for a moose permit in the same area in Teton County for the past seven years, I finally hit the jackpot in the summer of 2000. This area has few permits and is hard to hunt, but has produced big moose in the past. In early October a large winter storm moved into the state. This could be perfect, but it could also shut down the area completely for the rest of the season if it was severe enough. I decided I'd better hunt now even though the season was to remain open until mid-November. It's been my experience that it's nearly impossible to find big bulls early in the season, especially when it's warm. That, plus the fact you would need a string of packhorses to get the meat out quickly, makes early trophy hunting difficult.

I could tell at 4:30 a.m., being it was Friday the 13th, the day would be full of unexpected surprises. We were hunting just north of Jackson Hole in my home state of Wyoming. I've hunted elk and moose in the area for 40 years and still marvel at its ruggedness and beauty. As we left the main road, it was still dark and it began to snow heavily, and I mean heavily. One minute the road was clear and within ten minutes the snow was 12-inches deep. After driving for 10-12 miles we began gaining elevation and found the snow "bumper" deep.

My hunting companions were my daughter Kimberleigh and her boyfriend Art Nellermoe. Art is young and strong and I needed a packhorse. I've hunted elk and moose on horseback many times, but I feel you can hunt and find more moose sign traveling on foot. Of course, it may mean you spend a day or two of backbreaking work carrying out the meat, and if you are lucky enough, the antlers and cape.

After traveling about as far as we could go, it began to get light and I remarked, "This is the type of day that keeps most elk and moose bedded down, but sometimes in bad storms larger old bulls will travel great distances to get to lower wintering areas."

The area we finally stopped at was called Moose Meadows. The snow was deep, but new, so it was still fairly easy walking. I knew within a day or so it would be impossible to get around without snowshoes. After a while I heard Art say, "Moose! Big, big moose!" We were behind a group of trees with a clearing all around so we had to stay put until I could figure out how to move closer. From my position, I could see what first looked like elk antlers through the heavy snowfall and bushes. The antlers had long points and were very wide, but had a lot of snow on them hiding the palms. The bull's body was also covered with snow. I was behind a tree and asked Art, "Are you sure it looks like a bull moose?" He said yes, and then, even though we were about 275 yards away, the moose turned around and looked our way, which gave me my first clear view. I was stunned when he shook himself just like a dog and came out in full view. He was indeed a moose, and a very large one with a massive rack. For years I've wanted to take a 40-inch moose and knew this area had a potential for one that big. Big Wyoming moose are so rare anymore that you need to study the areas years in advance and spend many summer months scouting.

Old moose are very smart, live alone in high country, and have keen hearing and smell. And don't believe for a minute they can't see well. When full grown they aren't afraid of anything, and under most conditions packs of wolves and grizzly bears pose no threat. You can find young ones everywhere and they appear dumb.

The bull stared our way and never moved a muscle for at least 20 to 25 minutes. I wanted to get closer to get a good neck or head shot, but could not move without spooking him, and believe me when spooked, they can travel for miles. This was a once-in-a-lifetime moment and I did not want to blow it. I did feel I could place a shot in the heart/lung area if he turned and I moved to the right side of a nearby tree for a rest. When I barely moved, even at that distance, he turned and started to move off. I got a good heart shot off in that split second, and the 7mm Remington Magnum anchored him after he took just a step or two.

By the time we got to the moose, it was starting to get dark and we were a very nervous threesome. This area is almost "overrun" with grizzly bear and in the past few years many hunters have had trouble with them, especially at the kill sites. There was a lot of dark timber and 10-foot high brush near the downed bull and we approached very carefully with our pepper spray canisters, 44 Magnum pistol, and my rifle at the ready. Art and Kim kept a watchful eye while a very nervous hunter worked as fast as he could. Hours later after using axes, saws, ropes, pulleys, winches, backpacks, a four-wheeler and just plain manpower, we got the moose loaded in the truck. It took us almost five hours to drive out and we had to use our winch more than once in the deep snow.

Kim kept telling me that the rack was 50 inches wide and definitely over the 40 inches I was looking for. I was so caught up just getting to the moose, cleaning it without bear trouble, and before darkness, we didn't notice we left our camera in the truck. With my daughter being there and darkness moving in, my attention was only on cutting up the moose and getting the heck out of there. To say I was nervous is an understatement. The grizzly bears are getting so bad that hunters have had to kill several this year, which is unfortunate. The hunters in Wyoming fear that elk and moose hunting may be closed in some areas because of the recent problems with the bears.

Later, after we got back to the road, I finally took a good look at the bull's rack. I was shocked to see that Kim was right and a tape showed the rack to be nearly 55 inches wide. Even in the darkness I could see the palms were wide and long for a Wyoming moose. We placed the moose in a trailer and when we stopped for the night at Signal Mountain Lodge, the manager told us to get the trailer out of there first thing in the morning because he didn't want a grizzly bear in his parking lot. So naturally all night long I was still thinking about bears.

The game check station south of Dubois said they had not seen a 50-inch moose in many years. It then dawned on me that my bull might qualify for the Boone and Crockett Club's records book.

The minute the taxidermist looked at it he said it would score in the 190s and the body was larger than any he had ever seen. The bull officially scored 177 points. The Wyoming Game and Fish laboratory later said the bull was 11-1/2 years old. During the long ride back to Casper, the horns rubbed against the trailer sides and a couple of inches broke off four different points. Boy, have I heard about that from everybody.

Getting my taxidermist to complete the mount in time to send it to the 24th Big Game Awards held in Springfield, Missouri, was a riot. He only does one or two Alaska moose mounts a year, but up to ten Wyoming moose every year. He tried the largest Wyoming form he had, but finally had to order in an additional Alaska moose form. The mount has a measurement of over 19 inches from the eyes to the nose and

WYOMING MOOSE
Third Award - 177
▼ ▼ ▼ ▼ ▼
JAMES E. JONES

the brisket is extremely wide. I don't know what he weighed, but the meat processor said he processed over 600 pounds. I owe special thanks to the man many people know as the best taxidermist in the Rocky Mountain area, Lewis Ray. Ray's Taxidermy has been doing trophy heads since 1958 and Lewis once owned the former World's Record "typical" mule deer he found in a bar in Jackson Hole, Wyoming, some 40 years ago. I don't think anyone else could have done what he did in such a short time. Thanks Lewis!

I also want to thank my "spotter" and "packhorse" Art with whom I felt comfortable while watching for bear. It was 1968 that I last spent time with such an individual I felt I could depend upon in a tight spot.

Lastly, my new hunting partner of the past few years, Kim, has seen what hard work and dedication can bring. She likes to hunt, but more importantly, respects the magnificent animals, like deer, elk and moose. Both Kim and my son Mike respect guns, know how to use them, and appreciate the opportunities our wildlife gives us to hunt them. All of these animals are special and almost every hunter I know is a better man or woman for it. ▲▲▲

New World's Record

Photograph by Cliff White

TROPHY STATS

▼ ▼ ▼ ▼ ▼

Category
mountain caribou

Score
453

Location
Prospector Mt., Yukon Territory - 1998

Hunter
C. Candler Hunt

Length of Main Beam
Right: 48^2/$_8$ Left: 49^5/$_8$

Inside Spread
45^6/$_8$

Width of Brow Palm
Right: 13^1/$_8$ Left: 4

Number of Points
Right: 23 Left: 21

Photograph by Jack Reneau

C. Candler Hunt accepting his plaque and medal from Randy Byers, Chair of the Big Game Records Committee.

MOUNTAIN CARIBOU
First Award - 453

▼ ▼ ▼ ▼ ▼ ▼ ▼ ▼

C. Candler Hunt

When Candler Hunt made the decision to hunt Dall's sheep in Yukon Territory, he had no intention of hunting mountain caribou. Although earlier in his career he had hunted elk, bear, and whitetail, sheep hunting was now his only passion. Candler had no idea that this sheep hunt would net him a New World's Record mountain caribou.

Candler's sheep hunt in September of 1998 had been a wonderful experience. At home in Madison, Georgia, Candler had spent countless hours researching and checking outfitter references. He had chosen to hunt with outfitter Tim Mervin in an area northwest of Whitehorse. For days, Candler and his 24-year old guide, Jake Gunson, had been riding, walking, and glassing. Candler took his Dall's sheep on the fourth day of hunting.

It was a nice ram, and Candler was thrilled to add it to his collection. As far as he was concerned, this hunt was over. He had harvested the animal he wanted. Jake asked Candler whether he wanted to hunt caribou on the way back to the airstrip. "Caribou really don't turn me on," admitted Candler, "but I'm having so much fun, I'll give it a try." The weather had been very pleasant. Temperatures had been in the 50s and 60s during the day, and down in the 20s at night. It was beautiful country—low mountains scattered with rocks and moss. Although they were above treeline, the altitude was less than 5,000 feet and it wasn't hard to acclimate. Besides, he had paid for a mountain caribou. The only Dall's sheep hunt Tim Mervin had offered him was a combination hunt.

The following day, Candler, Jake, and a young wrangler named Bradley Malfair, rested in sheep camp. While Jake was working on the sheep cape, a young bull caribou passed near the camp, but other than that lone animal, the three men did not see or hear any caribou. For the next two days, Candler, Jake, and Bradley looked for caribou, moving down slightly in elevation and in the general direction of the landing strip where a Cessna 206 had dropped them off a week earlier. In two days, they saw only a few cows and calves.

The next morning, the hunt was cut short by a thunderstorm that forced them back into camp for the rest of the day. The storm broke up by early evening and the three men rode to a high point from which they could glass the area. "I think I see a caribou about a mile away, across the valley and on top of that far ridge," Bradley said. As he continued peering through his binoculars, Bradley changed his mind. "No . . . I'm sorry, it's a moose." Candler and Jake had seen sign of moose, and decided to get a better look. They put a spotting scope on the animal, and immediately determined this was a big caribou. Candler and Jake mounted their horses, leaving Bradley on the top of the ridge to tell them, with hand signals, if the bull started to move.

It took about 45 minutes of riding through thick cover and across a large creek. At the base of the ridge, they tethered the horses and quietly hiked up the ridge. As they neared the top, they saw the bull. He was about 300 yards away, almost in the exact spot where they hoped to find him. The animal was facing them, calmly grazing, and totally unaware of their presence.

Photograph courtesy of C. Candler Hunt

The author with his mountain caribou scoring 453 points making it the new World's Record.

There was little cover, so they stayed on their bellies, crawling a few more yards to get as close as they could without spooking the bull. Candler placed the animal in the cross hairs of his Ruger Model 77 featherweight .270, hoping that the animal would move into position for a broadside shot. "Don't look at the antlers," cautioned Jake, "and stay calm." Jake's advice was well taken. This bull was much bigger than anything they had anticipated and Candler was having a hard time controlling his excitement. Even though Candler and Jake had little experience with caribou, they knew the rack on this bull was magnificent.

The wait was agonizing! Finally, after five minutes or so—which felt like an hour to Candler—the bull moved and presented him with a broadside 300-yard shot. The shot appeared good, but it was not enough to drop the big animal instantly. He fired two more shots before the bull went down for good.

When they approached the bull their amazement for the bull's tremendous rack was overwhelming. They both had plenty of practice scoring sheep, but it was no help in field measuring this bull. They tried scoring the caribou a few times, and kept coming up with a rough score of 400. They knew this was not accurate. Even expert measurers agree that scoring a big caribou rack is extremely difficult unless one does it on a regular basis.

"I think he's too big for a shoulder mount," Jake concluded. "For something this big," Candler added, "there's no room in my house for even a head mount! Let's just take the meat and antlers."

After the antlers had dried for 60 days, an official measurer for the Boone and Crockett Club measured Candler's mountain caribou. It was given an entry score of 453-4/8 points. The 24th Awards Judges' Panel gave the bull an official score of 453 points making it the new World's Record mountain caribou.

Not a bad deal for a guy who only wanted a Dall's sheep! ▲▲▲

Photograph by Cliff White

TROPHY STATS

▼ ▼ ▼ ▼ ▼

Category
mountain caribou

Score
$416^7/_8$

Location
Arctic Red River, Northwest
Territories - 1999

Hunter
E. Royce Gunter, Jr.

Length of Main Beam
Right: 51 Left: $50^3/_8$

Inside Spread
$38^7/_8$

Width of Brow Palm
Right: $13^2/_8$ Left: $^1/_8$

Number of Points
Right: 20 Left: 13

Photograph by Jack Reneau

E. Royce Gunter, Jr., accepting his plaque
and medal from Randy Byers, Chair of the
Big Game Records Committee.

BOONE AND CROCKETT CLUB'

MOUNTAIN CARIBOU
Second Award - 416⁷/₈

▼ ▼ ▼ ▼ ▼ ▼ ▼ ▼ ▼

E. ROYCE GUNTER, JR.

Our mountain caribou hunting excursion in Northwest Territories began on the evening of March 12, 1999, at the Hilton Hotel in Reno, Nevada. That evening my younger brother Jay and I attended the Nevada Bighorn Unlimited (NBU) banquet with our good friend August Tedeschi, and about 15 other friends. NBU is a non-profit organization that has been raising funds to support programs and habitat improvement projects for the "wild sheep" of Nevada for over 20 years.

Late during the evening, a "Trophy Mountain Caribou Hunt" for two, donated by Arctic Red River Outfitters (Mr.& Mrs. Kelly Hogan), was up for auction. My brother began bidding on the hunt. He had been interested in a caribou and/or moose hunt for some time, and decided to go for it. Our good buddy Gus was trying to get our attention during the bidding process; however, we were so intent on the auctioneer and the other associates involved in the auction, that we didn't hear his feeble plea, "Do you know that's a BACKPACK HUNT?" My brother and I, wanting to appear to be in control said, "Ya, Right-On!" Now let me say, I don't know what thoughts my brother had, but I will tell you, I remember mine, and trust me when I say they are not repeatable. At 55 years old, out of shape and not mentally prepared for an endurance marathon hunt, the only thought I could muster was "boy-howdy," as my nine-year old niece Maryann would say.

After calling Kelly Hogan a couple of days later, he sent us his eight-page packet delineating the sequence of events that we could expect and should be prepared for during our September hunt. The part of his document that caught my attention was a casual mention that, "Your guide will expect you to hike ten miles a day with 50 pounds in your backpack." To say the least, I decided it would be prudent to go on a weight reduction plan and start a workout regime. After a loss of over 50 pounds and four months of vigorous conditioning, I felt I was ready for the hunt.

On September 14th we departed (driving) for Edmonton, Ontario, where we boarded a Canadian Air flight to Yellowknife and then on to Norman Wells. Upon arrival in Norman Wells, we were picked up by the Mckenzie River Inn staff and transported to the motel for the evening. Although not exactly comparable to the Hilton, the accommodations were comfortable, and Monica (the owner) made our stay very enjoyable. That evening, after dinner, we met with other hunters in the lounge and had a great time visiting with folks from as far away as Austria, discussing all of our hunts, completed or pending.

The next morning, Saturday, September 18, 1999, we arose full of excitement and anticipation of getting out to our hunting camp, and also to winds that would not allow small plane transport. We hung out, sighted in our rifles, ran errands for Monica, ate, and mentally prepared for our hunt. Late that afternoon, about the time we accepted the fact that we would spend another night in Norman Wells, Monica received a radio call from North-Wright Air that we would fly in one hour. We were pumped! The next thing we knew, we were on a large Beechcraft single engine prop plane flying to the Arctic Red River Outfitter's base camp. Landing along the side of the Arctic Red River was quite an experience. The North-Wright Air pilot did a great job bouncing over the boulders.

Photograph courtesy of E. Royce Gunter

The author and his brother, Lifetime Associate Jay Gunter, with the award-winning mountain caribou scoring 416-7/8 points.

Upon landing, we were immediately surrounded by half a dozen guys from the base camp unloading and loading gear, meat, horns and antlers, and jesting with each other. Refreshing was the accent of these extreme northern Americans.

With only a couple of hours of daylight left, we thought we would spend the night at the Arctic Red River base camp; but we were wrong again in our assumption. Kelly told us to get down to the airstrip, "You're going to the hunting camp tonight, that way you can hunt tomorrow;" (Canadian law prohibits any hunting within 12 hours of being in the air). Unknown at that time, it was a lucky break for me. The next thing we knew we were in the hunting camp, via two Super Cubs, with our guide Al Klassen and packer Alex Oberg. That evening we all got acquainted while Al prepared moose steaks to perfection.

The next morning we arose to have breakfast and received instructions of how the hunt would occur and the parameters we should abide by. Don't misunderstand, these guidelines were directed toward hunter safety and Canadian law. After breakfast we went for a little jaunt to the west from camp (located at the northern most point of the Mckenzie Mountain range) to glass for caribou. About three miles from camp, Al spotted a herd on a ridge five miles to the west of our position. After watching them for a few minutes, Al thought it would be worth venturing toward them for a better look. We journeyed around the mountain to the south, for a couple of miles or more where we had a good vantage point, about three miles from the herd. The herd appeared to be all bulls (19 animals in total), although three were either very young bulls or possibly cows. One large bull and a smaller caribou stayed away from the herd. They were following, but stayed about a quarter of a mile behind, or off to the side. Al

MOUNTAIN CARIBOU
Second Award - 416⁷/₈

▼   ▼   ▼   ▼   ▼

E. ROYCE GUNTER, JR.

speculated this bull was a good one and he was interested in getting a better look, but with three miles of uphill tundra between the animals and us it wasn't a favorable situation. However, as the saying goes "nothing is forever." In an instant the main herd was running down the mountain quartering toward us, with the lone bull and his companion following, still at a distance from the herd. Al asked if we felt like running across the tundra for about a mile or so, just on the outside chance that we might be able to cut them off. Of course we agreed and were off and almost running toward the "No Name River." (My brother and I later named the river "the Cal-Neva River" as I am from California and he is from Nevada. Corny, but what the heck.)

The closer we got to the animals, the more excited Al became. He related to us that this was a good bull and that one of us had to take him. I wasn't really interested or excited about the bull as he appeared to me to be somewhat light on the top, and I also felt he should be my brother's bull, being this was his hunt. My brother said he did not want to shoot the first bull he saw on the first day of the hunt. I asked Al if he really felt this was a quality bull and he related that it was an exceptionally good bull, and was worth taking. The one thought that kept flashing through my mind was a comment made by Kevin Peterson of Reno (who had hunted with Arctic Red River Outfitters the year before) after my brother outbid him on this hunt at the NBU banquet. "You guys will have a great time, and if your guide says shoot, don't question him; shoot!"

Being my first caribou hunt and not having any experience judging the quality of caribou antlers (other than what I had read), I depended on Al's advice and told him I would take the animal.

We were probably 800 yards from the large bull and proceeded, post haste, toward the animal. My brother and Alex were falling a little behind us, as Al and I rushed up-river to the animals. We had to cross two or three creeks that were probably 100 feet wide and as deep as 16 to 18 inches. (In the eight-page instruction packet that Kelly had sent he mentioned the need to bring along Aqua-shoes for wading the creeks. I was not able to find a pair that was adequate to fit my size 15 feet, so I took along a pair of Teva sandals.). Now here I am, a few hundred yards from a "real good mountain caribou bull" that could be gone in an instant. The last thing I was about to do was to take off my backpack, dig through it to find my Tevas, sit down and take off my boots and socks, put my backpack on again and then proceed crossing the creek, just to keep my feet dry.

We had crossed the waterways and continued toward the bull and were within about 500 yards, when Al said, "Can you take him from here?" I responded that I thought I could and dropped my backpack on a rock and took a careful rest. My rifle was a Browning A-Bolt, .300 Winchester Magnum, stainless Stalker, with the BOSS system. I had reloaded my own ammo, and had worked up a load for this rifle with which I was very satisfied. I was getting 3,236 fps. of muzzle velocity from a 165-grain Barnes XLC hollow point boat tail, in front of 75-grains of IMR 4350 powder. I immediately realized the shot was not possible since I could see willows in the scope, between the bull and me. I told Al that we had to move further up the river, so I could get into position for a clear shot. The large bull stood his ground, standing at a 45-degree angle facing to his left, watching us. Al took off with me in close pursuit, backpack in one hand and rifle in the other, stumbling over boulders and logs, and through the riparian vegetation. Finally, after running about 100 yards upstream, we stopped and again I dropped my backpack over a rock and took a rest. The bull appeared to be about 400 yards and I had a clear shot, when all of a sudden the rest of the herd, which had been running around us, stopped and started feeding 200 yards in front of us; directly between us and the larger bull. I was now in position to shoot and had an itchy trigger finger when suddenly I heard Al say, "Don't shoot, don't shoot, you'll hit the wrong bull." I responded that I had the situation under control, as I was looking through my scope at two nice bulls between me and the target bull. After giving serious thought about what to do next, the front bull fed forward about six feet, which presented a clear shot (between them) at the large bull which was 200 yards beyond them. I did not hesitate to squeeze the trigger as soon as I had the cross hairs behind the bull's left shoulder. After the shot the bull immediately humped-up, indicating to me that I had made a good hit. Al said, "Hit him again, put him down." I had already chambered another round and was ready to shoot. I then moved the cross hairs a little to the left, onto the point of the shoulder and touched off another round. Upon impact of the bullet, the bull spun around 180 degrees to his right, falling and disappearing from sight.

I picked up my backpack and started toward the bull when my brother approached from the rear and said, "Why did you shoot him the second time? He was dead on his feet after the first shot." Al instantly responded, "I've tracked too many caribou 'dead on their feet' across the tundra seven or eight miles, before recovering them." We then crossed the No Name River, which was an easy enough task (once again I didn't take off my boots) and there was my caribou, the largest antlered animal I have ever harvested. Upon examination of the bull, Al's estimation was correct that it was a 400-class animal; it scored 416-7/8 points. Beyond my wildest dreams!

After photos we all went to work, skinning, butchering, deboning and packing all the meat in plastic garbage bags for the trip back to camp. We had approximately a five and a half-mile pack back to camp.

The remainder of out hunt was spent resting, shooting Ptarmigan and working on getting Jay his bull. On the fourth day of our hunt, Jay connected on a heavily palmated bull — a good bull, but not large enough to meet the minimum score to make the Boone and Crockett book.

Jay and I have had many memorable hunts and enjoyable camps, the pleasure of the camaraderie of good friends, and we have also been very fortunate to have harvested many good animals. Being in the extreme northwest of the Northwest Territories hunting in the northern most portions of the Mckenzie Mountains, is a wilderness experience beyond description. The feeling is probably on a small parallel with the experience of an astronaut landing on the moon.

Back at Norman Wells we got a good night's sleep, a good meal (at the Mckenzie River Inn) and prepared to return to Edmonton. We arrived as scheduled and departed for home. We had a scenic, safe, and uneventful trip home, with memories to last a lifetime. ▲▲▲

Moments in Measuring...

Photograph by Jack Reneau

Several Boone and Crockett Official Measurers from the Missouri Show-Me Big Bucks Club were on hand Saturday, June 16, 2001, for a whitetail deer scoring clinic hosted at Bass Pro Shops in Springfield, Missouri.

Photograph by Cliff White

TROPHY STATS

▼ ▼ ▼ ▼ ▼

Category
woodland caribou

Score
$351^2/_8$

Location
St. Anthony, Newfoundland - 1998

Hunter
Thomas D. Lund

Length of Main Beam
Right: $45^7/_8$ Left: $46^1/_8$

Inside Spread
$39^1/_8$

Width of Brow Palm
Right: $11^5/_8$ Left:

Number of Points
Right: 12 Left: 11

Photograph by Jack Reneau

Thomas D. Lund accepting his plaque and medal from Randy Byers, Chair of the Big Game Records Committee.

WOODLAND CARIBOU
First Award - 351²/₈

▼ ▼ ▼ ▼ ▼ ▼ ▼ ▼ ▼

THOMAS D. LUND

On October 9, 1998, T.J. Johnson, Steve Ehrlich, Tom Benson, Clark Linss, and I met at Los Angeles Airport for a 10:35 p.m. flight. By 2:30 p.m. the next day, Saturday, we had been on three different Air Canada aircrafts and found ourselves in Deer Lake, Newfoundland. This was where we joined up with Dick Witt, a friend of T.J.'s from White-Sulfur Springs, Montana.

Dick had been hunting for a week and had taken what I consider a very respectable woodland caribou. Dick's hunt for the caribou was with the outfitter, Roly Reid. Roly's camp on the Buchans Plateau was a helicopter fly-in camp with no other camps or hunters in the area.

Our hunt took place outside of Roddicton, which is near the northern tip of Newfoundland. We rented two vans at the Deer Lake airport and drove 3-1/2 hours to Roddicton. Our hunt was with Mayflower Outfitters, which was one of only two outfitters hunting in the area. They put us up in a fairly new one-building lodge on the shore of Lane's Pond, which is actually a fairly good size lake.

The accommodations were excellent and the food was good with more-than-you-could-eat portions. The guides were all very experienced and good people. All six of us had our own guide. We hunted from Monday, October 12th through Saturday, the 17th of October. The weather was great — quite cool but almost no rain.

When our hunt was over, I had taken a small 900-pound moose for meat. Steve Ehrlich had a 54-inch moose — a monster. T.J. Johnson had a 52-inch moose and Clark Linss had a 50-inch bull. Tom and Dick where holding out for a trophy moose, but never had the opportunity. Mayflower Outfitters invited them back to get their trophy at no charge.

As for caribou, Clark Linss and I held the only tags for that northern area. Clark got a nice caribou and I was real lucky. On the first morning hunting for caribou, my guide Trevor and I drove as far north from the lodge as we could go. We spotted what appeared to be a large-racked caribou, but we were at least over a mile from him so it was difficult to tell just how big. The wind off the north Atlantic was extremely cold. It was so cold I didn't want to get out of the truck, but Trevor convinced me we should get a closer look at this bull. I agreed and we were off. We walked the entire way through peat bogs, flooded with a foot and a half of ice cold water. We could not walk through the small water holes, because you would disappear.

It was a good thing we were dressed in full camo, since there was little cover and no place to hide on the peat bog. No trees, no rocks, no hills or outcroppings, just bog. We kept the wind in our favor and stood still if the caribou looked in our direction. These caribou apparently had not been hunted before and were not too concerned about us approaching.

The closer I got the bigger this caribou rack looked. His rack had only one shovel — I wanted two. He had only twenty plus points — I was hoping for 30 points. He was a big bull with long points, however, unlike most of the bulls I had seen. His rack was quite symmetrical and beautiful so I decided to take him.

Photograph courtesy of Thomas D. Lund

B&C Lifetime Associate, Thomas D. Lund, with his woodland caribou scoring 351-2/8 points. Despite the fact three to four inches were broken off one of points on the plane ride home, the bull still scored high enough to receive a First Award.

The closer I drew, the more concerned he became. I got to what I thought was 250 yards, which was about as close as I felt he was going to let me get. As I walked closer, he would herd his seven cows away from me. I found a mound of peat moss about a foot and a half out of the water and sat on it using my knee to rest my elbow for the shot. I was shooting a .375 H&H Magnum with a 300-grain Trophy Bonded bullet.

I squeezed off the first shot and hit him low in the chest — a lot lower than I was aiming. The bull didn't even flinch and went back to grazing. I shot three more times, before Trevor told me I was hitting well in front of him. I quickly adjusted for the next shot by holding two feet above his left shoulder and dropped him. It turned out that the range was more like 400 yards and my bullet had a 31-inch drop at that distance.

When I got to his side, he was even bigger than I had thought. He was magnificent! Later T.J. looked him over and said he would make the top of the Boone and Crockett records book. On the plane ride home, three to four inches were broken off one point. I had to wait until December 31, 1998, 60-days from the kill date, to have it measured by Boone and Crockett. Boy, was I excited. The bull's final score as determined by the 24th Awards Judges' Panel was 351-2/8 points. ▲▲▲

Photograph by Cliff White

TROPHY STATS

▼ ▼ ▼ ▼ ▼

Category
woodland caribou

Score
339^1/$_8$

Location
Watsons Brook, Newfoundland - 1998

Hunter
Harold E. Coons

Length of Main Beam
Right: 37^4/$_8$ Left: 38^4/$_8$

Inside Spread
38^2/$_8$

Width of Brow Palm
Right: 11^5/$_8$ Left: 8^7/$_8$

Number of Points
Right: 18 Left: 14

Photograph by Jack Reneau

Harold E. Coons accepting his plaque and medal from Randy Byers, Chair of the Big Game Records Committee.

BOONE AND CROCKETT CLUB'

WOODLAND CARIBOU
Second Award - 339 1/8

▼ ▼ ▼ ▼ ▼ ▼ ▼ ▼

HAROLD E. COONS

The golden flash of antlers in a brief exposure of morning sunlight drew our attention to the far side of a group of woodland caribou cows we had just been glassing. There, emerging from a tangle of sparkling frost-glazed spruce, was a magnificent stag, displaying his majesty for all to see.

As he circled his cows with pirouettes and menacing feints with his antlers, the stag gathered his harem and our attention as well. Framed against the evergreen backdrop and glistening in the brilliant morning sunlight, his massive rack looked as full and symmetrical as any we had seen all week. Guide Dennis Pilgrim and I quickly took positions behind the nearest tussock of rock and moss and deployed first binoculars, then my spotting scope for a closer look. Several ponds and small bogs lay down the glacier-carved drainage between us and him. From this range there was little danger of spooking him or his harem, but moments to witness God's natural wonders like this are precious, and the emotion impossible to capture with a camera. For more reasons than the size of his antlers we just had to have a closer look.

Photograph courtesy of Harold E. Coons

Harold's wife Judy and his guide, Dennis Pilgram, transport the caribou back to camp. Shortly after taking the bull a severe winter storm blanketed the area with snow and gusting winds.

After nearly a week of hunting and glassing literally hundreds of caribou, at least a dozen of which precipitated long, pensive sessions with the spotting scope, Friday morning brought us back to a washout near Big Brook. From there we could see the little fishing village of Boat Harbour a few miles to the north. From this same spot, at last light on Thursday (Thanksgiving 1998) we had seen caribou scattered like wind-driven snowballs over the ridges and bogs to our north. Because of the apparent size and color of some of the animals, Dennis decided to hunt the area the next day. Now, even though first light showed only scattered tracks in the fresh-fallen snow, and with no caribou visible, we began our hunt. Either they had all turned south before the snow or they were hidden in the undulating terrain between us and Boat Harbour.

My wife Judy took the pick-up several miles around the peninsula to the village, and Dennis and I started our hunt down through the hillocks and small bogs toward our rendezvous point,

Photograph courtesy of Harld E. Coons

After hunting for nearly a week and glassing hundreds of caribou, the author finally connected with this woodland caribou scoring 339-1/8 points.

some three to four miles distant. Two and a half hours later, with only a few does and calves and very few tracks seen, we were halfway to Boat Harbour. Either we had guessed entirely wrong, or a good number of caribou were condensed into an ever-smaller area ahead of us.

Descending into the head of a long drainage meandering toward the sea, we spotted the caribou mentioned in the beginning of this story. Seven or eight hundred yards separated us, most of the distance covered with either bog, tuckamore, or semi-frozen ponds. When the stag started following his ladies straight away from us, we knew we needed to close the gap as soon as possible before they got out of stalking range. The pressure was on.

As we closed the gap to the spot we had last seen the stag, four cows we had thought we passed at a safe distance spooked and ran directly toward our departing band, threatening to alarm them. But suddenly, another very respectable stag interrupted these cows and, using his rack as a prod, gathered them together and herded them off in a different direction.

Almost immediately "our" stag reappeared with his cows, coming back toward us, but with a clear intent of leaving the drainage in a direction that would put him and his band on high ground at the edge of a seemingly endless barren wasteland which, in seconds, would lead them out of reach. We would have to intercept them if at all possible.

BOONE AND CROCKETT CLUB

The only clear route was along the edge of a half-frozen pond that stretched three quarters of the way between us and the stag, using the brush at the pond's edge to camouflage our hurried stalk. I prayed the ice was frozen hard enough as we ran (with the rifle's chamber empty) to the opposite end of the pond.

WOODLAND CARIBOU
Second Award - 339¹/₈

▼ ▼ ▼ ▼ ▼

HAROLD E. COONS

On arriving at the planned intercept point, we saw that the cows were already sky-lined, ready to go out of sight. But where was our stag?

Fortunately, as the troupe had hurried to gain the high ground on these two thundering, panting pond gremlins, the lead had changed and Dennis spotted the great stag standing halfway up the hillside looking alternately at the departing cows and then in our direction.

From 200 yards there was no doubt that this one had "the right stuff." Because of the height of the cover, however, the shot would have to be from a standing position, stretched as high as I could reach — all the while panting from our run down the pond edge. Attempting such a shot through the windblown treetops was unconscionable and Dennis offered his jacket atop a nearby boulder as a padded rest. This gave me the height and stability I needed. At the report of the old Ruger it was evident the stag was hard hit and a second double lung shot anchored the monarch as he struggled to follow his departing harem.

In the time it took us to field dress the animal, hike one and a half hours to Boat Harbour, and return with Judy and the four-wheeler and sleigh, the weather had changed from mostly high overcast to cloudy and windy with occasional flurries. After pictures, we loaded the caribou on the sleigh with me riding on top.

As we began our trip out with our prize, a snow squall engulfed us. For a time the visibility was near zero and landmarks were indistinguishable. Trails made by woodcutters and berry pickers early in the fall were quickly obliterated and the barrens and bogs took on a monochrome appearance. Stops at several viewpoints along the way, waiting for visibility to improve, were necessary. It gave us all a new appreciation of the term "whiteout."

Within 500 yards of town, I suddenly became aware that I was riding the stag and that our old sleigh and I had parted company. The rough terrain and heavy load had caused it to come apart. After a good laugh, we loaded the stag on the four-wheeler with Dennis and Judy, and I hiked out, as happy and fulfilled with our experience as I could be. The half-hour trip in had become a one and one-half hour trip out, but it couldn't have been scripted better.

The long ride back to Tuckamore Lodge took us through thickening clouds, whiteouts, sleet, and gusting winds as Newfoundland's fickle weather lived up to its reputation. But she had also rewarded us richly. Combined with the heavy double shovel stag Judy took earlier in the hunt and the handsome bull moose our friend Dale Price harvested on Tuesday, this beautiful stag fulfilled all our dreams and prayers for a successful experience. On this Thanksgiving it gave all of us reason to give thanks to God for all His provisions for us.

Newfoundland, Tuckamore Lodge, outfitter Barb Genge and all the people we met on the Great Northern Peninsula — a great land, an outfitter who truly delivers, and wonderful, generous and friendly people. We'll be back! ▲▲▲

TROPHY STATS

▼ ▼ ▼ ▼ ▼

Category
woodland caribou

Score
359²/₈

Location
Main Brook, Newfoundland - Picked
up in 1996

Owner
Donated to the B&C National
Collection of Heads and
Horns by Gerard R. Beaulieu

Length of Main Beam
Right: 40¹/₈ Left: 42³/₈

Inside Spread
34³/₈

Width of Brow Palm
Right: 11¹/₈ Left: 11²/₈

Number of Points
Right: 18 Left: 13

Photograph by Cliff White

Photograph by Jack Reneau

**Robert H. Hanson accepting the plaque on
behalf of Gerard R. Beaulieu from Randy
Byers, Chair of the Big Game Records
Committee.**

WOODLAND CARIBOU
Certificate of Merit - 359²/₈

▼ ▼ ▼ ▼ ▼ ▼ ▼ ▼ ▼

B&C National Collection of Heads and Horns - Owner

Gerard Beaulieu has always been fascinated with nature's artwork and has been collecting woodland caribou antlers for over 20 years. Gerard found a set of locked antlers half submerged in a bog hole approximately ten miles north of Main Brook, Newfoundland, in 1996. The massive rack is typical for a 400-500 pound stag. It was locked to a rack scoring 299 points, also a records book stag.

Woodland caribou frequently have double shovels and with very prominent bez development, two bulls can lock antlers quite easily. Gerard has another set of locked antlers that he found in August, 1992 — a 290 point locked to a 296 point. He spotted them across a valley over a half mile away with his binoculars. He soon found himself running toward them full of excitement — at least the wind was right and he didn't blow the stalk! Gerard has also harvested a few record book caribou and feels that finding locked antlers is just a great thrill. ▲▲▲

Photograph by Cliff White

TROPHY STATS

▼ ▼ ▼ ▼ ▼

Category
woodland caribou

Score
316⁴/₈

Location
Parson's Pond, Newfoundland - 1999

Hunter
Frederick L. Gers, Jr.

Length of Main Beam
Right: 35⁵/₈ Left: 35

Inside Spread
26⁶/₈

Width of Brow Palm
Right: 14⁶/₈ Left: 7¹/₈

Number of Points
Right: 15 Left: 16

Photograph by Jack Reneau

Frederick L. Gers, Jr., accepting his plaque and medal from Randy Byers, Chair of the Big Game Records Committee.

274

WOODLAND CARIBOU
Honorable Mention - 316⁴/₈

▼ ▼ ▼ ▼ ▼ ▼ ▼ ▼ ▼

FREDERICK L. GERS, JR.

My son and I attended a sportsman show in Chantilly, Virginia, in February 1999, where we met Trevor Keough, owner and operator of Rock Camp Outfitters in Newfoundland, Canada. I had not thought of booking as I would be 76 years old in March 1999, but after talking to Trevor we booked a moose and caribou hunt for October 1999. I had never shot a moose and thought I would like to try.

We decided to drive to Newfoundland with my pickup, so I put a generator and a freezer in the bed to bring meat home. We drove to Sidney, Cape Briton Island, to catch a ferry over to Channel-Port aux Basques in Newfoundland. This is about 1,200 miles from my son's home in Fairfax, Virginia. I live in Lewistown, Pennsylvania. It is a six-hour ride on the ferry from Channel-Port aux Basques and then a two-to-three-hour drive to where we were to meet our outfitter at Peter Strides Pond. From Peter Strides Pond we flew by helicopter to the main camp, located by a lake with a huge rock on the horizon. We stopped here briefly and then flew to the spike camp to hunt moose for three days. While flying we could see small herds of caribou.

We hunted moose for three days. The first day my son had a shot at a moose and afterwards passed up a spike and a small bull. We had a discussion, as I kept telling him his .264 Winchester Mag. was too light, and even though he followed the one he shot at for a short ways, there was no sign of a hit. The second day my guide, Derrick Dominey and I set down in a clearing and I saw a moose about 200 yards through the woods. I could not see his head, but Derrick said it was a bull. I did not ask how big and took the shot. When we got to my bull he turned out to be a spike. Derrick saw the disappointment on my face and said what he would see that I got a chance at a good caribou.

That evening the helicopter flew us and my meat back to the main camp. After a good night's rest and a shower we had a hearty breakfast prepared by Mrs. Keough. The weather that day was

Photograph courtesy of Frederick L. Gers, Jr.

The author took the woodland caribou the year he turned 76. The bull scores 316-4/8 points.

in the 30s and very windy, with sleet and snow showers. Mrs. Keough said she was seeing a good bull with a herd of caribou across the lake from the camp and my guide decided we should look for him.

My son left with the outfitter and Derrick and I took the boat across the lake to hunt. We immediately started to see bulls with small herds feeding. A bull seems to gather cows around him and then guards them from other bulls as they feed and move slowly along.

Getting to within two to three hundred yards wasn't too hard, as long as we stayed down wind and when they looked at us we stopped until they resumed feeding. Before he left that morning, my son decided to take my advice and traded his .264 for my Browning .338. I also had my .30-06 along as a backup gun. Before the hunt started I had reloaded for all three guns and sighted them in at 200 yards.

We saw about six different herds, each with bulls, but Derrick kept saying that we could do better. Finally we saw a herd with a bull about 500 yards away. We worked up to within what I thought was 300 yards. Derrick said he was a good bull so I decided to try and take him from there. It was still very windy with occasional showers of sleet or snow. I fired and missed, but it did not alarm the bull or the herd. The second round did not go off and when I worked the action l could not chamber another round. We checked and the bullet was up in the chamber. I must have missed putting powder in the casing and the primer shoved the ball forward. We could not get it out. While we were deciding what to do the bull laid down followed by the rest of the herd. I asked Derrick to go back to camp and get my .30-06, while I stayed and watched the herd.

While Derrick was gone the wind, sleet and snow showers increased. I kept hoping the bull and his cows would stay until Derrick showed up with my backup rifle. As I lay there waiting I thought about the shot. I knew that I had loaded my .30-06 with 165-grain Spire Point Boat tail bullets and 58 grains of 760-ball powder. At 300 yards I would have a drop of seven inches. By the time Derrick arrived the bull was bedded, and we decided that he was closer to 400 yards, so we tried to get closer. The area has vegetation they call "tough brush." It was very thick and hard to get through unless you followed a caribou trail. It is anywhere from six inches to three feet high. We got to what we thought was 300 yards and I lay across the brush to shoot. After my first shot the bull took five or six steps and went down. I had shattered his heart.

Derrick had brought an ATV back with him so we dressed and boned the caribou, and took it back to camp. When my son got back he had shot a nice bull that was just two points from making the records book. ▲▲▲

Moments in Measuring...

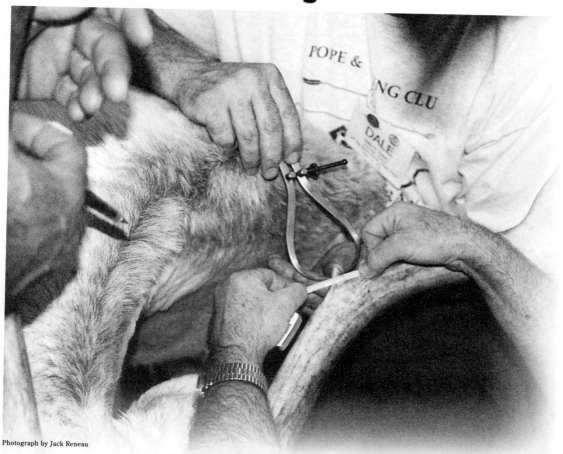

Photograph by Jack Reneau

Members of the 24th Awards Judges Panel use calipers and a measuring tape to determine whether or not the projection on this caribou antler qualifies as a scorable point. To be considered a scorable point, the projection must be at least one-half inch long, with length exceeding width at one-half inch or more of length.

New World's Record

Photograph by Cliff White

TROPHY STATS

▼ ▼ ▼ ▼ ▼

Category
    barren ground caribou

Score
    477

Location
    Iliamna Lake, Alaska - 1999

Hunter
    Daniel L. Dobbs

Length of Main Beam
    Right: $55^5/8$ Left: $57^7/8$

Inside Spread
    $38^3/8$

Width of Brow Palm
    Right: $4^5/8$ Left: $18^5/8$

Number of Points
    Right: 17 Left: 25

Photograph by Jack Reneau

Daniel L. Dobbs accepting his plaque and medal from Randy Byers, Chair of the Big Game Records Committee.

BARREN GROUND CARIBOU
First Award - 477

▼ ▼ ▼ ▼ ▼ ▼ ▼ ▼

DANIEL L. DOBBS

Dan Dobbs' only desire was to take a ten-foot bear. But in the end, he had so much more—a new World's Record barren ground caribou to be exact. Dan had been dreaming of shooting a really big bear nearly all his life. He had already set aside a place in his trophy room for the mount. He hadn't thought much about caribou until he signed up for an Alaska brown bear hunt that included caribou.

Dan is an independent timber consultant, an occupation that takes him into the woods on a regular basis to assess the value of growing hardwood trees for landowners wanting to sell their timber. Most of the time he hunts local whitetail deer, so the bear hunt was a big undertaking for him. For years Dan saved for this trip. In 1998, he began calling outfitters who advertised bear hunts in outdoor magazines. Dan talked to 30 to 40 outfitters about the location and logistics of their hunts. Then he called 30 to 40 references that were given to him by the outfitters.

When outfitter Chris Goll's client sent Dan a video of one of his fishing and hunting adventures, Dan was convinced this was the area he wanted to hunt. It was a short fishing video, but the quantity and size of brown bear in the background was very impressive. When he called to sign up, Goll offered him a bear hunt in combination with a caribou.

On September 16, 1999, Dan was full of anticipation and just a little bit nervous. This would be only the second time he had flown on an airplane, and it was a very long flight from his home in West Virginia. With a connection through Anchorage, he flew to Iliamna Lake, which is on the Alaska Peninsula. From there, he flew in a Beaver floatplane to Rainbow River Lodge to meet Goll and his guide, and to get organized for the flight to bear camp. His goal was to be hunting on September 18th, the opening day of bear season. After the bear hunt, he would fly to another camp for caribou.

The first glitch occurred when his luggage did not arrive in Iliamna. Apparently this happens all the time due to the number of fishermen and hunters coming to the area, and the huge amount of gear that the commercial airlines transport. Fortunately his luggage showed up the next day, but high winds prevented him from flying to spike camp.

Dan harvested a nice bear the next day. He was happy, even though it was not the enormous animal he had hoped for. Dan told himself that the hunt was not over, and he vowed to "make up for it with a big caribou." Little did he know what the future had in store for him. Dan began to focus on his next challenge: harvesting a barren ground caribou.

He would be hunting animals from the Alaska Peninsula North herd, which had a population of close to 10,000 in 1998. This herd is believed to be an offshoot of the huge Mulchatna herd located directly to the north, which is the largest herd in Alaska (220,000 animals in 1998). Dan and assistant guide Mark Freshwaters traveled by floatplane for about 45 minutes to a small lake and set up a comfortable spike camp. Dan noticed fire pits and other signs of previous use. Mark, who relies solely on stoves, said the fire pits were probably from self-guided hunters; for guided hunts, you must hire a guide provided by the outfitter who manages the concession.

Barren ground caribou camps are chosen for their proximity to traditional migration corridors.

The author with his award-winning barren ground caribou taken on a combination hunt. The 24th Awards Program Judges Panel scored the bull at 477 points making it the highest scoring caribou in the records book and a new World's Record for the barren ground category.

To ensure a successful hunt, a hunter must carefully study these corridors and the timing of the migration. This is "intercept" hunting, and you have to be at the right place at the right time. In the summer, caribou are high in the mountains where it is cool and insect-free. In September, as the rut begins and the weather turns cold, the caribou move down from the mountains, in large and small groups, following well-worn trails to winter ranges along the coast.

In addition to migration, there are other factors that can make it hard to get a shot at a good bull. Caribou evade predators (mainly wolves) by using speed and endurance, "clumping" together and leaving vast amounts of space empty, and using sudden, unpredictable shifts in position. They meander at a pace faster than any man can run for a sustained distance, and therefore trying to get in range by following a large bull on foot is often a hopeless undertaking.

This type of "intercept" hunting has been described as feast or famine. For Dan and Mark so far it had been famine. There were no caribou on the move. In fact, the only caribou that Dan had seen after several days were the 20 or so animals that were grazing near the campsite when the floatplane landed. The weather, which was very cold and windy, only added discomfort to disappointment.

After a couple of days, a few caribou finally began moving down from the mountains and into a draw four to six miles away from their camp. The two men saw some small bulls Dan could shoot, but he was trying not to settle for another average animal.

The morning of the fourth day, Dan walked from camp to the top of a hill they had been using as a vantage point. From there, they had a good view of the draw and the broad valley where the caribou were traveling. After Mark finished washing the breakfast dishes, he joined Dan on the top of the hill.

They saw quite a few caribou coming through the draw and decided to hike another three-quarters of a mile to get a closer look.

After a few minutes of glassing, Mark cried, "there is your caribou!" The bull he spotted was a little less than a mile away. Dan studied the caribou through his binoculars. His antlers were unbelievable! Dan was a little mesmerized by the sight of the big bull. A caribou bull, many would agree, is one of the most striking and beautiful of all American game animals. Outdoor writer Jack O'Connor, in his book *The Art of Big Game Hunting in North America* (1967) may have described them best:

"In the fall just before the rut their gray-brown bodies gleam as sleek as the hide of a seal, their powerful white necks shine in the sun, and their fantastic, palmated, many-pointed antlers rise above beautifully mounded heads with long, handsome faces, and flaring nostrils. When they are frightened, they raise their little white tails and go off with a high, springing trot so graceful as to make the gait of the finest horse seem lumpish and clumsy."

There was no time for further glassing. Given the direction the bull was headed, Dan would not be able to get close enough for a shot from where they were. Mark quickly assessed the situation. In order to get a shot, the men needed to go back to where they began—on top of the hill three-quarters of a mile away. "We have to hurry," Mark warned, "or we will lose him. He's moving very fast." The two men left their packs on the ground and ran as fast as they could back to the hill where they started. They stayed on the backside of a ridge for cover, hoping that the caribou would not see them or change his angular course toward the hill.

It was a very demanding three-quarter of a mile sprint for Dan. He tried to protect his .338-.378 Weatherby Magnum. It was brand new, and Dan knew it had enough punch to do the job. The rifle had a new scope, a Zeiss 3-12 x 56mm with an illuminated reticule. He tried hard to catch his breath and stay upright in the soft, wet, lumpy tundra. Both men scrambled up the hill, and dropped to the ground just moments before the bull arrived. The bull was following a ravine, and they could see the tips of his antlers just above the hill's crest. As he moved out of the ravine, more and more of his antlers became visible. Dan's excitement mounted. He was very close to the large bull, but the animal couldn't see him. There was no confusion about the size of this incredible animal!

At 90 yards, the bull stepped into full view. Dan squeezed the trigger, driving the bullet into his front shoulder. The bull continued to move in a circle, so he shot again. This time the bull dropped, and the two men were ecstatic. The antlers were not very wide, but they seemed to have everything else for a high score. "This caribou will make the Boone and Crockett Records Book," Mark announced as the men admired the magnificent animal. "No way!" Dan responded, silently hoping Mark really knew what he was talking about.

As Mark went back to retrieve the daypacks, Dan returned to camp to get his camcorder and a backpack to carry the meat. They enjoyed taking pictures and videos of the big bull, and ate lunch while they talked about the stalk. As they began caping and deboning, a couple of bears started moving toward them. Dan took the precaution of moving the antlers and cape about 75 yards uphill from the carcass before making the first trip back to camp. As anticipated, the bears were on the caribou carcass when Dan and Mark returned for the prize antlers.

Dan's caribou was officially scored at 477 points by the 24th Awards Program Judges Panel in Springfield, Missouri, making it the new World's Record barren ground caribou and the largest caribou ever taken out of the five species recognized by the Boone and Crockett Club.

Dan goes on to say his only wish was he could go to Alaska every year and to every hunter that on the dullest day in a blink of an eye that one magnificent animal could appear as long as you spend the time. ▲▲▲

Photograph by Cliff White

TROPHY STATS

▼ ▼ ▼ ▼ ▼

Category
  barren ground caribou

Score
  438$^7/8$

Location
  Three Arm Bay, Alaska - 2000

Hunter
  Heber Simmons, Jr.

Length of Main Beam
  Right: 51$^3/8$ Left: 50$^6/8$

Inside Spread
  47$^3/8$

Width of Brow Palm
  Right: 16$^6/8$ Left: $^1/8$

Number of Points
  Right: 19 Left: 15

Photograph by Jack Reneau

Heber Simmons, Jr., accepting his plaque
and medal from Randy Byers, Chair of the
Big Game Records Committee.

282

BOONE AND CROCKETT CLUB

BARREN GROUND CARIBOU
Second Award - 438$^7/_8$

▼ ▼ ▼ ▼ ▼ ▼ ▼ ▼ ▼

HEBER SIMMONS, JR.

The wind was blowing hard straight into our faces as Tim Booch, my guide, and I crawled on our bellies up a little ridge. A perfect stalking wind! Tim stuck his head up behind a rock and immediately turned around to me with a huge smile on his face and said, "The big bull is just across a little gully feeding broadside to us!" I whispered, "Get out of the way so I can take him!" I crept up beside Tim and saw the monster bull at close range for the first time. The bull was feeding 66 yards away facing to my left totally unaware that we were anywhere close. I pushed the safety to the off po-

Three Arm Bull

sition on my .338 rifle, lined up a spot just behind his left shoulder, and pulled the trigger to send the 225 grain. Barnes-X bullet on its way. There was a loud "Whomp" as the bullet hit its mark and the bull did not even move or acknowledge being hit. I bolted another shell into my rifle and shot again at the same spot. After that shot, the bull turned around and started walking away to my right. A third shot behind the right shoulder put him down on the ground for the first time and he never moved again. The thoughts of the entire stalk and hunt crowded my mind at that moment, for I had accomplished the goal that I had set for myself before I left home in Jackson, Mississippi — a Boone and Crockett barren ground caribou bull!

Our hunting party was composed of our guide Tim Booch of Aleutian Islands Guide Service, Jim Hlay from Westerville, Ohio, and myself. We had met in Anchorage, Alaska, and taken the Reeve Aleutian Air flight from there to Adak Island, about 1,300 miles west of Anchorage in the Aleutian Islands, arriving on Monday night, September 18, 2000. I knew that we were in for a real experience when I saw the sign at the Adak airport saying, "Welcome to Adak. Birthplace of the winds!" Rarely have I seen a sign more accurate or prophetic of what we would encounter.

We were supposed to leave for camp the next day on a chartered fishing boat, but actually did not leave the dock until the middle of Thursday afternoon due to the strong wind and high waves. The captain of the boat told us of seeing some big bulls at a certain cove and, after a council of war, we decided to stop there and stay in a nearby U.S. Fish & Wildlife cabin. The trip to the cabin was uneventful, but beautiful, allowing us to see the Aleutian Islands at their sunny and calm best! We arrived as dusk fell and moved all of our gear into our home away from home.

The next morning dawned sunny and mild, with the temperature in the low 40s. We hiked out of camp into the surrounding country full of anticipation in search of the big bulls that we knew were there. Even though we covered a lot of ground that day and glassed as much territory as possible, we did not find any bulls that met our criteria. Another council of war was held and we decided to try to call the boat on the VHF radio and ask them to move us to our original destination at Three Arm Bay. We were successful and before dark we were at our new destination and in another cabin. We knew that we had made the correct decision when we pulled into the bay and saw at least 40 caribou feeding on the hillside just above the cabin. Needless to say, our excitement and anticipation levels soared that night.

Saturday, September 23rd dawned cloudy, with a light, misty rain and the wind beginning to blow, but our hearts were glad with high hopes as we left the cabin at dawn. At 9:00 a.m. we spotted a herd of

Photograph courtesy of Heber Simmons, Jr.

The author missed this bull with his first two shots and got a rifleman's crease over his right eye from the recoil, but he continued the stalk. Two and a half hours later he finally put the bull on the ground. The award-winning barren ground caribou scores 438-7/8 points.

caribou and stalked to within 250 to 300 yards of the main bunch. After setting up my spotting scope, we looked over the five biggest bulls in the group. Jim selected the bull that fulfilled his wish, a good, mature, heavy-horned bull with a snow-white mane. About that time, Tim became very nervous because the wind was picking up in velocity and really swirling around.

I told Tim that I kept seeing the long points of a bull just over the ridge, but that I could not see the entire rack and wanted to wait until he worked our way. Finally, after an eternity of time (actually about 20 minutes), the bull turned and walked over the rise directly toward us. As his huge rack came into view, I said, "There is the one I came to Adak to get!"

Tim looked at the bull and said, "WOW!" He said that he thought the bull would score about 450 B&C points. Needless to say, that would put him high in the Book and was just what I wanted.

By this time, Jim's bull had fed to within 120 yards of us and mine was standing broadside at 260 yards. Tim told us to both shoot at the count of three, which we did. Jim's bull went down immediately with a terrific shot and I missed with my .338 Winchester from a prone position. My bull started running to my right and I rolled over and took a second shot. Missed again! Not only did I miss with both shots, the recoil from the second shot gave me a rifleman's crease over my right eye from the scope hitting me. My eyes and face were immediately covered with blood. Tim, who was looking at my bull through his binoculars, excitedly told me, "Shoot again, Heber, you missed both times!" He turned around to see why I was not shooting at the running bull and gasped at the sight of the blood all over my face from the cut. The combination of the rainwater and the blood, plus the stun of the blow, made an interesting and vivid combination. I told Tim to not worry about me and to keep his eyes on the bull, for we were going to get him before the sun set

BARREN GROUND CARIBOU
Second Award - 438⁷/₈

Second Award - 438$^7/_8$

▼ ▼ ▼ ▼ ▼

HEBER SIMMONS, JR.

today. As we watched the entire herd run off to the west into the wind, I tried to get the bleeding from my cut forehead under control.

While waiting for the caribou to calm down, we went to Jim's beautiful bull and rejoiced that he had been successful. Needless to say, Jim was ecstatic because the bull truly filled his criteria. We took some quick pictures and then headed off after my bull, telling Jim that we would be back sometime before dark — we hoped!

When we spotted them again, the herds had gone about two miles across a valley and had settled down and were feeding. Tim and I skirted the side of the valley using the terrain for cover, and headed for the herd. Every time we would raise our heads above a ridge and look, the herd was still there. Our excitement level was building as we closed the distance between us and the big bull. All the time I was mentally kicking myself in the rear-end for missing two shots that I should have made. One thing I have learned about hunting is that no one is successful all of the time and there is nothing like a missed shot or two to teach one about humility. We literally crawled the last 200 yards on our bellies, hardly daring to raise our heads to follow our pre-determined path to a little knoll of dirt and rocks.

As you know, we were successful and the bull was on the ground! The first two shots that I missed were at 10:00 a.m. and the time was now 12:45 p.m. We had tracked him for over two and half-hours before we finally put him on the ground.

As Tim and I approached the bull we were both in awe, for he looked huge on the ground. We took some photographs, did the preliminary cleaning and headed back to help Jim with his bull. Alaskan rules state that you must first remove all of the meat from an animal before you can take out the antlers. We adhered to the rule to the letter of the law, but it took us until Monday night to get all of the meat from both caribou back to the cabin. I must admit that I was extremely nervous about leaving the head, but realized that no one was around to take it and there were no animals big enough to move it.

We scored the antlers at the cabin and we came up with a green score of 447-6/8 points. Tim had estimated 450 when we first saw the bull. I told him, with tongue in cheek humor, that he was going to have to do better in the future.

The wind blew harder and harder, the rain came down in horizontal sheets, and we remained isolated in the cabin. In fact, the wind blew so hard that the building literally shook from the force. Finally, about noon on Thursday, the fishing boat picked us up and took us back to the village of Adak. There were two flights a week between Adak and Anchorage, one on Monday and the other on Thursday. Luckily, the flight to Anchorage was 12 hours late and we were able to make this flight. We had spent an extra three days on the front end of the hunt and another four days on the tail end due to the strong wind and general bad weather, but Jim and I both wound up with great bulls.

After all of the anticipation and preparation, we had a great trip to one of the most isolated places on earth, shared the experience with new friends, and accomplished what we set out to do. One cannot ask more from a hunting trip! ▲▲▲

Photograph by Cliff White

TROPHY STATS

▼ ▼ ▼ ▼ ▼

Category
  barren ground caribou

Score
  414^6/$_8$

Location
  Post River, Alaska - 1998

Hunter
  Shawn A. Lar

Length of Main Beam
  Right: 47^6/$_8$ Left: 48^2/$_8$

Inside Spread
  33^2/$_8$

Width of Brow Palm
  Right: 12^4/$_8$ Left: 2^4/$_8$

Number of Points
  Right: 17 Left: 16

Photograph by Jack Reneau

Shawn A. Lar accepting his plaque and medal from Randy Byers, Chair of the Big Game Records Committee.

BARREN GROUND CARIBOU
Third Award - 414⁶/₈

▼ ▼ ▼ ▼ ▼ ▼ ▼ ▼ ▼

SHAWN A. LAR

The final steps into camp meant fording a bone-chilling glacial stream, but I didn't bother to find a good crossing. My dad was standing on the far shore waiting to inspect the caribou antlers draped over my shoulders.

All through my adolescent years in central Montana, Dad took me hunting and we often wondered what it would be like to hunt in far away places. As I grew older the thought of us sharing a trip to Alaska turned into an obsession.

An Unlikely Trophy

As years passed, the idea seemed to be no more than another dream hunters have as they pass the time on a stand.

Our break came in January 1998. I swapped hunting stories for a year with a coworker, Ace Sommerfeld, who spent most of his adult life roaming across Alaska. He suggested concentrating on a valley deep in the Alaska Range. "It's a great place for an economical, do-it-yourself hunt," he said.

Now that I was committed, I worked on convincing my dad we could do it. When he was onboard I rounded up two more hunters. Roger Day, who lives a couple blocks from Dad in Musselshell, who jumped at the chance and Harlan "Ace" Erskine, from nearby Helena, Montana. We offered to pay Ace's way, and he agreed to tag along. Another tremendous advantage came when Dave Sullivan agreed to assist. David is a pilot who lives in Anchorage, Alaska, and is Ace's long-time hunting partner.

Getting into the Alaskan wilderness was going to be a complicated matter. We got off the plane in Anchorage at 10:00 a.m. on August 28th, 1998, and drove 100 miles north to Talkeetna, a village along the Susitna River. Our party then split up, with four of us flying out to a large gravel airstrip on the lower Post River. The Cessna 185 took two of us per trip. In the meantime, Ace directed the Piper Super Cub pilot to a sandbar strip 25 miles upstream that was marked by two pieces of fluorescent tape. Then the hopping began. It took six trips to get all hunters and gear assembled at the strip, which would be our hunting headquarters for the next week.

We didn't pick the lonely valley to test a pilot's endurance. The variety of game was the major factor. "You can find caribou, moose, and black bears, all legal to hunt without a guide," Ace said. For our party, four caribou and a moose seemed to be a reasonable goal. I wouldn't hesitate to shoot a mature black bear if the opportunity presented itself. On the final trip Dave flew in just before dark with the last load of gear to help make a comfortable camp, and spotted a bull moose just before landing.

There was little time to search for game the first night at camp, but it didn't make much difference; we couldn't fly and hunt in the same day. I was able to take a few minutes and survey the general landscape. The valley seemed endless and searching the entire surroundings looked impossible. A million gullies, ridges, false ridges, and lofty basins in the neighbor-

Photograph courtesy of Ace Sommerfed.

A view of camp with Dave Sullivan's plane on the right. Dave brought in a load of gear and supplies that helped make camp more comfortable.

ing peaks could hide the Chinese army. Small glaciers occupy many of the high basins, and snowfields streaked across the autumn-colored slopes.

The valley floor was about three miles across with the Post River cutting a meandering swath from side to side. It is a typical glacial stream with many sandbars and dry washes. To walk a straight line up the valley we'd be forced into fording the muddy current over and over.

Dry washes make walking tolerable as they allow you to avoid most of the muskeg and brush that blanketed the valley. Brush-covered knolls rising above the river banks provide excellent lookout points. Moose concentrated on willow-choked creek beds on the eastern side of the valley, and caribou showed up anywhere open ground could be scanned.

Our plan of approach was to hunt caribou on the western side of the valley for two days, and keep an eye peeled for moose on the eastern slopes as we hunted. Moose wouldn't open until September 1st, and we hoped to have a couple caribou "hanging" and a moose pegged by then.

Day one produced enough rain to drown the Chinese army. Despite everyone getting out and working different parts of the valley, no one saw a bull worthy of taking on the first day. The moose situation wasn't so bleak. Dave and I put the spotting scope on a bull across the river that appeared to have a 50 inch spread, the minimum Alaska requires for non-resident hunters.

There were several cow moose scattered across the far slopes, and we hoped the bull would stay put a few days. The hunt for caribou continued on the western slopes and adjoining valleys running into the main watershed. A multitude of wolf tracks, and scattered sightings of cows and small bulls told us mature bull caribou were going to be hard to find. "These caribou are local animals from the Rainy Pass herd," Dave said. "It's a small herd compared to the swarms in other parts of the state. If the main body is moving through your hunting area it's hard to single out a bull," Ace said. "If they are working a valley two watersheds away, you have to search every inch of the valley to find big bulls."

The first day of moose season came and went without success. The bull we had spotted earlier apparently left the valley. That day Dave flew out and left us to our own devices. The highlight of my days with him was watching a grizzly bear work its way across a mountain.

Caribou began to filter into camp despite the absence of big bulls. The temptation to bag mediocre trophies caught up with Dad first, and Roger and Harlan brought in two bulls the next day.

I was the final holdout on caribou. Ace and I gave up on moose, and put our energy into bringing home a big caribou. We figured our only chance was to explore the high basins lining the eastern side of the valley. With three days to hunt we left camp before daybreak under a crisp, starlit sky. It was the first day of sunlight in four days. Temperatures hovered around 15°, and puddles were iced over.

Fourteen hours and 12 miles of hiking turned up more cow moose and a herd of medium sized bull caribou in terrain Ace said would make a Dall's sheep proud. He mentioned that either wolves were pushing them into the upper reaches of the draws, or they were working their way into other regions.

Whatever the answer, we were encouraged by finding a herd of bulls. At least we felt we had the right idea. One of the airy basins may be hiding the prize our legs ached for. Another day and many more miles failed to yield big bulls. The summer training Ace insisted on was paying off. I kept in step with a partner who understood the rigors of tough Alaska Range hunting, but my Achilles tendon got scraped to the point where every step was painful.

I hobbled into camp with one day and one basin left. A good night's sleep and a lot of Advil would have to see me through another day. In the morning I considered staying in the warmth of the sleeping bag, but before I was fully awake I shook Ace out of his backcountry slumber. "Let's give it one last effort," I said. "It could be our lucky day."

Dad got up and made sure we left camp with bellies full of warm oatmeal and a good lunch. I borrowed Roger's boots that were a size or two larger than mine, and didn't lace them tight hoping for a little ankle relief.

We crossed the river and headed for a long basin that curved out of sight. It would take three hours to reach it, and all day to hike to its head. Half way to the basin's mouth we spotted caribou and binoculars revealed mature bulls. At this time of year mature bulls were losing velvet and antlers were either polished brown or blood red.

We didn't need the spotting scope for this herd. We knew without a close look that this was the break we worked so hard for. At least ten mature bulls milled about on the mountain above us; one in ten should be big enough to make my trip successful. We pushed hard through good cover until we were half a mile from the herd.

Vegetation on the upper slopes made stalking tricky, and we decided it would be better for me to continue alone while Ace monitored the bulls' movements through the spotting scope. I spent most of the next two hours getting familiar with the ground insects of interior Alaska.

Photograph courtesy of Ace Sommerfed.

The author, Shawn Lar, with his barren ground caribou scoring 414-6/8 points. This photo helps you appreciate the length of the rear points.

By making a steady crawl upward I was able to keep the herd in sight by occasionally raising up just enough for a look.

When the distance was down to 500 yards a peculiar bush caught my attention. To my astonishment, it could walk. A tremendous bull we hadn't seen from below was bullying every adversary in his way. I doubled my caution and inched closer to my goal. At 150 yards, I couldn't get any closer. Most of the herd was in plain sight as I prepared to shoot.

Nine bulls fed and intermingled in front of me oblivious to my presence. None of them measured up to the "bush" I'd spotted earlier. The minutes passed and I began to have my doubts. Maybe it wasn't as big as I thought. A couple of the other bulls were starting to look pretty darn good. The big bull could have run the smaller bulls off and left the other bulls. With these thoughts running full tilt through my mind, I heard a sharp clash of antlers. Bulls I couldn't see were sparing in a depression somewhere in front of me. Seven days of caribou hunting taught me they would hold a few moments after they determined I wasn't a wolf or bear and I decided it was time to show myself.

When I rose out of my prone position I realized the brush was barely knee-high. Suddenly the bulls bunched up and moved 50 yards uphill. The big bull came into sight, stopped to identify the disturbance, and I shot it in the chest. Two more shots were required to bring the large animal down.

I let out a yell that would've awakened the Chinese army. Actually, the shots and whoops reached camp four miles away, and brought Harlan to our aid. All I could do for half an hour until Ace reached me was stare at the magnificent bull. It was the most difficult and most impressive animal I'd ever taken.

Ace had his own story to tell. Soon after we split up he spotted the bull and considered trying to catch up to me and warn me of the monster on the mountain. In the end he sat tight and let fate take its course. He wasn't sure if I'd done things right until he saw the bull at my feet. We did the customary hop-n-hug, and went to work.

Harlan joined us just in time to put some of the load in his pack. I was so excited my feet never bothered me on the hike to camp. Seeing my dad's nod of approval made the entire week worth the effort. Everyone shared in the excitement of bringing a first-class trophy back to Montana. Ace told us Rainy Pass caribou are shunned by trophy hunters because they don't compare to bulls in the Nelchina or Alaska Peninsula herds, but this bull looked big... really big!

Dave flew in the next morning and concurred. Boone and Crockett experts would have the final say, but it appeared by rough measure the bull was headed for the book. Back in Talkeetna folks at the airport gathered to see the rack we strapped to the top of the load. I've placed several animals in Montana's record books, but walking up to the big bull remains the biggest hunting thrill of my life. When I plan my next dream hunt, I can do so knowing they come true once in a while. ▲▲▲

BARREN GROUND CARIBOU
Third Award - 414⁶/₈
▼ ▼ ▼ ▼ ▼

SHAWN A. LAR

Photograph by Cliff White

TROPHY STATS

▼ ▼ ▼ ▼ ▼

Category
Central Canada barren ground caribou

Score
407

Location
MacKay Lake, Northwest Territories -
1997

Hunter
Daniel J. Gartner

Length of Main Beam
Right: 55^6/$_8$ Left: 55

Inside Spread
34^5/$_8$

Width of Brow Palm
Right: 16^2/$_8$ Left: ^{1}/$_8$

Number of Points
Right: 23 Left: 18

Photograph by Jack Reneau

**Daniel J. Gartner accepting his plaque and
medal from Randy Byers, Chair of the Big
Game Records Committee.**

BOONE AND CROCKETT CLUB

CENTRAL CANADA
BARREN GROUND CARIBOU
First Award - 407

▼ ▼ ▼ ▼ ▼ ▼ ▼ ▼

DANIEL J. GARTNER

September 15, 1997

Everyone's excitement level rose as our plane climbed out of Yellowknife, Northwest Territories, heading for MacKay Lake. From the plane we watched the trees slowly disappear from the massive rock stretches broken with a scattering of lakes. As we neared MacKay Lake, we could see caribou trails interlaced across the landscape, some carved into the stone. These trails were obviously used over the ages. We

Quest for a Booner with a Bow

spotted a moose just outside of Yellowknife, then a black bear. A little further north brought sightings of caribou, white manes shining in the afternoon sun. Everyone was pumped; we've finally reached the tundra.

Our landing was pretty smooth on a strip 65 miles from the Arctic Circle. Gary Jaeb, Owner of True North Safaris, greeted us. He has two caribou camps on MacKay Lake - the main camp, MacKay Lake Lodge, and Barberton Bay. His crew unloaded our gear, then loaded up the hunters and their gear leaving camp for their ride back to Yellowknife. We were astonished by the big pile of caribou racks ready to leave camp. The previous week was apparently very successful.

This was my first trip to MacKay Lake, but not my first bow hunt for caribou. In August 1995, I took my first archery caribou. We had chased bulls for ten miles and I finally took an evenly balanced, velvet racked, bull. Although this bull was not very big, I was extremely happy. The next day I took a bull with my rifle that green scored 378 points. The following year I would be a little more selective with my bow.

In August 1996, the first day out in the field, I stalked a bull for about an hour and a half. A 60-yard double lung shot rewarded me with a 349-5/8 Pope & Young bull. The end of the week brought me a 339-2/8 bull. Both of these bulls were recorded in the velvet category with Pope & Young.

My next hunt would be for hard antler racks, which brought me to MacKay Lake. On the morning of September 16, my hunting partner James Powless and I left camp with our guide, Patrick. We proceeded north from camp, occasionally seeing a few caribou on the distant horizons. As we followed the shoreline we came around a point and spotted a herd of about 150 animals with some real nice bulls, but Patrick just kept going toward the end of the bay. Evidently he knew of a great crossing area.

Once we landed on shore, Patrick started us hiking up the ridge toward a group of caribou we had spotted a mile away. While on our trek across the tundra a wolverine ran across in front of us and stopped to check us out. He stood about 200 yards and displayed the white blaze on his chest. What a magnificent sight and animal!

Photograph courtesy of Daniel J. Gartner

The author told his hunting partners not to shoot the first bull they saw. Fortunately he didn't heed is own advice and took this caribou on the first day of his hunt. The bull scores 407 points and received a First Award at the 24th Big Game Awards Banquet.

During the next two to three hours, I stalked to within bow range of some bulls, but I didn't see anything I wanted. Patrick pointed to the east and we could see at least 1,000 caribou coming toward us. They were spread out a half-mile wide and were in sight as far as we could see. James and I decided to set-up in the rocks ahead of the approaching herd. We passed up several animals and then split up to cover more trails. Not long after settling in again a 335-class bull came right up to me and presented a quartering away shot. I drew my bow and released. My shot placement was perfect and he ran about 40 yards and went down. After seeing me take my bull James came over and we decided to video him shooting a bull while the herd was still moving through the area. He took a 370-7/8 bull at 45 yards — good enough to rank number 13 with Pope & Young.

With more caribou in sight, we split up again. I saw every size and shape of rack you could imagine over the next couple of hours. There were several 400 class bulls, but they were all out of bow range. I was passing up shots on 375 plus bulls because there were larger bulls coming behind them. The action was unbelievable! I was trapped, hiding in the rocks waiting for the caribou to pass, so I wouldn't spook the whole herd. They were so close I could hear them eating grass. Finally a break in the action presented an opportunity to relocate to another position. I spotted a monster bull and tried to intercept him, but couldn't get close enough as he went by at 80 yards. I then decided to creep up to the crossing the big bull had just used and waited. Before long another group of big bulls started to pass by me at 17 yards. After five or six animals passed, a giant bull presented me with a broadside shot. The arrow passed completely through him and he ran about 200 yards before going down. That bull ranks number two all-time Pope & Young — quite a bull with only one shovel!

CENTRAL CANADA BARREN GROUND CARIBOU
First Award - 407
▼   ▼   ▼   ▼   ▼
DANIEL J. GARTNER

What a day! We saw over 10,000 caribou in a six-hour period. I knew that I would get some ribbing from the other hunters for tagging out the first day, especially since I told them not to shoot the first one. From experience, I know that you always see a bigger bull!

Later in the week, James took another archery bull, scoring 346-6/8 points. Three of the four bulls we harvested made Boone and Crockett Club minimum scores. What a great hunt!

The week brought great fishing, trophy grayling, and lots of lake trout. Ptarmigan and Arctic hares were abundant and we were treated to sightings of wolves and grizzly bear. We were very lucky that the weather cooperated, making it possible for such a once-in-a-lifetime experience. ▲▲▲

Photograph by Cliff White

TROPHY STATS
▼ ▼ ▼ ▼ ▼

Category
Central Canada barren ground caribou

Score
398^6/8

Location
Little Marten Lake, Northwest
Territories - 1998

Hunter
William J. Mills

Length of Main Beam
Right: 48^6/8 Left: 50^2/8

Inside Spread
38^2/8

Width of Brow Palm
Right: 6^5/8 Left: 12^2/8

Number of Points
Right: 20 Left: 25

Photograph by Jack Reneau

William J. Mills accepting his plaque and
medal from Randy Byers, Chair of the Big
Game Records Committee.

CENTRAL CANADA BARREN GROUND CARIBOU
Second Award - 398⁶/₈

▼ ▼ ▼ ▼ ▼ ▼ ▼ ▼

WILLIAM J. MILLS

We began our hunt September 10, 1998, with Adventures Northwest out of Northwest Territory. After arriving in Yellowknife, we picked up our license and tags from our outfitter who had already obtained them for us. From there it was an hour and a half flight to Little Martin Lake where the main camp was located.

Our camp had heated wall tents with wood floors, running water, hot showers, and an excellent cook tent with plenty of great food.

After putting away our gear and checking our rifles to make sure they were properly sighted in after such a long fight, the rest of the day was spent getting acquainted and ready for the hunt. On the second day I was paired with Mike Markham from Washington State. Our guide was an Inuit Eskimo by the name of Jack. We started our hunt by taking a 40-minute boat ride up the lake.

We saw several herds of caribou with a few good trophies in each herd. Mike decided to take a bull out of one of the first herds we spotted. He made a good 220-yard shot and had his first caribou. While Jack and Mike were skinning and cleaning Mike's bull, I took my pack to a nearby ridge to glass.

After glassing for about an hour, I spotted what I thought was a trophy-class bull on the other side of the lake. He was scraping and rubbing in the brush to get the velvet off his antlers. I video taped this big guy for about another hour while he did his work. Shortly another herd came down the hill toward the lake, at which time the big bull joined this small herd. Much to my surprise, the whole herd came down the hill toward the lake, ran into the lake, and headed straight toward me. It looked like they were going to come within about 300 yards from where I was sitting. When I saw this I decided to work my way over to where I thought they would come out of the lake. I had guessed right, and when they came out and started feeding, I picked the big bull out again for a clear 150-yard shot. I leveled, and with one shot from my .300 Dakota I put one load right behind the shoulders. When he went down, he didn't even wiggle.

I knew I had taken a big bull by comparison to the others we'd seen and Mike's bull, but score-wise I didn't know how big until we got a tape on him. He ended up scoring 398-6/8 points. What an animal! ▲▲▲

Photograph by Cliff White

TROPHY STATS
▼ ▼ ▼ ▼ ▼

Category
Quebec-Labrador caribou

Score
415⁷/₈

Location
Minto Lake Island, Quebec - 1999

Hunter
Curt M. Coleman

Length of Main Beam
Right: 59⁴/₈ Left: 55⁶/₈

Inside Spread
44

Width of Brow Palm
Right: 10²/₈ Left: 14²/₈

Number of Points
Right: 20 Left: 22

Photograph by Jack Reneau

Curt M. Coleman accepting his plaque and medal from Randy Byers, Chair of the Big Game Records Committee.

QUEBEC-LABRADOR CARIBOU

First Award - 415⁷/₈

▼ ▼ ▼ ▼ ▼ ▼ ▼ ▼ ▼

CURT M. COLEMAN

When my dad, Mike Coleman, and my uncle, Gary Coleman, came home from their first caribou hunting trip, Dad was very excited about going back up north. He returned from this trip in mid September 1997. The very next week he called Umiujaq Outfitters located in Umiujaq, Nunavik in Northern Quebec. The earliest we could get in for a trip was September 1999, so we had plenty of time to prepare. This time it would be my dad, uncle Gary, my younger brother Mitch, and myself. The 30-hour drive to Radisson where we would fly out to our base camp seemed a little much, but later turned out to be worth every mile. I had never been on a big game hunt before with the exception of the whitetail deer I chase around the foothills of southeastern Ohio. I knew that Quebec is nothing like Ohio, but I figured that would be half the fun.

After arriving in Radisson we got all our tags and instructions. The next morning we loaded up the planes and headed north for Minto Lake Island. Our base camp consisted of three buildings and an outhouse. Two of the buildings were the hunters' bunkhouses, each holding eight people, even though we only had 12 hunters in the camp. The third bunk house was the utility/meat locker/guide building. The guides were Donald Laduc and Ben. Both of them were really funny to be around and good guides. Donald was a little more American acting than Ben — he spoke English better and related with the hunters more. He could joke around with just about anybody and understand everything you said. Ben could understand English, but didn't know all the right words to communicate back in English. Both knew a lot about caribou and the tundra.

The first three days of the hunt were pretty amazing even though we had not seen any caribou. The country is beautiful. I had never seen anything that compared to it. All that open ground that stretched on and on, looking like it never ended. I didn't even think I was on the same planet as the rest of world. When a person is up that far north there are no sounds but nature. No cars, traffic, security lights, or loud people who want me to quit hunting. One thing that was definite is that there were a lot of weather changes. It snowed, rained, hailed, and went from cold to warm off and on the entire trip. By the third day I was getting a little worried about the caribou. Then around two or three in the afternoon I saw my first herd of caribou. They were a long way off, but were heading our way. My hunting partner, uncle Gary, and I got set up on a bottleneck on one of the many shelves that were on the rocky hills. To our surprise the caribou went below us about 70 yards. Since we were hunting with bows at the time, it left us out of luck. It wasn't but five minutes later the loud shockwave of my brother's Model 700 muzzleloader rung out. I quickly snuck around to a lower shelf to see my brother's fatally wounded bull staggering down by the lakeshore. The walk to the animal felt like it took forever. Forty-five minutes to be exact, even though the bull only traveled 30 yards after the shot.

The author with his award-winning bull taken on his first caribou hunt. The animal scored 415-7/8 points.

Packing his bull out was a lot of work, but it was work none of us minded.

The next morning we awoke to strong gusty winds and cold rain. That day our little family group harvested three bulls: two bow kills and my dad successfully tried his hand at the muzzleloading.

I awoke the next morning to everyone in the cabin drinking coffee and looking out the windows at the lake. The lake was rough. I mean dangerously rough, and it was pouring down rain. Later in the morning we left in pairs. After a 40-minute boat ride across the rough lake we arrived at a little cove that was calm enough to beach the boat. As Gary and I got off the boat, a slight fog drifted in making it even more difficult to see. Donald tied the boat off to a small tree on the bank. He started to take us to the spot he had picked about 200 yards up a trail. While still on the trail Donald knelt to the ground and said, "Cow." I looked up and there was a cow about 100 yards above us on the rocky slope. I froze and never moved an inch until the cow turned and headed over the hill. We hurried to the nearest cover because we knew other caribou would follow. Just as soon as I got behind a big rock I saw a pair of antlers coming up the hillside. A nice, probably 300-class bull strolled along the same path as the cow. It was too late to get a shot at that bull, but I got ready for another one. Just then another bull stepped into sight as good as the first one. Just as I was to squeeze the trigger I saw the big tops of the antlers of another bull sticking up over the rocks. When this bull stepped out into the open I could tell that he was bigger than the other bulls, but I had no idea how big. The other caribou started to go straight up the hill in front of the big bull. I got my scope on him and had a good quartering away shot. I felt confident with the shot and guessed the caribou to be about 150 yards away. As I squeezed the trigger the bull turned to go uphill. The shot was very effective; the bull staggered for about 30 seconds and fell down. I watched him until he stopped moving. I heard Donald say that it was a very big bull. I still didn't understand what I had just taken. When I was about 50 feet away from the bull I saw half of his antlers sticking up over a big rock. That's when my heart started beating fast and the adrenalin started to flow — I knew he was something special.

I was so pumped up when I was carrying the hindquarters back to the boat (about 400 yards) I made it back before Donald had finished cutting the last quarter. The best carry was the head. I put the rack over my shoulder and headed to the boat. I don't even remember that last trip. I just remember thinking that I hope Dad and Mitch were seeing caribou. As I put the antlers in the boat I saw Gary up on the hill and he waved; I knew he would get one. He always pulls through. The ride back to camp was short and when I hit the beach the guys in camp swarmed around my bull and me. They all shook my hand and looked at the bull; it was a pretty cool moment. Later when I heard the boat coming I could see the antlers in it and then I saw it was Mitch. He had a very

QUEBEC-LABRADOR CARIBOU
First Award - 415⁷/₈

▼ ▼ ▼ ▼ ▼

Curt M. Coleman

nice bull, and when he jumped out of the boat he was grinning from ear to ear. I didn't know it at the time, but Donald had told him I shot a little bull. It took Mitch about five seconds to see my bull and he knew Donald was messing with him. Donald took the boat back after Dad. Mitch told me that Dad had a nice bull down too. After Dad returned the only person left out was Gary. After about two hours, Donald returned with him. He had a nice bull too and that made it final. We were done — 12 hunters, 20 bulls. Two Pope and Young bulls and one Boone and Crockett. It was a great hunt and a very neat experience. Maybe one of these days I can go back — even though it will be very hard to beat my old record, but everyone needs goals. ▲▲▲

Photograph by Cliff White

TROPHY STATS
▼ ▼ ▼ ▼ ▼

Category
Quebec-Labrador caribou

Score
397⁵/₈

Location
Lake Rigouville, Quebec - 1998

Hunter
James M. Parker

Length of Main Beam
Right: 51⁴/₈ Left: 49⁴/₈

Inside Spread
50⁷/₈

Width of Brow Palm
Right: 11⁶/₈ Left: ¹/₈

Number of Points
Right: 20 Left: 15

Photograph by Jack Reneau

James M. Parker accepting his plaque and medal from Randy Byers, Chair of the Big Game Records Committee.

QUEBEC-LABRADOR CARIBOU
Second Award - 397⁵/₈

▼ ▼ ▼ ▼ ▼ ▼ ▼ ▼ ▼

James M. Parker

My plans for my first big game adventure started in the spring of 1996 at the sportsmen's show in Pontiac, Michigan. After talking with several outfitters, I decided upon Safari Nordik, outfitting in Quebec, Canada. I made the reservation for two of my friends and me for September 1997. As time went by our group grew to seven. The final group consisted of Jack Homsher and Tom Robinson, both from Phoenix, Doug Caldwell from Wisconsin, Al Livingston from Missouri, and Gene Wheeler, Mike Apr, and myself from Michigan. Over the next year, as the anticipation of the hunt grew, so did our phone bills.

Finally the day came when we all met at my house to pack and make the drive to Montreal where we would meet with the outfitter and fly into the camp. It was about three in the afternoon and everyone was at my house loading their gear into the trailer. The phone rang and it was Kathy from Safari Nordik. She called to inform us that they would like us to delay our hunt until the following year. This was because there had been unusually warm weather and the caribou hadn't migrated to the area. Since the migration had been very slow, they were not seeing any animals and they were concerned about showing us a quality hunt. Kathy said we could still make the trip, but they recommended we wait for better conditions next year. I then had the task of delivering the bad news. Naturally the news was not taken well. We had a great deal of discussion, but we all agreed that they could have said nothing and taken us to camp, knowing full well that there were no animals in the area of any of their camps. We concluded this might be a blessing in disguise. Several of the guys called Safari Nordik back and after talking to them we all decided that going the following year was the best option. I have to admit that it was very disappointing and a huge let down after all the hype that we had built up between us.

As another year passed and it got closer to September, our spirits began to build for the second time. Several days prior to us meeting once again at my house, I called the outfitter to make sure we were still a go. They assured me that everything was fine and they were looking forward to meeting us in Montreal. Once everyone arrived at my house, you could see on their faces that the group still had reservations. I assured them I had talked to the outfitter and everything was fine. That night I had a big fish fry for all the guys and there was a lot of laughing and joking about our upcoming hunt. The next morning we got up and packed the trailer with all our gear. After lunch we finally took off for Canada.

After two days on the road we arrived at the hotel in Montreal and met with the representative from Safari Nordik. While at the hotel, we ran into some hunters coming out of camps with different outfitters, and to be totally honest it didn't look good. We didn't meet anyone that had taken their limit of two caribou. In fact, some of the guys were coming out empty-handed. Our spirits remained high and we were not going to let a poor report bring us down.

Jack Homsher, one of seven hunters who traveled to Lake Rigouville with James M. Parker for a Quebec-Labrador hunting adventure, watches the horizon for any sign of caribou.

The representative from Safari Nordik gave us our airline tickets for the flight from Montreal to Fort Chimo. From there we would take another plane into camp. We got to Fort Chimo and ran into some more hunters who did not have very good luck either. Again, they were with different outfitters. We did run into one group from Safari Nordik and they hadn't done very well. But Safari Nordik had offered them a return trip where the only cost would be the plane ride from Montreal to the camp. We where impressed that Safari Nordik was willing to do that.

We finally boarded a twin engine Otter loaded with our 60 pounds of gear per man and lifted off for camp. After about an hour flight, the Otter touched down directly on the tundra in front of camp, which was situated on the shore of a large lake. Our spirits perked back up again when we met the group heading back to Fort Chimo — they had all tagged out. Next, we met our guides and the camp leader. The camp consisted of floored tents with an oil furnace. For sleeping, there were three tents that each held eight men. There was also a tent for the guides and the cook, and a kitchen tent. We even had a shower with hot water! They had a big generator in camp for power so we had electricity until 10 p.m., and then they fired it back up again at 6 a.m.

We all drew numbers for our guides and there were three hunters per guide. Al Livingston, Jack Homsher, and I drew a guide by the name of Perry. I could tell by the way Perry acted that we were going to be in for a fun hunt. After the guide selection we had dinner and got settled into our tents. Later we had a meeting where the guides went over the rules, answered our questions, and gave us an update on the animals in the area. After the update it looked like we would be in for a hard hunt. They were truthful and told us that they were not seeing that many animals. Caribou were in the area. We would just have to hunt hard for them.

On our first morning Jack, Al, and I met with Perry after breakfast and loaded up the boat to go to the other end of the lake. The wind was blowing hard and it was overcast with the temperature around 40°. As we crossed the lake Perry spotted a small herd of caribou so we headed toward shore. As we approached they started to move inland, so Al tried to take a shot. Even though the boat was stopped the wind was blowing so hard a shot was almost impossible. He did shoot twice and missed, so Perry moved the boat to shore. We all got out and let Al have the first shot. But his gun jammed and Perry waved us forward. I went over to Perry and Jack went up the hill to cut the caribou off. There was one nice animal in the bunch, but I couldn't get a good shot. There was another animal standing broadside and I asked Perry what he looked like. He said that the bull was an adult, but nothing special and asked me if I wanted to try to shoot him. I decided to try a shot, but he was about 400 yards away and the wind was blowing so hard it was difficult to hold the gun steady. I finally settled in for a shot, which hit him in the neck and down he went.

Little did we know this would be the last herd of caribou we would see for four days. We hunted and walked a lot of miles over the next four days, but all we saw was tundra. Everyone in camp was getting anxious because the outfitter was not moving us. The camp leader was in contact every day with the outfitter and they said the animals should be there the next day. They knew a herd of caribou had crossed the Leaf River and since they can travel 40 miles a day, they should show up any day at our camp. By Thursday we had not seen any animals and we were getting very depressed. It didn't look like the outfitter was doing anything to correct the situation. Fortunately he was working on it; we just didn't know it. They flew a plane over the hunting area, but couldn't find anything, so they decided it was time to move our party. There were two camps south of us and they were doing well. They decided to move our group to another camp that was named Rigouville. This camp was between the two camps directly to the south. At lunch on Friday we were told to pack up the camp for the move. As we broke camp our spirits went up like a rocket since we were moving, and our hunt was also going to be extended by one day. At 4 p.m. the planes showed up to move us to the new camp.

On the way into the new camp we saw some animals from the air, which was a promising sight. That was all it took for us to be ready to go again. Saturday morning dawned bright and clear and everyone took off for their hunting areas. Perry, Jack, Al, and I went across a lake and inland about two miles to set up and watch for caribou. I located myself on a ridge looking down into a valley that overlooked a sea of tundra. We had been sitting and watching for quite awhile when all off a sudden I saw a herd of caribou coming around a ridge a mile away. I yelled for Al and he came to where I was sitting. I told him to set his backpack down on the ridge so I could see it from a distance and that I was going to try to head the herd off. To try and intercept the herd I had to go through a small stand of timber and then about half a mile onto the tundra. Unfortunately, when I came out onto the tundra the herd was nowhere in sight. Tired and disappointed, I turned and went back to where I had left Al. At that time Jack and Perry showed up and we told them what had happened and we discussed how fast caribou could disappear.

As we were talking Perry spotted another group of caribou coming over the same ridge and said we needed to go cut them off. I thought to myself, "Right, I just tried that and it didn't work!" Nevertheless, Jack and I took off with Perry, heading up the ridge after the herd. This time when we came out of the woods we kept going up the ridge, which is what I should have done the first

Photograph courtesy of James M. Parker

James M. Parker, left, with his guide Perry Buckle and James' Quebec-Labrador caribou scoring 397-5/8 points. James along with his six hunting partners were all successful on this caribou hunt in 1998.

time. As we walked, or to be more accurate I should say ran, I looked over to my left and spotted the herd. I told Perry, "There they are." We stopped as they passed about 100 yards in front of us. Perry pointed to the third caribou and said he had nice tops. As the caribou stepped clear of the rest of the herd I pulled up on him only to find my scope had fogged from the heat built up from the hike. Wearing a raincoat over my hunting jacket didn't help! Fortunately, the animals didn't pay any attention to us while I was clearing my scope. The one I wanted was standing broadside so I took the shot, which dropped him instantly. When we got to my bull, I couldn't believe my eyes. I had never shot anything that large. I remember Perry and I holding the up the antlers, looking at each other and grinning from ear to ear. Perry kept telling me I had taken a really a nice animal. At the time, I didn't realize just how nice he was.

Perry caped and quartered him for the pack trip down to the boat, which was about two miles away. I took the antlers and cape and Perry took some of the meat. By the time we returned to the ridge, Jack and Al had both filled their tags with nice bulls, so we had three more animals to pack to the boat. Luckily, another guide showed up and helped us quarter the bulls. We all loaded our backpacks with meat and started down the ridge back to the boat. One of the other boats was coming by so Al was able to hitch a ride back to camp. The guides told Jack and me to walk along the lake toward camp while they went back for the rest of the meat. Jack and I walked along the edge of the lake totally exhausted, but so pumped up we were like two kids in a candy store. We had heard a lot of shooting, but had no idea how well the group had done. At dinner we found out that as a group we only needed two

QUEBEC-LABRADOR CARIBOU
Second Award - 397 5/8

▼ ▼ ▼ ▼ ▼

JAMES M. PARKER

more animals to be completely tagged out. The next morning Tom was the only one left in our group with a tag. He left camp after breakfast and about lunchtime we heard a shot. We knew that had to be Tom, so our group of seven was now done. There was another group in the camp and they all took two caribou apiece.

Since the other guys in camp had left their animals in the area where they had shot them, they now had a two-mile hike to look forward to the next morning. When Tom left to go finish his hunt they all had to go retrieve their animals. While they were gone Jack and I did a little fishing. We caught and released several nice Lake trout. When we got back to camp the other guys were coming in with their animals. I didn't realized how big my bull was until all the others were brought in. The antlers of my bull overshadowed everything else in the camp and I realized then that I had something really special.

We had just one more night in camp and the next morning was very busy. We had to repack and then help get the animals ready to go. Two planes came in and picked us up around lunchtime and flew us back to Fort Chimo. From there we caught a flight back to Montreal. We had used a 15-foot trailer to haul our gear up to Montreal. It must have been quite a sight watching us load all the antlers and meat into the trailer. We stayed the night in Montreal then drove back to my house in Michigan.

On our trip back there was a lot of laughing and joking about the entire hunt. Everyone in the group was exhausted, but extremely happy with the results of the trip. This was truly the hunt of a lifetime for all of us. ▲▲▲

Photograph by Cliff White

TROPHY STATS
▼ ▼ ▼ ▼ ▼

Category
Quebec-Labrador caribou

Score
396⁵/₈

Location
Innuksuak River, Quebec - 2000

Hunter
Michel Labbe

Length of Main Beam
Right: 47⁷/₈ Left: 50⁴/₈

Inside Spread
46³/₈

Width of Brow Palm
Right: 13⁴/₈ Left: 5²/₈

Number of Points
Right: 20 Left: 12

QUEBEC-LABRADOR CARIBOU
Third Award - 396⁵/₈

▼ ▼ ▼ ▼ ▼ ▼ ▼ ▼ ▼

MICHEL LABBE

On September 25, 2000, we were scheduled to break our spike camp on Lake Inukshuk operated by Arctic Adventures. A single engine Otter and Beaver were on their way to camp from Fort Chimo to pick up all the gear and the three guests I was guiding for the past week. With all work completed on the campsite and two unfilled tags attached to my caribou hunting permit, I borrowed Steve Ashton's .270 Winchester Featherweight Classic rifle equipped with a 2.5-8 power Leupold scope and five rounds of ammunition. I hiked the hill behind camp accompanied by Bill Carrette, cameraman working for producer/host Steve McInnis of Adventures North, who broadcasts weekly on the Outdoor Channel.

The caribou were in full migration and I was very excited glassing many mature bulls. My guiding experience has taught me to always get the big picture and I started glassing further out when a spectacular rack came into view about a half mile away. I told Bill to follow me and keep very low so we wouldn't spook any of the animals around us. We got positioned ourselves behind some boulders and waited for the group of animals to approach within shooting range. As the bull approached, I zoomed in the scope, chambered a round and told Bill to start filming. At about 200 yards the bull presented me with a prefect shot. I sighted the crosshairs and squeezed. The bullet was well placed and my trophy bull did not take another step.

I have guided caribou hunters for the past 14 years and this bull's rack was the most impressive I have ever seen. ▲▲▲

Photograph by Cliff White

TROPHY STATS

▼ ▼ ▼ ▼ ▼

Category
    pronghorn

Score
    92^6/$_8$

Location
    Harney County, Oregon - 2000

Hunter
    Sam Barry

Length of Horn
    Right: 16^6/$_8$ Left: 17^3/$_8$

Circumference of Base
    Right: 7^5/$_8$ Left: 7^4/$_8$

Length of Prong
    Right: 7^5/$_8$ Left: 7^1/$_8$

Photograph by Jack Reneau

**Sam Barry accepting his plaque and medal
from Randy Byers, Chair of the Big Game
Records Committee.**

BOONE AND CROCKETT CLUB

PRONGHORN
First Award - 92⁶/₈

▼ ▼ ▼ ▼ ▼ ▼ ▼ ▼

SAM BARRY

Having grown up on a small cattle ranch in eastern Oregon's John Day Valley, my exposure to big game hunting came at an early age. By the time I was six, I was accompanying parents and other family members and friends on mule deer hunts. I could hardly wait until I turned 12 to begin hunting big game myself. Looking back, it doesn't seem possible that I have been actively pursuing eastern Oregon's various species of big game, varmints, and game birds for 32 years. I have accumulated many fond memories of exciting and successful, and some not so successful, hunts with family and friends. It has been my good fortune to take some nice mule deer bucks and several good bull elk over the years. With the exception of one elk-hunting trip to Idaho, all of my hunting experiences have taken place in eastern Oregon's diverse landscape.

Prior to this year, my last Oregon pronghorn buck tag was drawn in 1974. It was my first pronghorn hunt and it took place the summer after graduation from high school. On the first morning of the hunt, accompanied by my older brother Wayne, I harvested the first buck we saw. He measured an even 12 inches and was taken at less than 200 yards with one shot from my new Remington 700 ADL .30-06 rifle. Over the following 26 years, I have accompanied numerous friends and relatives on pronghorn hunts in different areas in Oregon, serving variously as spotter, gutter, skinner, packer, and camp cook. My wife Agnes was lucky enough to draw a tag on her very first attempt in 1984. She made a great shot on a buck that measured approximately 12-4/8 inches, besting me by about 4/8ths of an inch, and put me in second place for bragging rights in our household for the next 16 years.

Since that first hunt, with the exception of four years attending dental school, I have applied continuously for an Oregon pronghorn buck tag in various units. I was never successful, even though other hunting partners had drawn several tags in the same period of time. After being unlucky for so long, I was about ready to give up on ever drawing another Oregon tag and considered planning for an out-of-state pronghorn hunt, but persistence eventually paid off. After 26 years and accumulating the maximum number of preference points, I finally drew my second Oregon buck pronghorn tag in 2000.

My hunt took place in southeastern Oregon's expansive and sparsely populated high desert country of Harney County. Harney is the largest county in Oregon and, at 10,200 square miles, is larger than several states. It lies at the northern boundary of the Great Basin. This is a beautiful and unique part of Oregon in which my family and I have spent considerable time exploring, viewing wildlife, varmint hunting, and visiting friends who live there. It is a semi-arid region with an average annual precipitation between 9 and 11 inches. Elevations vary from 4,000 feet to nearly 10,000 feet above sea level. The main forms of vegetation vary from irrigated meadows, grasslands, sagebrush, and greasewood to juniper and aspen trees. Ascending in altitude, one goes from marshy valleys through greasewood/sagebrush flats, rolling, grassy sagebrush hills, rocky plateaus, rimrock canyons, and finally into the mountains. In addition to the natural water supplies, the BLM and local ranchers have developed extra water holes throughout the region. Further range enhancements have included removal of the native sagebrush in large areas and replacing it with grass seedlings. These range improvements, coupled with local landowners' hayfields and grazing practices, provide excellent habitat and forage for wildlife.

The excitement of drawing the tag was somewhat dampened when I realized that I was to be in southern Florida on business the entire week before the hunt and would not return to Oregon until Sunday night of the opening weekend. The season lasted only nine days and I would miss the first three days of the hunt, as it would take all day Monday to finish packing and travel to the hunt area. It became imperative to complete any scouting before I departed for Florida. To make matters worse, the very dry, hot summer with temperatures still in the low to mid 90s created extremely high fire danger conditions in eastern Oregon. There were threats of closure of public lands and the pronghorn hunting season if the conditions did not improve.

My brother Wayne and son Brian, age eight, accompanied me on two different weekends to scout the area and visit with local ranchers, some of whom we knew from previous trips to the area. After stopping at several different ranches, we were able to obtain permission to hunt areas of their private land that are interspersed among the large tracts of BLM land and were given good tips on where to focus our scouting efforts. Our scouting goals, besides locating some nice bucks, were to learn the roads that access the different hunting areas, familiarize ourselves with the terrain and property boundaries, and locate sources of water. For our scouting trips, I stocked up on USGS topographical 7.5 minute quadrangle maps. As fine optics are essential for locating game, I borrowed my wife's "prized" Swarovski SLC 8x30 binoculars (knowing full well if I did not return them in good condition I would never hear the end of it) to go along with my Nikon Spotter XL spotting scope.

On our first scouting trip we spent one hot day in July looking over some of the area. Numerous pronghorn were spotted, but the biggest buck we saw was estimated at 14 inches. We definitely felt we could do better. It was still six weeks before the start of the season. Conditions would certainly change and the pronghorn would move accordingly, plus we had a lot more area to look over. For now we were content with making connections with the landowners and becoming familiar with the terrain.

The first weekend in August found us on our second scouting trip. Again, pronghorn appeared to be plentiful with good numbers of average sized bucks in the 10 to 14-inch range. We eventually spotted a bachelor group of eleven bucks bedded down at midday. As we glassed them from about 400 yards, we spotted a huge buck bedded in the center of the group. Using the terrain to our advantage we moved in for a closer look; most of the bucks remained bedded as we approached to within 200 yards. The one buck definitely stood out in size from the others.

This large buck, we felt, definitely had record book potential even though we have had only limited experience field judging really large pronghorns. At that time we were not completely familiar with the Boone and Crockett scoring system. This buck appeared to have longer prongs and greater mass to his horns than any other buck we had seen while scouting. He was very symmetrical with a white ivory tip visible on one side. We estimated his length at 16 inches with a six- to seven-inch prong. I decided I would be more than happy with a buck like this and hopefully, with enough time and luck, we could find him again when it counted. Finally, the group of bucks spotted us and stood up and trotted off. This allowed us to note the larger overall body size of the large buck compared to the other bucks.

As we moved on and were still recovering from the excitement of our find, we spotted another buck feeding by himself in a small valley about 1/2 mile from the group of eleven. This buck was another tremendous animal in the 16-inch class. We did not feel he had quite the mass of the other buck we had seen 20 minutes earlier, but he was close. Now we were really excited, knowing that two trophy class animals were using this area with less than three weeks to go before the season opener. I was trying not to be too optimistic, however, since I would miss the first part of the hunt. Other hunters could possibly kill one or both bucks, or at least chase them out of the area before I returned from Florida.

PRONGHORN
First Award - 92⁶/₈

SAM BARRY

The rifle I chose for the hunt was one that has served me well over the years. It was the same .30-06 that I had used 26 years ago on my first pronghorn hunt. Since then the old rifle has been customized with a 26-inch Douglas barrel and the scope upgraded to a Leupold Vari-X III 2.5-8. It is extremely accurate and consistently shoots 1/2 to 3/4-inch five shot groups at 100 yards with 165-grain Nosler Partition handloads.

On Sunday morning, August 20th, I arose in Boca Raton, Florida, at 5:00 a.m. It had been a restless night anticipating a hunt that had started the day before without me. To my delight, the flight from Ft. Lauderdale to Portland was on schedule. I made an unsuccessful attempt to sleep on the plane. Arriving in Pendleton, Oregon, at 6:30 p.m. and tired from the trip, I finished packing, loaded the pickup and trailer, and tried sleeping. The next morning I had to return phone calls and take care of customer problems before I finally hit the road for the hunt. I hitched up my utility trailer and pulled out of my driveway only to discover that in my haste I had forgotten to raise the trailer jack. Now the jack was bent backwards and unusable. I wondered what else would go wrong. I hoped this was not an indication of what the rest of the hunting trip was going to be like. Two hours later, I picked up my brother Wayne.

I was still suffering from the effects of jet lag and the previous day's six-hour drive when my hunt finally started on Tuesday morning, the fourth day of the hunting season. Shortly after daylight we started seeing pronghorn. I made a short stalk on the first herd we spotted only to find a small 12 to 13-inch buck feeding with a dozen does. Using our optics, we spotted several other small herds of 12 to 20 pronghorn that morning, containing only small bucks. Early in the afternoon we spotted a nice 14 to 15-inch buck with heavy horns and two does at 300 yards. I was tempted to end the hunt, but elected to pass since this was my first day and I hoped that at least one of the larger bucks we had seen on our second scouting trip was still around. To finish off the day, I took a long hike to check out some plateaus and basins that lay between the next major drainage and us. One of the ranchers had told us that it was a good area for an old buck to hide. I got a lot of exercise, but saw only four does and a little buck.

Wednesday started much like Tuesday — several small herds with little bucks. Late in the morning we got a quick look at what we thought was a very nice buck with three does on the run. They disappeared into a juniper thicket before we could tell much about the buck. Since we were in good pronghorn habitat I spent the next several hours hunting in the same general direction that the buck was headed. Having no luck locating him and with a blister starting on my left heel, I headed back to meet my brother. For my efforts, however, I only managed to see a smaller buck with four does and one lone doe. As the day progressed we saw five more bucks, none of which

The author waited 26 years to draw his Oregon pronghorn tag. He took this award-winning buck which scores 92-6/8 points and is a new state record in Oregon. It is the only pronghorn in the top five that is not from Arizona.

were bigger than 14 inches. Late that afternoon we spotted what we thought was the large buck feeding with a group of about 30 does, at least a half mile or more away. We were hoping this was the one we were looking for. Being so late in the day, having sore feet from two days of hiking, the terrain not ideal for stalking, not being certain if this was "the buck," and with four days remaining to hunt, we decided to pass until the next morning. We did not want to take a chance at spooking them off at dusk.

The next morning, we headed for the basin where we had left the large buck with its harem the night before. The day was clear, sunny, warm, and calm, making for ideal hunting conditions. On our way we saw another really nice buck with 15-inch horns and good mass. It was a difficult decision, but I decided to take a chance and pass on this buck until we checked the basin where we had seen the big buck the evening before. Arriving at the basin, we again spotted the herd with what appeared to be the buck we were looking for. They were feeding along at 800 to 1,000 yards on the opposite side of the valley. Again, it was in an area where it would be extremely difficult to stalk very close to them.

After studying the buck with the spotting scope for quite awhile, we were confident that this was one of the big animals we had seen on our second scouting trip. Using the terrain to our best advantage, we decided to take a chance at not being spotted while they were busy feeding. We made our way off the ridge to a patch of taller grass, hoping that they would eventually feed closer to us. For approximately the next hour or more the buck and his harem continued to feed. They would move closer to us for awhile then move farther away, as if they were taunting us. Several times a doe broke from the herd running in the opposite direction from us. I thought each time that we had been detected, and that the entire herd would take off and follow the doe. But each time the buck would take after the doe, turn her back toward the herd, hook at her rump with his horns, and drive her back into the group.

Finally, the herd made its way to within 200 yards. The buck surrounded himself with the does and offered no clear shot. I was getting more nervous by the second, fearing that they would see us and bolt, making for a very difficult running shot, or no shot at all. At approximately 9:00 a.m., the buck was finally clear of the does and presented me with a clear, broadside shot. I placed the reticule on the center of his shoulder and squeezed the trigger. Down he went. The always reliable Nosler had done its job for me once more.

As we walked up to the buck, I was overwhelmed with excitement. He was a tremendously heavy-horned buck, taller than we had estimated, and should make the Records Book. He looked even bigger now than before. At the time I had no idea that he would be a potential new World's Record. I truly did not know what a trophy I really had until stopping at my mother's place in John Day, Oregon on my way home. A family friend, Carl Stout, an avid hunter, came by to see the buck. Being a surveyor by trade, he loves to measure things and he immediately took his tape to the horns. He informed me that this was an extraordinary pronghorn and I needed to have him officially scored.

Glenn Abbott of Sandy, Oregon, a Boone and Crockett Club official measurer, contacted me the following week to green score the buck. When he saw it he was shocked at its size. The green score was 95 even. He took multiple photographs from various angles to send to Boone and Crockett for a verification of the measurement locations before his final measurement. His prongs were low and the second circumference measurement fell into the area of the prong's swelling. In the last three years, Glenn has measured eight pronghorn bucks taken in Harney County that have scored over 80 points. He returned to my home after the 60-day drying period and scored my buck at 94-6/8 points, easily a new Oregon record and potentially a New World's Record. The BUCK of a lifetime! In Springfield, Missouri, the 24th Awards Judges' Panel officially scored the buck at 92-6/8 points, just 6/8 points below the World's Record.

I look forward to hunting pronghorn in Oregon again someday, if I am fortunate enough to draw another tag. I am also eagerly anticipating many years of hunting with my son Brian and daughter Katie, both of whom have passed their hunter education classes and are excited about learning to hunt. Katie has already informed me that she is going to apply for a pronghorn tag in 2001 when she turns 12 years old.

No doubt about it. Waiting 26 years to draw my second Oregon buck pronghorn tag was definitely worth it!. ▲▲▲

New World's Record
Sagamore Hill Award

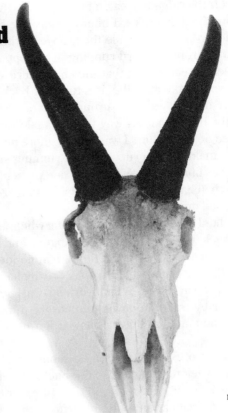

Photograph by Cliff White

TROPHY STATS
▼ ▼ ▼ ▼ ▼

Category
Rocky Mountain goat

Score
56^6/8

Location
Bella Coola, British Columbia - 1999

Hunters
G. Wober & L. Michalchuk

Owner
Gernot Wober

Length of Horn
Right: 11^7/8 Left: 10^6/8

Circumference of Base
Right: 6^4/8 Left: 6^4/8

Greatest Spread
8^7/8

Photograph by Jack Reneau

Gernot Wober accepting his plaque and medal from Randy Byers, Chair of the Big Game Records Committee.

316

ROCKY MOUNTAIN GOAT
First Award - 56⁶/₈

▼ ▼ ▼ ▼ ▼ ▼ ▼ ▼

Gernot Wober & Lawrence Michalchuk - Hunters
Gernot Wober - Owner

It all started on September 4, 1999, when Lawrence Michalchuk needed to find a new goat hunting partner after his wife announced she could not accompany him on his next hunt. Lawrence and I have known each other for eight years and have spent many hours hunting and fishing together. I was not surprised to hear his voice on the other end of the phone. "Can you leave tomorrow?" he asked.

Work was not a problem — I had been unable to find work as a mining exploration geologist for almost six months. But how was my relatively new girlfriend going to take the news that I was leaving that afternoon to go goat hunting? I put on my most loving attitude, drove to her shop at the ski resort, and mentioned my plans. Within the hour I phoned Lawrence to tell him I would arrive on Sunday at noon.

I drove nearly 500 miles from my home near Kamloops to reach Lawrence's home in Bella Coola, British Columbia. Not entirely prepared on such short notice, I borrowed longjohns, a backpack, Thermarest, raingear, and fleece pants to round out my skinny supplies. We packed homemade granola bars, trail mix, and Mr. Noodles packages for food, as well as a tent, small stove, and our bow hunting gear. Dividing the load between us, we each had approximately 60 pounds of gear to haul up the trail for a planned seven-day hunt.

From the trailhead, we slogged our way uphill for eight wet hours, climbing approximately 5,000 feet over five miles of trail. In retrospect, the only pleasant fact about the hike was that it was overcast and cool, and the view as we climbed out of the Bella Coola valley was spectacular. Low clouds draped themselves along the steep walls of the green valley and fog moved up and down the slopes as the wind changed.

Photograph courtesy of Gernot Wober

Lawrence Michalchuk standing on a goat trail along the edge of a plateau overlooking the Bella Coola Valley.

The main Bella Coola valley, which is tucked into the Coast Mountains about 250 miles west of Williams Lake, boasts some of the most magnificent views in British Columbia. Lush green valley

Photograph courtesy of Gernot Wober

Looking south with clouds in the main Bella Coola Valley, the hunters made their first camp in the flats of this wet cirque.

bottoms host great salmon rivers such as the Atnarko and Talchako, where grizzly bear roam freely. Rows of large mountain peaks line the main valley, rising from sea level to over 8,000 snow-capped feet. Blacktail deer and mule deer follow trails along valleys and steep mountain slopes. Recently, the cougar population has been increasing and wolves seem to be thriving as well.

Canadian heritage abounds as one hikes along the nearby Alexander Mackenzie Trail. Native petroglyphs can be visited along Thorsen Creek, and the rock where Alexander Mackenzie carved his name in granite in 1793 can be reached by boat on the Bentick Arm from Bella Coola harbor.

We pitched our tent in what seemed to be the only dry 10 square feet for miles around. Fall rains had saturated the ground, and small lakes and ponds were everywhere. We were centrally located in an area that held Rocky Mountain goat, with only a few miles between the locations Lawrence wanted to check out. Lawrence had been up in this area hunting for goat numerous times and knew the terrain very well.

We had a few hours before dark so we pushed our weary legs a little farther, walked to the closest spot overlooking the Bella Coola valley, and started glassing for goats. Along the edge of this east-west trending valley, it is very precipitous, well-vegetated, and perfect habitat for goat. We eventually spotted what looked to be a lone goat and probably a billie. We walked a small ridge parallel to the one the goat was on until we were 150 yards away from him. Lawrence put the spotting scope on the goat and said that it looked fairly large and was probably worth pursuing.

We both backed away slowly, walked around to the top of the ridge and started down to get closer. As we crept down small ledges without much cover, the goat spotted us and was staring directly at us from approximately 60 yards. Lawrence motioned that he was going to climb back up the ledges with the hope that the goat would watch him and allow me to get within bow range. The ruse seemed to work as I got to within 40 yards. I was directly above him with a steep downhill shot.

As I made the shot, I saw the arrow sail directly for the goat and then deflect off a small tree just in front of him. I missed! The goat bounded down the rock walls into the steep gully.

ROCKY MOUNTAIN GOAT
First Award - 56⁶/₈

▼ ▼ ▼ ▼

GERNOT WOBER & LAWRENCE MICHALCHUK

Tuesday morning we debated whether we should go back after the same goat we had seen or try somewhere else. We decided to head north to a cirque in which Lawrence had seen lots of goat activity before. Two hours of fast walking found us along the edge of a very steep walled cirque from which we could glass a large valley. We spotted eight goats in pairs and singles on a number of different ridges and ledges well over a mile away. Several seemed quite large, although we were still too far away to be certain they were billies.

Unless we could get a lot closer, determining whether these animals were billies would be impossible. Both sexes have black, well-polished horns; the nanny's horns are generally longer with narrow bases and a wide spread, while the billy's have larger bases and heavier overall circumference measurements. On average, body size is not a reliable indicator. Later that day, Lawrence made a stalk on a goat that appeared to be a billie until the very last instant. I watched him creep toward the goat carefully trying to see over rises and rocks until he was within 10 yards of the animal. He took an arrow from his quiver, readied for the shot, and suddenly froze. I took a step forward and realized, as Lawrence had, that this was a very large nanny.

By afternoon, we were quite a distance from camp so we thought it best to head back the way we came. We stopped to see if some of the goats we had spotted earlier had moved into a more favorable position. Looking over the steep edge on our side of the valley, Lawrence noticed a goat standing in thick brush approximately 50 feet up from the base of a cliff. As he looked through the scope, Lawrence said, "the bases of those horns are the biggest I've ever seen. Too bad we can't get to him from here." We watched the big goat for a while and then headed back toward camp. At the time, neither of us knew we had spotted a potential World's Record.

For the next two days we spotted and stalked numerous animals. I managed to deflect my arrows off more twigs and miss two shots on decent billies. At night as we cooked our meager dinners, all we could talk about was the large goat we had seen and the problems of accessing the area he was in. Lawrence was convinced that the goat was the largest he had ever seen in 16 years of hunting and I realized that thoughts of stalking it were consuming him. We discussed moving camp closer to the valley the goat was in but knew we couldn't climb down the cliffs at the headwall.

Friday morning brought a thick frost, but also the promise of sun for the first time in four days. After we had dried out and were comfortable again, we started hiking back to the truck. Lawrence and I had discussed things the evening before and reached a consensus that we should go after the big goat. The only way to get to him was to head home, get rid of most of our gear to lighten our loads, and start the grueling hike up the valley from the bottom. We headed to Lawrence's place looking forward to a change of socks, a hot shower, and to eating something other than sweet granola bars and Mr. Noodles.

The next day, we thrashed up a sidehill full of slide alder and devil's club for five hours to get up the new valley. Slide alder is nasty business. It grows sideways and upward 10 to 15 feet, and there is never a clearing through it—you simply climb on it or under it, often at the same time. Devil's club is aptly named for its toxic barbed needles that work their way into your skin until sufficient festering

Photograph courtesy of Gernot Wober

Gernot Wober with his award-winning Rocky Mountain goat taken in the Bella Coola Valley. The billy's final score ties the current World's Record at 56-6/8 points.

pops them out. As we had passed through a mature timber stand in the lower part of the valley, we noticed grizzly bear claw marks high up on the trees and clumps of hair stuck in the sap. It made us a little nervous, and we hoped the bear was in the lower valley looking for fish.

We almost turned back twice when the terrain and vegetation had us asking each other just what the heck we were doing here (whose brilliant idea was this anyway?). I pushed on, encouraging Lawrence to follow, but I was soon at wit's end and very frustrated with the thick brush. Next, it was Lawrence's turn to encourage me, pushing me to reach the next ridge. Finally, it appeared that the vegetation was giving way to rocky slide chutes, and we knew we were closer to our goal.

By noon, we were across the valley about a mile from the spot we had seen Mr. Big. At first we didn't see any activity, but as we were eating our lunch, Lawrence whispered, "He's there!" We watched him in the spotting scope and were amazed once again at how obviously big the billie seemed. Another billie was about 500 yards up the valley from him and we noticed that both goats had been watching our progress up the south slope for quite some time. The large billie was in exactly the same spot where we had seen him days before.

Lawrence had his bow and I carried his .270 (I had given up on bowhunting.) We agreed that Lawrence would get the first shot with his bow and if he couldn't get a shot, I could try with his bow one more time or just shoot with the rifle. We dropped down to the valley creek where we cached our large packs next to some huge boulders, which served as a good landmark. After crossing the creek, we climbed up the slide, staying hidden in the slide alder, then proceeded on our hands and knees for about an hour through tall wet grass and stinging nettles. About 100 yards from where we last saw the goat, we noticed numerous trails and tunnels through the grass where he had been feeding. The billie had a veritable grocery store to feed from with very little competition. As luck would have it, he had come down off his perch and was feeding at the base of a cliff.

Lawrence took the lead with his bow and we continued forward even slower, keeping a willow bush between the goat and us. We arrived at the base of the cliff and there was no sign of the billie! We stared at each other for a second; not wanting to admit that we had spooked him then continued our stalk. Lawrence climbed up the cliff a little ways and then moved right, following some small ledges. I moved sideways and to the right, staying in the grassy talus so I could keep a larger area of the cliff in view.

Lawrence crossed above me to the right and started gesturing emphatically that the goat was right there in the thick bushes on the cliff. I couldn't see the Billy yet so I scrambled up to where Lawrence was frantically pointing. I put the scope of the .270 up and sure enough I could make out the goat's vague outline at 70 yards. I told Lawrence I had a shot, though it was chancy through a bush. Lawrence told me to keep the scope on the billy, and he was going to try and sneak around the other side and get a bow shot at him. I watched Lawrence stalk around to the other side and then he went out of sight. Both the goat and I heard the muffled scrapes and rockfall that Lawrence couldn't help but make on the steep terrain.

After about 25 minutes of trying not to pull the trigger, I heard Lawrence yell, "just shoot him." Microseconds later the echo of the rifle shot was ringing through the valley and the goat dropped out of sight. All was silent. "Did you get him?" Lawrence shouted. "I think so," I replied, as I waited a minute longer to see if the goat was going to reappear for another shot.

As Lawrence climbed down from his perch, I crawled up on all fours to where I last saw the goat. The bed created by the goat was huge. We could have pitched a tent on the platform created in the bushes. The billy had obviously made this home for quite some time. He had an unrestricted view of most of the valley. I glanced over the edge of the bed and spotted the white fur of the goat in bushes 10 feet below. I carefully scrambled down to him and poked him with the rifle to make sure he was dead.

I had not expected the body to be so large; the billy appeared to weigh between 350 and 400 pounds. The horns were bigger than anything I had seen in my short goat hunting career. "Is it a small one?" Lawrence yelled from the base of the cliff. I knew he was being facetious—he knew it was a large billy, but just how big was the question. All I could reply was, "nope!"

Lawrence yelled back that he had just fallen 30 feet and didn't really feel like climbing up to where I was. "We've got to take the cape off up here so come on up," I shouted. By the time Lawrence scrambled his way up the cliff to where I was, I had tied a rope from a stunted spruce to the goat's head just to make sure we didn't lose it over the edge. "HOLY GOAT!" was all that Lawrence could say over and over again. "You don't know what you just shot!" was all the variation to the first theme that he could muster.

We took photos as best we could where the goat lay, as dragging the goat back up to his bed was impossible. We took the cape and the head off and let the body slip over the cliff. We clambered down the cliff to the goat's body and continued to roll the carcass all the way down to the creek in the valley bottom. We quickly deboned the hindquarters and took out the back straps, packing as much as we could carry. The blowflies found us right away and we had to fight to keep the eggs out of the meat. We carried the meat to our packs by the boulders and made camp under the overhang of the largest one. We started a fire and walked back to the goat carcass to pull off a rack of ribs and cut some steaks from the front end. Two hours later our socks were dry and we were feasting on what we knew was a very large goat.

Sunday morning we were well rested and ready for the long thrash back through the slide alder to get home. Five hours later, we made it to the truck and were on our way to Lawrence's home. After unpacking, I skinned out the goat's head and we green scored the horns. Knowing that the horns would shrink a little with drying, we conservatively measured the horns rounding some of the measurements downward. After we added all the totals and took off the deductions we ended up with a score of 58-2/8". The size of the billy we had just shot started sinking in after we realized that the goat might be in contention for the World's Record.

After the compulsory 60-day drying period, an official measurer for the Boone and Crockett Club measured the horns. With an official score of 56-6/8 points, the goat ties the current World's Record Rocky Mountain goat taken in 1949 in the Babine Mountains of British Columbia. What is intriguing is that the left horn had 1-1/8 inches broken off from the tip and could have scored even higher. ▲ ▲ ▲

Photograph by Cliff White

TROPHY STATS

▼ ▼ ▼ ▼ ▼

Category
Rocky Mountain goat

Score
54

Location
Flathead County, Montana - 1998

Hunter
Jason D. Beatty

Length of Horn
Right: $12^3/_8$ Left: $11^7/_8$

Circumference of Base
Right: 6 Left: 6

Greatest Spread
$9^2/_8$

ROCKY MOUNTAIN GOAT
Second Award - 54

▼ ▼ ▼ ▼ ▼ ▼ ▼ ▼ ▼

Jason D. Beatty

In the summer of 1998 I was lucky enough to draw a Rocky Mountain goat tag. The previous year I drew a bighorn sheep tag and was successful on the hunt. It was also a relatively easy hunt. Since my sheep hunt was easy I thought my goat hunt would be the same. Boy was I wrong! My dad has taken me into some pretty tough hunting spots, so I should have known better.

The district I drew the goat tag for was the Middle Fork of the Flathead River, which is located next to Glacier National Park, in northern Montana. The Middle Fork was about a one and a half-hour drive north from our home.

My dad did the homework. He spoke to different people about the area and poured over maps. Late that summer we headed out on a scouting trip. He had received a pretty good tip from a man who used to hunt the area. We scouted one time and did see one good billie.

On our first day we walked through the wooded terrain for about two hours, until we got to a point where we could glass the mountain. We glassed and looked for almost the entire day. As we were heading back we would occasionally stop and look back. One time we did see one goat, but it was getting too late in the day to try and get closer. The next day we went back to the same place and didn't see an animal.

The next Saturday, we decided to try a different spot and saw two goats. On Sunday we returned to the same area and couldn't find anything. Our goat season isn't very long and you can only hunt on weekends. I was starting to get a little nervous.

On the third weekend we saw nothing either day. We did have an interesting experience however, or should I say a scary experience. As we hiked up the side of the mountain, we were looking around and glassing. Dad stopped suddenly and told me, I better find some cover. "Suck yourself up close to the side." There was a big rock coming down on us. A rock about the size of a truck tire came rolling down, bouncing off the side of the mountain. It in turn, loosened other rocks, and we were caught in a small rockslide. It was really frightening. I've never been in a rockslide before, and don't care to be in another one.

Dad kept trying to talk me into staying overnight on the trail, but I kept telling him no. There was a lot of bear activity that year, so I wasn't about to stay out overnight.

On Saturday morning of the last weekend, we headed out again. Dad told me to pack a big lunch because we'd be going out early and hiking in the dark. It was getting late in the season and snow was on the ground. We returned to the first place we had seen a goat. While glassing, we spotted two goats, one off to the right and one to the left. The one on the right was so high it would have been a steep climb to get to him. My dad was carrying the binoculars, so he asked me which one I wanted. I picked the one on the right since he was the closest. We packed up and hiked for at least two and a half-hours. He was straight up and the only thing on the other side of him was blue sky. In order not to expose ourselves, we had to keep backtracking. When we got about 250 yards from him, we stopped. He was bedded down on the top of a rock and all we could see was the top of his back.

Dad kept an eye on him through his binoculars and knew he was a big one, but he didn't tell me how big. I guess he didn't want me to get too nervous. He told me that we needed to get parallel with him and get a good rest. As I started to move, the goat stood up. Dad said, "Go ahead and take your shot right here." I shot and hit him a little low. The shot didn't put him down for good, but it did knock him off his feet. He started rolling down the steep mountainside toward us. We were standing on a very narrow trail with a steep cliff on the other side. I just knew he was going to roll down the cliff and we would have to go all the way down to the bottom and find him, probably with a broken horn. We got lucky when he stopped, right on the edge, with his head hanging over the side. I quickly finished him with a shot to his neck. Boy, was that close! We knew he was a nice big one, but didn't realize how big.

There was no time to stand around. We had to pack him up and head out. It was getting late and we had to get out before dark. We hustled down the mountain and back to the truck. I thought to myself, boy am I lucky.

On the way home I couldn't believe I was so lucky to get a goat this year and a sheep last year. My ram scored high enough to get in the Records Book and now I have a goat that could make the book. I really couldn't believe it.

We took my goat to the taxidermy shop in Columbia Falls. On first sight, Mark Stanley, the taxidermist, felt it was the new state record. We weren't quite as sure as he was, but it sounded great.

If you've never been on a goat hunt you may not realize how tough it can be. It really amazes me how they can survive where they do. I know one thing for sure, if it wasn't for my dad's hunting abilities and his help, I would never have taken this goat. So, thanks Dad! I also had a little extra help. My grandma, Dad's mom, passed away in August so she didn't get to see my goat. She would have been so excited. I do feel she was with me on the hunt, so I know she knows. ▲▲▲

Moments in Measuring...

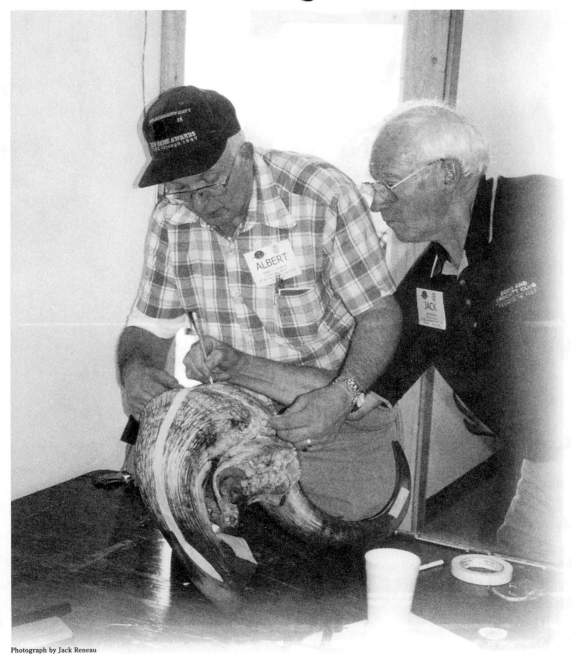

Photograph by Jack Reneau

Albert C. England and Jack Graham mark the center line of the boss for measuring the length of the horn on M.R. James' First Award muskox. The bull scores 126-2/8 points and was taken with bow.

TROPHY STATS

▼ ▼ ▼ ▼ ▼

Category
 Rocky Mountain goat

Score
 $52^4/_8$

Location
 Kittitas County, Washington - 1998

Hunter
 James L. Hawk, Jr.

Length of Horn
 Right: $10^5/_8$ Left: $10^1/_8$

Circumference of Base
 Right: 6 Left: 6

Greatest Spread
 $6^7/_8$

Photograph by Jack Reneau

James L. Hawk, Jr., accepting his plaque
and medal from Randy Byers, Chair of the
Big Game Records Committee.

ROCKY MOUNTAIN GOAT
Third Award - 52⁴/₈

▼ ▼ ▼ ▼ ▼ ▼ ▼ ▼ ▼

JAMES L. HAWK, JR.

On and off for the past 15 years I have submitted my entry for a goat permit in Washington State. For the last four years I've made sure to enter each year so I could accumulate points and increase my chances of being drawn. In August 1998, my persistence finally paid off and I was drawn for a goat tag in the Blazed Ridge Unit.

I didn't have much time for scouting because at the FNAWS banquet in February of that year I bought a caribou hunt in Alaska. I was leaving the 24th of August for a week of hunting.

Opening day for goat hunting was Sunday, September 13, and three of my friends, Don, Dave, and Dennis went out with me to look for goats. It was clear and hot, and in no time at all we spotted a lone goat that looked good through the spotting scope. After watching the goat for 20 minutes we decided to make a try for it. He was standing on a rock jutting out of the trees. After two hours of hiking and sliding backwards we made it up above where we had last seen the goat, but he was nowhere to be seen. We had lost him in the trees and rocks. As we circled around the ridge on our way back down we saw another goat. Unfortunately, he had spotted us first, and was quickly off his rock and into the timber. We had been busy looking at fresh cougar tracks and had missed our second opportunity in just under four hours. Maybe this wasn't going to be as easy as I thought.

The next weekend I went out by myself. It was raining, so I spent most of the day glassing and waiting for the clouds to lift. Late in the day I spotted two goats, one by the treeline and the other on the rocks about a half mile up on the ridge. The sky was clearing so

Photograph courtesy of James L. Hawk, Jr.

The author's hunting partner, Dave Gobel, backing down the ravine to recover the downed Rocky Mountain goat.

I decided to come back the next day and give the rocks a chance to dry. The next morning there were three men already up there. Two of them were up in the rocks and I stayed back to watch them with the other member of their party. He had taken his goat the week before, a dry nanny with 9 1/2-inch needle sharp horns. I was a little disappointed that I hadn't made it to

The author with his award-winning Rocky Mountain goat taken in Kittitas County, Washington, in 1998. He had spotted the goat twice earlier on the ledge of a 400-foot rock wall. Days later the goat was taken at the base of the rock wall. It scores 52-4/8 points.

the trailhead first and decided to head over to another valley, which I had found years earlier that always held goats. By late afternoon I had made it into the valley, and sure enough there were goats everywhere. I spotted eleven goats in all. Five nannies and their four kids were at one end of the ridge and two billies were further down on the ridge. The billy, which I ended up getting two weeks later, was hanging out on the north face of the cliff. He was on a ledge in the middle of a sheer 400-foot rock wall. I waited until sunset but the goat never left the ledge. As I was hiking back I was hoping my luck would soon change. I figured this was a good-sized goat, but had no idea at the time how good. The following weekend my friend Dennis and I went back to the canyon and got within 40 yards of the nanny and kids, but the two billies never came up to the top of the ridge. Three days later I went back, but the goat I had my eye on still wouldn't leave the ledge. I didn't even try for him because I knew if I shot him I'd never be able to get him down from the ledge.

I was starting to get a little anxious. I had been hunting for three weekends in a row, including several days during the week, and already had done a week of hunting in Alaska. I figured my understanding wife of one year, Jill, wasn't going to put up with my hunting adventures much longer this season.

ROCKY MOUNTAIN GOAT
Third Award - 52⁴/₈

▼ ▼ ▼ ▼ ▼

JAMES L. HAWK, JR.

On October 3, 1998, my friend Dave and I went back to the same valley, hoping that luck would be on our side this time. We got to the trailhead before sunrise. There was enough light to see because of the fresh snowfall the night before. By the time we hiked into the valley it had begun to snow and visibility was poor. It took several hours, but when the clouds lifted we spotted the five nannies and four kids on the opposite ridge, but the two billies were not with them. As we worked our way back up the ridge we saw a goat lying by himself at the base of the cliff. As we hurried to get into position for a shot we could see a snow shower was moving in. As I took off my jacket and was about to lie down I happened to look to the right and saw another goat walking away along the base of the cliff. We quickly glassed the two goats to determine which one had bigger horns. Both goats were about 200 yards away in opposite directions. Luckily, I remembered that two weeks earlier when I had seen these same two goats close together one had a much bigger body. I could tell the second goat walking away was the bigger one. I laid down, got a solid rest, and squeezed off the first shot from my .30-06. The 150-grain bullet hit him high behind his front shoulders.

He dropped down part way, but was up in a flash and moving out. I shot twice more, but shot too high. On my fourth shot I aimed at the bottom of his chest since I was about four or five hundred feet above him. This one hit him solid behind his front shoulders. He tumbled down the steep slope about 200 yards before he stopped. Dave looked at me and said "You shot him and it's your tag; you're on your own." I hoped he was joking.

We took a long rope from our packs and tied it off to a tree just above a rock ravine. We left our guns and took just our meat packs down with us. We wrapped the rope around one arm and backed down the ravine. Dave went first; not that I was nervous, I just wanted to make sure the knot I had tied around the tree would hold, and it did. Once we made it down to the goat we saw just how big he actually was. We figured he must have weighed between 300 and 350 pounds. We skinned out the entire goat and then boned all the meat off the animal. Now we had before us the tough task of packing about 100 pounds each in our packs off the ridge. It was nightfall as we got out, more dead than alive. I was thankful to have a good friend with a strong back to help me.

I took the goat to Bruce at SeaTac Taxidermy. He green scored him over 54 inches and I was shocked! The old state record from 1966 was 52-6/8 points. The hard part was waiting the required 60-day drying period. I hoped there wouldn't be much shrinkage. In early December, Russ Spalding, a volunteer and official measurer for the Boone and Crockett Club, scored it at 54-2/8 points. In Springfield, Missouri, the 24th Awards Judges' Panel gave the billy an official score of 52-4/8 points. His longest horn is 10-5/8 inches. The other one was broken and only measures 10-1/8 inches with 6 inch bases. If it wasn't for the help of good friends and my great and understanding wife, I may not have had my hunt of a lifetime. ▲▲▲

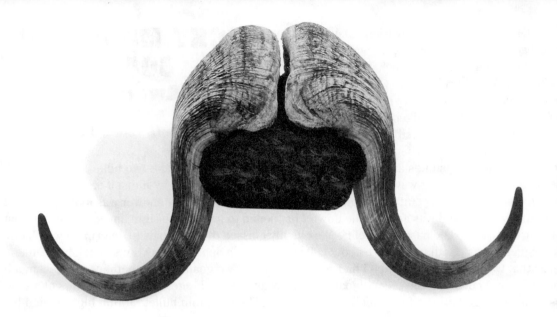

TROPHY STATS

▼ ▼ ▼ ▼ ▼

Category
muskox

Score
126²/₈

Location
Kugaryuak River, Northwest
Territories - 2000

Hunter
M.R. James

Length of Horn
Right: 29²/₈ Left: 29⁴/₈

Width of Boss
Right: 10⁵/₈ Left: 11

Greatest Spread
27⁷/₈

**M.R. James accepting his plaque and medal
from Randy Byers, Chair of the Big Game
Records Committee.**

MUSKOX
First Award - 126²/₈

▼ ▼ ▼ ▼ ▼ ▼ ▼ ▼ ▼

M.R. JAMES

"No closer!" cautioned my Inuit guide Charlie Bolt, raising his rifle just in case. "Shoot now. Shoot the white-horned bull."

"Easier said than done," I mumbled to myself. Over 50 yards of frozen, windswept tundra still stretched between us and the two huge muskox that stood facing us, pawing at the snow menacingly while lowering their heavy-horned heads as if contemplating an imminent charge. What would have been a simple shot for any rifleman was next to impossible for a savvy bowhunter. Even if the buffeting crosswind miraculously failed to affect my arrow's flight and accuracy, I knew from four decades of bowhunting experience that a frontal shot on such a large animal would be pure folly. Too much thick hair and hide, tough muscle, and dense bone stood between my shaving-sharp broadhead and the bull's vitals. Somehow I had to cut the remaining distance by nearly half and work myself into position for a broadside shot - preferably without further provoking my obviously worried guide or the two agitated bulls. Fair chase bowhunting for muskox, I was quickly discovering, can be an exercise in frustration. My hunting partner, Bob Ehle of Pennsylvania, and I had lost a full day of hunting to the fickle Arctic weather gods. Then, after locating two good bachelor bulls just after dawn on our first clear day afield, we parked the snow machines and began our stalk only to watch in stunned disbelief as the twin bulls instantly whirled and galloped away upon catching sight of us. Time after frustrating time throughout the long day, stalk after fruitless stalk, we tried and failed to move within good bow range. Fifty to 60 yards was as close as we could get. That's tempting yardage, but impractical in bitter cold, wind-whipped shooting conditions. The last we saw of "our" two trophy bulls they were disappearing over a ridgeline a couple of miles away - still running!

Leg weary, wind-burned, and emotionally drained, Bob and I returned to our comfy tent camp that night with a much better appreciation of the daunting task facing us. However, despite our disappointment, we agreed it hadn't been worth the risk of wounding and losing one of those great shaggy beasts — or forcing our guides to finish off a poorly hit bull with a bullet. We'd do it our way or no way.

The next morning we climbed into our enclosed sleds that were roped behind the guides' snow machines and headed out across a great flat that resembled a snow-covered moonscape. Soon we cut the meandering trail of two big nomadic bulls made sometime the previous night. After a hurried and animated conference, our excited guides turned their snowmobiles to follow the tracks. One hour passed. Two. Three. The sunny but frigid morning slipped slowly away as we paralleled the bulls' trail, our hopes soaring each time we approached a promising ridge, but falling each time we topped the rise only to see more empty tundra stretching endlessly ahead of us. It seemed as if we were following tundra phantoms, not flesh and blood creatures whose ancestors have tracked across these same icy wastelands since prehistoric times.

Riding in a bouncing wooden sled across miles of frozen tundra is a bone–jarring, tooth-rattling experience. Our base camp was perhaps 90 to 100 miles from the small village of Kugluktuk on the shores of the Arctic Ocean - and how far we ranged from camp in our daily search for *oomingmak*, the

Photograph courtesy of M.R. James

The author with his award-winning archery bull scoring 126-2/8 points.

bearded one, is anyone's guess. All I knew was it would be a long hike back to civilization in the event of any mechanical breakdowns. But there was obvious comfort in hunting in pairs and in knowing a radio was our link to the outside world.

It was late March. Already several days had passed since I winged north from my Montana home, overnighted in Yellowknife, and met my hunting companion and two other muskox hunters who had also booked a hunt with veteran north country outfitter Fred Webb. Together we caught a morning flight to Coppermine to embark on what was an unforgettable adventure. I was discovering, just as every muskox hunter I knew had told me, the appeal of this hunt lies in the overall experience. In this stark, frozen land. In the native guides whose knowledge of the Arctic and its wildlife is amazing. In testing oneself in an unfriendly environment where wind and bitter cold are constant companions. In finding a unique creature that is a true survivor in an inhospitable world, a special animal largely unchanged since Stone Age hunters pursued the forebears of these same beasts armed only with flint-tipped spears.

Back to the present, our whining snowmobiles crested yet another ridge - and there they were! The two bulls, dark dots against a sea of frozen white, were plodding on perhaps a mile ahead. The Inuits quickly braked their machines and held a brief conference while Bob and I studied the distant bulls through our binoculars.

Then we were off again, Bob and his guide veering to the left while Charlie steered his snowmobile in a looping arc to the right. Moments later we eased to a stop just below a ridgeline. As Charlie shouldered his pack and rifle, I stretched ride-stiffened muscles and pulled my bow once to make certain the rough ride or sub-zero cold hadn't rendered it useless. And then we were moving to the top of the ridge and beyond, dropping into a shallow bowl where the bulls should appear.

BOONE AND CROCKETT CLUB

And suddenly the bulls were there. But this time there was no turning and running. This time when these two old bulls spotted us moving slowly down the frozen rise they simply stopped and turned to face us, waiting and watching without apparent concern. It wasn't until we'd closed the distance to perhaps half a hundred yards that they began to paw the snow and shake their wooly heads. That's precisely when Charlie readied his rifle and warned we'd moved close enough for me to shoot the white-horned bull.

Turning, I shook my head. "Closer," I said. "Can't shoot. Too far." And with each word I took another cautious step closer to the waiting bulls.

Shaking his hooded head, Charlie moved after me. "Close enough," he insisted. "Shoot now." "Can't," I said again. "Too far."

At 40 yards I raised my tinted goggles and slipped the mitten off my shooting hand, slowly easing to my knees to study the muskox, with my worried guide crouching just behind me. The bulls still offered only an impossible head-on shot. Cautiously, I inched closer still, not taking my eyes from the shaggy apparitions looming before me, wispy guard hairs fluttering in the whipping crosswind.

Although I would have preferred to close the distance by another 5 to 10 yards, I sensed this was as near as I could get without inviting real trouble. Staring at two agitated muskox occasionally pawing the snow — with only some 100 feet of empty air between us — I couldn't help but recall Fred Webb's story of one rifle-toting client who had been charged, trampled, and injured when he violated a bull's perceived "safety zone." I certainly didn't want to have to explain how I came to get hoofprints all over my snow parka.

Speaking softly, I asked Charlie to move slowly to my left. If the bulls concentrated on my guide and turned to face him as he eased sideways, maybe I could get the broadside shot I needed. And the tactic worked perfectly, except when the bulls turned my white-horned bull was perfectly screened by his traveling companion. And even when Charlie moved behind me and edged to my right, the bigger bull wouldn't turn far enough to present me with the shot I needed for a quick, clean kill. Talk about a frustrating standoff!

As my mind raced for some solution, I spotted Bob and his guide watching the unfolding drama from a ridgeline maybe 150 yards away. A new idea struck me and I motioned Bob to circle around and approach from behind us. Within 10 minutes he was kneeling beside me, listening as I quickly explained what I had in mind while Charlie and Bob's Inuit guide warily eyed the increasingly nervous bulls, rifles ready for instant action in case the bulls charged.

Wishing Bob good luck, I carefully got to my feet and began sidling to my left. On cue, the two bulls turned as I moved and moments later I saw Bob draw, hold, and release. His arrow caught the second bull mid-body, angling forward. Immediately the mortally hit bull spun and lunged away in a spray of hoof-churned snow. My white-horned bull trailed close behind.

Bob's arrow quickly weakened the lumbering bull. He labored to the nearest ridgetop before pausing to bed down while his companion paced close beside him. Trailing quickly after them, Charlie and I ducked out of sight and crept closer. When I finally rose to peer over the ridge, Bob's bull lay only 20 short yards away. My bull was standing just behind him, stubbornly refusing to leave. And when he turned and strode into the clear, he was perfectly broadside. My arrow struck him just behind the right foreleg, its 3-blade broadhead burying deep in the off shoulder.

The huge white-horned bull spun in a tight circle and mere seconds later collapsed beside Bob's bull. Our frustrating, memorable, once in a lifetime Arctic adventure was over. Not only had we collected two great big game trophies, we'd done it our way — a very special way. ▲▲▲

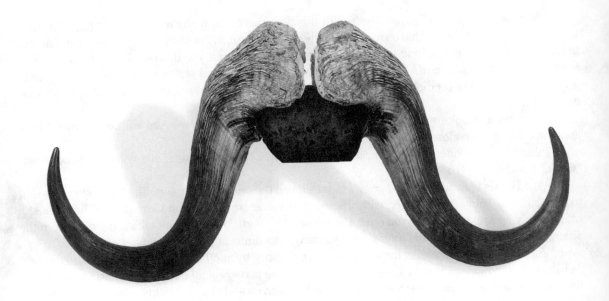

TROPHY STATS

▼ ▼ ▼ ▼ ▼

Category
   muskox

Score
   125

Location
   Coppermine, Northwest
   Territories - 1998

Hunter
   William L. Cox

Length of Horn
   Right: 28^6/$_8$ Left: 28^7/$_8$

Width of Boss
   Right: 11^1/$_8$ Left: 11^3/$_8$

Greatest Spread
   29^1/$_8$

Photograph by Jack Reneau

William L. Cox accepting his plaque and medal from Randy Byers, Chair of the Big Game Records Committee.

BOONE AND CROCKETT CLUB

MUSKOX
Second Award - 125

▼ ▼ ▼ ▼ ▼ ▼ ▼ ▼ ▼

WILLIAM L. COX

The story for this muskox hunt was not available.

TROPHY STATS

▼   ▼   ▼   ▼   ▼

Category
muskox

Score
124⁴/₈

Location
Kugaryuak River, Northwest Territories - 2000

Hunter
Ronald G. McKnight

Length of Horn
Right: 30 Left: 29⁷/₈

Width of Boss
Right: 10²/₈ Left: 10¹/₈

Greatest Spread
29⁴/₈

MUSKOX
Third Award - 124⁴/₈

▼ ▼ ▼ ▼ ▼ ▼ ▼ ▼

RONALD G. McKNIGHT

My Inuit guide said we were on the Coppermine River, but looking around all I could see was snow and ice. I couldn't tell where we were. All was brilliant white in the clear, sunny, but very, cold light.

How I got here is the beginning of this story. Like all good adventures, this one began with a dream. Then came the savings plan mixed with good research, procuring more good equipment and hooking up with a good (and dependable) hunting partner. In this latter category, I am blessed. My longtime friend, Bob Anderson of Casper, Wyoming, has hunted near and far with me for many years. He is always game for a new adventure, is adaptable, does not complain, and his favorite line is "We'll either get a good one or we won't." And when we don't, it is okay, because we have shared another special time in the wilds.

As we stepped off the small Canadian plane into the crisp, -15° air at Kugluktuk at noon on March 19, 2000, it happened exactly like Webb Outfitting (NWT) LTD. had promised. We were greeted by Fred and Martin, loaded into a vintage pickup, and rushed down to the provincial government office where we secured all necessary paperwork to begin our muskox hunt. And, with continued honed efficiency, we were soon changed into our arctic gear and standing on the ice at Coronation Bay. The handmade sleds were soon loaded, guides

Photograph courtesy of Ronald G. McKnight

The author with his muskox taken after days of hunting in the arctic cold. The bull scores 124-4/8 points.

assigned and the snow machines warming up. It was gloriously sunny and a balmy -20°, when we left with our guides. After three hours of steady travel and many miles, the sky began to darken, the ceiling dropped to nearly zero, and everything was shades of gray and white. Visibility was only a few yards. I KNEW it had been too good of a beginning! Our guides had been watching the sky, the sun and the horizon all along our journey — obviously keeping track of our position. But with no visibility, they wisely called a halt as it was not smart and too dangerous to continue. We hastily set up "Who Knows Where Camp #1." The wind was blowing like hell, and without the late afternoon sun the thermometer had dropped to -37°. We had to tie the tents to the sleds and snow machines to keep them from blowing away. The floor of the tents

The tents at "Who Knows Where Camp #1" were secured to the sleds and snow machines to keep them from blowing away. The floors of the tents were made of caribou hides.

consisted of caribou hides lying on the ice and upon these we settled down to an early supper of freeze-dried surprise (tasted great!), hot tea and frozen Eskimo bread. The storm died down a few hours before dark, so we hunted and glassed from the series of ridges behind camp, but no muskox.

Early the next morning we were blessed with clear, but still colder weather. Our savvy Inuit guides decided that we must hunt in pairs for safety. We began our second day of hunting and continued all day employing the following scenario. Approach a ridge, sneak up the back-side, glass until the binoculars froze to our cheeks, back off, thaw out, and move to the next ridge. That was our day, along with short rests for hot tea. We were having a great time. At nearly dark, we stopped in a sheltered swale for a rest and hot tea. The day's tally was one solitary snowshoe hare. The land is stark with little cover except for rocky outcrops and rolling hills. Everything else was frozen snow and ice. I was thinking that it is a true miracle that animals can live, and even thrive in this land. It was very cold as the sun dipped below the low hills, and we were again encamped for the night. This night would prove to be the coldest, or was I losing my patience with the constant cold? All I know is that I slept little and was glad to be up and moving around again in the morning. It was still before dawn when my guide, John Kolioktak thawed our bread on the Coleman stove and melted snow. Soon warm fluids and nourishment revived our spirits.

On the trail of muskox this day was exciting, but difficult. It was very cold and my mustache (go to the high arctic clean shaven!) was frozen to my balaclava, my cheeks, and even to my goggles. We hunted some 30 miles and saw only a half dozen arctic foxes. We spent most of our time glassing from a ridgetop where there were fresh muskox tracks and scat. In the early afternoon we finally located about 40 muskox feeding in a long valley five miles distant. A strategy was decided and we dropped over a low saddle and moved the snow machines along a parallel valley, stopping quite distant from the herd. At every opportunity we glassed and confirmed that were are at least eight big bulls in the herd.

MUSKOX
Third Award - 124⁴/₈
▼ ▼ ▼ ▼ ▼

RONALD G. McKNIGHT

Bob got the first shot on this hunt. After a final stop to catch our breath and to get our "muskox fever" under control, check and load our rifles, it was time to finish the climb to the ridgetop. It took nearly a half hour in unpleasant cold before the bull that Bob had chosen stepped clear. One shot from his trusty .300 and the bull was down. The muskox separated into three groups and two bulls, big bulls, broke over a near ridge. I liked the odds, so John and I ran up the ridge and flopped down behind a small boulder frozen on the skyline. I placed the crosshairs behind the shoulder of the lead bull and squeezed off a shot. It was true, and no follow-up shot was necessary. The muskox died quickly and both Bob and I had the ultimate trophies of a lifetime.

Bob and his guide, and John and I had to work very quickly to remove the heads and capes before the carcasses froze solid. This was accomplished after two hours had passed and four or five pairs of cloth gloves had frozen stiff! The carcasses were then loaded on the sled for the meat larder and we encamped for another cold but happy night on the ice and snow. A long day was needed to reach the safety of Kugluktuk, and a hot shower and hot meal at the Enokhok Inn. A whiskey on the rocks never tasted so good!

Bob and I had a great adventure and harvested two great bulls that scored well up in the all-time records book. They will forever be coveted memories of our high arctic adventure. ▲▲▲

Photograph by Cliff White

TROPHY STATS

▼ ▼ ▼ ▼ ▼

Category
muskox

Score
123²/₈

Location
Norman Wells, Northwest Territories - 1999

Hunter
Darcy Hernblad

Length of Horn
Right: 27 Left: 27²/₈

Width of Boss
Right: 10⁵/₈ Left: 10⁴/₈

Greatest Spread
25⁴/₈

BOONE AND CROCKETT CLUB

MUSKOX
Fourth Award - 123²/₈

▼ ▼ ▼ ▼ ▼ ▼ ▼ ▼ ▼

DARCY HERNBLAD

This was a hunting trip that I had dreamed about for years. I was lucky enough to have my name pulled in a drawing for one of two muskox tags for resident hunters of the Northwest Territories, Canada. I started doing my homework to find out the best time of year to go, as I had an eight-month window to hunt. The area where I would hunt, according to the draw rules, was east of a community called Norman Wells and west of Great Bear Lake.

I had never hunted this area before. I found out only one muskox had ever been taken in this area since the start of the draws several years earlier. This didn't bother me, as I knew I would love the hunt whether I saw a muskox or not. I also had no problems deciding on a hunting partner for this trip. I called my good friend, John Kowerchuk, with whom I had done several hunts. We both guide together at a caribou camp in Northwest Territories. I explained I had drawn for a muskox hunt around the Norman Wells area and asked if he would like to go with me. He instantly replied, "I'll start packing my stuff right away." John is one of those hunting partners you can count on for anything. We decided we were going to drive to Norman Wells, via all season road and winter road. We both live in Yellowknife, Northwest Territories, and the road trip would be 650 kilometers of all season road and 250 kilometers of winter road. We later found out that it is one of the worst roads in the world, or at least we thought so. It was mandatory that you carry chains before you drive on this road. We decided to hunt the last week of February 1999 since the winter road closed in mid April of every year.

Photograph courtesy of Darcy Hernblad

There were trees in the area, but they were sparse. The author ended up taking his bull high up on a ridge near Lenin Lake.

When the day finally came to leave for the hunt we were all packed and ready for anything. The first part of the road was fine. The last part of the winter road was tearing the front end of my truck apart; however, all I could think about was the muskox hunt and nothing else mattered. NOTHING! We arrived in Norman Wells at 10 o'clock that night and stayed at a friend's house, who just happened to have drawn a muskox tag in this area a few years earlier.

The author with his self-guided muskox scoring 123-2/8 points taken between Norman Wells and Great Bear Lake in Northwest Territories. The bull charged the hunter and presented a broadside shot at just 40 yards.

The next day we were up early and on our way. I was so excited I didn't sleep too well even after driving all day. The temperature was approximately -15°C, which for this area at this time of year was very pleasant. It could have easily been -40°C.

On the first day of the hunt toward late afternoon, John had spotted a muskox high up on a ridge near Lenin Lake. John mentioned to me that since this muskox was by himself he was probably a real big, old bull and was separated from the herd. We were about three miles away when we spotted him, so it was hard to judge his size and we decided to get a closer look. All dressed in white camouflage, we blended in with the terrain well. This terrain was completely open with no trees, but had dips and valleys that worked to our advantage. There were trees in the area but they were sparse. The snow in the open areas where this muskox was located was fairly easy to walk on as the wind had blown it into a hard crust. The snow in and around the wooded areas required the use of snowshoes since it was very soft. There were times we had to keep changing back and forth as the snow conditions changed as we moved forward. After a lengthy walk we got to an area where we could get a better look at the muskox with the use of binoculars. Now I was getting excited, and I knew this was going to be a day to remember. When I focused in with my binoculars I could not believe what I was seeing; it was a huge muskox with a boss that was dominant, even from a long way back on his head. John stated, "Do your thing, Darcy, and I'll come in slowly behind you since there is no cover and he has a good view for about a 1,000 yards in all directions." I stayed low, moving slowly and relied on my snow-white suit, slow moving and the slight wind advantage. Every time I looked at the bull I could not believe how majestic he looked standing there all by himself. I kept thinking I had to get to about 400 yards to be comfortable to shoot; however, if I could get within 200 yards it would even be better. As I kept moving up slowly I was getting tired from crawling on my hands and knees, but kept pressing on. I eventually got within 70 yards of the muskox; however, the muskox was now facing me, which did not leave me with a good clean shot with my .300 Winchester Magnum.

MUSKOX
Fourth Award - 123²/₈

▼ ▼ ▼ ▼ ▼

Darcy Hernblad

As I stayed crunched down I was trying to figure out a way to get a good shot. I decided to stand up and let the muskox see me and as he would turn to run I would be able to place a shot in the heart or lung areas. Well, this is not exactly what happened. The muskox was so startled when he saw me he let out a loud snort and decided to charge. He came straight at me and just when I was about to pull the trigger he stopped, let out another loud snort and turned his body sideways. I could not believe I was going to be this lucky. I now had a trophy muskox standing sideways in front of me at 40 yards. It did not take me long to figure out that I had better pull the trigger. With one close range shot the muskox fell to his knees, the excitement was outstanding. I shouted at John, and he was shouting at me, "You got him!"

John was moving quickly in my direction and I had my thumb up in the air to show the excitement I was feeling. We both could not believe the size of the boss on this muskox. At this time we both knew we had something special. I then said to John, "This muskox is yours as much as it is mine."

I could not believe our hunt was over so fast, and it was coming to an end before either us wanted it to. We did all the caping and the work required to take care of the meat and remaining hide, and then we radioed in for a pick up. The next day we spent visiting people in Norman Wells and getting all the paper work done at the wildlife office. The following day we were on our way home over the roughest road in the world with big smiles on our faces. My truck was making funny noises now from pounding so hard on the road on the way up, but I did not care as the muskox in the back was all I needed to keep the smile on my face, which lasted for weeks. ▲▲▲

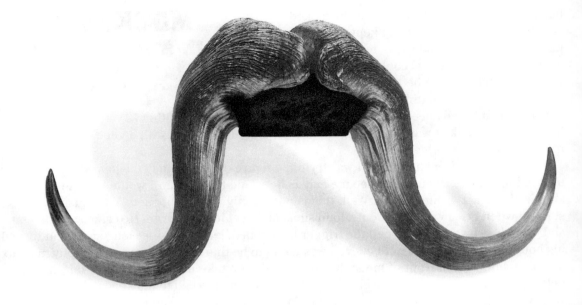

TROPHY STATS

▼ ▼ ▼ ▼ ▼

Category
muskox

Score
123

Location
Cambridge Bay, Northwest Territories - 2000

Hunter
Raymond L. Howell, Sr.

Length of Horn
Right: $29^{1}/_{8}$ Left: $28^{7}/_{8}$

Width of Boss
Right: $10^{2}/_{8}$ Left: $10^{3}/_{8}$

Greatest Spread
$28^{2}/_{8}$

MUSKOX
Fifth Award - 123

▼ ▼ ▼ ▼ ▼ ▼ ▼ ▼ ▼

RAYMOND L. HOWELL, SR.

I scheduled the hunt with Jerome and Halina Knap of Canadian North Outfitters. My goal was to try to harvest a Boone and Crockett muskox with my bow. Jerome told me that I should hunt the Kent Peninsula with the Inuits, as they were very experienced bow hunting guides.

As I left Edmonton, Canada and flew into Yellowknife, the pilot told us that the temperature was minus 20 degrees and when I stepped off the plane and walked to the terminal I thought to myself, "This isn't so bad." After re-boarding the plane, we flew into Cambridge Bay. The pilot now announced that it was -35°! As I stepped onto the runway, I thought to myself, "You really did it now." I was wearing a thin jacket and no long johns. The wind was blowing so hard that I believed within the first few seconds off the plane every hair on my body was frozen. I took my luggage into the restroom and immediately put on proper clothing.

For several months I had prepared for this hunt by locating the right type of clothing that would withstand wind chills of -90°, which I believe it was the day I stepped off the airplane in Cambridge Bay. My choice of clothing was a combination from Cabelas and Northern Outfitters. I had done a lot of alterations on my clothing in order to give me enough clearance on my chest and bow arm to assure me of the accuracy needed for at least a 40-yard shot. I had talked to several bow hunters who had hunted in extreme cold conditions and everyone had a different way of setting up their bows so that lubricants wouldn't freeze. I called my good friend Terry Ragsdale at PSE and asked what he knew about cold-weather hunting. He told me not to worry about changing anything on my bow. It would perform as well at 100° above as it would at 100° below zero. This was based on the research that PSE had done in the past.

Shortly after my arrival, the weather in Cambridge Bay became so severe that we couldn't fly into the small village near the Kent Peninsula for the next two days. We were forced to stay in a little hotel in town. Finally, they announced that the weather was clear enough to fly and when we arrived at the airport, I took pictures of the plane as they were loading it with our gear, and was thinking to myself that it's so cold outside that I can't believe the plane doesn't just snap in two!

After arriving in the village, I met my guide Peter and his family. All the children in the village were excited to meet us and they were playing and jumping on us as if we were part of their family. The amazing thing to me was watching the kids play in the sub-zero temperatures. They would take their sleds and run up and down the snow-covered hills all day.

My home for the week was a small cabin with a round barrel stove, and after unpacking I was eager to check out my archery equipment. I quickly found out that I could only put on my under-garments inside and the outerwear had to be put on after going outside, otherwise I would start sweating and then freeze when I did get outside. I was disoriented in the cold wind with my space-suit type clothing, but my main concern was that my bow had not been damaged during my travels. The weather conditions were good and my guides wanted to leave as soon as possible to their pre-scouted areas to start looking for muskox. I told my guide Pete I was not going hunting until I knew

After months of locating the right type of clothing and equipment for the arctic hunt, the author took this award-winning muskox scoring 123 points.

my bow was shooting accurately. He walked over and picked up a piece of 1-inch thick plywood and started walking away from me. I wasn't quite sure at first what he was doing. He put the plywood in the snow about 30 yards from where I was standing. When he got back to me he said, "There's your target." I told him that I wanted to shoot with the wind and not into the cross wind because it would make my arrow do all sorts of "funny" things.

There was a 55-gallon drum about 25 yards downwind from where we were standing. I asked Pete if it was okay if I stuck a hole in it rather than shoot at the plywood. I could tell by the expression on his face that he didn't think I was "dealing with a full deck." I picked a spot on the drum and released an arrow, and to Pete's surprise, it was a pass through.

My first day of the hunt was a real learning exercise. When I took my lunch out, I found that my cookies and sandwiches were frozen so hard that if I had dropped them on the ground they would have shattered. We had to dunk them into a cup of hot tea so that we could eat them. Three dunks and my tea was ice cold! I accidentally stuck my index finger (covered only by my thin under glove) into the cup of tea and it froze immediately! It took hours to get the feeling back into the tip of my finger. I wouldn't make that mistake again.

I believed the toughest part of the muskox hunt was going to be the sled ride pulled by a snowmobile. A close friend of mine who had been on a muskox hunt the previous year told me his horror story of riding on this type of sled. Another person told me that he and his friends were on a muskox hunt and had been urinating blood for five days after returning home from their hunt

because of the pounding sled rides. For my first 15 minutes of riding in the sled I thought that it wasn't as bad as what I had been told. After a couple of hours of the constant pounding over the waves of snow I realized it was as bad or worse. My insides were being turned inside out. I didn't know if I would be able to stand up to this kind of torture for the entire hunt. I was observing the snowmobile rider and how he was able to go over the bumps and it wasn't bothering him. I took my large duffel bag and sat on it as if I were riding a horse, or a snowmobile, and that immediately ended my problem and I began to enjoy a little relief.

I saw several muskox on this hunt. Every day we were finding different herds. On this particular day I was glassing from a high point about 1,000 yards away from a herd that had several good bulls in it. The terrain was a series of snow-covered, rolling hills with some flat open areas. I used the wind and some of the large boulders to my advantage to stalk within a hundred yards of the herd. At that point the herd was slowly grazing in the opposite direction and I told Peter that they were still too far away to get a good shot. He told me to move very slowly toward the herd. As I stepped out from behind the boulders, I couldn't believe that the herd didn't run off. But as I slowly made my way toward them, some of the herd began forming circles, facing outward. Two bulls left the herd and went back into the rocky area, so I decided to stalk the larger of the two. The huge rocks gave me the opportunity to stalk within a comfortable shooting range of about 35 yards.

As I released, my 104-pound PSE Gorilla performed perfectly! The 655-grain Easton arrow, tipped with a 150-grain, two-bladed Thunderhead, completely passed through the mountain of hair. The bull didn't know what happened. He took a couple of steps forward and collapsed. It was a very humane harvest. As I approached the bull, I couldn't believe his awesome size! I took out my camera, which I had kept close to my body in order to keep the batteries from freezing. We took a few pictures, then immediately began skinning the bull. You could see the frost forming on the hide as we peeled it back from the meat. I couldn't believe the guides could skin and quarter these animals barehanded in sub-zero temperatures. It didn't take them long before we were packed and on our way back to camp where a warm stove and some hot food awaited us. The bull was officially scored at 123 points by the 24th Awards Judges' Panel. ▲▲▲

TROPHY STATS

▼ ▼ ▼ ▼ ▼

Category
desert sheep

Score
178⁶/₈

Location
Sonora, Mexico - 2000

Hunter
George R. Harms

Length of Horn
Right: 35⁶/₈ Left: 36²/₈

Circumference of Base
Right: 15⁷/₈ Left: 16

Greatest Spread
25²/₈

DESERT SHEEP
First Award - 178⁶/₈

▼ ▼ ▼ ▼ ▼ ▼ ▼ ▼ ▼

GEORGE R. HARMS

As told by Craig Martin of Tucannon Outfitters

George Harms wanted to harvest a ram that would contend for a new World's Record archery desert bighorn. With patience and perseverance, he achieved the true essence of what it means to be a big game trophy hunter.

After 60 days of drying, George Harms' ram scored 178-6/8 points, a potential new World's Record archery desert bighorn.

It was the start of a normal day. In the morning, it was knock the January frost off the tent, grab a bite to eat by the fire, shoulder our packs, and head out on foot before daylight. On our first stop, we spotted three rams feeding. One of them was in the 180 class — an impressive desert ram, to say the least. We positioned Pancho and Felipe, our spotters, above the unsuspecting rams to keep an eye on the bedded ram and assist with our stalk.

As we crept closer, I kept watching our spotters for hand signals. They indicated that we were very close, and the 180 ram was still bedded, so we continued to inch closer. John Lewton, our videographer, had the film rolling, and George was ready to draw his bow, given the opportunity. We were able to get within ten yards before we checked to find him looking right at us. It would have been a perfect scenario, had it not been for some brush that blocked a clean shot. George searched for an opening, but the ram was gone in an instant!

That was just one of the many stalks we made on that January 2000 trip. For a lot of my clients, it would have been over on the first day. The frequent encounters with rams in the high 170s and low 180s would have been a rifle hunter's dream come true. But this particular tag holder, George Harms, wanted to harvest a ram that would contend for a new archery record.

Our hunt took place in the history rich biosphere reserve of Tiburon Island, where the ram density is higher than any other population of Desert bighorn. The island is part of the Seri Indian Territory, in the Gulf of California, located west of the city of Hermosillo, in the Sonora Republic. Just a year earlier, John Lewton and I had assisted George on a rifle hunt on this island, where he connected with a beautiful ram that scored 182-3/8 points.

George had assembled a formidable crew to assist in his new task. He hired me, Craig Martin of Tucannon Outfitters, videographer John Lewton of Cape Horn Taxidermy, and Dave Mattausch of SCI. We were accompanied by numerous hires of the Seri Government, including Pancho Lopez Nomero, age 63, with 175 desert rams to his credit and Felipe Rodrigues Garcia, a full-time biosphere biologist with his heart and soul in his job. We were also assisted by Seri Indians, Martin Enrique Barnett, Humberto Romero, and David Lopez just to name a few. All were excellent spotters and very eager to please. None of them would hesitate to shoulder a heavy pack and travel all night to bring in supplies.

Our January hunt ended after 14 days without success, so we rescheduled to return to Tiburon at the end of March. This time, George had 19 days to fulfill his dream. George, John,

Photograph courtesy of George R. Harms

George R. Harms and his videographer John Lewton with Harms' award-winning desert bighorn ram scoring 178-6/8 points. Harms hunt consisted of two trips lasting several weeks. He was finally able to get a clean shot after stalking within 20 yards of the sheep.

and I were the only three men on this second hunt, and we were fortunate to be joined by biologist Fernando Colchero of Mexico City.

March 23, 2000, began just like the earlier hunt. Before daybreak, we started alternating intense glassing with hikes through the broken terrain. Soon we came upon a lone ram that we guessed would be an archery record contender. Martin stayed behind to watch the bedded ram, while we moved closer to get a better look. By the time we got back into view of the ram's bed, he had grazed over a small ridge into a ravine. Fernando and I moved around, bringing the ram into view again. This time he was bedded in a much better position and I signaled back to Pancho, Felipe, George, and John to move into position for a stalk. When they reached my position we discussed the situation and John and George continued the stalk on their own. Meanwhile, the ram got up and began feeding again, moving deeper into the ravine. I signaled for George and John to move to a position on a rim of rocks. Soon John located the ram, which was feeding toward them, but was still out of bow range. Time crept painfully slow as they waited for the ram to feed closer. I could see George, and knew from his body language that he was going over his mental checklist, preparing for the shot.

At 20 yards, and directly below John and George, the ram pawed at the ground to prepare his bed. In unison, John and George quietly stood up, John rolling his video and George with his bow drawn. Again, there was some brush between the hunter and his prey. This time, though, George managed to locate an opening in the brush, and the arrow traveled cleanly through, connecting in the ram's spine. The ram went down on his knees and within seconds rolled over and expired. It was a dream come true for George Harms, an accomplished hunter who understood the significance of such a magnificent animal, and who possessed the stamina to pursue that dream. There was no doubt in my mind that he had earned this ram by holding out for a true record trophy. Many hunters would have taken a lesser specimen, but by George's patience and perseverance, he achieved the true essence of what it means to be a big game trophy hunter. ▲▲▲

DESERT SHEEP
First Award - 178$^6/_8$

▼ ▼ ▼ ▼ ▼

GEORGE R. HARMS

TROPHY
FIELD PHOTOS
FROM THE 24TH
AWARDS PROGRAM

B&C Associate Archie Nesbitt took this Atlantic walrus in Foxe Basin, Northwest Territories, with a 95# bow on a 20' x 20' ice flow. Archie's walrus scores 95-4/8 and is one of only two Atlantic walrus entered in the Boone and Crockett records program taken by modern day hunters.

BOONE AND CROCKETT CLUB'

Photograph courtesy of Julie L. Hopkins

Photograph courtesy of Brian L. Ross

Photograph courtesy of Jeffrey T. Mardis

TOP: Julie Hopkins was hunting Coues' whitetail deer in the Tumacacori Mountains in Arizona when this magnificent typical buck, scoring 110-6/8 points, stepped into an opening she was watching. She dropped it with one shot from her .30-06 at nearly 300 yards. **LEFT:** Brian Ross, a 17-year-old Washington state hunter, drew a once in a lifetime permit and took this Wyoming moose on Gleason Mountain in Pend Oreille County, Washington, with a .30-06. It scores 147-6/8. **RIGHT:** This barren ground caribou scoring 400-4/8 was taken by Jeffrey Mardis north of the King Salmon River on a drop camp hunt while hunting with Matt Hentrick and Joe Moore.

Photograph courtesy of James E. Vance

Photograph courtesy of Donald W. Jacklin

Photograph courtesy of Terry L. Fretz

TOP: B&C Associate James E. Vance hunted with Robert J. Seeds of Cougar Mountain Outfitters and took this tom in Upper Lopez Canyon in Rio Arriba County, New Mexico. This cougar scores 15-1/16. LEFT: B&C Associate Don Jacklin hunted the Sonoran Desert floor in Mexico for four hot, grueling days before spotting this 174 point desert sheep. RIGHT: This rare wood bison was taken by B&C Associate Terry Fretz near Sekulmun Lake, Yukon Territory, in 2000. Pictured with the bull are his outfitter Tim Mervin and guide Dave. It scores 116-6/8 points.

Photograph courtesy of Richard N. Kimball

B&C Associate Richard Kimball was guided on his 1997 whitetail hunt in White Fox, Saskatchewan, by Kevin Tourano. Richard's non-typical buck scored 205 points.

Kerry Rogers found this black bear feeding on a beechnut ridge during New York's early bear season in 1986. A 100 yard shot from his Remington 760 .30-06 bagged this outstanding 21-2/16 bruin for Kerry. The New York State Department of Environmental Conservation Big Game Unit aged this bear at 28 3/4 years.

Photograph courtesy of Brian B. Bingham

Photograph courtesy of Chad R. Collins

Photograph courtesy of Robert J. Maslowski

TOP: Big Chino Wash in Yavapai County, Arizona, produced this massive pronghorn, scoring 89-4/8 points, for B&C Associate Brian Bingham in 1999. He took it with his 7mm Magnum. LEFT: B&C Associate Chad Collins made the records books when he harvested this impressive 8x8 point buck, scoring 170 points, near Lake City, Minnesota. He dropped it at 30 yards with his 12 gauge shotgun. RIGHT: Robert Maslowski was hunting with Fred Webb and Sons in 1996 when he connected with this Central Canada barren ground caribou bull that scores 360-3/8 points. Robert was hunting 140 air miles north of Yellowknife, Northwest Territories, near Courageous Lake.

Photograph courtesy of Kent Deligans

Photograph courtesy of James A. Cook

Photograph courtesy of Freeman R. Bell

TOP: B&C Associate Kent Deligans and the grizzly bear he took during the 1995 season near Taku River, British Columbia. This bear, which scores 23-6/16 points, was officially aged at 18.5 years old. LEFT: B&C Associate James Cook scored big when he harvested this very symmetrical 7x7 typical American elk, scoring 391-5/8 points, in Tooele County, Utah, in 1999. RIGHT: A very satisfied Freeman Bell proudly displays the heavy-beamed typical buck he took near Meadow Lake, Saskatchewan, in 1997. It scores 181-3/8 points.

Photograph courtesy of George F. Dennis

B&C Associate George Dennis passed up over 40 desert bighorns in 6 days in 1999 before filling his tag with this truly impressive ram. At 169 points, it is the largest sheep to come out of Unit 15B, Mohave County, Arizona, that year.

B&C Associate Kelvin Finney's Rocky Mountain goat was taken near Bitch Creek, British Columbia, while hunting with guide and B&C Official Measurer, Ed Swanson of Cranbrook, British Columbia. Kevin's billy scored 48-6/8 points.

Photograph courtesy of Dan E. McBride

Photograph courtesy of Harold J. Humes

Photograph courtesy of Stephen J. McGrath

TOP: B&C Lifetime Associate Dan McBride filled his 1999 Wyoming mule deer tag with this typical buck that he harvested in Carbon County near Baggs. Dan's buck scores 183-3/8 points. LEFT: This 10 year old Dall's sheep was taken in 1998 in the Mackenzie Mountains, Northwest Territories, by Rusty Humes. It scores 161-4/8 points with no deductions. RIGHT: B&C Associate Stephen McGrath had little doubt this large grizzly would make the records book when he located it in a cutover area near Babine Lake, British Columbia, in 1999. It scores 24-10/16 points.

Photograph courtesy of Lee R. Anderson, Jr.

Photograph courtesy of Francois Brunet

Photograph courtesy of Linda J. McBride

TOP: Lee Anderson and his hunting companions with Lee's desert sheep shortly after he harvested it in the Marble Mountains of San Bernardino County, California, in 1997. It scores 171-6/8 points. LEFT: B&C Associate Francois Brunet was hunting near Dominion Lake, Quebec, in 1987 with his hunting companion Jean Pierre Lacelle when he harvested this typical whitetail scoring 161 points. RIGHT: B&C Associate and veteran pronghorn hunter Linda McBride with her fourth records book buck. Linda took this trophy, which scores 80 points, while hunting with her husband, Dan, North of Sierra Blanca in Hudspeth County, Texas, in 1999.

Photograph courtesy of Brad White

B&C Associate Brad White had an outstanding hunt with Fred Webb and Sons Outfitters in 1997 near Courageous Lake, Northwest Territories. Brad's Central Canada barren ground caribou scores 366-2/8.

Photograph courtesy of Jack L. Blachly

B&C Associate Jack Blachly hunted with guide Peter Katiak in 1999 to take this fine muskox 40 miles from Kugluktuk, Nunavut, Canada. This outstanding bull scored 122-4/8 points.

Photograph courtesy of Monte D. Matheson

Photograph courtesy of James A. Algerio

Photograph courtesy of Scott A. Wilkinson

TOP: B&C Associate Monte Matheson with the Roosevelt's elk he took four miles north of Smith River, California, in 2000. Monte's bull scores 340-7/8 points. LEFT: In spite of the fact that both tips of this billy's horns were broken off, it still scores 47-4/8 points. It was taken by James Algerio in Elko County, Nevada, 2000. RIGHT: B&C Associate Scott Wilkinson and his father pursued this Columbia blacktail buck for a year on their own cattle ranch five miles east of Mount Hamilton, Stanislaus County, California, before catching up with it in 1998. It scores 152-5/8 points.

Photograph courtesy of Randy Pittman

Photograph courtesy of Velma Smith

Photograph courtesy of Troy Cummins

TOP: B&C Associate Randy Pittman harvested this Dall's sheep, which scores 171-1/8 points, in the scenic and rugged mountains along the Blackstone River, Yukon Territory, in 1998. This full curl ram was 12 years old. LEFT: Christopher Lake, Saskatchewan, was the site of B&C Associate Velma Smith's trophy black bear hunt during Spring 2000. This bruin, which scores 20-7/16 points, also qualifies for the Pope and Young Club's records book. RIGHT: Troy Cummins was hunting on horseback in the snowy Cassiar Mountains, British Columbia, in 1999, when he took this exceptional mountain caribou. In spite of the fact that it is missing the left brow palm, it still makes the all-time records book at 398 points.

BOONE AND CROCKETT CLUB

Photograph courtesy of Dan H. Gildner

B&C Associate Dan Gildner took this outstanding typical mule deer buck in Lincoln County, Nevada in November 1999. The buck scores 190-1/8 points.

Ranch Foreman and guide, Mathew Herbeck, guided Don Mayes and Kay Magee on their 1998 moose hunts at the Root Ranch in Idaho's Frank Church Wilderness. After their hunts, Matthew took this Wyoming moose scoring 156 points on Whimstick Creek just a mile from the ranch.

Photograph courtesy of David R. Harrow

Photograph courtesy of David L. Hussey

Photograph courtesy of Robin L. McDonald

TOP: B&C Associate David Harrow was wearing his lucky B&C hat when he harvested this whopper pronghorn, scoring 82-6/8 points, in Socorro County, New Mexico, in 1998. Dave has six pronghorns in the Club's records books. LEFT: There were over 50 inches of snow on the ground when B&C Associate David Hussey took this muskox near Rendez-vous Lake, Northwest Territories, in 1998. It scores 105-6/8 points. RIGHT: B&C Associate Robin McDonald had no doubts this non-typical whitetail buck, which scores 197-1/8 points, was a keeper when it stepped out onto a cutline he was watching near Rocky Mountain House, Alberta, in 1998.

Photograph courtesy of Douglas D. Closner

Photograph courtesy of Joseph P. Ambrose

Photograph courtesy of Fred D. Ruland

TOP: Douglas Closner with the magnificent barren ground caribou bull he harvested in 1997 near Dillingham, Alaska, along the Chichitnok River. This bull scores 395-2/8 points. LEFT: Alberta is known for producing trophy bighorn sheep, and B&C Associate Joseph Ambrose was fortunate to take this one while hunting with Wild Horse Outfitters at Washout Creek in 1998. It scores 180-7/8 points. RIGHT: This typical mule deer buck, which makes the all-time records book with a score of 192-6/8 points, was taken by B&C Associate Fred Ruland in Burro Canyon near Trinidad, Colorado, in 1997. The all-time minimum score for mule deer was lowered to 190 points in 1994.

Photograph courtesy of Leo W. Mack, Jr.

Leo W. Mack's bison scoring 115-6/8 was taken in Utah's Henry Mountains in 1997.

Photograph courtesy of Larry J. Kruse

Boone and Crockett Lifetime Associate Larry Kruse took this typical Coues' whitetail on Rancho Bellotal in Sonora, Mexico, in January 1999. Larry's buck scores 111-3/8. Since he took this great buck, Larry has moved on to the great hunting grounds in the sky. After his death his good friends and hunting companions collected the funds required for Larry to be forever remembered in the annals of the Boone and Crockett Club as a lifetime associate.

Photograph courtesy of Charles A. LeKites

Photograph courtesy of Jeffery K. Harrow

Photograph courtesy of Drew E. Kline

TOP: It was sunny, clear, and -20° Fahrenheit when B&C Associate Charles LeKites caught up with this trophy muskox near Kikerk Lake, Northwest Territories, in 1999. It scores an impressive 120 points. LEFT: B&C Associate Jeffery K. Harrow has taken five records book pronghorns in three different states during the last 6 years. Jeffery took this buck, scoring 81-2/8 points, in Socorro County, New Mexico, in 1999. RIGHT: B&C Associate Drew Kline was hunting in a heavy downpour when he took this woodland caribou near the Rogers River, Newfoundland, in 1998. It scores 328-7/8 points.

Photograph courtesy of Russell W. Hews

Photograph courtesy of James D. Jurad

Photograph courtesy of Robert G. Ferrero

TOP: Russell Hews took this Wyoming moose, scoring 147-4/8 points, with a .300 Winchester Magnum near Gun Sight Pass in Teton County, Wyoming, in 1999. LEFT: This full-curl Stone's sheep, scoring 165-2/8 points, was taken by B&C Associate James Jurad near the Kechika River, British Columbia, in 1999. RIGHT: B&C Associate Robert Ferrero displays the typical mule deer, scoring 194-4/8 points, he harvested in Kane County, Utah, in 1999. Velvet has to be removed before a trophy can be officially measured for the B&C records book.

Photograph courtesy of Jesse Dutchik

Jesse Dutchik's cougar scoring 15-12/16 was invited to the 24th Boone and Crockett Big Game Awards in Springfield, Missouri. Unfortunately Jesse was not able to get the big cat's skull to Springfield in time for it to be Panel scored. Jesse took this great cat with a .32 Winchester Special while hunting with David Dutchik of Cochrane, Alberta.

The Three Lakes area of Mitkof Island, Alaska, produced this Sitka blacktail buck for Scott Newman in 1998. Scott's buck scoring 102-3/8 was taking with a .270 using 130 grain bullets.

Photograph courtesy of Todd R. Guthrie

Photograph courtesy of Michael E. Read

Photograph courtesy of William R. Pritchard

TOP: After spending seven days in Cold Bay, Alaska, waiting for the weather to clear, Alaskan guide, Richard Guthrie, flew in a remote camp on Alaska's Unimak Island from which he, his son Todd, and Richard Bettas hunted for Todd's ten-foot Alaska brown bear. Expert flying by his father, perseverance and good old fashioned hard work enabled Todd Guthrie to take this great bear scoring 26-2/16 points. LEFT: Michael Read made the all-time records book with this typical whitetail he took in Stafford County, Kansas, in 2000. It scores 171-1/8 points. RIGHT: B&C Associate William Pritchard took this desert sheep in Sonora, Mexico, that scores 169-6/8 points.

Photograph courtesy of William J. Smith

Photograph courtesy of Lee Wahlund

Photograph courtesy of J.R. Dienst

TOP: Persistence paid off for B&C Associate William J. Smith when he took this great non-typical mule deer on the Jicarilla Indian Reservation, New Mexico, in 1998. This buck scores a total of 233-2/8 points. LEFT: B&C official measurer Lee Wahlund has taken six record book trophies in six different categories, including this handsome typical Coues' whitetail buck that scores 108-6/8 points. Lee took this buck in Sonora, Mexico, during the 1999 hunting season. RIGHT: The Acoma Indian Reservation in New Mexico, produced this massive 6x6 typical American elk for B&C Associate J.R. Dienst. This bull scores 382-3/8 points.

Photograph courtesy of Rick G. Ferrara

B&C Associate Bud Willis of Folding Mountain Outfitters was Rick Ferrara's guide when he took this outstanding Stone's sheep near Toad River, British Columbia. Rick's ram scored 170-7/8.

Photograph courtesy of Don F. MacLean

Don MacLean had two inches of snow for his hunt when he took this great Alberta non-typical whitetail buck late in November 1997. The buck was taken near Chipman, Alberta and scored 196-7/8.

Photograph courtesy of Roger G. Nitzsche

Photograph courtesy of W. Ken French

Photograph courtesy of Jason J. Gisi

TOP: B&C Associate Roger Nitzsche was hunting with outfitter John Cassidy and John's hounds when he took this huge tom, scoring 15-7/16 points, on Bryant Creek, Alberta, in 1999. LEFT: B&C Associate Ken French with the large Alaska brown bear, scoring 27-2/16 points, he took during a 2000 brown bear hunt on the Cinder River, Alaska Peninsula, Alaska. Its left ear was nearly torn off, probably the result of an earlier scrap with another bear. RIGHT: The Hell Hole area near the legendary Aravaipa Canyon produced this full-curl desert ram, scoring a whopping 178-2/8 points, for B&C Associate Jason Gisi during Arizona's 1998 sheep hunting season.

Photograph courtesy of Thomas R. Drake

Photograph courtesy of Josh B. Johns

Photograph courtesy of Davin J. Jaatteenmaki

TOP: This Alaska-Yukon moose, scoring 236-5/8 points, was taken in the Buckstock Mountains, Alaska, by B&C Associate Thomas Drake (left) in 2000. It has 22 countable points and a greatest spread measurement of 73-3/8 inches. LEFT: Josh Johns was extremely fortunate to draw a coveted Montana bighorn sheep tag in 1998. He harvested this ram, which scores 182-4/8 points, on Walling Reef. RIGHT: Quartz Creek, British Columbia, yielded this records book Rocky Mountain goat, scoring 48-2/8 points, to Davin Jaatteenmaki in 1998.

Photograph courtesy of Joseph H. Snyder

After flying into base camp on Karluk Lake on Kodiak Island, Anchorage, Alaska, resident, Joseph Snyder, took this Alaska brown bear while hunting from a spike camp some three miles from his base camp. Joseph hunted with a .338 Winchester. His bear scored 28 points.

Photograph courtesy of Mitch S. Crouser

Photograph courtesy of D. Cody Kelch

Photograph courtesy of Joseph C. Hinderman

TOP: Harney County, Oregon, produced this non-typical mule deer for Mitch Crouser in 1998. It has a total of 19 points on both antlers and scores 230-4/8 points. LEFT: Avid youth hunter and B&C Associate David Kelch was 10 years old when he dropped this non-typical whitetail, scoring 201-2/8 points, in Lorain County, Ohio. RIGHT: Joseph Hinderman and the mountain caribou bull, scoring 399 points, he harvested in the Cassiar Mountains, British Columbia, in 1997, with a 71# Black Widow recurve. It is the third largest mountain caribou ever recorded by the Pope & Young Club.

Photograph courtesy of David F. Myrup

British Columbia's Ram Mountain produced this Canada moose scoring 192-4/8 points for B&C Associate and veteran muzzleloading hunter, David Myrup of Sandy, Utah. David took this bull with a .50 caliber muzzle loader.

B&C Associate Clifford Graham with an exceptional Rocky Mountain goat he tagged on the third day of a backpack hunt along the Taku River, British Columbia, in 1999. This billy made B&C's records book with a score of 51 points.

Photograph courtesy of Warren L. Strickland

Photograph courtesy of Cerene J. Paul

Photograph courtesy of Jody M. Anderson

TOP: Warren Strickland took this Alaska-Yukon moose with a bow on the MacMillan River, Yukon Territory, in 1998. It scores 225-4/8 points. LEFT: B&C Associate Cerene Paul completed his grand slam in 1998 with this desert bighorn. Cerene was hunting in the Black Mountains, Arizona, when he caught up with this ram that scores 168-6/8 points. RIGHT: This non-typical whitetail buck was taken in 1998 by Jody Anderson. Jody took his B&C buck in Pierce County, Wisconsin, during the archery season with a compound bow. It scores 195-6/8 points.

Photograph courtesy of Hogan H. MacCarty

Photograph courtesy of John D. Gordon

Photograph courtesy of Craig R. Droke

TOP: B&C Associate Hogan MacCarty harvested two black bears in 1998, including this big boar that scores 20-1/16 points. Hogan took it with her .270 Winchester near the Peace River in Alberta. LEFT: B&C Associate John Gordon with the trophy pronghorn he took after a brief stalk in Wildlife Management Unit 148 near the South Saskatchewan River, Alberta, in 2000. John's buck scores 82-2/8 points. RIGHT: B&C Associate Craig Droke with the Baker County, Oregon, bighorn sheep he harvested in 2000. This ram's right horn was charred and missing a large chip at its base, indicating it may have been hit by lightening. Craig's ram scores 184-3/8 points.

Photograph courtesy of Adan Alvarez

Adan Alvarez with the non-typical whitetail buck he took on the world famous King Ranch in Kleberg County, Texas, in 1998. This buck has a total of 56-2/8 inches of abnormal points and scores 239-4/8 points.

TABULATIONS OF RECORDED TROPHIES 24TH AWARDS PROGRAM 1998-2000

TABULATIONS OF RECORDED TROPHIES IN THE 24TH AWARDS ENTRY PERIOD

The trophy data shown herein have been taken from score charts in the Records Archives of the Boone and Crockett Club for the 24th Awards Program, 1998-2000. Trophies listed are those that meet minimum score and other stated requirements of trophy entry for the period.

The final scores and rank shown in the book are official, except for trophies shown with an asterisk. An asterisk is assigned to trophies accepted in this Awards Program with entry scores that were subject to verification by the 25th Awards Program Judges Panel. The asterisk can be removed (except in the case of a potential new World's Record) by submitting two additional, independent scorings by official measurers of the Boone and Crockett Club. The Records Committee of the Club will review the three scorings available (original, plus two additional) and determine which, if any, will be accepted in lieu of the Judges' Panel measurement.

When the score has been accepted as final by the Records Committee, the asterisk will be removed in future editions of the all-time records book, *Records of North American Big Game*, and other publications by the Boone and Crockett Club. In the case of a potential new World's Record, the trophy must come before a Judges' Panel. Only a Judges' Panel can certify a new World's Record and finalize its score. Asterisked trophies are shown at the end of the listings for their category. They are not ranked, as their final score is subject to revision by a Judges' Panel or by the submission of additional scorings, as described above.

Note that "PR" preceding the date of kill indicates "prior to" the year shown for kill.

The scientific and vernacular names, and the sequence of presentation, follows that suggested in the Revised Checklist of North American Mammals North of Mexico, 1979 (J. Knox, et al; Texas Tech University, 14 December 1979.)

TROPHY BOUNDARIES

Many of the categories recognized in the Boone and Crockett Club's North American Big Game Awards Program are based upon subspecies differences. In nature, subspecies freely interbreed where their ranges overlap, thus necessitating the setting of geographic boundaries to keep them, as well as hybrids, separate for records-keeping purposes.

Geographic boundaries are described for a number of categories. These include: brown and grizzly bear; Atlantic and Pacific walrus; American, Roosevelt's, and tule elk; mule, Columbia, and Sitka blacktail deer; whitetail and Coues' deer; moose; and caribou. Pertinent information is included in the trophy data listings that follow, but the complete, detailed description for each is to be found in the latest edition of *Measuring and Scoring North American Big Game Trophies*, 2nd Edition, revised 2000.

In addition to category specific boundaries, all trophies must be from North America, north of the south border of Mexico, to be eligible. For pelagic trophies such as walrus and polar bear, they must be from Canada, Greenland, and the United States of America side of the International Date Line to be eligible.

Trophy boundaries are set by the Boone and Crockett Club's Records of North American Big Game Committee, working with the latest and best available information from scientific researchers, guides, hunters, and other parties with serious interest in our big game resources. Boundaries are set so that it is highly unlikely specimens of the larger category or hybrids can be taken within boundaries set for the smaller category, thus upsetting the rankings of the smaller category. Trophy boundaries are revised as necessary to maintain this separation of the categories.

BLACK BEAR

Ursus americanus americanus and related subspecies

Minimum Score 20

World's Record 23 10/16

Score	Greatest Length of Skull Without Lower Jaw	Greatest Width of Skull	Locality	Hunter	Owner	Date Killed	Rank
22 13/16	14	8 13/16	Luzerne Co., PA	Joseph E. Mindick	Joseph E. Mindick	1998	1
22 8/16	13 11/16	8 13/16	Schuylkill Co, PA	Elwood W. Maurer	Elwood W. Maurer	1997	2
22 7/16	13 14/16	8 9/16	Owl River, AB	Dan B. Pence	Dan B. Pence	1999	3
22 4/16	14 1/16	8 3/16	Woodridge, MB	Peter U. Funk	Peter U. Funk	2000	4
22 3/16	13 12/16	8 7/16	Menominee Co., MI	James W. Henney	James W. Henney	2000	5
22 2/16	13 15/16	8 3/16	Ashland Co., WI	Kris J. Freimuth	Kris J. Freimuth	1998	6
22 2/16	13 13/16	8 5/16	Delta Co., CO	James B. George	James B. George	1998	6
22 1/16	13 12/16	8 5/16	Snake Lake, MB	Edward J. Blair	Edward J. Blair	2000	8
22	13 11/16	8 5/16	Lycoming Co., PA	John T. Zerbe	John T. Zerbe	1997	9
22	13 4/16	8 12/16	Burntwood River, MB	Ken R. Malehorn	Ken R. Malehorn	1998	9
22	13 12/16	8 4/16	Kuiu Island, AK	Ricky Smith	Ricky Smith	1999	9
21 15/16	13 14/16	8 1/16	Schuylkill Co., PA	Glen J. Hendricks	Glen J. Hendricks	1998	12
21 15/16	14	7 15/16	Santa Barbara Co., CA	Eliseo Pizano	Eliseo Pizano	1998	12
21 15/16	13 14/16	8 1/16	Bronson Lake, SK	Daniel Valette	Daniel Valette	2000	12
21 14/16	13 15/16	7 15/16	Polk Co., MN	Picked Up	MN Dept. of Natl. Resc.	1996	15
21 14/16	13 14/16	8	Weldon, SK	Ron S. Bodnarchuk	Ron S. Bodnarchuk	1998	15
21 14/16	13 10/16	8 4/16	Lackawanna Co., PA	Jeff J. Kozar	Jeff J. Kozar	1998	15
21 14/16	13 10/16	8 4/16	Lake of the Woods, ON	Greg D. Daniels	Greg D. Daniels	1999	15
21 14/16	14	7 14/16	Hyde Co., NC	Gurnwood L. Radcliff, Jr.	Gurnwood L. Radcliff, Jr.	1999	15
21 14/16	14 1/16	7 13/16	Point Lookout, AK	Mark L. Wilson	Mark L. Wilson	2000	15
21 13/16	13 3/16	8 10/16	Sullivan Co., NY	Thomas V. Schields	Thomas V. Schields	1998	21
21 13/16	13 10/16	8 3/16	Kupreanof Island, AK	Peter D. Rowe	Peter D. Rowe	1999	21
21 13/16	13 10/16	8 3/16	Nut Mt., SK	Earl Smith	Earl Smith	1999	21
21 13/16	13 8/16	8 5/16	Rusk Co., WI	Robert A. Brunkow	Robert A. Brunkow	2000	21
21 12/16	14 1/16	7 11/16	Tyrrell Co., NC	Jim Williams	Jim Williams	1995	25
21 12/16	13	8 12/16	Green Co., NY	Edward B. Rivenburg, Jr.	Edward B. Rivenburg, Jr.	1997	25
21 12/16	13 10/16	8 2/16	Fishing Lake, AB	LeRoy C. Haug	LeRoy C. Haug	1998	25
21 12/16	13 8/16	8 4/16	Pike Co., PA	Jeffrey N. Lee	Jeffrey N. Lee	1998	25
21 12/16	13 4/16	8 8/16	Ventura Co., CA	Loren C. Nodolf	Loren C. Nodolf	1998	25
21 11/16	13 5/16	8 6/16	Luzerne Co., PA	Gerard E. Dessoye	Gerard E. Dessoye	1997	30
21 11/16	13 13/16	7 14/16	Hyde Co., NC	Gary D. McMahan	Gary D. McMahan	1998	30
21 11/16	13 9/16	8 2/16	Riding Mt., MB	Mike Minshull	Mike Minshull	1998	30
21 11/16	13 8/16	8 3/16	Huntingdon Co., PA	Marty W. Snyder	Marty W. Snyder	1998	30
21 11/16	13 6/16	8 5/16	Bronson Forest, SK	Rhodney N. Honeycutt	Rhodney N. Honeycutt	1999	30
21 11/16	13 9/16	8 2/16	Paradise Hill, SK	Kolby Morrison	Kolby Morrison	1999	30

BLACK BEAR

Ursus americanus and related subspecies

Score	Greatest Length of Skull Without Lower Jaw	Greatest Width of Skull	Locality	Hunter	Owner	Date Killed	Rank
21 10/16	13 3/16	8 7/16	Pike Co., PA	Reynold L. Morey	Reynold L. Morey	1998	36
21 10/16	13 1/16	8 9/16	Chelan Co., WA	Robin L. Radach	Robin L. Radach	1999	36
21 9/16	13 1/16	8 8/16	Simonette River, AB	Kirk G. Garner	Kirk G. Garner	1997	38
21 9/16	13	8 9/16	Carbon Co., PA	Elwood P. Yaich	Elwood P. Yaich	1997	38
21 9/16	13 1/16	8 8/16	Prince of Wales Island, AK	David K. Mueller	David K. Mueller	1998	38
21 9/16	13 7/16	8 2/16	Oconto Co., WI	Todd E. Lackey	Todd E. Lackey	2000	38
21 8/16	13 5/16	8 3/16	Two Hills Lake, AB	Lional L. Rogers	Lional L. Rogers	1997	42
21 8/16	13 7/16	8 1/16	Sullivan Co., NY	Frederick A. DeBoer	Frederick A. DeBoer	1998	42
21 8/16	13 4/16	8 4/16	Jefferson Co., PA	Lanny L. Kunselman	Lanny L. Kunselman	1998	42
21 8/16	14 1/16	7 7/16	Washington Co., NC	Don W. Noah	Don W. Noah	1998	42
21 8/16	13 4/16	8 4/16	Burnett Co., WI	Daniel R. Sylte	Daniel R. Sylte	1998	42
21 7/16	13 1/16	8 6/16	Montmorency Co., MI	R. Dennis Desgrange	R. Dennis Desgrange	1996	47
21 7/16	13 8/16	7 15/16	Clinch Co., GA	Danny Hinson	Danny Hinson	1997	47
21 7/16	13 10/16	7 13/16	Poplarfield, MB	Stephen C. Mills	Stephen C. Mills	1999	47
21 7/16	13 6/16	8 1/16	Burnett Co., WI	Craig M. Wyszynski	Craig M. Wyszynski	1999	47
21 7/16	13 1/16	8 6/16	Mendocino Co., CA	Ronald L. Koch	Ronald L. Koch	2000	47
21 6/16	13 4/16	8 2/16	Clearfield Co., PA	Barry R. Henry	Barry R. Henry	1997	52
21 6/16	13 6/16	8	Otter Lake, MB	Timothy J. Laha	Timothy J. Laha	1997	52
21 6/16	13 3/16	8 3/16	McBride Lake, SK	Dennis H. Hextall	Dennis H. Hextall	1999	52
21 6/16	13 3/16	8 3/16	Tehama Co., CA	Picked Up	Matthew A. Reno	2000	52
21 5/16	13 3/16	8 2/16	Rusk Co., WI	James J. Heberlein	James J. Heberlein	1990	56
21 5/16	13 1/16	8 4/16	Beltrami Co., MN	Deloris M. Ekstrom	Deloris M. Ekstrom	1997	56
21 5/16	13 4/16	8 1/16	Washington Co., NC	Michael T. McCorquodale	Michael T. McCorquodale	1997	56
21 5/16	13 4/16	8 1/16	Gunnison Co., CO	Brian Curtis	Brian Curtis	1998	56
21 5/16	13 5/16	8	Aitkin Co., MN	W.E. Haeg & M.K. Kiekow	Wayne E. Haeg	1998	56
21 5/16	13 6/16	7 15/16	Wolf Lake, AB	Thomas G. Lester	Thomas G. Lester	1998	56
21 5/16	13 2/16	8 3/16	El Capitan Peak, AK	Steven R. Martin	Steven R. Martin	1998	56
21 5/16	13 1/16	8 4/16	Red Deer River, SK	William A. Pace	William A. Pace	1998	56
21 5/16	13 1/16	8 4/16	Gila Co., AZ	Richard S. Rosenberg	Richard S. Rosenberg	1998	56
21 5/16	13 5/16	8	Hyde Co., NC	Thomas C. Rowland III	Thomas C. Rowland III	1998	56
21 5/16	13 3/16	8 2/16	Mono Co., CA	Gregory W. Brackett	Gregory W. Brackett	1999	56
21 4/16	12 14/16	8 6/16	Graham Co., AZ	Tommie Harendt	Tommie Harendt	1996	67
21 4/16	13	8 4/16	Roanoke Co., VA	Chester A. Scott	Chester A. Scott	1996	67
21 4/16	13 12/16	7 8/16	Mille Lacs Co., MN	James Schug	James Schug	1998	67
21 4/16	13 10/16	7 10/16	Hyde Co., NC	Daniel A. Hoffler	Daniel A. Hoffler	1999	67

21 4/16	13	8 4/16	Mink Creek, MB	Leonard R. Bull	Leonard R. Bull	2000	67
21 4/16	13 6/16	7 14/16	Prince of Wales Island, AK	Brian Crawford	Brian Crawford	2000	67
21 4/16	13 4/16	8	Sanpete Co., UT	Justin Rasmussen	Justin Rasmussen	2000	67
21 3/16	13 8/16	7 11/16	Georgetown Co., SC	Picked Up	SC Dept. of Natl. Resc.	1994	74
21 3/16	13 5/16	7 14/16	Rappahannock Co., VA	Michael A. Presgraves	Michael A. Presgraves	1997	74
21 3/16	12 15/16	8 4/16	Presque Isle Co., MI	Brian M. Zdanowski	Brian M. Zdanowski	1997	74
21 3/16	13 6/16	7 13/16	Bayfield Co., WI	Michael R. Cunningham	Michael R. Cunningham	1999	74
21 3/16	13 3/16	8	Pine Falls, MB	Fred L. Souders	Fred L. Souders	1999	74
21 3/16	12 13/16	8 6/16	Pike Co., PA	Mathew J. Wierzbowski	Mathew J. Wierzbowski	1999	74
21 3/16	13 1/16	8 2/16	Desbergeres Lake, QC	Chris S. Carson	Chris S. Carson	2000	74
21 3/16	12 13/16	8 6/16	Big River, SK	Warren K. Dugan	Warren K. Dugan	2000	74
21 3/16	13	8 3/16	Gila Co., AZ	Fred Peters	Fred Peters	2000	74
21 2/16	12 12/16	8 6/16	Hamilton Co., NY	Kerry Rogers	Kerry Rogers	1986	83
21 2/16	13 8/16	7 10/16	Burnett Co., WI	Bill Klugow	Bill Klugow	1988	83
21 2/16	13 8/16	7 10/16	Jones Co., NC	Forrest P. Boone	Forrest P. Boone	1997	83
21 2/16	13 9/16	7 9/16	Hyde Co., NC	Steve Hyde	Steve Hyde	1997	83
21 2/16	13	8 2/16	Wadena Co., MN	Wade A. Kern	Wade A. Kern	1997	83
21 2/16	13 3/16	7 15/16	Pike Co., PA	William S. Sinclair	William S. Sinclair	1997	83
21 2/16	13	8 2/16	Nez Perce Co., ID	Brice J. Barnes	Brice J. Barnes	1998	83
21 2/16	13 6/16	7 12/16	Hyde Co., NC	Michael B. Davis	Michael B. Davis	1998	83
21 2/16	13	8 2/16	Aroostook Co., ME	Linda L. Harlow	Linda L. Harlow	1998	83
21 2/16	13 1/16	8 1/16	Carrot River, SK	Dan S. Meske	Dan S. Meske	1998	83
21 2/16	13 4/16	7 14/16	Lintlaw, SK	Donald Schemenauer	Donald Schemenauer	1998	83
21 2/16	13 2/16	8	High Prairie, AB	Chris P. Thomas	Chris P. Thomas	1998	83
21 2/16	12 12/16	8 6/16	Las Animas Co., CO	Roger L. Bell	Roger L. Bell	1999	83
21 2/16	13 2/16	8	Lac La Biche, AB	Ralph R. Brausen	Ralph R. Brausen	1999	83
21 2/16	13 2/16	8	Washburn Co., WI	Jesse M. Hill	Jesse M. Hill	1999	83
21 2/16	13 4/16	7 14/16	Wexford Co., MI	Michael D. Horton	Michael D. Horton	1999	83
21 2/16	13 2/16	8	Washburn Co., WI	Paul C. Arnold	Paul C. Arnold	2000	83
21 2/16	13 5/16	7 13/16	Smoky River, AB	James S. Eason	James S. Eason	2000	83
21 2/16	13 4/16	7 14/16	Kittitas Co., WA	John J. Heinz	John J. Heinz	2000	83
21 1/16	12 13/16	8 5/16	Okanogan Co., WA	Jeffery G. Randall	Jeffery G. Randall	2000	83
21 1/16	13 5/16	7 12/16	Flatbush, AB	Tom McFadzen	Tom McFadzen	PR 1988	103
21 1/16	13 7/16	7 10/16	Ventura Co., CA	Thomas J. Weir	Thomas J. Weir	1996	103
21 1/16	13	8 1/16	Swan River, MB	Richard Barrett	Richard Barrett	1998	103
21 1/16	13 3/16	7 14/16	St. Louis Co., MN	Joseph A. Benedict	Joseph A. Benedict	1998	103
21 1/16	13 8/16	7 9/16	Ventura Co., CA	Kevin D. Colvard	Kevin D. Colvard	1998	103
21 1/16	13	8 1/16	Tyrell Co., NC	Marion K. DuPree	Marion K. DuPree	1998	103
21 1/16	12 15/16	8 2/16	Iosco Co., MI	Nicholas E. Uithol	Nicholas E. Uithol	1998	103
21 1/16	12 13/16	8 4/16	Greenlee Co., AZ	Derek W. Doran	Derek W. Doran	1999	103
21 1/16	12 15/16	8 2/16	Poplarfield, MB	Stephen R. Mills	Stephen R. Mills	1999	103
21 1/16	13 7/16	7 10/16	Douglas Co., WI	Larry J. Selzler	Larry J. Selzler	1999	103
21 1/16	12 12/16	8 5/16	Prince of Wales Island, AK	Dennis Dix, Jr.	Dennis Dix, Jr.	2000	103

BLACK BEAR

Ursus americanus and related subspecies

Score	Greatest Length of Skull Without Lower Jaw	Greatest Width of Skull	Locality	Hunter	Owner	Date Killed	Rank
21 1/16	13 8/16	7 9/16	Rennell Sound, BC	Philip Giesbrecht	Philip Giesbrecht	2000	103
21 1/16	12 15/16	8 2/16	Little Fishing Lake, SK	Gilbert Groseth	Gilbert Groseth	2000	103
21 1/16	13 7/16	7 10/16	Saddle Hills, AB	Terry D. Hagman	Terry D. Hagman	2000	103
21	13 1/16	7 15/16	Pine Co., MN	Donald J. Lorentz	Donald J. Lorentz	1993	117
21	13	8	Makinak, MB	Robert C. Missler	Robert C. Missler	1996	117
21	13 2/16	7 14/16	Tioga Co., PA	Melvin D. Noll	Melvin D. Noll	1997	117
21	13 1/16	7 15/16	Tehama Co., CA	Kenneth A. Wilson, Sr.	Kenneth A. Wilson, Sr.	1997	117
21	12 12/16	8 4/16	Mendocino Co., CA	Ralph Allino	Ralph Allino	1998	117
21	13 3/16	7 13/16	Wadena Co., MN	Darrell A. Anderson	Darrell A. Anderson	1998	117
21	12 13/16	8 3/16	Montezuma Co., CO	Joe W. Brunner	Joe W. Brunner	1998	117
21	13	8	Mendocino Co., CA	Peter M. Hoyle	Peter M. Hoyle	1998	117
21	13 13/16	7 3/16	Sidney Lake, SK	Donald Wright	Donald Wright	1998	117
21	13 3/16	7 13/16	Fergus Co., MT	Ross C. Roe, Jr.	Ross C. Roe, Jr.	1999	117
21	13 3/16	7 13/16	Beaver River, SK	Jason Toews	Jason Toews	1999	117
21	13 4/16	7 12/16	Beaver River, SK	Paul J. Allgyer	Paul J. Allgyer	2000	117
21	12 15/16	8 1/16	Porcupine Plain, SK	Kirby Fruin	Kirby Fruin	2000	117
21	12 7/16	8 9/16	Beavervale Creek, BC	Brett J. McAllister	Brett J. McAllister	2000	117
21	12 11/16	8 5/16	Onion Lake, SK	Lannon Nault	Lannon Nault	2000	117
20 15/16	13 2/16	7 13/16	Rio Blanco Co., CO	Jack Thompson	Jack Thompson	1970	132
20 15/16	13 6/16	7 9/16	Coconino Co., AZ	Burgh K. Johnson	Burgh K. Johnson	1997	132
20 15/16	13 2/16	7 13/16	Lewis Co., WA	Roy A. Lane	Roy A. Lane	1997	132
20 15/16	13 4/16	7 11/16	Marinette Co., WI	Joe J. Schlies	Joe J. Schlies	1997	132
20 15/16	13 2/16	7 13/16	Pondera Co., MT	Doug W. Calfrobe	Emerson Calfrobe	1998	132
20 15/16	13	7 15/16	Newton Co., AR	Shon Chastain	Shon Chastain	1998	132
20 15/16	13	7 15/16	Iron Co., MI	Christopher J. DeBrito	Christopher J. DeBrito	1998	132
20 15/16	12 11/16	8 4/16	Clyde Creek, BC	Mark A. Nucci	Mark A. Nucci	1999	132
20 14/16	13 4/16	7 10/16	Westmoreland Co., PA	Gary R. Sever	Gary R. Sever	1997	140
20 14/16	13 4/16	7 10/16	Prince of Wales Island, AK	Brenn R. Hill	Brenn R. Hill	1998	140
20 13/16	12 15/16	7 14/16	Rusk Co., WI	Eldon E. Berg	Eldon E. Berg	1997	142
20 13/16	12 14/16	7 15/16	Umatilla Co., OR	Justin D. Ward	Justin D. Ward	1997	142
20 13/16	12 14/16	7 15/16	Bernalillo Co., NM	Chris Zamora	Chris Zamora	1997	142
20 13/16	12 14/16	7 15/16	Gila Co., AZ	Larry G. Isley	Larry G. Isley	1998	142
20 13/16	13 4/16	7 9/16	Potter Co., PA	Gregory G. Minnich	Gregory G. Minnich	1998	142
20 13/16	13 3/16	7 10/16	Sawyer Co., WI	Vincent A. Volkey	Vincent A. Volkey	1998	142
20 13/16	13 4/16	7 9/16	Virden, MB	Orville K. Brown	Orville K. Brown	1999	142

20 13/16	13	7 13/16	McKean Co., PA	Gerald A. Gauthier	Gerald A. Gauthier	1999	142
20 13/16	12 12/16	8 1/16	Fremont Co., CO	Frank J. Kovacich	Frank J. Kovacich	1999	142
20 13/16	12 13/16	8	Sawyer Co., WI	Carl J. Kujac	Carl J. Kujac	1999	142
20 13/16	12 13/16	7 14/16	Kupreanof Island, AK	Richard D. Selby	Richard D. Selby	1999	142
20 13/16	12 15/16	7 15/16	Forest Co., WI	Bryan G. Van Lanen	Bryan G. Van Lanen	1999	142
20 13/16	12 14/16	7 14/16	Otter Creek, SK	Matthew J. McLean	Matthew J. McLean	2000	142
20 12/16	12 15/16	7 15/16	Kake, AK	Edward M. Wojtys	Edward M. Wojtys	1996	155
20 12/16	12 13/16	7 13/16	Lake Co., MN	Kent T. Engle	Kent T. Engle	1997	155
20 12/16	13 1/16	7 11/16	Gila Co., AZ	Brent Barstow	Brent Barstow	1998	155
20 12/16	12 11/16	8 1/16	Oconee Co., SC	Tony B. Cantrell	Tony B. Cantrell	1998	155
20 12/16	12 13/16	7 5/16	Kern Co., CA	Peter C. Nalos	Peter C. Nalos	1998	155
20 12/16	13 4/16	7 12/16	Beltrami Co., MN	Craig A. Dahl	Craig A. Dahl	1999	155
20 11/16	12 12/16	7 7/16	Waterhen River, MB	Claire T. Martin	Claire T. Martin	1999	163
20 11/16	12 11/16	8	Union Co., OR	Allen L. Cook	Allen L. Cook	2000	163
20 11/16	12 15/16	7 11/16	Cass Co., MN	William P. Beckvall	William P. Beckvall	1997	163
20 11/16	13 4/16	7 6/16	Mahnomen Co., MN	Richard Barten	Richard Barten	1998	163
20 11/16	12 11/16	7 8/16	Pierceland, SK	Stephen F. Kowalczyk	Stephen F. Kowalczyk	1998	163
20 11/16	13	7 8/16	Idaho Co., ID	Bernard E. Patynski	Bernard E. Patynski	1998	163
20 11/16	13 5/16	7 4/16	Ventura Co., CA	Robert J. Colla, Sr.	Robert J. Colla, Sr.	1999	163
20 11/16	13 3/16	7 10/16	Lycoming Co., PA	Eric P. Droege, Jr.	Eric P. Droege, Jr.	1999	171
20 11/16	13 3/16	7 4/16	Hyde Co., NC	Ronald G. Leadbeater, Jr.	Ronald G. Leadbeater, Jr.	1999	171
20 10/16	13 6/16	7 6/16	Mendocino Co., CA	Jared E. Johnson	Jared E. Johnson	2000	171
20 10/16	13	7 13/16	St. Jean Lake, QC	Clifford J. Allison, Jr.	Clifford J. Allison, Jr.	1995	171
20 10/16	13 6/16	7 6/16	Pike Co., PA	Thomas E. Engvaldsen	Thomas E. Engvaldsen	1997	171
20 10/16	12 13/16	7 14/16	Hudson Bay, SK	Dairl Hicks	Dairl Hicks	1997	171
20 10/16	13 4/16	7 11/16	Riding Mt., MB	Robert E. Butler	Robert E. Butler	1998	171
20 10/16	12 15/16	7 14/16	Langlade Co., WI	Joel C. McOlash	Joel C. McOlash	1998	171
20 10/16	12 13/16	7 14/16	Oconto Co., WI	Ronald F. Thomson	Ronald F. Thomson	1998	171
20 10/16	12 12/16	7 12/16	Pennington Co., MN	Jeffrey H. Kohlhase	Jeffrey H. Kohlhase	1999	171
20 10/16	12 12/16	8	Augusta Co., VA	W.A. Koontz	W.A. Koontz	1999	171
20 10/16	12 14/16	8 3/16	Beaver Co., UT	David J. Edwards	David J. Edwards	2000	182
20 9/16	12 10/16	7 10/16	Prince of Wales Island, AK	Dennis R. Laird	Dennis R. Laird	2000	182
20 9/16	12 6/16	7 12/16	Cocagne River, NB	David W. Wells	David W. Wells	2000	182
20 9/16	12 15/16	7 14/16	Rio Arriba Co., NM	Robert J. Seeds	Robert J. Seeds	1997	182
20 9/16	12 13/16	7 11/16	Idaho Co., ID	Rickey M. Davis	Rickey M. Davis	1998	182
20 9/16	12 11/16	7 4/16	Langlade Co., WI	Mark E. Kropp	Mark E. Kropp	1998	182
20 9/16	13 5/16	7 5/16	Logjam Creek, AK	Ralph E. Stewart	Ralph E. Stewart	1998	182
20 9/16	12 13/16	7 12/16	Pine Co., MN	Henry D. Vernon	Henry D. Vernon	1998	182
20 9/16	12 10/16	7 15/16	Union Co., PA	Jackson D. Wetzel	Jackson D. Wetzel	1998	182
20 9/16	12 15/16	7 10/16	Florence Co., WI	Todd M. Frisbie	Todd M. Frisbie	1999	182
20 9/16	12 13/16	7 12/16	Oconto Co., WI	Theodore A. Huchro	Theodore A. Huchro	1999	182
20 9/16	12 9/16	7 15/16	Vesta Bay, AK	Rhonda E. Cook	Rhonda E. Cook	2000	182
20 8/16	12 9/16	7 15/16	Thurston Co., WA	Michael D. Lytle	Michael D. Lytle	1995	191

BLACK BEAR

Ursus americanus americanus and related subspecies

Score	Greatest Length of Skull Without Lower Jaw	Greatest Width of Skull	Locality	Hunter	Owner	Date Killed	Rank
20 8/16	12 10/16	7 14/16	Becker Co., MN	Gill S. Gigstead, Jr.	Gill S. Gigstead, Jr.	1996	191
20 8/16	12 14/16	7 10/16	Kittitas Co., WA	Brennan D. Earhart	Brennan D. Earhart	1997	191
20 8/16	12 9/16	7 15/16	Price Co., WI	Terry J. Zellner	Terry J. Zellner	1997	191
20 8/16	12 6/16	8 2/16	Cook Inlet, AK	Keith Blair	Keith Blair	1998	191
20 8/16	12 10/16	7 14/16	Douglas Co., WI	Dale A. Wilhelmson	Dale A. Wilhelmson	1998	191
20 8/16	12 14/16	7 10/16	Lake Co., MN	George D. Foede	George D. Foede	1999	191
20 8/16	12 14/16	7 14/16	Dolores Co., CO	Woody Ott	Woody Ott	1999	191
20 8/16	13 2/16	7 6/16	Mistatim, SK	David R. Prunty	David R. Prunty	1999	191
20 8/16	12 2/16	8 6/16	Eagle Lake, ON	William C. Weitkemper	William C. Weitkemper	1999	191
20 8/16	12 10/16	7 14/16	Boise Co., ID	Rodney L. Pylican	Rodney L. Pylican	2000	191
20 7/16	12 10/16	7 13/16	Hubbard Co., MN	David H. Sanson	David H. Sanson	1997	202
20 7/16	13	7 7/16	The Pas, MB	Rex L. Hockett	Rex L. Hockett	1998	202
20 7/16	12 12/16	7 11/16	Lake Co., MT	Andy Larsson	Andy Larsson	1998	202
20 7/16	12 13/16	7 10/16	Siskiyou Co., CA	R.J. Simington	R.J. Simington	1998	202
20 7/16	12 14/16	7 9/16	Sanders Co., MT	Samuel J. Valore	Samuel J. Valore	1998	202
20 7/16	13	7 7/16	Hyde Co., NC	Jay Jackson	Jay Jackson	1999	202
20 7/16	12 5/16	8 2/16	Christopher Lake, SK	Velma L. Smith	Velma L. Smith	2000	202
20 6/16	12 10/16	7 12/16	Iron Co., WI	Kendal Durham	Kendal Durham	1993	209
20 6/16	12 8/16	7 14/16	Ventura Co., CA	Donald R. Allison	Donald R. Allison	1996	209
20 6/16	12 9/16	7 13/16	Mendocino Co., CA	Picked Up	Chris Brennan	1997	209
20 6/16	12 14/16	7 8/16	Shawano Co., WI	Walter R. Grunewald	Walter R. Grunewald	1997	209
20 6/16	12 7/16	7 15/16	Peace River, AB	Randall W. Pierce	Randall W. Pierce	1998	209
20 6/16	12 4/16	8 2/16	Lincoln Co., WI	James R. Porath	James R. Porath	1998	209
20 6/16	12 8/16	7 14/16	Tingley Creek, BC	David J. Schwemler	David J. Schwemler	1998	209
20 6/16	12 14/16	7 8/16	Barron Co., WI	Robert J. Capra	Robert J. Capra	1999	209
20 6/16	12 14/16	7 8/16	Klakas Inlet, AK	Andrew J. Fierro	Andrew J. Fierro	1999	209
20 6/16	12 13/16	7 9/16	Bayfield Co., WI	John E. Hendrickson	John E. Hendrickson	1999	209
20 6/16	13	7 6/16	Clinton Co., PA	John B. Melora, Sr.	John B. Melora, Sr.	1999	209
20 6/16	12 3/16	8 3/16	Rio Arriba Co., NM	W. Michael Whatley	W. Michael Whatley	1999	209
20 6/16	12 4/16	8 2/16	McLeese Lake, BC	Shelley K. Willet	Shelley K. Willet	1999	209
20 6/16	12 7/16	7 15/16	Prince of Wales Island, AK	Bernie Hildebrand	Bernie Hildebrand	2000	209
20 6/16	12 12/16	7 10/16	Nez Perce Co., ID	Dirk T. Williams	Dirk T. Williams	2000	209
20 5/16	12 11/16	7 10/16	McKean Co., PA	James T. Furness	James T. Furness	1996	224
20 5/16	12 9/16	7 12/16	Mendocino Co., CA	John T. Corrigan	John T. Corrigan	1997	224
20 5/16	12 6/16	7 15/16	Arrostook Co., ME	Jerry R. Simpson	Jerry R. Simpson	1997	224

20 5/16	12 12/16	7 9/16	Piney, MB	Darrell R. Wallace	Darrell R. Wallace	1997	224
20 5/16	13 1/16	7 4/16	Price Co., WI	Robert A. Armstrong	Robert A. Armstrong	1998	224
20 5/16	13 1/16	7 8/16	Chilako River, BC	Herb Klima	Herb Klima	1998	224
20 5/16	12 9/16	7 12/16	Twoforks River, SK	Don Mason	Don Mason	1998	224
20 5/16	12 11/16	7 10/16	Rio Arriba Co., NM	Robert J. Seeds	Robert J. Seeds	1998	224
20 5/16	12 1/16	7 1/16	Klickitat Co., WA	Kevin E. Vaughn	Kevin E. Vaughn	1998	224
20 5/16	12 10/16	7 11/16	Western Arm, NF	Eric H. Boley	Eric H. Boley	1999	224
20 5/16	12 9/16	7 12/16	Nez Perce Co., ID	Gregory L. Bryant	Gregory L. Bryant	1999	224
20 5/16	12 13/16	7 8/16	Idaho Co., ID	Tina M. Mattice	Tina M. Mattice	1999	224
20 5/16	12 9/16	7 12/16	Gila Co., AZ	Caleb J. Miller	Caleb J. Miller	1999	224
20 5/16	12 10/16	7 11/16	Prince of Wales Island, AK	Ricky S. Brown	Ricky S. Brown	2000	224
20 5/16	12 5/16	8	Granite Lake, NF	Carl A. Portner, Jr.	Carl A. Portner, Jr.	2000	224
20 4/16	13 1/16	7 4/16	Lane Co., OR	Rik Warden	Rik Warden	2000	224
20 4/16	12 13/16	7 7/16	Forest Co., WI	James B. Siegel	James B. Siegel	1992	240
20 4/16	12 6/16	7 14/16	Curry Co., OR	Richard A. Stoutenburgh	Richard A. Stoutenburgh	1992	240
20 4/16	12 15/16	7 5/16	Langlade Co., WI	Mike H. Bodden	Mike H. Bodden	1995	240
20 4/16	12 12/16	7 8/16	Price Co., WI	Brian J. Heimbaugh	Brian J. Heimbaugh	1996	240
20 4/16	12 12/16	7 8/16	Otero Co., NM	Michael Z. Summers	Michael Z. Summers	1997	240
20 4/16	12 8/16	7 12/16	Kuiu Island, AK	Ray Epps	Ray Epps	1998	240
20 4/16	12 11/16	7 9/16	Caribou Co., ID	Andrew J. Ford	Andrew J. Ford	1998	240
20 4/16	12 12/16	7 8/16	Menominee Co., MI	Diane D. Maul	Diane D. Maul	1998	240
20 4/16	13 2/16	7 2/16	Porcupine Mts., MB	Deborah T. Perone	Deborah T. Perone	1998	240
20 4/16	12 1/16	8 3/16	Vancouver Island, BC	Terry D. Romans	Terry D. Romans	1998	240
20 4/16	12 8/16	7 12/16	Pueblo Co., CO	Richard S. West	Jarred West	1998	240
20 4/16	12 8/16	7 12/16	White Lake, ON	Rick Lingo	Rick Lingo	1999	240
20 4/16	12 8/16	7 12/16	Blowhole Bay, BC	George G. Matthews	George G. Matthews	1999	240
20 4/16	12 8/16	7 12/16	Foleyet, ON	Mark Rodgers	Mark Rodgers	1999	240
20 4/16	12 3/16	8 1/16	Johnson Co., WY	Michael J. Smith	Michael J. Smith	1999	240
20 4/16	12 10/16	7 10/16	Bayfield Co., WI	Jeffery L. Senske	Jeffery L. Senske	1999	240
20 3/16	12 12/16	7 8/16	Duchesne Co., UT	Rick R. Sorensen	Rick R. Sorensen	2000	240
20 3/16	12	8 3/16	Clark Co., WA	Lawrence T. Nelson	Lawrence T. Nelson	1994	257
20 3/16	12 10/16	7 9/16	Venango Co., PA	Terry E. Groger, Jr.	Terry E. Groger, Jr.	1995	257
20 3/16	12 7/16	7 12/16	Clinton Co., PA	Gregory J. Cence	Gregory J. Cence	1997	257
20 3/16	12 6/16	7 13/16	Granby River, BC	Rob McGregor	Rob McGregor	1997	257
20 3/16	12 12/16	7 7/16	Granite Peak, BC	Roy Gerrath	Roy Gerrath	1998	257
20 3/16	12 14/16	7 5/16	Duck Mountain, SK	Ron Vandermeulen	Ron Vandermeulen	1998	257
20 3/16	12 4/16	7 15/16	Turtle Lake, SK	Douglas L. Bowen	Douglas L. Bowen	1999	257
20 2/16	13 1/16	7 2/16	Saskatoon, SK	Alan J. Mershman	Alan J. Mershman	1999	257
20 2/16	13 1/16	7 2/16	Craven Co., NC	Darrell J. Musselman	Darrell J. Musselman	1999	257
20 2/16	12 9/16	7 10/16	Elk Co., PA	Timothy P. Schall	Timothy P. Schall	1999	257
20 2/16	13	7 3/16	Likely, BC	Allen A. Campsall	Allen A. Campsall	2000	257
20 2/16	12 11/16	7 7/16	Oconto Co., WI	Dale W. Schindel	Dale W. Schindel	1996	268
20 2/16	12 8/16	7 10/16	Bleu Lake, QC	H. James Blamy	H. James Blamy	1997	268

Ursus americanus americanus and related subspecies

Score	Greatest Length of Skull Without Lower Jaw	Greatest Width of Skull	Locality	Hunter	Owner	Date Killed	Rank
20 2/16	12 8/16	7 10/16	Smoothrock Falls, ON	Matthew S. Emkow	Matthew S. Emkow	1998	268
20 2/16	12 9/16	7 9/16	McKean Co., PA	John E. Higgins	John E. Higgins	1998	268
20 2/16	12 7/16	7 11/16	Berthelot Lake, QC	Rickie L. Savage	Rickie L. Savage	1998	268
20 2/16	12 12/16	7 6/16	Moffat Co., CO	Delbert L. Schmidt	Delbert L. Schmidt	1998	268
20 2/16	12 9/16	7 9/16	Bayfield Co., WI	Howard E. Schwamer	Howard E. Schwamer	1998	268
20 2/16	11 15/16	8 3/16	Polk Co., WI	Chad L. Alden	Chad L. Alden	1999	268
20 2/16	13 2/16	7	Beaufort Co., NC	Darrell Pritchard	Darrell Pritchard	1999	268
20 2/16	12 11/16	7 7/16	Cass Co., MN	Gary M. Scheuble	Gary M. Scheuble	1999	268
20 2/16	12 8/16	7 10/16	Oneida Co., WI	Jeff J. Schoenecker	Jeff J. Schoenecker	1999	268
20 2/16	12 9/16	7 9/16	Gogebic Co., MI	Michael A. Zacharias	Michael A. Zacharias	1999	268
20 2/16	12 11/16	7 7/16	Chitek Lake, SK	Wayne B. Six	Wayne B. Six	2000	268
20 1/16	12 4/16	7 13/16	Green Lake, SK	Jack Culpepper	Jack Culpepper	1994	281
20 1/16	12 1/16	8	Lake of the Woods, ON	Ned A. Haas	Ned A. Haas	1996	281
20 1/16	12 10/16	7 7/16	Wallowa Co., OR	Trent E. Hafer	Trent E. Hafer	1996	281
20 1/16	12 11/16	7 6/16	San Bernardino Co., CA	Nick A. Sahagun	Nick A. Sahagun	1996	281
20 1/16	12 4/16	7 13/16	Huerfano Co., CO	Charles M. Betters	Charles M. Betters	1997	281
20 1/16	12 7/16	7 10/16	Mendocino Co., CA	Chris Brennan	Chris Brennan	1997	281
20 1/16	12 11/16	7 6/16	Snohomish Co., WA	Paul D. Givler	Paul D. Givler	1997	281
20 1/16	12 12/16	7 5/16	Oxford Co., ME	Gary J. Russell	Gary J. Russell	1997	281
20 1/16	12 11/16	7 6/16	Sullivan Co., PA	Brian H. Brandt	Brian H. Brandt	1998	281
20 1/16	12 10/16	7 7/16	Mahnomen Co., MN	Eugene R. Langenfeld	Eugene R. Langenfeld	1998	281
20 1/16	12 8/16	7 9/16	Peace River, AB	Hogan H. MacCarty	Hogan H. MacCarty	1998	281
20 1/16	12 10/16	7 7/16	Riding Mt., MB	Charles G. Seamon	Charles G. Seamon	1998	281
20 1/16	12 14/16	7 3/16	Burnett Co., WI	Bradley K. Alden	Bradley K. Alden	1999	281
20 1/16	12 7/16	7 10/16	Thorne Bay, AK	James L. Davis	James L. Davis	1999	281
20 1/16	12 6/16	7 11/16	Graham Co., AZ	Richard R. Kereny	Richard R. Kereny	1999	281
20 1/16	12 10/16	7 7/16	Port Hardy, BC	Ernest T. Lyons	Ernest T. Lyons	1999	281
20 1/16	12 8/16	7 9/16	Fremont Co., WY	William Rouse	William Rouse	1999	281
20	12 1/16	7 15/16	Baraga Co., MI	Clayton H. Bohto	Clayton H. Bohto	1980	298
20	12 4/16	7 12/16	Mendocino Co., CA	Bret Chappell	Bret Chappell	1994	298
20	12 9/16	7 7/16	Price Co., WI	David A. Pepper	David A. Pepper	1995	298
20	12 9/16	7 7/16	Rockingham Co., VA	Michael W. Myers	Michael W. Myers	1996	298
20	12 6/16	7 10/16	Tehama Co., CA	David Bucini	David Bucini	1997	298
20	12 9/16	7 7/16	Cairn Mt., AK	Delery Guillory	Delery Guillory	1997	298
20	12 9/16	7 7/16	Kane Lake, SK	Richard A. Jacobs	Richard A. Jacobs	1997	298

Rank			Locality	Hunter	Date	Score
20	12 12/16	7 4/16	Otero Co., NM	John T. Philley	1997	298
20	12 5/16	7 11/16	Elliot Lake, ON	A. Hunter Wilson	1997	298
20	12	8	Wawa, ON	Kirk M. MacDonald	1998	298
20	12 14/16	7 2/16	Rockingham Co., VA	Ray A. Miller	1998	298
20	12 8/16	7 8/16	Shaheen Creek, AK	Felix A. Nieves	1998	298
20	12 9/16	7 7/16	Douglas Co., OR	Quinn Norton	1998	298
20	12 9/16	7 7/16	Nestor Falls, ON	Ben F. Rutten	1998	298
20	12 4/16	7 12/16	McKean Co., PA	Rickey R. Ashton	1999	298
20	12 8/16	7 8/16	Oneida Co., WI	Kevin M. Hansen	1999	298
20	12 5/16	7 11/16	Bowron River, BC	Ian B. Murray	1999	298
20	12 5/16	7 11/16	Big Creek, AK	Kim S. Randrup	2000	298
20	12 14/16	7 2/16	Star Lake, SK	Michael J. Wachowski	2000	298
20	12 6/16	7 10/16	Chilako River, BC	David V. Webber	2000	
23*	14 8/16	8 8/16	Montmorency Co., MI	Sharon L. Agren	1997	

* Final score subject to revision by additional verifying measurements.

GRIZZLY BEAR

Ursus arctos horribilis

Minimum Score 23   New World's Record 27 5/16

Score	Greatest Length of Skull Without Lower Jaw	Greatest Width of Skull	Locality	Hunter	Owner	Date Killed	Rank
27 5/16	16 11/16	10 10/16	Toklat River, AK	David F. Malzac	David F. Malzac	1998	1
26 10/16	16 14/16	9 12/16	Kaltag, AK	Roger D. Hooten	Roger D. Hooten	1999	2
26 9/16	16 6/16	10 3/16	Anvik River, AK	Thomas M. Sharko	Thomas M. Sharko	1999	3
26 7/16	16 7/16	10	Lone Mt., AK	Jon D. Seifert	Jon D. Seifert	2000	4
26 3/16	16 1/16	10 2/16	Marys Igloo, AK	Mark W. Kelso	Mark W. Kelso	1998	5
26 2/16	15 12/16	10 6/16	Seal Oil Creek, AK	Ronald O. North	Ronald O. North	1997	6
26 2/16	16 9/16	9 9/16	Simonette River, AB	Picked Up	Mikal Christensen	1998	6
26 1/16	15 11/16	10 6/16	Nunavulnuk River, AK	Kenneth S. Orrison	Kenneth S. Orrison	2000	8
25 13/16	15 13/16	10	Knights Inlet, BC	Kenneth R. Hamer	Kenneth R. Hamer	1998	9
25 12/16	16 6/16	9 6/16	Smithers, BC	Troy N. Ginn	Troy N. Ginn	1995	10
25 12/16	16 7/16	9 5/16	Taku River, BC	David J. Leslie	David J. Leslie	1998	10
25 9/16	15 10/16	9 15/16	Bitter Creek, BC	Dennis R. Beebe	Dennis R. Beebe	1998	12
25 9/16	15 15/16	9 10/16	Anvik River, AK	Gene A. Ott	Gene A. Ott	1999	12
25 8/16	16 8/16	9	Roscoe Creek, BC	Robert Strebel	Robert Strebel	1997	14
25 8/16	15 12/16	9 12/16	Grayling, AK	David G. Imm	David G. Imm	1998	14
25 8/16	15 11/16	9 13/16	Squirrel River, AK	Robert H. McKay	Robert H. McKay	2000	14
25 8/16	15 10/16	9 14/16	Andreafsky Hills, AK	Kenneth L. Wallach	Kenneth L. Wallach	2000	14
25 7/16	15 13/16	9 10/16	Bob Quinn Lake, BC	Patrick Kennedy	Patrick Kennedy	1998	18
25 7/16	16 9/16	8 14/16	Chiroskey River, AK	Jonathan G. Schiller	Jonathan G. Schiller	2000	18
25 6/16	15 3/16	10 3/16	American River, AK	Casey D. Simon	Casey D. Simon	2000	20
25 5/16	15 10/16	9 11/16	Alaska Range, AK	Andrew J. Klejka	Andrew J. Klejka	1998	21
25 4/16	15 14/16	9 6/16	Noatak River, AK	A. Dean Chelton	A. Dean Chelton	1999	22
25 2/16	15 6/16	9 12/16	Banner Creek, AK	Randall K. Russell	Randall K. Russell	1999	23
25 1/16	15 15/16	9 2/16	Tatshenshini River, BC	James C. Ranck	James C. Ranck	1998	24
25 1/16	15 14/16	9 3/16	Nulato River, AK	Heath Sisk	Heath Sisk	2000	24
25	15 11/16	9 5/16	Klinaklini River, BC	George P. Mann	George P. Mann	1999	26
24 14/16	15 8/16	9 6/16	Buckland River, AK	Norbert D. Bremer	Norbert D. Bremer	1999	27
24 12/16	16	8 12/16	Stupendous Mt., BC	Malcolm R. Bachand	Malcolm R. Bachand	1999	28
24 12/16	15 15/16	8 13/16	Noatak River, AK	Christian J. Johnson	Christian J. Johnson	1999	28
24 12/16	15 14/16	8 14/16	Beaver Inlet, BC	Peter G. Klaui	Peter G. Klaui	2000	28
24 11/16	15 6/16	9 5/16	Cheeneetnuk River, AK	Charles R. Schlindwein	Charles R. Schlindwein	1999	31
24 10/16	15 2/16	9 8/16	Bond Sound, BC	Marvin S. Maki	Marvin S. Maki	1997	32
24 10/16	15 14/16	8 12/16	Babine Lake, BC	Stephen J. McGrath	Stephen J. McGrath	1999	32
24 9/16	15 8/16	9 1/16	Mosquito Fork, AK	Richard C. Swisher	Richard C. Swisher	1996	34
24 9/16	15 11/16	8 14/16	Eleven Mile Creek, BC	Clint Cartier	Clint Cartier	1999	34

Score			Locality	Hunter	Hunter	Year	Rank
24 9/16	15 12/16	8 13/16	Ungalik River, AK	William F. Kneer, Jr.	William F. Kneer, Jr.	1999	34
24 9/16	14 13/16	9 12/16	Ungalik River, AK	Steven A. Persson	Steven A. Persson	1999	34
24 8/16	15 8/16	9	Yukon River, YT	Roger D. Hanover	Roger D. Hanover	1994	38
24 8/16	15 1/16	9 7/16	Tezzeron Creek, BC	Ken Graham	Ken Graham	1996	38
24 7/16	15 2/16	9 5/16	Kelly River, AK	Robert H. Mace	Robert H. Mace	1998	40
24 6/16	15 6/16	9	Kelly River, AK	David T. Klein	David T. Klein	1999	41
24 6/16	15 6/16	9	Stikine River, BC	Frank D. Amoretto	Frank D. Amoretto	2000	41
24 6/16	15 8/16	8 14/16	Koyuk River, AK	Terry J. Fricks	Terry J. Fricks	2000	41
24 6/16	15 7/16	8 15/16	Otter Creek, AK	George A. Schiller	George A. Schiller	2000	41
24 5/16	15 3/16	9 2/16	Quesnel Lake, BC	Michael D. Bright	Michael D. Bright	1999	45
24 5/16	15	9 5/16	Flambeau River, AK	Anthony S. Gorn	Anthony S. Gorn	1999	45
24 5/16	15 6/16	8 15/16	Nass River, BC	Steve Pereira	Steve Pereira	1999	45
24 2/16	15 3/16	8 15/16	Chalco Creek, BC	Mark A. Nucci	Mark A. Nucci	1999	45
24 2/16	15 6/16	8 12/16	Wood River, AK	Evan L. Wheeler	Evan L. Wheeler	1999	48
24 1/16	15 6/16	8 11/16	Majuba Lake, BC	Scott E. Edwards	Scott E. Edwards	1997	48
23 15/16	15 6/16	8 9/16	Moose Lake, BC	William J. Mills	William J. Mills	1998	50
23 15/16	15 2/16	8 13/16	Noatak, AK	Julie M. Richards-Lees	Julie M. Richards-Lees	1999	51
23 14/16	14 13/16	9 1/16	Etivluk River, AK	Charles D. Day	Charles D. Day	1998	51
23 9/16	14 8/16	9 1/16	Chandler River, AK	David G. Phillips	David G. Phillips	1997	53
23 6/16	14 13/16	8 9/16	Taku River, BC	Kent Deligans	Kent Deligans	1995	54
23 6/16	14 2/16	9 4/16	Ratchfort Creek, BC	Johannes Mayr	Johannes Mayr	1995	55
23 4/16	14 9/16	8 11/16	Canning River, AK	Phillip J. Williams	Phillip J. Williams	1988	55
23 4/16	14 3/16	9 1/16	Blackwater Lake, BC	Kurt B. Futrell	Kurt B. Futrell	1999	57
23 3/16	14 7/16	8 12/16	Anaktuvuk River, AK	Gary K. Rohanna	Gary K. Rohanna	1997	57
23 2/16	14 10/16	8 8/16	Felix Harbour, YT	Ronald A. Kober	Ronald A. Kober	1998	59
23 1/16	14 5/16	8 12/16	Taku River, BC	Kent Deligans	Kent Deligans	1994	60
23 1/16	14 12/16	8 5/16	Black Martin Creek, BC	Joe Kolida	Joe Kolida	1999	61
26 6/16*	16 5/16	10 1/16	Iron Creek, AK	Scott Dunavin	Scott Dunavin	1998	61

* Final score subject to revision by additional verifying measurements.

ALASKA BROWN BEAR

Ursus arctos middendorffi and certain related subspecies

Minimum Score 26

World's Record 30 12/16

Score	Greatest Length of Skull Without Lower Jaw	Greatest Width of Skull	Locality	Hunter	Owner	Date Killed	Rank
30 3/16	18 5/16	11 14/16	Aliulik Pen., AK	Michael L. Ward	Michael L. Ward	1999	1
29 14/16	18 6/16	11 8/16	Uyak Bay, AK	John E. Schuchart	John E. Schuchart	1998	2
29 5/16	18 6/16	10 15/16	Seal Islands, AK	Larry G. Collinson	Larry G. Collinson	1999	3
29 4/16	18 8/16	10 12/16	Alaska Pen., AK	Peter K. Berga	Peter K. Berga	2000	4
28 13/16	17 8/16	11 5/16	Uganik Bay, AK	R. Dale Ziegler	R. Dale Ziegler	1998	5
28 10/16	17 10/16	11	Kejulik River, AK	Robert D. Gibbs	Robert D. Gibbs	1999	6
28 8/16	17 2/16	11 6/16	Muklung Hills, AK	Phillip T. Stringer	Phillip T. Stringer	1998	7
28 8/16	17 8/16	11	Sturgeon River, AK	Bill C. Sapa	Bill C. Sapa	1999	7
28 8/16	18 1/16	10 7/16	Cold Bay, AK	Robert B. Johnson	Robert B. Johnson	2000	7
28 8/16	17 3/16	11 4/16	Dog Salmon River, AK	Wesley J. Streed	Bell Mus. of Natl. Hist.	1996	10
28 7/16	17 15/16	10 8/16	David River, AK	Charles J. Watkins	Charles J. Watkins	1997	10
28 7/16	17 10/16	10 13/16	Halibut Bay, AK	Richard B. Sapa	Richard B. Sapa	1998	10
28 7/16	18 6/16	10 1/16	Unimak Island, AK	A. Timothy Toth	A. Timothy Toth	2000	10
28 6/16	16 15/16	11 7/16	Deadman Bay, AK	Isidro Lopez del Bosque	Isidro Lopez del Bosque	1998	14
28 6/16	17 8/16	10 14/16	Unimak Island, AK	Rusty Hall	Rusty Hall	1999	14
28 6/16	17 6/16	11	Sandy Cove, AK	Brian D. Hayes	Brian D. Hayes	1999	14
28 5/16	17 8/16	10 13/16	Afognak Island, AK	Daniel M. Vogel	Daniel M. Vogel	1997	17
28 4/16	17 10/16	10 10/16	Herendeen Bay, AK	J. Wayne Heaton	J. Wayne Heaton	1998	18
28 4/16	17 4/16	11	Sturgeon River, AK	Mark Freshwaters	Mark Freshwaters	1999	18
28 4/16	17 4/16	11	Frazer Lake, AK	Terry L. Christiansen	Terry L. Christiansen	2000	18
28 4/16	18 4/16	10	Meshik River, AK	Stan W. Newding	Stan W. Newding	2000	18
28 3/16	17 2/16	11 1/16	Foul Bay, AK	Robert L. Hales	Robert L. Hales	1997	22
28 3/16	17 3/16	11	Sandy River, AK	J.V. Lattimore III	J.V. Lattimore III	1998	22
28 3/16	17	11 3/16	Kodiak Island, AK	John W. Wilson	John W. Wilson	2000	22
28 2/16	17 4/16	10 14/16	Rude River, AK	Karl Strenger	Karl Strenger	1997	25
28 2/16	17 10/16	10 8/16	Cold Bay, AK	Foster V. Yancey III	Foster V. Yancey III	1998	25
28 1/16	17	11 1/16	Olga Bay, AK	James Azevedo	James Azevedo	1994	27
28 1/16	17	11 1/16	Afognak Island, AK	John P. Burke	John P. Burke	1997	27
28 1/16	17 4/16	10 13/16	Deadman Bay, AK	Javier Lopez del Bosque	Javier Lopez del Bosque	1997	27
28 1/16	17 6/16	10 11/16	Olga Lake, AK	Brian A. Marang	Brian A. Marang	1998	27
28 1/16	17 6/16	10 11/16	Karluk Lake, AK	Buck Siler	Buck Siler	1999	27
28	17 2/16	10 14/16	Grayback Mt., AK	David L. Bathke	David L. Bathke	1998	32
28	17 9/16	10 7/16	Unimak Island, AK	Jon A. Shiesl	Jon A. Shiesl	1999	32
28	17 1/16	10 15/16	Karluk Lake, AK	Joseph H. Snyder	Dana M. Snyder	1999	32
27 14/16	17 7/16	10 7/16	Uganik Bay, AK	L. Dale Gaugler	L. Dale Gaugler	1998	35

			Location	Name	Year	Rank
27 14/16	17	10 14/16	Olga Bay, AK	Thomas J. Stolsky	1999	35
27 7/16	17 5/16	10 2/16	Kahiltna River, AK	Michael P. Sokoloski	1999	37
27 5/16	16 9/16	10 12/16	Chichagof Island, AK	Dale E. Dunn	1999	38
27 5/16	15 14/16	11 7/16	Kodiak Island, AK	Dexter W. White	2000	38
27 3/16	17 7/16	9 12/16	Clark Bay, AK	Stanley W. Scruggs	1995	40
27 2/16	17	10 2/16	Kodiak Island, AK	Richard O. Burns, Jr.	2000	41
27 2/16	17	10 2/16	Cinder River, AK	W. Ken French	2000	41
27 1/16	16 14/16	10 3/16	Orca Bay, AK	Blake A. Trangmoe	1999	43
27	17 7/16	9 9/16	Big Creek, AK	Dexter Yokom, Jr.	1978	44
26 15/16	16 13/16	10 2/16	Cold Bay, AK	Hal N. Signett	2000	45
26 14/16	17 1/16	9 13/16	Naknek River, AK	Gary E. Jones	1998	46
26 12/16	16 8/16	10 4/16	Chilkoot Lake, AK	Vladimir L. Benda	1999	47
26 12/16	16 12/16	10	Halibut Bay, AK	Jerry R. Hall	1999	47
26 7/16	16 4/16	10 3/16	Hoonah Sound, AK	Robert E. Welsh	1998	49
26 7/16	16 9/16	9 14/16	Meshik River, AK	Steven E. Nocket	1999	49
26 5/16	16 12/16	9 9/16	Nushagak River, AK	Earl J. Fairman, Jr.	1997	51
26 5/16	16 3/16	10 2/16	Alaska Pen., AK	Mark D. Farnam	1998	51
26 3/16	16 1/16	10 2/16	Young Creek, AK	Kitty M. Peiffer	1998	53
26 3/16	16 5/16	9 14/16	Admiralty Island, AK	Chester J. Fincke	2000	53
26 2/16	16 1/16	10 1/16	Unimak Island, AK	Todd R. Guthrie	1999	55
26	16 4/16	9 12/16	Freshwater Bay, AK	Rondo A. Ihde	1998	56

POLAR BEAR

Ursus maritimus

Minimum Score 27

World's Record 29 15/16

Score	Greatest Length of Skull Without Lower Jaw	Greatest Width of Skull	Locality	Hunter	Owner	Date Killed	Rank
27 6/16*	17 1/16	10 5/16	Home Bay, NT	Antonius Rensing	Antonius Rensing	2000	

* Final score subject to revision by additional verifying measurements.

Felis concolor hippolestes and related subspecies

Minimum Score 14 8/16

World's Record 16 4/16

Score	Greatest Length of Skull Without Lower Jaw	Greatest Width of Skull	Locality	Hunter	Owner	Date Killed	Rank
15 15/16	9 5/16	6 10/16	Hinton, AB	Roy LePage	Roy LePage	1999	1
15 13/16	9 4/16	6 9/16	Carbon Co., UT	Anthony J. Berardi	Anthony J. Berardi	1999	2
15 12/16	9 3/16	6 9/16	Idaho Co., ID	Dave Hiatt	Dave Hiatt	1994	3
15 10/16	9 2/16	6 8/16	Idaho Co., ID	Bill Daugherty	Bill Daugherty	1998	4
15 9/16	9 1/16	6 8/16	Idaho Co., ID	Dave Hiatt	Dave Hiatt	1997	5
15 9/16	9 1/16	6 8/16	Mesa Co., CO	Darryl Powell	Darryl Powell	1997	5
15 9/16	8 15/16	6 10/16	Lincoln Co., MT	Hershel E. Landon, Jr.	Hershel E. Landon, Jr.	1999	5
15 8/16	9 2/16	6 6/16	Grant Co., OR	Joe L. West	Joe L. West	1992	8
15 8/16	9 4/16	6 4/16	Mount Skinner, BC	Jeff S. Ashe	Jeff S. Ashe	1997	8
15 8/16	9 3/16	6 5/16	Flat Creek, AB	A. Paul Kroshko	A. Paul Kroshko	1998	8
15 8/16	9 2/16	6 6/16	Rio Arriba Co., NM	Robert J. Seeds	Robert J. Seeds	1999	8
15 7/16	8 15/16	6 8/16	Bryant Creek, AB	Roger G. Nitzsche	Roger G. Nitzsche	1999	12
15 6/16	9 2/16	6 4/16	Lemhi Co., ID	Robert G. Barningham	Robert G. Barningham	1998	13
15 6/16	9 3/16	6 3/16	Lemhi Co., ID	Larry C. Ward	Larry C. Ward	1999	13
15 6/16	9 3/16	6 3/16	Washington Co., UT	Eugene E. Hafen	Eugene E. Hafen	2000	13
15 5/16	9	6 5/16	Clearwater Co., ID	Donald W. Jacklin	Donald W. Jacklin	1997	16
15 5/16	9	6 5/16	Granite Co., MT	Luke J. Bergey	Luke J. Bergey	1998	16
15 5/16	8 15/16	6 6/16	Costilla Co., CO	Edward Deckes	Edward Deckes	2000	16
15 5/16	9 2/16	6 3/16	Pearson Ridge, BC	Joseph F. Kenny III	Joseph F. Kenny III	2000	16
15 4/16	8 15/16	6 5/16	Idaho Co., ID	Dave Hiatt	Dave Hiatt	1993	20
15 4/16	9 1/16	6 3/16	Monte Lake, BC	Marc Simard	Marc Simard	1996	20
15 4/16	8 14/16	6 6/16	Moyie Lake, BC	Robert C. Faiers	Robert C. Faiers	1997	20
15 4/16	9 1/16	6 3/16	Broadwater Co., MT	Kevin D. Harms	Kevin D. Harms	1998	20
15 4/16	8 15/16	6 5/16	Flathead Co., MT	Carleton L. Mocabee	Carleton L. Mocabee	1998	20
15 4/16	8 15/16	6 5/16	Idaho Co., ID	Thomas J. Schank	Thomas J. Schank	1998	20
15 4/16	9 4/16	6	Colfax Co., NM	Robert E. Darmitzel	Robert E. Darmitzel	1999	20
15 4/16	8 12/16	6 8/16	Andreen Creek, BC	Roland M. Larrabee	Roland M. Larrabee	1999	20
15 3/16	8 13/16	6 6/16	Nez Perce Co., ID	Steavon C. Hornbeck	Steavon C. Hornbeck	1984	28
15 3/16	8 15/16	6 4/16	Echo Lake, BC	Terry S. Wasylyszyn	Terry S. Wasylyszyn	1995	28
15 3/16	9 1/16	6 2/16	Maze Lake, BC	Eric Petosa	Eric Petosa	1997	28
15 3/16	8 15/16	6 4/16	Idaho Co., ID	Jesse J. Higgins	Jesse J. Higgins	1998	28
15 3/16	9 4/16	5 15/16	Tooele Co., UT	Kevin J. Hunt	Kevin J. Hunt	1998	28
15 3/16	8 14/16	6 5/16	Valley Co., ID	Kenneth Leavitt	Kenneth Leavitt	1998	28
15 3/16	8 11/16	6 8/16	Hinton, AB	Danny Ljubsa	Danny Ljubsa	1998	28
15 3/16	8 11/16	6 8/16	Carbon Co., MT	Lynn R. McKittrick	Lynn R. McKittrick	1998	28

COUGAR OR MOUNTAIN LION

Felis concolor hippolestes and related subspecies

Score	Greatest Length of Skull Without Lower Jaw	Greatest Width of Skull	Locality	Hunter	Owner	Date Killed	Rank
15 3/16	8 15/16	6 4/16	Rio Arriba Co., NM	Robert J. Seeds	Robert J. Seeds	1998	28
15 3/16	8 13/16	6 6/16	Clearwater Co., ID	James J. Backman	James J. Backman	1999	28
15 3/16	8 15/16	6 4/16	Lake Co., MT	Robert C. Hartwig	Robert C. Hartwig	1999	28
15 3/16	8 14/16	6 5/16	McLean Creek, AB	Neil G. Johnson	Neil G. Johnson	1999	28
15 3/16	8 13/16	6 5/16	Pondera Co., MT	Felix W. Parks	Felix W. Parks	1985	40
15 2/16	8 11/16	6 7/16	Kootenai Co., ID	Lawrence L. Booher	Lawrence L. Booher	1997	40
15 2/16	8 14/16	6 4/16	Mineral Co., MT	Timothy R. Brant	Timothy R. Brant	1997	40
15 2/16	8 14/16	6 4/16	Rocky Mountain House, AB	Dennis J. Tucker	Dennis J. Tucker	1997	40
15 2/16	8 15/16	6 3/16	Chelan Co., WA	John A. Barnes	John A. Barnes	1998	40
15 2/16	8 14/16	6 4/16	Chain Lakes, AB	Tom Foss	Tom Foss	1998	40
15 2/16	8 15/16	6 3/16	Dry Lake, BC	David L. Hartin	David L. Hartin	1998	40
15 2/16	8 13/16	6 5/16	Cynthia, AB	Martin Lang	Martin Lang	1998	40
15 2/16	8 13/16	6 5/16	La Plata Co., CO	Brad F. Pfeffer	Brad F. Pfeffer	1999	40
15 2/16	8 14/16	6 4/16	Montezuma Co., CO	Terry D. Amrine	Terry D. Amrine	1999	40
15 2/16	8 14/16	6 4/16	Mineral Co., MT	Darren Crusch	Darren Crusch	1999	40
15 2/16	8 13/16	6 5/16	Lemhi Co., ID	Henry K. Leworthy	Henry K. Leworthy	1999	40
15 2/16	9	6 2/16	Montrose Co., CO	Steven R. Hickok	Steven R. Hickok	2000	40
15 1/16	9 1/16	6	Union Co., NM	Arthur E. Ashcraft	Arthur E. Ashcraft	1999	53
15 1/16	8 10/16	6 7/16	Grand Co., CO	Paul T. Jones	Paul T. Jones	1999	53
15 1/16	8 15/16	6 2/16	Rio Arriba Co., NM	James E. Vance	James E. Vance	1999	53
15 1/16	8 13/16	6 4/16	Mill Creek, AB	Luke Semenoff	Luke Semenoff	2000	53
15	8 13/16	6 3/16	Clallam Co., WA	Michael A. Reaves	Michael A. Reaves	1993	57
15	8 13/16	6 3/16	Flathead Co., MT	Larry D. Dahlke	Larry D. Dahlke	1996	57
15	8 12/16	6 4/16	Bonner Co., ID	Shawn Frederickson	Shawn Frederickson	1997	57
15	8 12/16	6 4/16	Bonner Co., ID	W. David Howton	W. David Howton	1997	57
15	8 13/16	6 3/16	Invermere, BC	Dave Lougheed	Dave Lougheed	1997	57
15	8 14/16	6 2/16	Missoula, Co., MT	Mick T. Waletzko	Mick T. Waletzko	1997	57
15	8 13/16	6 3/16	Clearwater River, AB	Mark S. Coles	Mark S. Coles	1998	57
15	8 12/16	6 4/16	Crowsnest Pass, AB	Jeff B. Davis	Jeff B. Davis	1998	57
15	8 13/16	6 3/16	Benewah Co., ID	Donald L. Houk	Donald L. Houk	1998	57
15	8 12/16	6 4/16	Las Animas Co., CO	Barry G. Hasten	Barry G. Hasten	1999	57
15	8 14/16	6 2/16	Archuleta Co., CO	Harry M. Hocker	Harry M. Hocker	1999	57
15	8 15/16	6 1/16	San Juan Co., UT	Gary E. Huff	Gary E. Huff	1999	57
15	8 9/16	6 7/16	Flathead Co., MT	Joe R. Kuzmic	Joe R. Kuzmic	1999	57
15	8 13/16	6 3/16	Lincoln Co., MT	Michael L. Lieffring	Michael L. Lieffring	1999	57

15	8 12/16	6 4/16	Robert A. Marod	Ravalli Co., MT	Robert A. Marod	1999	57
14 15/16	8 13/16	6 2/16	Stefan Scheinost	Utah	Eddie Scheinost	1974	72
14 15/16	8 13/16	6 2/16	R. Terry Anderson	Union Co., OR	R. Terry Anderson	1993	72
14 15/16	8 12/16	6 3/16	Shawn M. Conrad	Missoula Co., MT	Shawn M. Conrad	1998	72
14 15/16	8 12/16	6 3/16	Rick Pasutto	Kelowna, BC	Rick Pasutto	1998	72
14 15/16	8 15/16	6	Derrill W. Herman	Beaver Lake, AB	Derrill W. Herman	1999	72
14 14/16	9	5 14/16	Paul N. Harvey	Archuleta Co., CO	Paul N. Harvey	1998	77
14 14/16	8 12/16	6 2/16	Robert J. Pacini	Kane Co., UT	Robert J. Pacini	1998	77
14 14/16	8 10/16	6 4/16	Randy L. Pfaff	Fremont Co., CO	Randy L. Pfaff	1999	77
14 13/16	8 9/16	6 4/16	Terry D. Braden	Jeff Davis Co., TX	Terry D. Braden	1998	80
14 13/16	8 13/16	6	Ike Carpenter	Latah Co., ID	Ike Carpenter	1998	80
14 13/16	8 11/16	6 2/16	Ray C. Clements	Union Co., OR	Ray C. Clements	1998	80
14 13/16	8 9/16	6 4/16	Roland E. Deane, Jr.	Gallatin Co., MT	Roland E. Deane, Jr.	1998	80
14 13/16	8 10/16	6 3/16	Steve L. Lewis	Madison Co., MT	Steve L. Lewis	1998	80
14 13/16	8 15/16	5 14/16	Steve W. Chin	Rio Blanco Co., CO	Steve W. Chin	1999	80
14 13/16	8 11/16	6 1/16	Mark A. Miller	Missoula Co., MT	Mark A. Miller	1997	80
14 12/16	8 11/16	6 1/16	H. Allen Hoffman	Clearwater Co., ID	H. Allen Hoffman	1998	86
14 12/16	8 10/16	6 2/16	Kevin L. Kendrick	Lincoln Co., MT	Kevin L. Kendrick	1998	86
14 12/16	8 11/16	6 1/16	John L. Piotrowski	Custer Co., CO	John L. Piotrowski	1998	86
14 12/16	8 10/16	6 2/16	Ronald J. Finnegan	Sheridan Co., WY	Ronald J. Finnegan	1999	86
14 12/16	8 12/16	6	Dave Kennedy	Salt Lake Co., UT	Dave Kennedy	1999	86
14 12/16	8 13/16	5 15/16	Jim Miller, Jr.	McCarren Creek, BC	Jim Miller, Jr.	1999	86
14 11/16	8 10/16	6 1/16	Kurt R. Folke	Washington Co., ID	K.R. Folke & J. Farnam	1998	86
14 11/16	8 12/16	5 15/16	Steve T. Letcher	Washington Co., UT	Steve T. Letcher	1998	93
14 11/16	8 9/16	6 2/16	Scott C. Quinn	Custer Co., ID	Scott C. Quinn	1998	93
14 11/16	8 12/16	5 15/16	John W. Scurfield	Clearwater River, AB	John W. Scurfield	1999	93
14 11/16	8 10/16	6 1/16	Edward J. Deichmeister	Hawkeye Creek, AB	Edward J. Deichmeister	2000	93
14 10/16	8 10/16	6	Aileen A. Klein	Madison Co., MT	Aileen A. Klein	1996	93
14 10/16	8 12/16	6	Danny J. Townsend	Rio Blanco Co., CO	Danny J. Townsend	1996	98
14 10/16	8 10/16	5 14/16	David A. Little	Sullivan Creek, AB	David A. Little	1997	98
14 10/16	8 12/16	6 2/16	Michael B. Stevens	Teton Co., WY	Michael B. Stevens	1997	98
14 10/16	8 8/16	6	James Collings	Allison Creek, AB	James Collings	1998	98
14 10/16	8 10/16	5 14/16	Terry D. Hagman	Harold Creek, AB	Terry D. Hagman	1998	98
14 10/16	8 12/16	5 14/16	Douglas A. Brown	Idaho Co., ID	Douglas A. Brown	1999	98
14 9/16	8 11/16	6 1/16	Harley L. Johnson	Boulder Co., CO	Harley L. Johnson	1993	98
14 9/16	8 8/16	6 2/16	Shannon D. O'Sullivan	Clallam Co., WA	Shannon D. O'Sullivan	1997	105
14 9/16	8 7/16	6 1/16	Michael R. Treinen	Costilla Co., CO	Michael R. Treinen	1997	105
14 9/16	8 8/16	6 3/16	Keith D. Bergum	Elko Co., NV	Keith D. Bergum	1998	105
14 9/16	8 6/16	6 3/16	David E. Serbonich	Park Co., WY	David E. Serbonich	2000	105
14 8/16	8 5/16	6	Trent E. Hafer	Wallowa Co., OR	Trent E. Hafer	1992	105
14 8/16	8 8/16	5 14/16	Curtis J. Babler	Idaho Co., ID	Curtis J. Babler	1997	110
14 8/16	8 10/16	5 14/16	Thomas A. Hunt	Garfield Co., UT	Thomas A. Hunt	1998	110
14 8/16	8 10/16	5 14/16	Robert D. Owens	Rio Blanco Co., CO	Robert D. Owens	1998	110

COUGAR OR MOUNTAIN LION

Felis concolor hippolestes and related subspecies

Score	Greatest Length of Skull Without Lower Jaw	Greatest Width of Skull	Locality	Hunter	Owner	Date Killed	Rank
14 8/16	8 11/16	5 13/16	Rio Blanco Co., CO	Dennis L. Roehl	Dennis L. Roehl	1999	110
14 8/16	8 9/16	5 15/16	Humboldt Co., NV	David R. Pasinski	David R. Pasinski	2000	110
16*	9 7/16	6 9/16	Tongue Creek, AB	T. Klassen & J.D. Gordon	T. Klassen & J.D. Gordon	1999	
15 14/16*	9 6/16	6 8/16	Wheeler Co., OR	John Rhoden	John Rhoden	1996	
15 12/16*	9 5/16	6 7/16	Lesueur Creek, AB	Jesse Dutchik	Jesse Dutchik	1999	

* Final score subject to revision by additional verifying measurements.

BOONE AND CROCKETT CLUB'S

ATLANTIC WALRUS

Odobenus rosmarus rosmarus

Minimum Score 95

World's Record 118 6/8

The geographical boundary for Atlantic walrus is basically the Arctic and Atlantic coasts south to Massachusetts. More specifically the Atlantic walrus boundary in Canada extends westward to Mould Bay of Prince Patrick Island, to just east of Cape George Richards of Melville Island and to Taloyoak, Nunavut Province (formerly known as Spence Bay, Northwest Territories); and eastward to include trophies taken in Greenland.

Score	Entire Length of Loose Tusk R.	L.	Circumference of Base R.	L.	Circumference at the Third Quarter R.	L.	Locality	Hunter	Owner	Date Killed	Rank
98 2/8 *	24	23 1/8	7 2/8	6 6/8	5	5 2/8	Bencas Island, NT	James A. Bush, Jr.	James A. Bush, Jr.	1997	
95 4/8 *	22	22 2/8	6 5/8	6 7/8	5 1/8	5 2/8	Foxe Basin, NT	Archie J. Nesbitt	Archie J. Nesbitt	1996	

* Final score subject to revision by additional verifying measurements.

PACIFIC WALRUS

Odobenus rosmarus divergens

Minimum Score 100

World's Record 147 4/8

The geographical boundary for Pacific walrus is: That portion of the Bering Sea east of the International Dateline; south along coastal Alaska, including the Pribilof Islands and Bristol Bay; extending eastward into Canada to the southwest coasts of Banks and Victoria Islands and the mouth of Bathurst Inlet in Nunavut Province (formerly known as Northwest Territories).

Score	Entire Length of Loose Tusk R.	L.	Circumference of Base R.	L.	Circumference at the Third Quarter R.	L.	Locality	Hunter	Owner	Date Killed	Rank
132 2/8	33 2/8	33 6/8	8 6/8	9	6 6/8	7	Bering Sea, AK	Unknown	R. & C. Ballow	PR 1971	1
129 4/8	36 5/8	34 6/8	7 4/8	7 6/8	6 4/8	6 1/8	Cape Seniavin, AK	Picked Up	Herman C. Meyer	1993	2
128 2/8	32 2/8	32 2/8	9	9	9 1/8	9 1/8	Nome, AK	Native American	Charles A. LeKites	1968	3
124 6/8	31 3/8	31	8 6/8	8 6/8	5 7/8	6	Bering Sea, AK	Unknown	R. & C. Ballow	PR 1971	4
122 2/8	30 5/8	31 4/8	8 5/8	8 7/8	5 6/8	5 6/8	Alaska	Unknown	R. & C. Ballow	1996	5
115 2/8	28 5/8	28	7 7/8	8	5 4/8	5 6/8	Port Heiden, AK	Picked Up	Shawn R. Andres	1997	6
137*	37 1/8	36 4/8	8 4/8	8 3/8	6 4/8	6 4/8	Port Moller, AK	Picked Up	Jim Miller	1999	

* Final score subject to revision by additional verifying measurements.

AMERICAN ELK - TYPICAL ANTLERS

Cervus elaphus nelsoni and related subspecies

Minimum Score 360 World's Record 442 5/8

Score	Length of Main Beam R	Length of Main Beam L	Inside Spread	Circumference at Smallest Place Between First and Second Points R	Circumference at Smallest Place Between First and Second Points L	Number of Points R	Number of Points L	Locality	Hunter	Owner	Date Killed	Rank
425 3/8	56 7/8	60 2/8	54 6/8	10 3/8	10 7/8	6	7	Nye Co., NV	Jerry McKoen	Jerry McKoen	1999	1
397 5/8	57 5/8	57 2/8	62 2/8	9 1/8	9 2/8	6	7	Socorro Co., NM	Richard E. Westwood	Richard E. Westwood	1998	2
397 3/8	57 3/8	58 6/8	48 3/8	8 4/8	8 6/8	7	7	Coconino Co., AZ	Lonzo H. Shields	Lonzo H. Shields	1998	3
396 4/8	53 3/8	53 2/8	37 4/8	9 2/8	9 1/8	6	7	Gila Co., Ariz.	Dan J. Agnew	Dan J. Agnew	1997	4
396	58 5/8	59 6/8	45 2/8	9 2/8	8 4/8	6	6	Billings Co., ND	Paige M. Burian	Paige M. Burian	1997	5
395 4/8	50 2/8	51 4/8	49 6/8	10	10 3/8	6	7	Millard Co., UT	Philip K. Tuttle	Philip K. Tuttle	1999	6
395	56 4/8	54 3/8	39 4/8	9 5/8	9 4/8	7	6	Childs Lake, MB	Irvin Funk	Irvin Funk	1998	7
393 4/8	57	56	46 6/8	9 7/8	9 2/8	6	6	Blaine Co., ID	Darren K. Spiers	Darren K. Spiers	2000	8
393 2/8	55 2/8	56 2/8	43 2/8	8 6/8	9	6	6	Catron Co., NM	Robert M. Miller	Robert M. Miller	1997	9
392 4/8	51 5/8	57 1/8	44 2/8	8 6/8	9	6	7	Gallatin Co., MT	Christopher R. Hann	Christopher R. Hann	2000	10
391 5/8	59 2/8	59 7/8	54 7/8	9 7/8	9	7	7	Tooele Co., UT	James A. Cook	James A. Cook	1999	11
389 4/8	49 5/8	48 5/8	49	8 4/8	8 6/8	6	6	Morgan Co., UT	Robert Farrell	Robert Farrell	1999	12
389	56 2/8	54 5/8	36 2/8	10 3/8	10 6/8	6	6	Otero Co., NM	Larry Stifflemire	Larry Stifflemire	1999	13
388	54 6/8	54	41 6/8	9 2/8	9 1/8	7	6	Beaver Co., UT	Daniel Carter	Daniel Carter	1998	14
387 6/8	52 7/8	52 5/8	39 4/8	8 3/8	8 3/8	6	6	Apache Co., AZ	John A. Cardwell	John A. Cardwell	1998	15
387 5/8	53 5/8	55 4/8	39 7/8	10 3/8	10 3/8	7	7	Douglas Co., CO	Picked Up	CO Div. of Wildl.	1999	16
387	60 4/8	60 1/8	38 2/8	7 1/8	7 3/8	6	6	Apache Co., AZ	Picked Up	Donald H. McBride	1998	17
386 4/8	49 2/8	50 6/8	39	10 4/8	11 2/8	6	6	Navajo Co., AZ	Johnny Bliznak	Johnny Bliznak	1998	18
386 1/8	58 2/8	58 3/8	45 1/8	8 3/8	8 2/8	7	7	Powder River Co., MT	Darrell L. Brabec	Darrell L. Brabec	1999	19
385 6/8	54 7/8	53 2/8	44 6/8	9 5/8	9 3/8	7	7	Billings Co., ND	James A. Feser	James A. Feser	1998	20
385 6/8	55 3/8	55 6/8	50	8 5/8	8 4/8	7	6	Beaverhead Co., MT	Raymond F. Ford, Jr.	Raymond F. Ford, Jr.	1998	20
385	52 4/8	51 4/8	41 4/8	8 5/8	9 6/8	6	6	Jefferson Co., CO	Thomas E. Tietz	Thomas E. Tietz	1997	22
385	56 4/8	59 4/8	47	9	9 4/8	6	6	Park Co., WY	Kelly Preuit	Kelly Preuit	1999	22
384 6/8	55 5/8	56 2/8	42 4/8	9	8	6	6	Sublette Co., WY	Jerry W. Cover	Jerry W. Cover	2000	24
384 1/8	55 7/8	56 7/8	48 1/8	9 1/8	9 3/8	6	7	Gilpin Co., CO	William C. Wheeler	James W. Wheeler	1850	25
383	53 4/8	52	44 6/8	8 1/8	8 2/8	6	6	Garfield Co., UT	Jeffery H. Starr	Jeffery H. Starr	1998	26
382 5/8	52 3/8	52	38 1/8	8 6/8	9 2/8	6	6	Butte Co., ID	Paul E. Harrell	Paul E. Harrell	1997	27
382 3/8	58	58 3/8	43 5/8	8 3/8	8 4/8	6	6	Valencia Co., NM	J.R. Dienst	J.R. Dienst	1998	28
382	58	56 7/8	50 4/8	7 7/8	8	6	6	Iron Co., UT	Douglas Ellett	Douglas Ellett	1998	29
381 7/8	57 1/8	56 6/8	40 7/8	9 7/8	10	7	7	Idaho Co., ID	Charles E. Carver	Charles E. Carver	1998	30
381 2/8	50 6/8	49 2/8	41	9 5/8	9 2/8	7	7	Apache Co., AZ	Gerald Tenigieth	Donald H. McBride	1996	31
381 1/8	50 1/8	51 5/8	43 1/8	8 6/8	8 3/8	7	7	Gila Co., AZ	Steve J. Rico	Steve J. Rico	1999	32
381	59 1/8	61	38 6/8	10 3/8	10	6	6	Garfield Co., UT	Joseph T. Jantorno	Joseph T. Jantorno	2000	33
380 6/8	56 2/8	56 2/8	40	8 3/8	7 7/8	6	6	Unknown	Unknown	Bill Lyons, Jr.	PR 1990	34

AMERICAN ELK - TYPICAL ANTLERS

Cervus elaphus nelsoni and related subspecies

Score	Length of Main Beam R.	L.	Inside Spread	Circumference at Smallest Place Between First and Second Points R.	L.	Number of Points R.	L.	Locality	Hunter	Owner	Date Killed	Rank
380 6/8	57	54 3/8	47 2/8	7 5/8	7 3/8	7	7	Coconino Co., AZ	John C. McClendon	John C. McClendon	1995	34
380 3/8	57	58	34 5/8	8 4/8	8 4/8	6	6	Millard Co., UT	Pam Smith	Pam Smith	1999	36
380 1/8	59 6/8	59 3/8	41 5/8	7 7/8	8 5/8	6	6	Yavapai Co., AZ	Chris J. Dunn	Chris J. Dunn	1997	37
380 1/8	48 2/8	49 7/8	41 3/8	8 7/8	9 4/8	7	6	Coconino Co., AZ	Gerald J. Berkel	Gerald J. Berkel	1998	37
380 1/8	49 1/8	51 1/8	41 7/8	10 5/8	10 3/8	6	6	Moffat Co., CO	Dale L. Harthan	Dale L. Harthan	1998	37
379 6/8	51 7/8	53 1/8	38 4/8	9 5/8	8 5/8	6	6	Millard Co., UT	Darwin B. Johnson	Darwin B. Johnson	2000	40
379 4/8	58 1/8	58 4/8	41 6/8	8 2/8	7 5/8	7	6	Coconino Co., AZ	Dwight Crump	Dwight Crump	1997	41
379 2/8	54 5/8	53 5/8	41 2/8	9 4/8	9 6/8	6	6	Millard Co., UT	Timothy D. Park	Timothy D. Park	1996	42
378 7/8	51 7/8	50 5/8	45 7/8	8 4/8	8 6/8	7	6	Grant Co., NM	Picked Up	David Palmer	1986	43
378 7/8	56 7/8	56 1/8	45 5/8	9 4/8	9 1/8	6	6	Elko Co., NV	Roger T. Mering	Roger T. Mering	1999	43
378 4/8	52 4/8	52 4/8	43 6/8	8 5/8	9 3/8	7	7	Catron Co., NM	Terry K. Miller	Terry K. Miller	1997	45
378 4/8	53 4/8	51 6/8	38 4/8	9 4/8	9 4/8	6	6	Johnson Co., WY	Richard G. Pallister	Richard G. Pallister	1998	45
378 3/8	56	54 5/8	50 7/8	7 5/8	8 1/8	7	6	Panther River, AB	Allen A. Meyer	Allen A. Meyer	1993	47
377 4/8	57 4/8	55 1/8	37 4/8	9 5/8	9 3/8	6	6	Idaho	Unknown	Dale S. Rasmus	1973	48
377	57 2/8	57 5/8	41 2/8	9 3/8	9 5/8	6	7	San Juan Co., UT	Bob W. Mitchell	Bob W. Mitchell	1998	49
377	52 5/8	54 6/8	38 2/8	9 2/8	9 3/8	7	7	Dawes Co., NE	John Walker	John Walker	1998	49
376 7/8	50 2/8	51 3/8	44 3/8	9 6/8	9 5/8	6	6	Red Deer River, AB	Donald E. Charlton	Donald E. Charlton	1999	51
376 5/8	51 2/8	52 3/8	43 3/8	8 2/8	7 6/8	6	6	Unknown	Unknown	Charles F. Seibold	PR 1978	52
376 3/8	53 1/8	53 2/8	53 5/8	8 6/8	8 5/8	8	7	White Pine Co., NV	William R. Balsi, Jr.	William R. Balsi, Jr.	1999	53
376	53 3/8	54 6/8	43	7 4/8	7 5/8	6	6	Unknown	Unknown	Raymond A. Hanken	PR 1999	54
375 3/8	54 5/8	54 7/8	55 6/8	9 5/8	10	6	6	Sevier Co., UT	Lannce Sudweeks	Lannce Sudweeks	1999	55
375 2/8	58 2/8	57 6/8	43 2/8	9 1/8	9 4/8	6	6	Broadwater Co., MT	James A. Davies	James A. Davies	1998	56
375	59 4/8	58	42	8 6/8	9	8	7	Cibola Co., NM	Archie J. Nesbitt	Archie J. Nesbitt	1997	57
373 2/8	58	58	41 4/8	9 1/8	9	6	6	Wallowa Co., OR	Unknown	Dexter Yokom, Jr.	PR 1960	58
373	55 1/8	55 2/8	38 2/8	10 1/8	9 3/8	7	7	Brule Lake, AB	Adriaan Mik	Adriaan Mik	1998	59
372 4/8	54 4/8	51	46 2/8	7 7/8	7 2/8	7	6	Catron Co., NM	Mark A. Knaupp	Mark A. Knaupp	1998	60
371 2/8	48 3/8	49 2/8	40 2/8	9	9 4/8	6	6	Carbon Co., UT	Jody W. White	Jody W. White	2000	61
371 1/8	52	53 5/8	55 5/8	8 6/8	8 3/8	6	6	Madison Co., MT	Jim Gilstrap	Jim Gilstrap	1961	62
370	53 3/8	55 4/8	43 5/8	9	8 4/8	6	7	Teton Co., WY	Richard L. Pharr	Richard L. Pharr	1995	63
369 2/8	56	53 2/8	38 5/8	10 2/8	10 1/8	7	9	Gila Co., AZ	Gilbert T. Adams III	Gilbert T. Adams III	1999	64
368 2/8	50 7/8	50 6/8	40 2/8	9 2/8	9 2/8	6	6	Elko Co., NV	James D. Currivan	James D. Currivan	1998	65
367	57 2/8	57 2/8	40	8 3/8	8 7/8	6	6	Navajo Co., AZ	Robert L. Pagel, Sr.	Robert L. Pagel, Sr.	1998	66
366 5/8	52 3/8	55 3/8	42 7/8	10 4/8	9	6	7	Elko Co., NV	William R. Balsi, Sr.	William R. Balsi, Sr.	1999	67
366 3/8	50 7/8	52	40 5/8	10 2/8	10 2/8	6	6	Albany Co., WY	Kenneth Atkinson	Kenneth Atkinson	1990	68

Score	Main Beam R	Main Beam L	Inside Spread	Circ. R	Circ. L	Pts. R	Pts. L	Locality	Hunter	Owner	Date	Rank
366 3/8	53	53 2/8	42 7/8	9 7/8	10 5/8	6	6	Stillwater Co., MT	Eric N. Svenson	Eric N. Svenson	1999	68
366 2/8	52 4/8	52	48 6/8	8 6/8	8 4/8	6	7	Park Co., WY	Larry L. Hedderman	Larry L. Hedderman	1997	70
366 1/8	53 3/8	55 1/8	43 1/8	8	7 7/8	6	5	Park Co., WY	Claude A. Archuleta	Claude A. Archuleta	1998	71
365 7/8	53 6/8	53 7/8	40 1/8	9	10 5/8	6	7	Billings Co., ND	Henry P. Heintz	Henry P. Heintz	1998	72
365 3/8	55 1/8	54 3/8	47 2/8	7 6/8	8 2/8	7	6	Dolores Co., CO	Renay Neely	Renay Neely	1973	73
365 1/8	58 1/8	58 6/8	51 1/8	7 7/8	8 1/8	6	6	Carbon Co., UT	Michael J. Rodriguez	Michael J. Rodriguez	1998	74
364 7/8	58 5/8	56 6/8	43 7/8	7 6/8	8	5	5	Gallatin Co., MT	William C. Zimmerman, Jr.	William C. Zimmerman, Jr.	1967	75
364 6/8	53 5/8	52 3/8	43	8 5/8	8 4/8	6	6	Crook Co., OR	J. & S. Halsey	Jim Halsey	1975	76
364 6/8	45 7/8	48	41 4/8	9 4/8	9 2/8	8	9	Whitefox River, SK	S. Clifford & R. Fredin	S. Clifford & R. Fredin	1998	76
364 1/8	48 6/8	50 7/8	40 2/8	8 5/8	8 5/8	8	6	Benewah Co., ID	Wallace O. Darkow	Wallace O. Darkow	1998	78
364	50 2/8	51 1/8	42 2/8	8 2/8	8 2/8	6	7	Madison Co., MT	Robert C. Carter	Robert C. Carter	1960	79
363 5/8	54 5/8	55	43 1/8	9 2/8	9 1/8	6	7	Sierra Co., NM	Roy L. Walk	Roy L. Walk	2000	80
363 1/8	54 2/8	54 1/8	46 1/8	7 5/8	7 6/8	6	7	Kittitas Co., WA	Al Bundt	Arlington Fire Dept.	1935	81
362 3/8	52 2/8	52 6/8	32 5/8	8 4/8	9 1/8	6	6	Gila Co., AZ	Brent S. Ruttle, Sr.	Brent S. Ruttle, Sr.	1997	82
362 3/8	51 4/8	52 1/8	41 5/8	8 6/8	9 1/8	6	6	Juab Co., UT	Loren K. Farnsworth	Loren K. Farnsworth	1999	82
362 1/8	50	50 3/8	41 1/8	8 1/8	8 5/8	7	7	Las Animas Co., CO	Tom C. Smith	Tom C. Smith	1996	84
362 1/8	54 1/8	52 7/8	44 1/8	8	7 6/8	6	6	Elko Co., NV	Daniel V. Basanez	Daniel V. Basanez	1999	84
362 1/8	55	56 4/8	40 1/8	9 2/8	8 7/8	6	7	Custer Co., SD	Daniel P. Hartmann	Daniel P. Hartmann	1999	84
362	50 2/8	51 1/8	36 4/8	8 4/8	8 6/8	8	7	Rio Grande Co., CO	Joseph D. Medina	Joseph D. Medina	1998	87
361 7/8	44 3/8	50 7/8	43	8 3/8	8 4/8	6	7	Elko Co., NV	Molly B. Wolf	Molly B. Wolf	1999	88
361 4/8	51 3/8	50 4/8	42 1/8	9 2/8	9 1/8	6	7	Jackson Co., CO	John R. Goemmel	John R. Goemmel	1965	89
361	52 4/8	53 4/8	37 4/8	10 4/8	10	6	6	Valley Co., MT	Gaylord Hagen	Gaylord Hagen	1962	90
361	53 1/8	53 1/8	39 7/8	8 4/8	8 5/8	7	6	Teton Co., WY	Nicholas W. Seador	Nicholas W. Seador	1997	90
361	50 3/8	51	40	8 2/8	8	7	6	Park Co., WY	David Weaver	David Weaver	1998	90
360 4/8	48 3/8	49	39 2/8	8 4/8	8 2/8	6	6	Wallowa Co., OR	Rob Quaempts	Rob Quaempts	1999	93
360	50	48	36 6/8	9 2/8	9 2/8	6	7	White Pine Co., NV	Dennis D. Bowman	Dennis D. Bowman	1997	94
411 2/8*	61 4/8	61 1/8	45 6/8	10 2/8	9 2/8	6	6	Coconino Co., AZ	Picked Up	Thomas J. Wagner	1999	
404*	63 3/8	61 2/8	41 6/8	8 2/8	8 1/8	6	6	Gila Co., AZ	William H. Tilley	William H. Tilley	1998	
400 4/8*	59 1/8	58 5/8	47 4/8	10	11 2/8	6	6	Lincoln Co., NV	W. Steve Perry	W. Steve Perry	1999	

* Final score subject to revision by additional verifying measurements.

AMERICAN ELK - NON-TYPICAL ANTLERS

Cervus elaphus nelsoni and related subspecies

Minimum Score 385   World's Record 465 2/8

Score	Length of Main Beam R	L	Inside Spread	Circumference at Smallest Place Between First and Second Points R	L	Number of Points R	L	Locality	Hunter	Owner	Date Killed	Rank
450 6/8	59	52 6/8	39 4/8	9 1/8	9 3/8	8	8	Apache Co., AZ	Alan D. Hamberlin	Alan D. Hamberlin	1998	1
420 4/8	52	55 5/8	36 2/8	10 4/8	10 4/8	8	9	Kern Co., CA	Brad Peters	Brad Peters	2000	2
419 4/8	55 5/8	56	38 7/8	9 6/8	9 1/8	8	8	Yakima Co., WA	Jim R. Coe	James P. Walter	1932	3
410 3/8	48 3/8	52 5/8	45 1/8	10 6/8	11	7	8	Hill Co., MT	Brendan V. Burns	Brendan V. Burns	2000	4
409 3/8	52 6/8	53	42 2/8	9 3/8	9 4/8	7	8	Coconino Co., MT	Brent V. Trumbo	Brent V. Trumbo	2000	5
408 5/8	53 2/8	52 3/8	45 6/8	9 4/8	9 4/8	8	6	Petroleum Co., MT	Riley T. McGiboney	Riley T. McGiboney	1998	6
406 4/8	53	53 3/8	39 6/8	10 5/8	10 5/8	8	6	Elko Co., NV	Randy Blackwell	Randy Blackwell	1999	7
403 6/8	64 1/8	63 6/8	40	9 4/8	9 7/8	6	8	Greenlee Co., AZ	Valentino J. Pugnea	Valentino J. Pugnea	1997	8
403 5/8	50 1/8	50 5/8	44 3/8	6 6/8	7 6/8	8	8	Catron Co., NM	Picked Up	Jack Diamond	1999	9
401 4/8	48 6/8	47 7/8	32 6/8	9 1/8	9 7/8	7	10	Dauphin Lake, MB	Picked Up	Cabela's	1998	10
401	49 1/8	49 2/8	40 6/8	9 2/8	8 6/8	8	8	Cache Co., UT	Picked Up	L. Dwight Israelsen	1959	11
398 3/8	52 2/8	51 3/8	37 6/8	8 7/8	9 3/8	8	9	Adams Co., ID	Unknown	Delvin L. Watkins	1955	12
398 3/8	48 2/8	47 7/8	37 3/8	8 3/8	8 3/8	10	9	Klickitat Co., WA	Ron Whitmire	Roger Kuhnhousen	1999	12
398 1/8	53 4/8	52 2/8	42 5/8	7 7/8	8 3/8	8	8	White Pine Co., NV	Brian D. Harwood	Brian D. Harwood	1998	14
398	49	53 4/8	38 1/8	9	9 6/8	8	9	Graham Co., AZ	George R. Harms	George R. Harms	1998	15
397 5/8	50 4/8	50 2/8	43	10	9 5/8	8	8	Greenlee Co., AZ	Gerald D. Spivey, Sr.	Gerald D. Spivey, Sr.	1997	16
397 2/8	54 7/8	55	39 6/8	9 7/8	9 6/8	7	8	Billings Co., ND	Larry J. Fitterer	Larry J. Fitterer	1999	17
396 3/8	54 7/8	54 3/8	54 4/8	11 1/8	10 4/8	8	6	Apache Co., AZ	Herman C. Meyer	Herman C. Meyer	1995	18
396 3/8	41 6/8	44	40 2/8	10 7/8	10 4/8	8	8	Pasqua Hills, SK	Wilfred Richer	Wilfred Richer	1998	18
396	52 7/8	51 4/8	38	9 4/8	9 2/8	7	6	Apache Co., AZ	Jay A. Kellett	Jay A. Kellett	1998	20
395 5/8	49 5/8	48	44 7/8	9 2/8	9 1/8	8	7	Fremont Co., ID	James E. Hoover	D.J. Hollinger & B. Howard	1976	21
394 3/8	55 5/8	49 7/8	42 5/8	9 7/8	9 6/8	8	7	Hill Co., MT	Picked Up	Gerald Small	1900	22
390 3/8	47 1/8	46 4/8	46 3/8	9 1/8	9 3/8	8	7	Unknown	Unknown	W. Scott Smith	1900	23
389	55 4/8	58 2/8	40 6/8	8 3/8	8 1/8	8	8	Juab Co., UT	Russell Jones	Russell Jones	1998	24
388 5/8	51 6/8	52	38 4/8	9 7/8	9 7/8	8	9	White Pine Co., NV	Patrick J. Juhl	Patrick J. Juhl	1998	25
387 4/8	53	52 5/8	49 2/8	10 3/8	11 2/8	6	9	Lincoln Co., NV	Cory L. Lytle	Cory L. Lytle	1998	26
387 4/8	53 3/8	53 2/8	35 4/8	9	9 7/8	7	7	Coconino Co., AZ	James B. Herrick	James B. Herrick	1999	26
385 5/8	50 4/8	49 7/8	43 5/8	11 7/8	11 6/8	7	8	Petroleum Co., MT	Gregory A. Herrin	Gregory A. Herrin	1997	28
385 2/8	56	55 5/8	42	10 6/8	10 7/8	8	7	Navajo Co., AZ	Truman D. Collins	Truman D. Collins	1998	29
415 2/8*	49 1/8	51 7/8						Apache Co., AZ	Blair Anderson	Blair Anderson	1999	

* Final score subject to revision by additional verifying measurements.

ROOSEVELT'S ELK

Cervus elaphus roosevelti

Minimum Score 275　　　　　　　New World's Record 396 5/8

Roosevelt's elk includes trophies from: west of Highway I-5 in Oregon and Washington; Del Norte, Humboldt and Trinity Counties, California, as well as that portion of Siskiyou County west of I-5 in Northern California; Afognak and Raspberry Islands of Alaska; and Vancouver Island, British Columbia.

Score	Length of Main Beam R.	L.	Inside Spread	Circumference at Smallest Place Between First and Second Points R.	L.	Number of Points R.	L.	Locality	Hunter	Owner	Date Killed	Rank
396 5/8	46 3/8	46 7/8	32 3/8	8 7/8	9 5/8	10	9	Campbell River, BC	Karl W. Minor, Sr.	Karl W. Minor, Sr.	1997	1
372 1/8	53 4/8	55 4/8	37 3/8	8 6/8	8 1/8	8	8	Del Norte Co., CA	Robert H. Gaynor	Robert H. Gaynor	2000	2
372	47 4/8	49 5/8	34 5/8	8 6/8	8 4/8	8	8	Humboldt Co., CA	Scot A. Christiansen	Scot A. Christiansen	2000	3
360 5/8	51 4/8	50 3/8	36	8 4/8	9	8	10	Clatsop Co., OR	Tod L. Reichert	Tod L. Reichert	2000	4
359 7/8	49 2/8	53 5/8	43 2/8	7	7 2/8	7	6	Tillamook Co., OR	Floyd Crandel	James O. Acock	PR 1960	5
356 4/8	48 4/8	49 7/8	35 2/8	9 3/8	9 2/8	7	7	Davie River, BC	Larry A. Russak	Larry A. Russak	1999	6
353 5/8	53 3/8	53	35 5/8	9	9 2/8	8	8	Coos Co., OR	Hank Shields	Glenn Shields	1951	7
345 1/8	47	47 2/8	41 2/8	9 5/8	8 6/8	7	7	Bonanza Lake, BC	Wanda LeBlanc	Wanda LeBlanc	1999	8
342 2/8	44	46 2/8	35 1/8	9 4/8	10	7	7	Memekay River, BC	David H. Todd	David H. Todd	1998	9
341 6/8	47 3/8	44 1/8	40 2/8	9 7/8	10 2/8	7	9	Vancouver Island, BC	Archie J. Nesbitt	Archie J. Nesbitt	1997	10
340 7/8	45 5/8	44 7/8	35 1/8	9 3/8	8 5/8	7	7	Del Norte Co., CA	Monte D. Matheson	Monte D. Matheson	2000	11
338 7/8	49 6/8	50 4/8	43	8	7 4/8	7	7	Humboldt Co., CA	Paul E. Benoit	Paul E. Benoit	2000	12
338 1/8	54 4/8	49 1/8	32	7	8 1/8	8	8	Humboldt Co., CA	Ric Rhoades	Ric Rhoades	1984	13
338	50 7/8	48 3/8	36 2/8	9 6/8	10 7/8	6	9	Muchalat Lake, BC	Joshua D. Fyfe	Joshua D. Fyfe	1998	14
336 5/8	38	39 1/8	34 7/8	10 3/8	10 1/8	6	8	Jefferson Co., WA	L. & T. McClanahan	Larry McClanahan	1965	15
335 2/8	51 1/8	51 6/8	40 1/8	11 3/8	10 3/8	6	7	Benton Co., OR	Gary W. Kinman	Gary W. Kinman	1997	16
335 1/8	48 3/8	48 5/8	39 3/8	9	9 1/8	7	8	Humboldt Co., CA	Everett J. Goodale	Everett J. Goodale	2000	17
326 4/8	48 1/8	51 2/8	42 3/8	7	7 2/8	6	6	Douglas Co., OR	Lawrence Smith	Jody Smith	1958	18
325 2/8	45 4/8	41 2/8	43 5/8	8 5/8	8 3/8	8	7	Del Norte Co., CA	Michael McCollum	Michael McCollum	1999	19
324 4/8	52 6/8	51	39 7/8	9 1/8	8 7/8	6	7	Polk Co., OR	Ronald G. Smith	Ronald G. Smith	1998	20
322 7/8	53	51 5/8	42 5/8	9 4/8	9 2/8	8	6	Curry Co., OR	Dallas E. Ettinger	Dallas E. Ettinger	1993	21
320 2/8	44 5/8	44 5/8	29 3/8	7 5/8	8	8	6	Tillamook Co., OR	A. Wegler	Joseph Doerfler	PR 1950	22
319 5/8	42 7/8	42	35 6/8	8 4/8	8 5/8	9	7	Grays Harbor Co., WA	Gary D. Schurr	Gary D. Schurr	1996	23
318	43 5/8	43 4/8	30 6/8	9	8 5/8	7	7	Sucwoa River, BC	Barry Naimark	Barry Naimark	1998	24
315 2/8	41 6/8	43	39 6/8	8 6/8	8 2/8	7	7	Columbia Co., OR	David A. Evenson	David A. Evenson	1998	25
313 3/8	50 3/8	50 3/8	41 3/8	9 6/8	9 5/8	6	6	Del Norte Co., CA	Richard L. Smith	Richard L. Smith	1998	26
311 4/8	44 5/8	44 6/8	44 3/8	9 2/8	8 4/8	7	7	Clatsop Co., OR	Delmer A. Johnson	Casey Johnson	1957	27
311 2/8	47 1/8	46 4/8	32 2/8	9 3/8	9	7	8	Clatsop Co., OR	Don L. Twito	Don L. Twito	1956	28
308 5/8	49 1/8	47 4/8	37 7/8	12 1/8	11 2/8	6	5	Douglas Co., OR	George Kellis	Bob Wilkes	1952	29
308 4/8	46 1/8	44 6/8	36 2/8	6 5/8	6 6/8	6	7	Clatsop Co., OR	Earnest A. Stevens	Donald J. Stevens	PR 1964	30
307 4/8	49 7/8	48 1/8	34	10 1/8	11 7/8	7	7	Del Norte Co., CA	Richard L. Butler	Richard L. Butler	1998	31

ROOSEVELT'S ELK

Cervus elaphus rooseveli

Score	Length of Main Beam R.	L.	Inside Spread	Circumference at Smallest Place Between First and Second Points R.	L.	Number of Points R.	L.	Locality	Hunter	Owner	Date Killed	Rank
307 2/8	48 1/8	45 7/8	39 7/8	9 1/8	8 2/8	7	7	Siskiyou Co., CA	Bill Kleaver	Bill Kleaver	1997	32
305 7/8	41 7/8	44	34 5/8	9 6/8	9	7	7	Gold River, BC	Cory C. Hanley	Cory C. Hanley	1998	33
305 4/8	47 2/8	47	37 3/8	7 6/8	7 2/8	6	6	Tillamook Co., OR	Patrick E. Windle	Patrick E. Windle	1995	34
305 2/8	43 2/8	43 6/8	35 2/8	8 4/8	8 5/8	7	7	Pacific Co., WA	Michael M. McHale	Michael M. McHale	1975	35
304 3/8	45 2/8	49 2/8	42 1/8	9 2/8	9 1/8	6	6	Clallam Co., WA	Harry E. Reed	Harry E. Reed	1997	36
301 1/8	40 6/8	40 2/8	39	8 3/8	7 7/8	7	8	Pacific Co., WA	Larry D. Hart	Larry D. Hart II	1969	37
300 3/8	45 7/8	44 5/8	40 2/8	8 5/8	9 2/8	7	8	Lincoln Co., OR	Donald V. Miles	Donald V. Miles	1996	38
300 2/8	40	39 5/8	33 2/8	8 1/8	9 2/8	7	8	Yamhill Co., OR	Timothy R. Bainter	Timothy R. Bainter	1997	39
300 1/8	47 3/8	48 6/8	34	8 3/8	8 4/8	6	6	Del Norte Co., CA	Paul H. Kunzler	Paul H. Kunzler	1999	40
299	47 6/8	46 2/8	33 3/8	8 6/8	7 7/8	7	6	Del Norte Co., CA	Glenn W. Ng	Glenn W. Ng	2000	41
298 6/8	44 6/8	45	33 1/8	9 1/8	9 6/8	6	7	Conuma River, BC	Monty A. Klein	Monty A. Klein	1998	42
297 5/8	45 6/8	44 6/8	39 7/8	8 3/8	8 1/8	6	6	Del Norte Co., CA	Ronald F. Cibart	Ronald F. Cibart	2000	43
295 1/8	42 6/8	43 5/8	33 5/8	9 3/8	9	6	6	Washington Co., OR	Eric T. Sahnow	Eric T. Sahnow	1996	44
293 1/8	42 7/8	44	41 4/8	8	8 3/8	6	6	Douglas Co., OR	Bruce K. Moore	Tadd K. Moore	1998	45
290 5/8	43 7/8	43 2/8	34 3/8	8	8 7/8	7	8	Clatsop Co., OR	James H. Thrower	James H. Thrower	1998	46
287 6/8	44 6/8	41 2/8	37 4/8	7 7/8	7 4/8	6	6	Clatsop Co., OR	Weslie J. Rud	Weslie J. Rud	1998	47
282	44 2/8	46 4/8	41 5/8	7 4/8	10 1/8	6	6	Douglas Co., OR	Ray Cole	Ray Cole	1953	48
280 5/8	43 3/8	44 3/8	35 6/8	7 5/8	7 3/8	6	6	Lane Co., OR	Roger A. Moore	Roger A. Moore	1998	49
278 5/8	40 4/8	42 7/8	38 7/8	8 2/8	8	8	8	Columbia Co., OR	Thomas A. Cieloha	Thomas A. Cieloha	1999	50
275 7/8	42 2/8	43 7/8	29 3/8	8	8 6/8	6	7	Raspberry Island, AK	Guy C. Powell	Guy C. Powell	1958	51
376 1/8*	43 5/8	45 4/8	39 2/8	9 6/8	9 5/8	8	8	Bonanza Lake, BC	Richard D. Smith	Richard D. Smith	1995	
372*	49 1/8	47 3/8	41	7 4/8	7 5/8	9	8	Columbia Co., OR	Picked Up	R.E. & T.D. Walker	PR 1940	

* Final score subject to revision by additional verifying measurements.

TULE ELK

Cervus elaphus nannodes

Minimum Score 270   New World's Record 351

Tule elk are from selected areas in California. For a complete description of the boundary, check the Official Measurer's manual, *Measuring and Scoring North American Big Game Trophies*, 2nd Edition, Revised 2000.

Score	Length of Main Beam R.	L.	Inside Spread	Circumference at Smallest Place Between First and Second Points R.	L.	Number of Points R.	L.	Locality	Hunter	Owner	Date Killed	Rank
351	48 6/8	47 4/8	51 3/8	7 1/8	6 4/8	9	9	Solano Co., CA	Quentin Hughes	B&C National Collection	1990	1
346 6/8	48	49 4/8	37 4/8	7 5/8	6 7/8	8	8	Sonoma Co., CA	Christian Weise	Harry Weise	1851	2
341 4/8	49 5/8	52 2/8	48 3/8	7 6/8	7 5/8	8	7	Solano Co., CA	Alvin M. Wallen	Alvin M. Wallen	1990	3
330 1/8	52 3/8	52 4/8	38 4/8	7 6/8	7 2/8	9	7	Solano Co., CA	Tod L. Reichert	Tod L. Reichert	1999	4
319 2/8	47 6/8	43	44 7/8	6 6/8	7 4/8	8	7	Solano Co., CA	H. James Tonkin, Jr.	H. James Tonkin, Jr.	1992	5
317 3/8	51 5/8	49 6/8	39 4/8	7 4/8	7 4/8	9	8	Solano Co., CA	Donald L. Potter	Donald L. Potter	1996	6
315 4/8	46 4/8	48 7/8	39 7/8	7 6/8	7 2/8	7	7	Solano Co., CA	David G. Paullin	David G. Paullin	1994	7
308 6/8	40 4/8	42 4/8	52	8 1/8	8 1/8	8	6	San Luis Obispo Co., CA	Ray M. Tonkin	Ray M. Tonkin	1999	8
277	42 5/8	42 5/8	40 7/8	8	8	6	7	Mendocino Co., CA	Scott L. Brothers	Scott L. Brothers	1995	9
273 4/8	37	43 6/8	42	7 2/8	7 3/8	7	7	San Luis Obispo Co., CA	Rex Baker	Rex Baker	2000	10
403*	45 6/8	43 1/8	37 6/8	10 3/8	9 5/8	10	12	Solano Co., CA	Picked Up	CA Dept. of Fish & Game	1995	
365*	48	47 3/8	41 3/8	8 4/8	8 6/8	9	8	Solano Co., CA	Bryce Evans	Bryce Evans	1997	
324 6/8*	43 6/8	44 2/8	40 4/8	8 4/8	8 1/8	10	9	Solano Co., CA	David L. Newsom	David L. Newsom	1991	
311 4/8*	41 5/8	40 4/8	38 3/8	8 7/8	7 7/8	10	10	Solano Co., CA	Paul D. Osmond	Paul D. Osmond	1999	

* Final score subject to revision by additional verifying measurements.

MULE DEER - TYPICAL ANTLERS

Odocoileus hemionus hemionus and certain related subspecies

Minimum Score 180 World's Record 226 4/8

Score	Length of Main Beam R.	L.	Inside Spread	Circumference at Smallest Place Between Burr and First Point R.	L.	Number of Points R.	L.	Locality	Hunter	Owner	Date Killed	Rank
212 7/8	27 1/8	26 6/8	28 4/8	4 5/8	4 6/8	5	5	Garfield Co., CO	Errol R. Raley	Errol R. Raley	1971	1
206 6/8	28 1/8	27 4/8	26	6 1/8	6 2/8	7	7	Sonora, MX	Jack Gurley	Jack Gurley	1998	2
206 1/8	25 7/8	25 5/8	22 1/8	5 7/8	6	5	5	Coconino Co., AZ	Unknown	Danny Hopper	PR 1949	3
202 1/8	27 1/8	27 1/8	21 1/8	5 3/8	5 4/8	5	5	Deschutes Co., OR	Ray Cole	Ray Cole	1946	4
201 1/8	26 5/8	27 5/8	25 2/8	5 1/8	5	6	6	Sonora, MX	Bruce K. Kidman	Bruce K. Kidman	1998	5
201	25 4/8	25 4/8	25 6/8	4 7/8	5 1/8	5	5	Wallowa Co., OR	Ross Bennett	Ross Bennett	1959	6
201	24 7/8	26	23 1/8	5 2/8	5 1/8	6	5	Idaho	Unknown	Bruce D. Ringsmith	PR 1960	6
200 7/8	26 5/8	26	26 3/8	5 6/8	5 4/8	6	6	Colorado	Robert E. Lee, Jr.	Kent Lee	1956	8
200 7/8	27 7/8	27	26 7/8	5 4/8	5 6/8	5	5	Baker Co., OR	Hans C. Finke	Hans C. Finke	1998	8
200 6/8	27 7/8	25 3/8	25	4 7/8	5 1/8	5	7	Eagle Creek, SK	Ronald S. Cordes	Ronald S. Cordes	1998	10
200 6/8	25 1/8	24 7/8	26	5	5 1/8	5	6	Caribou Co., ID	Beaver Fillo	Beaver Fillo	2000	10
200 5/8	27 7/8	28	27 5/8	5 2/8	5 2/8	6	6	Rio Arriba Co., NM	Larry L. Panzy	Larry L. Panzy	1998	12
199 6/8	29	27 4/8	24 7/8	4 6/8	4 6/8	5	5	Mesa Co., CO	Picked Up	Darryl Powell	PR 1975	13
199 6/8	26 5/8	27	20	5 4/8	5 3/8	4	4	Harney Co., OR	Chris Schweizer	Chris Schweizer	1995	13
199 5/8	28 3/8	27 3/8	22 3/8	5 5/8	5 6/8	5	5	Unknown	Unknown	Pat Powell	PR 1950	15
199 5/8	30 5/8	29 5/8	27 5/8	5	5	6	7	Lake Co., OR	B. Keene & D. Keene	Bill Keene	1968	15
199 5/8	25 4/8	26 2/8	28 6/8	5	5	5	6	Highvale, AB	Gordon Kulak	Gordon Kulak	1997	15
199 3/8	25 7/8	25 1/8	23 4/8	5 5/8	5 6/8	4	6	Uncompahgre Natl. For., CO	Floyd Whitner	Jerome Burlingame	PR 1933	18
199 2/8	25 1/8	25 4/8	19 4/8	5	4 6/8	5	5	Elmore Co., ID	Picked Up	Judi L. Williams	1998	19
198 5/8	25 6/8	27 4/8	25 5/8	4 4/8	4 4/8	5	5	Montezuma Co., CO	Mary Ann Ott	Mary Ann Ott	1968	20
198 5/8	22 2/8	22 4/8	26 5/8	5 6/8	5 2/8	7	7	Sonora, MX	Jerry W. Willeford	Jerry W. Willeford	1998	20
198 5/8	26 5/8	28 6/8	28 2/8	4 5/8	4 5/8	6	6	Malheur Co., OR	Troy Cummins	Troy Cummins	2000	20
197 7/8	29 3/8	28 7/8	29 1/8	5 3/8	5 4/8	5	5	Rio Arriba Co., NM	Picked Up	Robert J. Seeds	1999	23
197 5/8	27	27	23 7/8	5 1/8	5 3/8	5	5	Unknown	Unknown	Robert E. Oldroyd	1963	24
197 5/8	26 7/8	26	27 6/8	5 2/8	5 2/8	7	6	S. Saskatchewan River, SK	Robert H. Boeschen	Robert H. Boeschen	1998	24
197 4/8	28 3/8	28 7/8	26	5 4/8	5 3/8	7	5	Rio Arriba Co., NM	Travis Amarillo	Travis Amarillo	1999	26
197 1/8	27 1/8	28 1/8	24 3/8	5	4 7/8	7	7	Colorado	Kenneth W. Knox	Kenneth W. Knox	PR 1980	27
197	25 1/8	26	25 2/8	4 7/8	4 6/8	5	5	Lincoln Co., MT	Darvin R. Chambliss	Darvin R. Chambliss	1998	28
196 7/8	27	27 6/8	21 2/8	5 2/8	5 2/8	6	6	Teton Co., ID	Dennis Barker	Dennis Barker	1986	29
196 7/8	25 5/8	24 2/8	26 3/8	4 4/8	4 3/8	5	5	Rio Arriba Co., NM	Robert J. Seeds	Robert J. Seeds	1998	29
196 6/8	27 2/8	26 6/8	27 2/8	5 2/8	5 3/8	6	6	Malheur Co., OR	Dan L. Erwert	Dan L. Erwert	1992	31
196 5/8	24 7/8	23 7/8	23 7/8	5	5 1/8	6	6	Washington Co., ID	Phillip J. Wilson	Phillip J. Wilson	1958	32
196 5/8	24 4/8	24 7/8	25 5/8	4 7/8	4 7/8	7	5	Wyoming	Unknown	Richard C. Birch	PR 1980	32
196 5/8	26 5/8	27 5/8	22 5/8	5 1/8	5 1/8	5	5	Hayes Creek, BC	Dave Legg	Robert H. Legg	1982	32

Score						R	L	Locality	Hunter	Owner	Date	Rank
$196^{5}/_{8}$	28	$26^{5}/_{8}$	$31^{2}/_{8}$	$5^{1}/_{8}$	$5^{1}/_{8}$	5	6	Deschutes Co., OR	Robert E. Byrd	Robert E. Byrd	PR 1984	32
$196^{4}/_{8}$	$25^{4}/_{8}$	27	27	$5^{6}/_{8}$	$5^{1}/_{8}$	6	5	Park Co., WY	Keith G. Larsen	Keith G. Larsen	1997	36
$196^{4}/_{8}$	$24^{3}/_{8}$	$26^{7}/_{8}$	$24^{2}/_{8}$	$4^{7}/_{8}$	$5^{6}/_{8}$	5	5	Bonneville Co., ID	Louis H. Griffin	Louis H. Griffin	1998	36
$196^{4}/_{8}$	$26^{4}/_{8}$	26	$24^{1}/_{8}$	$5^{4}/_{8}$	$5^{4}/_{8}$	6	7	Gooding Co., ID	Gary D. Loghry	Gary D. Loghry	1999	36
$196^{4}/_{8}$	$26^{3}/_{8}$	$29^{2}/_{8}$	$22^{4}/_{8}$	$5^{3}/_{8}$	$5^{3}/_{8}$	7	7	Rio Arriba Co., NM	Alan Vicenti	Alan Vicenti	1999	36
$196^{1}/_{8}$	$26^{3}/_{8}$	$27^{4}/_{8}$	$23^{3}/_{8}$	$5^{7}/_{8}$	$5^{6}/_{8}$	6	5	Blackwater River, BC	Dale Harrison	Dale Harrison	1998	40
196	$25^{5}/_{8}$	$27^{5}/_{8}$	22	$5^{3}/_{8}$	$5^{2}/_{8}$	5	5	Sevier Co., UT	Picked Up	Wade L. Eakle	1976	41
196	26	$26^{1}/_{8}$	$23^{2}/_{8}$	$5^{3}/_{8}$	5	6	6	Sounding Creek, AB	William F. Potosky	William F. Potosky	1998	41
$195^{5}/_{8}$	28	$27^{7}/_{8}$	$24^{7}/_{8}$	$5^{5}/_{8}$	$5^{4}/_{8}$	6	6	Lake Co., OR	Betty L. Morris	Betty L. Morris	1963	43
$195^{4}/_{8}$	$28^{5}/_{8}$	$27^{6}/_{8}$	$27^{2}/_{8}$	$4^{4}/_{8}$	$4^{3}/_{8}$	5	5	Gunnison Co., CO	Celso Rico, Jr.	Celso Rico, Jr.	1981	44
$195^{4}/_{8}$	$25^{6}/_{8}$	$27^{4}/_{8}$	$20^{3}/_{8}$	$5^{4}/_{8}$	$5^{4}/_{8}$	6	7	Harris Creek, BC	Al Hunt	Al Hunt	1986	44
$194^{7}/_{8}$	$24^{7}/_{8}$	$25^{6}/_{8}$	$23^{5}/_{8}$	$5^{4}/_{8}$	$5^{1}/_{8}$	7	10	Mesa Co., CO	JoReva Wellborn	JoReva Wellborn	1949	46
$194^{7}/_{8}$	$28^{3}/_{8}$	$28^{2}/_{8}$	$21^{1}/_{8}$	$5^{4}/_{8}$	$6^{1}/_{8}$	5	5	Kamloops Lake, BC	Donald E. Meeks	Donald E. Meeks	PR 1987	46
$194^{6}/_{8}$	$25^{2}/_{8}$	$25^{3}/_{8}$	$22^{1}/_{8}$	$4^{7}/_{8}$	$4^{7}/_{8}$	6	5	Adams Co., ID	Stanley Branstetter	Stanley Branstetter	1984	48
$194^{6}/_{8}$	26	$25^{6}/_{8}$	$22^{6}/_{8}$	$5^{1}/_{8}$	$5^{1}/_{8}$	5	5	Rio Arriba Co., NM	Jordan A. Pearlman	Jordan A. Pearlman	1998	48
$194^{5}/_{8}$	$27^{1}/_{8}$	$26^{6}/_{8}$	$31^{5}/_{8}$	$5^{1}/_{8}$	5	6	7	Idaho	Harold K. Layher	Rod Stewardson	PR 1950	50
$194^{5}/_{8}$	$26^{7}/_{8}$	$26^{7}/_{8}$	$23^{5}/_{8}$	$4^{7}/_{8}$	$4^{6}/_{8}$	7	6	Montezuma Co., CO	Tom G. Broderick	Tom G. Broderick	1990	50
$194^{4}/_{8}$	$22^{4}/_{8}$	$22^{7}/_{8}$	$22^{3}/_{8}$	$5^{1}/_{8}$	$5^{2}/_{8}$	6	5	Kane Co., UT	Robert G. Ferrero	Robert G. Ferrero	1999	52
$194^{2}/_{8}$	$24^{2}/_{8}$	24	25	$5^{5}/_{8}$	$5^{5}/_{8}$	5	5	Siskiyou Co., CA	Hap Hottenstein	Judy G. Cottini	PR 1950	53
$194^{2}/_{8}$	$27^{4}/_{8}$	$27^{2}/_{8}$	$26^{4}/_{8}$	$5^{1}/_{8}$	$5^{1}/_{8}$	6	6	Mesa Co., CO	Frank J. Moore	Frank J. Moore	1999	53
$194^{1}/_{8}$	$27^{3}/_{8}$	$23^{5}/_{8}$	$23^{5}/_{8}$	$4^{7}/_{8}$	$4^{7}/_{8}$	5	5	Bone Creek, SK	Kevin R. Whyte	Kevin R. Whyte	1998	55
$194^{1}/_{8}$	$22^{4}/_{8}$	$23^{7}/_{8}$	$22^{1}/_{8}$	$5^{1}/_{8}$	$5^{3}/_{8}$	6	5	Gooding Co., ID	Jeff L. Basterrchea	Jeff L. Basterrchea	1999	55
194	$26^{4}/_{8}$	$25^{7}/_{8}$	25	5	$4^{5}/_{8}$	6	6	Lemhi Co., ID	Andrew W. Jones	Benjamin C. Jones	1979	57
194	$26^{3}/_{8}$	$28^{7}/_{8}$	$23^{4}/_{8}$	$4^{6}/_{8}$	$4^{6}/_{8}$	5	6	Grand Co., CO	Bill Britt	Larry Underwood	PR 1980	57
$193^{7}/_{8}$	$25^{5}/_{8}$	$27^{2}/_{8}$	$26^{7}/_{8}$	$5^{2}/_{8}$	$5^{2}/_{8}$	5	5	S. Saskatchewan River, SK	Belinda M. Guckert	Belinda M. Guckert	1998	59
$193^{6}/_{8}$	24	$24^{1}/_{8}$	$22^{6}/_{8}$	$5^{1}/_{8}$	$5^{1}/_{8}$	5	5	Yuma Co., CO	John M. McAteer	John M. McAteer	1997	60
$193^{5}/_{8}$	$23^{3}/_{8}$	$23^{7}/_{8}$	$19^{1}/_{8}$	5	$4^{7}/_{8}$	5	6	Sublette Co., WY	Paul Carter, Jr.	Paul Carter, Jr.	1966	61
$193^{5}/_{8}$	$25^{7}/_{8}$	$25^{7}/_{8}$	$22^{2}/_{8}$	$4^{7}/_{8}$	$4^{6}/_{8}$	5	5	Kane Co., UT	Jeffrey L. Janisch	Jeffrey L. Janisch	1993	61
$193^{4}/_{8}$	$26^{6}/_{8}$	$27^{2}/_{8}$	$29^{1}/_{8}$	$5^{2}/_{8}$	$5^{2}/_{8}$	8	7	Iron Co., UT	Gordon L. Farnsworth	Gordon L. Farnsworth	1966	63
$193^{4}/_{8}$	$24^{5}/_{8}$	$25^{7}/_{8}$	$20^{3}/_{8}$	$5^{1}/_{8}$	$5^{1}/_{8}$	5	5	Unknown	Unknown	Ron Boehm	1995	63
$193^{4}/_{8}$	$25^{7}/_{8}$	$25^{5}/_{8}$	$22^{2}/_{8}$	$4^{4}/_{8}$	$4^{3}/_{8}$	5	6	Cassia Co., ID	Picked Up	David R. Harrow	1998	63
$193^{3}/_{8}$	$25^{5}/_{8}$	$24^{4}/_{8}$	$18^{5}/_{8}$	$5^{2}/_{8}$	$5^{3}/_{8}$	6	5	Frenchman River, SK	Brian M. Irish	Brian M. Irish	1998	66
$193^{2}/_{8}$	$28^{2}/_{8}$	$28^{3}/_{8}$	$28^{2}/_{8}$	$4^{6}/_{8}$	$4^{4}/_{8}$	7	6	Eagle Co., CO	Robert D. Pape	Rory Pape	1959	67
$193^{2}/_{8}$	$26^{7}/_{8}$	$26^{4}/_{8}$	$26^{4}/_{8}$	$5^{1}/_{8}$	5	6	5	Delta Co., CO	Kenneth R. French	Kenneth R. French	1979	67
$193^{2}/_{8}$	$23^{7}/_{8}$	$24^{4}/_{8}$	$22^{4}/_{8}$	$5^{1}/_{8}$	$5^{1}/_{8}$	4	4	Lincoln Co., WY	Greg E. Morris	Greg E. Morris	2000	67
$193^{1}/_{8}$	25	$25^{5}/_{8}$	$23^{4}/_{8}$	$5^{4}/_{8}$	$5^{3}/_{8}$	7	5	Sublette Co., WY	Edward E. Hall, Jr.	Edward E. Hall, Jr.	1958	70
$193^{1}/_{8}$	$26^{7}/_{8}$	$26^{2}/_{8}$	27	$5^{2}/_{8}$	$5^{1}/_{8}$	6	5	Arizona	Unknown	Aly M. Bruner	PR 1970	70
$193^{1}/_{8}$	$28^{4}/_{8}$	$28^{5}/_{8}$	$23^{1}/_{8}$	$5^{5}/_{8}$	$5^{5}/_{8}$	6	8	Suffern Lake, SK	Dan C. McKinnon	Dan C. McKinnon	1998	70
193	$24^{4}/_{8}$	$24^{5}/_{8}$	$22^{3}/_{8}$	$5^{6}/_{8}$	$5^{4}/_{8}$	4	4	Lincoln Co., WY	David K. Halverson	David K. Halverson	1997	73
$192^{7}/_{8}$	$27^{2}/_{8}$	27	$24^{7}/_{8}$	$5^{3}/_{8}$	5	6	6	Bonneville Co., ID	Max L. Christensen	Terrel M. Christensen	1965	74
$192^{7}/_{8}$	$26^{3}/_{8}$	$26^{3}/_{8}$	$26^{3}/_{8}$	$5^{4}/_{8}$	$5^{4}/_{8}$	8	9	Rio Arriba Co., NM	J. Ed Morgan	J. Ed Morgan	1966	74
$192^{6}/_{8}$	24	$23^{6}/_{8}$	$24^{5}/_{8}$	5	$5^{6}/_{8}$	7	7	Montezuma Co., CO	Jay N. Cruzan	Jay N. Cruzan	1988	76
$192^{6}/_{8}$	$24^{2}/_{8}$	25	$23^{7}/_{8}$	$5^{5}/_{8}$	$5^{4}/_{8}$	6	6	Las Animas Co., CO	James S. Kent	James S. Kent	1995	76

MULE DEER - TYPICAL ANTLERS

Odocoileus hemionus hemionus and certain related subspecies

Score	Length of Main Beam R.	L.	Inside Spread	Circumference at Smallest Place Between Burr and First Point R.	L.	Number of Points R.	L.	Locality	Hunter	Owner	Date Killed	Rank
192 6/8	26 7/8	26 4/8	22 4/8	5 3/8	5 3/8	6	5	Las Animas Co., CO	Fred D. Ruland	Fred D. Ruland	1997	76
192 6/8	24 6/8	25	22 1/8	4 7/8	5	6	7	Elbow, SK	Rick E. Hawkes	Rick E. Hawkes	1998	76
192 5/8	25 6/8	25 4/8	20 5/8	5 2/8	5 2/8	4	4	Grand Co., CO	Erwin R. Palmer	Erwin R. Palmer	1961	80
192 4/8	26 6/8	25 5/8	21 2/8	5 1/8	5 1/8	6	6	Idaho	Unknown	Alan C. Ellsworth	PR 1990	81
192 4/8	25 6/8	25 5/8	24	5 2/8	5 4/8	5	5	Apache Co., AZ	Bobby L. Beeman	Bobby L. Beeman	1991	81
192 3/8	25 6/8	25 7/8	27 6/8	4 4/8	4 4/8	5	5	Idaho	Unknown	Daniel Woodbridge	PR 1972	83
192 3/8	25 6/8	25 5/8	22 1/8	5 1/8	5	5	5	Grant Co., OR	Norman O. Peters	Norman O. Peters	1980	83
192 3/8	24 5/8	25 4/8	23	5 2/8	5 2/8	5	4	Kane Co., UT	Picked Up	Danny C. Stratton	1990	83
192 3/8	25	27	23 7/8	5	5 1/8	5	6	Rio Arriba Co., NM	Levi Pesata	Levi Pesata	1998	83
192 3/8	25	24 1/8	26 2/8	5 2/8	5 4/8	5	7	Camas Co., ID	Brian T. Storey	Brian T. Storey	1999	83
192 3/8	23 1/8	23 1/8	20 6/8	4 5/8	4 5/8	5	6	Teton Co., WY	Vance S. Welch	Vance S. Welch	2000	83
192 2/8	26 3/8	25 7/8	24 3/8	5 4/8	5 3/8	6	7	Archuleta Co., CO	John Richardson	John Richardson	1965	89
192 2/8	25 3/8	26 1/8	19 5/8	4 7/8	4 7/8	5	6	Grant Co., OR	Paul D. Bennett	Paul D. Bennett	1968	89
192 2/8	25 7/8	26 2/8	21 6/8	4 4/8	4 5/8	5	6	Grant Co., OR	Larry T. Palmer	Larry T. Palmer	1990	89
192 2/8	25 2/8	26 6/8	25 6/8	4 7/8	5	5	5	San Juan Co., NM	Picked Up	Rogelio D. Couder, Jr.	1996	89
192 2/8	25 2/8	25 2/8	24 6/8	5 1/8	4 7/8	6	5	Grizzly Bear Creek, AB	Andy P. Charchun	Andy P. Charchun	1998	89
192 1/8	24 3/8	25 2/8	23 2/8	4 5/8	4 6/8	5	5	Dorothy, AB	David A. McIver	David A. McIver	1997	94
192	24 4/8	24 4/8	24 7/8	5 4/8	5 5/8	6	5	Wasco Co., OR	Jeffrey R. Davis	Jeffrey R. Davis	1998	95
191 7/8	27	26 7/8	22 1/8	4 7/8	5	6	5	Beaver Mt., BC	Earl Miller	Glenn Miller	1921	96
191 7/8	27 6/8	26	29 5/8	5 6/8	5 5/8	5	4	Moffat Co., CO	Howard Hageman	Aly M. Bruner	1963	96
191 6/8	28 4/8	28 2/8	27	5	5	6	7	Teton Co., WY	Jesse Barker	Rex N. Barker	1963	98
191 6/8	24 6/8	25 4/8	26 4/8	5 1/8	5 1/8	6	5	Unknown	Unknown	Richard C. Birch	PR 1980	98
191 6/8	26	26 4/8	21 3/8	5 6/8	5 6/8	7	7	Kane Co., UT	Edward A. Tognetti	Edward A. Tognetti	1997	98
191 5/8	27 5/8	27 6/8	24 7/8	5 2/8	5 2/8	5	5	Union Co., OR	Picked Up	Jon Anderson	1978	101
191 4/8	21 7/8	23	18 1/8	5	5	6	6	Fraser River, BC	Gerard Fournier	Gerard Fournier	1997	102
191 4/8	26 1/8	25 1/8	23 7/8	6 1/8	6	8	7	Kane Co., UT	Robert J. Pacini	Robert J. Pacini	1998	102
191 3/8	26	26	20 3/8	6	5 6/8	5	5	Cornwell Mt., BC	Don Bundus	John D. Bundus	1963	104
191 1/8	27 7/8	27 3/8	22 4/8	5	5 1/8	6	6	Grand Co., CO	Lloyd A. Palmer	Lloyd A. Palmer	1959	105
191	28 1/8	26 7/8	26 4/8	4 7/8	5	4	7	Colorado	Unknown	Craig C. Christenson	PR 1961	106
191	24 1/8	24 4/8	21 4/8	5	5	5	5	Lincoln Co., WY	Eric E. Andersen	Eric E. Andersen	1999	106
190 7/8	24 6/8	25 5/8	27 7/8	5 2/8	5 3/8	5	5	Apache Co., AZ	Thomas B. Anderson	Thomas B. Anderson	1997	108
190 7/8	26 1/8	26 2/8	23 1/8	5 3/8	5 2/8	5	5	Riske Creek, BC	David Novak	David Novak	1997	108
190 6/8	24 4/8	24 2/8	20 2/8	5 4/8	5 3/8	5	5	Rio Arriba Co., NM	James G. Biela	James G. Biela	1977	110
190 6/8	26 2/8	25 4/8	25 1/8	4 6/8	4 7/8	5	6	Lincoln Co., WY	Dave Doney	Dave Doney	1986	110

190 6/8	22 7/8	22 6/8	20 1/8	4 5/8	4 5/8	5	6	Moyie River, BC	Robert C. Faiers	Robert C. Faiers	1998
190 6/8	24 1/8	24	20	4 6/8	4 4/8	5	5	Fly Hill, BC	Randy Bellows	Randy Bellows	1999
190 6/8	25 4/8	25 4/8	26 3/8	5 1/8	5 1/8	6	5	Lincoln Co., WY	Terry D. Goff	Terry D. Goff	2000
190 5/8	26	26	21 4/8	5	5 1/8	7	5	Rock Creek, BC	Herb Killback	Doug Killback	1963
190 5/8	24 3/8	24 4/8	23 3/8	5 1/8	5 3/8	5	5	Nez Perce Co., ID	Richard A. Galles	Richard A. Galles	PR 1964
190 5/8	27 3/8	26 4/8	27	4 6/8	5	4	7	Coconino Co., AZ	Stephen M. Milano	Stephen M. Milano	1997
190 4/8	24	25 1/8	23 4/8	4 6/8	4 6/8	5	5	Arapahoe Co., CO	Ted Swanson	Michael D. Swanson	PR 1960
190 4/8	23 1/8	23 7/8	21 7/8	4 6/8	4 7/8	5	6	Washoe Co., NV	Susan M. Ambrose	Susan M. Ambrose	1998
190 4/8	26	25 5/8	25 7/8	5 2/8	5 2/8	5	7	Colfax Co., NM	Campbell A. Griffin, Jr.	Campbell A. Griffin, Jr.	1999
190 4/8	25 6/8	25 6/8	27 4/8	5 2/8	5 2/8	5	6	Lincoln Co., WY	Gerald R. Tadina	Gerald R. Tadina	2000
190 3/8	25 4/8	25 6/8	31 3/8	4 6/8	4 6/8	6	6	Garfield Co., CO	Bert Jones	Bert Jones	1951
190 3/8	26 1/8	23	26 6/8	5	5 1/8	5	5	Coconino Co., AZ	Seth A. Brunsvold	Seth A. Brunsvold	1998
190 2/8	27 6/8	26 7/8	21 6/8	5 4/8	5 1/8	7	6	Humboldt Co., NV	Kevin M. Budney	Kevin M. Budney	1999
190 1/8	25 6/8	23 6/8	21 3/8	4 6/8	4 5/8	5	5	Lincoln Co., MT	Alfred A. Abrahamson	Alfred A. Abrahamson	1991
190 1/8	28	27 3/8	24 7/8	5 4/8	5 4/8	8	8	Archuleta Co., CO	John P. Parsons	John P. Parsons	1998
190 1/8	24 6/8	25 1/8	23 5/8	4 6/8	4 6/8	5	5	Rio Arriba Co., NM	Gary Rasche	Gary Rasche	1998
190 1/8	23 2/8	23 5/8	24 2/8	6 1/8	5 7/8	6	5	Lake Co., OR	Barbara K. Shaw	Barbara K. Shaw	1998
190 1/8	24 3/8	25	24 3/8	4 5/8	4 5/8	6	8	Custer Co., ID	Unknown	Aly M. Bruner	PR 1999
190 1/8	24 6/8	23 7/8	25 7/8	4 4/8	4 4/8	5	6	Lincoln Co., NV	Dan H. Gildner	Dan H. Gildner	1999
190	24 2/8	25 7/8	26 5/8	5 4/8	5 2/8	5	5	Lassen Co., CA	Terry M. Schmitt	Terry M. Schmitt	1998
190	26 4/8	25 5/8	20 6/8	5 2/8	5 1/8	8	8	Rio Arriba Co., NM	Picked Up	Larry L. Panzy	1999
189 6/8	25 4/8	26	24 2/8	5 1/8	5 2/8	5	5	Duschene Co., UT	H. Glade Evans	H. Glade Evans	1959
189 4/8	24 5/8	26	21 4/8	5 4/8	5 4/8	5	5	Blaine Co., ID	Ken Twito	Ken Twito	1976
189 4/8	28	25 7/8	23 2/8	5 1/8	5 1/8	5	6	Rio Arriba Co., NM	Jackie Cassador	Jackie Cassador	1998
189 2/8	28 3/8	27 1/8	24 6/8	4 5/8	4 5/8	6	5	Routt Co., CO	James M. Malonis	James M. Malonis	1997
189	24 3/8	25 1/8	26 7/8	5 3/8	5 3/8	5	5	Sublette Co., WY	Randy P. Kirkwood	Randy P. Kirkwood	1998
188 7/8	24 1/8	25	24 7/8	5 2/8	4 7/8	8	8	S. Saskatchewan River, SK	Barry Miller	Barry Miller	1996
188 7/8	29 3/8	28 3/8	27 7/8	5 4/8	5 4/8	5	6	Humboldt Co., NV	Randy R. Tassi	Randy R. Tassi	1999
188 5/8	25 6/8	26 3/8	27 2/8	4 4/8	4 7/8	5	5	Las Animas Co., CO	Picked Up	Carl J. Wohlfert	1991
188 5/8	24 4/8	25 1/8	27 1/8	6	5 7/8	5	5	Weld Co., CO	James D. Fox	James D. Fox	1998
188 2/8	26 4/8	25 1/8	25 4/8	5 1/8	5 2/8	6	6	Gunnison Co., CO	James J. Wilmes, Jr.	James J. Wilmes, Jr.	1998
188 1/8	23 4/8	23 5/8	21 6/8	4 6/8	4 5/8	8	6	Cypress Hills, AB	Glenn C. MacLeod	Glenn C. MacLeod	1998
188 1/8	26 1/8	25 4/8	26 1/8	5 2/8	5 4/8	6	5	Malheur Co., OR	Mark E. Richards	Mark E. Richards	1998
188	22	24 4/8	25	5 4/8	5 6/8	5	7	Eagle Co., CO	Steve Evanow	Steve Evanow	1989
187 7/8	23 2/8	23 1/8	21 7/8	5 4/8	5 4/8	5	5	Montezuma Co., CO	Jerry L. DeFrenchi	Jerry L. DeFrenchi	1988
187 7/8	25 6/8	25 5/8	25 3/8	5 1/8	5 1/8	8	5	Washington Co., ID	Seward P. Mellon	Seward P. Mellon	1996
187 7/8	26 6/8	26 6/8	23 5/8	5 2/8	5 2/8	5	5	Park Co., CO	Drew L. Wright	Drew L. Wright	1998
187 6/8	27 3/8	26 6/8	27 3/8	5 3/8	5 6/8	5	6	Sheridan Co., NE	Jerry J. Cuddy	Jerry J. Cuddy	1998
187 6/8	24 2/8	23 5/8	25 3/8	4 3/8	4 3/8	4	4	Carbon Co., WY	Brian McCulloch	Brian McCulloch	1999
187 5/8	24 2/8	25 5/8	29 6/8	4 4/8	4 4/8	7	7	Adams Co., ID	Roy Eastlick	Roy Eastlick	1980
187 4/8	26 2/8	26 2/8	27 3/8	5 1/8	5	5	5	Madison Co., MT	Jim Gilstrap	Jim Gilstrap	1960
187 3/8	24 7/8	27	21 6/8	4 7/8	4 7/8	6	6	Garfield Co., UT	Jacob E. Coffman	Rick Brereton	1962
187 3/8	24 3/8	25 1/8	22 6/8	4 5/8	4 7/8	5	6	La Hache Lake, BC	Ross Curry	Ross Curry	1987

MULE DEER - TYPICAL ANTLERS

Odocoileus hemionus hemionus and certain related subspecies

Score	Length of Main Beam R.	L.	Inside Spread	Circumference at Smallest Place Between Burr and First Point R.	L.	Number of Points R.	L.	Locality	Hunter	Owner	Date Killed	Rank
187 2/8	24 6/8	25 6/8	19 7/8	5	5 1/8	6	6	San Juan Co., UT	Bart Christensen	Bart Christensen	1998	155
187 2/8	21 4/8	23	21 4/8	4 3/8	4 3/8	5	5	Eagle Co., CO	Timothy J. Molitor	Timothy J. Molitor	1999	155
187 1/8	23 3/8	24 1/8	24 6/8	4 3/8	4 4/8	5	5	Ravalli Co., MT	Jack E. Popham	Jack E. Popham	1971	157
187 1/8	24	24 6/8	22 6/8	4 7/8	4 7/8	6	5	Bannock Co., ID	L. Dwight Israelsen	L. Dwight Israelsen	2000	157
186 7/8	25 3/8	23 6/8	23 2/8	4 7/8	5	6	4	Elko Co., NV	Don R. Aschenbach	Don R. Aschenbach	1986	159
186 7/8	23 5/8	24	21	5 1/8	5 1/8	6	5	Sonora, MX	James P. Baumgartner	James P. Baumgartner	1998	159
186 6/8	27 2/8	27 2/8	23 3/8	5 4/8	5	6	6	Mesa Co., CO	L. Jack Lyon	L. Jack Lyon	1952	161
186 6/8	24 6/8	24 3/8	23 2/8	5 2/8	5 3/8	6	6	Larimer Co., CO	Gerald D. Rice	Gerald D. Rice	1962	161
186 4/8	27	26 3/8	21 4/8	4 5/8	4 5/8	5	5	Lake Co., OR	Moran L. Baker	Moran L. Baker	1956	163
186 4/8	27 6/8	26 6/8	28 4/8	4 6/8	4 6/8	6	6	San Juan Co., NM	Craig A. Bock	Craig A. Bock	1994	163
186 3/8	26	26 2/8	24 3/8	5 1/8	5 2/8	5	5	Montezuma Co., CO	Duane Calhoon	Duane Calhoon	1976	165
186 2/8	24 1/8	25 2/8	25	5	5	5	5	Eagle Co., CO	Robert D. Pape	Rory Pape	1960	166
186 2/8	27 7/8	27 2/8	22	5 4/8	5 2/8	6	5	Pine River, BC	Doug Field	Doug Field	1990	166
186 2/8	25 3/8	23 3/8	23 4/8	5 2/8	5 2/8	5	5	Baker Co., OR	William D. Ross	William D. Ross	1995	166
186 1/8	25 2/8	25 4/8	25 2/8	5 3/8	5 3/8	5	5	Gallatin Co., MT	James E. Montgomery	James E. Montgomery	1998	170
186 1/8	28 6/8	28 1/8	26 2/8	6 4/8	6	8	7	Grant Co., OR	Michael R. DePretto	Michael R. DePretto	1998	170
186 1/8	22 7/8	24 1/8	22 7/8	5 1/8	5 1/8	5	5	Caribou Co., ID	John Tautin, Jr.	John Tautin, Jr.	1998	170
186	21 7/8	20 4/8	20 7/8	4	4	5	5	Elmore Co., ID	Billy Knox	Billy Knox	2000	173
186	24 4/8	24 4/8	24 4/8	5 1/8	5 1/8	6	6	Rio Blanco Co., CO	Kelly W. Brown	Kelly W. Brown	1999	173
185 7/8	24 4/8	26	27 1/8	5 3/8	5 4/8	5	7	Washakie Co., WY	Joe L. Sanchez	Joe L. Sanchez	1999	175
185 6/8	25 7/8	24 6/8	26 5/8	5	4 7/8	6	5	Crook Co., WY	George L. Cooper	George L. Cooper	1999	176
185 6/8	25 7/8	26	24	5 1/8	5 1/8	7	5	Peers Creek, BC	Tony MacInnes	Tony MacInnes	1994	176
185 6/8	21 7/8	24 4/8	24	4 4/8	4 3/8	5	5	Douglas Co., CO	Bruce E. Ritts	Bruce E. Ritts	1998	176
185 4/8	26	24	30 6/8	6	5 7/8	5	5	Sheridan Co., WY	Gary A. Roebling	Gary A. Roebling	1999	179
185 4/8	24 4/8	24 4/8	20 5/8	4 5/8	4 7/8	6	6	Niobrara Co., WY	Robert J. Holmes, Jr.	Robert J. Holmes, Jr.	1999	179
185 4/8	25 6/8	24	25 5/8	4 6/8	4 6/8	4	5	Grant Co., WA	David P. McBrayer	David P. McBrayer	1999	179
185 1/8	27 1/8	27 3/8	24 1/8	5	5 4/8	8	8	Ferry Co., WA	Unknown	Robert D. Jones	PR 1958	181
185 1/8	24 7/8	24 4/8	26 2/8	5 1/8	4 7/8	5	6	Slope Co., ND	Lawrence J. Wolfgram	Lawrence J. Wolfgram	1961	181
185 1/8	24 2/8	24 5/8	24 3/8	4 5/8	4 5/8	5	5	Mesa Co., CO	Stanley J. Capelli, Sr.	Stanley J. Capelli, Sr.	1970	181
185 1/8	26 3/8	25 6/8	23 3/8	4 6/8	4 6/8	5	4	Washoe Co., NV	Alton R. Parker	Alton R. Parker	1998	181
185	26 7/8	25 6/8	25 1/8	5 2/8	5 1/8	6	5	Mohave Co., AZ	Chris H. Darnell	Chris H. Darnell	1994	185
185	26 4/8	27 1/8	25	4 6/8	4 6/8	5	5	Rio Arriba Co., NM	Terry R. Chapman	Terry R. Chapman	2000	185
184 7/8	26 2/8	25 6/8	25 5/8	4 5/8	4 5/8	5	6	Fremont Co., WY	Ronald E. Krause, Jr.	Ronald E. Krause, Jr.	2000	187
184 6/8	25	24 3/8	22 4/8	4 6/8	4 4/8	4	5	Elko Co., NV	Jared L. Aschenbach	Jared L. Aschenbach	1986	188

Score								Locality	Owner	Hunter	Date	Rank
184 6/8	28 1/8	26 2/8	24 2/8	4 5/8	4 6/8	5	5	Consort, AB	Raymond J. Benik	Raymond J. Benik	1998	188
184 6/8	25 7/8	25 3/8	27 2/8	5 7/8	6 2/8	5	5	Lincoln Co., NV	Jelindo A. Tiberti II	Jelindo A. Tiberti II	1998	188
184 6/8	26	25 1/8	21 6/8	4 5/8	4 5/8	6	8	Sublette Co., WY	Jeff R. Brock	Jeff R. Brock	1999	188
184 5/8	27 2/8	28 1/8	25	5 4/8	5 4/8	7	5	Fremont Co., ID	Paul C. Truxal	Paul C. Truxal	1966	192
184 5/8	24 6/8	25 6/8	22 1/8	4 6/8	4 5/8	6	8	Carbon Co., WY	Wesley R. Millar	Wesley R. Millar	2000	192
184 4/8	26 2/8	26 2/8	20 4/8	5 2/8	5 2/8	6	6	McKenzie Co., ND	Brian Freed	Brian Freed	1990	194
184 4/8	24 4/8	24 4/8	24 1/8	4 7/8	4 7/8	5	5	Baker Co., OR	Hans C. Finke	Hans C. Finke	1999	194
184 3/8	25 3/8	25 5/8	25 5/8	4 6/8	4 7/8	6	6	Klamath Co., OR	Lester A. Loraditch	Donnie J. Allen	1988	196
184 3/8	22 4/8	21 7/8	18 5/8	4 3/8	4 4/8	5	5	Lincoln Co., WY	Picked Up	Jon E. Sonnenschein	1999	196
184 2/8	25 1/8	25 4/8	23	4 7/8	4 7/8	7	7	Coconino Co., AZ	Frederick G. March	Frederick G. March	1997	198
184 1/8	24	25	21 7/8	4 5/8	4 4/8	6	5	Umatilla Co., OR	Joseph Overstreet	Joseph Overstreet	1998	199
184	24 6/8	24 5/8	25 6/8	4 7/8	4 7/8	5	6	Eagle Co., CO	Randy L. Motzner	Randy L. Motzner	1997	200
183 7/8	27 2/8	27	24 5/8	5 4/8	5 6/8	5	5	Unknown	Unknown	Donnie J. Allen	PR 1996	201
183 7/8	25 4/8	24 7/8	26 3/8	4 4/8	4 5/8	5	5	Sonora, MX	Lou E. Misterly, Jr.	Lou E. Misterly, Jr.	1997	201
183 5/8	25 4/8	24 5/8	23 1/8	4 6/8	4 6/8	5	5	Utah	John Murko	Ron Boehm	1960	203
183 5/8	25	26 1/8	23 5/8	5 3/8	5 3/8	6	8	Klickitat Co., WA	Larry W. Lyons	Larry W. Lyons	1996	203
183 5/8	25 4/8	24 3/8	23	5 1/8	5 1/8	6	6	Eagle Co., CO	Jack T. Baumstark, Sr.	Jack T. Baumstark, Sr.	1998	203
183 5/8	23 2/8	24 4/8	24 2/8	4 2/8	4 2/8	6	5	Montezuma Co., CO	Jerry L. DeFrenchi	Jerry L. DeFrenchi	1999	203
183 4/8	24 3/8	24 4/8	26 2/8	4 7/8	4 7/8	5	5	Camas Co., ID	Dallas E. Smith	Dallas E. Smith	2000	207
183 3/8	25 6/8	24 3/8	22 1/8	5	4 7/8	5	5	Adams Co., WA	L.A. McBroom	L.A. McBroom	1998	208
183 3/8	23 2/8	24 3/8	21 2/8	4 4/8	4 2/8	6	6	Carbon Co., WY	Dan E. McBride	Dan E. McBride	1999	208
183 3/8	22	23 6/8	25	5 4/8	5 3/8	6	6	Montezuma Co., CO	Mike J. Maass	Mike J. Maass	2000	208
183 2/8	24 7/8	24 2/8	24 5/8	4 6/8	4 7/8	5	5	Lincoln Co., WY	Danny S. Adams	Danny S. Adams	1996	211
183 2/8	24 4/8	24 4/8	20 3/8	5 4/8	5	6	7	Morgan Co., UT	Richard W. Reed	Richard W. Reed	1998	211
183 1/8	25 3/8	25 6/8	28	5 3/8	5 5/8	6	7	Elmore Co., ID	Frank W. Trimble	Frank W. Trimble	1980	213
183 1/8	25 4/8	25	21 4/8	4 7/8	5	5	6	Mesa Co., CO	Billy E. Green	Billy E. Green	1986	213
183	24 4/8	25	25 4/8	4 4/8	4 4/8	5	5	Summit Co., UT	Robert J. Margolis	Robert J. Margolis	2000	215
182 6/8	23 4/8	23 2/8	24 6/8	4 6/8	4 6/8	5	5	Bear Lake Co., ID	Chad Hulme	Chad Hulme	1976	216
182 6/8	24 5/8	24 4/8	25 7/8	5 2/8	5 2/8	6	6	Malheur Co., OR	George A. Applegate	George A. Applegate	1995	216
182 5/8	26 7/8	25 5/8	29 1/8	4 5/8	4 4/8	7	7	Kane Co., UT	Van M. Gardner	Van M. Gardner	1997	218
182 4/8	25 1/8	25 1/8	21	4 2/8	4 3/8	5	5	Modoc Co., CA	Delmore R. Pomeroy	Delmore R. Pomeroy	1959	219
182 4/8	23 3/8	24	21 6/8	5 1/8	5 1/8	6	5	Wallowa Co., OR	Dexter Yokom, Sr.	Dexter Yokom, Jr.	1965	219
182 3/8	24 6/8	24 3/8	24 4/8	5	5	6	6	Uravan, Co.	Eugene Schladoer	Keven Sterling	1966	221
182 1/8	23 4/8	25 4/8	23 3/8	4 4/8	4 4/8	6	6	Sublette Co., WY	Edison D. Dearing, Jr.	Edison D. Dearing, Jr.	1961	222
182 1/8	25 5/8	25 1/8	20 4/8	5	4 7/8	6	6	Klamath Co., OR	Lester W. Todd	Lester W. Todd	1971	222
182 1/8	25 1/8	26	21 3/8	4 3/8	4	5	4	Box Elder Co., UT	Tyler D. Pugsley	Tyler D. Pugsley	1999	222
182	24 3/8	23 5/8	20 4/8	4 5/8	4 4/8	5	5	Morgan Co., UT	Randolph W. Reed	Randolph W. Reed	1999	225
181 6/8	23 5/8	26 6/8	22 5/8	5 2/8	5 5/8	8	6	Sublette Co., WY	Larry G. Dearing	Larry G. Dearing	1961	226
181 6/8	24 5/8	26	29 6/8	4 5/8	5	4	5	Routt Co., CO	Boyd Danielson	Lance C. Jones	PR 1964	226
181 6/8	23 1/8	23 3/8	26 2/8	6 2/8	5 7/8	7	8	Beaver Co., UT	Larry Maycock	Larry Maycock	1969	226
181 6/8	24 3/8	24 6/8	24 1/8	4 3/8	4 4/8	6	6	Washington Co., CO	Ronald E. Markow	Ronald E. Markow	1991	226
181 4/8	25 1/8	24 4/8	22	4 1/8	4 1/8	5	5	Delta Co., CO	Bob K. Carter	Bob K. Carter	1998	226
181 4/8	26 2/8	26 3/8	26	5 1/8	4 7/8	8	5	Elmore Co., ID	Scott E. Pylican	S.E. & R.L. Pylican	1990	231

MULE DEER - TYPICAL ANTLERS

Odocoileus hemionus hemionus and certain related subspecies

Score	Length of Main Beam R.	L.	Inside Spread	Circumference at Smallest Place Between Burr and First Point R.	L.	Number of Points R.	L.	Locality	Hunter	Owner	Date Killed	Rank
181 4/8	24 4/8	24 6/8	19 6/8	4 7/8	4 7/8	5	5	Fallon Co., MT	Timothy S. Norgard	Timothy S. Norgard	1999	231
181 3/8	22 2/8	22 5/8	23 7/8	4 5/8	4 6/8	5	5	Carbon Co., WY	Gary K. Dye	Gary K. Dye	1990	233
181 2/8	24 1/8	23 5/8	20	4 6/8	4 4/8	7	5	Humboldt Co., NV	Steve T. Nolan	Steve T. Nolan	1997	234
181 2/8	26 3/8	22 7/8	26 5/8	5 1/8	5 1/8	6	6	Teton Co., WY	Michael T. Letsch	Michael T. Letsch	1999	234
181	23 2/8	24 2/8	21 5/8	6 2/8	6 1/8	7	5	Bethune, SK	Ronald N. Riche	Ronald N. Riche	1998	236
181	22	22 4/8	22 5/8	5 2/8	5 1/8	5	5	Summit Co., CO	Grant A. Warfield	Grant A. Warfield	1999	236
180 7/8	22 1/8	23 5/8	20 3/8	4 4/8	4 5/8	5	5	Rosebud Co., MT	Shawn Green	Scott J. Studiner	1984	238
180 6/8	23	22 4/8	22 6/8	4 3/8	4 4/8	5	5	Vermilion River, AB	Frederick M. These	Frederick M. These	1998	239
180 5/8	24 1/8	23 4/8	20 6/8	4 3/8	4 3/8	6	5	Crook Co., OR	Brad Edwards	Josh A. Edwards	PR 1990	240
180 5/8	23 3/8	24	20 4/8	4 3/8	4 4/8	5	5	Grand Co., CO	Ryan G. Firth	Ryan G. Firth	1997	240
180 5/8	25 1/8	24 2/8	24 3/8	4 6/8	4 7/8	5	5	Decatur Co., KS	Andrew L. Bird	Andrew L. Bird	1999	240
180 5/8	24 7/8	24 7/8	27 3/8	5	5	6	5	Sonora, MX	Peter W. Spear	Peter W. Spear	1999	240
180 4/8	24 4/8	24 6/8	25 4/8	5 3/8	5 3/8	6	5	Bannock Co., ID	Thomas Taylor	Thomas Taylor	1968	244
180 4/8	27	26 4/8	26 7/8	4 4/8	4 4/8	4	5	Montezuma Co., CO	Jerry L. DeFrenchi	Jerry L. DeFrenchi	1986	244
180 4/8	23 7/8	24 5/8	24 7/8	4 4/8	4 5/8	6	5	Malheur Co., OR	Jimmy R. Belnap	Jimmy R. Belnap	1998	244
180 3/8	27 5/8	27 2/8	24 2/8	5 3/8	5 4/8	6	5	Lake Co., OR	Wilbur Chandler	Dave Hakola	1939	247
180 3/8	25 3/8	25 1/8	22 6/8	4 4/8	4 4/8	7	5	Niobrara Co., WY	Jeffery A. Crites	Jeffery A. Crites	1997	247
180 3/8	23 4/8	22 5/8	23 4/8	4 5/8	4 5/8	4	4	Bear Lake Co., ID	Mike E. Nelson	Mike E. Nelson	1999	247
180 2/8	27 6/8	27 4/8	30 1/8	5 1/8	5 1/8	7	6	Coconino Co., AZ	Max Tait	Max Tait	1950	250
180 2/8	24 6/8	26 5/8	22 6/8	4 6/8	4 5/8	5	5	Malheur Co., OR	Stephen F. Hay	Stephen F. Hay	1998	250
180 1/8	24 2/8	26 2/8	22 3/8	5 6/8	5 6/8	5	5	Douglas Co., CO	Patrick G. Diesing	Patrick G. Diesing	1987	252
180 1/8	27 7/8	26 5/8	29 4/8	5 4/8	5 2/8	6	7	Jackson Co., CO	Darren F. Mumma	Darren F. Mumma	1998	252
180	25 7/8	25 7/8	21 2/8	5	5 2/8	5	5	Gilpin Co., CO	Arthur Nichols	Byron T. Sayers	1958	254
180	23 7/8	25 3/8	20 4/8	5 4/8	5 2/8	8	6	Sublette Co., WY	Edison D. Dearing, Jr.	Edison D. Dearing, Jr.	1960	254
180	22 4/8	22 7/8	19 2/8	5	5 2/8	5	5	Campbell Co., SD	Kevin L. Schaefbauer	Kevin L. Schaefbauer	1998	254
180	24 5/8	26 1/8	24	4 6/8	4 4/8	4	4	Niobrara Co., WY	Gerald C. Brown	Gerald C. Brown	1999	254
218 4/8 *	27 5/8	27 5/8	29 5/8	5 5/8	5 5/8	6	5	S. Saskatchewan River, SK	Lars Svenson	Larry Svenson	PR 1950	
215 3/8 *	29 6/8	30 1/8	36 1/8	5 4/8	5 3/8	5	5	Delta Co., CO	Robert L. Ingels	Fred Ferganchick	1958	
203 4/8 *	27 3/8	26 7/8	21 3/8	5 1/8	5	8	7	Montezuma Co., CO	Olen J. Hicks	Olen J. Hicks	1999	

* Final score subject to revision by additional verifying measurements.

MULE DEER - NON-TYPICAL ANTLERS

Odocoileus hemionus hemionus and certain related subspecies

Minimum Score 215 World's Record 355 2/8

Score	Length of Main Beam R.	L.	Inside Spread	Circumference at Smallest Place Between Burr and First Point R.	L.	Number of Points R.	L.	Locality	Hunter	Owner	Date Killed	Rank
288 7/8	26 3/8	26 5/8	28 5/8	4 6/8	4 2/8	16	12	Sweetwater Co., WY	Walter Boam	D.J. Hollinger & B. Howard	PR 1940	1
287 6/8	21 1/8	19 7/8	18	6	6 1/8	14	24	Blaine Co., ID	Tim Weary	D.J. Hollinger & B. Howard	1942	2
280 2/8	24 6/8	25 6/8	27 5/8	4 5/8	4 6/8	13	12	Cache Co., UT	Mr. Orr	L. Dwight Israelsen	1969	3
274 3/8	28 7/8	29 2/8	26	5 6/8	5 3/8	12	12	Unknown	Unknown	Buckhorn Mus. & Saloon, Ltd.	PR 1960	4
273 2/8	25 5/8	26 2/8	27 4/8	5 3/8	5 4/8	14	15	Richland Co., MT	Joe Berzel	Matthew Berzel	1955	5
269 6/8	22 7/8	24 2/8	26	6 4/8	6 2/8	13	14	Morgan Co., CO	Picked Up	Aly M. Bruner	1987	6
269 6/8	27 6/8	26 7/8	22 5/8	4 7/8	5	17	12	Sherman Co., OR	James G. Petersen	James G. Petersen	1998	6
268	28 1/8	31 2/8	26 3/8	5 5/8	5 4/8	14	9	Bonneville Co., ID	Picked Up	D.J. Hollinger & B. Howard	1979	8
265 2/8	25 5/8	24 5/8	24 5/8	6 2/8	5 6/8	14	13	Wheeler Co., NE	Leo Dwyer	Leo Dwyer	1959	9
257 5/8	23 5/8	23 7/8	22 6/8	4 7/8	4 7/8	16	10	Manning, AB	Victor Mercier	David Mercier	1946	10
257 2/8	26	27 5/8	29 5/8	6 1/8	6 2/8	12	11	British Columbia	Carl Balantine	Tony MacInnes	PR 1950	11
256 2/8	24 6/8	24 1/8	21 6/8	4 5/8	4 4/8	12	11	Oneida Co., ID	S. Tracey Davis	S. Tracey Davis	1998	12
256	25 6/8	26	25	5	5 2/8	11	19	Jefferson Co., OR	Spencer Darrar	Gail McDougall	1953	13
255 3/8	26 3/8	28	23	5 4/8	5 6/8	10	11	Peace River, BC	C.C. Brandt	N. Peace Hist. Soc.	1930	14
252 6/8	25 6/8	24 4/8	22 4/8	4 7/8	5	14	12	Beaver Co., UT	Picked Up	Rance Rollins	1980	15
252 1/8	27 3/8	27 1/8	24 4/8	5 5/8	5 3/8	11	11	Delta Co., CO	John W. Stockemer	John W. Stockemer	1969	16
251 6/8	28 2/8	27 3/8	25 2/8	5 4/8	6	10	11	Ouray Co., CO	Bruce Phillips	T. Larry Pope	PR 1985	17
251	25 6/8	26	29 4/8	4 7/8	5 2/8	16	13	Crook Co., OR	Herrel C. Throop	Gerald L. Throop	1935	18
251	28 3/8	28	26 7/8	6 1/8	5 5/8	12	12	Cache Co., UT	John Reynolds	D. J. Hollinger & B. Howard	1960	18
250 7/8	27 4/8	27 3/8	29 3/8	5 4/8	5 6/8	12	14	Unknown	Unknown	Buckhorn Mus. & Saloon, Ltd.	PR 1965	20
249 1/8	25 2/8	23 4/8	19 2/8	5 4/8	5 5/8	13	16	Jackson Co., OR	Meryl Loy	Marvin M. Loy	1938	21
249 1/8	25 3/8	25 6/8	27 6/8	4 5/8	4 5/8	12	12	Shoshone Co., ID	Jim Brines	D.J. Hollinger & B. Howard	1962	21
248	24	26	18 1/8	4 7/8	4 7/8	11	11	Treasure Co., MT	Orville Campbell	David E. Campbell	1948	23
247 4/8	26 1/8	27 1/8	23 1/8	5 4/8	5 5/8	11	8	Sevier Co., UT	Unknown	D.J. Hollinger & B. Howard	PR 1960	24
246 5/8	25 3/8	25 6/8	23	5 4/8	5 5/8	13	17	Empress, AB	George Servage	Richard Bonnett	1987	25
246	24 3/8	24 6/8	27 3/8	5 3/8	5 4/8	15	13	Owyhee Co., ID	Douglas W. Pittman	Douglas W. Pittman	1998	26
245 7/8	28 4/8	25 6/8	22 4/8	5	5 1/8	18	15	Dolores Co., CO	Picked Up	Mike Gassman	1984	27
244 2/8	21 6/8	20 6/8	17 2/8	6	6	5	5	Mariposa Co., CA	Donald E. Nelson	Donald E. Nelson	1968	28
244	25 6/8	25 6/8	28 7/8	5 1/8	5	9	10	Mohave Co., AZ	Eric P. McCormick	Eric P. McCormick	1998	29
243 7/8	26 7/8	27 2/8	26 3/8	5	5 3/8	13	13	Iron Co., UT	R. Kenneth Benson	Kendall L. Benson	1968	30
243 6/8	25	24 6/8	22 3/8	5 6/8	5 3/8	8	11	Moose Creek, BC	Hartley Blatz	Hartley Blatz	1992	31
243 1/8	21 6/8	24 4/8	21 5/8	5 4/8	5 5/8	11	12	Mohave Co., AZ	Joe H. Heffelfinger	Joe H. Heffelfinger	1997	32
243	29 4/8	29 6/8	18	5 7/8	5 7/8	15	12	Oregon	Donald Mikkonen	Kevin J. Huserik	1950	33
242 3/8	27 1/8	27 2/8	23 4/8	5	4 7/8	12	12	Sanpete Co., UT	Elwin Shelley	Elwin Shelley	1966	34

MULE DEER - NON-TYPICAL ANTLERS

Odocoileus hemionus hemionus and certain related subspecies

Score	Length of Main Beam R.	L.	Inside Spread	Circumference at Smallest Place Between Burr and First Point R.	L.	Number of Points R.	L.	Locality	Hunter	Owner	Date Killed	Rank
241 7/8	25 4/8	24	24 3/8	5 4/8	5 4/8	7	13	Malheur Co., OR	Unknown	Daniel Woodbridge	PR 1938	35
241 4/8	27 6/8	28 1/8	22 3/8	6 4/8	6 6/8	8	13	Gooding Co., ID	Robert L. Fossceco	Robert L. Fossceco	1997	36
241 4/8	26 3/8	26 3/8	23 2/8	5 7/8	5 7/8	10	11	Colfax Co., NM	Andrew J. Ortega	Andrew J. Ortega	1998	36
241 3/8	23 1/8	23 6/8	19 5/8	5 2/8	5 3/8	11	13	Sublette Co., WY	Larry G. Isley	Larry G. Isley	1999	38
241 2/8	23 3/8	24 3/8	21 2/8	5 5/8	5 6/8	12	11	Lumby, BC	Bill Shunter	Bill Shunter	1964	39
240 2/8	25 2/8	25 4/8	19 4/8	4 7/8	4 7/8	9	9	Rio Arriba Co., NM	J.B. Meyers, Jr.	J.B. Meyers, Jr.	1971	40
240 1/8	24 6/8	25 2/8	27 7/8	5 5/8	5 4/8	11	14	Sanpete Co., UT	Elwin Shelley	Elwin Shelley	1972	41
239 7/8	28 1/8	27 2/8	26 2/8	5 4/8	5 4/8	9	10	Blaine Co., ID	Unknown	D.J. Hollinger & B. Howard	PR 1975	42
239 6/8	27 6/8	26 6/8	27 4/8	5 2/8	5 1/8	13	13	La Plata Co., CO	David Blake	David Blake	1977	43
239 6/8	25	24 6/8	23	5 4/8	5 2/8	11	11	Carbon Co., UT	Michael R. Tryon	Michael R. Tryon	1998	43
239 3/8	24 2/8	24 7/8	20 6/8	6	5 5/8	8	11	Teton Co., WY	Gary C. Livingston	Gary C. Livingston	1990	45
239 2/8	28 3/8	27 2/8	28 1/8	4 7/8	4 6/8	8	8	Grant Co., OR	Harry A. Dew	Derral A. Dew	1971	46
239 2/8	27 6/8	26 5/8	24	5 4/8	5 3/8	8	8	Mohave Co., AZ	Douglas B. Bundy	Douglas B. Bundy	1995	46
238 7/8	24 1/8	27 5/8	29 2/8	5	5 1/8	8	12	Crook Co., OR	Derral A. Dew	Derral A. Dew	1969	48
238 7/8	24 4/8	26 6/8	29 5/8	5 4/8	5 6/8	9	8	Mohave Co., AZ	Rachelle Iverson	Rachelle Iverson	1997	48
238 5/8	26 4/8	25 2/8	19 5/8	5 3/8	5 2/8	10	12	Utah Co., UT	Jacob E. Coffman	Rick Brereton	1952	50
238 2/8	27	26 3/8	21 7/8	6	5 7/8	12	8	Churn Creek, BC	Burt Collins	Corky Collins	PR 1920	51
238	24 4/8	28 1/8	22 6/8	5 1/8	5 1/8	10	11	Fremont Co., WY	Hank Hammond	Ralph E. White	1943	52
237 7/8	26 6/8	26 2/8	21 2/8	5 3/8	4 7/8	8	11	Gunnison Co., CO	Herbert Hild III	Herbert Hild III	1996	53
237 6/8	26 2/8	26 2/8	22 4/8	4 5/8	4 5/8	14	12	Carbon Co., WY	Terry L. Younce	Terry L. Younce	1969	54
237 5/8	26 2/8	27 2/8	26	6 6/8	6 4/8	11	11	Pitkin Co., CO	Dennis G. Muth	Dennis G. Muth	1981	55
237 3/8	27 3/8	26 3/8	30 5/8	6 3/8	6	9	9	Harney Co., OR	Culver Page	Aly M. Bruner	1927	56
237 3/8	25 4/8	24 1/8	22 4/8	5	5 1/8	12	10	Douglas Co., CO	Unknown	D.J. Hollinger & B. Howard	PR 1970	56
237 2/8	27 2/8	24 4/8	23 5/8	5 4/8	6 5/8	8	15	Chelan Co., WA	Louis Brown	Kim S. Scott	1940	58
237 2/8	25 5/8	24	21	4 2/8	4 3/8	15	9	Golden Valley Co., ND	Palmer Georgeson	Palmer Georgeson	1965	58
237 2/8	26 7/8	27 6/8	22 1/8	6 2/8	6 1/8	11	10	Colorado	Unknown	Aly M. Bruner	PR 1996	58
237	25 2/8	25 7/8	28 7/8	4 4/8	5 2/8	11	14	Colorado	Lillia Winkler	Mike Sheppeard	1982	61
236 7/8	24 5/8	24 4/8	23	5 1/8	5 4/8	9	12	Wallowa Co., OR	Unknown	Ken Moore	1940	62
236 7/8	24	24 7/8	22 3/8	4 4/8	4 5/8	10	8	Forty Mile Co., AB	Merle Klaudt	Merle Klaudt	1998	62
236 3/8	25 3/8	24 6/8	25	5 6/8	6	10	12	Coconino Co., AZ	Johnny C. Parsons	Johnny C. Parsons	1997	64
236 2/8	27 5/8	27 2/8	23	6	6	12	9	Rio Arriba Co., NM	Picked Up	Pat Powell	2000	65
236	26	26 6/8	21 2/8	5 4/8	5 4/8	11	10	Deschutes Co., OR	Ray Cole	Ray Cole	1951	66
235 6/8	24	26 5/8	27 3/8	5 2/8	5 4/8	14	12	White Pine Co., NV	Roland J. DiSanza	Roland J. DiSanza	1968	67
235 6/8	27 4/8	28	30 2/8	4 7/8	4 7/8	10	10	Montezuma Co., CO	Picked Up	Tom G. Broderick	1992	67

Score								Locality	Hunter	Owner	Date	Rank
235 4/8	24	24 5/8	21 1/8	4 6/8	4 5/8	9	12	Rio Arriba Co., NM	J.B. Meyers, Jr.	J.B. Meyers, Jr.	1969	69
235 3/8	27 4/8	29 2/8	27 4/8	5 3/8	5 4/8	6	10	Missoula Co., MT	Mitchel Rasmussen	Mitchel Rasmussen	1978	70
235 2/8	25 4/8	29 2/8	24 6/8	4 7/8	4 7/8	8	13	Lincoln Co., WY	Steven M. James	Steven M. James	1991	71
235 2/8	24 7/8	23	27 7/8	5 4/8	5 4/8	9	11	Yuma Co., CO	Dusty T. Walters	Dusty T. Walters	1998	71
235 1/8	25 7/8	25 5/8	23 3/8	5 2/8	5 2/8	9	11	Clark Co., ID	James E. Gabettas	James E. Gabettas	1999	73
235	25 4/8	25 2/8	22	5	5	9	10	Iron Co., UT	Don C. Higgins	Don C. Higgins	1988	74
234 6/8	23 4/8	24 3/8	21	5	5	8	11	Lincoln Co., NV	George J. Brown	George J. Brown	1998	75
234 3/8	25 4/8	27 4/8	25 7/8	4 7/8	5	9	12	Powell Co., MT	John D. Simons	John D. Simons	1978	76
234 3/8	25 1/8	25 2/8	25 1/8	5 5/8	5 2/8	8	8	Williams Lake, BC	Dean Mace	Dean Mace	1998	76
234 2/8	25	24 4/8	18 2/8	4 6/8	4 7/8	14	12	Delta Co., CO	Picked Up	Robert A. Kaufman	1980	78
234 1/8	28 7/8	29 1/8	33 4/8	6	6 3/8	8	6	Lake Co., OR	Unknown	Donnie J. Allen	1960	79
234 1/8	25 6/8	27 2/8	25 7/8	5 7/8	6	10	8	Larimer Co., CO	David R. Cheeseman	David R. Cheeseman	1986	79
234	23 1/8	22 7/8	25 6/8	5	5	9	11	Rio Arriba Co., NM	Alan Vicenti	Alan Vicenti	1994	81
233 7/8	27 3/8	26 4/8	25 5/8	6	5 5/8	13	10	Deschutes Co., OR	Mr. Matteson	Lisa I. Thomas	1960	82
233 5/8	23 2/8	24	20 7/8	4 4/8	5 2/8	11	11	Carbon Co., WY	William S. Nelson	William S. Nelson	1998	83
233 3/8	25	26 7/8	19 6/8	5 4/8	5 5/8	10	10	Cassia Co., ID	James J. Knoll	James J. Knoll	1986	84
233 2/8	26	25 4/8	22	5	4 7/8	9	9	Beaton River, BC	Dwayne Shawchek	Dwayne Shawchek	1992	85
233 2/8	26 1/8	28 1/8	26 2/8	5 2/8	5 2/8	8	7	Rio Arriba Co., NM	William J. Smith	William J. Smith	1998	85
232 6/8	23 6/8	22 4/8	28 5/8	4 6/8	4 7/8	13	11	Park Co., WY	Eddie Schwager	Bill Clark	1949	87
232 5/8	22 5/8	21	19 3/8	5 4/8	6	13	14	Scott Co., KS	Michael A. Kershner	Michael A. Kershner	1999	87
232 3/8	22 4/8	23 4/8	20 4/8	5 4/8	5 2/8	10	13	Hayes Co., NE	Delbert Fornoff	Christopher G. Fornoff	1959	89
232 2/8	25 3/8	25 7/8	25 3/8	5	5 2/8	11	13	Eagle Creek, SK	Joe W. Schmidt	Joe W. Schmidt	1997	90
232 2/8	25 4/8	25 6/8	25 6/8	4 5/8	4 7/8	9	8	Garfield Co., CO	Allen O. Downie, Jr.	Allen O. Downie, Jr.	2000	91
231 7/8	26 5/8	26 6/8	25 1/8	4 4/8	4 6/8	11	12	Utah Co., UT	John Fast	Tony Mol	PR 1949	92
231 4/8	24 4/8	24 6/8	26 3/8	5 2/8	5 2/8	8	10	Elmore Co., ID	RA Thorpe & B. Wippel	Robert A. Thorpe	2000	93
231 3/8	28	28 1/8	35	5 5/8	5 5/8	10	10	Camas Co., ID	Jack Omohundro	Aly M. Bruner	1960	94
231 1/8	21	14 5/8	20 5/8	6 6/8	6 6/8	10	10	Cochrane, AB	Helmut Schock	Helmut Schock	1995	95
230 7/8	21 7/8	21 3/8	16 3/8	5 4/8	5 7/8	12	9	Faulkland, BC	Unknown	D.J. Hollinger & B. Howard	PR 1960	96
230 4/8	26 7/8	27 2/8	23 2/8	5 1/8	5	9	10	Harney Co., OR	Mitch S. Crouser	Mitch S. Crouser	1998	97
230 1/8	25	24	24 5/8	4 4/8	4 5/8	8	12	Wallowa Co., OR	Cloyd R. Ream	Cloyd R. Ream	1999	98
230	27 2/8	26 7/8	20 6/8	4 6/8	5	10	9	Buck Lake, AB	William Meyer	Bill Landals	PR 1910	99
230	23 3/8	22 7/8	22 6/8	5 1/8	5	10	11	Coconino Co., AZ	Wayne W. Montgomery	Virginia M. Reed	PR 1940	99
230	27 1/8	25 4/8	22 7/8	4 6/8	4 6/8	11	7	Garfield Co., CO	Unknown	Jack Thompson	PR 1978	99
229 3/8	22 3/8	22 6/8	18 1/8	5 6/8	5 4/8	16	14	Chelan Co., WA	Ray Sweet	Brian R. Hedden	1945	102
228 2/8	27 2/8	28 2/8	19 6/8	4 5/8	4 6/8	11	11	Mesa Co., CO	Mathew M. Gilson	Mathew M. Gilson	1998	103
227 7/8	28	26 2/8	24 1/8	5 6/8	5 7/8	8	11	Waterton Park, AB	Walter Foster	D.J. Hollinger & B. Howard	1934	104
227 5/8	27 5/8	27 5/8	21 3/8	5	4 7/8	12	12	Wallowa Co., OR	Tony Pallis	Keith D. Pratt	1979	104
227 5/8	22 4/8	21 5/8	19 2/8	5 2/8	4 7/8	14	10	Weber Co., UT	Billie F. Peterson	Dale S. Peterson	PR 1956	106
226 3/8	26 1/8	25 7/8	22	5 1/8	5 3/8	12	13	Klamath Co., OR	Picked Up	Robert G. Jones	1988	107
225 3/8	24 4/8	27 2/8	27 1/8	5 6/8	5 6/8	12	6	Beaver Co., UT	G. Wilford Guthrie	Stephen L. Sessions	1941	108
225 3/8	25 3/8	24 7/8	24	5 2/8	5 2/8	10	10	Oregon	Unknown	Alan J. Sturm	PR 1970	108
224 6/8	26 4/8	25 7/8	28 2/8	5 1/8	5 1/8	10	6	Nye Co., NV	Candyce A. Ward	Candyce A. Ward	1998	110
223 2/8	26 3/8	26 3/8	24 2/8	4 6/8	4 7/8	7	7	Morgan Co., UT	David F. Myrup	David F. Myrup	1986	111

MULE DEER - NON-TYPICAL ANTLERS

Odocoileus hemionus hemionus and certain related subspecies

Score	Length of Main Beam		Inside Spread	Circumference at Smallest Place Between Burr and First Point		Number of Points		Locality	Hunter	Owner	Date Killed	Rank
	R.	L.		R.	L.	R.	L.					
223 2/8	23 3/8	25	20 3/8	5 4/8	5 4/8	9	10	Moffat Co., CO	Bradley D. Herman	Bradley D. Herman	1999	111
222 7/8	25 6/8	25 2/8	24 4/8	5	5	10	12	Klamath Co., OR	William E. Chastain	Violet L. Chastain	1936	113
222 7/8	27 5/8	30 1/8	31 1/8	4 7/8	5	7	11	Red Willow Co., NE	Philip J. Blum	Philip J. Blum	1998	113
221 7/8	26 1/8	25 6/8	24 6/8	4 7/8	4 7/8	10	10	Grant Co., OR	Verlin Turner	Verlin Turner	1986	115
220 6/8	26 2/8	27 6/8	24 1/8	5	5	10	10	Mesa Co., CO	John O. Garvin	John O. Garvin	1962	116
220 5/8	27 2/8	29	22 3/8	5 4/8	5 6/8	10	8	Rio Blanco Co., CO	Anthony L. Weiss	Anthony L. Weiss	1974	117
220 2/8	25 4/8	25 4/8	22 3/8	5 2/8	5 3/8	8	8	Garfield Co., CO	Calvin Turner	Calvin Turner	1966	118
220 1/8	25 3/8	25	25	5	5 1/8	10	12	Fremont Co., WY	Albert Wagner, Jr.	Albert Wagner, Jr.	1966	119
220 1/8	25 5/8	26 2/8	25 7/8	5	5 1/8	10	10	Sublette Co., WY	Doug Leininger	Doug Leininger	1998	119
219 7/8	25 7/8	26 2/8	23 1/8	4 7/8	4 7/8	8	8	Utah Co., UT	Martin R. Cole	Martin R. Cole	1978	121
218 5/8	25 3/8	26	22 4/8	4 7/8	5	7	8	Diefenbaker Lake, SK	Murray D. Murdoch	Murray D. Murdoch	1999	122
218 2/8	24 2/8	25 6/8	23 1/8	7	6 4/8	11	9	Randall Co., TX	Jerry G. Curtis	Jerry G. Curtis	1999	123
218 1/8	26	26 6/8	21 3/8	4 4/8	4 6/8	8	7	Wyoming	Jean L. Nickel	John C. Nickel	PR 1986	124
218	26	26 1/8	25 2/8	5 1/8	5 2/8	5	5	Blackwater River, BC	Henry Harrison	Dale Harrison	1982	125
217 3/8	23 6/8	23 6/8	22 1/8	4 3/8	4 3/8	7	7	Moffat Co., CO	Art Biggs	Joseph C. Schilling	PR 1950	126
217 3/8	26 2/8	26 1/8	21 6/8	5 2/8	5 1/8	7	11	Linn Co., OR	Stanley A. Benson	Stanley A. Benson	1978	126
217 3/8	22	21 5/8	19 6/8	5 1/8	5 1/8	11	12	Morgan Co., UT	Kirt H. Richins	Kirt H. Richins	1997	126
216 7/8	24	24 3/8	17 4/8	4 7/8	4 7/8	12	9	Missoula Co., MT	Eino Hill	Fred R. Willis	PR 1940	129
216 7/8	23	22 2/8	24 1/8	4	4 2/8	10	11	Lemhi Co., ID	Herbert Williams	Avery Williams	1979	129
216 3/8	28 2/8	24	28 1/8	5 3/8	5 4/8	9	12	Princeton, BC	Unknown	Ted Hardin	PR 1940	131
216 2/8	23 2/8	22 2/8	23	5 2/8	5 4/8	9	9	Wyoming	Unknown	Steve F. DePaul	PR 1970	132
216 1/8	26 1/8	26	29 7/8	5 2/8	5 4/8	7	6	Umatilla Co., OR	James W. Parry	James W. Parry	1968	133
216	24 5/8	24 5/8	29 6/8	7 2/8	6 2/8	8	9	Harney Co., OR	Unknown	William D. Ross	PR 1935	134
216	21 3/8	21 5/8	19 7/8	4 1/8	4 2/8	7	7	Jefferson Co., CO	Picked Up	Troy Cunningham	1999	134
215 4/8	22 2/8	22 6/8	21 3/8	4 5/8	4 5/8	11	8	Camas Co., ID	Wade R. Steffenhagen	Wade R. Steffenhagen	1999	136
320 2/8 *	25 2/8	24 4/8	16 3/8	7	6	28	25	Trinity Valley, BC	Herb Banister	Charles Banister	1943	
257 4/8 *	25 1/8	25 6/8	21 6/8	6 1/8	6	9	12	Mohave Co., AZ	Sam S. Jaksick, Jr.	Sam S. Jaksick, Jr.	1999	

* Final score subject to revision by additional verifying measurements.

BOONE AND CROCKETT CLUB'S

COLUMBIA BLACKTAIL DEER

Odocoileus hemionus columbianus

Minimum Score 125

World's Record 182 2/8

Score	Length of Main Beam R.	L.	Inside Spread	Circumference at Smallest Place Between Burr and First Point R.	L.	Number of Points R.	L.	Locality	Hunter	Owner	Date Killed	Rank
178 4/8	23	23 6/8	23 2/8	4 5/8	4 7/8	5	5	Jackson Co., OR	Picked Up	Mervyn R. Thomson	PR 1950	1
167	23	23	20	4 2/8	4 3/8	5	5	Jackson Co., OR	Riley F. Bean	Riley F. Bean	1958	2
162 2/8	25	24	19 1/8	4 4/8	4 6/8	6	5	Jackson Co., OR	Norman J. Shanklin	Norman J. Shanklin	1979	3
158 1/8	24 7/8	24 1/8	17	4 6/8	4 6/8	7	6	Campbell Creek, BC	Barry Thoen	Barry Thoen	1968	4
157 7/8	23	22	17 7/8	4 2/8	4 3/8	5	5	Tillamook Co., OR	Oscar L. Scudder	Lloyd W. Scudder	1954	5
157 7/8	20 6/8	21 3/8	20 5/8	4 2/8	4 2/8	5	5	Mendocino Co., CA	William Torcato	William Torcato	1999	5
157	21 2/8	21 2/8	18 6/8	4 4/8	4 4/8	5	5	Alameda Co., CA	Ramona L. Torcato	Ramona L. Torcato	1997	7
156 4/8	20 6/8	22 4/8	18	5 3/8	5 2/8	6	5	Mendocino Co., CA	Picked Up	D.M. & J. Phillips	1958	8
156 3/8	25 6/8	23 5/8	21 7/8	4 3/8	5 2/8	5	4	Siskiyou Co., CA	Henry Klope	William T. Klope	PR 1939	9
154	22 6/8	21	16	4 5/8	4 6/8	6	5	Trinity Co., CA	Robert E. Blanc	Robert E. Blanc	1984	10
152 5/8	21 7/8	20 4/8	20 5/8	4 4/8	4 5/8	5	5	Stanislaus Co., CA	Scott A. Wilkinson	Scott A. Wilkinson	1998	11
151 6/8	24 6/8	25	23 6/8	4 1/8	4 2/8	3	4	Stanislaus Co., CA	Scott A. Wilkinson	Scott A. Wilkinson	2000	12
151 2/8	23	22 4/8	19 2/8	5 2/8	5 2/8	5	5	Mendocino Co., CA	Tommy E. Thompson	Tommy E. Thompson	1994	13
151 1/8	22 1/8	22 6/8	19 3/8	4 4/8	4 4/8	6	8	Marion Co., OR	Chad A. Richardson	Chad A. Richardson	1997	14
150 7/8	21	22 5/8	16 4/8	4 5/8	4 5/8	7	7	Jackson Co., OR	Andy Wilkins	Andy Wilkins	1998	15
150 1/8	22 7/8	22	24 4/8	4 6/8	4 3/8	5	6	Mendocino Co., CA	Brock B. Perry	Brock B. Perry	2000	16
149 6/8	20	20 4/8	18 4/8	3 7/8	4	5	5	Mendocino Co., CA	Robert Whiting	Ted T. Daly, Jr.	PR 1988	17
149 5/8	24 2/8	23 1/8	17 5/8	5	4 7/8	6	5	Whatcom Co., WA	Bruce V. Seton	Bruce B. Seton	1942	18
148 6/8	21 2/8	22 1/8	22 4/8	4 1/8	4 2/8	7	5	Trinity Co., CA	David E. Evanow	David E. Evanow	1998	19
148 4/8	24 4/8	24 1/8	22 4/8	4 6/8	5	5	5	Washington Co., OR	Floyd Gray	Joe G. Papasadero	PR 1945	20
147 5/8	20 5/8	21 3/8	20 3/8	4 4/8	4 4/8	6	6	Siskiyou Co., CA	James A. Swortzel	James A. Swortzel	2000	21
147 4/8	21 4/8	21 4/8	18	4 4/8	4 5/8	6	6	Jackson Co., OR	Steve S. Richardson	Steve S. Richardson	1997	22
147 3/8	20 2/8	21 1/8	19 2/8	4 4/8	4 4/8	6	6	Humboldt Co., CA	Bill C. Byron	Bill C. Byron	1997	23
147 3/8	21 7/8	22 5/8	18 5/8	5	5	4	4	Mendocino Co., CA	Paul D. Osmond	Paul D. Osmond	1998	23
147 3/8	22 5/8	21 5/8	18 3/8	4 6/8	4 6/8	6	5	Linn Co., OR	Dean Bowers	Dean Bowers	1999	23
147 1/8	19 4/8	20 2/8	15	4 3/8	4 5/8	5	7	Siskiyou Co., CA	Lowell Wolfe	Larry R. Wolfe	1946	26
147 1/8	19 6/8	17 7/8	17 1/8	5 1/8	4 6/8	5	5	Lane Co., OR	Jeff Heater	Jeff Heater	1978	26
146 5/8	23	23	17 4/8	4	3 6/8	6	7	Trinity Co., CA	Gary M. Ireland	Gary M. Ireland	1997	28
146 2/8	22 5/8	23 3/8	23 1/8	4 3/8	4 3/8	6	5	Trinity Co., CA	Craig L. Brown	C.L. & J.L. Brown	1993	29
145 1/8	21 5/8	21 6/8	16	4 6/8	4 4/8	7	6	Lewis Co., WA	Wenzel Tauscher	John L. Tauscher	1946	30
145	21 7/8	20 6/8	20	4 5/8	4 5/8	5	6	Trinity Co., CA	Dennis A. Nilsen	Dennis A. Nilsen	1997	31
144 6/8	20 7/8	21 4/8	22	4 3/8	4 4/8	5	5	Trinity Co., CA	Craig L. Brown	C.L. & J.L. Brown	1996	32
144 6/8	21 6/8	21 3/8	18 7/8	4 7/8	4 4/8	6	5	Mendocino Co., CA	John D. Tuso	John D. Tuso	1998	32
143 4/8	21 1/8	21 2/8	18	4 4/8	4 2/8	5	5	Trinity Co., CA	Dennis A. Nilsen	Dennis A. Nilsen	1994	34

COLUMBIA BLACKTAIL DEER

Odocoileus hemionus columbianus

Score	Length of Main Beam R.	L.	Inside Spread	Circumference at Smallest Place Between Burr and First Point R.	L.	Number of Points R.	L.	Locality	Hunter	Owner	Date Killed	Rank
143 3/8	21 4/8	21 5/8	20 1/8	4 3/8	4 3/8	5	5	Shasta Co., CA	David E. Smith	David E. Smith	1977	35
143 3/8	21	19 6/8	17 1/8	4 7/8	4 6/8	5	5	Trinity Co., CA	Joy L. Brown	C.L. & J.L. Brown	1991	35
142 6/8	21 4/8	21 4/8	21 6/8	4 4/8	4 2/8	5	5	Mendocino Co., CA	Thomas J. Fetzer	Thomas J. Fetzer	1998	37
142 5/8	21 6/8	20 5/8	17 5/8	4 4/8	4 4/8	5	5	Lane Co., OR	Byron J. Hoeper	Byron J. Hoeper	1995	38
142 4/8	23 4/8	23 4/8	18 4/8	3 4/8	3 4/8	9	5	Jackson Co., OR	Brian V. Morris	D.M. & J. Phillips	1991	39
142 2/8	21 4/8	20 7/8	20 4/8	4	4	5	5	Trinity Co., CA	Derek W. Harrison	Derek W. Harrison	1997	40
142 2/8	22 3/8	22 5/8	21 6/8	4 2/8	4 2/8	5	5	Mendocino Co., CA	Michael D. Callahan	Michael D. Callahan	1998	40
142 2/8	22 7/8	22 3/8	22	4 2/8	4 4/8	5	5	Mendocino Co., CA	George A. Deffterios	George A. Deffterios	2000	40
142 1/8	22 6/8	21 4/8	14 7/8	4 2/8	4 2/8	5	4	Knight Inlet, BC	Andrew M. Rippingale	Andrew M. Rippingale	1998	43
142	21 3/8	21 4/8	18	4 4/8	4 4/8	5	5	Jackson Co., OR	Riley F. Bean	Riley F. Bean	1970	44
141 6/8	20 2/8	19 6/8	15 4/8	4 5/8	4 6/8	5	5	Mendocino Co., CA	Dennis Bartolomei	Dennis Bartolomei	1996	45
141 4/8	21 2/8	22 4/8	15 5/8	4 5/8	4 4/8	6	7	Trinity Co., CA	Larry Brown	C.L. & J.L. Brown	1986	46
141	18 4/8	18 6/8	13	4 4/8	4 3/8	5	5	Santa Clara Co., CA	Charles Nesler	Ben W. Mazzone	1957	47
141	21	20 4/8	17 6/8	4 1/8	4 1/8	5	5	Jackson Co., OR	Philip W. Sandquist	Philip W. Sandquist	1993	47
141	22 6/8	22 2/8	16 6/8	4 2/8	4 3/8	5	5	Yamhill Co., OR	Danny J. Moen	Danny J. Moen	1997	47
140 7/8	18	19 1/8	16 1/8	4 4/8	4 4/8	5	5	Mendocino Co., CA	John T. Corrigan	John T. Corrigan	1997	50
140 7/8	24	23 5/8	22 5/8	4 2/8	4 2/8	5	4	Colusa Co., CA	John H. Knight	John H. Knight	1998	50
140 6/8	21 3/8	21 5/8	20 2/8	4 6/8	4 7/8	6	5	Clackamas Co., OR	Casey Johnson	Casey Johnson	1997	52
140 6/8	19 7/8	20 5/8	16 4/8	5 1/8	5 3/8	5	5	Trinity Co., CA	Russell A. Nickols	Russell A. Nickols	1999	52
140 1/8	20 6/8	20 1/8	19 7/8	5	5	5	6	Lane Co., OR	Jacob S. Huck	Jacob S. Huck	1971	54
140 1/8	21 4/8	21 4/8	20 1/8	4 6/8	4 6/8	5	5	Trinity Co., CA	Craig L. Brown	C.L. & J.L. Brown	1986	54
139 7/8	21 5/8	21	20 1/8	4	3 6/8	5	5	Mendocino Co., CA	Howard H. Bowles	Howard H. Bowles	1998	56
139 4/8	19 2/8	18 6/8	19	4 6/8	4 5/8	5	5	Mendocino Co., CA	Ronald G. Malvino	Ronald G. Malvino	1993	57
139 4/8	21 4/8	22 4/8	15	5 4/8	6	5	5	Trinity Co., CA	Wayne C. Evans	Wayne C. Evans	1997	57
139 3/8	22	22 6/8	16 7/8	5	5 2/8	5	5	San Mateo Co., CA	Daniel R. Caughey III	Daniel R. Caughey III	1995	59
139 3/8	20 3/8	20	17 1/8	4 3/8	4 4/8	5	5	Lake Co., CA	Steven K. Farr	Steven K. Farr	1997	59
139 2/8	21 5/8	22 5/8	19 2/8	4 6/8	4 3/8	6	3	Lane Co., OR	Hubert Simmions	Jeff Heater	1978	61
139 2/8	22 4/8	22 1/8	22 3/8	5 1/8	5 3/8	5	5	Trinity Co., CA	Joy L. Brown	C.L. & J.L. Brown	1993	61
138 7/8	20 2/8	18 4/8	18 7/8	4	3 7/8	5	5	Trinity Co., CA	Picked Up	C.L. & J.L. Brown	1995	63
138 7/8	22 6/8	21 1/8	17 2/8	6 1/8	6 3/8	6	7	Clark Co., WA	Thomas Holland	Thomas Holland	1997	63
138 5/8	21 1/8	20 4/8	16 7/8	3 6/8	3 6/8	5	5	Lake Co., CA	Frank J. Bush	Frank J. Bush	1997	65
138 3/8	22	21 2/8	19 1/8	4 1/8	3 6/8	5	4	Mendocino Co., CA	Glenn A. Zane	Glenn A. Zane	1998	66
138 2/8	20 6/8	21	19 6/8	4	3 7/8	5	5	Shasta Co., CA	David E. Smith	David E. Smith	1979	67
138	19 7/8	20	20 1/8	3 7/8	3 6/8	4	4	Siskiyou Co., CA	Jeff Mitola	Jeff Mitola	1997	68

Score						L	R	Locality	Hunter	Owner	Date	Rank
137 7/8	22 5/8	22 1/8	16 5/8	4 7/8	4 5/8	4	4	Douglas Co., OR	Pat Johnsrud	Pat Johnsrud	1973	69
137 7/8	19 3/8	19 3/8	16 1/8	4 5/8	4 5/8	5	5	Trinity Co., CA	Craig L. Brown	C.L. & J.L. Brown	1989	69
137 6/8	20 1/8	20 4/8	19 6/8	4 4/8	4 4/8	5	6	Trinity Co., CA	Loran G. August	Loran G. August	2000	69
137 5/8	19 4/8	20 7/8	14 2/8	3 5/8	3 4/8	5	5	Douglas Co., OR	Barry Smith	Barry Smith	1998	72
137 5/8	21 1/8	19 7/8	17 3/8	4 6/8	4 6/8	4	4	Shasta Co., CA	Vern A. Ferguson	Vern E. Ferguson	PR 1960	73
137 5/8	19 5/8	17	17 7/8	4 4/8	4 4/8	5	5	Mendocino Co., CA	Ronald L. Christensen	Ronald L. Christensen	1992	73
137 5/8	21 6/8	22 2/8	15 4/8	4 7/8	4 5/8	4	4	Linn Co., OR	Robert E. Ryan	Robert E. Ryan	1993	73
137 5/8	23 2/8	23	17 5/8	4 5/8	4 5/8	6	6	Jefferson Co., WA	Karl K. Stueve	Karl K. Stueve	1997	73
137	22 6/8	22 2/8	15 4/8	4 4/8	4 3/8	4	4	Trinity Co., CA	Robert J. King	Robert J. King	1997	77
137	19 4/8	18 1/8	18 4/8	3 6/8	3 5/8	5	5	Mendocino Co., CA	Robert Flanagan	Robert Flanagan	1979	77
136 6/8	23 7/8	25	22	4 7/8	5 1/8	6	6	Josephine Co., OR	Roxie Smith	Aly M. Bruner	1940	79
136 6/8	18 6/8	18 7/8	15 4/8	4	4	5	5	Clackamas Co., OR	Edward L. Farmer, Sr.	Edward L. Farmer, Sr.	1996	79
136 5/8	22 7/8	22	16 7/8	4 5/8	4 4/8	4	4	Lincoln Co., OR	Leonard L. Wilson	Leonard L. Wilson	1997	81
136 5/8	20 2/8	20	18 7/8	3 3/8	3 3/8	4	4	Trinity Co., CA	Autumn L. Brown	C.L. & J.L. Brown	2000	81
136	21 1/8	20 5/8	19 4/8	4 7/8	4 4/8	5	5	Mendocino Co., CA	Anthony J. Grech	Anthony J. Grech	1998	83
135 6/8	19 7/8	20	17 6/8	4 2/8	4 1/8	5	5	Trinity Co., CA	Bill Baker	Bill Baker	2000	84
135 5/8	22 4/8	21 5/8	20 1/8	3 7/8	3 7/8	5	5	Napa Co., CA	Richard H. August	Richard H. August	1988	85
135 4/8	21 1/8	21 1/8	17 1/8	4 7/8	4 5/8	5	5	Humboldt Co., CA	Daniel M. Geisinger	Daniel M. Geisinger	2000	85
135 3/8	21 2/8	21 1/8	15 4/8	4 5/8	4 5/8	5	5	Mendocino Co., CA	Jace Comfort	Jace Comfort	1998	87
135 2/8	19 2/8	20	16 1/8	4 6/8	4 3/8	5	5	Humboldt Co., CA	Melvin J. Domko	Melvin J. Domko	1982	88
135 1/8	19 4/8	19 4/8	17	4 1/8	4 1/8	5	5	Humboldt Co., CA	Kirk D. Younker	Kirk D. Younker	1998	89
135 1/8	19 3/8	18 2/8	15 5/8	3 6/8	3 4/8	5	5	Trinity Co., CA	James A. Swortzel	James A. Swortzel	1996	90
135 1/8	19 1/8	19 7/8	17 7/8	4 3/8	4	5	5	Mendocino Co., CA	Bradley E. Nolan	Bradley E. Nolan	1998	90
135	19 1/8	20	19	3 7/8	3 7/8	5	5	Josephine Co., OR	Picked Up	Bruce D. Ringsmith	1990	92
135	20 3/8	20 5/8	15 6/8	4 7/8	4 1/8	5	5	Humboldt Co., CA	Kevin G. Fay	Kevin G. Fay	1998	92
134 2/8	20 6/8	22 2/8	15 3/8	4	4	6	6	Mendocino Co., CA	Wilbur Boettcher	Wilbur Boettcher	1997	94
133 4/8	17	18 3/8	17 2/8	3 5/8	3 5/8	5	5	Lane Co., OR	William J. Gardner, Jr.	William J. Gardner, Jr.	1996	95
133 1/8	20 5/8	18 6/8	13 6/8	4 4/8	4 4/8	6	6	San Mateo Co., CA	Robert L. Conley	Robert L. Conley	1968	96
132 7/8	21 5/8	20 1/8	16	5	5	5	5	Santa Clara Co., CA	Daniel R. Caughey III	Daniel R. Caughey III	1998	97
132 6/8	19 6/8	20 1/8	11	4 2/8	4 2/8	5	5	Trinity Co., CA	Ben W. Mazzone	Ben W. Mazzone	1995	98
132 1/8	20 2/8	22	21 1/8	4 4/8	4 4/8	4	4	Trinity Co., CA	Craig L. Brown	C.L. & J.L. Brown	1991	99
132 1/8	20	20 2/8	13 7/8	3 7/8	3 7/8	5	5	Mendocino Co., CA	Donald W. Biggs	Donald W. Biggs	1999	99
131 7/8	20 6/8	22	20 5/8	3 7/8	3 7/8	4	4	Trinity Co., CA	Jerrold M. King	Jerrold M. King	1999	101
131 6/8	19 7/8	18 4/8	16	4 7/8	4 7/8	5	5	Trinity Co., CA	Craig L. Brown	C.L. & J.L. Brown	1991	102
131 6/8	20 3/8	21	14 2/8	4 1/8	4 2/8	6	6	Tehama Co., CA	David A. Rosin	David A. Rosin	1998	102
131 3/8	21 3/8	21 1/8	15 7/8	4 2/8	4 2/8	5	5	Curry Co., OR	Ron N. Crook	Ron N. Crook	1991	104
131 1/8	17 3/8	18	15 1/8	5 6/8	5 6/8	4	4	San Mateo Co., CA	Daniel R. Caughey III	Daniel R. Caughey III	1995	105
131	19 6/8	20	16 3/8	3 3/8	3 4/8	5	5	Jackson Co.,OR	Duane M. Bernard	Duane M. Bernard	1997	106
131	21	21 2/8	20 6/8	3 7/8	3 5/8	6	6	Humboldt Co., CA	Robert J. King	Robert J. King	1997	106
130 7/8	21	21	15 1/8	4 2/8	4 4/8	4	4	Siskiyou Co., CA	John J. Flores	John J. Flores	1997	108
130	19	18 6/8	18 6/8	4	4	5	5	Sonoma Co., CA	Jeff J. Konnoff	Jeff J. Konnoff	1999	109
129 7/8	19 2/8	15 3/8	15 5/8	3 6/8	3 7/8	6	5	Jackson Co., OR	Chris Sandquist	Chris Sandquist	1997	110
129 6/8	18	18 3/8	13 2/8	4 1/8	4 2/8	5	5	Tillamook Co., OR	Joshua C. Parkin	Joshua C. Parkin	1998	111

COLUMBIA BLACKTAIL DEER

Odocoileus hemionus columbianus

Score	Length of Main Beam R.	Length of Main Beam L.	Inside Spread	Circumference at Smallest Place Between Burr and First Point R.	Circumference at Smallest Place Between Burr and First Point L.	Number of Points R.	Number of Points L.	Locality	Hunter	Owner	Date Killed	Rank
129 5/8	23	22 6/8	18 6/8	3 7/8	4 1/8	7	7	Trinity Co., CA	Charles Burden	Charles Burden	1998	112
129 1/8	16 7/8	17 1/8	15 1/8	4 4/8	4 3/8	5	5	Mendocino Co., CA	Jill M. Shaul	G.R. Shaul	1997	113
129	21 5/8	20 4/8	21	4 5/8	4 4/8	5	4	Trinity Co., CA	David E. Evanow	David E. Evanow	1998	114
128 1/8	19 6/8	20 7/8	15 7/8	4 3/8	4 1/8	5	5	Thurston Co., WA	Wayne E. Rikerd	Wayne E. Rikerd	1971	115
127 3/8	20 5/8	20	16 3/8	3 6/8	4 2/8	4	5	Trinity Co., CA	Paul J. Reuter	Paul J. Reuter	1998	116
127 2/8	20 1/8	19 4/8	18 2/8	4	4	5	5	Mendocino Co., CA	Rodney D. Fitch	Rodney D. Fitch	1997	117
126 3/8	19 1/8	19 4/8	15 3/8	4 1/8	4 1/8	5	5	Napa Co., CA	Bruce D. Ringsmith	Bruce D. Ringsmith	1971	118
126 2/8	19 6/8	20 6/8	14 4/8	4 6/8	4 7/8	5	6	Skamania Co., WA	David A. Roberts	David A. Roberts	1998	119
126 1/8	21	21	17 5/8	4 4/8	4 6/8	4	4	Cowlitz Co., WA	Jason R. Olson	Jason R. Olson	1998	120
125 1/8	19 3/8	19 3/8	14 3/8	4 2/8	4	5	5	Pierce Co., WA	Dennis M. Collins	Dennis M. Collins	1973	121
125 1/8	18 3/8	19 2/8	15 3/8	4	4	5	5	Lane Co., OR	Wesley D. Long	Wesley D. Long	1999	121
179*	25	24 5/8	19 4/8	4 7/8	5 1/8	5	5	Coos Co., OR	Robert E. Irving	Robert E. Irving	1953	

* Final score subject to revision by additional verifying measurements.

SITKA BLACKTAIL DEER

Odocoileus hemionus sitkensis

Minimum Score 100

World's Record 133

Sitka blacktail deer includes trophies from coastal Alaska and Queen Charlotte Islands of British Columbia.

Score	Length of Main Beam R.	L.	Inside Spread	Circumference at Smallest Place Between Burr and First Point R.	L.	Number of Points R.	L.	Locality	Hunter	Owner	Date Killed	Rank
121 6/8	18 1/8	18 5/8	16	4 4/8	5	5	5	Dall Island, AK	James F. Baichtal	James F. Baichtal	1998	1
115 1/8	17 5/8	16 6/8	14 7/8	4 2/8	4 6/8	5	5	Thomas Bay, AK	Eli Lucas	Eli Lucas	1997	2
109 5/8	16 4/8	16 6/8	15 1/8	3 5/8	3 6/8	5	5	Thorne River, AK	James F. Baichtal	James F. Baichtal	1999	3
109 1/8	16 4/8	17 4/8	13 5/8	3 6/8	3 4/8	5	5	Kizhuyak Bay, AK	Leonard J. Schwarz	Leonard J. Schwarz	1998	4
108 7/8	15 3/8	16	15 3/8	4	3 7/8	5	5	Red Bay, AK	Steve Geary	Steve Geary	1997	5
108 6/8	18 2/8	18 1/8	15 4/8	3 7/8	3 7/8	4	5	Port Lyons, AK	Ronald W. Taylor	Ronald W. Taylor	1996	6
106 7/8	16 2/8	16 2/8	14 3/8	3 5/8	3 5/8	5	5	Afognak Island, AK	Robert J. Barck, Jr.	Robert J. Barck, Jr.	1998	7
106 3/8	17 3/8	17 2/8	14 5/8	4	3 6/8	4	5	Kelp Bay, AK	Travis D. Peterson	Travis D. Peterson	1998	8
105 6/8	18 1/8	17 7/8	15 6/8	4 3/8	4 1/8	4	4	Kodiak Island, AK	Kyle J. Carlisle	Kyle J. Carlisle	1997	9
105 6/8	17 1/8	16 2/8	13 2/8	3 4/8	3 4/8	5	5	Uganik Bay, AK	H. Arthur Peck	H. Arthur Peck	1998	9
104	18	18 6/8	13 2/8	3 6/8	3 5/8	5	5	Kiliuda Bay, AK	Timothy C. Moore	Timothy C. Moore	1998	11
103	17 7/8	17 2/8	15	3 7/8	4 2/8	4	5	Olga Bay, AK	Joseph J. Vaness	Joseph J. Vaness	1997	12
102 3/8	18 6/8	18 4/8	15 3/8	3 7/8	3 5/8	4	4	Mitkof Island, AK	Scott D. Newman	Scott D. Newman	1998	13
101 4/8	15 6/8	17 6/8	13 4/8	3 7/8	4	5	4	Uganik Bay, AK	Andrew J. Fierro	Andrew J. Fierro	1997	14
121 5/8*	19 3/8	19 2/8	16 6/8	4	4	5	6	Grassy Lake, AK	Picked Up	Janet B. Clark	1983	
110 7/8*	18 2/8	16 2/8	14 3/8	3 5/8	3 7/8	5	5	Aliulik Pen., AK	Andrew R. Rios	Andrew R. Rios	1993	
110 3/8*	15 6/8	16 5/8	15 7/8	3 2/8	3 4/8	4	5	Three Saints Bay, AK	Louis Lashley	Louis Lashley	1997	

* Final score subject to revision by additional verifying measurements.

WHITETAIL DEER - TYPICAL ANTLERS

Odocoileus virginianus virginianus and certain related subspecies

Minimum Score 160   World's Record 213 5/8

Score	Length of Main Beam R.	L.	Inside Spread	Circumference at Smallest Place Between Burr and First Point R.	L.	Number of Points R.	L.	Locality	Hunter	Owner	Date Killed	Rank
197 6/8	30	26 7/8	18 7/8	5 7/8	6	7	10	Kenosha Co., WI	Keith S. Brossard	Keith S. Brossard	1999	1
195 5/8	29 4/8	27 5/8	18 7/8	4 6/8	4 7/8	9	8	Rock Island Co., IL	Kent E. Anderson	Kent E. Anderson	1999	2
193 7/8	25 2/8	25 2/8	21 5/8	4 7/8	4 7/8	7	6	Van Buren Co., IA	W. Eugene Zieglowsky	W. Eugene Zieglowsky	1997	3
193 3/8	25 6/8	24 5/8	19 1/8	5 6/8	5 5/8	8	8	Witchekan Lake, SK	Marcel Tetreault	Marcel Tetreault	1998	4
192 6/8	26	27	19 2/8	5 6/8	5 6/8	6	6	Washington Co., NE	Robert E. Wackel	Robert E. Wackel	1961	5
192 3/8	26 7/8	26 7/8	18 5/8	4 6/8	5 1/8	5	6	Jennings Co., IN	Walter M. Johnson	Walter M. Johnson	1997	6
192 2/8	26 7/8	26 7/8	18 4/8	5 4/8	5 4/8	5	5	Mills Co., IA	John Chase	John Chase	1997	7
191 7/8	29	27	20 5/8	5 1/8	5 1/8	6	5	Monroe Co., IA	Picked Up	Troy Amoss	1986	8
191 4/8	30 7/8	30 4/8	22 3/8	5 7/8	5 2/8	9	7	Monroe Co., GA	Buck Ashe	Buck Ashe	PR 1962	9
191 4/8	28 5/8	28 5/8	21 2/8	4 6/8	4 6/8	5	5	Henry Co., IL	Keith Hamerlinck	Keith Hamerlinck	1999	9
190 7/8	29 5/8	29 4/8	24 3/8	4 6/8	4 4/8	6	6	Leduc, AB	Robert J. Kowalyshyn	Robert J. Kowalyshyn	1997	11
190 6/8	30	30 2/8	20 6/8	5 1/8	5 2/8	7	7	Union Co., IN	John R. Ison, Jr.	John R. Ison, Jr.	1997	12
190 4/8	28 2/8	29 1/8	24 3/8	5 5/8	5 5/8	8	8	Menard Co., IL	Dwaine E. Heyen	Dwaine E. Heyen	1997	13
189 3/8	25 5/8	26	18 1/8	5 3/8	5 2/8	7	7	Lewis Co., KY	Jim Cooper	Jim Cooper	1999	14
189 2/8	28 5/8	27 1/8	18 4/8	4 3/8	4 3/8	5	5	Buchanan Co., VA	Jerry L. James	Jerry L. James	1999	15
188 7/8	28 2/8	28 7/8	19 4/8	6	6 1/8	6	6	Clark Co., IL	Larry Shaw	Larry Shaw	1998	16
188 3/8	28 3/8	29 1/8	22 4/8	4 7/8	5	10	10	Montgomery Co., IL	Travis L. Hartman	Travis L. Hartman	1999	17
188	26 2/8	27 2/8	19 1/8	5 7/8	5 6/8	8	7	N. Saskatchewan River, AB	Darrel J. Patera	Darrel J. Patera	1999	18
187 7/8	28	28 3/8	21 2/8	5	5	7	8	Bayfield Co., WI	Simon Jacobs	Jon Jacobs	1951	19
187 5/8	27 1/8	27 2/8	20 5/8	5 5/8	5 4/8	5	5	Pickaway Co., OH	Jeffrey M. Bragg	Jeffrey M. Bragg	1999	20
187 5/8	28 2/8	29	23 3/8	5 4/8	5	8	8	Greene Co., IA	Chris Jones	Chris Jones	1999	20
187 4/8	25 4/8	27 4/8	25 4/8	4 2/8	4 4/8	6	7	Warren Co., MO	Gary D. Schuster	Gary D. Schuster	1998	22
187 3/8	24 7/8	25 2/8	23 3/8	5 3/8	5	6	8	St. Francis Co., AR	Andy Anderson	Andy Anderson	1998	23
187 2/8	27 1/8	26 4/8	24 2/8	5 2/8	5 3/8	6	8	Wandering River, AB	Jason L. Hayes	Jason L. Hayes	1999	24
187	29 2/8	28	25 5/8	5 6/8	5 7/8	6	6	Geary Co., KS	Jack Swenson	Brad Sowter	1997	25
186 5/8	27	26 5/8	22 1/8	5 2/8	5 2/8	5	5	Kelvington, SK	David Martin	David Martin	1999	26
186 5/8	27 1/8	26 4/8	21 4/8	4 4/8	4 3/8	7	8	Buffalo Co., WI	Kenneth H. Shane	Kenneth H. Shane	2000	26
186 4/8	28 3/8	28 6/8	24 3/8	5 4/8	5 4/8	6	7	Appanoose Co., IA	Picked Up	Robert Walker	1998	28
186 2/8	25 1/8	24 4/8	18	5 2/8	5 2/8	6	6	White Co., IN	Samuel T. Young	Samuel T. Young	1997	29
186	28	27 7/8	19 1/8	5 4/8	5 4/8	6	6	Macoupin Co., IL	Picked Up	Darrell Baker	1998	30
185 7/8	28 2/8	27 7/8	23 7/8	4 4/8	4 5/8	5	5	Queen Annes Co., MD	Walter J. Lachewitz, Jr.	Walter J. Lachewitz, Jr.	1998	31
185 6/8	26 3/8	26 2/8	20 7/8	5	5 2/8	8	8	Bryan Co., OK	Larry D. Luman	Larry D. Luman	1997	32
185 5/8	26	27 5/8	19 5/8	6	5 4/8	5	5	Johnson Co., IN	Michael J. Arney	Michael J. Arney	1998	33
185 4/8	27 1/8	27 2/8	22 2/8	4 7/8	5	6	8	Brisco, BC	Baptiste Paul	Winston Wolfenden	1914	34

Score								Locality	Hunter	Owner	Date Killed	Rank
185 3/8	23 1/8	27 2/8	23 7/8	5 1/8	5 5/8	7	9	Morris Co., KS	Gregory A. Glasgow	Gregory A. Glasgow	1998	35
185 2/8	24 7/8	27	23 2/8	5 7/8	5 3/8	6	5	Mercer Co., IL	Richard L. McCaw	Richard L. McCaw	1997	36
184 4/8	27 3/8	26 4/8	20	4 6/8	4 7/8	6	6	Echo Lake, SK	Dale McKay	Dale McKay	1997	37
184 4/8	27 7/8	26 7/8	19 2/8	5 3/8	5 3/8	5	6	Eagle Creek, SK	Preston Haanen	Preston Haanen	1999	37
184 4/8	30 1/8	30 7/8	19 6/8	5 2/8	5 3/8	4	7	McHenry Co., IL	Russell A. Lovins	Russell A. Lovins	1999	37
184 3/8	27 6/8	28	23	5 6/8	5 4/8	8	6	Reno Co., KS	Michael Denney	Michael Denney	1991	40
184 3/8	26 3/8	27 1/8	23 7/8	5 2/8	5 1/8	6	6	Porcupine Plain, SK	Lee Krantz	Lee Krantz	1998	40
184 2/8	28 4/8	29 4/8	21 2/8	5	5	5	5	McLeod River, AB	Clifford L. Haddock	Clifford L. Haddock	1998	42
184 1/8	31	30 2/8	22	5 6/8	5 7/8	7	7	Montgomery Co., OH	Glenn Parks	Glenn Parks	1999	43
184	27 6/8	25 6/8	24 6/8	4 6/8	4 6/8	6	6	Douglas Co., WI	David H. Johnson	David H. Johnson	1998	44
183 7/8	27 7/8	27 5/8	20 2/8	5 2/8	5 1/8	5	6	Muhlenberg Co., KY	James E. Brewer	James E. Brewer	1997	45
183 7/8	29 3/8	27 3/8	22 5/8	5 1/8	5 1/8	6	5	Washington Co., KS	Rick B. Novak	Rick B. Novak	1997	45
183 6/8	27 4/8	27 1/8	22 2/8	5 2/8	5 3/8	6	7	Franklin Co., KS	Picked Up	B&C National Collection	1994	47
183 4/8	26 4/8	27 1/8	24	4 6/8	4 7/8	7	7	Douglas Co., WI	Michael Head	Michael Head	1999	48
183 3/8	29 1/8	29 6/8	20 4/8	5	5	6	6	Coos Co., NH	Frank Thurston	Frank Thurston	1997	49
183 3/8	26 6/8	26 7/8	21 1/8	4 7/8	5 2/8	6	9	Nemaha Co., KS	Roy D. Rissky	Roy D. Rissky	1998	49
183 1/8	26 3/8	25 6/8	22 1/8	4 6/8	4 6/8	7	7	Cass Co., MO	Gerald E. Lemmer	Gerald E. Lemmer	1997	49
183	26	24 7/8	18 2/8	5 6/8	5 6/8	5	5	Lincoln Co., NE	Kevin L. Wood	Kevin L. Wood	1999	51
182 6/8	29 7/8	29 4/8	20 1/8	4 3/8	4 5/8	7	9	Wayne Co., IA	Donald P. Greenlee	Donald P. Greenlee	1997	52
182 6/8	26	26	18 4/8	4 4/8	4 5/8	6	5	Kelvington, SK	Roger D. Bibee	Roger D. Bibee	1999	53
182 6/8	26 7/8	26 1/8	19	4 6/8	4 6/8	5	5	Roanoke Co., VA	Dwayne E. Webster	Dwayne E. Webster	1999	53
182 4/8	26 3/8	26 4/8	15 4/8	5	5 4/8	6	6	Jackson Co., IN	Rocky Deakin	Rocky Deakin	1999	53
182 4/8	27	28 4/8	19 2/8	4 2/8	4 2/8	6	6	Franklin Co., IL	Tim Broy	Tim Broy	1985	56
182 4/8	25 5/8	25 7/8	18 4/8	4 5/8	4 6/8	6	6	Maverick Co., TX	Christopher J. Roswell	Christopher J. Roswell	1997	56
182 4/8	26 3/8	26 5/8	24 6/8	5 3/8	5 2/8	6	5	Wells Co., IN	Matt Roush	Matt Roush	1999	56
182 2/8	29	25 7/8	18 7/8	5 2/8	5 1/8	6	7	Bonnyville, AB	Jim Baik	Jim Baik	1998	60
182	25	24 1/8	22 6/8	5 7/8	5 7/8	5	6	Henderson Co., IL	Nicky J. Clark, Jr.	Nicky J. Clark, Jr.	1999	61
181 6/8	28 7/8	30 4/8	24	5 6/8	5 6/8	7	5	Cando, SK	Karl Oliver	Karl Oliver	1998	62
181 5/8	24 1/8	24	17 7/8	5	5 1/8	5	5	Fulton Co., IL	George S. Hadsall	George S. Hadsall	1999	63
181 5/8	25 7/8	25 5/8	19 7/8	7	7	7	9	Dixon Co., NE	Kirk C. Kneifl	Kirk C. Kneifl	1999	63
181 3/8	26 3/8	27	19 7/8	5 1/8	5 2/8	7	8	Meadow Lake, SK	Freeman R. Bell	Freeman R. Bell	1997	65
181 2/8	30	30 1/8	20	4 3/8	4 3/8	6	5	Pike Co., IL	Stephen J. Smith	Stephen J. Smith	1973	66
181 2/8	28 4/8	28 5/8	18	4 7/8	5	5	5	Sangamon Co., IL	Sean Shymansky	Sean Shymansky	1997	66
181 2/8	28 3/8	26 5/8	19 7/8	5 5/8	6 1/8	8	8	Fawcett Lake, AB	Robert Neimor	Robert Neimor	1998	66
181 1/8	27 4/8	27 1/8	19	5 7/8	6	7	6	Henry Co., MO	William C. Buckner	William C. Buckner	1997	69
181 1/8	26 4/8	27 1/8	19 3/8	5 4/8	5 3/8	5	5	Avoyelles Parish, LA	Donald A. Riviere	Donald A. Riviere	1998	69
181 1/8	29 5/8	28 5/8	18 4/8	5 7/8	5 7/8	6	6	St. Clair Co., IL	Dean R. Billhartz	Dean R. Billhartz	1999	69
181 1/8	25 7/8	25 6/8	20 1/8	5 5/8	5 4/8	8	7	Manitowoc Co., WI	Ronald R. Rieth	Ronald R. Rieth	1999	69
180 7/8	25 5/8	26	21 1/8	5 1/8	5	8	8	Clayton Co., IA	Robert M. Hefel	Robert M. Hefel	1998	73
180 6/8	27 2/8	26 5/8	17 6/8	4 7/8	4 4/8	8	5	Anne Arundel Co., MD	Paul H. Anderson, Jr.	Paul H. Anderson, Jr.	1995	74
180 6/8	28 3/8	28 5/8	16 4/8	5 4/8	5 4/8	8	6	Linn Co., MO	Picked Up	Doug D. Davis	1998	74
180 6/8	29 6/8	27 1/8	22 5/8	4 6/8	4 5/8	6	5	Horse Lake, SK	Cheryl Kaban	Cheryl Kaban	1999	74
180 6/8	23 4/8	25 2/8	24 6/8	5 4/8	5 6/8	6	6	Drayton Valley, AB	Peter Underwood	Peter Underwood	1999	74

WHITETAIL DEER - TYPICAL ANTLERS

Odocoileus virginianus virginianus and certain related subspecies

Score	Length of Main Beam R.	L.	Inside Spread	Circumference at Smallest Place Between Burr and First Point R.	L.	Number of Points R.	L.	Locality	Hunter	Owner	Date Killed	Rank
180 5/8	23	23 7/8	19 3/8	4 1/8	4 1/8	7	7	Waterhen, MB	Craig R. Zmijewski	Craig R. Zmijewski	1996	78
180 5/8	25 6/8	27	19 7/8	4 5/8	4 5/8	5	5	Cedar Co., IA	Bobby Smith	William H. Lilienthal	1998	78
180 5/8	25 1/8	25 2/8	18 1/8	5 3/8	5 3/8	6	7	Coles Co., IL	H. Lee Adams	H. Lee Adams	1999	78
180 5/8	28 3/8	28 3/8	17 3/8	4 5/8	4 5/8	5	5	Ashe Co., NC	William Price	William Price	1999	78
180 4/8	26 4/8	27	19 2/8	5 4/8	5 3/8	5	5	Washburn Co., WI	Timothy J. Clare	Timothy J. Clare	1998	82
180 4/8	25 5/8	25 5/8	22 5/8	5	5	6	7	Olmsted Co., MN	Thomas C. Kroening	Thomas C. Kroening	1998	82
180 3/8	25 4/8	23 6/8	21 1/8	5 5/8	5 5/8	6	5	Wapiti River, AB	Terry D. Hagman	Terry D. Hagman	1997	84
180 3/8	30 7/8	28 5/8	21 4/8	4 6/8	4 7/8	6	8	Westchester Co., NY	Richard L. Johnson	Richard L. Johnson	1998	84
180 2/8	26 7/8	26 6/8	18 7/8	4 7/8	4 7/8	6	6	Wayne Co., KY	Green Hamlin	Green Hamlin	1966	86
180 2/8	28 2/8	26 6/8	21 4/8	6 1/8	6 7/8	5	5	Cedar Co., IA	Roger Schoene	Beth Tucker	PR 1981	86
180 1/8	26 7/8	25 5/8	18 4/8	4 3/8	4 5/8	6	5	Rice Co., MN	Picked Up	Stephen L. Albers	1998	88
180 1/8	27 3/8	28	22 7/8	4 2/8	4	5	5	Medina Co., OH	Stephen F. DeMeulenaere	Stephen F. DeMeulenaere	1998	88
180 1/8	28 2/8	27 1/8	19 6/8	4 5/8	4 5/8	7	7	Boone Co., MO	Benjamin K. Betz	Benjamin K. Betz	1999	88
180 1/8	30 2/8	29 1/8	23 5/8	5 4/8	5 2/8	8	9	Waukesha Co., WI	Kevin A. McNeven	Kevin A. McNeven	2000	88
180	23 3/8	22 7/8	17 4/8	6	6	5	7	Moose Mt. Prov. Park, SK	Robin Hilts	Robin Hilts	1997	92
180	26	26	19	5 1/8	5	5	5	Redberry Lake, SK	Steven Hupaelo	Steven Hupaelo	1998	92
179 7/8	28 4/8	27 7/8	23 7/8	4 6/8	4 7/8	6	6	Valley Co., NE	Leonard L. Krason	Leonard L. Krason	1998	94
179 7/8	25 4/8	27 5/8	21 2/8	5 5/8	5 6/8	7	9	Pasquia Hills, SK	Jeffrey S. Metzler	Jeffrey S. Metzler	1998	94
179 6/8	25 2/8	25 3/8	22 3/8	5 5/8	5 4/8	7	5	Plamondon, AB	Edmond Bourassa	Edmond Bourassa	1998	96
179 6/8	26 4/8	25 4/8	21 2/8	5	4 7/8	6	6	Warren Co., OH	Rex A. Gill	Rex A. Gill	1998	96
179 6/8	25 6/8	26 5/8	21	6 1/8	5 5/8	5	5	Osage Co., KS	Ronald D. Fine	Ronald D. Fine	1999	96
179 6/8	26 7/8	27 7/8	19 6/8	4 6/8	5 2/8	8	6	Madison Co., OH	Robert E. Hunter II	Robert E. Hunter II	1999	96
179 5/8	25 5/8	25 3/8	20 6/8	4 3/8	4 3/8	5	6	Handhill Lakes, AB	D. Troutman & G. Amendt	Dave Troutman	1996	100
179 4/8	25 2/8	25 2/8	19 4/8	5 2/8	5 6/8	5	5	Macoupin Co., IL	Kurt A. Bohl	Kurt A. Bohl	1997	101
179 4/8	25	24 7/8	21	4 7/8	5	7	6	Maverick Co., TX	Lee M. Bass	Lee M. Bass	1998	101
179 3/8	24 6/8	24 6/8	20 3/8	5 7/8	5 7/8	6	6	High Prairie, AB	Walter J. Malysh	Walter J. Malysh	1997	103
179 3/8	26 5/8	25 7/8	18 7/8	6 1/8	6 2/8	5	8	Warren Co., IN	Steven B. Childress	Steven B. Childress	1999	103
179 2/8	25 7/8	24 2/8	19 4/8	4 7/8	4 7/8	6	7	Vernon Lake, AB	Del Kirchmayer	Del Kirchmayer	1997	105
179 2/8	28	27 7/8	19 4/8	5 2/8	5 1/8	6	6	Blaine Co., OK	Matt Parker	Matt Parker	1999	105
179 1/8	24 6/8	25 1/8	19 3/8	4 4/8	4 6/8	6	6	Fulton Co., IL	Jerry D. Manning	Jerry D. Manning	1977	107
179	23	23 1/8	16 5/8	3 5/8	3 5/8	8	9	La Salle Co., TX	Charles Duffy	Emory C. Thompson	PR 1941	108
179	29 2/8	29 1/8	19 6/8	5	5 1/8	6	7	McLean Co., IL	Ryan B. Bottles	Ryan B. Bottles	1999	108
179	26 3/8	26 3/8	18 2/8	5 2/8	5 3/8	5	5	St. Croix Co., WI	Kelly A. Geraghty	Kelly A. Geraghty	1999	108
178 7/8	28 3/8	27 6/8	22	5	5 1/8	6	5	Brown Co., IL	Joseph V. Barnett	Joseph V. Barnett	1988	111

Score	Main Beam R.	Main Beam L.	Inside Spread	Circ. R.	Circ. L.	Pts. R.	Pts. L.	Locality	Pts.	By Whom Killed	Owner	Date	Rank
178 5/8	26 6/8	26 7/8	17 3/8	4 5/8	4 6/8	5	5	Taylor Co., GA	5	W. Michael Layfield	W. Michael Layfield	1997	112
178 5/8	25 4/8	25	17 5/8	4 4/8	4 5/8	6	6	Blueberry Creek, AB	6	Mark E. Wolney	Dennis Wolney	1997	112
178 5/8	27 1/8	27 1/8	22 7/8	5 4/8	5 3/8	6	6	Peoria Co., IL	5	Steven M. DeSmet	Steven M. DeSmet	1998	112
178 5/8	26	26 5/8	20 3/8	5 1/8	5 3/8	5	5	Cedar Co., IA	6	Michael M. Hatzky	Michael M. Hatzky	1999	112
178 5/8	26 2/8	28	19 3/8	4 4/8	5 1/8	6	6	Morgan Co., GA	5	Brent McCarty	Brent McCarty	1999	112
178 5/8	26 4/8	25 2/8	18 2/8	5	5	6	6	Hemphill Co., TX	5	Cliff Norris	Cliff Norris	1999	112
178 4/8	28 2/8	28	22 6/8	4 2/8	4 2/8	5	5	Lincoln Co., WA	5	Melvin Scheuss	Gary H. Wilcox	1951	118
178 4/8	26 3/8	25 4/8	23	4 6/8	4 6/8	6	6	Jack Fish Lake, SK	6	Michael J. Frawley	Michael J. Frawley	1997	118
178 4/8	27 6/8	28 4/8	20 6/8	5 7/8	5 7/8	7	7	Cass Co., IA	6	Mark A. Funk	Mark A. Funk	1997	118
178 3/8	29 4/8	29 7/8	19 5/8	5 2/8	5 2/8	5	5	Mitchell Co., GA	9	Ricky C. Dowis	Ricky C. Dowis	1997	121
178 3/8	29 1/8	28 2/8	17 4/8	4 3/8	4 3/8	7	7	De Kalb Co., MO	6	Merrill Hall	Merrill Hall	1997	121
178 3/8	24 7/8	25	19 1/8	5 2/8	5 3/8	5	5	Marion Co., IA	7	Lyle E. Palmer	Lyle E. Palmer	1998	121
178 2/8	28 3/8	28 7/8	19 4/8	5 3/8	5 4/8	8	8	Kanabec Co., MN	6	Lennie L. Henning	Lennie L. Henning	1999	124
178 2/8	27 6/8	27 1/8	21 5/8	5 6/8	5 4/8	8	8	Warren Co., IL	7	Picked Up	Tory Mills	1999	124
178 2/8	28 7/8	28 7/8	21 6/8	4 7/8	5	4	4	Yorkton, SK	9	Wayde Morley	Wayde Morley	1999	124
178 1/8	26 5/8	26 2/8	20 7/8	5 1/8	5 1/8	5	5	Coteau Hills, SK	4	Trevor A. Broom	Trevor A. Broom	1997	127
178 1/8	25 5/8	25 3/8	19 5/8	6 1/8	5 6/8	6	6	De Kalb Co., MO	5	Kendall J. Weigand	Kendall J. Weigand	1998	127
178 1/8	26 7/8	27	21 3/8	4 2/8	4 2/8	6	6	Morgan Co., IL	6	Clark K. Dirden	Clark K. Dirden	1999	127
178 1/8	28 2/8	28 6/8	22 3/8	5 2/8	5 2/8	7	7	Wheeler Co., NE	7	Raymond M. Gay	Raymond M. Gay	1999	127
178	28 2/8	26 5/8	18 2/8	4 5/8	5	5	5	Crawford Co., Wi	5	Picked Up	David G. Mueller	1992	131
178	28	28 6/8	19 2/8	4 4/8	4 4/8	5	5	Sweet Grass, SK	7	Leo J. Lefevre	Leo J. Lefevre	1999	131
177 7/8	25 1/8	25 3/8	18 5/8	5	5	5	5	Pettis Co., MO	5	Michael J. Macafree	Michael J. Macafree	1997	133
177 7/8	25 2/8	26 5/8	18 1/8	5 3/8	5 1/8	6	6	Jefferson Co., IA	5	John J. Oberhaus	John J. Oberhaus	1997	133
177 7/8	24 2/8	24 7/8	19 7/8	4 4/8	4 5/8	5	5	Sioux Narrows, ON	6	Michael Christopher	Michael Christopher	1999	133
177 6/8	25 3/8	25 2/8	20 2/8	5 1/8	5 1/8	5	5	Vernon Co., MO	5	Darrell Chapman	Darrell Chapman	1997	136
177 5/8	26 4/8	26 6/8	18 4/8	5 1/8	5 1/8	5	5	Schuyler Co., IL	5	Archie D. Stagner	Archie D. Stagner	1997	137
177 5/8	26 2/8	25 4/8	20 1/8	4 3/8	4 3/8	5	5	Buffalo Co., WI	6	Mark T. Gleiter	Mark T. Gleiter	1998	137
177 4/8	28 4/8	28 5/8	19 2/8	4 5/8	4 5/8	6	6	St. Lawrence Co., NY	6	Timothy B. Lucas	Timothy B. Lucas	1997	139
177 4/8	27 6/8	26 5/8	18 6/8	4 4/8	4 4/8	9	9	Arborfield, SK	9	Tyler Johnson	Terry L. Amos	1998	139
177 3/8	26 1/8	25	20	5 1/8	5 1/8	7	7	Jefferson Co., WI	7	John L. Hausz	John L. Hausz	1996	141
177 3/8	26 6/8	26 5/8	18 7/8	5 1/8	5 1/8	5	5	Gove Co., KS	5	Daniel L. Arndt	Daniel L. Arndt	1997	141
177 3/8	27 7/8	28 2/8	23 1/8	5 2/8	5 2/8	5	5	Woodson Co., KS	6	Terry S. Wells	Terry S. Wells	1998	141
177 2/8	26	27	19 4/8	5 4/8	5 3/8	5	5	Mills Co., IA	5	James H. Roberts	James H. Roberts	1998	144
177 2/8	25 6/8	24 4/8	20 2/8	4 7/8	4 7/8	6	6	Webb Co., TX	6	Gordon Still	Gordon Still	1999	144
177 1/8	25 2/8	25 4/8	21 1/8	4 5/8	4 3/8	5	5	Marshall Co., MN	7	Dennis W. Severson	Dennis W. Severson	1954	146
177 1/8	28 4/8	26 6/8	20 2/8	5 1/8	5	6	6	Washington Co., IA	6	Ernest Aronson	Ernest Aronson	1985	146
177	26 2/8	26 2/8	18 4/8	4 3/8	4 5/8	5	5	Rapides Co., LA	5	H. Glenn Feazell	H. Glenn Feazell	1997	148
177	29 2/8	27 6/8	19 2/8	5 2/8	5 2/8	6	6	Nicholas Co., KY	6	Jim D. Whisman	Jim D. Whisman	1998	148
176 6/8	27	26	22 2/8	5 3/8	5 3/8	6	6	Mozart, SK	6	Frank Prisciak	Frank Prisciak	1997	150
176 6/8	26 5/8	26 5/8	19 4/8	5 2/8	5 2/8	5	5	River Glade, NB	5	Dennis Halliday	Dennis Halliday	1998	150
176 6/8	28 6/8	28	19 6/8	5 1/8	5 1/8	5	5	Cottonwood Co., MN	5	Cory S. Paplow	Cory S. Paplow	1999	150
176 6/8	26 2/8	26 2/8	19 6/8	4 7/8	5 2/8	7	7	Little Quill Lake, SK	5	Jonathan Rorquist	Jonathan Rorquist	1999	150
176 5/8	26 1/8	25 7/8	18 7/8	4 6/8	4 6/8	6	6	St. Louis Co., MN	6	Unknown	Allen Valley	PR 1970	154

WHITETAIL DEER - TYPICAL ANTLERS

Odocoileus virginianus virginianus and certain related subspecies

Score	Length of Main Beam R.	L.	Inside Spread	Circumference at Smallest Place Between Burr and First Point R.	L.	Number of Points R.	L.	Locality	Hunter	Owner	Date Killed	Rank
176 5/8	26	26	17 1/8	5 2/8	5 3/8	8	7	White Co., AR	Dickie P. Duke	Dickie P. Duke	1996	154
176 5/8	25 7/8	26 3/8	20 5/8	5 5/8	5 4/8	6	5	Wilbarger Co., TX	Owen P. Carpenter III	Owen P. Carpenter III	1999	154
176 4/8	28 3/8	28	18 3/8	4 6/8	5 6/8	7	10	Muscatine Co., IA	Tim S. Kroul	Tim S. Kroul	1997	157
176 4/8	26 2/8	25 3/8	22 4/8	4 2/8	4 1/8	5	6	Refugio Co., TX	William M. Murphy	William M. Murphy	1997	157
176 4/8	22 5/8	24 3/8	19 2/8	5 3/8	5 3/8	7	7	Oldman Lake, AB	John Proud	John Proud	1997	157
176 4/8	28 7/8	28 4/8	18 5/8	5 3/8	5 3/8	6	6	Columbiana Co., OH	Blane A. Wade	Blane A. Wade	1997	157
176 4/8	30 1/8	31 3/8	25 2/8	5 4/8	5 5/8	5	6	Long Sault, ON	Robert Archambault, Jr.	Robert Archambault, Jr.	1998	157
176 4/8	27 2/8	28 2/8	20 7/8	4 7/8	4 5/8	7	8	Saline Co., IL	John D. Jackson	John D. Jackson	1999	157
176 4/8	28 5/8	28 5/8	22 4/8	5 1/8	5 2/8	6	5	Ashland Co., WI	Thomas J. Warren	Thomas J. Warren	1999	157
176 3/8	24 5/8	24 5/8	16 1/8	5	5	6	6	Juneau Co., WI	Paul F. Beall	Paul F. Beall	1997	164
176 3/8	28 7/8	27 5/8	21 2/8	5	5	6	6	Adams Co., IL	Lawrence Walton	Lawrence Walton	1997	164
176 2/8	25 5/8	25 5/8	20 6/8	4 6/8	4 6/8	5	6	Vermilion River, AB	Edwin J. Bowman	Edwin J. Bowman	1997	166
176 2/8	28 5/8	30 3/8	20 4/8	4 7/8	4 5/8	7	7	Wayne Co., IL	Kent A. Ochs	Kent A. Ochs	1997	166
176 2/8	29 4/8	29	15 5/8	5 6/8	5 5/8	5	6	Aitkokan, ON	Robert G. Schlingmann	Robert G. Schlingmann	1998	166
176 2/8	25 5/8	26 4/8	18 7/8	4 5/8	4 6/8	6	6	Meyers Lake, SK	Trent Derkatz	Trent Derkatz	1999	166
176 2/8	27 2/8	27 1/8	19 1/8	4 6/8	4 7/8	7	5	Foam Lake, SK	Stanley Kaban	Stanley Kaban	1999	166
176 2/8	26 2/8	25 7/8	20	5	5	5	5	Worth Co., MO	David Shipman	David Shipman	1999	166
176 2/8	27 4/8	27 2/8	21 2/8	4 4/8	4 4/8	6	7	Nueva Leon, MX	Al Mendoza	Al Mendoza	2000	166
176 1/8	26 4/8	27 3/8	24 3/8	5 1/8	5	5	5	Monroe Co., MS	J.D. Hood	Michael D. Steadman	1972	173
176 1/8	25 4/8	27	19 1/8	4 7/8	4 6/8	5	5	Southampton Co., VA	Samuel B. Drewry, Jr.	Samuel B. Drewry, Jr.	1997	173
176 1/8	24 2/8	23 2/8	17 1/8	4 7/8	4 7/8	6	7	Webb Co., TX	Robert L. Hixson, Jr.	Robert L. Hixson, Jr.	1997	173
176 1/8	28 2/8	27 7/8	20 6/8	4 2/8	4 1/8	6	6	Maverick Co., TX	Steve E. Holloway	Steve E. Holloway	1997	173
176 1/8	28 6/8	28 1/8	20 2/8	4 5/8	4 6/8	6	7	Linn Co., IA	Rudolph C. Ashbacher	Rudolph C. Ashbacher	1998	173
176 1/8	25 7/8	26 4/8	24 2/8	5	5	7	8	Lenore Lake, SK	Emile Creurer	Emile Creurer	1998	173
176 1/8	24 3/8	24	17 7/8	4 6/8	4 7/8	6	6	Adams Co., IL	Thomas M. Foote	Thomas M. Foote	1998	173
176 1/8	25 1/8	24 5/8	16 7/8	5	5 1/8	7	8	Gentry Co., MO	Frank L. Thomas	Frank L. Thomas	1998	173
176 1/8	24 3/8	26 3/8	20 3/8	4 7/8	4 7/8	6	6	Pike Co., MO	Christopher C. Clamors	Christopher C. Clamors	1999	173
176	26 4/8	26	23	4 2/8	4 3/8	5	6	Green Lake Co., WI	Timothy S. Judas	Timothy S. Judas	1997	182
175 7/8	26 7/8	26 3/8	16 5/8	5 2/8	4 7/8	8	10	Brown Co., IL	Mark W. West	Mark W. West	1997	183
175 7/8	25 7/8	25 6/8	20	5 4/8	5 4/8	6	5	Shipman, SK	William L. Cox	William L. Cox	1998	183
175 6/8	26 3/8	27 3/8	22	5 3/8	5 2/8	5	5	Davis Co., IA	Kendall M. Palmer	Kendall M. Palmer	1997	185
175 5/8	26 1/8	26 4/8	24 1/8	4 5/8	5 5/8	5	5	Itasca Co., MN	Art R. Swanson	LeRoy R. Swanson	1945	186
175 5/8	26 3/8	25 6/8	18 5/8	5 5/8	5 5/8	6	5	Leoville, SK	Frank J. Tucek, Jr.	Frank J. Tucek, Jr.	1998	186
175 5/8	23 6/8	23 2/8	16 3/8	4 3/8	4 6/8	7	7	Cedar Co., IA	Picked Up	Rory Peterson	1999	186

175 4/8	28 4/8	28 4/8	22 2/8	4 3/8	4 3/8	5	5	Allamakee Co., IA	William Moody	William Moody	1997	189
175 4/8	24 6/8	24 3/8	20 2/8	5 6/8	5 5/8	5	7	Meyers Lake, SK	Picked Up	Chad Nickeson	1997	189
175 4/8	28 3/8	27 4/8	21 2/8	5 1/8	5 3/8	6	5	Hart Co., KY	Randy Ray	Randy Ray	1998	189
175 4/8	26 2/8	25	15 2/8	4 7/8	4 7/8	5	5	Kaposvar Creek, SK	Scott W. Soyka	Scott W. Soyka	1999	189
175 4/8	27 1/8	26 3/8	19 3/8	4 6/8	4 6/8	7	6	Preble Co., OH	Jerry W. Jones	Jerry W. Jones	2000	189
175 3/8	27 7/8	25 7/8	19 5/8	5 3/8	5 3/8	6	6	Satellite Hill, BC	Bill Shunter	Bill Shunter	1990	194
175 3/8	27 7/8	26 4/8	21 2/8	4 6/8	4 5/8	6	9	Fayette Co., IA	Donald Massman	Phyllis Massman	1991	194
175 3/8	27 3/8	26 5/8	17 5/8	5 5/8	5 7/8	8	5	Monona Co., IA	William Jones	B.A. Tucker	1991	194
175 3/8	25 4/8	25	21	4 6/8	4 5/8	6	6	Linn Co., KS	Lloyd L. Wilson III	Lloyd L. Wilson III	1995	194
175 3/8	25 2/8	26 1/8	20 6/8	6	6 2/8	8	8	Shelby Co., IN	Timothy D. Taggart	Timothy D. Taggart	1999	194
175 3/8	26 6/8	26 6/8	20 1/8	5 7/8	5 7/8	6	7	Chickasaw Co., IA	Dennis P. Troyna	Dennis P. Troyna	1999	194
175 2/8	28 3/8	27 4/8	21 2/8	4 3/8	4 6/8	6	6	Henderson Co., KY	Donald K. White	Donald K. White	1987	200
175 2/8	27 4/8	26 7/8	21 7/8	5 4/8	5 3/8	6	5	Richland Co., IL	Cory A. Ristvedt	Cory A. Ristvedt	1997	200
175 2/8	25 3/8	25 4/8	20 4/8	4 6/8	4 7/8	5	6	Johnson Co., IA	George J. Hebl	George J. Hebl	1999	200
175 2/8	25 4/8	25 4/8	22 6/8	4 6/8	4 6/8	6	7	Piatt Co., IL	Jerry Rudisill	Jerry Rudisill	1999	200
175 1/8	30 1/8	30 4/8	22 5/8	5 1/8	4 7/8	6	6	Hardin Co., OH	Tracey H. Seiler	Tracey H. Seiler	1999	205
175 1/8	22 7/8	23 6/8	19 7/8	4 7/8	4 7/8	7	6	Dimmit Co., TX	Ray Perry	Ray Perry	1976	205
175 1/8	29	27 7/8	19 1/8	5	5	5	5	Hardin Co., OH	Donald O. Braun	Donald O. Braun	1997	205
175 1/8	26 2/8	28 4/8	23 6/8	5 1/8	5 1/8	6	6	Huron Co., OH	Keith B. Keysor	Keith B. Keysor	1999	205
175	25 7/8	27 1/8	19 5/8	4 2/8	4 1/8	6	7	Spokane Co., WA	Michael G. McBride	Michael G. McBride	1999	209
175	28 2/8	28 7/8	20 2/8	5 6/8	5 6/8	7	6	Peace River, BC	Shane Pallister	Unknown	PR 1980	209
175	27 7/8	27 4/8	19 3/8	4 6/8	4 7/8	6	6	Gregory Co., SD	Ken Dooley	Ken Dooley	1996	209
175	26 2/8	26	23 2/8	5	5	6	5	Crittenden Co., KY	Steve L. Clark	Steve L. Clark	1997	209
175	27 3/8	27 1/8	22 4/8	4 7/8	5 2/8	6	6	Lac La Biche, AB	Ronald N. Carpenter	Ronald N. Carpenter	1998	209
175	26 5/8	27 3/8	18 3/8	5 1/8	5	6	6	Butler Co., KY	Stevie Henderson	Stevie Henderson	1998	209
175	27	26 4/8	21 4/8	5 3/8	5 1/8	6	5	Echo Lake, SK	Kelvin E. Karpinski	Kelvin E. Karpinski	1998	209
175	26 6/8	26 1/8	19	5 1/8	5 1/8	8	6	Union Co., IA	Luke A. Bradley	Luke A. Bradley	1999	209
175	28 7/8	28 3/8	21 6/8	5 2/8	5 2/8	5	5	Maverick Co., TX	John A. Cardwell	John A. Cardwell	1999	209
175	27 2/8	26 5/8	22 4/8	4 6/8	4 5/8	7	6	Washington Co., NE	Allan K. Wical	Allan K. Wical	1999	209
174 6/8	28 2/8	28	18 6/8	6	5 6/8	6	5	Adams Co., MS	Jeremy E. Boelte	Jeremy E. Boelte	1997	218
174 6/8	27 6/8	27 6/8	18 6/8	4 5/8	4 6/8	6	5	Union Co., IL	Dirk A. Hernandez	Dirk A. Hernandez	1997	218
174 6/8	25 3/8	25 7/8	21 2/8	4 5/8	4 5/8	7	6	Franchere, AB	Franklin B. Janz	Franklin B. Janz	1997	218
174 6/8	27	27	20 2/8	4 1/8	4 2/8	5	5	Ray Co., MO	Douglas Kirk	Douglas Kirk	1997	218
174 6/8	26 3/8	26 6/8	19	5 2/8	5 3/8	6	6	Desha Co., AR	James F. Finch	James F. Finch	1999	218
174 5/8	25 1/8	24 6/8	18 3/8	4 7/8	4 5/8	5	7	Leavenworth Co., KS	Mark R. Wegner	Mark R. Wegner	1999	218
174 5/8	23	23 2/8	17 7/8	4 7/8	5	8	8	Lincoln Co., MO	William Ziegelmeyer	Ronald Ziegelmeyer, Sr.	1968	224
174 5/8	25 6/8	25 3/8	18 1/8	5	4 7/8	5	6	Lyon Co., KS	Joshua W. Koch	Joshua W. Koch	1997	224
174 5/8	25 6/8	26 2/8	20 7/8	4 6/8	4 5/8	5	5	Jumping Deer Creek, SK	Doug Blaha	Doug Blaha	1998	224
174 4/8	26 2/8	27 2/8	16 1/8	5	5	6	6	Stafford Co., KS	Darin J. Brummer	Darin J. Brummer	1995	227
174 4/8	27 3/8	28 3/8	23 2/8	5 1/8	5 2/8	8	7	Massac Co., IL	Josh A. Bowman	Josh A. Bowman	1997	227
174 4/8	29 2/8	29	28 3/8	5 6/8	5 2/8	7	8	Unknown	Unknown	Aly M. Bruner	PR 1997	227
174 4/8	30 1/8	28 6/8	22 5/8	5 3/8	5 3/8	8	6	Randolph Co., IL	William S. Simmons	William S. Simmons	1998	227
174 4/8	27 3/8	27 7/8	22 4/8	5	5	7	5	Jackson Co., IA	Ted B. Howell	Ted B. Howell	1999	227

WHITETAIL DEER - TYPICAL ANTLERS

Odocoileus virginianus virginianus and certain related subspecies

Score	Length of Main Beam R.	L.	Inside Spread	Circumference at Smallest Place Between Burr and First Point R.	L.	Number of Points R.	L.	Locality	Hunter	Owner	Date Killed	Rank
174 3/8	27 1/8	27 2/8	15 5/8	4 4/8	4 3/8	7	7	Texas	Unknown	Buckhorn Mus. & Saloon, Ltd.	PR 1956	232
174 3/8	27 6/8	27 3/8	22 3/8	5 1/8	5 1/8	5	5	Osage Co., KS	Evans Woehlecke	Evans Woehlecke	1997	232
174 3/8	24 4/8	24	22 7/8	4 6/8	4 5/8	6	7	Cynthia, AB	Camillo J. Baratto	Camillo J. Baratto	1998	232
174 3/8	25 2/8	25 3/8	16 1/8	4 1/8	4 2/8	6	6	Outagamie Co., WI	Alan B. Conger	Alan B. Conger	1998	232
174 3/8	26 7/8	26 7/8	18 5/8	4 7/8	5	6	7	Sullivan Co., NY	Domenick A. DeMaria	Domenick A. DeMaria	1998	232
174 3/8	26 5/8	26 5/8	21 7/8	4 2/8	4	5	5	Johnson Co., IA	Picked Up	Steve Scharf	1998	232
174 3/8	26	26	22	5 5/8	5 7/8	7	5	Allamakee Co., IA	Clinton C. Mohn	Clinton C. Mohn	1999	232
174 2/8	27 2/8	28 1/8	20 2/8	5 4/8	5 3/8	5	5	Langlade Co., WI	Lyman Aderman	David C. Aderman	PR 1963	239
174 2/8	25 3/8	25 3/8	21	4 6/8	4 6/8	5	5	Mt. Pleasant, NS	Garth Hirtle	Garth Hirtle	1993	239
174 2/8	27 3/8	27 2/8	19 4/8	5	4 6/8	5	5	Sussex Co., DE	J.R. Cropper	J.R. Cropper	1997	239
174 2/8	28 1/8	27 5/8	23 1/8	5	5 1/8	8	5	Jefferson Co., IA	James W. Ferguson	James W. Ferguson	1997	239
174 2/8	26 6/8	26 1/8	23 5/8	4 5/8	4 4/8	7	8	Pulaski Co., KY	Ishmael R. Helton	Ishmael R. Helton	1998	239
174 2/8	25 5/8	26	21 6/8	5 3/8	5 2/8	5	5	Lake of the Prairies, MB	Stephen Davies	Stephen Davies	1999	239
174 2/8	23 3/8	23 5/8	18	5 6/8	5 4/8	7	7	Montgomery Co., MO	S. Douglas Lensing	S. Douglas Lensing	1999	239
174 2/8	24 1/8	24	16 4/8	4 6/8	4 6/8	6	6	Moosomin, SK	Jim Toth	Jim Toth	1999	239
174 1/8	25	25 2/8	23 3/8	5 1/8	5	6	5	Renville Co., MN	Galen Kodet	Galen Kodet	1970	247
174 1/8	25 4/8	24 5/8	21 5/8	5 1/8	5 1/8	6	5	Dubuque Co., IA	James E. Beecher	James E. Beecher	1998	247
174 1/8	26 4/8	25 7/8	18 1/8	5 2/8	5 3/8	7	7	Allamakee Co., IA	Hugh E. Conway	Hugh E. Conway	1998	247
174 1/8	25 5/8	25	18 4/8	4 7/8	4 7/8	7	5	Johnson Co., NE	Fred Leuenberger	Fred Leuenberger	1998	247
174 1/8	25 7/8	25 2/8	16 4/8	4 7/8	5	6	8	Clayton Co., IA	Milo Rolfe	Milo Rolfe	1998	247
174 1/8	27 1/8	27 4/8	20 1/8	4 5/8	4 4/8	5	5	Coahuila, MX	Wayne Glover	Wayne Glover	1999	247
174 1/8	24 1/8	23 4/8	19 1/8	5	5 2/8	7	5	Dallas Co., MO	Otis Villines	Otis Villines	1999	247
174	29 2/8	28	21 2/8	5 2/8	5	5	5	Fayette Co., IA	Charles Schott	Charles Schott	1982	254
174	28	25 6/8	18 2/8	5 7/8	5 4/8	8	5	Eaton Co., MI	Rodney S. Brown	Connie Brown	1984	254
174	26 4/8	26	18	4 6/8	4 6/8	5	5	Marion Co., KS	Gerald W. Lock	Gerald W. Lock	1997	254
174	27 6/8	26 1/8	23	5 3/8	5 3/8	4	5	Allen Co., IN	James L. Harden	James L. Harden	1998	254
174	27 7/8	28	20 2/8	5 3/8	5 2/8	6	6	Lake Co., IN	Picked Up	Howard Munson	1998	254
174	25 6/8	26 1/8	23 5/8	4 3/8	4 4/8	6	6	Battle River, AB	Jeff White	Jeff White	1998	254
174	24 1/8	24 1/8	16	4 4/8	4 3/8	6	7	Pierce Lake, SK	James W. Beresford	James W. Beresford	1999	254
174	23 6/8	21 7/8	17 5/8	4	3 7/8	8	8	Allamakee Co., IA	Richard Gaunitz	Richard Gaunitz	1990	254
173 7/8	23 6/8	24 4/8	21 3/8	5 3/8	5 2/8	5	5	Johnson Co., IA	Unknown	Ruth Waters	1990	261
173 7/8	28	30 1/8	24 3/8	4 5/8	4 5/8	6	6	Appanoose Co., IA	Tim G. Anderson	Tim G. Anderson	1997	261
173 7/8	29 2/8	26 1/8	21 7/8	4 2/8	4 6/8	6	8	Webster Co., KY	Glenn R. Cummings	Glenn R. Cummings	1997	261

BOONE AND CROCKETT CLUB'S

Score	Main Beam R	Main Beam L	Inside Spread	Circ. R	Circ. L	Points R	Points L	Locality	By Whom Killed	Owner	Date Killed	Rank
173 7/8	27 6/8	26 6/8	18 4/8	5 6/8	5 6/8	4	6	Wilbarger Co., TX	John T. Wright	John T. Wright	1998	261
173 7/8	24 1/8	23 2/8	22 5/8	5 3/8	5 3/8	5	5	Unknown	Unknown	Terry L. Amos	PR 1999	261
173 7/8	28 3/8	28 6/8	24 5/8	4 3/8	4	7	7	Grant Parish, LA	Dwayne H. Robertson	Dwayne H. Robertson	1999	261
173 7/8	29 5/8	28 6/8	22 3/8	4 5/8	4 7/8	5	7	Union Co., IA	David Wetsch	David Wetsch	1999	261
173 6/8	24 7/8	24 6/8	18 2/8	4 6/8	4 7/8	6	6	Jasper Co., IA	Danny E. Keuning	Danny E. Keuning	1992	269
173 6/8	28 3/8	27 7/8	20 7/8	5 1/8	5 1/8	6	6	Louisa Co., IA	Todd J. Parsons	Todd J. Parsons	1994	269
173 6/8	28 4/8	28	25	5 2/8	5 1/8	6	6	Green Lake Co., WI	Steven J. Coda	Steven J. Coda	1997	269
173 6/8	27 2/8	28	19 2/8	4 4/8	4 4/8	5	5	Reno Co., KS	James E. Dye	James E. Dye	1997	269
173 6/8	24 4/8	25	17 4/8	4 3/8	4 1/8	6	6	Allen Co., KS	Dewey L. Lewis	Dewey L. Lewis	1997	269
173 6/8	27 1/8	27	24 4/8	5	5	6	5	McHenry Co., IL	Richard E. Pope	Richard E. Pope	1997	269
173 6/8	27 4/8	26 4/8	21 2/8	5 1/8	5 1/8	5	6	Brown Co., IL	Michael P. Postema	Michael P. Postema	1997	269
173 6/8	26 5/8	26 5/8	20 7/8	5	5	7	7	Allamakee Co., IA	Joseph Lieb	Joseph Lieb	1998	269
173 6/8	26 1/8	26 5/8	21 3/8	5 6/8	5 6/8	6	7	Cherokee Co., IA	Robert L. Lundquist	Robert L. Lundquist	1998	269
173 6/8	24	24 3/8	21	5 2/8	5 3/8	7	5	Good Spirit Lake, SK	Blair Sawka	Blair Sawka	1998	269
173 5/8	26 2/8	26 2/8	17 4/8	5	4 6/8	5	5	Morgan Co., OH	Daniel Clemens	Daniel Clemens	1997	279
173 5/8	26 1/8	26	20 1/8	4 5/8	4 5/8	5	5	La Salle Co., TX	Jeff S. Golbow	Jeff S. Golbow	1997	279
173 5/8	26 4/8	26	20	4 6/8	4 6/8	8	5	Kankakee Co., IL	Tim Lynch	Tim Lynch	1999	279
173 4/8	25 1/8	25 1/8	18 6/8	4 5/8	4 5/8	6	6	Porcupine Plain, SK	Picked Up	Terry L. Amos	PR 1997	282
173 4/8	25 7/8	25 6/8	19 2/8	4 1/8	4 1/8	5	5	La Salle Co., TX	James K. Haney	James K. Haney	1997	282
173 4/8	26	26 1/8	18 4/8	4 3/8	4 3/8	5	5	Rusk Co., WI	Jody Lebal	Jody Lebal	1998	282
173 4/8	24 6/8	25	17 1/8	6	6	6	5	Sweet Grass, SK	Steven Riley	Steven Riley	1998	282
173 4/8	27 6/8	27 6/8	15 2/8	4 6/8	4 5/8	7	6	Logan Co., KY	Jesse Wolf	Jesse Wolf	1998	282
173 4/8	27 4/8	29 3/8	22	4 5/8	4 5/8	5	5	Appanoose Co., IA	Randy Andreini	Randy Andreini	1999	282
173 4/8	25 2/8	25 5/8	17 7/8	5	5	7	7	St. Louis Co., MN	Gerald R. Fausone	Gerald R. Fausone	1999	282
173 4/8	30	28 4/8	23 2/8	4 7/8	4 7/8	6	5	Monroe Co., IA	Glen A. McElroy	Glen A. McElroy	1999	282
173 4/8	28 1/8	27 4/8	21	4 2/8	4 2/8	5	5	Chisago Co., MN	Robert C. Palmer	Robert C. Palmer	1999	282
173 3/8	26 6/8	26 5/8	17 5/8	5 4/8	5 4/8	5	5	Grant Parish, LA	Michael G. Hicks	Michael G. Hicks	1997	291
173 3/8	26 2/8	26 2/8	23	5 1/8	5 1/8	8	8	Linn Co., KS	Vernon L. Morrell, Jr.	Vernon L. Morrell, Jr.	1997	291
173 3/8	26 5/8	26 4/8	20 1/8	5 6/8	5 6/8	5	7	Prowers Co., CO	Les F. Ohlhauser	Les F. Ohlhauser	1997	291
173 3/8	26 1/8	26 3/8	21 5/8	5 2/8	5	5	5	Jones Co., IA	Todd J. Rollinger	Todd J. Rollinger	1997	291
173 3/8	25 7/8	27 2/8	20 3/8	4 7/8	5	6	7	Noble Co., OH	David W. Heeter	David W. Heeter	1998	291
173 2/8	27 4/8	26 4/8	19 7/8	5 1/8	5	6	6	Gage Co., NE	Harold G. McPheron	Harold G. McPheron	1998	291
173 2/8	24 4/8	24 4/8	21 2/8	5 4/8	5 4/8	6	8	Unknown	Unknown	Neal T. Rietveld	PR 1960	297
173 2/8	25	24 2/8	19	5 2/8	5	5	5	Butler Co., MO	Marcus O. Milligan	Marcus O. Milligan	1997	297
173 2/8	26 5/8	26 5/8	24 6/8	4 1/8	4	5	5	Pickaway Co., OH	Timothy S. Ritchie	Timothy S. Ritchie	1997	297
173 2/8	22 4/8	22 4/8	15	5 1/8	5 1/8	6	6	Pope Co., IL	James W. Sanderson	James W. Sanderson	1997	297
173 2/8	25 2/8	24 3/8	23 2/8	5 2/8	5	5	5	Marion Co., IA	Joseph C. Laird	Joseph C. Laird	1998	297
173 2/8	24 2/8	24 1/8	17 2/8	4 4/8	4 4/8	6	6	Chautauqua Co., NY	Brian Whalen	Brian Whalen	1998	297
173 2/8	26 2/8	26 6/8	22	5	5	7	7	Preble Co., OH	Gary H. Vest	Gary H. Vest	1999	297
173 1/8	30	30 5/8	23	5 2/8	5 2/8	7	7	Brown Co., OH	Michael P. Nunnelley	Michael P. Nunnelley	1995	304
173 1/8	25 5/8	24 2/8	23 3/8	4 3/8	4 3/8	5	5	Buffalo Co., WI	Thomas J. Johnson	Thomas J. Johnson	1997	304
173 1/8	23 5/8	24 1/8	13 7/8	4 6/8	4 4/8	6	6	Torch River, SK	Debbie Karle	Debbie Karle	1999	304
173 1/8	25	25 3/8	19 1/8	4 7/8	5	5	5	Clermont Co., OH	Alton L. Cornett	Alton L. Cornett	2000	304

WHITETAIL DEER - TYPICAL ANTLERS

Odocoileus virginianus virginianus and certain related subspecies

Score	Length of Main Beam R.	L.	Inside Spread	Circumference at Smallest Place Between Burr and First Point R.	L.	Number of Points R.	L.	Locality	Hunter	Owner	Date Killed	Rank
173	25 7/8	25 3/8	16 7/8	5	5 4/8	6	8	Adair Co., OK	Louis C. Mattler	Louis C. Mattler	1995	308
173	26 6/8	26 5/8	17 6/8	4 4/8	4 4/8	8	6	Macoupin Co., IL	Dickie A. Spurgeon	Dickie A. Spurgeon	1995	308
173	27 1/8	26 5/8	23 4/8	5	5 1/8	6	8	Christian Co., KY	Mark C. Morris	Mark C. Morris	1997	308
173	25 6/8	25 2/8	19 6/8	4 7/8	4 7/8	6	6	Allamakee Co., IA	Thomas E. Peters	Thomas E. Peters	1997	308
173	24 3/8	24 5/8	18	4 2/8	4 2/8	6	6	St. Marie Lake, QC	Philippe Gratton	Philippe Gratton	1998	308
173	28 6/8	29 3/8	16 5/8	5 7/8	5 6/8	7	6	Itaska Co., MN	Robert W. Bourman	Robert W. Bourman	1999	308
173	27 7/8	28 2/8	19 6/8	4 6/8	4 6/8	7	7	Preble Co., OH	Jeffery T. Haeseker	Jeffery T. Haeseker	1999	308
172 7/8	25	26	18 3/8	4 5/8	4 5/8	6	5	Estevan, SK	Brent Barreth	Brent Barreth	1998	315
172 7/8	25 2/8	24 2/8	19 1/8	4 5/8	4 6/8	5	5	Jackson Co., WI	Donald R. Anderson	Donald R. Anderson	1999	315
172 7/8	28 3/8	27 6/8	29	5	5 2/8	6	5	Donley Co., TX	Barrett W. Thorne	Barrett W. Thorne	1999	315
172 7/8	29 1/8	29 1/8	19 7/8	5 4/8	6	5	7	Buffalo Co., WI	Robert H. Becker	Robert H. Becker	2000	315
172 6/8	25 6/8	24 7/8	23 4/8	4 2/8	4 2/8	5	5	Texas	Unknown	Thomas P. Kosub	PR 1945	319
172 6/8	24 4/8	21	18 6/8	5	5	5	5	Biggar, SK	Roy Polsfut	Roy Polsfut	1989	319
172 6/8	28	28 1/8	24 4/8	4 1/8	4 2/8	5	5	Russell Co., KS	Mark A. Heinz	Mark A. Heinz	1997	319
172 6/8	27 2/8	28 2/8	23 4/8	4 6/8	4 5/8	5	5	Franklin Co., ME	Michael W. Auger	Michael W. Auger	1998	319
172 6/8	25	25 6/8	19 1/8	6 3/8	6 3/8	5	8	McLean Co., IL	Picked Up	Matt Cheever	1998	319
172 6/8	27 5/8	28 3/8	22 2/8	5 6/8	5 6/8	7	6	Morrison Co., MN	Leroy R. Zimmerman	Leroy R. Zimmerman	1998	319
172 6/8	24 7/8	25 7/8	18 4/8	5 4/8	5 2/8	7	7	Northampton Co., NC	L. Thomas Baird	L. Thomas Baird	1999	319
172 6/8	25 4/8	25 2/8	18 1/8	5 7/8	5 5/8	7	9	Lost Bay, ON	Peter Marcinuk	Peter Marcinuk	1999	319
172 5/8	30 4/8	28 5/8	18 7/8	4 7/8	5	5	4	Jones Co., IA	Johnny S. Cook	Johnny S. Cook	1997	327
172 5/8	26	26 1/8	22 3/8	5	5 1/8	6	6	Smith Co., KS	Jonathan D. Weavers	Jonathan D. Weavers	1998	327
172 5/8	24 3/8	22 5/8	18 3/8	5 1/8	4 7/8	7	7	Treasure Co., MT	Ted K. Welchlin	Ted K. Welchlin	1998	327
172 5/8	24 5/8	25 1/8	25 1/8	4 5/8	4 5/8	5	5	Adams Co., WI	Picked Up	Vernon J. Williams, Jr.	1998	327
172 5/8	25 5/8	27	21 7/8	4 6/8	4 5/8	6	5	Kipling, SK	Tim Davies	Tim Davies	1999	327
172 4/8	26 5/8	25 6/8	20 6/8	4 4/8	4 6/8	9	8	Mason Co., TX	Earl E. Allen	Allen Family	PR 1926	332
172 4/8	25 4/8	25 4/8	18 2/8	5 6/8	5 4/8	5	5	McLennan, AB	Gordon Ristow	Gordon Ristow	1995	332
172 4/8	27 1/8	27 2/8	24	4 6/8	4 6/8	5	5	Muscatine Co., IA	John D. Russell	John D. Russell	1997	332
172 4/8	22 4/8	23 2/8	16 6/8	5 1/8	5 1/8	7	7	Athabasca, AB	Christopher Sawchyn	Christopher Sawchyn	1997	332
172 4/8	26 6/8	25 7/8	18 4/8	4 7/8	5	6	6	Evansburg, AB	Dana Baksa	Dana Baksa	1998	332
172 4/8	26 2/8	25	17 6/8	5 2/8	5 4/8	6	6	St. Clair Co., MI	Djura Drazic	Djura Drazic	1998	332
172 4/8	25 6/8	25 1/8	20	5	4 7/8	6	5	Fir River, SK	Andrew Dyess	Andrew Dyess	1998	332
172 4/8	28	26 3/8	19 3/8	4 7/8	4 7/8	6	9	Piscataquis Co., ME	James A. Nicols, Jr.	James A. Nicols, Jr.	1998	332
172 4/8	28 4/8	28 2/8	19 5/8	4 2/8	4 1/8	5	6	Fayette Co., IA	Rick L. Taylor	Rick L. Taylor	1998	332
172 4/8	28	27 7/8	20	5 4/8	5 5/8	9	8	Putnam Co., IN	M.R. Abner & C. Yates	M.R. Abner & C. Yates	1999	332

172 4/8	24 5/8	25 4/8	21 1/8	5	5	7	5	Dubuque Co., IA	Steven W. Berkley	Steven W. Berkley	1999	332
172 4/8	27 2/8	26	19	4 7/8	4 7/8	6	7	Adair Co., MO	Eldon L. Grissom, Sr.	Eldon L. Grissom, Sr.	1999	332
172 4/8	27 5/8	28 6/8	21 5/8	4 3/8	4 2/8	6	6	Haywood Co., TN	Mark S. Powell	Mark S. Powell	1999	332
172 3/8	28 1/8	28 4/8	22 5/8	4 3/8	4 3/8	5	6	Fulton Co., GA	Michael Gregory	Lee E. Johnson	1986	345
172 3/8	25	25 2/8	22 5/8	5	4 7/8	6	6	Des Moines Co., IA	Colin J. Gerst	Colin J. Gerst	1997	345
172 3/8	25 6/8	27 4/8	19 3/8	5 6/8	5 6/8	6	7	Monroe Co., NY	Picked Up	Joseph Masci	1997	345
172 3/8	28	27 5/8	22 2/8	5	4 7/8	7	5	Iowa Co., WI	Bruce E. Schuelke	Bruce E. Schuelke	1997	345
172 3/8	26 7/8	25 7/8	17 7/8	4 7/8	4 6/8	5	5	Hart Co., KY	Terry Avery	Terry Avery	1999	345
172 2/8	27 5/8	27 6/8	19 4/8	4	4 2/8	5	5	Scott Co., IA	Patrick D. Willhoite	Patrick D. Willhoite	1999	350
172 2/8	27 6/8	26 5/8	20 2/8	4 4/8	4 4/8	5	5	Ashland Co., WI	Arnold D. Miller	Arnold D. Miller	1994	350
172 2/8	27	27 2/8	19 6/8	4 5/8	4 6/8	6	6	Randolph Co., MO	Edward L. Sneed	Edward L. Sneed	1997	350
172 2/8	27 2/8	27 4/8	22 6/8	4 7/8	4 6/8	5	5	Wabasha Co., MN	John K. Gusa	John K. Gusa	1998	350
172 2/8	28 4/8	28 7/8	18 6/8	4 5/8	4 7/8	7	6	Talbot Co., MD	Jack W. Jones	Jack W. Jones	1998	350
172 2/8	26 1/8	25	20	5	5	6	5	Knox Co., OH	David K. Palmer	David K. Palmer	1998	350
172 2/8	28 3/8	28 2/8	19 6/8	4 4/8	4 4/8	4	4	Frio Co., TX	Thomas W. Burell	Thomas W. Burell	1999	350
172 2/8	27 4/8	28	20 2/8	4 7/8	5 1/8	6	6	Peoria Co., IL	Heye H. Peters, Jr.	Heye H. Peters, Jr.	1999	350
172 2/8	26 5/8	26 1/8	19 6/8	5 1/8	4 7/8	5	5	Vernon Co., WI	Ronald J. Stilwell	Ronald J. Stilwell	1999	350
172 1/8	26	25 5/8	18	4 3/8	4 6/8	6	6	Baraga Co., MI	Gust Varlen	Bass Pro Shops F. & W. Mus.	1945	359
172 1/8	27 2/8	26 7/8	21	5 2/8	5 2/8	7	7	Jefferson Co., IA	Joe F. Arndt	Joe F. Arndt	1997	359
172 1/8	26 3/8	26 1/8	20 1/8	5	5 3/8	6	6	Keokuk Co., IA	Ric L. Bishop	Ric L. Bishop	1997	359
172 1/8	25 2/8	25 2/8	17 2/8	4 1/8	4 2/8	5	5	Wabasha Co., MN	Michael R. Klagge	Michael R. Klagge	1997	359
172 1/8	25 4/8	25 7/8	24	4 5/8	4 5/8	6	6	Pipestone Creek, SK	Clayton Roberts	Clayton Roberts	1997	359
172 1/8	27 2/8	27	18 4/8	5	5	6	6	Todd Co., MN	Kenneth J. Ostendorf	Kenneth J. Ostendorf	1998	359
172	25 5/8	24 1/8	22 5/8	4 4/8	4 4/8	6	6	Monroe Co., IA	Jeffrey A. Butler	Jeffrey A. Butler	1999	359
172	27 5/8	27 5/8	20	5 2/8	5 1/8	8	7	Kankakee Co., IL	Darrel L. Duby	Darrel L. Duby	1999	359
172	28 4/8	28 4/8	17 5/8	4 5/8	4 6/8	4	4	Crooked Lake, SK	Gil Mountney	Gil Mountney	1999	359
172	26 2/8	25 6/8	22 7/8	5 3/8	5 3/8	5	5	Lake Co., IL	Derrell W. Listhartke	Derrell W. Listhartke	1999	359
172	28	28 2/8	19 5/8	4 7/8	4 7/8	9	10	Otter Tail Co., MN	Paul W. Wagner	Paul W. Wagner	2000	359
172	26 2/8	26 2/8	20	4 5/8	4 4/8	7	5	Fayette Co., IA	Robert Goad	Robert Goad	1987	369
172	26 3/8	26 5/8	20 7/8	5 2/8	5 4/8	6	6	Kenedy Co., TX	Lee M. Bass	Lee M. Bass	1996	369
172	26 2/8	26 2/8	19 2/8	4 6/8	4 6/8	5	5	Delaware Co., IA	Charles E. Fessler	Charles E. Fessler	1997	369
172	24 4/8	26	18 4/8	5	4 7/8	5	5	Avoyelles Parish, LA	Richard J. Dupuy, Jr.	Richard J. Dupuy, Jr.	1998	369
172	23 3/8	23 3/8	19 4/8	5 6/8	5 5/8	7	5	Little Red River, SK	Peter LoPiccolo	Peter LoPiccolo	1998	369
172	25 4/8	25 4/8	20 4/8	5 4/8	5 4/8	9	7	Jefferson Co., IA	Brandon Slaubaugh	Brandon Slaubaugh	1998	369
172	27 5/8	29 6/8	21 2/8	4 7/8	5 1/8	6	6	Pasquia Hills, SK	Easton C. Kapeller	Easton C. Kapeller	1999	369
171 7/8	26 4/8	25 6/8	17 4/8	6	6	6	6	Menominee Co., MI	Karl Schwartz	Bass Pro Shops F. & W. Mus.	1974	377
171 7/8	24 7/8	25 6/8	21 7/8	5 1/8	5 1/8	5	5	Todd Co., MN	Picked Up	Del Halverson	1991	377
171 7/8	24 4/8	24 4/8	17 5/8	4 4/8	4 4/8	6	6	Maverick Co., TX	William H. Whitley	William H. Whitley	1997	377
171 7/8	25 5/8	25 2/8	18 3/8	5	5	5	5	Romance, SK	Cameron Kirzinger	Cameron Kirzinger	1999	377
171 7/8	27 4/8	26 7/8	19 6/8	5 4/8	5 5/8	6	5	Essex Co., MA	Michael G. Prescott	Michael G. Prescott	1999	377
171 6/8	26 7/8	25 5/8	19 5/8	5 3/8	5 4/8	5	5	Moniteau Co., MO	Randy Wilson	Randy Wilson	1999	377
171 6/8	23 5/8	24 4/8	16 7/8	4 5/8	4 5/8	7	7	Chinook, AB	Ian Proudfoot	Ian Proudfoot	1996	383
171 6/8	27 3/8	28	21 7/8	5 7/8	6 2/8	5	4	Hamilton Co., OH	Donald R. Johnson	Donald R. Johnson	1997	383

WHITETAIL DEER - TYPICAL ANTLERS

Odocoileus virginianus virginianus and certain related subspecies

Score	Length of Main Beam R.	L.	Inside Spread	Circumference at Smallest Place Between Burr and First Point R.	L.	Number of Points R.	L.	Locality	Hunter	Owner	Date Killed	Rank
171 6/8	28 6/8	28 3/8	20 4/8	4 3/8	4 3/8	8	5	S. Saskatchewan River, SK	Garry Kennon	Garry Kennon	1997	383
171 6/8	23 6/8	24	20	5 4/8	5 4/8	5	5	Big Horn Co., WY	Thomas D. Dixon	Thomas D. Dixon	1998	383
171 6/8	26 2/8	24 4/8	23	4 6/8	4 6/8	5	7	Tamarack Lake, MB	John L. Duncan II	John L. Duncan II	1998	383
171 6/8	25 3/8	25 2/8	17 6/8	5 2/8	5 2/8	7	7	Winona Co., MN	James J. Heberlein	James J. Heberlein	1998	383
171 6/8	26	25	16 3/8	5 2/8	5 3/8	6	8	Dakota Co., MN	Vincent A. LaCroix	Vincent A. LaCroix	1998	383
171 6/8	25 7/8	26 2/8	19 4/8	5 6/8	5 6/8	5	5	Hart Co., KY	Paul A. Miller	Paul A. Miller	1998	383
171 6/8	25 6/8	25 1/8	16 2/8	4 7/8	4 6/8	5	5	Dunn Co., WI	David J. Tuschl, Sr.	David J. Tuschl, Sr.	1998	383
171 6/8	25 3/8	25 7/8	18 5/8	5 1/8	5 2/8	5	6	Cookson, SK	Bry Loyd	Bry Loyd	1999	383
171 5/8	26 5/8	24 5/8	18 4/8	5	5 2/8	7	6	Clayton Co., IA	Chris M. Borcherding	Chris M. Borcherding	1997	393
171 5/8	27 6/8	27 6/8	20 4/8	6 1/8	6 2/8	6	6	Pottawatomie Co., KS	Kevin P. Devader	Kevin P. Devader	1997	393
171 5/8	26	26 5/8	19 5/8	4 6/8	4 6/8	5	5	Grundy Co., IL	Joseph A. Gray	Joseph A. Gray	1997	393
171 5/8	23 3/8	23 6/8	15 4/8	5 2/8	5 4/8	6	6	Strasbourg, SK	Donald A. Williamson	Donald A. Williamson	1998	393
171 5/8	26 5/8	26 6/8	17 4/8	5 2/8	5 2/8	6	5	Swan Lake, MB	John Gidney	John Gidney	1999	393
171 5/8	28 7/8	28	20 1/8	5 2/8	5 4/8	5	5	Atchison Co., MO	Frank Hackworth	Frank Hackworth	1999	393
171 5/8	25 5/8	27 1/8	18 5/8	5	5	5	5	Marion Co., KY	Francis M. Hutchins	Francis M. Hutchins	1999	393
171 5/8	28 3/8	27 2/8	19 5/8	5 4/8	5 4/8	7	6	Paradise Valley, AB	Dale Luedtke	Dale Luedtke	1999	393
171 4/8	24 7/8	25 2/8	22 3/8	4 7/8	5	5	6	Cass Co., NE	Alvin H. Baller	Alvin H. Baller	1971	401
171 4/8	28 1/8	28 5/8	20 6/8	4 4/8	4 3/8	5	5	Dimmit Co., TX	Kenneth P. Crawford	Kenneth P. Crawford	1997	401
171 4/8	24 5/8	27 1/8	16 4/8	4 6/8	4 6/8	6	6	Pierceland, SK	Stacer Helton	Stacer Helton	1997	401
171 4/8	25 3/8	26	19 1/8	5 5/8	5 6/8	6	6	Talbot Co., MD	William D. Collison	William D. Collison	1998	401
171 4/8	25 5/8	26 1/8	21 4/8	4 7/8	5	5	5	Scott Co., IA	William H. Fahrenkrog	William H. Fahrenkrog	1998	401
171 4/8	26	25 1/8	21	5 2/8	5 1/8	5	5	Edson, AB	Ted E. Mortimer	Ted E. Mortimer	1998	401
171 4/8	26 2/8	27 5/8	22 2/8	4 6/8	4 3/8	5	5	Raleigh Co., WV	Omar O. Burns	Omar O. Burns	1999	401
171 4/8	24 6/8	24 5/8	17 6/8	6 3/8	6 3/8	9	7	Tallahatchie Co., MS	Ricky Lee	Ricky Lee	1999	401
171 3/8	26 6/8	26 7/8	22 5/8	4 5/8	4 5/8	5	7	Dorchester Co., MD	Mark S. Bronder	Mark S. Bronder	1995	409
171 3/8	24 3/8	24 2/8	17 5/8	5 1/8	5 1/8	6	7	Boundary Co., ID	Donald B. Vickaryous	Donald B. Vickaryous	1995	409
171 3/8	27 4/8	25 5/8	19 6/8	5 5/8	5 3/8	6	9	Glaslyn, SK	Brian Huscroft	Brian Huscroft	1996	409
171 3/8	26 3/8	25 5/8	18 3/8	4 4/8	4 4/8	5	5	Buffalo Co., WI	Dave K. Kitzman	Dave K. Kitzman	1996	409
171 3/8	28 5/8	27 2/8	21 3/8	5 1/8	5 3/8	4	4	Oregon Co., MO	Dale Conner	Scott D. Lindsey	1996	409
171 3/8	26 6/8	27 3/8	19 7/8	5	5	9	5	Trempealeau Co., WI	Heidi A. Daffinson	Heidi A. Daffinson	1997	409
171 3/8	26	26 3/8	20 1/8	4 4/8	4 6/8	5	5	Monroe Co., IA	Michael L. DeMoss	Michael L. DeMoss	1997	409
171 3/8	27 2/8	27	17 7/8	4 7/8	4 7/8	5	5	Charles Co., MD	Patrick E. Langley	Patrick E. Langley	1997	409
171 3/8	24 6/8	26 2/8	25 5/8	5 4/8	5 2/8	5	5	Wayne Co., OH	Ivan R. Schlabach	Ivan R. Schlabach	1997	409
171 3/8	27 7/8	26 2/8	18 2/8	4	4 1/8	5	6	Nemaha Co., KS	Paul L. Steinlage	Paul L. Steinlage	1997	409

Score	Main Beam R	Main Beam L	Spread	Spread	Circ. R	Circ. L	Pts. R	Pts. L	Locality	Hunter	Owner	Date	Rank
171 3/8	24 4/8	24 2/8	17 4/8	21 4/8	5	5 1/8	7	8	Hamilton Twp., ON	Peter Francis	Peter Francis	1998	409
171 3/8	27	26 7/8	21 5/8	21 5/8	6	5 7/8	5	6	Breathitt Co., KY	Kenneth J. Minks	Kenneth J. Minks	1998	409
171 3/8	27 2/8	28 5/8	22 7/8	22 5/8	4 7/8	4 7/8	6	6	Little Manitou Lake, SK	Bruce Soderberg	Bruce Soderberg	1998	409
171 3/8	27 4/8	27 5/8	17 7/8	21 1/8	5 1/8	5 1/8	5	5	Monroe Co., MO	Shelton Wheelan	Shelton Wheelan	1999	409
171 2/8	26 6/8	27	21 1/8	21 3/8	6	5 4/8	6	6	Alger Co., MI	John Peterson	Bass Pro Shops F. & W. Mus.	1948	423
171 2/8	26 3/8	25 5/8	19 5/8	21 1/8	4 5/8	5 7/8	6	5	S. Saskatchewan River, SK	Cheri Boeschen	Cheri Boeschen	1997	423
171 2/8	27 6/8	26 4/8	20 4/8	22 5/8	5 1/8	4 6/8	5	5	Logan Co., IL	Brian M. Laubenstein	Brian M. Laubenstein	1997	423
171 2/8	25 6/8	24 5/8	18 2/8	19 4/8	5 2/8	4 7/8	5	5	Benton Co., IA	Timothy McLaud	Timothy McLaud	1997	423
171 2/8	23 3/8	24 6/8	18 6/8	21 2/8	5	5	5	5	Cowan, MB	Scott P. Nigbor	Scott P. Nigbor	1998	423
171 2/8	24 6/8	25 4/8	18	21	4 3/8	4 3/8	5	6	Ashtabula Co., OH	Gene E. Clemens	Gene E. Clemens	1999	423
171 2/8	26 1/8	26 5/8	21	21 5/8	5 5/8	5 7/8	6	6	Green Lake Co., WI	Richard Waters	Richard Waters	1999	423
171 1/8	26 4/8	25 3/8	17 4/8	21	4 2/8	4 2/8	6	6	La Salle Co., TX	Unknown	F. Gus Reinarz	PR 1980	430
171 1/8	25 4/8	26 4/8	17 3/8	20 4/8	4 4/8	4 4/8	5	6	Scotland Co., MO	Joseph Frye	Joseph Frye	1997	430
171 1/8	23 7/8	23 4/8	19 3/8	22 4/8	5 1/8	5 1/8	5	5	Ringgold Co., IA	Darren Martin	Darren Martin	1998	430
171 1/8	25 2/8	24 6/8	18 4/8	21 6/8	5	5 4/8	8	5	Sauk Co., WI	David K. Zimmerman	David K. Zimmerman	1999	430
171 1/8	26 2/8	27 2/8	20 5/8	22 4/8	5 3/8	5 4/8	5	5	Stafford Co., KS	Michael E. Read	Michael E. Read	2000	430
171	24	24	23 3/8	24 1/8	4 3/8	4 3/8	7	6	Pipestone Co., MN	Scott A. Crawford	Scott A. Crawford	1995	435
171	26 5/8	25 5/8	19 4/8	22 5/8	5 4/8	5 4/8	7	7	Lawrence Co., IL	Picked Up	Michael E. Neikiek	1996	435
171	25 5/8	26 1/8	21 2/8	23 5/8	5 3/8	5 2/8	8	7	Knox Co., MO	Herbert J. Wedemeier	Herbert J. Wedemeier	1997	435
171	26 1/8	26	21	23 1/8	5 1/8	5	7	8	Palo Alto Co., IA	Paul R. Demiter	Paul R. Demiter	1998	435
171	28 5/8	28	19	22 1/8	4 5/8	4 6/8	7	7	Becker Co., MN	Jeff D. Holmer	Jeff D. Holmer	1998	435
171	26 4/8	27	20 4/8	23 3/8	4 4/8	4 5/8	6	6	St. Clair Co., MI	James R. Hurd, Jr.	James R. Hurd, Jr.	1998	435
171	25 7/8	26 2/8	22 4/8	22 1/8	4 5/8	4 7/8	7	7	Washington Co., ME	William S. Lawrence	William S. Lawrence	1998	435
171	28 2/8	28 7/8	17 6/8	22 5/8	4	4 1/8	6	6	Clark Co., OH	Louis J. Graham	Louis J. Graham	1999	435
171	24 2/8	23 7/8	16 5/8	21 1/8	4 5/8	4 6/8	6	4	Gooseberry Lake, SK	Terry R. McGillicky	Terry R. McGillicky	1999	435
171	26 2/8	26 6/8	22 4/8	22 7/8	4 3/8	4 1/8	6	7	Callaway Co., MO	Jeff M. Sumpter	Jeff M. Sumpter	1999	435
170 7/8	25 5/8	25 5/8	20 5/8	23 4/8	4 6/8	4 6/8	7	7	Texas	Unknown	Larry D. Bollier	PR 1970	445
170 7/8	26 3/8	26 5/8	23 5/8	24 5/8	4 5/8	4 4/8	7	7	Des Moines Co., IA	Timothy Verhey	Timothy Verhey	1992	445
170 7/8	25 4/8	25 4/8	21 1/8	22 2/8	5	5	5	5	Price Co., WI	David A. Pritzl	David A. Pritzl	1994	445
170 7/8	24 4/8	24 5/8	25 1/8	26 6/8	4 7/8	4 5/8	5	5	Ostenfeld, MB	Karl E. Mistelbacher	Karl E. Mistelbacher	1995	445
170 7/8	28 7/8	27 4/8	21 3/8	22 6/8	5	4 7/8	5	5	Charles Co., MD	Richard L. Albright	Richard L. Albright	1997	445
170 7/8	27 5/8	28 1/8	21 1/8	21 7/8	5 1/8	5 2/8	6	6	Dane Co., WI	Alison J. Baake	Alison J. Baake	1997	445
170 7/8	25 1/8	25 3/8	22 5/8	24 6/8	4 6/8	4 6/8	5	5	Hamilton Co., NE	Clint J. Ochsner	Clint J. Ochsner	1997	445
170 7/8	25 5/8	26	18 1/8	22 4/8	5	5	6	5	Worth Co., MO	Duane Hostikka	Duane Hostikka	1998	445
170 7/8	23 3/8	23 3/8	19 7/8	22 3/8	4 7/8	4 7/8	7	6	Shelby Co., IL	Robert A. Howell	Robert A. Howell	1998	445
170 7/8	26 7/8	26 3/8	19 4/8	21 6/8	4 6/8	4 6/8	5	5	Parry Sound, ON	Gary Jackson	Gary Jackson	1998	445
170 7/8	25 3/8	25 4/8	15 5/8	20 5/8	4 4/8	4 5/8	6	5	Loon Lake, SK	James D. Schatz	James D. Schatz	1998	445
170 7/8	24	24 3/8	19 2/8	22 4/8	4 5/8	4 6/8	6	6	Spencer Co., IN	Jamie L. Waninger	Jamie L. Waninger	1999	445
170 6/8	28 6/8	28 2/8	25 6/8	25 2/8	5	5 2/8	4	4	Phelps Co., MO	Dave Gabel	Dave Gabel	1996	457
170 6/8	30	29	19 6/8	23 6/8	5 4/8	5 4/8	5	5	Grant Co., WI	Randall J. Ertz	Randall J. Ertz	1997	457
170 6/8	26	25	20 7/8	22 7/8	4 7/8	4 6/8	6	6	Montgomery Co., IA	Steve Philby	Steve Philby	1997	457
170 6/8	26 4/8	25 7/8	18 6/8	23 5/8	4 6/8	5 5/8	5	5	Sullivan Co., MO	Rodney A. Raley	Rodney A. Raley	1997	457
170 6/8	27 1/8	27 3/8	18 6/8	22 6/8	5 4/8	—	5	5	Adams Co., IL	Steven A. Schwartz	Steven A. Schwartz	1997	457

WHITETAIL DEER - TYPICAL ANTLERS

Odocoileus virginianus virginianus and certain related subspecies

Score	Length of Main Beam R.	L.	Inside Spread	Circumference at Smallest Place Between Burr and First Point R.	L.	Number of Points R.	L.	Locality	Hunter	Owner	Date Killed	Rank
170 6/8	27	25 3/8	20 4/8	5 2/8	5 1/8	5	6	Rock Co., WI	Dan Davis	Dan Davis	1998	457
170 6/8	26 5/8	26 6/8	18	5	4 6/8	7	6	Waukesha Co., WI	Jonathan A. Denk	Jonathan A. Denk	1998	457
170 6/8	22 7/8	21 7/8	17	4 4/8	4 4/8	6	7	Waskesiu Lake, SK	Edwin W. Ehler	Edwin W. Ehler	1999	457
170 6/8	25 3/8	24 2/8	19 6/8	5 3/8	5 6/8	5	6	Columbia Co., WI	Robert J. Kau	Robert J. Kau	1999	457
170 6/8	23	22 4/8	17 6/8	6 1/8	5 5/8	5	5	Isle of Wight Co., VA	Picked Up	David A. Reece	1999	457
170 5/8	28 7/8	28 2/8	19 5/8	4 6/8	4 6/8	7	7	Lowndes Co., GA	Jack L. Garrison	Jack L. Garrison	1983	467
170 5/8	28 1/8	27 5/8	21 3/8	5 1/8	4 7/8	5	5	Monona Co., IA	Unknown	George Waters	1993	467
170 5/8	27 4/8	27 5/8	22	5 2/8	5 1/8	8	7	Eagle Creek, SK	Perry Haanen	Perry Haanen	1995	467
170 5/8	26 2/8	27 6/8	23 6/8	5 2/8	5 1/8	8	6	Paddle River, AB	Dwayne C. Moore	Dwayne C. Moore	1997	467
170 5/8	24 2/8	25 3/8	17 3/8	4 5/8	4 5/8	6	6	Washington Co., ME	David Shaffner	David Shaffner	1997	467
170 5/8	26 6/8	27 5/8	20 1/8	5 3/8	5 3/8	6	5	Williamsburg Co., SC	A. Hugh Gaskins	A. Hugh Gaskins	1998	467
170 5/8	27 7/8	26 4/8	19 3/8	5	5 5/8	5	5	Highland Co., OH	Harold D. Jewett	Harold D. Jewett	1998	467
170 5/8	29	27 4/8	21 1/8	5 1/8	5 1/8	5	6	Adams Co., IL	Randy J. Kurz	Randy J. Kurz	1998	467
170 5/8	25 7/8	25 6/8	23 1/8	4 7/8	4 5/8	5	5	Clayton Co., IA	Jerry E. Morris	Jerry E. Morris	1998	467
170 5/8	25 7/8	26	19 5/8	5 2/8	5 2/8	5	5	Kenosha Co., WI	Gary Schaetten	Gary Schaetten	1999	467
170 5/8	26 2/8	25 5/8	20 6/8	5	5	5	5	Toole Co., MT	Cody P. Voermans	Cody P. Voermans	1999	467
170 4/8	25 2/8	24 7/8	17 6/8	4 7/8	5	5	5	Taylor Co., IA	Picked Up	Jim Haas	1987	478
170 4/8	24 2/8	23 3/8	21	5 6/8	5 6/8	8	8	Swan Plain, SK	Chris Halsey	Chris Halsey	1997	478
170 4/8	28 7/8	27 7/8	19	5 6/8	5 5/8	7	6	Hopkins Co., KY	Luther T. Mincy, Jr.	Luther T. Mincy, Jr.	1997	478
170 4/8	28 1/8	28	22 2/8	5 2/8	5 3/8	5	5	Lucas Co., IA	Rick L. Mitchell	Rick L. Mitchell	1997	478
170 4/8	24 2/8	23 7/8	19 3/8	5 2/8	5 3/8	6	5	Marion Co., IL	Louis P. Williams, Jr.	Louis P. Williams, Jr.	1997	478
170 4/8	28 2/8	28 4/8	22 6/8	4 4/8	4 4/8	6	6	Dimmit Co., TX	Joe E. Coleman	Joe E. Coleman	1998	478
170 4/8	25 7/8	26	19 2/8	4 5/8	4 7/8	7	6	Rooks Co., KS	Shawn Sammons	Shawn Sammons	1998	478
170 4/8	28 1/8	26 4/8	21 2/8	5 2/8	5 3/8	5	5	Dunn Co., WI	Richard H. Damro	Richard H. Damro	1999	478
170 4/8	26 6/8	27 1/8	21 7/8	5 2/8	5	6	6	Marinette Co., WI	Randy J. Willms	Randy J. Willms	1999	478
170 3/8	24 2/8	25	24 4/8	6	5	6	6	Madison Parish, LA	Stephens M. White, Sr.	Stephens M. White, Jr.	1945	487
170 3/8	26	25 6/8	18 7/8	4 6/8	5	5	5	Lake Rosseau, ON	Picked Up	Philip Giroday	PR 1994	487
170 3/8	23 2/8	23 4/8	21 5/8	4 7/8	4 7/8	7	6	Smeaton, SK	Samuel D. Singer	Samuel D. Singer	1997	487
170 3/8	24 7/8	24 6/8	17 5/8	4 2/8	4 1/8	5	5	Throckmorton Co., TX	Ken W. Youngblood	Ken W. Youngblood	1997	487
170 3/8	25 2/8	25	20 2/8	4 7/8	5 2/8	8	6	Wayne Co., KY	Kelvin Casada	Kelvin Casada	1998	487
170 3/8	26 6/8	27 2/8	22 4/8	6	5 5/8	6	6	Jo Daviess Co., IL	Cliff Perry	Cliff Perry	1998	487
170 3/8	26	25 6/8	18 7/8	5 5/8	5 6/8	6	6	E. Carroll Parish, LA	David L. Roselle	David L. Roselle	1998	487
170 3/8	23 7/8	23 3/8	21 3/8	5 6/8	5 7/8	5	5	Turtle Ford, SK	Gordon E. Janz	Gordon E. Janz	1999	487
170 3/8	28 6/8	27 6/8	19 7/8	4 7/8	4 7/8	7	6	Houston Co., MN	Picked Up	MN Dept. of Natl. Resc.	1999	487

Score	Main Beam R	Main Beam L	Inside Spread	Circ. R	Circ. L	Points R	Points L	Locality	Hunter	Owner	Date	Rank
170 2/8	26 6/8	26 2/8	19 4/8	4 5/8	4 7/8	5	5	Scotts Bluff Co., NE	Russel C. McKeehan II	Russel C. McKeehan II	1996	496
170 2/8	24 3/8	24 5/8	23	4 6/8	4 7/8	6	5	Pike Co., IL	Michael E. Kennedy	Michael E. Kennedy	1997	496
170 2/8	27	27 4/8	19 7/8	5 5/8	5 6/8	7	5	Rusk Co., WI	Fredrick J. Marcon	Fredrick J. Marcon	1997	496
170 2/8	26 7/8	26 2/8	19 3/8	4 7/8	5 2/8	6	6	Clayton Co., IA	Randy D. Reck	Randy D. Reck	1997	496
170 2/8	24	24 6/8	18 6/8	4 3/8	4 4/8	6	6	Davis Co., IA	Richard C. Riggenbach	Richard C. Riggenbach	1997	496
170 2/8	24 7/8	28	21 4/8	4 6/8	4 6/8	6	6	Hamilton Co., IN	James P. Tomasik	James P. Tomasik	1997	496
170 2/8	24 7/8	25	20	4 7/8	4 7/8	5	6	Esterhazy, SK	Sidney W. Golling	Sidney W. Golling	1998	496
170 2/8	26 3/8	26 1/8	18 4/8	5 1/8	5 3/8	8	8	Hubbard Co., MN	Michael E. Greetan	Michael E. Greetan	1998	496
170 2/8	28 1/8	27	21 6/8	5 3/8	5 3/8	7	4	Hancock Co., IL	James E. Lenix	James E. Lenix	1998	496
170 2/8	27 3/8	27 6/8	20	4 6/8	4 7/8	5	5	Tobin Lake, SK	Trevor Rehaluk	Trevor Rehaluk	1998	496
170 2/8	27 7/8	27 1/8	19 2/8	4 6/8	4 5/8	4	5	Walworth Co., WI	Dale Wilson	Dale Wilson	1998	496
170 2/8	27 6/8	26 2/8	20 4/8	5 7/8	5 6/8	6	5	Battle River, AB	Jeff Golka	Jeff Golka	1999	496
170 2/8	26 3/8	25 4/8	24	4 3/8	4 2/8	5	5	George Lake, AB	Susan G. Isaacs	Susan G. Isaacs	1999	496
170 2/8	24 6/8	25	18 4/8	4 3/8	4 6/8	6	6	Langlade Co., WI	Jay P. Konetzke	Jay P. Konetzke	1999	496
170 2/8	24	25 1/8	21	4 4/8	4 5/8	5	5	Clark Co., KS	Ray Morais	Ray Morais	1999	496
170 2/8	25	25 5/8	19 2/8	5 6/8	5 3/8	5	5	Unknown	Unknown	Manuel F. Nunez	PR 1999	496
170 2/8	26	25 3/8	16 4/8	5 5/8	5 1/8	7	5	Christian Co., KY	Brian K. Oatts	Brian K. Oatts	1999	496
170 1/8	25 3/8	24 5/8	17 1/8	4 4/8	4 5/8	6	6	Putnam Co., MO	Ralph J. Shoultz	Otteline Shoultz	1973	513
170 1/8	24 6/8	24 4/8	18 4/8	5 2/8	5 2/8	6	6	Cowley Co., KS	Mitchell D. Payne	Mitchell D. Payne	1996	513
170 1/8	22 7/8	22 7/8	17 5/8	4 1/8	4 1/8	5	5	Maverick Co., TX	Donald Gann	Donald Gann	1997	513
170 1/8	23 4/8	23 2/8	17 7/8	5	5 3/8	7	6	Cochin, SK	John M. Hanger II	John M. Hanger II	1997	513
170 1/8	27 2/8	26 5/8	19 2/8	4 2/8	4 1/8	7	7	Kleberg Co., TX	Robert Nichols III	Robert Nichols III	1997	513
170 1/8	26 1/8	26 4/8	17 1/8	4 2/8	4 2/8	6	6	Gates Co., NC	William W. Parker III	William W. Parker III	1997	513
170 1/8	28 5/8	29 1/8	22 3/8	5 1/8	5 3/8	5	5	Hart Co., KY	Paul B. Wilson	Paul B. Wilson	1997	513
170 1/8	29 1/8	26 6/8	16 1/8	5 4/8	5 4/8	4	4	Brown Co., IL	Todd D. Carlton	Todd D. Carlton	1998	513
170 1/8	26 6/8	28 3/8	20 5/8	4 4/8	4 4/8	6	6	Hart Co., KY	Doug Fields	Doug Fields	1998	513
170 1/8	28 3/8	23 6/8	18 1/8	4 5/8	4 5/8	6	6	Kenedy Co., TX	Jarred W. Peeples	Jarred W. Peeples	1998	513
170 1/8	23 6/8	28 1/8	17 2/8	4 2/8	4 4/8	6	6	Taylor Co., GA	Joseph J. Ryals	Joseph J. Ryals	1998	513
170 1/8	28 1/8	27 1/8	22 7/8	5	5	5	5	Keya Paha Co., NE	Picked Up	Teresa A. Bammerlin	1999	513
170 1/8	27	23 4/8	18 3/8	4 4/8	4 4/8	6	6	Unknown	Unknown	Martin E. Cahoon	PR 1999	513
170 1/8	23 7/8	28 2/8	19 1/8	5 5/8	5 6/8	7	5	Saginaw Co., MI	Mario VanderMeulen	Mario VanderMeulen	1999	513
170	27	26 5/8	19 2/8	4 7/8	5	5	5	Emo, ON	Jack Booth	Jack Booth	1986	527
170	27 1/8	27 1/8	23	5 1/8	5 2/8	5	5	Wabamun Lake, AB	John Nagtegaal	John Nagtegaal	1990	527
170	27 1/8	25 2/8	21 6/8	5 3/8	5 3/8	5	5	Desha Co., AR	Ben J. Miller	Ben J. Miller	1994	527
170	26 5/8	25 4/8	20 5/8	6 2/8	6 2/8	8	5	Pike Co., IL	Perry Stanley	Perry Stanley	1996	527
170	26 4/8	23 7/8	22 2/8	4 6/8	4 6/8	5	5	Washington Co., WI	Alan R. Gehl	Alan R. Gehl	1997	527
170	24 4/8	25 1/8	17	4 2/8	4 2/8	5	5	Allamakee Co., IA	Lloyd O. Griffith	Lloyd O. Griffith	1998	527
170	27 1/8	25 4/8	19	4 6/8	4 7/8	5	5	Whiteside Co., IL	Arlyn D. Hamstra	Arlyn D. Hamstra	1998	527
170	24 6/8	23 7/8	19 2/8	4 7/8	4 4/8	5	5	Kane Co., IL	Bradley J. Lundsteen	Bradley J. Lundsteen	1998	527
170	26 5/8	27 3/8	20 5/8	5	4 5/8	6	6	Cherokee Co., IA	Ben R. Puttmann	Ben R. Puttmann	1998	527
170	27 3/8	24 5/8	20 2/8	4 6/8	4 5/8	5	5	Wakaw Lake, SK	Nolan Balone	Nolan Balone	1999	527
170	24 5/8	25 6/8	20 7/8	4 5/8	5 3/8	5	5	Cedar Co., IA	Ronald R. Cain	Ronald R. Cain	1999	527
170	25 1/8	25 1/8	18 2/8	5 3/8	4 5/8	7	7	Wabasha Co., MN	Chad R. Collins	Chad R. Collins	1999	527

WHITETAIL DEER - TYPICAL ANTLERS

Odocoileus virginianus virginianus and certain related subspecies

Score	Length of Main Beam R.	L.	Inside Spread	Circumference at Smallest Place Between Burr and First Point R.	L.	Number of Points R.	L.	Locality	Hunter	Owner	Date Killed	Rank
170	26 2/8	26 6/8	20 2/8	4 7/8	4 7/8	7	5	Pratt Co., KS	Ronald R. George	Ronald R. George	1999	527
170	29 3/8	28 6/8	18	4 6/8	4 7/8	6	6	Neosho Co., KS	Frank L. Pechacek	Frank L. Pechacek	1999	527
169 6/8	27 2/8	28 1/8	22 6/8	5 4/8	5 1/8	7	5	Coahoma Co., MS	Steven R. Williams	Steven R. Williams	1998	541
169 4/8	28 2/8	28 6/8	14 3/8	4 7/8	5 2/8	6	5	Boone Co., KY	Tim Adams	Tim Adams	1998	542
169 4/8	24 4/8	25	20 6/8	4 1/8	4 1/8	5	5	Sheho, SK	Trevor Walchuk	Trevor Walchuk	1999	542
169 3/8	26 7/8	26 6/8	19 3/8	5 4/8	5 3/8	6	6	Woods Co., OK	Paul L. McElveen	Paul L. McElveen	1995	544
169 3/8	24 3/8	24	19 5/8	5 2/8	5 4/8	6	8	Clark Co., KS	Kevin E. Shafer	Kevin E. Shafer	1999	544
169 3/8	25 6/8	25 6/8	18 4/8	5	5 1/8	6	7	Christian Co., KY	Kelly Slone	Kelly Slone	1999	544
169 2/8	23	24 2/8	19 2/8	5 2/8	5 1/8	5	5	Kittson Co., MN	Frederick G. Johnson	Frederick G. Johnson	1991	547
169 1/8	26 1/8	26 5/8	17 3/8	5 4/8	5 6/8	5	5	Door Co., WI	Timothy M. Buhr	Timothy M. Buhr	1997	548
169 1/8	23 5/8	23 2/8	19 3/8	4 7/8	4 7/8	9	7	Holt Co., MO	Bruce A. Medsker	Bruce A. Medsker	1997	548
169	24 5/8	24 5/8	20 6/8	4 6/8	4 5/8	6	6	Dickinson Co., IA	Ronny Hartwig	Ronny Hartwig	1973	550
169	24 4/8	24 5/8	22 4/8	4 1/8	4 3/8	5	5	Hidalgo, MX	Ray J. Guarisco	Ray J. Guarisco	1995	550
169	28	27 3/8	16 2/8	5 4/8	5 4/8	9	8	Washington Co., IN	Harold Mutter	Harold Mutter	1998	550
169	30 2/8	28 2/8	19 4/8	4 7/8	5	6	8	Rockbridge Co., VA	Richard J. Lowe, Jr.	Richard J. Lowe, Jr.	1999	550
168 7/8	24 3/8	25 1/8	20 5/8	4 5/8	4 4/8	7	6	Dimmit Co., TX	David M. Shashy	David M. Shashy	1997	554
168 7/8	27 4/8	26 6/8	17 3/8	5 3/8	5 2/8	7	5	Brooks Co., GA	Mickey Tillman	Mickey Tillman	2000	554
168 6/8	27 3/8	27 1/8	18 2/8	4 5/8	4 5/8	6	6	Grafton Co., NH	Warren F. Parker	Warren F. Parker	1959	556
168 6/8	25 4/8	25 4/8	22	5 4/8	5 5/8	5	5	Marathon Co., WI	Anthony Locascio	Anthony Locascio	1997	556
168 6/8	26 5/8	26 3/8	18 6/8	4 7/8	4 6/8	6	6	Coos Co., NH	Bernard Petrie	Bernard Petrie	1998	556
168 5/8	27	27 3/8	18 7/8	5	4 7/8	5	7	Amherst Co., VA	Ronald P. Leary	Ronald P. Leary	1997	559
168 5/8	23 7/8	23 5/8	20 3/8	5 2/8	5 3/8	7	7	Avoyelles Parish, LA	Michael G. Willis	Michael G. Willis	1997	559
168 4/8	24 2/8	24 7/8	19 6/8	5 1/8	5 1/8	5	5	Clark Co., IL	Dane E. Thompson	Dane E. Thompson	1997	561
168 3/8	25 7/8	26	19 1/8	4 4/8	4 6/8	5	5	Rockcastle Co., KY	Brent Boone	Brent Boone	1998	562
168 3/8	27 2/8	27 5/8	21 1/8	5	5	6	6	Outagamie Co., WI	Rodney R. Schutt	Rodney R. Schutt	1998	562
168 2/8	28 5/8	27 6/8	21 2/8	5 2/8	5 1/8	6	6	Dewey Co., OK	Chad E. Kisinger	Chad E. Kisinger	1996	564
168 2/8	24 3/8	24 5/8	16	4 4/8	4 5/8	8	8	Moose Mt., SK	Barry Adair	Barry Adair	1997	564
168 2/8	22 6/8	24	18 4/8	4 4/8	4 4/8	9	6	Casey Co., KY	Andrew Weddle	Andrew Weddle	1998	564
168 2/8	25 2/8	24 2/8	18	5 4/8	5 1/8	6	6	Iowa Co., WI	Craig A. Christians	Craig A. Christians	1999	564
168 2/8	25 2/8	24 5/8	19 2/8	4 3/8	4 2/8	5	5	Richland Co., WI	Bud G. Williams	Bud G. Williams	1999	564
168 1/8	26 6/8	26 6/8	19 2/8	5	5	6	5	Franklin Co., NY	James W. Demers	James W. Demers	1997	569
168 1/8	27 2/8	26 6/8	18 7/8	4 4/8	4 3/8	5	6	Boyle Co., KY	Chris Douglas	Chris Douglas	1997	569
168 1/8	24 5/8	25 1/8	17 7/8	4 4/8	4 5/8	6	6	Monroe Co., OH	Dan Rush	Dan Rush	1997	569
168 1/8	25	22 4/8	19 1/8	5	5	6	5	Harvey Co., KS	Derrick W. Dollar	Derrick W. Dollar	1998	569

Score	Main Beam R.	Main Beam L.	Inside Spread	Circ. R.	Circ. L.	Pts. R.	Pts. L.	Locality	Owner	Hunter	Date	Rank
168	26 4/8	26 6/8	19 4/8	4 4/8	4 4/8	5	5	Monroe Co., IA	Jason Morgan	Jason Morgan	1995	573
167 7/8	27	26 6/8	22 4/8	5 2/8	5 2/8	8	7	Bayfield Co., WI	Charles L. Weiss	Charles L. Weiss	1996	574
167 7/8	27	26 6/8	20 4/8	4 2/8	4 2/8	5	6	Merrimack Co., NH	Picked Up	NH Fish & Game Dept.	1998	574
167 6/8	24 5/8	25 4/8	21	5	5	4	4	Bannoc, SK	Joe Dillon	Joe Dillon	1998	576
167 5/8	25	24 7/8	20 1/8	4 4/8	4 4/8	6	6	Preble Co., OH	Robert D. Ballinger	Robert D. Ballinger	1999	577
167 4/8	27 2/8	27 4/8	20 2/8	4 5/8	4 4/8	6	5	Ontario Co., NY	Jeremy Thomas	Jeremy Thomas	1997	578
167 4/8	27 1/8	27	22 2/8	5 3/8	5 1/8	6	6	Waupaca Co., WI	Daniel P. Hauk	Daniel P. Hauk	1998	578
167 4/8	27	26 1/8	19 4/8	5	5 1/8	6	5	Trigg Co., KY	Terry Mitcheson	Terry Mitcheson	1998	578
167 4/8	26 7/8	25 7/8	18 5/8	5 1/8	5 1/8	5	4	Metcalfe Co., KY	Tony E. Shockley	Tony E. Shockley	1998	578
167 4/8	24 3/8	30 6/8	19 6/8	5	4 2/8	8	6	Dougherty Co., GA	Bobby L. Joiner	Bobby L. Joiner	1998	578
167 4/8	30 2/8	26	19 6/8	4 2/8	4 4/8	5	6	Preeceville, SK	Gerald Swiderski	Gerald Swiderski	1999	578
167 3/8	26 1/8	26 6/8	19 6/8	4 4/8	4 3/8	5	5	Buffalo Co., WI	Jay J. Snopek	Jay J. Snopek	1999	585
167 3/8	27 5/8	26 2/8	21 2/8	4 6/8	5	5	6	Breckinridge Co., KY	Ronald D. Keen	Ronald D. Keen	2000	585
167 3/8	26	26 2/8	17 5/8	4 4/8	4 4/8	6	6	Hancock Co., IL	Trevor G. Akers	Trevor G. Akers	1996	585
167 3/8	25	26	20 5/8	4	4 4/8	7	6	Telfair Co., GA	David A. Rawlins	David A. Rawlins	1997	585
167 3/8	26 3/8	26 2/8	24 3/8	4 5/8	4 2/8	8	7	Miami Co., KS	Curtis W. Hrabe	Curtis W. Hrabe	1997	585
167 2/8	23 7/8	22 3/8	18 7/8	4 6/8	5 2/8	7	7	Alexander Co., IL	Tom M. Swanson	Tom M. Swanson	1998	590
167 2/8	26 7/8	25 1/8	18 5/8	4	4 4/8	5	7	Meade Co., KY	William V. Gilbert	William V. Gilbert	1998	590
167 2/8	26	27 5/8	19 6/8	4 3/8	4 2/8	5	5	Macon Co., MO	Spencer A. Barron	Spencer A. Barron	1969	590
167 2/8	24 1/8	24 5/8	18 4/8	4 2/8	4 5/8	5	5	Douglas Co., WI	Mark E. Henck	Mark E. Henck	1997	590
167 2/8	25 3/8	24 6/8	16 6/8	4 7/8	5 3/8	6	5	Rappahannock Co., VA	Edwin Lillis	Edwin Lillis	1998	590
167 2/8	27 2/8	25 4/8	17 6/8	5 1/8	6	7	7	Kent Co., MD	F. David Black	F. David Black	1998	590
167 1/8	24 5/8	27 6/8	18 7/8	5 3/8	5 2/8	5	5	Fountain Co., IN	Joe R. Coffing	Joe R. Coffing	1999	596
167 1/8	25 7/8	26	22 2/8	5 4/8	4 7/8	7	7	Oakland Co., MI	Chris C. Goodwin	Chris C. Goodwin	1999	596
167 1/8	27 7/8	25 7/8	17 7/8	4 5/8	5 1/8	5	5	Breckinridge Co., KY	Ben Whitfill	Ben Whitfill	1997	596
167	26 1/8	27 7/8	21 3/8	5 2/8	5 1/8	6	6	Clermont Co., OH	Johnie R. Wardrup	Johnie R. Wardrup	1998	599
166 7/8	24 7/8	26 1/8	23 7/8	4 4/8	5 3/8	8	8	St. Mary's Co., MD	Bryan R. Thrush	Bryan R. Thrush	1999	600
166 7/8	24 7/8	24 2/8	17 7/8	4 2/8	5 1/8	6	6	Davidson Co., TN	A. Wade Daugherty	A. Wade Daugherty	1999	600
166 7/8	23 4/8	24 4/8	19 1/8	4 5/8	4 6/8	5	5	Hinds Co., MS	Edwin F. Schmidt IV	Edwin F. Schmidt IV	1997	600
166 7/8	24 7/8	25 4/8	19 1/8	5 3/8	4 1/8	7	7	Kingman Co., KS	Ted Z. Stryhas	Ted Z. Stryhas	1997	600
166 7/8	26 6/8	26 3/8	21 7/8	6	5 3/8	5	5	Jersey Co., IL	William P. O'Neal	William P. O'Neal	1998	600
166 6/8	24	22 7/8	19 5/8	4 7/8	6	6	6	Umatilla Co., OR	Doug Coverdale	Doug Coverdale	1999	604
166 6/8	26	28 2/8	20 2/8	5 1/8	4 7/8	5	5	Jefferson Co., MO	Eli Parkhurst	Eli Parkhurst	1966	605
166 5/8	25	24 6/8	16	5 3/8	5 1/8	8	6	Douglas Co., WI	Robert W. Strauch	Robert W. Strauch	1997	605
166 5/8	28 6/8	27 6/8	18 5/8	4 6/8	5 1/8	6	6	Todd Co., KY	Douglas Gibson	Douglas Gibson	1998	607
166 4/8	25 5/8	25 5/8	17	4 5/8	4 6/8	5	6	La Salle Co., TX	Thomas E. Baine	Thomas E. Baine	1999	607
166 4/8	25 6/8	26 4/8	21 1/8	5 7/8	5 7/8	6	7	Adams Co., OH	Mitchell Baker	Mitchell Baker	1997	609
166 3/8	26 5/8	29 5/8	21 4/8	5 2/8	5 2/8	7	6	St. Croix Co., WI	John J. Wilson	John J. Wilson	1998	609
166 3/8	26 4/8	28 2/8	17 1/8	5 1/8	5 1/8	5	5	Marinette Co., WI	Wayne M. Blickhahn	Wayne M. Blickhahn	1962	611
166 2/8	27	26 1/8	20 4/8	4 6/8	4 6/8	4	4	Atchison Co., MO	Vernie A. Rhoades	Vernon F. Rhoades	1989	611
166 2/8	25 2/8	26 1/8	19 2/8	4 1/8	3 7/8	6	6	McMullen Co., TX	Jim Arnold	Jim Arnold	1997	611
166 2/8	24 4/8	23 4/8	18 4/8	5 3/8	5 1/8	5	5	Keya Paha Co., NE	Aaron A. Gruber	Aaron A. Gruber	1999	611
166 1/8	24 3/8	24 5/8	19 2/8	6	6	7	6	Wayne Co., KY	Douglas Watson	Douglas Watson	1998	615

WHITETAIL DEER - TYPICAL ANTLERS

Odocoileus virginianus virginianus and certain related subspecies

Score	Length of Main Beam R.	L.	Inside Spread	Circumference at Smallest Place Between Burr and First Point R.	L.	Number of Points R.	L.	Locality	Hunter	Owner	Date Killed	Rank
166 1/8	24 2/8	26 2/8	18 4/8	5	5 2/8	7	6	Clark Co., IL	Brett A. Higginbotham	Brett A. Higginbotham	1999	615
166 1/8	27 2/8	27 1/8	21 5/8	5 2/8	5	4	5	Hardin Co., KY	Ella M. Moore	Ella M. Moore	1999	615
166	26 5/8	25 4/8	19	5 7/8	5 5/8	4	4	The Dirt Hills, SK	Gordon Popescul	Gordon Popescul	1998	618
166	25 6/8	28	20	5 3/8	5 4/8	6	5	Steuben Co., NY	Justin Schwabe	Justin Schwabe	1998	618
166	26 1/8	24 6/8	18 4/8	5	5 1/8	5	6	Coshocton Co., OH	William R. Warther	William R. Warther	1999	618
165 6/8	26 4/8	26 2/8	20 2/8	4 5/8	4 3/8	5	5	Jim Hogg Co., TX	Byron Kibby	Byron Kibby	1974	621
165 6/8	23 3/8	23 5/8	19 4/8	4 5/8	4 6/8	6	6	Clay Co., WV	Brian A. Rickmers	Brian A. Rickmers	1997	621
165 6/8	25 5/8	27 1/8	19 4/8	5 1/8	5	5	5	Cass Co., MN	Brent M. Beimert	Brent M. Beimert	1998	621
165 6/8	28 4/8	28 4/8	18 1/8	5 3/8	5 2/8	6	6	Jersey Co., IL	David A. Balaco	David A. Balaco	1999	621
165 5/8	26 3/8	25 3/8	17 4/8	5 3/8	5 6/8	7	8	Flatbush, AB	Grant Horosko	Grant Horosko	1997	625
165 5/8	26 4/8	24 5/8	17	5 2/8	5 1/8	6	6	Cooper Co., MO	Daniel L. Twenter	Daniel L. Twenter	1997	625
165 5/8	24 1/8	25 6/8	17 5/8	4 3/8	4 4/8	7	6	Coal Co., OK	Gary D. Bruhwiler	Gary D. Bruhwiler	1999	625
165 5/8	25 3/8	25	18	4 2/8	4 2/8	5	6	Clay Co., AR	Richard Catt	Richard Catt	1999	625
165 4/8	27 3/8	26 2/8	25 5/8	5 4/8	5 4/8	7	6	Clay Co., SD	Howard W. Bresaw	Howard W. Bresaw	1970	629
165 4/8	30 5/8	29 6/8	18 6/8	4 6/8	4 7/8	6	6	Bedford Co., VA	T.A. Phillips	Loretta P. Harrison	1976	629
165 4/8	25 7/8	25 4/8	23 4/8	4 5/8	4 5/8	5	5	Halifax Co., VA	Howard S. Elliott	Howard S. Elliott	1997	629
165 4/8	26	26 3/8	20	5 1/8	5 1/8	5	5	Hart Co., KY	Clarence K. Merideth	Clarence K. Merideth	1997	629
165 3/8	28 4/8	28 3/8	19 5/8	4 5/8	4 5/8	8	6	Hillsborough Co., NH	John P. Coulter	John P. Coulter	1998	633
165 3/8	23 6/8	23 5/8	17 3/8	5 5/8	5 6/8	5	5	McHenry Co., IL	Jared A. Gratz	Jared A. Gratz	1998	633
165 3/8	25 1/8	25 5/8	17 5/8	4 3/8	4 3/8	4	4	Rolette Co., ND	Scott G. Moen	Scott G. Moen	1999	633
165 2/8	28 6/8	28 6/8	21	5 6/8	6	7	9	St. Louis Co., MN	Harold Wilkins	James P Wilkerson	1974	636
165 2/8	25 7/8	25 1/8	16 2/8	5 1/8	5 2/8	4	4	Vernon Co., MO	George Brannan	George Brannan	1990	636
165 2/8	27 2/8	24 2/8	23	4 4/8	4 3/8	6	5	St. Croix Co., WI	Ron W. Nelson	Ron W. Nelson	1995	636
165 2/8	23	25 4/8	21	4 4/8	4 5/8	5	5	Lincoln Co., MO	Ronald D. Olson	Ronald D. Olson	1996	636
165 2/8	25 1/8	24 5/8	18	4 1/8	4 2/8	5	5	Roane Co., WV	Robert L. Fitzwater	Robert L. Fitzwater	1998	636
165 2/8	25	24 7/8	19 4/8	4 1/8	4 1/8	5	5	Carroll Co., IA	Gary T. Riesselman	Gary T. Riesselman	1999	636
165 1/8	25 4/8	26 1/8	17 3/8	5 5/8	5 7/8	5	5	Sawyer Co., WI	Shawn A. Campbell	Shawn A. Campbell	1998	642
165 1/8	25 5/8	24 5/8	17 7/8	5 4/8	5 3/8	5	5	Bay Co., MI	Terry L. Horner	Terry L. Horner	1998	642
165 1/8	25 2/8	25 2/8	16 3/8	4 4/8	4 4/8	6	6	Hillsborough Co., NH	Leon W. Nelson	Leon W. Nelson	1998	642
165 1/8	23 2/8	21 5/8	19 7/8	4 5/8	4 6/8	6	6	Oconto Co., WI	Thomas M. Wagner	Thomas M. Wagner	1998	642
165 1/8	25	23 6/8	22	4 2/8	4 3/8	6	6	Worth Co., GA	Leon McDonald	Leon McDonald	1999	642
165 1/8	24 3/8	25	16 7/8	4 4/8	4 2/8	6	6	Adams Co., NE	Michael T. Roth	Michael T. Roth	1999	642
165 1/8	25 6/8	26	19 7/8	5 3/8	5 5/8	6	6	Fort-a-Corne, SK	Steve Clifford	Steve Clifford	2000	642
165 1/8	27 6/8	28	20 5/8	4 5/8	4 5/8	6	5	Buffalo Co., WI	Gary L. Fleishauer	Gary L. Fleishauer	2000	642

454

Score							Location	Name	Name	Year	Score
165	26 7/8	25 7/8	17 6/8	4 7/8	5	6	5	Copiah Co., MS	William M. Campbell	William M. Campbell	1997	650
165	26	26 3/8	17 6/8	5 2/8	5 2/8	5	5	Pike Co., IL	George R. Metcalf	George R. Metcalf	1998	650
165	25 5/8	25 4/8	18 7/8	5 4/8	5 3/8	5	6	Oconto Co., WI	Brian R. Belongea	Brian R. Belongea	1999	650
165	25	25	18	4 2/8	4 2/8	5	5	Westmoreland Co., PA	Robert E. Duff, Jr.	Robert E. Duff, Jr.	1999	650
165	22 2/8	22 5/8	17 6/8	5	5	5	5	Crow Wing Co., MN	Michael J. Dullinger	Michael J. Dullinger	1999	650
164 7/8	24 6/8	23 5/8	15 3/8	4 4/8	4 5/8	6	6	Kewaunee Co., WI	William J. Derenne	William J. Derenne	1998	655
164 7/8	24 5/8	24 6/8	16 5/8	4 5/8	4 5/8	5	5	St. Charles Co., MO	Adam C. Bethmann	Adam C. Bethmann	1999	655
164 6/8	24 5/8	23 4/8	18 2/8	3 7/8	4	5	5	Flathead Co., MT	Stephen Holladay	Stephen Holladay	1990	657
164 6/8	22 4/8	23	18 7/8	4 4/8	4 4/8	7	5	Dimmit Co., TX	Stuart W. Stedman	Stuart W. Stedman	1997	657
164 6/8	25 5/8	24 7/8	18 6/8	4 4/8	4 5/8	5	5	Worth Co., GA	Alan D. Brightwell	Alan D. Brightwell	1998	657
164 6/8	23	23	17 4/8	4 3/8	4 2/8	6	6	Dodge Co., NE	Douglas W. Hoffman	Douglas W. Hoffman	1998	657
164 6/8	26 2/8	25 5/8	20 6/8	5 2/8	5 4/8	6	5	Brown Co., WI	Cecil J. Skenandore	Cecil J. Skenandore	1998	657
164 6/8	26 7/8	26 7/8	22	4 4/8	4 3/8	6	5	Racine Co., WI	Thomas A. Wendt	Thomas A. Wendt	1998	657
164 5/8	25 5/8	25 5/8	23 4/8	4 5/8	4 5/8	6	7	Morrison Co., MN	Bruce D. Edberg	Bruce D. Edberg	1977	663
164 5/8	27 2/8	26	20 1/8	4 7/8	5 1/8	6	5	St. Joseph Co., IN	Scott G. Johnson	Scott G. Johnson	1998	663
164 5/8	27 2/8	26 6/8	21 7/8	5 3/8	5 4/8	7	8	Brown Co., IL	Larry O. Greene	Larry O. Greene	1999	663
164 4/8	23 3/8	24 2/8	21 1/8	5 1/8	5 2/8	5	5	Pepin Co., WI	Oliver J. Grotthus	Oliver J. Grotthus	1999	663
164 4/8	27 3/8	26 3/8	24 2/8	4 5/8	4 5/8	6	6	Pope Co., MN	Myron A. Forbord	Myron A. Forbord	1972	667
164 4/8	24 1/8	24	19	5 4/8	5 2/8	6	7	La Crosse Co., WI	Donald K. Earley	Donald K. Earley	1999	667
164 4/8	25 5/8	25 5/8	20	5 1/8	5 1/8	6	6	Ruby Lake, SK	George M. O'Brien	George M. O'Brien	1999	667
164 3/8	28 6/8	28 4/8	22 6/8	5 1/8	5 1/8	8	4	Nemaha Co., KS	Gerald R. Uphaus	Gerald R. Uphaus	1997	671
164 2/8	24 7/8	26 2/8	21 4/8	5	5 1/8	7	5	Dubuque Co., IA	Richard R. Herbst	Richard R. Herbst	1999	671
164 2/8	30	29 7/8	26 1/8	5	4 7/8	6	6	Anne Arundel Co., MD	Douglas M. Christensen	Douglas M. Christensen	1998	673
164 1/8	23 4/8	24 1/8	18 2/8	5	5	4	4	Logan Co., KY	Anthony D. Shoemake	Anthony D. Shoemake	1999	673
164 1/8	26 3/8	25 6/8	17 6/8	5	5	5	6	Shawano Co., WI	Keith Wilcox	Keith Wilcox	1997	675
164 1/8	23 1/8	22 4/8	17 5/8	5 1/8	4 4/8	8	7	Noble Co., OK	Patrick O. Pollman	Patrick O. Pollman	1998	675
164 1/8	26 4/8	27 2/8	20 3/8	5 2/8	5 1/8	5	5	Calumet Co., WI	Scott D. Bonlander	Scott D. Bonlander	1998	675
164 1/8	24 7/8	24 3/8	17 7/8	5	5 3/8	5	5	Woodward Co., OK	Ricky Lamascus	Ricky Lamascus	1998	675
164 1/8	25 4/8	25 4/8	16 7/8	4 2/8	4 2/8	8	6	Eriksdale, MB	Alan D. Long	Alan D. Long	1998	675
164 1/8	25 7/8	26 2/8	19 1/8	4 6/8	4 6/8	6	6	Lake Co., IN	J. Michael Tapper	J. Michael Tapper	1998	675
164 1/8	26 1/8	25 4/8	21 2/8	5	4 7/8	6	6	Vernon Co., WI	Todd M. Anderson	Todd M. Anderson	1999	675
164	25 4/8	25 1/8	18 3/8	4 7/8	4 5/8	6	5	Vernon Co., WI	Troy D. Oldenburg	Troy D. Oldenburg	1999	682
164	26 6/8	27 1/8	18	4 7/8	5	7	7	Saline Co., MO	David L. Cramer	David L. Cramer	1978	682
164	25 7/8	27 1/8	20 7/8	4 7/8	4 7/8	6	6	Lancaster Co., PA	Wade A. Conrad	Wade A. Conrad	1997	682
164	25 2/8	25 7/8	17	5 1/8	5 2/8	5	5	Guernsey Co., OH	Robert R. Crawford	Robert R. Crawford	1999	682
163 7/8	25 1/8	24 6/8	23	4 6/8	4 7/8	6	5	Webb Co., TX	William W. Lloyd	William W. Lloyd	1999	686
163 7/8	24	24 2/8	18 7/8	4 1/8	3 7/8	7	6	Brooks Co., TX	Timothy C. Brady	Timothy C. Brady	1997	686
163 7/8	24 7/8	25 7/8	19 2/8	5	5	8	7	Oakland Co., MI	Michael L. Senia	Michael L. Senia	1999	686
163 7/8	23 5/8	23 5/8	21 3/8	5 3/8	5 3/8	6	5	Spiritwood, SK	Richard P. Smith	Richard P. Smith	1999	686
163 6/8	29 5/8	29 2/8	24	4 6/8	4 4/8	5	5	Macon Co., IL	Jerry J. Wilson	Jerry J. Wilson	1999	686
163 6/8	25 5/8	25 2/8	19 2/8	5	5 1/8	5	5	Gage Co., NE	Robert S. Ulmer	Robert S. Ulmer	1998	690
163 6/8	24 1/8	24 4/8	21	4 6/8	4 6/8	5	5	Shawano Co., WI	Donald A. Juers	Donald A. Juers	1999	690
163 6/8	23 5/8	24 2/8	18 2/8	4 1/8	4 2/8	6	6	Henry Co., KY	Richard Nadicksbernd	Richard Nadicksbernd	1999	690

WHITETAIL DEER - TYPICAL ANTLERS

Odocoileus virginianus virginianus and certain related subspecies

Score	Length of Main Beam R.	L.	Inside Spread	Circumference at Smallest Place Between Burr and First Point R.	L.	Number of Points R.	L.	Locality	Hunter	Owner	Date Killed	Rank
163 6/8	28 4/8	27	19	4 7/8	4 7/8	4	4	Todd Co., MN	Jacob J. Slabaugh	Jacob J. Slabaugh	1999	690
163 5/8	26 3/8	29	21	4 6/8	4 4/8	8	6	Vermilion Co., IL	James D. Rueter	James D. Rueter	1992	694
163 5/8	24 5/8	24 5/8	17 5/8	4 4/8	4 5/8	6	6	Shelby Co., MO	Suzanne S. von Thun	Suzanne S. von Thun	1996	694
163 5/8	25 1/8	26 1/8	24 1/8	4 7/8	4 4/8	5	5	Cass Co., MI	Thomas M. Boynton	Thomas M. Boynton	1997	694
163 5/8	24 4/8	24 1/8	23 7/8	4 4/8	4 4/8	5	5	Young Co., TX	Jeffery D. Hill	Jeffery D. Hill	1997	694
163 5/8	25	24 4/8	20	4 7/8	4 6/8	7	7	Iowa Co., WI	Ryan F. Lipska	Ryan F. Lipska	1997	694
163 5/8	25 6/8	26 3/8	19 2/8	4 6/8	4 6/8	6	6	Meadow Lake, SK	Lewis E. Hartenstine	Lewis E. Hartenstine	1998	694
163 5/8	25 4/8	26 2/8	19 5/8	4 7/8	4 5/8	6	5	Madison Co., MT	Lia S. Ballou	Lia S. Ballou	1999	694
163 5/8	24 7/8	25 5/8	21 1/8	4 2/8	4 2/8	5	5	Dubuque Co., IA	Jamey M. Streif	Jamey J. Streif	1999	694
163 5/8	24 5/8	24 3/8	19 5/8	5 6/8	6	6	6	Coffey Co., KS	James C. Gilliam	James C. Gilliam	2000	694
163 4/8	24 7/8	24 1/8	16 7/8	4 6/8	4 7/8	6	6	Wapello Co., IA	Sean E. Ide	Sean E. Ide	1989	703
163 4/8	24 4/8	24 2/8	18 4/8	4 2/8	4 2/8	6	6	Coahuila, MX	Thomas F. Priestly	Thomas F. Priestly	1997	703
163 4/8	25 6/8	24 6/8	19 1/8	4 7/8	4 7/8	6	5	Swan Hills, AB	Sandro Trulli	Sandro Trulli	1997	703
163 4/8	27 6/8	27 1/8	19 1/8	5 3/8	5 3/8	6	6	Sawyer Co., WI	Lawrence J. Burger	Lawrence J. Burger	1998	703
163 4/8	23 4/8	23 2/8	16	4	4 1/8	6	6	Coahuila, MX	Myron Cole	Myron Cole	1998	703
163 4/8	27 4/8	26 3/8	21 2/8	4 6/8	4 6/8	5	5	Hancock Co., ME	Robert L. Wright	Robert L. Wright	1998	703
163 4/8	27 3/8	29	19 5/8	4 2/8	4 2/8	6	6	Jefferson Co., WI	Nathan J. Hrobsky	Nathan J. Hrobsky	1999	703
163 3/8	25	26	18 3/8	4 5/8	4 5/8	4	4	Latah Co., ID	Steven J. Funke	Steven J. Funke	1997	710
163 3/8	25	24 7/8	17 1/8	5 1/8	5 1/8	5	5	Boone Co., KY	John R. Stephenson	John R. Stephenson	1997	710
163 3/8	26 4/8	26 7/8	21 4/8	5 1/8	4 6/8	7	6	Jackson Co., IA	Doug J. Lange	Doug J. Lange	1999	710
163 3/8	25 3/8	24 4/8	21 5/8	4 3/8	4 6/8	8	9	Montgomery Co., MO	Roy L. Smith	Roy L. Smith	1999	710
163 2/8	27 3/8	26 1/8	20	5 1/8	5 1/8	7	6	Reno Co., KS	Larry D. Kerschner	Larry D. Kerschner	1990	714
163 2/8	26 7/8	25 7/8	19 6/8	4 6/8	4 6/8	6	6	Dimmit Co., TX	Phil Barnes	Phil Barnes	1997	714
163 2/8	27 3/8	28 2/8	20 6/8	5	5 2/8	6	7	Geauga Co., OH	Bruce A. Powell	Bruce A. Powell	1997	714
163 2/8	24 7/8	27	22 4/8	5 6/8	5 5/8	5	4	Adams Co., IL	Leslie E. Voorhis	Leslie E. Voorhis	1998	714
163 1/8	24 5/8	25 2/8	16 7/8	5	5	5	5	Elkhart Co., IN	Joseph J. Leszczynski	Joseph J. Leszczynski	1984	718
163	26 3/8	27	22 5/8	5 1/8	4 6/8	6	8	Buffalo Co., WI	Laine W. Lahndt	Laine W. Lahndt	1994	719
163	26 4/8	25 7/8	18 7/8	5 3/8	5 5/8	7	8	Effingham Co., IL	Todd J. Bloemer	Todd J. Bloemer	1995	719
163	22 5/8	21 5/8	18 4/8	4 4/8	4 6/8	6	6	Spotsylvania Co., VA	Ricky Hairfield	Ricky Hairfield	1997	719
163	25 3/8	24 1/8	18 2/8	4 6/8	4 6/8	6	6	Stafford Co., KS	Robert G. Williams, Jr.	Robert G. Williams, Jr.	1997	719
163	26 4/8	25 2/8	19 7/8	4 7/8	5	6	5	Washington Co., IA	Joseph Goodell	Joseph Goodell	1998	719
163	23 4/8	24 6/8	18 5/8	4 5/8	4 7/8	6	7	Jo Daviess Co., IL	Dennis D. Wurster	Dennis D. Wurster	1998	719
163	27 3/8	27 5/8	19 6/8	4 3/8	4 5/8	4	6	Jones Co., IA	Ryan F. Frasher	Ryan F. Frasher	1999	719
162 7/8	27	26 4/8	20 6/8	4 7/8	5 4/8	6	6	Crawford Co., KS	Joe E. Aquino	Joe E. Aquino	1994	726

Score	Length of Main Beam R	Length of Main Beam L	Inside Spread	Circumference R	Circumference L	Points R	Points L	Locality	Hunter	Owner	Date	Rank
162 7/8	23 3/8	23 3/8	18 5/8	5 1/8	5 2/8	6	5	Plymouth Co., IA	Brandon S. Youngstrom	Brandon S. Youngstrom	1998	726
162 7/8	22 6/8	24 1/8	17 7/8	5 7/8	5 3/8	6	5	Keya Paha Co., NE	Thomas E. Watkins	Thomas E. Watkins	1999	726
162 6/8	25 5/8	25 6/8	17 6/8	4 6/8	4 6/8	5	5	Lake Winnipeg, MB	Rodney M. Wozniak	Rodney M. Wozniak	1993	729
162 6/8	25 2/8	25 6/8	22 4/8	4 4/8	4 3/8	5	5	Christian Co., KY	Greg Abner	Greg Abner	1997	729
162 6/8	25 7/8	28 1/8	20 4/8	5 2/8	5 2/8	5	5	Kandiyohi Co., MN	Eric R. Strand	Eric R. Strand	1998	729
162 6/8	26 2/8	25 4/8	21	5 2/8	5 3/8	5	6	Crawford Co., WI	Wayne C. Martin	Wayne C. Martin	1999	729
162 6/8	25 1/8	25 5/8	16 4/8	4 5/8	4 4/8	8	7	Penobscot Co., ME	Phil McTigue	Phil McTigue	1999	729
162 5/8	23 6/8	24 7/8	20	4 6/8	4 5/8	6	5	Suffolk Co., NY	Robert A. Catalano	Robert A. Catalano	1997	734
162 5/8	25 4/8	26 3/8	19 6/8	4 6/8	4 5/8	6	5	Rice Co., KS	James R. Henderson	James R. Henderson	1997	734
162 5/8	23 1/8	23	18 1/8	4 3/8	4 4/8	5	4	Harper Co., OK	Larry A. Beatty	Larry A. Beatty	1998	734
162 5/8	26 4/8	26	19 5/8	6 2/8	6 5/8	4	4	Marion Co., KY	Jody E. Yates	Jody E. Yates	1998	734
162 5/8	25 5/8	23 5/8	23 1/8	4 3/8	4 4/8	5	5	Kiskatinaw River, BC	Dan Hachey	Dan Hachey	1999	734
162 4/8	27	26 4/8	18	4 1/8	4 1/8	6	6	Fillmore Co., MN	Todd R. Johnson	Todd R. Johnson	1999	739
162 3/8	24 4/8	24 3/8	15 5/8	4 4/8	4 5/8	6	6	Wood Co., WI	Aldro M. Johnson	Jim Johnson	1945	740
162 3/8	26 6/8	27 2/8	19	4 1/8	4 2/8	6	5	Hillsborough Co., NH	Gary A. Sullivan	Gary A. Sullivan	1973	740
162 3/8	25 5/8	24 3/8	19 3/8	5	4 6/8	5	6	Dane Co., WI	Ronald E. Goodrich	Ronald E. Goodrich	1997	740
162 3/8	24	24 7/8	17 2/8	4 2/8	4 2/8	4	6	Oakland Co., MI	Matthew A. Jameson	Matthew A. Jameson	1997	740
162 3/8	27 1/8	26 1/8	21	5 2/8	5 3/8	6	6	George Lake, AB	Shannon D. Kuzik	Shannon D. Kuzik	1998	740
162 3/8	24 7/8	23 5/8	21 1/8	5 2/8	5 2/8	6	6	Christian Co., KY	John W. Blankenship	John W. Blankenship	1999	740
162 2/8	26 5/8	25 4/8	19 6/8	4	4	5	6	Jackson Co., WI	Wallace Crober	John E. Hendrickson	1955	746
162 2/8	25	24 4/8	18 1/8	4 7/8	4 7/8	6	7	Wadena Co., MN	James K. Mell	James K. Mell	1997	746
162 2/8	30	28 7/8	23 5/8	4 3/8	4 6/8	5	6	Geauga Co., OH	Anthony J. Misseri	Anthony J. Misseri	1997	746
162 2/8	23 2/8	22 4/8	18 4/8	4 5/8	4 6/8	6	6	Peace River, AB	Thomas E. Baine	Thomas E. Baine	1998	746
162 2/8	25 3/8	25 6/8	18 5/8	5 2/8	5 1/8	5	5	Grant Co., WI	David A. Berther	David A. Berther	1998	746
162 2/8	27 2/8	27 6/8	18 6/8	5 4/8	5 4/8	6	6	Penobscot Co., ME	David Willey	David Willey	1998	746
162 2/8	23 5/8	22 2/8	20	5 2/8	5 1/8	6	6	Guthrie Co., IA	James J. Cowan	James J. Cowan	1999	746
162 1/8	24 4/8	24 3/8	17 5/8	4 7/8	4 6/8	5	7	Rusk Co., WI	Richard T. Cowan	Richard T. Cowan	1997	753
162 1/8	22 2/8	19 5/8	18 3/8	3 7/8	3 7/8	6	7	Clark Co., AR	Terry B. Kinser	Terry B. Kinser	1998	753
162 1/8	25 1/8	25	19 2/8	4 3/8	4 3/8	6	6	Bayfield Co., WI	Kevin S. Mytko	Kevin S. Mytko	1998	753
162 1/8	25	24	18 1/8	4 4/8	4 3/8	8	8	Callaway Co., MO	Thomas L. Wekenborg	Thomas L. Wekenborg	1999	753
162	25 1/8	25 4/8	19 4/8	4 4/8	4 4/8	5	6	Rainy Lake, ON	Rick Johnson	Rick Johnson	1990	757
162	27 5/8	26 4/8	22 2/8	5 3/8	5 4/8	4	4	Calhoun Co., MI	George Satterfield	George Satterfield	1995	757
162	26 1/8	26 1/8	23 5/8	5 2/8	5 3/8	7	7	Beckham Co., OK	John B. Bullard	John B. Bullard	1997	757
162	26 7/8	27	20 6/8	5 3/8	5 2/8	5	5	Coahoma Co., MS	Duncan F. Williams	Duncan F. Williams	1997	757
162	24 5/8	24 2/8	19 5/8	5 4/8	5 4/8	6	6	Pierceland, SK	Frank J. Fatti, Sr.	Frank J. Fatti, Sr.	1998	757
162	24	24 1/8	18 4/8	4 4/8	4 5/8	6	5	Brown Co., KS	Ronnie W. Gossett	Ronnie W. Gossett	1998	757
162	25 2/8	24 7/8	17 2/8	4 3/8	4 2/8	6	6	Henderson Co., KY	Alan C. Taylor	Alan C. Taylor	1998	757
162	24 7/8	23 6/8	16 6/8	4 6/8	4 5/8	6	5	Clayton Co., IA	Michael A. Bries	Michael A. Bries	1999	757
161 7/8	24	23 6/8	18 5/8	3 7/8	4	5	5	Terrell Co., TX	S. Randall Hearne	S. Randall Hearne	1997	765
161 7/8	27 4/8	27 1/8	19 1/8	4 2/8	4 2/8	6	6	Webster Co., MO	Jack J. Hubbell	Jack J. Hubbell	1997	765
161 7/8	23 2/8	22 2/8	20 1/8	4 4/8	4 4/8	5	5	Salem Co., NJ	Don R. D'Antonio	Don R. D'Antonio	1998	765
161 6/8	28 2/8	27 3/8	18 4/8	4 1/8	4 2/8	5	5	Shawano Co., WI	Todd W. Davis	Todd W. Davis	1999	768
161 6/8	25 6/8	23 2/8	22 1/8	5	5	5	6	Hancock Co., ME	Daniel D. Pert	Daniel D. Pert	1999	768

WHITETAIL DEER - TYPICAL ANTLERS

Odocoileus virginianus virginianus and certain related subspecies

Score	Length of Main Beam R.	L.	Inside Spread	Circumference at Smallest Place Between Burr and First Point R.	L.	Number of Points R.	L.	Locality	Hunter	Owner	Date Killed	Rank
161 6/8	24	23 7/8	16	4 3/8	4 4/8	7	6	King Co., TX	Mike Stewart	Mike Stewart	1999	768
161 5/8	24 4/8	25 1/8	19 1/8	4 6/8	4 5/8	5	5	Jackson Co., IA	Robert R. Gross	Robert R. Gross	1995	771
161 5/8	26 2/8	26 5/8	21	5 2/8	5 2/8	7	5	Todd Co., KY	Brian P. Stratton	Brian P. Stratton	1996	771
161 5/8	26 5/8	26 7/8	20 1/8	4 5/8	4 6/8	6	8	Woodward Co., OK	Gregory K. Crouse	Gregory K. Crouse	1997	771
161 5/8	27 1/8	24 7/8	16 7/8	4 3/8	4 6/8	8	5	Warren Co., MO	Nathan T. Maune	Nathan T. Maune	1997	771
161 5/8	26 4/8	28 2/8	19 4/8	5 2/8	5	4	6	Platte Co., MO	Kelly C. Thompson	Kelly C. Thompson	1997	771
161 5/8	25 2/8	25 3/8	19 1/8	4 5/8	4 4/8	5	5	Randolph Co., MO	Dennis M. Hodgson	Dennis M. Hodgson	1998	771
161 5/8	25 4/8	25 3/8	18 7/8	4 3/8	4 5/8	5	6	Bayfield Co., WI	Donald R. Lahti	Donald R. Lahti	1998	771
161 5/8	23 4/8	22 5/8	19 1/8	5 1/8	5 2/8	5	7	Washington Co., NE	Aaron T. Rosholm	Aaron T. Rosholm	1998	771
161 4/8	25 4/8	25 4/8	17 4/8	5	5	5	5	Price Co., WI	Fred J. Wisnewski	Fred J. Wisnewski	1955	779
161 4/8	26 6/8	26	18 5/8	4 1/8	4	6	6	Callaway Co., MO	Michael J. Bernskoetter	Michael J. Bernskoetter	1996	779
161 4/8	26 2/8	26 1/8	19	5	4 7/8	5	5	Callaway Co., MO	Tad R. Smith	Tad R. Smith	1997	779
161 4/8	26 3/8	27 1/8	21 3/8	4 4/8	4 4/8	6	7	Worth Co., MO	Paul D. Watson	Paul D. Watson	1997	779
161 4/8	24 4/8	26	17 6/8	4 5/8	4 4/8	7	6	Waupaca Co., WI	Anthony J. Burton	Anthony J. Burton	1998	779
161 4/8	26 5/8	27	17 3/8	4 6/8	4 6/8	10	6	Oconto Co., WI	Richard L. Rosio	Richard L. Rosio	1998	779
161 4/8	24 5/8	25	20 2/8	4 4/8	4 5/8	5	5	Washtenaw Co., MI	Gordon E. Berenson	Gordon E. Berenson	1999	779
161 4/8	25	24 6/8	17 4/8	4 7/8	4 7/8	5	7	Dawson Co., MT	Picked Up	Gregory R. Stroh	2000	779
161 3/8	24 4/8	23 4/8	20 7/8	4 5/8	4 3/8	5	5	Idaho Co., ID	Douglas Lamm	Douglas Lamm	1978	787
161 3/8	26 5/8	26	21 3/8	4	4	5	5	Campbell Co., VA	Julian A. McFaden III	Cynthia McFaden	1992	787
161 3/8	27 2/8	28 2/8	17 7/8	5 2/8	5	7	7	Lake Co., MN	Jacob Ahonen	Jacob Ahonen	1997	787
161 3/8	25 3/8	25	16 4/8	4 4/8	4 4/8	5	6	Lowndes Co., GA	Picked Up	John Reed, Jr.	1997	787
161 3/8	28 6/8	30 6/8	20 5/8	5	5	4	4	Ross Co., OH	John P. Blesedell III	John P. Blesedell III	1998	787
161 3/8	25	25	16 7/8	5 2/8	5 2/8	6	7	McHenry Co., IL	Timothy L. Harkness	Timothy L. Harkness	1998	787
161 3/8	24 5/8	25 1/8	17 5/8	4 6/8	4 7/8	7	6	Lancaster Co., NE	Fred P. Matulka	Fred P. Matulka	1998	787
161 3/8	26 4/8	26	18 7/8	4 7/8	4 5/8	4	5	Ohio Co., KY	Bruce A. Russell	Bruce A. Russell	1999	787
161 3/8	26 2/8	26 2/8	18 5/8	5 1/8	5	6	5	Herkimer Co., NY	Jerry Selbach	Jerry Selbach	1999	787
161 3/8	25 2/8	25 4/8	17 7/8	5	4 7/8	5	5	Marion Co., KY	Delayne Smothers	Delayne Smothers	1999	787
161 2/8	24	24	18 6/8	5	5 1/8	5	5	Carroll Co., MO	James E. Parker	James E. Parker	1993	797
161 2/8	24 6/8	25	18 2/8	4 6/8	4 5/8	5	5	La Salle Co., IL	Thomas L. Sroka	Thomas L. Sroka	1996	797
161 2/8	24 6/8	23 5/8	18 1/8	4 3/8	4 4/8	8	5	Louisa Co., IA	Jeffrey D. McKinney	Jeffrey D. McKinney	1997	797
161 2/8	25 7/8	27 5/8	22 6/8	5 3/8	5 2/8	5	5	Comanche Co., KS	Marvin R. Schwein	Marvin R. Schwein	1999	797
161 2/8	22 3/8	21	18 2/8	4 5/8	4 7/8	4	4	Langlade Co., WI	Timothy A. Zahurones	Timothy A. Zahurones	1999	797
161 2/8	25	26 5/8	17 4/8	5 1/8	4 7/8	7	7	Williamson Co., TN	James R. Brown	James R. Brown	2000	797
161 1/8	27 1/8	26 3/8	26 3/8	4 3/8	4 4/8	6	5	Maverick Co., TX	D.L. Doyle	Pat Doyle	1952	803

Score								Locality	Hunter	Owner	Date	Rank
161 1/8	23 2/8	23 2/8	16 5/8	4 7/8	4 6/8	9	7	Coahoma Co., MS	Terry L. Dulaney	Terry L. Dulaney	1984	803
161 1/8	26 7/8	26	21	4 6/8	4 6/8	6	7	Pennington Co., MN	Eric Hoven	Eric Hoven	1991	803
161 1/8	26 4/8	26 5/8	20	5 2/8	5 4/8	9	6	Iron Co., WI	Bryan L. Bellows	Bryan L. Bellows	1995	803
161 1/8	24 6/8	24 6/8	18 3/8	4 7/8	4 6/8	6	5	Monroe Co., NY	Dane R. Edwards	Dane R. Edwards	1999	803
161 1/8	26 3/8	26 6/8	18 5/8	4 4/8	4 1/8	6	6	Parker Co., TX	Donald C. Stanley	Donald C. Stanley	1999	803
161	25 6/8	27 1/8	21 4/8	5 2/8	5 2/8	6	5	Dominion Lake, QC	Francois Brunet	Francois Brunet	1987	809
161	25 7/8	25	15 6/8	5	5 3/8	5	5	Sullivan Co., MO	Monty W. Gordon	Monty W. Gordon	1998	809
161	26 4/8	25 6/8	19 7/8	4 7/8	5	6	5	Louisa Co., IA	David W. Hotz	David W. Hotz	1998	809
161	26 7/8	26 3/8	17 4/8	4 6/8	4 5/8	5	5	St. Croix Co., WI	Mark H. Johnson	Mark H. Johnson	1998	809
161	23 4/8	24 4/8	20 6/8	4 5/8	4 7/8	5	5	Waldo Co., ME	Kenneth E. Bailey	Kenneth E. Bailey	1999	809
161	21 4/8	22 2/8	17 5/8	4 7/8	5	6	6	Piscataquis Co., ME	Randy J. Butterfield	Randy J. Butterfield	1999	809
160 7/8	25 1/8	27 7/8	18 1/8	5	5 1/8	5	5	Clearwater Co., MN	John Veit	Thomas R. Forbes	PR 1905	815
160 7/8	25 4/8	24 4/8	17 1/8	4 4/8	4 5/8	5	5	Natchitoches Parish, LA	Amos R. Bradley	Amos R. Bradley	1998	815
160 7/8	23	23 2/8	17 3/8	5 1/8	5 1/8	5	6	Porter Co., IN	Timothy J. Mocabee	Timothy J. Mocabee	1998	815
160 6/8	24 3/8	24 7/8	17 4/8	4 5/8	4 6/8	6	6	Orange Co., IN	Dwight C. Beaty	Dwight C. Beaty	1995	818
160 6/8	24 6/8	24 6/8	21 2/8	5	5	5	5	Knox Co., MO	James A. Baker	James A. Baker	1997	818
160 6/8	24 2/8	25 2/8	21 5/8	4 6/8	4 6/8	6	6	Dooly Co., GA	Jarrod Brannen	Jarrod Brannen	1997	818
160 6/8	25 3/8	25 4/8	19 2/8	4	4	6	6	Chippewa Co., WI	Richard Hunziker	Richard Hunziker	1998	818
160 6/8	22 2/8	24	22 2/8	5 1/8	5 1/8	5	5	Marshall Co., IL	Aron W. Shofner	Aron W. Shofner	1998	818
160 6/8	25 1/8	25 1/8	21 6/8	6 3/8	6 3/8	4	4	Sussex Co., DE	Richard A. Davis	Richard A. Davis	1999	818
160 5/8	24	24 2/8	18 7/8	4 7/8	4 7/8	7	7	Texas	Unknown	Buckhorn Mus. & Saloon, Ltd.	PR 1956	824
160 5/8	23 5/8	22 2/8	23 1/8	3 6/8	4	5	5	Harlan Co., NE	Wesley K. Mason	Wesley K. Mason	1997	824
160 5/8	25	24 7/8	19	5	5	7	5	Bienville Parish, LA	William J. Mooney	William J. Mooney	1998	824
160 5/8	24 7/8	24 7/8	17 1/8	4 7/8	5	5	5	Torch River, SK	Wes Shahan	Wes Shahan	1998	824
160 4/8	28 2/8	27 6/8	20 6/8	4 5/8	4 7/8	5	5	Jackson Co., WI	Clarence R. Rezin	Vivian Rezin	1945	828
160 4/8	25 6/8	26 3/8	25	5	4 6/8	8	8	Webb Co., TX	Melvin Huth	F. Gus Reinarz	PR 1959	828
160 4/8	24 5/8	24 3/8	18 4/8	4 3/8	4 3/8	5	5	Okanogan Co., WA	Michael D. Treadwell	Michael D. Treadwell	1996	828
160 4/8	24 2/8	25	20 3/8	4 5/8	4 4/8	6	5	Athens Co., OH	T. Jeff Daugherty	T. Jeff Daugherty	1997	828
160 4/8	25 3/8	23 6/8	18 5/8	5 1/8	5	7	5	Porter Co., IN	Donald M. Dolph	Donald M. Dolph	1997	828
160 4/8	25 5/8	26	20 4/8	4 6/8	4 5/8	5	5	Dooly Co., GA	Joe V. Fraser	Joe V. Fraser	1997	828
160 4/8	25	25 4/8	19 3/8	4 3/8	4 4/8	6	6	Chariton Co., MO	Rodney J. Gladbach	Rodney J. Gladbach	1997	828
160 4/8	25 1/8	24 1/8	18 3/8	4	4	6	5	Rockcastle Co., KY	Lonnie G. Brumett	Lonnie G. Brumett	1998	828
160 4/8	25 6/8	26	18 2/8	4 6/8	4 6/8	7	7	Shelby Co., TN	Ben L. Daniel	Ben L. Daniel	1998	828
160 4/8	24 4/8	25	20 2/8	4 4/8	4 4/8	5	6	Dimmit Co., TX	Stuart W. Stedman	Stuart W. Stedman	1998	828
160 4/8	23 5/8	23 3/8	18	5	5	5	5	Dawson Creek, BC	Craig Bahm	Craig Bahm	1999	828
160 3/8	23 7/8	24 2/8	19 2/8	5 3/8	5 4/8	6	6	Warren Co., IA	David L. Schaffer	David L. Schaffer	1999	828
160 3/8	23 4/8	23	15 5/8	4 2/8	4 1/8	5	5	Manitowoc Co., WI	Wayne J. Blaha	Wayne J. Blaha	1997	840
160 3/8	27 4/8	26	19 6/8	5	5 1/8	5	5	Vermilion Co., IL	John E. Hubbard	John E. Hubbard	1997	840
160 3/8	22	21 2/8	18 1/8	3 7/8	4 2/8	6	6	Mille Lacs Co., MN	Scott J. Schmit	Scott J. Schmit	1997	840
160 3/8	26 2/8	25 5/8	22 7/8	5 2/8	5 2/8	4	4	Fayette Co., OH	Matthew S. Buell	Matthew S. Buell	1998	840
160 3/8	24 5/8	24 4/8	18 3/8	5	5 1/8	5	5	Catahoula Parish, LA	Julius L. Lovasz	Julius L. Lovasz	1998	840
160 3/8	23 5/8	23 7/8	17 5/8	4 2/8	4 2/8	5	5	Ralls Co., MO	John E. Robinson	John E. Robinson	1998	840

WHITETAIL DEER - TYPICAL ANTLERS

Odocoileus virginianus virginianus and certain related subspecies

Score	Length of Main Beam R.	L.	Inside Spread	Circumference at Smallest Place Between Burr and First Point R.	L.	Number of Points R.	L.	Locality	Hunter	Owner	Date Killed	Rank
160 3/8	25 7/8	21 1/8	18 5/8	4 7/8	5	6	5	Washburn Co., WI	Larry R. Melton	Larry R. Melton	1999	840
160 3/8	27 2/8	27 4/8	20 5/8	4 7/8	4 7/8	5	5	Oneida Co., NY	Charles E. Roberts	Charles E. Roberts	1999	840
160 3/8	24 5/8	27 5/8	17 3/8	4 2/8	4 2/8	5	6	Lincoln Co., ME	Picked Up	David Teele	1999	840
160 2/8	24 5/8	25 5/8	18 4/8	5 6/8	5 5/8	4	4	Penobscot Co., ME	Peter K. Smith	Peter K. Smith	1997	849
160 2/8	24 6/8	26	17 6/8	4 7/8	4 6/8	5	5	Outagamie Co., WI	Matthew R. Heimann	Matthew R. Heimann	1998	849
160 2/8	27 1/8	26 5/8	19	5	5	5	5	Hillsdale Co., MI	Jeffrey D. Gier	Jeffrey D. Gier	1999	849
160 2/8	25 4/8	27	19 1/8	4 4/8	4 4/8	7	6	Outagamie Co., Wi	Jason Mathis	Jason Mathis	1999	849
160 2/8	22 5/8	22 5/8	16 6/8	4 7/8	4 7/8	5	5	Swan River, MB	Ronald D. McMahan	Ronald D. McMahan	1999	849
160 2/8	24	25 4/8	16 6/8	5 2/8	5 3/8	6	7	Daviess Co., MO	Larry J. Pagel	Larry J. Pagel	1999	849
160 2/8	27	24 4/8	18 4/8	3 5/8	4	5	5	Polk Co., WI	Jack B. Wilson	Jack B. Wilson	1999	849
160 1/8	28 4/8	27 3/8	16 5/8	4 6/8	4 5/8	5	5	Calhoun Co., GA	Alan Lee	Alan Lee	1979	856
160 1/8	24 1/8	25 3/8	19	4 2/8	4 2/8	7	5	Switzerland Co., IN	Joseph W. Bacon	Joseph W. Bacon	1997	856
160 1/8	26 1/8	26 7/8	17 3/8	4 2/8	4 2/8	5	5	Brooks Co., GA	Carl L. Doane, Jr.	Carl L. Doane, Jr.	1997	856
160 1/8	22 7/8	23 5/8	18	4 4/8	4 4/8	6	5	Latimer Co., OK	Johnny M. Freeman	Johnny M. Freeman	1997	856
160 1/8	23 6/8	25 4/8	22 7/8	3 7/8	4	5	5	Allamakee Co., IA	Chris Schoh	Chris Schoh	1997	856
160 1/8	23	23 1/8	19 5/8	5	5	5	6	Esson, AB	Peter M. Konopacky	Peter M. Konopacky	1998	856
160 1/8	23 7/8	23 5/8	18 3/8	5 2/8	5 3/8	5	6	Dubuque Co., IA	Stephen M. Seipp	Stephen M. Seipp	1998	856
160 1/8	23 4/8	23 4/8	16 7/8	4 3/8	4 3/8	6	6	Koochiching Co., MN	Robert W. Barnes	Robert W. Barnes	1999	856
160 1/8	25 5/8	24 3/8	20 3/8	4 4/8	4 6/8	5	5	Rawlins Co., KS	James Brennan	James Brennan	1999	856
160 1/8	25	26 2/8	22 4/8	6 1/8	6	7	6	Schuyler Co., IL	Michael S. Helsley, Jr.	Michael S. Helsley, Jr.	1999	856
160 1/8	23 2/8	23	18 6/8	5 4/8	5 2/8	7	7	Champaign Co., IL	Matthew M. Pacunas	Matthew M. Pacunas	1999	856
160 1/8	27 3/8	28 6/8	20 3/8	5 3/8	5 3/8	4	5	Rockingham Co., NH	Picked Up	Tod Rinfret	1999	856
160 1/8	27	26 5/8	21 5/8	4 6/8	4 6/8	5	5	Calumet Co., WI	David E. Schaefer	David E. Schaefer	1999	856
160	25 7/8	24	20 5/8	3 7/8	4 1/8	6	6	Goliad Co., TX	Michael V. Stewart	Michael V. Stewart	1964	869
160	24 6/8	24 3/8	19 6/8	4 3/8	4 4/8	6	6	Roosevelt Co., MT	Kurt D. Rued	Kurt D. Rued	1983	869
160	28	27 2/8	20 3/8	4 4/8	4 4/8	6	4	Charles Co., MD	David A. Anderson	David A. Anderson	1997	869
160	25 6/8	24 6/8	21 6/8	4 2/8	4 3/8	5	5	Geauga Co., OH	Monte H. Curtis	Monte H. Curtis	1997	869
160	26 3/8	26 3/8	18 2/8	4 7/8	5	7	7	Noble Co., OH	Mark A. Hudak	Mark A. Hudak	1997	869
160	21 2/8	22 1/8	19 6/8	4 4/8	4 4/8	7	10	Oldham Co., KY	James W. Lunsford	James W. Lunsford	1997	869
160	24 2/8	23 7/8	19 5/8	5	4 4/8	8	6	Outagamie Co., WI	Kevin L. Lohrenz	Kevin L. Lohrenz	1998	869
160	24 4/8	25 2/8	15 4/8	6 4/8	6 4/8	6	7	Oldham Co., KY	Richard D. Mangum	Richard D. Mangum	1998	869
160	28	27 2/8	20 3/8	4 2/8	4 2/8	6	7	Lafayette Co., WI	Eric J. Straehl	Eric J. Straehl	1998	869
160	25 3/8	26 2/8	21	5 2/8	5 2/8	6	5	Carroll Co., NH	Joe Nye	Joe Nye	1999	869
160	25 1/8	25 2/8	20 2/8	5	5 1/8	5	6	Defiance Co., OH	Ellis M. Reynolds	Ellis M. Reynolds	1999	869

								Locality	Hunter	Owner	Date
198 7/8*	24 6/8	25 3/8	18 1/8	5	5	6	6	Moose Mountain Lake, SK	Mark Hordeski	Mark Hordeski	1999
195 6/8*	26 2/8	26 4/8	20	5	4 6/8	6	6	Good Spirit Lake, SK	Carl L. Sawchuk, Sr.	Carl A. Sawchuk, Jr.	1954

* Final score subject to revision by additional verifying measurements.

WHITETAIL DEER - NON-TYPICAL ANTLERS

Odocoileus virginianus virginianus and certain related subspecies

Minimum Score 185   World's Record 333 7/8

Score	Length of Main Beam R.	L.	Inside Spread	Circumference at Smallest Place Between Burr and First Point R.	L.	Number of Points R.	L.	Locality	Hunter	Owner	Date Killed	Rank
266 1/8	26 6/8	27	20 4/8	6 4/8	7 1/8	17	16	Pike Co., MO	Randy J. Simonitch	Randy J. Simonitch	2000	1
259	16 2/8	15 3/8	15 6/8	5 4/8	5 3/8	16	11	Frio Co., TX	William B. Brown	Bettie B. Brown	PR 1967	2
257 1/8	29 4/8	27 4/8	23 2/8	6 2/8	5 6/8	20	14	Marion Co., KS	Jamie L. Remmers	Bass Pro Shops F. & W. Mus.	1997	3
254 3/8	23 3/8	24 2/8	20	4 3/8	4 4/8	13	13	McHenry Co., ND	Austin Dugan	James K. Dugan	1940	4
251 4/8	27 3/8	22 1/8	19 3/8	6 6/8	6 5/8	15	14	Hendricks Co., IN	Timothy J. Goode	Bass Pro Shops F. & W. Mus.	1980	5
248 4/8	26 1/8	26 3/8	22 3/8	5 5/8	6	12	14	Wellwood, MB	Paul A. Adriaansen	Paul A. Adriaansen	1999	6
248 1/8	27 5/8	28 3/8	20 2/8	7 7/8	7 2/8	14	12	Crawford Co., KS	Bruce Jameson	Bass Pro Shops F. & W. Mus.	1989	7
247 3/8	23 5/8	24 7/8	24 6/8	5 3/8	5 1/8	12	13	Vernon Co., WI	Arnold N. Stalsberg	Arnold N. Stalsberg	1998	8
245 7/8	28 2/8	26 6/8	18 5/8	6 2/8	6 4/8	13	15	Kankakee Co., IL	Lawrence G. Ekhoff	Lawrence G. Ekhoff	1999	9
245 5/8	28	25 7/8	18 4/8	4 6/8	4 7/8	17	16	Marshall Co., IA	Don L. Boucher	Don L. Boucher	1996	10
244	28 7/8	28 3/8	20 1/8	7	6 4/8	15	11	Morris Co., KS	Burt Nichols	Brad Sowter	1997	11
240 3/8	28 7/8	28 2/8	20 4/8	5	5	13	13	Pine Lake, AB	Edwin R. Pick	Edwin R. Pick	1997	12
239 4/8	26 1/8	25 7/8	19 6/8	6 5/8	6 5/8	13	12	Glasyn, SK	Mark Schumlick	Mark Schumlick	1997	13
239 4/8	26 6/8	25 1/8	19 4/8	5 1/8	5	13	13	Kleberg Co., TX	Adan Alvarez	Adan Alvarez	1998	13
239 2/8	25 5/8	26 4/8	22 4/8	7 1/8	6 6/8	13	9	Prowers Co., CO	Scott M. Tenold	Scott M. Tenold	1997	15
239	25 3/8	25 1/8	17	5 3/8	5 6/8	16	12	Pawnee Co., NE	Danny C. Boliver	Danny C. Boliver	1996	16
238 6/8	25 4/8	18 6/8	21	6 5/8	6 3/8	13	15	Schuyler Co., IL	Kenneth B. Robertson	Kenneth B. Robertson	1997	17
238 3/8	24 2/8	23 2/8	13 2/8	6	5 6/8	12	15	Prairie Co., AR	William Dooley	William Dooley	1999	18
238 1/8	31	28 4/8	21	6 1/8	5 7/8	10	17	Lewis Co., KY	Tom D. Fetters, Sr.	Tom D. Fetters, Sr.	1998	19
237 3/8	27 3/8	28 3/8	23 2/8	6 2/8	6 3/8	14	11	Wayne Co., IA	Picked Up	Brad Sowter	1998	20
237 3/8	25	24 7/8	17 6/8	5 6/8	5 1/8	17	15	Delaware Co., OK	Charles A. Tullis	Charles A. Tullis	1998	20
237 3/8	24 7/8	24 6/8	16 3/8	5 1/8	5 1/8	13	10	Monroe Co., IA	Larry V. Zach	Larry V. Zach	2000	20
236 5/8	26	26 3/8	21 4/8	6	6 1/8	12	14	Pope Co., MN	Douglas D. Vesledahl	Douglas D. Vesledahl	1961	23
236 3/8	25 6/8	25 6/8	18 4/8	5 6/8	5 6/8	9	13	Bayfield Co., WI	Unknown	Jean B. Schultz	1998	24
235 5/8	30 7/8	29 7/8	21 4/8	5 4/8	5 7/8	17	13	Nemaha Co., KS	Picked Up	James R. Matlock	PR 1998	25
235	25 5/8	24 3/8	22 2/8	4 7/8	4 7/8	13	14	Daviess Co., MO	Justin K. Moore	Justin K. Moore	1997	26
234 7/8	27 3/8	29 2/8	20 7/8	5 3/8	5 7/8	8	13	Coffey Co., KS	Danny L. Hawkins	Danny L. Hawkins	1999	27
234 1/8	29 6/8	29 2/8	19 7/8	4 7/8	4 6/8	13	10	Lewis Co., KY	Joey Smith	Joey Smith	1997	28
233 7/8	27 6/8	30 1/8	21 4/8	5 6/8	5 6/8	10	13	Blueberry Mt., AB	William Shumaker	William Shumaker	1994	29
232 5/8	23 7/8	24 1/8	18 2/8	7 2/8	6	12	13	Fulton Co., IL	Carl B. Brown	Carl B. Brown	1997	30
231 5/8	26 1/8	26	20 3/8	5 4/8	5 2/8	16	11	Wayne Co., WV	Charles I. McLaughlin	D.J. Hollinger & B. Howard	1997	31
231 5/8	26 6/8	27 5/8	23	6 1/8	6 1/8	10	9	Battle River, SK	Kevin Rowswell	Kevin Rowswell	1998	31
231 2/8	25	25 2/8	17 5/8	8 1/8	5 7/8	21	12	Muscogee Co., GA	Blakely H. Voltz	Blakely H. Voltz	1997	33
228 7/8	28 1/8	27 4/8	22 5/8	5 7/8	5 6/8	13	11	W. Feliciana Parish, LA	Tommy Rice	Tommy Rice	1998	34

Score	R. Main Beam	L. Main Beam	Inside Spread	R. Circ.	L. Circ.	R. Pts.	L. Pts.	Locality	Hunter	Owner	Date	Rank
228 4/8	26 7/8	26 2/8	19 1/8	6	5 3/8	12	11	Person Co., NC	Don C. Rockett	Don C. Rockett	1998	35
228	20	20	22 1/8	4 5/8	4 6/8	17	12	Hunt Co., TX	Tom Cole	Tom Cole	1997	36
228	23 2/8	23 3/8	18 1/8	5 5/8	5 6/8	13	12	Las Animas Co., CO	Brad C. Hardin	Brad C. Hardin	1998	36
227 1/8	22	23 4/8	19	6	5 1/8	15	13	Dunn Co., WI	David D. Dewey	David D. Dewey	1999	38
226 5/8	26 5/8	26	18 7/8	6 1/8	6	15	12	Shell Lake, SK	Marcel Proulx	DJ. Hollinger & B. Howard	1984	39
226 5/8	29	28 4/8	18 1/8	5 3/8	5 2/8	13	13	Licking Co., OH	John S. Blythe	John S. Blythe	1999	39
226 2/8	27 7/8	28 3/8	19 6/8	5 3/8	5 2/8	11	13	Fulton Co., IL	Picked Up	David L. Lidwell	1996	41
225 4/8	23 7/8	23 5/8	19 4/8	6 5/8	7	10	18	Greene Co., OH	Alan J. Meade	Alan J. Meade	1999	42
225 1/8	28 3/8	28 1/8	20 2/8	6	6	8	9	Winona Co., MN	Jeffrey S. Wilder	Jeffrey S. Wilder	1977	43
225 1/8	27	26 1/8	18 4/8	5 2/8	5 6/8	11	14	Holmes Co., OH	Chris G. Hider	Chris G. Hider	1998	43
224 5/8	25 7/8	27 4/8	19 3/8	5 2/8	5 2/8	10	8	Mercer Co., IL	Roger R. Roy	Roger R. Roy	1999	45
223 6/8	24	26 4/8	18 5/8	5	5 2/8	11	11	Jasper Co., IA	Picked Up	Bruce A. Sanburn	1997	46
223 5/8	26 2/8	26 3/8	19 6/8	5 1/8	5 1/8	12	11	St. Francis Co., AR	Tony Gore	Tony Gore	1999	47
223 4/8	25 5/8	26 3/8	20 1/8	5 5/8	6	16	16	Dickenson Co., VA	Picked Up	James A. Cox	1998	48
223	28 1/8	27 5/8	20 1/8	5 5/8	5 6/8	11	11	Jefferson Co., IN	Sam O. Leverett, Jr.	Sam O. Leverett, Jr.	1997	49
222 7/8	29 7/8	30 1/8	21 4/8	5	5	15	9	Morgan Co., KY	Denzil C. Potter	Denzil C. Potter	1999	50
222 5/8	24 5/8	24 2/8	20 7/8	5 6/8	5 4/8	10	10	Clark Co., IL	David E. Morris	David E. Morris	1997	51
222 4/8	25	25 2/8	25 2/8	6 4/8	6 3/8	12	12	Barber Co., KS	Michel M. Letourneau	Michel M. Letourneau	1999	52
222 3/8	28 1/8	27	18 4/8	6 6/8	6 3/8	12	11	Pickaway Co., OH	C. Joseph Schneider	C. Joseph Schneider	1998	53
221 7/8	27 3/8	27 1/8	21	5 7/8	5 6/8	10	10	Jefferson Co., IA	Jared L. Rebling	Jared L. Rebling	2000	54
221 2/8	25 5/8	25 6/8	19 1/8	5 1/8	5 2/8	11	11	Muhlenberg Co., KY	Mark A. Smith	Mark A. Smith	1998	55
220 7/8	26 4/8	26 4/8	22 4/8	5 6/8	5 6/8	10	9	Trego Co., KS	John M. Benewiat	John M. Benewiat	1999	56
220 5/8	22 1/8	23 6/8	16 6/8	4 3/8	4 3/8	10	15	Halfway River, BC	Bill Miller	Deb Fleet	PR 1934	57
220 4/8	29 2/8	29 2/8	20 2/8	5 1/8	5 6/8	8	8	Knox Co., OH	Richard E. Boyd	Richard E. Boyd	1995	58
220 4/8	27 4/8	26 3/8	20 3/8	4 5/8	4 6/8	14	14	Chitek Lake, SK	Douglas Falone	Douglas Falone	1998	58
220 3/8	26 2/8	26 7/8	21	5 5/8	5 4/8	10	10	Oktibbeha Co., MS	Dean E. Jones	Dean E. Jones	1976	60
220 2/8	26 6/8	27 5/8	20 2/8	4 7/8	4 6/8	9	9	Lewis Co., ID	Steavon C. Hornbeck	Steavon C. Hornbeck	2000	61
220 1/8	23 6/8	23 3/8	18 4/8	5 2/8	5 2/8	17	12	Iroquois Co., IL	John P. Boshears	John P. Boshears	1998	62
220	30 3/8	28 6/8	17 4/8	6 6/8	6 4/8	8	15	Allen Co., KS	Merril R. Lamb	Merril R. Lamb	1999	63
219 3/8	26 7/8	26 2/8	18	6	6	9	6	Fulton Co., IL	Christipher W. Schweigert	Christipher W. Schweigert	1998	64
219 2/8	27 3/8	27 3/8	17	6 2/8	5 1/8	8	10	Hinds Co., MS	Matt M. Woods	Matt M. Woods	1998	65
219 1/8	27 6/8	27 6/8	18 7/8	5 1/8	5 3/8	15	9	Bell Co., KY	Jeff D. Jackson	Jeff D. Jackson	1999	66
219	24 1/8	24 6/8	21	5 2/8	4 6/8	11	10	Van Buren Co., IA	James E. Garrels	Wayne G. Nevar	1988	67
218 6/8	26	27 7/8	21 7/8	4 4/8	7 4/8	10	8	Cass Co., IL	Stanley E. Walker	Stanley E. Walker	1998	68
218 5/8	29 5/8	30	21 5/8	7 3/8	5	11	7	Kansas	Unknown	Larry D. Bollier	PR 1997	69
217 4/8	27 4/8	27 6/8	23 5/8	5	5 3/8	8	8	Bethune, SK	Ronald N. Riche	Ronald N. Riche	1998	70
217 1/8	27 3/8	27 5/8	21 1/8	5 3/8	6 2/8	13	13	Butler Co., KY	Merle Raymer	Merle Raymer	1999	71
216 7/8	25 4/8	25 7/8	21	5 5/8	5	11	11	Lee Co., IL	Clifford L. Walter	Clifford L. Walter	1997	72
216 3/8	29 2/8	28 1/8	17 5/8	5	4 6/8	8	8	Jersey Co., IL	Walter L. Baker	Walter L. Baker	1998	73
216 3/8	29 1/8	28 3/8	21 7/8	6 2/8	7 1/8	9	9	Christian Co., IL	John R. Reese	John R. Reese	1998	73
216 3/8	26 3/8	27 1/8	26 3/8	4 4/8	4 4/8	12	8	Woodbury Co., IA	Picked Up	Helen Peterson	1999	73
216 1/8	27	27 6/8	17 7/8	5 6/8	5 7/8	10	11	Stephenson Co., IL	Steven M. Knopes	Steven M. Knopes	1999	76
215 7/8	26 2/8	26 7/8	21 4/8	6	5 5/8	10	10	Eau Claire Co., WI	Dale G. Planert	Dale G. Planert	1997	77

WHITETAIL DEER - NON-TYPICAL ANTLERS

Odocoileus virginianus virginianus and certain related subspecies

Score	Length of Main Beam R.	L.	Inside Spread	Circumference at Smallest Place Between Burr and First Point R.	L.	Number of Points R.	L.	Locality	Hunter	Owner	Date Killed	Rank
215 6/8	28 1/8	28 1/8	26 2/8	6 6/8	6 1/8	10	9	Mayerthorpe, AB	Gary F. Jamieson	Gary F. Jamieson	1998	78
215 5/8	21 6/8	22	15	5 7/8	6 2/8	14	15	Medicine Hat, AB	Dave Moore	Dave Moore	1998	79
215 1/8	29 2/8	28 1/8	21 7/8	5 4/8	5 4/8	11	10	Rusagonis River, NB	Art Appleby	Art Appleby	1998	80
215	24 2/8	23 3/8	22 2/8	5 3/8	5 2/8	8	10	Caldwell Co., KY	C.J. Brummett	C.J. Brummett	1998	81
214 7/8	26 3/8	24 6/8	21 1/8	5 1/8	6 4/8	9	13	Cass Co., MN	Glen W. Slagle, Sr.	Glen W. Slagle, Sr.	1959	82
214 4/8	25 4/8	25 4/8	22 2/8	5	5	12	9	Clearwater Co., ID	Don L. Twito	Don L. Twito	1975	83
214 3/8	30 2/8	29	22 7/8	5	5 1/8	11	12	Washington Co., ME	E. Colson Fales	E. Colson Fales	1999	84
214	24 1/8	25 3/8	19	6 3/8	6	10	13	Madison Co., IA	Merle Allen	Merle Allen	1998	85
214	25 2/8	26 1/8	19	5	5 2/8	9	6	Hancock Co., IL	Steven Guedesse	Steven Guedesse	1999	85
213 7/8	29 7/8	28 6/8	20	6 5/8	6 2/8	11	9	Greene Co., IL	Adam T. Hoene	Adam T. Hoene	1999	87
213 1/8	30 1/8	28	23 5/8	4 6/8	4 6/8	10	7	Kimble Co., TX	Henry B. Allsup	Frederica Wyatt	1941	88
213 1/8	25 4/8	24 7/8	19	7 4/8	8 1/8	10	10	Schuyler Co., IL	Todd A. Ritchey	Todd A. Ritchey	1997	88
212 5/8	27 3/8	27 6/8	19 5/8	5 5/8	5 5/8	9	6	Greenwood Co., KS	Picked Up	B&C National Collection	1998	90
212 5/8	24 6/8	23 1/8	19 6/8	6 1/8	6 7/8	12	11	Marshall Co., IL	Picked Up	Carl H. Kimble	1998	90
212 4/8	23 1/8	23 4/8	19 6/8	4 7/8	4 6/8	10	8	Swan Lake, MB	William A. Riel	William A. Riel	1997	92
212 2/8	29 7/8	27 7/8	21 4/8	5 2/8	5	13	8	Lane Co., KS	Picked Up	R & A. Johnson	1994	93
212 2/8	26 1/8	26 3/8	25 7/8	5 7/8	5 7/8	9	10	Two Hills, AB	Wesley I. Nikiforuk	Wesley I. Nikiforuk	1999	93
212 1/8	26	25 7/8	21 4/8	6 1/8	5 7/8	12	11	Clinton Co., MI	Kenneth V. Montgomery	Kenneth V. Montgomery	1997	95
212	28 4/8	27 7/8	24 5/8	6	6 1/8	7	8	Big Stone Co., MN	Picked Up	Danny L. Cole	1993	96
212	23 5/8	23	14 5/8	6 3/8	5 6/8	11	14	Madison Co., MS	Richard W. Parker	Richard W. Parker	1999	96
211 6/8	26 4/8	26 5/8	18 3/8	5	5	10	8	Green Co., WI	Kevin W. Bouers	Kevin W. Bouers	1999	98
211 5/8	27 3/8	26 6/8	26 2/8	5 2/8	5 1/8	12	7	Adair Co., IA	Bob C. Garside	Bob C. Garside	1998	99
211 4/8	24 5/8	24 4/8	18 3/8	5 5/8	6 2/8	10	12	Washington Co., WI	LeRoy Neu	LeRoy Neu	1999	100
211 3/8	27 3/8	27 5/8	22 2/8	5 4/8	5 6/8	10	9	Scotland Co., MO	Gary L. Childress	Gary L. Childress	1998	101
211 2/8	24 6/8	26 2/8	18 6/8	4 7/8	4 7/8	9	7	Pigeon Lake, AB	Jeff Strandquist	Jeff Strandquist	1997	102
211 2/8	24 5/8	24 2/8	23	4 7/8	4 6/8	8	9	Wells Co., ND	Robert Newman	Robert Newman	1961	103
211 1/8	24 2/8	24 6/8	17 2/8	5 4/8	5 1/8	15	11	Houston Co., MN	Daniel P. Gade	Daniel P. Gade	1998	103
211 1/8	27 1/8	28 5/8	20 4/8	5 6/8	6 2/8	11	9	Grady Co., OK	Bon D. Lentz	Bon D. Lentz	1999	103
211 1/8	27 4/8	25 7/8	20 6/8	5 6/8	5 3/8	10	10	Dearborn Co., IN	Chad M. Hornberger	Chad M. Hornberger	1997	106
211	27 3/8	27 7/8	25	5 1/8	5 1/8	9	8	Christian Co., IL	Jeffrey Tumiati	Jeffrey Tumiati	1997	106
210 7/8	26 7/8	26	19 5/8	6 3/8	6 2/8	9	10	Lac La Biche, AB	Render L. Crowder, Sr.	Render L. Crowder, Sr.	1998	108
210 7/8	23 4/8	19 4/8	15 5/8	5 3/8	7 2/8	12	11	Winona Co., MN	Donald D. Zenk	Donald D. Zenk	1998	108
210 6/8	25 2/8	26 2/8	23 6/8	5 3/8	5 4/8	14	11	N. Saskatchewan River, SK	Brent La Clare	Brent La Clare	1998	110
210 4/8	31	29 2/8	21	6	5 5/8	10	11	Allegan Co., MI	Bruce A. Maurer	Bruce A. Maurer	1997	111

Score							Locality	Owner	Hunter	Date	Rank
210 3/8	24 3/8	16	4 7/8	5	9	9	Adams Co., IL	Unknown	Chuck House	1897	112
210 3/8	30 4/8	24 4/8	5 4/8	5 2/8	8	9	Calhoun Co., IL	Timothy A. Moore	Timothy A. Moore	1999	112
210 3/8	24	16 2/8	6	8 4/8	7	10	Morgan Co., IL	Frankie Wildhagen	Frankie Wildhagen	1999	112
210 1/8	24	20 2/8	6 1/8	5 4/8	8	9	Leoville, SK	Ray J. Guarisco	Ray J. Guarisco	1994	115
210 1/8	24 6/8	19	5 5/8	6 1/8	8	12	Lac La Biche, AB	Otis W. Cowles	Otis W. Cowles	1998	115
210 1/8	22 6/8	19 2/8	5 1/8	5 1/8	9	7	St. Paul, AB	Richard C. Nelson	Richard C. Nelson	1999	115
210	22	13 5/8	4 4/8	5 3/8	10	8	Jefferson Co., IA	Jared L. Rebling	Jared L. Rebling	1998	118
210	29 4/8	31	5 7/8	5 6/8	10	12	Kingman Co., KS	Picked Up	Odie Sudbeck	1998	118
209 7/8	25 7/8	21 1/8	5 4/8	5 4/8	12	8	Adams Co., IA	Gregory L. Andrews	Gregory L. Andrews	1998	120
209 7/8	24 6/8	18 2/8	4 6/8	4 4/8	11	13	Waupaca Co., WI	Ryan A. Thiel	Ryan A. Thiel	1999	120
209 6/8	23 4/8	15 5/8	5 6/8	5 6/8	9	14	Morton, MB	Charles C. Dixon	Charles C. Dixon	1996	122
209 6/8	25 6/8	17 7/8	5 1/8	5 1/8	8	7	Sullivan Co., MO	Curt E. Richardson	Curt E. Richardson	1997	122
209 5/8	23 3/8	18 2/8	4 1/8	4 2/8	10	14	Logan Co., IL	Clint M. Awe	Clint M. Awe	1997	124
209 5/8	24 4/8	21	5 2/8	5 1/8	10	10	Livingston Co., MI	Michel A. LaFountain	Michel A. LaFountain	2000	124
209 2/8	25 6/8	20 4/8	5 2/8	5 3/8	9	11	De Witt Co., IL	Ronald L. Willmore	Ronald L. Willmore	1997	126
209 1/8	26	28 5/8	5 4/8	5 5/8	8	6	N. Saskatchewan River, SK	Gerald Hamel	Gerald Hamel	1986	127
209 1/8	25 4/8	26	6	6	11	9	Prowers Co., CO	Paul D. Mirley	Paul D. Mirley	1997	127
209 1/8	24 1/8	17 3/8	5 7/8	5 7/8	9	17	Waupaca Co., WI	Vince Burns II	Vince Burns II	1999	127
209	24 6/8	17	6 1/8	6	12	6	Saskatchewan	Unknown	Aly M. Bruner	PR 1996	130
209	28 7/8	17 4/8	6 1/8	6 3/8	12	10	Crawford Co., KS	Steven R. Burt	Steven R. Burt	1999	130
208 7/8	24 1/8	19 2/8	5	4 7/8	8	7	Anoka Co., MN	Picked Up	Becky Wozney	1998	132
208 6/8	24 4/8	21 5/8	4 2/8	4 3/8	7	6	Idaho	Unknown	Richard J. Dorchuck	PR 1975	133
208 6/8	22 3/8	19 1/8	6 7/8	5 3/8	12	7	Bartholomew Co., IN	Randy E. Cash	Randy E. Cash	1997	133
208 5/8	25 2/8	15 7/8	4 1/8	4 1/8	10	14	Haskell Co., OK	Michael B. Vail	Michael B. Vail	1999	133
208 5/8	25 1/8	17 6/8	4 7/8	5	16	14	Unknown	Unknown	Darryl Powell	PR 1980	136
208 4/8	22 2/8	13 4/8	4 5/8	4 5/8	16	13	Pontotoc Co., OK	S. Chris Snell	S. Chris Snell	1997	136
208 4/8	28 3/8	22 5/8	5 4/8	5 4/8	10	9	Grenfell, SK	Clayton Roberts	Clayton Roberts	1998	138
208 4/8	24 4/8	20 2/8	7 4/8	7 6/8	12	12	Lee Co., IA	Dennis L. Case	Dennis L. Case	1999	138
208 4/8	23 4/8	19 7/8	4 2/8	4 2/8	17	10	Pope Co., AR	Danny L. Reed	Danny L. Reed	1999	138
208 4/8	24 3/8	14 7/8	4 5/8	5 2/8	12	10	Pike Co., IL	Brian M. Rennecker	Brian M. Rennecker	1999	138
208 2/8	28 4/8	22 6/8	5 2/8	5 2/8	10	12	Saline Co., IL	Mark A. Sheldon	Mark A. Sheldon	1999	142
208 2/8	27 1/8	23 4/8	5 6/8	6	7	13	Rockingham Co., NH	Glenn R. Townsend	Glenn R. Townsend	2000	142
208	29	22 2/8	5 3/8	5 3/8	11	13	Sangamon Co., IL	Daniel R. Lusardi	Daniel R. Lusardi	1999	144
207 7/8	28 3/8	18 4/8	5 1/8	5 3/8	14	8	Union Co., AR	Unknown	Travis Worthington	1999	145
207 7/8	29 5/8	21 1/8	5 2/8	5 1/8	7	7	Warren Co., IA	Michael J. King	Michael J. King	1995	145
207 5/8	29 3/8	19 3/8	4 7/8	5 2/8	10	11	Ashland Co., WI	Carl W. Moebius, Sr.	Eric Moebius	1934	147
207 5/8	26 7/8	21	5 6/8	4 7/8	6	9	Dane Co., WI	William L. Myhre, Jr.	William L. Myhre, Jr.	1997	147
207 4/8	25 2/8	18 5/8	6 2/8	5 6/8	11	11	Fulton Co., IL	Jack L. Link	Jack L. Link	1999	147
207 4/8	26 4/8	19	5 2/8	5	10	8	Lewis Co., MO	Leonard G. Grant	Leonard G. Grant	1999	150
207 3/8	25 7/8	17 6/8	5 2/8	5 2/8	8	8	Lee Co., IA	Donald L. Butler	Donald L. Butler	1999	151
207 2/8	29 5/8	22 1/8	5 2/8	5 7/8	9	8	Clark Co., IL	Richard D. Ellington	Richard D. Ellington	1997	152
207 2/8	27 3/8	18 2/8	5 7/8	5 5/8	12	10	Pulaski Co., KY	Mark Jones	Mark Jones	1998	152
207 2/8	27 7/8	20 6/8	5 3/8	5 5/8	11	9	Wilkin Co., MN	Richard K. Christopher	Richard K. Christopher	1999	152

WHITETAIL DEER - NON-TYPICAL ANTLERS

Odocoileus virginianus virginianus and certain related subspecies

Score	Length of Main Beam R.	L.	Inside Spread	Circumference at Smallest Place Between Burr and First Point R.	L.	Number of Points R.	L.	Locality	Hunter	Owner	Date Killed	Rank
207 1/8	25 5/8	26 7/8	17 3/8	5 5/8	5 1/8	12	9	Clay Co., IA	Rodney W. Dean	Rodney W. Dean	1973	155
207 1/8	27 5/8	27 5/8	23 2/8	5 4/8	5 7/8	10	10	Montgomery Co., IA	Raymond E. Crouch	Raymond E. Crouch	1997	155
207 1/8	27 4/8	27 7/8	16 6/8	4 6/8	5	9	11	Ohio Co., KY	Rick Daugherty	Rick Daugherty	1997	155
207	26 3/8	23 6/8	18 4/8	5	5	10	9	Walworth Co., WI	Kurt Mohrbacher	Kurt Mohrbacher	1997	158
206 6/8	26	26 2/8	19 2/8	5 1/8	5	8	9	Fulton Co., IN	Lewis Polk	Robert E. VanMeter III	1960	159
206 6/8	27 5/8	24 1/8	16 6/8	6 4/8	6	6	14	N. Saskatchewan River, SK	David C. Pezderic	David C. Pezderic	1997	159
206 6/8	30 2/8	29 5/8	20 6/8	5 5/8	5 3/8	8	13	Hart Co., KY	Daniel Behr	Daniel Behr	1998	159
206 5/8	26	25 7/8	20 1/8	6	6 3/8	11	11	Guthrie Co., IA	Terry R. Adams	Terry R. Adams	1998	162
206 5/8	22	22 3/8	18 1/8	4 4/8	4 5/8	10	12	Stevens Co., WA	Dick E. Jones II	Dick E. Jones II	1998	162
206 2/8	29 3/8	28 6/8	20 5/8	6	5 7/8	6	8	Adair Co., MO	Charles M. Zeman	Charles M. Zeman	1997	164
205 7/8	25	25 6/8	21 6/8	5 5/8	6	8	9	Greene Co., IL	Ronald R. Okonek	Ronald R. Okonek	1998	165
205 7/8	31 3/8	31 4/8	22 5/8	6 1/8	6 3/8	10	7	McPherson Co., KS	Chad Doughman	Chad Doughman	1999	165
205 6/8	23 7/8	26 1/8	20	5 3/8	5 2/8	10	8	Hickman Co., KY	Jerry M. Evans	Jerry M. Evans	1998	167
205 4/8	26 6/8	26 4/8	19 6/8	6 3/8	6 2/8	11	8	Dodge Co., WI	John Steckling	John Steckling	1998	168
205 3/8	26	26 1/8	19 1/8	5 3/8	5 4/8	10	10	Freeborn Co., MN	Picked Up	Kevin J. Nelsen	1997	169
205 3/8	19 7/8	23 4/8	20	5 6/8	4 7/8	12	7	White Co., AR	Charles L. Marcum, Jr.	Charles L. Marcum, Jr.	1998	169
205 3/8	25	25 3/8	19 2/8	4 7/8	5 2/8	7	13	Winona Co., MN	James D. Vitcenda	James D. Vitcenda	1998	169
205 3/8	24 4/8	26 2/8	21	8 4/8	8	12	11	Kansas	Picked Up	Keith A. Baird	2000	169
205 2/8	25 6/8	27	21 2/8	5	5	9	9	Richland Co., MT	Loyd Salsbury	Marlo Salsbury	PR 1958	173
205 2/8	26 6/8	27 2/8	22 1/8	4 6/8	4 7/8	9	9	Bollinger Co., MO	Linda K. Peters	Linda K. Peters	1998	173
205	24 2/8	22 1/8	18	6 2/8	5 7/8	8	9	White Fox, SK	Richard N. Kimball	Richard N. Kimball	1997	175
205	26 3/8	24 4/8	22 4/8	4 5/8	4 4/8	8	9	Warren Co., IL	Jason A. Schwass	Jason A. Schwass	1997	175
205	27 4/8	26 2/8	21 6/8	5 7/8	5 7/8	10	9	Fulton Co., IL	Picked Up	Robert E. Burgard	1998	175
204 7/8	26 3/8	26 4/8	18 5/8	5 2/8	5 2/8	9	12	Yankton Co., SD	Daniel M. Rederick	Daniel M. Rederick	1998	178
204 5/8	29 5/8	30 4/8	20 3/8	5 6/8	4 4/8	7	6	Calhoun Co., IL	Chad Strickland	Chad Strickland	1999	179
204 4/8	25 3/8	25 1/8	20 1/8	5 5/8	5 5/8	12	10	Fisher Co., TX	Keith H. Prince	Keith H. Prince	1997	180
204 3/8	26 1/8	26 3/8	17 2/8	5 6/8	5 6/8	9	9	Montgomery Creek, SK	Don L. Davey	Don L. Davey	1997	181
204 3/8	27	24 3/8	16 2/8	5 1/8	4 7/8	11	12	Doniphan Co., KS	Robby L. Buford	Robby L. Buford	1998	181
204 3/8	23 5/8	23 6/8	18 5/8	5 4/8	6 2/8	8	10	Waushara Co., WI	Debra A. Schmalzer	Debra A. Schmalzer	1998	181
204 2/8	25 7/8	25 4/8	19 3/8	5 5/8	5 7/8	13	12	Winneshiek Co., IA	Benjamin Christopher	Benjamin Christopher	1999	184
204 1/8	29 1/8	28 4/8	22 1/8	6 2/8	6 1/8	10	9	O'Brien Co., IA	Roy Jalas	Delores Jalas	1961	185
204	26 2/8	26 4/8	22 6/8	5	5	12	8	Warren Co., IA	Jack J. Schuler, Jr.	Jack J. Schuler, Jr.	1997	186
204	25	26 6/8	22 6/8	4 6/8	5	9	11	Buffalo Pound Lake, SK	Jim Weatherall	Jim Weatherall	1997	186
203 6/8	25 1/8	23 6/8	24 1/8	6 1/8	6 5/8	6	14	Kendall Co., IL	Brian Carlson	Brian Carlson	1998	188

Score	Main Beam R	Main Beam L	Inside Spread	Circ. R	Circ. L	Points R	Points L	Locality	Hunter	Owner	Date	Rank
203 6/8	25 4/8	26 5/8	23 2/8	5 3/8	5 6/8	10	12	Neosho Co., KS	Michael J. Hentzen	Michael J. Hentzen	1999	188
203 6/8	23 2/8	23 7/8	17 7/8	5 7/8	5 4/8	15	14	Calloway Co., KY	John D. Morgan	John D. Morgan	1999	188
203 5/8	25 5/8	24 4/8	24 1/8	5 6/8	5 6/8	9	9	Buffalo Co., WI	Ronald J. Jilot	Ronald J. Jilot	1997	191
203 4/8	27 2/8	26 5/8	24	5 5/8	5 6/8	12	9	Ford Co., IL	Gary G. Tessdale	Gary G. Tessdale	1997	192
203 4/8	25 3/8	23 1/8	18 6/8	5 6/8	6	12	12	Clearwater Co., MN	Craig Maxwell	Craig Maxwell	1998	192
203 4/8	22 3/8	21 3/8	22 6/8	4 6/8	4 6/8	9	15	Hardin Co., KY	Odell Chambers	Odell Chambers	1999	192
203 3/8	24 6/8	20 1/8	18 3/8	6 4/8	7 3/8	10	11	Van Buren Co., IA	Robert R. McWilliams	Robert R. McWilliams	1981	195
203 3/8	29 3/8	28 4/8	21 3/8	6 3/8	6 3/8	12	7	Gallia Co., OH	Hoyle S. Foy, Sr.	Hoyle S. Foy, Sr.	1998	195
203 3/8	26	23 2/8	17 1/8	5 4/8	5 6/8	7	11	Red Pheasant Indian Res., SK	Douglas A. Salomon	Douglas A. Salomon	1998	195
203 2/8	25 2/8	25 1/8	21 6/8	4 1/8	4 2/8	9	8	Marshall Co., MN	Andrew Anderson	Elmer Anderson	1947	198
203 2/8	28	27 7/8	21	4 7/8	4 5/8	10	10	Preston Co., WV	Unknown	L. Keith Casteel	1952	198
203 2/8	23 2/8	23 5/8	22	5 2/8	5 3/8	8	9	Open Creek, AB	Dave Serhan	David Serhan	1995	198
203 1/8	25 7/8	26 1/8	24 5/8	5 2/8	6 1/8	8	8	N. Saskatchewan River, SK	Barrie Taylor	Barrie Taylor	1997	201
203 1/8	24 4/8	23 5/8	19 2/8	4 7/8	4 6/8	9	7	St. Clair Co., IL	Gary W. White	Gary W. White	1997	201
202 7/8	21 5/8	21 7/8	16 3/8	4	4	10	13	Fergus Co., MT	Daniel N. Balster	Daniel N. Balster	1998	203
202 7/8	26	26 1/8	17 6/8	5 1/8	4 7/8	8	6	Sioux Co., IA	Jason W. Davelaar	Jason W. Davelaar	1999	203
202 7/8	25 5/8	27	20 2/8	5 1/8	5 2/8	11	12	Adams Co., IL	Ben H. Myers	Ben H. Myers	1999	203
202 6/8	25 6/8	25 6/8	18 4/8	5 3/8	5 4/8	8	13	Fayette Co., IA	John M. McMillen	John M. McMillen	1983	206
202 5/8	24 5/8	24 7/8	17 4/8	4 1/8	4 1/8	9	10	Ripley Co., IN	James A. Leveille	James A. Leveille	1999	207
202 3/8	25 2/8	24 2/8	19 5/8	4 6/8	4 7/8	13	12	Allen Co., KS	John F. Pfeiffer	John F. Pfeiffer	1998	208
202 3/8	24	25 7/8	18 3/8	4 4/8	4 4/8	9	8	Houston Co., TX	Clint M. Croft	Clint M. Croft	1999	208
202 1/8	27 7/8	28 6/8	21 6/8	4 7/8	4 7/8	9	10	Holt Co., MO	Gary F. Hoeper	Gary F. Hoeper	1997	210
202 1/8	26	26 3/8	20	5 3/8	5 4/8	12	10	Whitefish Lake, AB	Bill Yaceyko	Bill Yaceyko	1997	210
202 1/8	26 7/8	26 7/8	24 4/8	6 5/8	6 4/8	8	11	Jewell Co., KS	Rex A. Morgan	Rex A. Morgan	1998	210
202 1/8	23 7/8	24 4/8	19 3/8	6 5/8	6 4/8	9	11	Wright Co., MN	Picked Up	Jacob Burley	1999	210
202	20 4/8	22 4/8	17 4/8	6	6 1/8	12	15	Macon Co., MO	Larry Allen	Bill J. Timms	1994	214
202	26 1/8	26 1/8	22 7/8	5 1/8	5 2/8	9	8	Guthrie Co., IA	Donald E. Jensen	Ronald E. Jensen	1995	214
202	27 4/8	27 1/8	20	5 6/8	6	8	8	Tippecanoe Co., IN	Stephen L. Burkhalter	Stephen L. Burkhalter	1997	214
201 6/8	28 4/8	28 3/8	20 5/8	4 5/8	4 4/8	8	9	Roseau Co., MN	Picked Up	Phillip C. Larson	1999	218
201 4/8	25 7/8	24 4/8	16 3/8	6 5/8	6 7/8	9	18	Unknown	Unknown	Ray Panaro	PR 1960	219
201 3/8	28 7/8	29 7/8	22	7	6 2/8	12	10	Shawnee Co., KS	J.S. Smith	J.S. Smith	1999	220
201 2/8	25 7/8	26 1/8	20 7/8	5 2/8	5 3/8	6	9	Mitchell Co., KS	Terry L. Fiala	Terry L. Fiala	1998	221
201 2/8	24 1/8	24 6/8	18 6/8	5	5	8	8	Dawes Co., NE	Cole Emmett	Cole Emmett	1998	221
201	23 6/8	25 7/8	21 4/8	5 4/8	5 3/8	12	5	Lorain Co., OH	D. Cody Kelch	D. Cody Kelch	1999	223
201	28 5/8	26 4/8	18 4/8	4 7/8	5	11	10	Becker Co., MN	Gill S. Gigstead, Jr.	Gill S. Gigstead, Jr.	1964	223
201	24 7/8	25 5/8	17 3/8	6 4/8	6 1/8	9	9	Guthrie Co., IA	Patrick N. Thompson	Patrick N. Thompson	1996	223
201	22 6/8	27 4/8	20 5/8	5 3/8	5 6/8	16	13	Delaware Co., OH	Charles W. Henderson	Charles W. Henderson	1997	223
200 7/8	25 7/8	26 4/8	21 1/8	4 5/8	4 6/8	11	13	Cooke Co., TX	Michael W. Lang	Michael W. Lang	1997	227
200 7/8	22 5/8	25 7/8	18 6/8	4 2/8	4 6/8	10	9	Lawrence Co., AR	E.B. Ivie	Jimmy Huskey	1928	227
200 7/8	26 7/8	26 4/8	15 6/8	4 4/8	5 4/8	9	13	Unknown	Unknown	Robert J. Werner	PR 1940	227
200 7/8	27 1/8	25 4/8	23 6/8	5 5/8	5 4/8	7	8	Muscatine Co., IA	William L. Brockert	William L. Brockert	1998	227
200 7/8	23 1/8	23 7/8	19 6/8	4 4/8	4 2/8	11	9	Langlade Co., WI	Jordan Halverson	Jordan Halverson	1998	227
200 5/8	27 2/8	25 5/8	20 6/8	5 4/8	5 2/8	7	8	Iowa Co., IA	Michael L. Ealy	Michael L. Ealy	1998	231

WHITETAIL DEER - NON-TYPICAL ANTLERS

Odocoileus virginianus virginianus and certain related subspecies

Score	Length of Main Beam R.	L.	Inside Spread	Circumference at Smallest Place Between Burr and First Point R.	L.	Number of Points R.	L.	Locality	Hunter	Owner	Date Killed	Rank
200 5/8	25 5/8	25 3/8	19 6/8	4 7/8	5	10	10	Woods Co., OK	Aaron R. Sheik	Aaron R. Sheik	1998	231
200 3/8	23 7/8	22 1/8	21 5/8	5	6 6/8	6	10	Keya Paha Co., NE	Charles V. Stroud	Charles V. Stroud	1998	233
200 3/8	24 7/8	25 1/8	15 3/8	4 7/8	4 7/8	9	9	Boone Co., MO	Kevin B. Sample	Kevin B. Sample	1999	233
200 2/8	28	28 5/8	25 3/8	5 6/8	5 6/8	7	7	La Salle Co., IL	James A. Carr	James A. Carr	1999	235
200	26 6/8	25 6/8	17 5/8	5 4/8	5 3/8	10	8	Baca Co., CO	David Sanford	David Sanford	1996	236
200	26 3/8	26 3/8	20 3/8	5 7/8	6	6	8	Otter Tail Co., MN	Timothy J. Kapphahn	Timothy J. Kapphahn	1998	236
200	26 3/8	26 3/8	21 2/8	4 7/8	4 7/8	10	8	Nance Co., NE	Gale Sup	Gale Sup	1998	236
200	24 1/8	23 3/8	23 1/8	5	5	8	9	Lake of the Prairies, SK	Phil Olshewski	Phil Olshewski	1999	236
199 5/8	27 5/8	27 2/8	19 2/8	6 2/8	5 5/8	9	10	Unknown	Unknown	Harley L. Johnson	PR 2000	240
199 3/8	24 2/8	23 4/8	17 2/8	5 3/8	5 3/8	10	8	Houston Co., MN	Picked Up	MN Dept. of Natl. Resc.	1997	241
199 3/8	25 6/8	25 4/8	19 1/8	5 2/8	5 1/8	9	9	Penobscot Co., ME	Robert Raymond	Robert Raymond	1997	241
199 3/8	24 6/8	24 3/8	16	5	5	11	8	Logan Co., KY	Michael D. Forrest	Michael D. Forrest	1998	241
199 3/8	26	24 1/8	28 1/8	5 1/8	5 2/8	8	9	Charette Lake, SK	Chris J. Weinkauf	Chris J. Weinkauf	1998	241
199 2/8	25 3/8	25 1/8	23 4/8	5 7/8	7 1/8	7	8	Shannon Co., MO	Charles Martin	Doug Masner	1996	245
199 2/8	26 1/8	26 3/8	18 1/8	5 2/8	5 3/8	11	11	Washtenaw Co., MI	Donald W. Bollinger	Donald W. Bollinger	1998	245
199 2/8	28 1/8	26 4/8	19 4/8	5 3/8	5 2/8	7	8	Clayton Co., IA	Shane M. Hass	Shane M. Hass	1998	245
199 1/8	23 5/8	24 1/8	24 4/8	4 6/8	4 7/8	11	10	Billings Co., ND	Jake Braun	Jake Braun	1949	248
199 1/8	23 3/8	23 2/8	22 5/8	5 5/8	5 6/8	9	8	Smoky Lake, AB	Helmuth Ritter	Helmuth Ritter	1992	248
199 1/8	25 2/8	24 3/8	19 4/8	5	5	8	8	Morgan Co., CO	Michael L. Furcolow	Michael L. Furcolow	1997	248
199	25 5/8	24 2/8	17 1/8	5 1/8	4 7/8	8	8	Qu'Appelle River, SK	Gilbert Brule	Gilbert Brule	1998	251
199	25 2/8	24 5/8	21 2/8	6	5 6/8	9	10	Hancock Co., ME	Dale Henderson	Dale Henderson	1998	251
199	25 5/8	24 1/8	18 5/8	5 3/8	5 3/8	13	13	Harrison Co., IA	Kody Wohlers	Kody Wohlers	1998	251
198 7/8	25 2/8	25 1/8	17 2/8	5 6/8	5 7/8	7	7	Pike Co., IL	James Kruczynski	James Kruczynski	1998	254
198 7/8	25 2/8	24 4/8	19 6/8	5 1/8	6 7/8	6	13	Fulton Co., IL	Todd L. DeGroot	Todd L. DeGroot	1999	254
198 6/8	20	20 6/8	17 4/8	4 3/8	4 3/8	9	19	Angelina Co., TX	B. Tyler Fenley	Daniel Fenley	1999	256
198 6/8	26 7/8	26 4/8	17 7/8	4 4/8	4 4/8	9	8	Butler Co., IA	Harlan Schmadeke	Harlan Schmadeke	1999	256
198 5/8	27 2/8	26 5/8	22 4/8	5 6/8	5 7/8	8	10	Morton Co., ND	Grant C. Starck	Grant C. Starck	1952	258
198 5/8	28 7/8	29 2/8	19 4/8	6 2/8	5 6/8	7	7	Ray Co., MO	Stephen D. Kirk	Stephen D. Kirk	1997	258
198 5/8	24 6/8	24 1/8	15 6/8	3 7/8	3 7/8	8	9	Clay Co., TX	Glenn M. Lucas	Glenn M. Lucas	1997	258
198 5/8	25 4/8	24 4/8	20 5/8	4 5/8	4 7/8	12	15	Oktibbeha Co., MS	Timothy P. Watson	Timothy P. Watson	1997	258
198 5/8	26 6/8	27 6/8	20 4/8	7 2/8	6	10	8	Des Moines Co., IA	Craig R. Belknap	Craig R. Belknap	1998	258
198 5/8	22	23 1/8	20 4/8	5 6/8	5 1/8	8	8	N. Saskatchewan River, SK	Robin McLean	Robin McLean	1998	258
198 5/8	23 7/8	24 1/8	22 1/8	5	5	9	7	Turtle Mt., MB	Charles C. Dixon	Charles C. Dixon	1999	258
198 5/8	23 7/8	24 6/8	20 2/8	4 6/8	4 6/8	10	10	Pulaski Co., MO	Donald R. McGraw	Donald R. McGraw	1999	258

198 4/8	25 3/8	24 6/8	17 4/8	4 2/8	4 4/8	14	9	Kleberg Co., TX	Glenn Thurman	Glenn Thurman	1994	266
198 4/8	25 5/8	25 2/8	17	5 3/8	5 2/8	11	8	Chautauqua Co., KS	Mark A. Shull	Mark A. Shull	1998	266
198 4/8	29 4/8	29 5/8	24 6/8	5 4/8	5 6/8	10	7	Macoupin Co., IL	Brett Bridgewater	Brett Bridgewater	1999	266
198 3/8	20 7/8	22 2/8	17 5/8	4 4/8	4 7/8	10	10	Nez Perce Co., ID	Milton R. Wilson	G. & J. Reed	1983	269
198 3/8	24 4/8	24 4/8	20 5/8	6 6/8	6 4/8	9	6	Sherburne Co., MN	David J. Valerius	David J. Valerius	1997	269
198 3/8	23 2/8	23 2/8	17 5/8	4 1/8	4 2/8	6	8	Pasqua Lake, SK	Trent Mattick	Trent Mattick	1998	269
198 2/8	27 2/8	28 7/8	21 3/8	5 6/8	5 7/8	8	9	Geauga Co., OH	Greg Raudenbush	Greg Raudenbush	1997	272
198 1/8	27 3/8	25 1/8	22 1/8	5	5	12	5	Kingman Co., KS	Harold W. Hellman	Harold W. Hellman	1997	273
198 1/8	25 1/8	25 2/8	19 1/8	4 2/8	4 2/8	11	8	Kootenai Co., ID	Luke D. Finney	Luke D. Finney	1998	273
198 1/8	25 2/8	25	16 4/8	5 4/8	5 4/8	8	9	Pike Co., IL	Picked Up	Sam Moore	1998	273
198	25 6/8	25 3/8	20 6/8	5 2/8	5 2/8	8	9	Mercer Co., OH	Werner H. Schmiesing	Werner H. Schmiesing	1979	276
197 7/8	26 3/8	27	20 4/8	4 6/8	4 6/8	10	7	Madison Co., IA	Scott R. Busch	Scott R. Busch	1997	277
197 7/8	26 2/8	27 2/8	19 6/8	7 1/8	6 1/8	10	7	Woods Co., OK	Steve Purviance	Steve Purviance	1997	277
197 7/8	25	24 7/8	18 6/8	5 2/8	5 2/8	10	8	Aitkin Co., MN	Thomas N. Sauro	Thomas N. Sauro	1998	277
197 7/8	26 2/8	26 3/8	17 7/8	5 6/8	5 5/8	7	6	Fishing Lake, SK	Nicole Hrycak	Nicole Hrycak	1999	277
197 6/8	27 2/8	26 3/8	18 2/8	5	4 6/8	6	8	Harrison Co., MO	Rod L. Shain	Rod L. Shain	1985	281
197 6/8	31 4/8	30 4/8	23	5 3/8	5 4/8	11	9	Fairfield Co., OH	Bob Sink	Bob Sink	1997	281
197 6/8	25 6/8	27 1/8	19 4/8	5 2/8	5 5/8	7	9	Fayette Co., IN	Boyd L. Lunsford	Boyd L. Lunsford	1998	281
197 6/8	27 3/8	28	20 4/8	5 5/8	5 7/8	6	10	Preble Co., OH	Larry E. Hickman	Larry E. Hickman	1999	281
197 5/8	27 4/8	27 1/8	21 1/8	4 7/8	5	9	9	Foam Lake, SK	Tom Taylor	Tom Taylor	1999	281
197 5/8	25 2/8	26 2/8	22 6/8	5 2/8	5	9	10	McDonough Co., IL	Ronald A. Edwards	Ronald A. Edwards	1998	286
197 5/8	26 5/8	27 1/8	17 1/8	5 2/8	5 1/8	9	7	Vermilion Co., IL	Thad E. Powell	Thad E. Powell	1998	286
197 4/8	26	27	19 5/8	6 4/8	6 3/8	8	9	Willow Creek, SK	Alan D. Hingson	Alan D. Hingson	1997	288
197 4/8	27 3/8	25	17 5/8	4 3/8	4 4/8	10	9	Dore Lake, SK	Arie Vandertweel	Arie Vandertweel	1997	288
197 4/8	25 6/8	27 3/8	20 5/8	5 3/8	5 4/8	8	12	Hopkins Co., KY	Erwin W. Brown	Erwin W. Brown	1998	288
197 3/8	22	21 4/8	17 6/8	3 6/8	3 6/8	11	10	Iowa Co., WI	Tim Capps	Tim Capps	1998	291
197 3/8	23 5/8	24 2/8	18 2/8	5 5/8	5 5/8	10	12	Athabasca, AB	Luke J. Leiterman	Luke J. Leiterman	1998	291
197 3/8	21 4/8	20 5/8	18 5/8	4 7/8	5 3/8	12	11	Koochiching Co., MN	Clinton Peredery	Clinton Peredery	1999	291
197 2/8	22 6/8	23 1/8	20	6 2/8	5 6/8	13	10	Starr Co., TX	John Erickson	Marc M. Jackson	1951	294
197 2/8	23 7/8	23 5/8	15 5/8	4 7/8	4 6/8	15	14	Winneshiek Co., IA	Matthew J. Arnold	Matthew J. Arnold	1997	294
197 2/8	26 3/8	26 2/8	22 1/8	4 6/8	4 4/8	10	11	Stephens Co., OK	Richard M. Blaess	Richard M. Blaess	1997	294
197 2/8	24 5/8	25	17 5/8	5	4 7/8	12	10	Piscataquis Co., ME	Bryan C. Walker	Bryan C. Walker	1997	294
197 2/8	28 2/8	28 6/8	20 6/8	5 7/8	5 7/8	8	6	Casey Co., KY	Penny Demar	Penny Demar	1998	294
197 2/8	25 2/8	23 3/8	15	5 6/8	5 6/8	9	12	Sanilac Co., MI	Ryan Elmore	Ryan Elmore	1998	294
197 2/8	27 7/8	26 5/8	19 2/8	5 6/8	5 6/8	11	9	Marion Co., IA	Charles E. Goodfellow	Charles E. Goodfellow	1998	294
197 1/8	24 3/8	26	23 4/8	5 4/8	4 6/8	9	7	Rocky Mountain House, AB	Larry J. Lautenbach	Larry J. Lautenbach	1998	294
197 1/8	27 5/8	27 1/8	18 3/8	5 3/8	5 6/8	9	10	Bartholomew Co., IN	Robin L. McDonald	Robin L. McDonald	1998	302
197 1/8	25 6/8	25 4/8	18	6	6	13	13	Clark Co., SD	C. Greg Caudill	C. Greg Caudill	1999	302
197 1/8	23 6/8	23 4/8	20 2/8	5 7/8	5 7/8	11	11	S. Saskatchewan River, SK	Marlin Maynard	Marlin Maynard	1999	302
197	24	23 3/8	17 3/8	5 5/8	5 4/8	8	7	Bayfield Co., WI	Barry Miller	Barry Miller	1999	302
197	28 2/8	28 2/8	19 5/8	5 6/8	5 4/8	7	7	Bureau Co., IL	Larry M. Nyhus	Larry M. Nyhus	1997	306
196 7/8	27	25	21 5/8	4 7/8	5 4/8	8	10	Winneshiek Co., IA	Steve M. Mazurek	Steve M. Mazurek	1995	307
196 7/8	28	28 2/8	22	5 6/8	6 1/8	7	11	Winneshiek Co., IA	David G. Baumler	David G. Baumler	1997	307

WHITETAIL DEER - NON-TYPICAL ANTLERS

Odocoileus virginianus virginianus and certain related subspecies

Score	Length of Main Beam R.	L.	Inside Spread	Circumference at Smallest Place Between Burr and First Point R.	L.	Number of Points R.	L.	Locality	Hunter	Owner	Date Killed	Rank
196 7/8	26 3/8	27 3/8	21 7/8	5 4/8	5 3/8	10	5	Chipman, AB	Don F. MacLean	Don F. MacLean	1997	307
196 7/8	25 6/8	25 6/8	20 6/8	7	6 5/8	7	8	Becker Co., MN	James A. Henderson	James A. Henderson	1998	307
196 7/8	27 5/8	28 4/8	24 1/8	5 2/8	5 7/8	8	8	Shawano Co., WI	Robert D. Little	Robert D. Little	1998	307
196 6/8	23 7/8	26 4/8	22 4/8	5 2/8	5 2/8	12	13	Porcupine Plain, SK	Picked Up	Terry L. Amos	PR 1997	312
196 6/8	25 2/8	25 2/8	18 2/8	4 7/8	5 1/8	8	12	Latimer Co., OK	Brian K. Paul	Brian K. Paul	1998	312
196 6/8	24 2/8	24	25 6/8	4 7/8	4 7/8	9	10	Whitefish Bay, ON	Matthew R. Rydberg	Matthew R. Rydberg	1998	312
196 5/8	19 2/8	18	18 4/8	5 1/8	5 1/8	15	13	Comanche Co., OK	R. Dewayne High	R. Dewayne High	1998	315
196 5/8	25	25 1/8	17 5/8	5 7/8	5 5/8	12	10	Henry Co., IA	Troy M. Matter	Troy M. Matter	1998	315
196 4/8	28 1/8	27	19 7/8	4 2/8	4 2/8	6	8	Buffalo Co., WI	Scott T. Beach	Scott T. Beach	1996	317
196 4/8	25 1/8	24 2/8	20 7/8	4 7/8	4 6/8	15	17	Charlotte Co., VA	Paul S. Wray	Paul S. Wray	1997	317
196 3/8	28 3/8	25 6/8	21 1/8	6	6	8	7	Belmont Co., OH	Brian R. Elston	Brian R. Elston	1999	319
196 3/8	22 5/8	23 7/8	18 5/8	5 2/8	5 2/8	11	7	Gregory Co., SD	Michael O. Jacobsen	Michael O. Jacobsen	1999	319
196 2/8	29 3/8	27	19 3/8	6 1/8	6 2/8	11	12	Pratt Co., KS	Travis D. Kolm	Travis D. Kolm	1997	321
196 2/8	27 5/8	25 2/8	17 7/8	5 5/8	6 6/8	11	16	Bourbon Co., KS	Picked Up	Odie Sudbeck	1999	321
196 1/8	27 3/8	27 2/8	21 3/8	5 6/8	7 2/8	10	10	Leduc, AB	Gordon Gulick	Gordon Gulick	1993	323
196 1/8	23 5/8	25 4/8	18 1/8	6	5 6/8	11	9	Pontotoc Co., OK	Bruce A. Hall	Bruce A. Hall	1999	323
196 1/8	26 4/8	26 2/8	18 6/8	4 6/8	4 6/8	7	8	Frio Co., TX	Orville W. Simmang, Sr.	Orville W. Simmang, Sr.	1999	323
196	22 3/8	24 5/8	16 5/8	5 1/8	5 2/8	13	10	Luce Co., MI	Herbert Miller, Sr.	Bass Pro Shops F. & W. Mus.	1945	326
196	25 1/8	25 5/8	16 1/8	4 1/8	4 4/8	11	11	Jasper Co., GA	Frank M. Pritchard	Frank M. Pritchard	1968	326
196	26 6/8	23 3/8	15 5/8	7 1/8	7	9	9	Cumberland Co., IL	Jeff A. Light	Jeff A. Light	1997	326
196	27 6/8	28 3/8	23 6/8	5 3/8	5 4/8	7	7	Washington Co., KS	Jeff W. Novak	Jeff W. Novak	1998	326
196	27 5/8	26 3/8	19 1/8	6	6 1/8	6	9	Fayette Co., OH	Sean C. Huff	Sean C. Huff	1999	326
195 7/8	25 6/8	25 4/8	15 1/8	5	5	9	11	Webster Parish, LA	Shannon Stanley	Shannon Stanley	1991	331
195 7/8	23	22 6/8	15 6/8	5 3/8	5 5/8	10	9	Unknown	Unknown	Larry D. Bollier	PR 1998	331
195 6/8	24 1/8	24 4/8	15 6/8	6 1/8	5 6/8	7	11	Ontonagon Co., MI	Andrew Pietila	Bass Pro Shops F. & W. Mus.	PR 1920	333
195 6/8	23 6/8	25	18 2/8	5 4/8	5 4/8	12	8	Vernon Co., WI	William T. Newman	William T. Newman	1997	333
195 6/8	29 1/8	29	21 3/8	5 1/8	4 7/8	7	8	Pierce Co., WI	Jody M. Anderson	Jody M. Anderson	1998	333
195 6/8	24 5/8	24 3/8	16 7/8	5 4/8	5 3/8	16	10	Putnam Co., MO	Douglas E. Gadberry	Douglas E. Gadberry	1998	333
195 6/8	24 4/8	23 5/8	21 3/8	4 4/8	4 5/8	8	7	Lake Co., MN	Corey A. Swartout	Corey A. Swartout	1998	333
195 5/8	27	25 7/8	19 7/8	4 6/8	5 1/8	10	8	Winneshiek Co., IA	Picked Up	Milan Kumlin	1990	338
195 5/8	26 3/8	26	18 1/8	4 7/8	5 1/8	7	8	Platte Co., MO	Lincoln A. Godfrey	Lincoln A. Godfrey	1999	338
195 5/8	28	21	21	4 4/8	4 6/8	9	10	Schuyler Co., MO	Jason McCartney	Jason McCartney	1999	338
195 4/8	24	23 7/8	20	5	5	9	8	Red Deer River, SK	Glen Gulka	Glen Gulka	1993	341

Score	Length of Main Beam R	Length of Main Beam L	Inside Spread	Circ.	Circ.	Points	Points	Locality	By Whom Killed	Owner	Date Killed	Rank
195 4/8	24	22	18 1/8	4 6/8	4 6/8	6	9	Lincoln Co., MO	David M. Thiemet	David M. Thiemet	1996	341
195 4/8	28	27 3/8	20 3/8	5 2/8	5 2/8	8	8	Jo Daviess Co., IL	Glen M. Volk	Glen M. Volk	1997	341
195 4/8	25 1/8	25 1/8	15 3/8	5 2/8	4 6/8	17	11	Natrona Co., WY	Picked Up	Ann Ginder	1998	341
195 4/8	23 3/8	23 3/8	23 3/8	5 4/8	5 3/8	8	9	Winneshiek Co., IA	Clair R. Malanaphy	Clair R. Malanaphy	1998	341
195 4/8	25 3/8	26 2/8	18 5/8	5 1/8	5 3/8	9	8	Grenfell, SK	Anthony Roberts	Anthony Roberts	1998	341
195 4/8	23	22 6/8	26 5/8	4 2/8	4 1/8	8	11	Hughes Co., OK	Mike K. Williams	Mike K. Williams	1998	341
195 4/8	25 5/8	24 6/8	23 4/8	5	5 1/8	11	8	Suffolk Co., NY	Eric Kowalski	Eric Kowalski	1999	341
195 4/8	25 2/8	25 5/8	18 4/8	6 6/8	6 3/8	13	7	Anderson Co., KS	H.C. Stokes	H.C. Stokes	1999	341
195 3/8	25 7/8	25 6/8	19 3/8	5 3/8	5 2/8	8	12	Allamakee Co., IA	Picked Up	Douglas A. Bartz	1998	350
195 3/8	25 1/8	25 2/8	17	5 1/8	5 1/8	9	10	Souris River, SK	Corinne Biette	Corinne Biette	1998	350
195 3/8	26 3/8	27 4/8	18 5/8	4 5/8	4 6/8	7	8	Pike Co., IL	Ray Yates	Ray Yates	1998	350
195 3/8	21 1/8	21 4/8	19 7/8	4 1/8	4 2/8	9	15	Johnson Co., GA	Picked Up	Jackie Bailey	1999	350
195 2/8	28 2/8	27 2/8	22 1/8	5 4/8	5 3/8	8	8	Pierce Co., WI	Jesse W. Sullivan	Jesse W. Sullivan	1999	355
195 2/8	26 2/8	24 6/8	18 1/8	5 7/8	5 4/8	6	9	Warren Co., OH	Ronald E. Lay	Ronald E. Lay	1995	355
195 2/8	24 4/8	23 5/8	16 6/8	5 6/8	5 7/8	8	9	Christian Co., KY	George Hilton, Jr.	George Hilton, Jr.	1997	355
195 2/8	24 2/8	24 4/8	19 6/8	4 2/8	4 3/8	7	8	Major Co., OK	Hoot M. Patterson	Hoot M. Patterson	1997	355
195 1/8	23 7/8	24 4/8	16 3/8	5	5	17	13	Dodge Co., WI	Michael Peirick	Michael Peirick	1999	359
195 1/8	24 7/8	24 3/8	17 5/8	5 5/8	5 4/8	8	8	Merrick Co., NE	Robert K. Betts	Robert K. Betts	1962	359
195 1/8	23 4/8	23 4/8	16 6/8	5	4 6/8	8	8	Crook Co., WY	John P. Barrows	John P. Barrows	1998	359
195 1/8	25 5/8	25 7/8	19 1/8	5 6/8	5 6/8	10	13	Parke Co., IN	Todd D. Farris	Todd D. Farris	1998	359
195	23 3/8	25 3/8	22 2/8	6 2/8	6	14	7	Buffalo Co., WI	Michael J. Barstad	Michael J. Barstad	1999	363
195	24 6/8	24 4/8	18 3/8	5 6/8	5 5/8	6	13	Dome Creek, BC	John Hale	John Charters	PR 1960	363
195	25	25	20 1/8	5 1/8	5 2/8	9	9	Allamakee Co., IA	Joey Richards	Teresa Waters	1991	363
195	25	25	18 7/8	5 3/8	5 1/8	8	7	Mitchell Creek, AB	Gord Moreau	Gord Moreau	1998	363
195	27 1/8	27 6/8	19 3/8	4 3/8	5 4/8	7	10	Lenawee Co., MI	Craig Rodosalewicz	Craig Rodosalewicz	1998	363
194 5/8	25 5/8	25 7/8	23 1/8	4 7/8	4 5/8	7	7	Dimmit Co., TX	J. Marvin Smith IV	J. Marvin Smith IV	1998	368
194	26 3/8	26 3/8	20 4/8	4 4/8	4 5/8	7	9	Reno Co., KS	Sam E. Bontrager	Sam E. Bontrager	1999	369
194	25 1/8	25 1/8	19 4/8	4 7/8	4 7/8	8	7	Lincoln Co., MT	Stephen Holladay	Stephen Holladay	1988	369
193 7/8	24 5/8	24 3/8	16 5/8	5 3/8	5 2/8	9	11	Porcupine Plain, SK	Jeff Unteriner	Terry L. Amos	1998	371
193 6/8	22 1/8	22 2/8	16 2/8	6 4/8	6 2/8	12	17	McBride Lake, SK	Patrick G. Stoia	Patrick G. Stoia	1999	372
193 5/8	23 1/8	22 3/8	18	5 4/8	5 5/8	9	8	Metcalfe Co., KY	David Dick	David Dick	1998	373
193 5/8	24 6/8	24 6/8	21 6/8	5 2/8	5 3/8	9	10	Vilas Co., WI	Unknown	Charles Glut	1998	373
193 5/8	26 3/8	26 3/8	20 1/8	4 5/8	4 7/8	6	9	High Level, AB	Richard Provencher	Richard Provencher	PR 1900	373
193 4/8	27 5/8	28 3/8	25 2/8	5 7/8	6 3/8	9	12	Bayfield Co., WI	Mark Kinney	Mark Kinney	1998	376
193 3/8	24 6/8	25 2/8	16	4 1/8	4 1/8	14	9	Warren Co., IN	Bill D. Wadkins	Bill D. Wadkins	1999	377
193 3/8	29 1/8	28 2/8	19	6	5 6/8	9	9	St. Mary's Co., MD	Ronald D. Cullember	Ronald D. Cullember	1999	377
193 3/8	25	25	17 6/8	5 4/8	5 7/8	10	9	Piscataquis Co., ME	Paul J. Amos	Paul J. Amos	1993	377
193 3/8	27 4/8	24	21 3/8	7	7 5/8	9	8	McHenry Co., IL	Michael W. Kaufmann	Michael W. Kaufmann	1998	377
193 2/8	25 2/8	23 6/8	18 5/8	5 5/8	6 1/8	9	11	Fulton Co., IL	James Crane	James Crane	1999	380
192 7/8	22 5/8	22 5/8	17 2/8	6 1/8	5 7/8	7	6	Bedford Co., VA	Claude J. Wilson, Jr.	Claude J. Wilson, Jr.	1997	381
192 6/8	27 7/8	26 7/8	20 2/8	6 1/8	5 7/8	10	9	Stark Co., IL	John H. Ford, Jr.	John H. Ford, Jr.	1998	382
192 6/8	26 5/8	24 1/8	20 5/8	5 7/8	5 2/8	11	8	Waukesha Co., WI	Curt Samanske	Curt Samanske	1998	382
192 4/8	24 1/8	26 3/8	19 6/8	4 7/8	4 7/8	7	8	Wapello Co., IA	Kennard C. Kaplan	Kennard C. Kaplan	1990	384

WHITETAIL DEER - NON-TYPICAL ANTLERS

Odocoileus virginianus virginianus and certain related subspecies

Score	Length of Main Beam R.	L.	Inside Spread	Circumference at Smallest Place Between Burr and First Point R.	L.	Number of Points R.	L.	Locality	Hunter	Owner	Date Killed	Rank
192 4/8	22	25	20 6/8	4 6/8	4 4/8	8	8	Lucas Co., IA	Brad S. Pruismann	Brad S. Pruismann	1999	384
192 2/8	26 5/8	27 2/8	18 5/8	4 5/8	4 4/8	6	7	Warren Co., IN	Sam L. Karras	Sam L. Karras	1998	386
192 1/8	25 5/8	26 4/8	21 6/8	6	5 5/8	11	8	Livingston Co., KY	John W. Layne	John W. Layne	1969	387
192	26 7/8	26 6/8	18 2/8	4 6/8	4 6/8	8	6	Todd Co., KY	Brian P. Stratton	Brian P. Stratton	1997	388
192	26	26 1/8	19 1/8	4 4/8	4 6/8	6	7	Montgomery Co., TN	John J. Teeter	John J. Teeter	1998	388
191 4/8	24	23 4/8	17 6/8	5 5/8	5 6/8	8	10	Tallahatchie Co., MS	Willie L. Carvan	Willie L. Carvan	1999	388
191 4/8	25 3/8	25 6/8	19 5/8	4 6/8	5 3/8	10	9	Holt Co., MO	Richard D. Wilson	Richard D. Wilson	1999	391
191 3/8	26 5/8	26	22 2/8	4 5/8	4 7/8	9	9	Lemhi Co., ID	Unknown	Aly M. Bruner	PR 1930	392
191 3/8	22	22 7/8	14 3/8	4 6/8	4 7/8	10	10	Webb Co., TX	Ken A. Harding	Ken A. Harding	1999	392
191 1/8	21 6/8	23 5/8	16 2/8	4 4/8	4 2/8	10	10	Fond du Lac Co., WI	Alan H. Woods	Alan H. Woods	1999	394
191	24 5/8	24 6/8	15 3/8	4 5/8	4 5/8	8	8	Cedar Co., IA	Chris E. Bergmann	Chris E. Bergmann	1997	395
191	23 2/8	23	19 4/8	4 6/8	4 6/8	8	9	Macon Co., MO	Gerald D. Bojarsky	Gerald D. Bojarsky	1997	395
190 7/8	24 2/8	27 2/8	20 5/8	5 6/8	5 6/8	12	9	Christian Co., KY	Joseph R. Tanner	Joseph R. Tanner	1999	397
190 6/8	25 6/8	25 2/8	20 3/8	5	5 2/8	11	8	Crawford Co., WI	James A. Moore	James A. Moore	1997	398
190 6/8	26 1/8	27	22 3/8	5 4/8	5 5/8	8	11	Howard Co., MO	Curtis Thornhill	Curtis Thornhill	1998	398
190 5/8	29 4/8	26	19 6/8	5 7/8	6	12	12	Bedford Co., VA	J.B. Karnes	Mrs. J.B. Karnes	1974	400
190 5/8	27 3/8	27 2/8	20 7/8	5 6/8	5 6/8	12	11	Worth Co., GA	George L. Houston	George L. Houston	1997	400
190 3/8	25 6/8	27 1/8	17 6/8	4 5/8	4 6/8	8	8	La Salle Co., TX	Raymond M. Otto	Raymond M. Otto	1997	402
190 3/8	29 2/8	30 5/8	25 1/8	5 7/8	5 5/8	10	9	McLean Co., IL	Dwight E. Johnson, Jr.	Dwight E. Johnson, Jr.	1998	402
190 3/8	25 2/8	25	21 2/8	4 3/8	4 3/8	9	11	Lewis Co., KY	Bobby J. Whitaker	Bobby J. Whitaker	1999	402
190 1/8	26 3/8	25 2/8	22 1/8	5 1/8	5	10	8	Livingston Co., IL	Daniel P. Olson	Daniel P. Olson	1995	405
190	25 6/8	26 3/8	19 1/8	5	5	9	10	Hunting Lake, SK	Walter J. Benton	Walter J. Benton	1997	406
189 4/8	27 5/8	27 5/8	20	5 6/8	5 7/8	7	11	Iron Co., WI	Bryan L. Bellows	Bryan L. Bellows	1994	407
189 4/8	22 7/8	23 4/8	15 4/8	6 2/8	6 4/8	9	7	Chipman, AB	Kenneth H. Jackson	Kenneth H. Jackson	1998	407
189 3/8	26 3/8	25 3/8	20	4 7/8	4 7/8	6	7	Tamaulipas, MX	Thomas A. Moy, Jr.	Thomas A. Moy, Jr.	1997	409
189 2/8	26 2/8	24 5/8	20 2/8	4 7/8	5 4/8	7	10	Northumberland Co., PA	Thomas E. Messinger	Thomas E. Messinger	1998	410
189 1/8	24 3/8	23 7/8	22 1/8	5	5	7	7	Ross Lake, AB	Lawrence Cahoon	Lawrence Cahoon	1967	411
189 1/8	22 7/8	23 5/8	16	4 5/8	4 5/8	9	7	Kent Co., DE	Barry D. Smith	Barry D. Smith	1996	411
189 1/8	24 4/8	22 1/8	16 6/8	5 2/8	5	11	8	Hodgeman Co., KS	Gary Tenbrink	Gary Tenbrink	1997	411
189	25 3/8	24 6/8	17 4/8	5 4/8	5 1/8	9	8	Waushara Co., WI	Anthony E. O'Kon	Anthony E. O'Kon	1999	414
188 6/8	23 1/8	23 2/8	17 6/8	4 3/8	4 3/8	10	10	St. Lawrence Co., NY	Timothy C. Besaw	Timothy C. Besaw	1999	415
188 3/8	24 3/8	26 6/8	19 7/8	5 6/8	5 3/8	8	7	Cass Co., IL	Jack O. McKenzie	Jack O. McKenzie	1997	416
188 3/8	25 2/8	26 3/8	17 1/8	5 1/8	5	7	9	New Haven Co., CT	Christopher K. Krista	Christopher K. Krista	1998	416
188 3/8	23	23 1/8	17 6/8	7 1/8	6 3/8	9	9	Clay Co., KS	Gail W. Steenbock	Gail W. Steenbock	1999	416

Score	Main Beam R	Main Beam L	Inside Spread	Circ. R	Circ. L	Points R	Points L	Locality	Hunter	Owner	Date Killed	Rank
188 1/8	26 5/8	28 1/8	22 1/8	4 7/8	5 1/8	6	10	Clay Co., IA	Bob Syndergarrd	Bob Syndergarrd	1984	419
187 7/8	27 2/8	28 1/8	27	5 4/8	5 3/8	7	8	Highland Co., OH	Larry M. Black	Larry M. Black	1995	420
187 7/8	28 2/8	27 4/8	27	5 2/8	5 7/8	8	9	Chisago Co., MN	Christopher L. Johnson	Christopher L. Johnson	1998	420
187 4/8	24 5/8	24 3/8	18 5/8	5 5/8	5 4/8	15	10	Grant Co., KY	Jon B. Good	Jon B. Good	1998	422
187 4/8	28 1/8	31 3/8	23 6/8	5 2/8	5 3/8	12	9	Huron Co., OH	Rodney L. Cook	Rodney L. Cook	1999	422
187 4/8	24 2/8	24 1/8	21 2/8	4 6/8	5 2/8	9	9	Pushmataha Co., OK	Clyde W. Gibbons	Clyde W. Gibbons	1999	422
187 3/8	26 5/8	27 6/8	22	5 6/8	5 6/8	7	7	Gogebic Co., MI	James W. Ansami	James W. Ansami	1998	425
187 2/8	27 3/8	27 3/8	23 5/8	4 3/8	4 3/8	8	7	Brooks Co., TX	Richard M. Pilgrim	Richard M. Pilgrim	1980	426
186 7/8	25 4/8	24 5/8	22 5/8	4 6/8	4 7/8	8	7	Marshall Co., IN	Matt J. Meyers	Matt J. Meyers	1997	427
186 7/8	28 5/8	26 5/8	25 2/8	4 7/8	4 5/8	5	7	Fayette Co., IN	William C. Powers II	William C. Powers II	1999	427
186 6/8	25 2/8	25 6/8	18 7/8	5 3/8	5	7	7	Adams Co., IL	Gregory D. Schutte	Gregory D. Schutte	1996	429
186 5/8	26 1/8	27 3/8	19 3/8	5 4/8	5 1/8	9	9	Brown Co., MN	Gerald W. Griebel	Gerald W. Griebel	1978	430
186 5/8	23 2/8	22 5/8	17 4/8	4 6/8	4 6/8	9	8	Ashtabula Co., OH	Wesley J. Gaul, Sr.	Wesley J. Gaul, Sr.	1992	430
186 5/8	25 6/8	22 4/8	19	6 7/8	7 5/8	12	10	Outagamie Co., WI	Picked Up	Chad Schroeder	1998	430
186 3/8	24 2/8	24 6/8	20 1/8	4 6/8	4 6/8	10	9	Custer Co., SD	Unknown	Brad F. Pfefer	1977	433
186 3/8	23 7/8	24 6/8	17	4 2/8	4 3/8	10	8	Daviess Co., MO	Michael E. Cross	Michael E. Cross	1998	433
186 2/8	24 5/8	26	19 4/8	5 3/8	5 5/8	9	7	Dickinson Co., KS	Orren L. Holt	Orren L. Holt	1999	435
186 1/8	25 2/8	27	17 4/8	6 2/8	6	10	7	Keya Paha Co., NE	Michael L. LeZotte	Michael L. LeZotte	1997	436
186 1/8	24 1/8	25 5/8	21 4/8	4 3/8	4 1/8	9	10	Mahoning Co., OH	Robert A. Schiele	Robert A. Schiele	1999	436
186	23 5/8	23 4/8	17 1/8	4 4/8	4 4/8	9	9	Flathead Co., MT	Bruce H. Louden	Bruce H. Louden	1988	438
186	24 7/8	24	21 3/8	5 3/8	5 3/8	7	7	Calhoun Co., MI	Leland D. Putnam	Leland D. Putnam	1997	438
185 7/8	26 7/8	27 5/8	22 7/8	4 6/8	4 7/8	8	10	Hancock Co., IL	Joshua T. Baird	Joshua T. Baird	1998	440
185 7/8	25 1/8	24 4/8	18 3/8	5 3/8	5 3/8	9	8	Becker Co., MN	Anthony J. Donner	Anthony J. Donner	1998	440
185 7/8	26 3/8	28	18 3/8	5 3/8	5 3/8	8	6	Todd Co., KY	Alan Mansfield	Alan Mansfield	1998	440
185 7/8	24	24 4/8	16 2/8	5 1/8	5 4/8	8	10	Dent Co., MO	Brent W. Young	Brent W. Young	1998	440
185 6/8	27 1/8	22 4/8	22 6/8	4 5/8	5	7	9	Charles Co., MD	Thomas M. Maddox	Thomas M. Maddox	1999	444
185 5/8	22 4/8	22 6/8	18 7/8	5	4 7/8	9	7	St. Ann Lake, AB	Brian Lehenki	Brian Lehenki	1997	445
185 4/8	24 5/8	24 3/8	19 7/8	4 6/8	4 7/8	8	9	Dawson Creek, BC	Doug Field	Doug Field	1993	446
185 4/8	23 5/8	23 4/8	17 5/8	5 1/8	5 2/8	9	9	Cass Co., NE	Joseph E. Woitzel	Joseph E. Woitzel	1998	446
185 4/8	20 4/8	22 6/8	17 2/8	6 2/8	5 7/8	11	10	Love Co., OK	Barry L. Bowker	Barry L. Bowker	1999	446
185 3/8	25 5/8	25	19 6/8	4 7/8	5	8	8	Kingman Co., KS	Robert L. Ciravolo	Robert L. Ciravolo	1998	449
185 3/8	23 6/8	23 7/8	17 7/8	5	5	8	7	Metcalf Co., KY	Picked Up	David Dick	1998	449
185 3/8	25 7/8	24 4/8	15 4/8	4 6/8	4 7/8	9	10	Madison Co., IA	Dwayne C. Bechtol	Dwayne C. Bechtol	1999	449
185 3/8	23 7/8	24 4/8	18	5	5	7	8	Clay Co., MN	Todd M. Landa	Todd M. Landa	1999	449
185 2/8	28 3/8	28 1/8	20 6/8	5 6/8	5 6/8	7	6	Porter Co., IN	David A. Bobrowski	David A. Bobrowski	1997	453
185 2/8	21 1/8	20 3/8	18 1/8	4 7/8	4 6/8	7	10	McIntosh Co., OK	Larry L. Burchfield	Larry L. Burchfield	1998	453
185 2/8	23 6/8	24 1/8	17 6/8	5	5	7	7	Jefferson Co., MS	Jeff D. Ingram, Jr.	Jeff D. Ingram, Jr.	1998	453
185 2/8	26 1/8	26	17 4/8	4	4 3/8	8	8	Oxford Co., ME	Michael R. Morris	Michael R. Morris	1999	453
185 1/8	24 1/8	24	21 1/8	5 2/8	5 4/8	8	8	Nez Perce Co., ID	Nick Roberson	Nick Roberson	1977	457
185 1/8	26 4/8	24 1/8	23 3/8	4 7/8	4 7/8	7	8	Columbia Co., WI	Wilfred Alt	Wilfred Alt	1997	457
185 1/8	26 3/8	27 2/8	21	5 2/8	5 1/8	7	8	Rock Co., WI	Lawrence O. Stomprude	Lawrence O. Stomprude	1998	457
185 1/8	26 4/8	24 2/8	19 1/8	5 4/8	5 6/8	7	5	Mills Co., IA	John R. McElvain	John R. McElvain	1999	457
185 1/8	26 1/8	24 2/8	19 4/8	5 6/8	5 6/8	7	8	Fayette Co., IA	Gerald Miller	Gerald Miller	1999	457

WHITETAIL DEER - NON-TYPICAL ANTLERS

Odocoileus virginianus virginianus and certain related subspecies

Score	Length of Main Beam R.	L.	Inside Spread	Circumference at Smallest Place Between Burr and First Point R.	L.	Number of Points R.	L.	Locality	Hunter	Owner	Date Killed	Rank
185	24 6/8	25 7/8	18 2/8	4 2/8	4 2/8	9	8	Itasca Co., MN	Fred Sandness	E.F. Anderson & H. Westrom	1912	462
185	26 6/8	26	20 1/8	4 7/8	4 5/8	11	8	St. Louis Co., MN	David A. Wuorinen	David A. Wuorinen	1999	462
261 5/8*	25 6/8	23	21 5/8	5 7/8	6	16	15	Park Co., WY	Bobby L. Beeman	Bobby L. Beeman	1998	
254 2/8*	26 3/8	25 1/8	19 1/8	5 6/8	5 6/8	13	11	Frenchman Butte, SK	Dwayne Erb	Dwayne Erb	1999	
252 6/8*	27 1/8	24 5/8	17 1/8	5 7/8	5 5/8	9	15	Sandy Lake, AB	Donald Brenneman	Donald Brenneman	1998	
251 6/8*	30 4/8	31 6/8	25 2/8	5 5/8	5 3/8	12	13	Fulton Co., IL	William K. Brown	William K. Brown	1999	

* Final score subject to revision by additional verifying measurements.

COUES' WHITETAIL DEER - TYPICAL ANTLERS

Odocoileus virginianus couesi

Minimum Score 100 — World's Record 144 1/8

Score	Length of Main Beam R	L	Inside Spread	Circumference at Smallest Place Between Burr and First Point R	L	Number of Points R	L	Locality	Hunter	Owner	Date Killed	Rank
126 6/8	20	18 7/8	17 6/8	4 7/8	5 1/8	5	5	Yavapai Co., AZ	Picked Up	Joshua E. Epperson	1999	1
124 6/8	16 7/8	17 1/8	15 1/8	3 7/8	4 1/8	7	6	Gila Co., AZ	Tommy T. Zienka	Tommy T. Zienka	1998	2
124	18 7/8	18 6/8	15	3 4/8	3 4/8	6	5	Sonora, MX	Joseph P. Kalt	Joseph P. Kalt	1998	3
122 5/8	20 5/8	20 6/8	15	4 4/8	4 4/8	5	4	Chihuahua, MX	Kirk Kelso	Kirk Kelso	1997	4
118 6/8	18	17 7/8	16 4/8	3 7/8	4	5	5	Chihuahua, MX	Alberto Trousselle	Alberto Trousselle	1996	5
117 4/8	18 1/8	18	15 6/8	4 3/8	4 1/8	4	4	Apache Co., AZ	Harry Neff	Harry Neff	1995	6
116 5/8	20 7/8	19 6/8	17 7/8	4 3/8	4 3/8	6	4	Greenlee Co., AZ	John R. Primasing, Jr.	John R. Primasing, Jr.	1997	7
115 1/8	18 3/8	18 1/8	13 1/8	4	4	5	5	Pima Co., AZ	Robert A. Finelli	Robert A. Finelli	1997	8
114 5/8	18 6/8	18 2/8	15 5/8	3 5/8	3 6/8	4	4	Pima Co., AZ	James A. Reynolds	James A. Reynolds	1984	9
114 4/8	17 5/8	18 3/8	14 4/8	4 1/8	4	4	5	Hidalgo Co., NM	Travis Darnell	W.B. Darnell	1986	10
114 3/8	17 2/8	18 5/8	13 3/8	3 7/8	4	5	4	Pima Co., AZ	James A. Reynolds	James A. Reynolds	1980	11
114 2/8	19 6/8	18 5/8	13 6/8	4 1/8	4 2/8	5	4	Pima Co., AZ	Steven E. Shooks	Steven E. Shooks	1998	12
113 7/8	19	18 7/8	14 3/8	4 2/8	4 2/8	4	5	Pima Co., AZ	James A. Reynolds	James A. Reynolds	1985	13
113 7/8	17 3/8	18 1/8	15 5/8	3 7/8	3 6/8	4	4	Pinal Co., AZ	James L. Boyd	James L. Boyd	1997	13
113 7/8	19 6/8	20 4/8	14 3/8	3 6/8	3 7/8	5	6	Santa Cruz Co., AZ	Picked Up	James A. Reynolds	1999	13
113 3/8	17 2/8	18 2/8	15 3/8	4 1/8	4 1/8	4	4	Navajo Co., AZ	Picked Up	Harry Neff	1999	16
113 2/8	18 3/8	18 1/8	14 2/8	4	4	5	4	Pima Co., AZ	James A. Reynolds	James A. Reynolds	1997	17
113	18 1/8	18 4/8	15 4/8	3 7/8	3 7/8	5	5	Pima Co., AZ	Jeffrey K. Volk	M.E. Duperret & J.K. Volk	1998	18
112 6/8	16 3/8	17	10 6/8	3 7/8	3 6/8	4	4	Sonora, MX	Lee Christmas	Lee Christmas	1999	19
112 4/8	19 6/8	19 1/8	12 6/8	3 4/8	3 3/8	4	4	Pima Co., AZ	Donald H. McBride	Donald H. McBride	1999	20
112 3/8	17 2/8	17 3/8	15 7/8	3 4/8	3 4/8	5	5	Pima Co., AZ	Robert H. Conway	Robert H. Conway	1998	21
112	18	18	12 4/8	3 7/8	3 6/8	5	5	Sonora, MX	Mark G. Mills	Mark G. Mills	1998	22
111 5/8	17 2/8	18 2/8	13 7/8	3 7/8	4 1/8	4	4	Pima Co., AZ	Kevin T. Murray	Kevin T. Murray	1996	23
111 3/8	17 4/8	17 4/8	14 1/8	3 7/8	4 1/8	5	4	Sonora, MX	Larry J. Kruse	Larry J. Kruse	1999	24
111	19 5/8	18 6/8	11 3/8	4 1/8	4 2/8	5	4	Sonora, MX	Jack Atcheson, Jr.	Jack Atcheson, Jr.	1998	25
111	17 6/8	17	14 6/8	4 1/8	4 2/8	5	4	Santa Cruz Co., AZ	David M. Yearin	David M. Yearin	1999	25
110 6/8	17 2/8	16 2/8	14 2/8	4 4/8	4 1/8	4	5	Pima Co., AZ	Rudolph B. Aguilar	Rudolph B. Aguilar	1998	27
110 6/8	17 4/8	17 5/8	13 1/8	4 2/8	4	4	4	Santa Cruz Co., AZ	Julie L. Hopkins	Julie L. Hopkins	1998	27
110 3/8	18 2/8	18 2/8	13 5/8	3 7/8	4	4	4	Santa Cruz Co., AZ	Michael G. Adams	Michael G. Adams	1998	29
110	19 1/8	18 6/8	18	4 3/8	4 3/8	5	6	Sonora, MX	Picked Up	David A. Miller	1998	30
110	15 5/8	15 7/8	13	4 3/8	4 2/8	5	6	Maricopa Co., AZ	Picked Up	L. Pangerl & B. Johnson	1998	30
108 6/8	20	19 1/8	16 4/8	3 6/8	3 7/8	4	4	Sonora, MX	Lee M. Wahlund	Lee M. Wahlund	1998	32
107 5/8	17	17 3/8	14 7/8	3 7/8	4	4	4	Sierra Co., NM	Lonnie Seipp	Lonnie Seipp	1999	33
105 6/8	18 5/8	18 4/8	14 2/8	3 5/8	3 5/8	4	4	Sonora, MX	David E. Evanow	David E. Evanow	1999	34

COUES' WHITETAIL DEER - TYPICAL ANTLERS

Odocoileus virginianus couesi

Score	Length of Main Beam R.	L.	Inside Spread	Circumference at Smallest Place Between Burr and First Point R.	L.	Number of Points R.	L.	Locality	Hunter	Owner	Date Killed	Rank
105 2/8	16 7/8	17 7/8	12 6/8	3 7/8	3 7/8	5	5	Sonora, MX	David A. Miller	David A. Miller	2000	35
105	17 5/8	17 5/8	12 6/8	3 7/8	3 7/8	5	4	Sonora, MX	Peter W. Spear	Peter W. Spear	1997	36
104 4/8	15 6/8	16	13 4/8	4 1/8	4 2/8	4	4	Cochise Co., AZ	Bruce Asbury	Bruce Asbury	1966	37
104 3/8	18	16 7/8	12 7/8	4	4	4	4	Sonora, MX	David A. Miller	David A. Miller	1998	38
104 2/8	15 4/8	17	11 6/8	3 4/8	3 4/8	5	5	Sonora, MX	Peeler G. Lacey	Peeler G. Lacey	1998	39
104 1/8	16	15	12 3/8	4	4 4/8	4	5	Pima Co., AZ	John B. Kerfoot	John B. Kerfoot	1993	40
102 4/8	17 3/8	16 6/8	13 4/8	4 3/8	4 4/8	4	5	Pima Co., AZ	Jared L. Baker	Jared L. Baker	1998	41
102 3/8	16 6/8	16 6/8	12 7/8	3 4/8	4	5	4	Sonora, MX	Arthur E. Ashcraft	Arthur E. Ashcraft	1997	42
101 4/8	15 1/8	14 6/8	12 2/8	4	4	5	5	Graham Co., AZ	Patrick J. Bernard	Patrick J. Bernard	1995	43
101 2/8	15 7/8	16 4/8	14 4/8	4	4	4	4	Pima Co., AZ	Kimball B. Taylor	Kimball B. Taylor	1992	44
100 4/8	17 2/8	16 4/8	12 6/8	3 5/8	3 6/8	4	4	Sonora, MX	David A. Miller	David A. Miller	1999	45
100 3/8	15 6/8	16 4/8	15 3/8	4 3/8	4 3/8	6	6	Maricopa Co., AZ	Gregory M. Moore	Gregory M. Moore	1994	46
100 3/8	16 7/8	16 3/8	15	3 4/8	3 3/8	4	5	Sonora, MX	David A. Miller	David A. Miller	1999	46
121 3/8*	20	19 5/8	13 4/8	4 4/8	4 4/8	7	5	Pima Co., AZ	William A. Ball	William A. Ball	1999	

* Final score subject to revision by additional verifying measurements.

COUES' WHITETAIL DEER - NON-TYPICAL ANTLERS

Odocoileus virginianus couesi

Minimum Score 105   New World's Record 186 1/8

Score	Length of Main Beam R.	L.	Inside Spread	Circumference at Smallest Place Between Burr and First Point R.	L.	Number of Points R.	L.	Locality	Hunter	Owner	Date Killed	Rank
186 1/8	17 6/8	16 5/8	18 2/8	4 5/8	4 6/8	8	8	Hidalgo Co., NM	Peter M. Chase	W.B. Darnell	1941	1
151 3/8	19 6/8	19 7/8	15 3/8	4 3/8	4 4/8	7	8	Pima Co., Ariz.	Picked Up	Patrick H. Taylor	1997	2
148 4/8	20 3/8	20 4/8	17 3/8	4 6/8	4 6/8	6	6	Sonora, MX	Bruce K. Kidman	Bruce K. Kidman	2000	3
147	18 6/8	19 6/8	16 6/8	5	4 5/8	10	7	Pima Co., AZ	James A. Reynolds	James A. Reynolds	1991	4
140 7/8	17	18	14	4 4/8	4 2/8	10	7	Santa Cruz Co., AZ	Randal W. Reaves	Randal W. Reaves	1998	5
124 3/8	19 4/8	19 5/8	16 2/8	4 3/8	4 1/8	5	8	Arizona	C. Touche	Alan C. Ellsworth	1977	6
121 6/8	12 5/8	18 5/8	14 2/8	4 2/8	4 3/8	7	9	Pima Co., AZ	Rene E. Rodriguez	Rene E. Rodriguez	1998	7
121 5/8	15 7/8	17 1/8	14 1/8	4	4	7	6	Pima Co., AZ	James A. Reynolds	James A. Reynolds	1979	8
121 2/8	17 2/8	17 2/8	15 3/8	4 2/8	4 4/8	6	7	Apache Co., AZ	Picked Up	Harry Neff	1998	9
120	19 3/8	18 4/8	13 6/8	4 2/8	4 2/8	5	5	Apache Co., AZ	Picked Up	Harry Neff	1998	10
115 5/8	18 4/8	18 1/8	13 1/8	4	3 6/8	5	6	Sonora, MX	Thomas Bowman	Thomas Bowman	2000	11
115 1/8	15 3/8	14 5/8	14 2/8	3 7/8	5	5	8	Sonora, MX	Harold K. Han, Jr.	Harold K. Han, Jr.	1999	12
113 6/8	17 2/8	18 6/8	13 7/8	3 4/8	4	6	5	Cochise Co., AZ	Robert D. Kelley	Robert D. Kelley	1997	13
106 2/8	18 5/8	17 3/8	15 3/8	4	4	7	6	Sonora, MX	David F. Myrup	David F. Myrup	1999	14
159*	18 4/8	18 1/8	15 5/8	5	7 7/8	7	7	Pima Co., AZ	Daniel D. King	International Wildlife Museum	1991	

* Final score subject to revision by additional verifying measurements.

CANADA MOOSE

Alces alces americana and Alces alces andersoni

Minimum Score 185

World's Record 242

Three categories of moose are recognized for records keeping, with boundaries based on geographic lines. Canada moose includes trophies from Newfoundland and Canada (except for Yukon Territory and Northwest Territories), Maine, Minnesota, New Hampshire, North Dakota, and Vermont.

Score	Greatest Spread	Length of Palm R.	L.	Width of Palm R.	L.	Circumference of Beam at Smallest Place R.	L.	Number of Normal Points R.	L.	Locality	Hunter	Owner	Date Killed	Rank
219 6/8	61 2/8	46 6/8	45	15 7/8	16	7 3/8	7 5/8	13	11	Kinaskan Lake, BC	Thomas E. Farmer	Thomas E. Farmer	1998	1
217 6/8	63 6/8	40 6/8	39 6/8	17 4/8	18 7/8	7 7/8	7 6/8	12	16	Meat Cove, NS	Picked Up	Shawn Hadley	1995	2
215 3/8	60 3/8	43 6/8	45 3/8	13 4/8	14 2/8	8 4/8	8 2/8	12	12	Kearl Lake, AB	Leo D. Paquin	Leo D. Paquin	1998	3
215 1/8	66 3/8	41 2/8	41	13 2/8	14 2/8	7 1/8	7 2/8	13	14	Prairie River, SK	John Horvath	John Horvath	1987	4
214 2/8	62 4/8	48 5/8	45	14	14 4/8	7 7/8	7 7/8	14	9	Nipekamew Lake, SK	Greg Cochran	Greg Cochran	1999	5
213 4/8	62 4/8	47 3/8	44 3/8	13 5/8	13 4/8	7 5/8	8	11	10	Tatshenshini River, BC	James C. Ranck	James C. Ranck	1998	6
212 5/8	63 1/8	44 2/8	42 1/8	13 2/8	14 4/8	7 3/8	7 4/8	12	12	Lake Co., MN	Randall J. Wise	Randall J. Wise	1998	7
211	63 2/8	41 1/8	42 2/8	18 5/8	15 6/8	7 6/8	7 4/8	16	10	Red Earth Creek, AB	M. Nathan Sabo	M. Nathan Sabo	2000	8
210 5/8	58 5/8	43	42 6/8	14 6/8	15	7 4/8	7 5/8	16	11	Billard Lake, MB	Kendall J. Bauer	Kendall J. Bauer	1998	9
209 1/8	53 7/8	43 2/8	43 4/8	13	11 4/8	6 7/8	7	16	17	Red Earth Creek, AB	Gabriel J. Plamondon	Gabriel J. Plamondon	1997	10
208 7/8	54 3/8	43	43 2/8	13 7/8	13 4/8	6 6/8	6 6/8	14	14	Hivon Lake, AB	R. George Crooker	R. George Crooker	1997	11
208 6/8	65 2/8	42 6/8	40 7/8	13 6/8	11 6/8	8 1/8	8 4/8	12	11	Coos Co., NH	Norma J. Taplin	Norma J. Taplin	1999	12
208 4/8	56 2/8	42 2/8	40 1/8	13 3/8	14 4/8	7 5/8	8 2/8	15	15	Notikewin, AB	Bruce Friedel	Bruce Friedel	1994	13
207 7/8	56 7/8	42 6/8	42 3/8	13 5/8	11 7/8	7 2/8	7 3/8	16	14	Buckley Lake, BC	John F. Abbott	John F. Abbott	1996	14
207 6/8	62	41 1/8	41 3/8	13 3/8	13 3/8	7 7/8	7 7/8	13	11	Bocquene Lake, AB	John M. Damberger	John M. Damberger	1998	15
207 5/8	54 7/8	40 4/8	41 6/8	16	15 6/8	7 2/8	7 1/8	13	13	Dease Lake, BC	Robert T. Ryan	Robert T. Ryan	1997	16
207 2/8	56 4/8	38 4/8	39 4/8	14 4/8	14 4/8	7 3/8	7 3/8	15	15	Rock Lake, BC	Timothy J. Koll	Timothy J. Koll	1999	17
206 6/8	61 6/8	43 4/8	40 6/8	15 6/8	14 5/8	7 5/8	7 1/8	10	10	Gordondale, AB	Chuck LeDuc	Chuck LeDuc	1975	18
206 6/8	68	39	35 4/8	14 2/8	16 4/8	7 5/8	7 6/8	12	12	Cook Co., MN	R.J. Parent, J. Parent, & R. Parent	Rick J. Parent	2000	18
205 7/8	59 5/8	41	37 3/8	15 4/8	15	8	7 6/8	14	13	Dease Lake, BC	Gordon E. Janz	Gordon E. Janz	1997	20
205 6/8	62 4/8	42 5/8	44	18 4/8	11 7/8	8 1/8	8 1/8	16	9	Piscataquis Co., ME	Steve Heath	Brian Ross	1997	21
205 1/8	58 1/8	43	43	14 4/8	24 3/8	8	8	8	6	Eddies Cove, NF	Floyd Lawless	F. & I. Lawless	1999	22
205	59	41 5/8	42	15	13 2/8	7 1/8	7 4/8	13	11	Dease Creek, BC	Bert Berry	Bert Berry	1997	23
205	61	37 4/8	41 2/8	13 5/8	17	7 7/8	7 7/8	13	13	Long Lake, ON	Randy H. Shell	Randy H. Shell	1998	23
204 6/8	64 6/8	42 7/8	45	11 6/8	10 2/8	7 7/8	8	10	11	Cassiar Mts., BC	Douglas Rehbein	Douglas Rehbein	1998	25
204 1/8	62 1/8	36	38 2/8	16 5/8	15 5/8	7 3/8	7 4/8	12	12	Cassiar Mts., BC	Roger B. Donahue, Jr.	Roger B. Donahue, Jr.	1995	26
204	58	39 4/8	39 4/8	14 5/8	15 3/8	7 1/8	6 7/8	12	12	Dease Lake, BC	Robert L. Hudman	Robert L. Hudman	1998	27
203 6/8	61 4/8	41 4/8	41	11 5/8	16 2/8	8 4/8	8 4/8	10	14	Somerset Co., ME	Fanado J. Pelotte	Fanado J. Pelotte	1998	28
203 2/8	60	42	44 6/8	14 6/8	15 2/8	6 7/8	7	8	11	Little Rancheria River, BC	G.E. & R.G. Lueck	George E. Lueck	1999	29
203 1/8	49 3/8	40 5/8	41	13 6/8	13 6/8	7 4/8	7 6/8	15	16	Hatin Lake, BC	Werner Wistuba	Werner Wistuba	1998	30

Score										Locality	Hunter	Year	Rank
203	53 2/8	43 3/8	42 6/8	12 2/8	13 1/8	7 7/8	8 1/8	12	13	Gladys River, BC	Spencer J. Vaa	1998	31
202 2/8	58	41 2/8	43	14	13	7 3/8	7 6/8	11	12	Somerset Co., ME	John A. Albee	1998	32
201 7/8	55 7/8	40 4/8	40	17 1/8	15 2/8	8 1/8	7 6/8	10	10	Turnagain River, BC	Rodney S. Marcum	1997	33
201 5/8	56 7/8	42 6/8	41 2/8	16 1/8	14 7/8	8 2/8	7 6/8	9	9	Rainbow Lake, BC	Kelly D. Voigt	1997	34
200 1/8	49 3/8	47 2/8	47 5/8	15	13	8 2/8	8 1/8	8	7	Disella Lake, BC	Bryant Dunn	1996	35
200 1/8	56 5/8	43 1/8	41 6/8	11	11 4/8	7 2/8	8	12	12	Ten Mile Lake, NF	David W. Chambers	1997	35
199 4/8	52 2/8	43 2/8	44	15	12	8 3/8	7 7/8	11	11	Dease River, BC	William J. Falcheck	1999	37
199 3/8	56 3/8	44 6/8	41 6/8	13 2/8	13	7 6/8	8 1/8	13	9	Kechika River, BC	Willy Tielen	1997	38
199	59 2/8	46 4/8	40 4/8	17 3/8	14	8	7 7/8	13	10	Coos Co., NH	Ross H. Marble	1998	39
198 4/8	51 6/8	39 2/8	39 3/8	14 2/8	14 5/8	7	6 7/8	13	14	Rainbow Lake, AB	David S. Stelter	1998	40
198 4/8	50 4/8	37 6/8	43 3/8	15	18 4/8	7 2/8	7 2/8	14	14	Carroll Co., NH	A. Jay Van Dyne	1998	40
198 1/8	61 3/8	39 3/8	38	13	11	8 5/8	8 3/8	12	11	Bolkow, ON	Terry Coutcher	1998	42
197 7/8	55 5/8	44 4/8	45 4/8	14 3/8	11 4/8	7 2/8	7 1/8	8	8	Somerset Co., ME	Richard G. Bernier	1999	43
197 3/8	55 3/8	40 7/8	43 4/8	11 5/8	14	7 4/8	7 7/8	11	14	Coos Co., NH	Armand L. Hebert	1998	44
197 3/8	51 3/8	42	42 7/8	13 4/8	12 5/8	7 4/8	7 3/8	12	11	Atlin Lake, BC	James R. Gall	1999	44
196 7/8	59 5/8	36 5/8	36 5/8	15 3/8	14 4/8	6 4/8	6 5/8	11	12	Cook Co., MN	M. Groven, M. Groven, R. Anderson, & P. Anderson	1999	46
196 6/8	48 2/8	37 3/8	37 1/8	17 5/8	16 6/8	6 7/8	7	14	14	Moberly Lake, BC	Picked Up	1997	47
196 3/8	55 7/8	43 2/8	43 1/8	10 2/8	12 1/8	7 3/8	7 4/8	10	12	Blackfox Mt., BC	Robert P. O'Connor	1999	48
196 2/8	60 6/8	41 6/8	37 2/8	13 3/8	13 4/8	10 1/8	10 5/8	11	9	Ottawa Lake, QC	Robert Durocher	1998	49
196 2/8	63	36 6/8	38 3/8	13	11 6/8	7 1/8	7 1/8	11	11	McGregor River, BC	Kevin D. Gull	1999	49
196 1/8	58 5/8	40 2/8	41 1/8	12	14 1/8	7 4/8	7 4/8	15	9	Cree Lake, SK	Greg G. Darby	1998	51
196 1/8	54 5/8	41 2/8	39	11 3/8	13 4/8	7 3/8	7 3/8	13	16	Kearl Lake, AB	Robert Paquin	1999	51
196	60 4/8	39 6/8	40 7/8	11 5/8	12 6/8	7 3/8	7 6/8	9	13	Big Sand Lake, MB	Ronald F. Mancl	1999	53
195 7/8	54 5/8	40	40	12 7/8	12 6/8	7 7/8	8 1/8	10	12	Franklin Co., ME	Matthew Duguay	1998	54
195 5/8	56 5/8	40	41 6/8	11 2/8	10 3/8	7 1/8	7 6/8	12	12	Kechika River, BC	Don Pedersen	1999	55
195 4/8	57 6/8	39	38 2/8	14 3/8	14	7 5/8	7 6/8	10	9	McKenzie Lake, ON	Larry N. Cornellier, Sr.	1997	56
195 4/8	59 2/8	40 2/8	39	12 4/8	17 2/8	7 2/8	7 1/8	11	10	Port au Port Bay, NF	Paul R. Pearsall	2000	56
195 1/8	56 5/8	39 2/8	39 4/8	14 1/8	12 6/8	7 2/8	7 2/8	12	10	Ludwig Creek, BC	John M. Hinkle, Jr.	1998	58
195	59	42 2/8	39 4/8	12	11 5/8	8 3/8	7 7/8	9	12	Loune Lake, ON	Douglas H. Campbell	1998	59
195	54 6/8	40 2/8	42	12	12 5/8	7	6 7/8	11	13	Keily Creek, BC	Dennis D. Church	1999	59
195	56 2/8	41 3/8	40 2/8	12 4/8	12 2/8	7	6 7/8	10	11	Kakwa River, AB	David J. Gochenaur	1999	59
193 6/8	53 6/8	38 7/8	41	14 4/8	12 6/8	7 3/8	7 4/8	13	11	Vista Lake, ON	Timothy P. Crosby	1999	62
193 6/8	57 6/8	36 6/8	36 2/8	13 6/8	15	7	7 3/8	11	11	Dease Lake, BC	Ronald L. Miller	1999	62
193 5/8	58 5/8	36 5/8	39 5/8	12 6/8	13	7 2/8	7 1/8	11	11	Leyond River, MB	J. Ross Singleton	1999	64
193 1/8	64 1/8	40 6/8	38 5/8	11 5/8	11 6/8	7 2/8	7 2/8	10	7	Dease Lake, BC	Don L. Miller	1999	65
192 5/8	56 5/8	36 5/8	40	12 2/8	14 4/8	9	8 1/8	11	14	Red Earth Lake, SK	Fred J. Williams	2000	66
192 4/8	57 2/8	37 4/8	38 6/8	12 6/8	14 4/8	6 7/8	6 7/8	11	11	Toad River, BC	David F. Myrup	1999	67
192 3/8	61 1/8	35 3/8	40 2/8	15 4/8	15 4/8	8 3/8	7 6/8	13	7	Franklin Co., ME	Caleb P. Kimball	1998	68
192 3/8	52 7/8	40	44 3/8	13 6/8	11 2/8	7 4/8	7 5/8	11	12	Aroostook Co., ME	Jason R. Chapman	1999	68
192 2/8	51 2/8	39 6/8	37 6/8	13 6/8	12 6/8	8	8	12	12	McGregor River, BC	Lyle G. Nesbitt	1998	70
191 7/8	64 5/8	34 5/8	38	12 5/8	12 4/8	7 2/8	7	11	10	Oxford Co., ME	Chris C. Farrington	2000	71
191 4/8	64 4/8	40 1/8	34 3/8	12 4/8	13 7/8	7 6/8	7 5/8	12	10	Wright Lake, ON	John R. Melhus	1991	72

CANADA MOOSE

Alces alces americana and *Alces alces andersoni*

Score	Greatest Spread	Length of Palm R.	L.	Width of Palm R.	L.	Circumference of Beam at Smallest Place R.	L.	Number of Normal Points R.	L.	Locality	Hunter	Owner	Date Killed	Rank
191	58	35 2/8	39	13 1/8	12 5/8	7 1/8	8 6/8	12	18	Ontario	Spencer V. Silverthorne	Holly A. Silverthorne	1955	73
191	55	39 6/8	42	10 6/8	11 7/8	7 4/8	7 5/8	10	10	Pinto Creek, AB	Charles A. Wisekal	Charles A. Wisekal	1998	73
190 4/8	62 6/8	37	35 4/8	11	11	7 3/8	7 3/8	11	10	Somerset Co., ME	Jack R. Tindall	Jack R. Tindall	1999	75
190 4/8	59 4/8	36 3/8	33	14 2/8	14 2/8	7 6/8	7 2/8	13	12	Oxford Co., ME	Earl R. Zinck	Earl R. Zinck	1999	75
190 3/8	56	36 2/8	36 2/8	12 6/8	12 7/8	8	8	11	13	Washington Co., ME	Brian D. LaFrance	Brian D. LaFrance	1999	77
190 2/8	56	38	40 1/8	12 6/8	12 6/8	8	7 3/8	9	9	Cook Co., MN	S.G. & L.G. Antolick	S.G. & L.G. Antolick	1999	78
190 2/8	61 6/8	41 4/8	43	9 2/8	12 6/8	7	7 4/8	7	10	Franklin Co., ME	Gene M. Casey, Sr.	Gene M. Casey, Sr.	1999	78
189 4/8	61	35 2/8	35 6/8	11 7/8	11 2/8	7 6/8	7 6/8	10	10	Coos Co., NH	Robert V. Berger	Robert V. Berger	1999	80
189 3/8	56 5/8	40 6/8	38 5/8	10 1/8	12 4/8	7 5/8	7 5/8	10	10	Stupart Lake, MB	James M. Hoffmann	James M. Hoffmann	2000	81
189 1/8	59 3/8	37 4/8	36 4/8	14 2/8	13 2/8	7 1/8	7 5/8	8	11	Longlegged River, ON	John Leopold	John Leopold	1970	82
189	55 4/8	36 4/8	38 6/8	13 3/8	12 7/8	7 3/8	7 5/8	11	10	McEwen Creek, BC	Stan Dutoff	Stan Dutoff	1996	83
188 6/8	52 6/8	36 5/8	34 6/8	13 2/8	13 2/8	6 4/8	6 5/8	14	14	Porcupine Plain, SK	Harvey D. Messner	Harvey D. Messner	2000	84
184 4/8	55	39 1/8	41	13 2/8	14 2/8	7 3/8	7 3/8	9	7	Ovington Creek, BC	Susan D. Lowe	Susan D. Lowe	1998	85
187 7/8	61 7/8	34 2/8	35 2/8	11 1/8	12 4/8	6 5/8	7 1/8	11	13	Commisaires Lake, QC	Henry Grubisich	Henry Grubisich	1971	86
187 7/8	55 1/8	34 7/8	37 3/8	15 1/8	14 2/8	6 7/8	6 6/8	11	12	Kechika River, BC	Janet E. Cameron	Janet E. Cameron	1997	86
187 6/8	60 2/8	35 4/8	36 2/8	13 1/8	11	6 7/8	6 6/8	11	11	Somerset Co., ME	James P. Burgess	James P. Burgess	1999	88
187 4/8	52	37 4/8	38 7/8	14 3/8	15 2/8	6 7/8	6 7/8	9	9	Cassiar Mts., BC	Scott P. Young	Scott P. Young	1999	89
187 4/8	58 2/8	35 3/8	36 4/8	11 4/8	11 5/8	7 7/8	7 6/8	12	10	Aroostook Co., ME	Thomas E. O'Neill	Thomas E. O'Neill	2000	89
187 3/8	52 7/8	38	35	13 2/8	12	7 2/8	7 2/8	13	13	Aroostook Co., ME	R Edwin Hamilton	Holly S. Hamilton	1999	91
186 5/8	64 1/8	34 1/8	38	13 1/8	12 5/8	7 4/8	7 1/8	11	7	Essex Co., VT	Stephen D. Hunn	Stephen D. Hunn	1996	92
186 4/8	51 6/8	36 2/8	37 2/8	12 3/8	12 2/8	6 7/8	7 1/8	12	12	Ptarmigan Lake, BC	Francis E. McMillon	Francis E. McMillon	1998	93
185 6/8	57 2/8	39 1/8	39 1/8	14	11 2/8	7	6 7/8	12	7	Gladys River, BC	Warren E. Reeves	Warren E. Reeves	1999	94
185 4/8	49 2/8	38	36 6/8	12 4/8	13 1/8	7	6 7/8	12	12	Chukachida River, BC	Dale C. Emmans	Dale C. Emmans	1997	95
185 3/8	56 5/8	38	36 4/8	12 2/8	11 6/8	7 1/8	7 3/8	9	11	Coos Co., NH	Robert A. Gallant	Robert A. Gallant	1999	96
185 2/8	53	37	41 4/8	10 5/8	11 6/8	7 4/8	7 4/8	12	11	Island Lake, AB	Philip Ramish	Philip Ramish	1998	97
185	56 2/8	42 1/8	35	12	12 4/8	7 7/8	8 1/8	10	11	Telegraph Creek, BC	Curtis J. Babler	Curtis J. Babler	1998	98
185	64	32 6/8	43 4/8	16 4/8	15 6/8	7 7/8	7 4/8	5	10	Aroostook Co., ME	Paul S. Milliken	Paul S. Milliken	1999	98
185	59 4/8	39 1/8	36 6/8	13 5/8	12 1/8	7 7/8	8	6	9	Savant Lake, ON	John W. Reck	John W. Reck	1999	98
220 6/8*	60 4/8	43 2/8	43 3/8	14 1/8	14 4/8	7 6/8	8 2/8	15	16	Aroostook Co., ME	Cynthia M. Higgins	Cynthia M. Higgins	2000	
217*	61 6/8	42 6/8	47 7/8	14 3/8	18 4/8	6 4/8	6 7/8	14	18	Franklin Co., ME	Clifford H. Damon	Clifford H. Damon	1997	
216*	61 4/8	37 5/8	43 3/8	17 6/8	17 4/8	8 1/8	8 6/8	16	14	Oxford Co., ME	Brian A. Martin	Brian A. Martin	1998	

* Final score subject to revision by additional verifying measurements.

ALASKA-YUKON MOOSE

Alces alces gigas

Minimum Score 210

World's Record 261 5/8

Alaska-Yukon moose includes trophies from Alaska, Yukon Territory, and Northwest Territories.

Score	Greatest Spread	Length of Palm R.	L.	Width of Palm R.	L.	Circumference of Beam at Smallest Place R.	L.	Number of Normal Points R.	L.	Locality	Hunter	Owner	Date Killed	Rank
256 6/8	78 2/8	49 6/8	50 5/8	17 3/8	18 2/8	7 5/8	7 6/8	16	15	Beluga River, AK	William G. Nelson	William G. Nelson	1997	1
245 2/8	70 4/8	46 4/8	44 4/8	22 2/8	19	8 1/8	7 7/8	16	16	Ruby Creek, AK	James W. Gelhaus	James W. Gelhaus	1997	2
241	74 2/8	42 7/8	47 3/8	18	20	7 4/8	7 6/8	15	16	Anvil Range, YT	Dawson H. Colby, Jr.	Dawson H. Colby, Jr.	2000	3
239 6/8	66 2/8	46 5/8	47 2/8	18 3/8	17 6/8	7 3/8	7 4/8	15	17	Yukon Territory	Nick Engles	Don C. Kirkpatrick	1967	4
239 2/8	69	49 4/8	50 2/8	16 1/8	15 5/8	8	8 1/8	14	12	Ladue River, AK	Tim N. Hand	Tim N. Hand	1997	5
239 1/8	64 1/8	49	50 7/8	17 5/8	18 4/8	7 7/8	8 1/8	14	13	Rabideux Creek, AK	Derrick G. Bell	Derrick G. Bell	1997	6
237 6/8	71 4/8	47 6/8	48 7/8	16 3/8	15 5/8	7 6/8	7 7/8	12	12	Selwyn Mts., YT	William J. Weaver	William J. Weaver	1970	7
237 6/8	72	44 2/8	50	18 3/8	21 6/8	7 6/8	8 2/8	13	16	Melozitna River, AK	Darrell C. Aplanalp	Darrell C. Aplanalp	1998	7
237 2/8	68 4/8	49	53 1/8	17 4/8	18	7 3/8	7 4/8	12	11	Tikchik River, AK	Mark T. Rule	Mark T. Rule	1999	9
236 5/8	73 3/8	49 6/8	47 6/8	15 7/8	15 1/8	7 6/8	7 7/8	11	11	Buckstock River, AK	Thomas R. Drake	Thomas R. Drake	2000	10
236 2/8	65 4/8	48 4/8	49	15 6/8	15 5/8	7 2/8	7 2/8	14	14	Lake Clark, AK	Robert J. Salome	Robert J. Salome	1998	11
235 4/8	66 4/8	46 4/8	45	20 3/8	19 2/8	8 2/8	8 4/8	13	12	Farewell Lake, AK	James M. Moore	James M. Moore	2000	12
234 4/8	68 4/8	46 1/8	46	18 7/8	18 1/8	7 7/8	8 2/8	11	15	Mt. Susitna, AK	Richard M. Young	Richard M. Young	1999	13
233 2/8	70 4/8	49 1/8	47 1/8	17 1/8	12 6/8	8 4/8	8 6/8	13	13	Koyukuk River, AK	Scott A. Shipman	Scott A. Shipman	1998	14
233 1/8	66 7/8	46 6/8	47 6/8	16	16 2/8	7 3/8	7 4/8	15	13	Yuki River, AK	Steven B. Spaulding	Steven B. Spaulding	1998	15
231 4/8	64 2/8	45 4/8	47 2/8	16 3/8	17	7 6/8	7 7/8	14	14	Ogilvie Mts., YT	Ken Taylor	Ken Taylor	1997	16
230 4/8	69 4/8	48 7/8	49 4/8	14 4/8	15 5/8	8 1/8	8 7/8	9	14	Tazimina River, AK	Gary L. Jacobs II	Gary L. Jacobs II	1998	17
230 4/8	63	45 4/8	47	17 4/8	17 4/8	7 6/8	8 1/8	13	17	Melozitna River, AK	Dennis M. Fuller	Dennis M. Fuller	1999	17
230 3/8	66 7/8	42 6/8	46 5/8	19	22 2/8	7 4/8	7 4/8	13	16	Innoko River, AK	Keith W. Arnold	Aly M. Bruner	1987	19
229 6/8	58 6/8	48 3/8	49 6/8	16 2/8	18	8 7/8	8 7/8	15	12	Kuskokwim River, AK	Theodore L. Hetrick, Jr.	Theodore L. Hetrick, Jr.	1999	20
229 2/8	65 6/8	45	45 1/8	14 6/8	15	8 2/8	8	14	16	Fortymile River, AK	Chuck Thorsrud	Chuck Thorsrud	1998	21
229 1/8	67 3/8	47 4/8	48 7/8	16 4/8	13 4/8	8	7 7/8	12	13	Mosquito Mt., AK	Gary L. Hebbert	Gary L. Hebbert	2000	22
229	75 4/8	47 2/8	44 4/8	18 6/8	16	8 5/8	8 5/8	10	13	Mulchatna River, AK	Charles A. LeKites	Charles A. LeKites	1999	23
229	65 6/8	43 3/8	44 5/8	15 7/8	15 7/8	7 3/8	7 4/8	15	15	Lake Clark, AK	Ronald W. Rogers	Ronald W. Rogers	2000	23
228 7/8	70 5/8	45 4/8	45 3/8	15 2/8	16 2/8	7 5/8	7 5/8	11	12	Mackenzie Mts., NT	Thomas N. Osso	Thomas N. Osso	2000	25
228 1/8	74 7/8	49 4/8	52	13	14 5/8	7 5/8	7 6/8	9	13	Jones River, AK	Dale J. Martin	Dale J. Martin	2000	26
227 6/8	66 6/8	48 6/8	49	14 7/8	14 2/8	8 4/8	8 4/8	9	10	Chekok Lake, AK	Don W. Noah	Don W. Noah	2000	27
227 5/8	64 3/8	44 5/8	50 3/8	15 4/8	15 3/8	7 5/8	7 7/8	14	16	Discovery Creek, AK	Joseph R. Weber	Joseph R. Weber	1998	28
227 4/8	61 2/8	46 2/8	45 6/8	14 4/8	15 1/8	7 7/8	8	15	15	Granite Mt., AK	Michael A. Mendenhall	Michael A. Mendenhall	1998	29
227 4/8	69	49	44 3/8	15 4/8	14 3/8	9 4/8	9 5/8	11	13	Wheeler Creek, AK	Stephen R. Vogler	Stephen R. Vogler	1999	29
226 6/8	71 2/8	44 4/8	43 5/8	15 4/8	14 4/8	7 5/8	7 5/8	12	12	McGrath, AK	Bryan T. Patterson	Bryan T. Patterson	1999	31
226 5/8	65 5/8	42 3/8	46 2/8	16 2/8	15 4/8	8 5/8	8 5/8	14	14	Manley Hot Springs, AK	Robert J. Fowler	Robert J. Fowler	1999	32

Alces alces gigas

Score	Greatest Spread	Length of Palm R.	L.	Width of Palm R.	L.	Circumference of Beam at Smallest Place R.	L.	Number of Normal Points R.	L.	Locality	Hunter	Owner	Date Killed	Rank
226 4/8	71 4/8	43	43	17 4/8	17 5/8	7	7	12	10	Alaska Pen., AK	Ben E. Meyers	Ben E. Meyers	1994	33
226 4/8	65	46	47 2/8	14 4/8	14 7/8	8 2/8	8 2/8	12	12	Fortymile River, AK	Alan Jubenville	Alan Jubenville	1998	33
226 3/8	61 5/8	41 6/8	42 6/8	15 3/8	17 5/8	7 3/8	7 2/8	18	19	Shale Lake, NT	Jerold B. Millendorf	Jerold B. Millendorf	1997	35
226	57	48 2/8	48	15 7/8	14 7/8	8 5/8	8 6/8	13	13	Koyukuk River, AK	Jack L. Brickner	Jack L. Brickner	1999	36
226	67	44 1/8	47 6/8	16	18 6/8	7 3/8	7 5/8	12	14	Innoko River, AK	John J. Cronin III	John J. Cronin III	1999	36
225 6/8	67 2/8	46 6/8	45 2/8	13 1/8	12 7/8	8 1/8	8 1/8	15	13	White River, AK	Dave L. Hanson	Dave L. Hanson	1998	38
225 5/8	66 5/8	44 3/8	47 7/8	16	15 5/8	8	8 1/8	14	12	Koyukuk River, AK	Michael S. Berg	Michael S. Berg	1997	39
225 5/8	65 5/8	46 2/8	44 5/8	15 5/8	15 2/8	8 1/8	9	15	12	Moody Creek, AK	Robert J. Kaseta	Robert J. Kaseta	1997	39
225 4/8	65 6/8	42 5/8	43 1/8	16 1/8	16 5/8	7 1/8	7 2/8	15	14	Caribou Hills, AK	Bill H. Baucum	Bill H. Baucum	1996	41
225 4/8	60 6/8	44 2/8	48 5/8	16 1/8	15 5/8	8 4/8	8 7/8	14	16	MacMillan River, YT	Warren L. Strickland	Warren L. Strickland	1998	41
225 3/8	66 3/8	45 1/8	44	14 7/8	14 7/8	7 5/8	7 7/8	13	15	Rainy Pass, AK	Michael H. Rivard	Michael H. Rivard	1997	43
225 2/8	66 6/8	46	43 5/8	15 6/8	16 4/8	8 3/8	8 3/8	12	12	Yanert, AK	Christopher J. Davis	Christopher J. Davis	1997	44
225 1/8	67 5/8	48	46 3/8	13 6/8	15 4/8	7 5/8	7 6/8	11	14	Aniak River, AK	Michael T. Williams	Michael T. Williams	1999	45
225	64 2/8	44 4/8	46 4/8	19	16 4/8	7 3/8	7 3/8	12	13	Koyukuk River, AK	Alan L. Earnest	Alan L. Earnest	1998	46
224 7/8	68 5/8	42 6/8	43 2/8	17 4/8	14 4/8	7 7/8	8 1/8	13	17	Wind River, YT	Chris P. Morton	Chris P. Morton	1997	47
224 6/8	67 6/8	47 4/8	48 1/8	20 4/8	13 5/8	7 3/8	7 3/8	13	11	Chilchitna River, AK	Mike Henry	Mike Henry	1999	48
224 2/8	63 4/8	49 6/8	49 3/8	14 4/8	13 5/8	7 3/8	7 5/8	11	10	Iliamna Lake, AK	Craig L. Halstead	Craig L. Halstead	1997	49
224 2/8	62	46 2/8	45 5/8	17	18 5/8	8 5/8	8 4/8	11	10	Koyukuk River, AK	Steven C. Tressler	Steven C. Tressler	1997	49
223 4/8	70 4/8	41 4/8	42	19 4/8	17 4/8	7 4/8	7 4/8	10	12	Naknek, AK	Robert H. Hanson	Robert H. Hanson	1969	51
222 6/8	61	44 3/8	41 7/8	16 2/8	15 4/8	7 4/8	7 4/8	16	16	Galena, AK	Daniel F. Wand	Daniel F. Wand	1995	52
222 6/8	59 6/8	44	44	15 3/8	14 7/8	7 5/8	7 5/8	15	17	Farewell Lake, AK	Pat Hurley	Pat Hurley	1999	52
222 1/8	57 5/8	48 4/8	46 4/8	15 4/8	19 4/8	8 2/8	8 2/8	12	12	Koyukuk, AK	Steve Purviance	Steve Purviance	1999	54
221 3/8	74 5/8	39 6/8	41 3/8	16 7/8	25 1/8	8 4/8	8 2/8	11	17	Cordova, AK	William T. Dungan	Larry D. Bollier	1979	55
221 2/8	65 4/8	43 7/8	47 2/8	15 4/8	15 6/8	7 4/8	7 4/8	11	14	Koyukuk River, AK	Richard Deem	Richard Deem	1999	56
221	66 4/8	41 6/8	42 2/8	14 4/8	16 1/8	8	8	13	15	Kuskokwim River, AK	Lucky Simpson	Lucky Simpson	1997	57
220 6/8	60 6/8	48 3/8	47 3/8	16 5/8	16 5/8	6 7/8	6 7/8	10	10	Bristol Bay, AK	Otto E. Olson	Otto E. Olson	1998	58
220 2/8	67 6/8	52 7/8	48	11 5/8	13 4/8	7 5/8	7 5/8	9	11	Ugashik Lake, AK	Jason C. Wrinkle	Jason C. Wrinkle	1997	59
220	65	43 1/8	41 3/8	15	15 2/8	7 3/8	7 7/8	14	15	Ess Lake, YT	Thomas L. Cope	Thomas L. Cope	1999	60
220	62 4/8	41 4/8	42 1/8	21	17	8 3/8	8 2/8	14	12	Aniak, AK	Dennison V. Peiffer	Dennison V. Peiffer	1999	60
219 7/8	66 5/8	44 2/8	42 2/8	17 3/8	17 4/8	7	7	10	10	Iliamna Lake, AK	Craig T. Wickman	Craig T. Wickman	1999	62
218 7/8	67 3/8	43	43	16 2/8	19 3/8	7 4/8	7 7/8	10	9	Koyukuk River, AK	James K. Wilkens	James K. Wilkens	1999	63
218 5/8	61 1/8	44 6/8	43 6/8	15 3/8	14	7 1/8	7	14	16	Koyukuk River, AK	Chris M. Kendrick	Chris M. Kendrick	1997	64
218 2/8	61 2/8	45 6/8	46 4/8	13 7/8	13 7/8	7 7/8	7 7/8	11	12	Noatak River, AK	Scott A. Wilkinson	Scott A. Wilkinson	2000	65
217 5/8	65 7/8	43 2/8	42 5/8	22 2/8	15 2/8	7	7 1/8	12	11	Mountain River, NT	Robert D. Jones	Robert D. Jones	1998	66

Score										Locality	Owner	Hunter	Date	Rank
217 4/8	70	45 3/8	45 3/8	13 2/8	16 6/8	7 5/8	7 5/8	8	11	September Lake, AK	Robert Boyd	Robert Boyd	1997	67
217 2/8	63 6/8	45 6/8	45 4/8	14 4/8	15 1/8	6 7/8	6 6/8	10	10	Buckland River, AK	Dennis C. Foster	Dennis C. Foster	2000	68
216 6/8	62 2/8	42 3/8	41 1/8	16 2/8	15 2/8	6 4/8	6 5/8	14	14	Aniak, AK	John Nutt	John Nutt	1997	69
216 3/8	69 1/8	42 6/8	40 6/8	16 1/8	15 6/8	7 2/8	7 1/8	10	11	Burnt Cabin Creek, AK	Mitchell S. Baxter	Mitchell S. Baxter	1999	70
216 3/8	60 5/8	45 7/8	43 5/8	13 1/8	14	8 1/8	8 2/8	14	14	Yukon River, AK	Stephen E. Melton, Jr.	Stephen E. Melton, Jr.	2000	70
215 6/8	68 6/8	39 4/8	42	13 5/8	13 4/8	8	8	14	13	Iliamna Lake, AK	Eugene L. Cole	Eugene L. Cole	1997	72
215 6/8	53	52 3/8	48 2/8	15 7/8	17 3/8	8 4/8	8 2/8	11	9	Huslia River, AK	Brad A. Graeter	Brad A. Graeter	1998	72
215 6/8	63 6/8	42 6/8	38 4/8	18 3/8	17	7 4/8	8 4/8	13	18	Lyman Hills, AK	Rick L. Thompson	Rick L. Thompson	1999	72
215 5/8	61 1/8	43 4/8	45 3/8	16 2/8	14 6/8	8 4/8	8 4/8	11	14	Innoko River, AK	Robert E. Richardson	Robert E. Richardson	1996	75
215 4/8	60 2/8	45 1/8	49	15	16 3/8	7 4/8	7 4/8	10	11	Yantarni Creek, AK	Vernon R. Anderson	Vernon R. Anderson	1998	76
214 7/8	60 3/8	44 5/8	44 2/8	14 2/8	16 2/8	8 6/8	8 6/8	10	12	Selawik River, AK	Lawrence M. Yacubian	Lawrence M. Yacubian	1997	77
214 2/8	64 2/8	45 4/8	46 4/8	15 6/8	18 5/8	8 2/8	8 6/8	6	8	Kitchatna River, AK	Robert M. Fisher	Robert M. Fisher	1999	78
214 1/8	66 1/8	45 4/8	42 4/8	14 4/8	15 6/8	7	7 2/8	10	10	Lake Clark, AK	Joe Hill	Joe Hill	1989	79
214	68 6/8	40 7/8	43 4/8	13 3/8	14 4/8	8 3/8	8 7/8	10	11	Tikchik Lake, AK	Edward A. Conkell	Edward A. Conkell	1998	80
213 3/8	64 7/8	46 1/8	47 4/8	18	12 5/8	7 4/8	8 1/8	8	11	Port Heiden, AK	Charles A. LeKites	Charles A. LeKites	1998	81
213 3/8	70 5/8	41 3/8	43 1/8	15 7/8	14 1/8	8 7/8	9	7	8	Twopete Mt., YT	Mark R. Zimmerman	Mark R. Zimmerman	1998	81
213	57 6/8	54 2/8	45 4/8	15 4/8	14 3/8	7 6/8	7 6/8	11	10	Joseph Creek, AK	James E. Herren	James E. Herren	1997	83
213	61 4/8	41 7/8	43 4/8	13 4/8	14 7/8	7 3/8	7 4/8	13	14	Iliamna, AK	G. Todd Ralstin	G. Todd Ralstin	1997	83
213	72 2/8	41 4/8	37 2/8	13 4/8	15	8 1/8	8 2/8	12	13	Gilroy Mt., AK	Chad W. Sienkiewicz	Chad W. Sienkiewicz	1997	83
212 6/8	65 6/8	41 2/8	44 2/8	14 4/8	19 4/8	9	8 6/8	10	12	Kaliakh River, AK	Hope N. Crites	Hope N. Crites	2000	86
212 4/8	66	38 6/8	40 3/8	13 7/8	14 6/8	7 5/8	7 6/8	13	13	Fortymile River, AK	Tim D. Hiner	Tim D. Hiner	1997	87
212 4/8	63	40 4/8	42 7/8	15	14 2/8	7 7/8	7 7/8	12	12	Lachbuna Lake, AK	Brian P. Burke	Brian P. Burke	2000	87
212 4/8	61 6/8	43 6/8	46 2/8	13 2/8	14 2/8	7 3/8	7 6/8	11	14	Buchanan Creek, AK	Jeffrey A. Whitaker	Jeffrey A. Whitaker	2000	87
212 3/8	63 5/8	43 6/8	41	15	17 6/8	7 7/8	7 3/8	11	11	Yanert Fork, AK	Phillip N. Kromm	Phillip N. Kromm	1999	90
212 1/8	66 3/8	42 7/8	44	15 1/8	12 4/8	7 4/8	7 4/8	11	10	Chunitna Creek, AK	Robert C. Bowers III	Robert C. Bowers III	1999	91
212	62	45 3/8	47 3/8	12 7/8	13 4/8	7 6/8	8	11	9	Mystic Lake, AK	Donald E. Reichel	Donald E. Reichel	1999	92
211 6/8	65 2/8	43 1/8	45 2/8	12	12 5/8	7 1/8	7 1/8	11	11	Swift River, AK	J.D. Felps & E.W. Holmes	J.D. Felps & E.W. Holmes	1999	93
211 5/8	63 5/8	44 4/8	38 7/8	16 3/8	15	7 1/8	7 4/8	13	14	Telaquana Lake, AK	Del Mar Waters	Del Mar Waters	2000	94
211 4/8	60 4/8	40 4/8	43	14 4/8	14 6/8	7 4/8	7 5/8	13	13	Melozitna River, AK	Randy L. Minzenmayer	Randy L. Minzenmayer	1997	95
210 7/8	60 7/8	45 1/8	45 1/8	12 6/8	12 5/8	7 2/8	7 2/8	10	10	Mosquito Creek, AK	Boby Slinkard	Boby Slinkard	2000	96
210 5/8	65 5/8	43 6/8	42	15 1/8	14 6/8	6 7/8	6 6/8	10	9	Koyukuk River, AK	Brian L. Allen	Brian L. Allen	1998	97
210 4/8	62	41 3/8	42 5/8	14 3/8	13 6/8	7 1/8	7 1/8	15	12	Becharof, AK	Roy C. Vande Hey	Roy C. Vande Hey	1998	98
210	63 6/8	40 6/8	40 3/8	15 5/8	16 5/8	7 1/8	7 4/8	10	10	Wood River, AK	Dan G. Janochoski	Dan G. Janochoski	1998	99
247 2/8*	71	48 2/8	49 2/8	20 2/8	21 7/8	8 2/8	8 1/8	17	12	Ogilvie Mts, YT	Dennis C. Campbell	Dennis C. Campbell	1998	
244 6/8*	78 2/8	45 3/8	46	16 1/8	17 4/8	7 6/8	8	14	15	Tsiu River, AK	John T. Portemont	John T. Portemont	1998	

* Final score subject to revision by additional verifying measurements.

WYOMING MOOSE

Alces alces shirasi

Minimum Score 140 World's Record 205 4/8

Wyoming (Shiras) moose includes trophies taken in Colorado, Idaho, Montana, Utah, Washington, and Wyoming.

Score	Greatest Spread	Length of Palm R.	L.	Width of Palm R.	L.	Circumference of Beam at Smallest Place R.	L.	Number of Normal Points R.	L.	Locality	Hunter	Owner	Date Killed	Rank
185 5/8	48 5/8	35 4/8	36 3/8	13 6/8	14 7/8	6 2/8	6 3/8	13	14	Bonneville Co., ID	Mary A. Isbell	Mary A. Isbell	2000	1
180 7/8	58 7/8	32 3/8	32 6/8	11 2/8	10 5/8	6	6	12	14	Missoula Co., MT	Picked Up	MT Dept. of Fish, Wildl., & Parks	1997	2
177 2/8	54 2/8	35 6/8	37 7/8	12	11 3/8	6 3/8	6 4/8	8	8	Shoshone Co., ID	April H. Preston	April H. Preston	1999	3
177	54 2/8	36 4/8	37 7/8	10 7/8	11 7/8	7	7 1/8	8	7	Teton Co., WY	James E. Jones	James E. Jones	2000	4
176 4/8	43 6/8	40	39	11 6/8	10	7 3/8	7 3/8	10	12	Madison Co., ID	Gerald D. Madsen	Gerald D. Madsen	1998	5
175 2/8	50 4/8	32 2/8	36 3/8	13 6/8	14 2/8	6 3/8	6 4/8	10	11	Larimer Co., CO	Thomas A. Thorson	Thomas A. Thorson	2000	6
175	51 4/8	38 2/8	33 4/8	12	10 2/8	7 2/8	7	13	11	Lewis & Clark Co., MT	James C. Johnson	James C. Johnson	1999	7
174 7/8	45 7/8	34 6/8	32 6/8	13 3/8	13 4/8	6 3/8	6 3/8	14	12	Teton Co., WY	William T. Jones	William T. Jones	2000	8
174 3/8	51 5/8	34 7/8	33 4/8	10 1/8	9 6/8	6 1/8	6 1/8	12	12	Caribou Co., ID	Leo E. Lish	Leo E. Lish	2000	9
171 5/8	49 3/8	36 2/8	32 2/8	12	12 4/8	6 7/8	7	10	10	Beaverhead Co., MT	George J. Wood	George J. Wood	2000	10
168 5/8	52 1/8	33 4/8	34 4/8	9 2/8	9 6/8	6 5/8	6 4/8	9	11	Bonneville Co., ID	Michael L. Adams	Michael L. Adams	1999	11
168 5/8	48 1/8	41 4/8	35 4/8	10 3/8	10 2/8	6 4/8	6 5/8	8	13	Summit Co., UT	Brandon E. Haws	Brandon E. Haws	2000	11
167 4/8	46 6/8	34 6/8	37 2/8	9 4/8	10 6/8	6 5/8	6 1/8	10	12	Bear Lake Co., ID	Tony Lloyd	Tony Lloyd	1992	13
167 4/8	44 2/8	34 4/8	35 2/8	11 6/8	13 2/8	6 3/8	6 4/8	9	9	Uinta Co., WY	David W. Black	David W. Black	1999	13
167 4/8	53 2/8	33 7/8	33	10 4/8	10	6 1/8	6 2/8	8	9	Teton Co., WY	Richard A. Hlavnicka	Richard A. Hlavnicka	2000	13
167 3/8	52 5/8	33 4/8	37	11 5/8	12 6/8	6 2/8	6 4/8	6	9	Idaho Co., ID	Antony G. Forrer	Antony G. Forrer	1998	16
167 2/8	50	34 1/8	34 1/8	11 3/8	12	6 1/8	6 1/8	8	7	Uinta Co., WY	Vanessa A. Bair	Vanessa A. Bair	2000	17
167 1/8	51 7/8	33 6/8	30 2/8	10 6/8	10 6/8	6 5/8	6 5/8	12	11	Boundary Co., ID	Robbie A. Piehl	Robbie A. Piehl	1998	18
165 2/8	47 6/8	32	31 4/8	11 1/8	11 2/8	6 4/8	6 1/8	10	11	Lincoln Co., MT	Roger L. Haas	Roger L. Haas	1997	19
165 2/8	48 6/8	30	31 5/8	11 6/8	12 3/8	6 6/8	6 4/8	10	10	Lincoln Co., MT	Chad M. Place	Chad M. Place	1998	19
164 7/8	42 7/8	33 2/8	34 2/8	10 2/8	11 6/8	6 6/8	6 4/8	11	12	Teton Co., WY	Roger L. Roraff	Roger L. Roraff	1997	21
164 5/8	52 5/8	29	33 6/8	10 7/8	11 6/8	6 1/8	6 2/8	10	11	Bonneville Co., ID	Robert Martineau	Robert Martineau	2000	22
164	53 4/8	30 5/8	33 7/8	9 4/8	9 6/8	6 1/8	6 3/8	9	9	Beaverhead Co., MT	Glenn M. Smith	Glenn M. Smith	1998	23
163 6/8	60	35 6/8	27	10 6/8	10 3/8	6 5/8	6 4/8	10	8	Carbon Co., WY	Rodney B. Weinman	Rodney B. Weinman	2000	24
162 7/8	48 5/8	30 4/8	30	10 2/8	9 7/8	6 7/8	6 2/8	11	11	Hot Springs Co., WY	Kenneth J. Kucera	Kenneth J. Kucera	1998	25
162 4/8	44	36 4/8	32	10 2/8	10 3/8	6	6 1/8	11	13	Bingham Co., ID	Larry D. Jaeger	Larry D. Jaeger	1998	26
162	49	31 5/8	32 4/8	9 3/8	9	6 7/8	6 7/8	9	10	Jackson Co., CO	Michael R. Tucker	Michael R. Tucker	1998	27
161 7/8	45 5/8	34	33 5/8	9 4/8	11 4/8	6 1/8	6	9	12	Weber Co., UT	Michael R. Pribbanow	Michael R. Pribbanow	2000	28
161 6/8	45 6/8	35 1/8	36 1/8	9 3/8	10 1/8	6 5/8	6 4/8	7	10	Sublette Co., WY	Robert W. Skorcz	Robert W. Skorcz	1996	29
161 5/8	51 3/8	32	35 1/8	8 1/8	10 1/8	6	6 4/8	9	11	Pend Oreille Co., WA	Seth Greenhaw, Jr.	Seth Greenhaw, Jr.	2000	30
161 4/8	47 2/8	31 2/8	31 6/8	10	11 3/8	5 7/8	5 7/8	10	11	Madison Co., ID	Archie Moe	Archie Moe	1998	31

Score									Locality	Owner	Hunter	Date	Rank
161 2/8	50 6/8	27 7/8	12	11 3/8	7	6 6/8	10	11	Jackson Co., CO	Wayne R. Kroft	Wayne R. Kroft	1999	32
161	48 6/8	38 1/8	8 1/8	9 2/8	6 5/8	7 2/8	8	9	Boundary Co., ID	Lon E. Merrifield	Lon E. Merrifield	2000	33
160 7/8	45 3/8	33 5/8	9 6/8	7 7/8	6 5/8	6 3/8	10	10	Madison Co., ID	Lisa M. Sherick	Lisa M. Sherick	1998	34
159 6/8	49 4/8	28 3/8	10 5/8	10 2/8	6 4/8	6 5/8	11	10	Sanders Co., MT	Robert A. Parker	Robert A. Parker	1997	35
159 4/8	47	33 4/8	12 5/8	9	6 3/8	6 2/8	11	9	Jackson Co., CO	Steven M. Weinberg	Steven M. Weinberg	1998	36
159 3/8	49 7/8	31 1/8	11 5/8	11 4/8	6 3/8	6 2/8	8	8	Clearwater Co., ID	Jeffrey D. Dunbar	Jeffrey D. Dunbar	1997	37
159 1/8	47 7/8	27 1/8	11 7/8	11 4/8	6	6	11	11	Grand Co., CO	Gerry A. Adair	Gerry A. Adair	1997	38
159 1/8	48 3/8	32	9 2/8	7 6/8	6 5/8	6 5/8	9	9	Teton Co., CO	Richard F. Karbowski	Richard F. Karbowski	1998	38
158 7/8	48 3/8	29 4/8	10 2/8	11	6 4/8	6 5/8	9	9	Latah Co., ID	Robert E. Bergquist	Robert E. Bergquist	1998	40
158 3/8	42 3/8	36	11	11 5/8	7 3/8	6 7/8	9	10	Pend Oreille Co., WA	Dustin L. Thomas	Dustin L. Thomas	1998	41
158 2/8	45	34 6/8	9 6/8	9 7/8	6 1/8	6 2/8	7	6	Shoshone Co., ID	Carl T. Bach	Carl T. Bach	1998	42
158 1/8	47 5/8	33 3/8	11	10 3/8	6	5 6/8	9	10	Bonneville Co., ID	John L. Pongrac	John L. Pongrac	1997	43
158	45 2/8	32 6/8	8 7/8	10 4/8	6 6/8	7	8	9	Flathead Co., MT	Larry T. Evens	Larry T. Evens	1997	44
157 7/8	50 5/8	29 2/8	9 7/8	10 3/8	6 5/8	6 4/8	8	12	Beaverhead Co., MT	Tom L. Ritzdorf	Tom L. Ritzdorf	1998	45
157 6/8	43 4/8	32 2/8	10	10 2/8	6 7/8	7 2/8	8	8	Weber Co., UT	Louis A. Kluesner	Louis A. Kluesner	1997	46
157 6/8	46 6/8	29 5/8	10 2/8	10 6/8	6 1/8	6 2/8	10	10	Summit Co., UT	Andreas Boehlendorf	Andreas Boehlendorf	2000	46
157 5/8	44 5/8	29 7/8	10 1/8	12 6/8	6 4/8	6 5/8	12	10	Weber Co., UT	Robert C. Chidester	Robert C. Chidester	1999	48
157 3/8	46 1/8	29 2/8	11 3/8	10 4/8	6 7/8	6 7/8	9	10	Flathead Co., MT	Scott George	Scott George	1998	49
156 6/8	44	29	9 2/8	9 4/8	6 2/8	6 2/8	10	10	Bonneville Co., ID	Charles J. Fritz	Charles J. Fritz	1997	50
156 5/8	39 2/8	34	10 4/8	10 4/8	6 3/8	6 3/8	6	6	Morgan Co., UT	Daniel J. Branagan	Daniel J. Branagan	2000	51
156 3/8	42 1/8	32	7 2/8	8 2/8	6 3/8	6 4/8	7	7	Lincoln Co., MT	Robert O. Calvert	Robert O. Calvert	1999	52
156 2/8	46	26 4/8	7 7/8	10 1/8	5 7/8	6 2/8	9	10	Sublette Co., WY	Gay M. Osler-Cook	Gay M. Osler-Cook	2000	53
156	49 3/8	26 2/8	13 2/8	11	6 4/8	6 4/8	12	11	Idaho Co., ID	James M. Cody	James M. Cody	1998	54
156	45 5/8	28	10 1/8	10	6 2/8	6 3/8	10	9	Sheridan Co., WY	Matthew J. Herbek	Matthew J. Herbek	1998	54
153 1/8	41	28	11 4/8	12	6 1/8	6 3/8	8	9	Sublette Co., WY	Bonnie J. Schuldt	Bonnie J. Schuldt	1997	56
153	49 6/8	31 2/8	11 6/8	11 6/8	5 4/8	5 5/8	10	11	Bear Lake Co., ID	Michael D. McConahay	Michael D. McConahay	1999	57
152 3/8	40 2/8	25 1/8	12 2/8	9 5/8	5 1/8	5 2/8	13	13	Weber Co., UT	Delwin G. Sparks	Delwin G. Sparks	1986	58
151 5/8	47 4/8	30	9 7/8	10 2/8	6 1/8	6 2/8	8	8	Gallatin Co., MT	Mark D. Becker	Mark D. Becker	1999	59
151 4/8	45 2/8	29 6/8	10	4 6/8	6	6	9	9	Sublette Co., WY	Glenn R. Olson	Glenn R. Olson	1994	60
151	45 6/8	27 7/8	12	11	6	6	10	10	Pend Oreille Co., WA	Frank M. Baber	Frank M. Baber	1999	61
150 6/8	47	27 4/8	9 4/8	10 5/8	6 2/8	6 1/8	7	6	Missoula Co., MT	Fred Abrams	Fred Abrams	1991	62
150 2/8	55 4/8	29 6/8	12 7/8	11 2/8	5 5/8	5 4/8	10	10	Uinta Co., WY	Janice M. Henderson	Janice M. Henderson	1998	63
150 2/8	46 2/8	27 7/8	10 3/8	9 5/8	5 7/8	6	10	9	Teton Co., WY	Greg P. Torlai	Greg P. Torlai	1998	63
149 6/8	46 3/8	28	8 5/8	10 2/8	5 7/8	6 2/8	8	10	Fremont Co., ID	John D. Bennett, Jr.	John D. Bennett	1952	65
149 6/8	43	28 4/8	9 7/8	4 6/8	6	5 7/8	6	4	Clearwater Co., ID	Kenneth J. Kincaid	Kenneth J. Kincaid	1992	65
149 6/8	46 1/8	29	11 4/8	12	6 2/8	6	10	10	Summit Co., UT	Wade V. Stockton	Wade V. Stockton	1998	65
149	46 1/8	31	9 6/8	9 6/8	5 6/8	5 7/8	8	7	Summit Co., UT	William E. Christensen	William E. Christensen	1999	68
148 3/8	49 7/8	27 4/8	9 4/8	9 4/8	6 3/8	5 7/8	10	10	Teton Co., WY	Dwaine R. Beebe	Dwaine R. Beebe	1999	69
148 2/8	48 2/8	26 7/8	9 4/8	9 4/8	6	6 3/8	10	10	Teton Co., WY	Don L. Twito	Don L. Twito	1992	70
148 1/8	48	25 5/8	8 3/8	7 5/8	5 6/8	5 7/8	10	8	Fremont Co., ID	Gale E. Burns	Gale E. Burns	1998	71
147 7/8	46 1/8	26 7/8	7 5/8	7 5/8	6 1/8	6 1/8	8	8	Weber Co., UT	Daniel E. Harris	Daniel E. Harris	1999	72
147 6/8	49 7/8	30 6/8	6 1/8	9 1/8	6 3/8	6 4/8	7	9	Pend Oreille Co., WA	Brian L. Ross	Brian L. Ross	1998	73
147 4/8	48 2/8	26 2/8	9 1/8	9 1/8	6 3/8	6 4/8	8	9	Teton Co., WY	Russell W. Hews	Russell W. Hews	1999	74

Alces alces shirasi

Score	Greatest Spread	Length of Palm R.	L.	Width of Palm R.	L.	Circumference of Beam at Smallest Place R.	L.	Number of Normal Points R.	L.	Locality	Hunter	Owner	Date Killed	Rank
146 5/8	48 3/8	29 4/8	30	6 3/8	6 2/8	6 4/8	6 3/8	7	7	Clearwater Co., ID	Rich W. Monteith	Rich W. Monteith	1999	75
146 5/8	44 1/8	28	27 3/8	9 4/8	9 4/8	6 3/8	6 4/8	9	8	Stevens Co., WA	Robert Vierra	Robert Vierra	1999	75
146 4/8	39	30 2/8	30 6/8	10 3/8	9 6/8	5 6/8	5 6/8	10	9	Sublette Co., WY	David R. May	David R. May	2000	77
146	50 4/8	22 6/8	24 5/8	9 4/8	10 6/8	6 4/8	6 5/8	6	9	Bear Lake Co., ID	RaeLynne C. Kunz	RaeLynne C. Kunz	1997	78
145 6/8	44	34 2/8	30 6/8	8 5/8	7 5/8	5 7/8	6	11	8	Sublette Co., WY	Verle L. Rademacher	Verle L. Rademacher	1999	79
145 2/8	42 4/8	28 2/8	28	10 6/8	10 4/8	6 4/8	6 3/8	9	7	Park Co., WY	Thomas A. Renner	Thomas A. Renner	1996	80
145 2/8	53 2/8	32 3/8	25	6 5/8	7	6 4/8	6 3/8	9	8	Park Co., WY	Andy Andrews	Andy Andrews	1999	80
145 1/8	44 1/8	28	29 2/8	8 3/8	9	6 1/8	6 4/8	9	10	Sublette Co., WY	Robert L. Beiermann	Robert L. Beiermann	1998	82
145	41	26 2/8	28 2/8	10 4/8	11 6/8	6 4/8	6 2/8	9	10	Weber Co., UT	Chelsea Talbot	Chelsea Talbot	1998	83
144 7/8	48 7/8	28	24	10 3/8	11 3/8	5 5/8	5 6/8	9	8	Rich Co., UT	Lewis J. Lowder	Lewis J. Lowder	1997	84
144 4/8	44	27 2/8	31	8 2/8	12 2/8	5 6/8	5 7/8	9	12	Caribou Co., ID	Lila J. Nelson	Lila J. Nelson	1997	85
144 4/8	44 4/8	26 6/8	26 5/8	8 7/8	8 3/8	6	6	9	9	Weber Co., UT	Leslie L. Janisch	James J. Janisch	1999	85
143 4/8	41 4/8	30 1/8	28 4/8	8 4/8	11	7	7	8	7	Bonneville Co., ID	Conrad Evanow	Conrad Evanow	1999	87
143 2/8	48 2/8	31	30	7 4/8	6 3/8	5 1/8	5 1/8	7	6	Lewis & Clark Co., MT	Rick Koepplin	Rick Koepplin	1998	88
143 2/8	44 2/8	35 1/8	28 4/8	8 7/8	7 2/8	7 2/8	6 6/8	10	7	Madison Co., MT	Adam R. Stuart	Adam R. Stuart	1999	88
143 1/8	41 5/8	29 7/8	28 6/8	10 2/8	10 1/8	6	5 7/8	7	6	Fremont Co., ID	Greg G. Painter	Greg G. Painter	1999	90
141 6/8	43 4/8	25 6/8	24 2/8	9 4/8	10 5/8	6 4/8	6 3/8	11	9	Weber Co., UT	Lee M. Wahlund	Lee M. Wahlund	1998	91
141 2/8	51 4/8	26 2/8	26 5/8	6 2/8	9 3/8	6 3/8	6 7/8	6	8	Shoshone Co., ID	Marvin E. Haagen	Marvin E. Haagen	2000	92
141 1/8	40 1/8	26 3/8	25 6/8	9 5/8	10 3/8	6 1/8	6 1/8	9	9	Sublette Co., WY	Fred W. Williams	Fred W. Williams	1998	93
140 4/8	43	26 5/8	32 3/8	8 3/8	11 1/8	5 6/8	5 6/8	8	9	Park Co., WY	Richard R. Fleming	Richard R. Fleming	1999	94
140 1/8	45 7/8	25 1/8	27 5/8	9	7 4/8	6 4/8	6 5/8	8	8	Mineral Co., MT	Jeff Elliott	Jeff Elliott	1998	95
140 1/8	49 1/8	26 4/8	27 7/8	5 5/8	7 7/8	6 3/8	6 4/8	8	8	Stevens Co., WA	Benjamin P. Conley	Benjamin P. Conley	2000	95
140	49 4/8	25 4/8	23 5/8	9 4/8	8	6 5/8	6 6/8	7	7	Jackson Co., CO	Ronald L. Elkins	Ronald L. Elkins	1999	97
178 2/8*	50	39 5/8	43 5/8	11 3/8	9 7/8	6 5/8	6 7/8	10	8	Missoula Co., MT	Edward M. Jungers	Edward M. Jungers	2000	
177 7/8*	57 3/8	35 3/8	37 3/8	11 1/8	10 3/8	6 4/8	6 5/8	8	11	Teton Co., WY	Shaun Rees	Shaun Rees	1999	

* Final score subject to revision by additional verifying measurements.

MOUNTAIN CARIBOU

Rangifer tarandus caribou

Minimum Score 360   New World's Record 453

Mountain caribou includes trophies from Alberta, British Columbia, southern Yukon Territory, and the Mackenzie Mountains of Northwest Territories.

Score	Length of Main Beam R.	L.	Inside Spread	Circ. at Smallest Place Between Brow and Bez Points R.	L.	Length of Brow Points R.	L.	Width of Brow Points R.	L.	Number of Points R.	L.	Locality	Hunter	Owner	Date Killed	Rank
453	$48^2/_8$	$49^5/_8$	$45^6/_8$	$6^3/_8$	$6^5/_8$	20	$17^1/_8$	$13^1/_8$	4	23	21	Prospector Mt, YT	C. Candler Hunt	C. Candler Hunt	1998	1
$416^7/_8$	51	$50^3/_8$	$38^7/_8$	$6^4/_8$	$6^2/_8$	$18^1/_8$	16	$13^2/_8$	$^1/_8$	20	13	Arctic Red River, NT	E. Royce Gunter, Jr.	E. Royce Gunter, Jr.	1999	2
416	$37^5/_8$	38	$37^7/_8$	$7^4/_8$	$6^7/_8$	$16^5/_8$	$15^3/_8$	12	$11^3/_8$	23	26	Little Rancheria River, BC	Brian T. Pelczar	Brian T. Pelczar	1996	3
$413^6/_8$	$50^5/_8$	$52^1/_8$	$34^1/_8$	$6^6/_8$	$7^4/_8$	$20^7/_8$	$17^5/_8$	$16^4/_8$	$2^5/_8$	26	17	Ethel Lake, YT	Russel Tait	Russel Tait	1999	4
$411^4/_8$	$48^3/_8$	$49^4/_8$	$29^6/_8$	$6^7/_8$	7	$15^5/_8$	20	$13^4/_8$	$12^5/_8$	18	23	Cassiar Mts., BC	Jeffery T. Redfearn	Jeffery T. Redfearn	1998	5
$408^5/_8$	$50^7/_8$	$50^6/_8$	$42^3/_8$	$7^1/_8$	$6^2/_8$	$18^2/_8$	19	$14^6/_8$	$10^2/_8$	15	14	Ramparts River, NT	Robert Gruszecki	Robert Gruszecki	1999	6
$405^1/_8$	45	$42^3/_8$	$34^1/_8$	$6^6/_8$	$6^5/_8$	17	$2^7/_8$	12	$^1/_8$	14	12	Cassiar Mts., BC	Robert H. Cobun	Robert H. Cobun	1998	7
$402^6/_8$	$51^1/_8$	$53^2/_8$	$48^7/_8$	$8^2/_8$	$7^1/_8$	$13^5/_8$	$20^3/_8$	$1^2/_8$	$12^3/_8$	13	13	Glenlyon Range, YT	C. Kelly Farmer	C. Kelly Farmer	1997	8
$401^3/_8$	$47^3/_8$	$47^2/_8$	$38^2/_8$	$7^4/_8$	$7^2/_8$	$15^2/_8$	2	$11^7/_8$	$^4/_8$	23	15	Arctic Red River, NT	Timothy F. McGinn	Timothy F. McGinn	2000	9
400	43	$41^7/_8$	$36^6/_8$	$8^5/_8$	$8^1/_8$	$16^6/_8$		9		18	21	Fire Lake, YT	Jonathan Thornberry	Jonathan Thornberry	1998	10
$399^3/_8$	$45^4/_8$	$45^4/_8$	47	$6^5/_8$	7	$18^3/_8$	$17^3/_8$	$12^3/_8$	8	17	14	Teslin River, BC	Abe J.N. Dougan	Abe J.N. Dougan	1998	11
399	$49^7/_8$	$51^5/_8$	$40^2/_8$	$6^6/_8$	$6^4/_8$	18	$10^5/_8$	$15^1/_8$	3	14	13	Cassiar Mts., BC	Joseph C. Hinderman	Joseph C. Hinderman	1997	12
$398^2/_8$	47	$47^5/_8$	$43^5/_8$	$6^2/_8$	$6^2/_8$	$9^4/_8$	$18^2/_8$	$^1/_8$	$12^6/_8$	15	16	Tuya Lake, BC	Jack Clary	Jack Clary	1999	13
398	$50^2/_8$	$48^2/_8$	$32^7/_8$	$7^7/_8$	8	$18^3/_8$		$15^2/_8$		20	16	Cassiar Mts., BC	Troy Cummins	Troy Cummins	1999	14
$396^2/_8$	$47^3/_8$	$46^3/_8$	$31^1/_8$	$8^6/_8$	$7^6/_8$	16	$15^1/_8$	$7^7/_8$	$9^1/_8$	19	19	Telegraph Creek, BC	John H. Johnson	Roger S. Johnson	1952	15
$394^3/_8$	$48^3/_8$	$51^1/_8$	$35^2/_8$	$6^2/_8$	$6^6/_8$	$21^4/_8$	$21^1/_8$	$7^6/_8$	13	15	16	Selwyn Valley, YT	Hans Berg	Hans Berg	1991	16
393	$47^1/_8$	$47^2/_8$	$34^4/_8$	$6^3/_8$	$6^1/_8$	$18^7/_8$	$18^4/_8$	$3^5/_8$	$12^6/_8$	12	15	Tay River, YT	Mark R. Zimmerman	Mark R. Zimmerman	1998	17
392	$47^5/_8$	$45^6/_8$	$40^6/_8$	$6^5/_8$	$6^7/_8$	$16^4/_8$	$15^7/_8$	$14^2/_8$	$4^1/_8$	21	17	Cassiar Mts., BC	H. Ross Mann	H. Ross Mann	2000	18
$391^3/_8$	$53^3/_8$	$54^1/_8$	$36^6/_8$	$6^4/_8$	$6^5/_8$	$3^2/_8$	$14^5/_8$	$10^7/_8$	$10^1/_8$	14	17	Tuya Lake, BC	John D. Frost	John D. Frost	1995	19
$391^3/_8$	$49^4/_8$	$48^7/_8$	$35^7/_8$	$6^6/_8$	$5^3/_8$	$16^7/_8$	$13^7/_8$	14	$^1/_8$	18	19	Dick Lake, BC	James R. Colosimo	James R. Colosimo	1996	19
$390^6/_8$	$46^6/_8$	$46^2/_8$	$44^2/_8$	$5^6/_8$	$5^3/_8$	$15^4/_8$	$4^7/_8$	$^1/_8$	$13^3/_8$	23	22	Mackenzie Mts., NT	Scott S. Snyder	Scott S. Snyder	1991	21
390	$46^1/_8$	$46^6/_8$	$44^7/_8$	$6^4/_8$	$6^4/_8$	$10^1/_8$	17	$14^3/_8$	$14^3/_8$	13	13	Teslin River, BC	Dan Stacey	Dan Stacey	1998	22
$388^5/_8$	$48^6/_8$	$47^4/_8$	$46^2/_8$	7	7	14	$10^2/_8$	$4^4/_8$	$^1/_8$	13	12	Blue River, BC	William J. Falcheck	William J. Falcheck	1999	23
$388^4/_8$	$55^5/_8$	$54^4/_8$	41	$6^2/_8$	6	$17^6/_8$	$18^7/_8$	$9^4/_8$	$10^7/_8$	16	17	Telegraph Creek, BC	Roger S. Johnson	Roger S. Johnson	1952	24
$385^2/_8$	$43^4/_8$	$41^3/_8$	$27^6/_8$	$8^2/_8$	$9^2/_8$	$16^1/_8$	$14^4/_8$	$8^1/_8$	$4^6/_8$	18	11	Ice Lake, YT	Jonathan Thornberry	Jonathan Thornberry	1997	25
$382^5/_8$	$47^4/_8$	$47^7/_8$	$46^3/_8$	$7^5/_8$	$7^3/_8$	$17^5/_8$	$7^1/_8$	$14^3/_8$	$^1/_8$	14	16	Cassiar Mts., BC	Ross H. Mann	Ross H. Mann	1997	26
378	$48^3/_8$	$46^4/_8$	$36^1/_8$	$6^5/_8$	$6^5/_8$	3	$18^7/_8$	$11^5/_8$	3	16	12	Cranswick River, NT	Amy Jo Peterson	Amy Jo Peterson	2000	27
375	$50^5/_8$	$49^1/_8$	$37^2/_8$	7	$7^1/_8$	4	$12^3/_8$	$^1/_8$	$^1/_8$	11	12	Ice Lakes, YT	Robert Lehet	Robert Lehet	1997	28
$374^5/_8$	$40^5/_8$	$38^1/_8$	$25^5/_8$	$5^6/_8$	$5^3/_8$	$15^2/_8$	$17^2/_8$	$10^2/_8$	$13^2/_8$	22	21	Mackenzie Mts., NT	Kevin D. Peterson	Kevin D. Peterson	1998	29
$374^5/_8$	47	$45^3/_8$	$26^5/_8$	$6^2/_8$	$6^3/_8$	$18^4/_8$	$12^2/_8$	$13^1/_8$	$^1/_8$	19	14	Mackenzie Mts., NT	Buck Taylor	Buck Taylor	1998	29
$374^1/_8$	$51^3/_8$	$49^7/_8$	$53^6/_8$	$5^5/_8$	$5^2/_8$	$18^7/_8$	$11^4/_8$	$7^6/_8$	$^1/_8$	10	10	Turnagain Lake, BC	Robert J. Pacini	Robert J. Pacini	1975	31

MOUNTAIN CARIBOU

Rangifer tarandus caribou

Score	Length of Main Beam R	L	Inside Spread	Circumference at Smallest Place Between Brow and Bez Points R	L	Length of Brow Points R	L	Width of Brow Points R	L	Number of Points R	L	Locality	Hunter	Owner	Date Killed	Rank
373 7/8	49	48 2/8	33 4/8	7 2/8	7 4/8	16	14 2/8	6 5/8	5	14	13	Rabbit River, BC	Adley Callison	Adley Callison	1986	32
371 7/8	47	47 3/8	37 4/8	6 2/8	6 2/8	5 6/8	19 2/8	1/8	13 4/8	13	18	Mackenzie Mts., NT	Joseph C. Hinderman	Joseph C. Hinderman	1995	33
371 7/8	49 6/8	49	34 3/8	6	6 2/8	14/8	18	1/8	14 7/8	15	19	Arctic Red River, NT	Richard F. Seifert	Richard F. Seifert	2000	33
371	44 6/8	46 3/8	39 7/8	6 1/8	6 1/8	15	15	6 6/8	4 1/8	11	14	Mackenzie Mts., NT	Felix W. Parks	Felix W. Parks	1998	35
370 3/8	39 2/8	38 6/8	31 6/8	7 6/8	10	16 4/8	21 1/8	7	13	13	14	Hayes Peak, BC	David L. Hussey	David L. Hussey	1997	36
370 2/8	46 4/8	49 2/8	34 6/8	6 6/8	6 3/8	17 2/8	16 6/8	10 5/8	3 7/8	12	13	Mountain River, NT	Sanford Gelzer	Sanford Gelzer	1997	37
367 3/8	46 3/8	48 4/8	38 1/8	6 4/8	6 5/8	5 7/8	17 1/8	2 6/8	13 4/8	11	17	Fire Lake, YT	J. Michael Thornberry II	J. Michael Thornberry II	1998	38
364 7/8	41 2/8	40 4/8	28 6/8	5 4/8	6	14 1/8	14 4/8	4 5/8	12 1/8	18	18	Godlin River, NT	Darrel L. Moberly	Darrel L. Moberly	1998	39
361 6/8	53 1/8	52 3/8	32 4/8	6 5/8	7 1/8	15	1 4/8	1 2/8	12	14	18	Fire Lake, YT	David A. Creamer	David A. Creamer	1998	40
361 2/8	44 7/8	43	39 7/8	6 4/8	7	7	17 4/8	1/8	13	17	20	Mountain River, NT	Brian L. Dam	Brian L. Dam	1999	41
361 1/8	45 1/8	45 2/8	31 5/8	6 2/8	7	3	15 2/8	1/8	8 7/8	16	17	Fire Lake, YT	F. David Thornberry	F. David Thornberry	1998	42
444*	44 2/8	45 2/8	36 1/8	6 6/8	6 6/8	13 7/8	20 4/8	4	15 6/8	17	21	Quiet Lake, YT	Russ Mercer	Robert A. VanSkyock	1965	
442 4/8*	44 2/8	45 5/8	38 3/8	8 3/8	8 2/8	14	19 5/8	8 2/8	18 6/8	19	25	Fortin Lake, YT	Kim Runions	Kim Runions	1994	
417 4/8*	49 7/8	49 5/8	37	6 1/8	6 2/8	16 4/8	15 6/8	11 4/8	10 4/8	18	23	Mountain River, NT	William E. Hosford	William E. Hosford	2000	

* Final score subject to revision by additional verifying measurements.

WOODLAND CARIBOU

Rangifer tarandus caribou

Minimum Score 265

World's Record 419 5/8

Woodland caribou includes trophies from Nova Scotia, New Brunswick, and Newfoundland

Score	Length of Main Beam R	L	Inside Spread	Circumference at Smallest Place Between Brow and Bez Points R	L	Length of Brow Points R	L	Width of Brow Points R	L	Number of Points R	L	Locality	Hunter	Owner	Date Killed	Rank
359 2/8	40 1/8	42 3/8	34 3/8	6 6/8	6 2/8	16 2/8	14	11 1/8	11 2/8	18	13	Main Brook, NF	Picked Up	Gerard R. Beaulieu	1996	1
351 2/8	45 7/8	46 1/8	39 1/8	6 1/8	6 1/8	15 2/8		11 5/8		12	11	St. Anthony, NF	Thomas D. Lund	Thomas D. Lund	1998	2
339 1/8	37 4/8	38 4/8	38 2/8	6 1/8	5 7/8	14 6/8	13 5/8	11 5/8	8 7/8	18	14	Watsons Brook, NF	Harold E. Coons	Harold E. Coons	1998	3
335 3/8	42	40	27 4/8	5 6/8	5 6/8	17 3/8	18 3/8	15 7/8	6 2/8	18	14	Main Brook, NF	George R. Stoner	George R. Stoner	1999	4
334 6/8	39 5/8	40 1/8	28 5/8	5 2/8	5 1/8	13 7/8	15 4/8	12 5/8	14 5/8	18	16	North Arm, NF	Dennis C. Frederick	Dennis C. Frederick	1999	5
334 6/8	36 2/8	35 3/8	33 6/8	4 6/8	5 1/8	15 2/8	15 7/8	12 7/8	14	23	24	Adies Pond, NF	Gerard R. Beaulieu	Gerard R. Beaulieu	2000	5
333 2/8	39 6/8	40 3/8	33 3/8	4 7/8	5	17 4/8	16 5/8	15 4/8	8	12	13	Cat Arm River, NF	William R. Reed	William R. Reed	1998	7
331 3/8	37 4/8	37	29	5 2/8	5 1/8	17 7/8	16 5/8	12 6/8	12 1/8	17	16	Gander River, NF	David W. Schrody	David W. Schrody	2000	8
331 1/8	39 1/8	35	28 3/8	5 7/8	6 3/8	16	15 2/8	9 4/8	13 2/8	20	18	Alexander Pond, NF	Charles M. Bloom	Charles M. Bloom	1999	9
330 3/8	37 1/8	38 6/8	38 6/8	5 3/8	5 5/8	17 1/8	16 6/8	7	13 4/8	17	20	Deer Lake, NF	Picked Up	Gerard R. Beaulieu	1997	10
329 2/8	34 6/8	35 2/8	26 6/8	6	6 2/8	15	16 6/8	11 3/8	17 5/8	19	21	Eddy's Cove, NF	Annie Larkin	Gerard R. Beaulieu	1999	11
328 7/8	39	36 3/8	19 5/8	6	6 6/8	13 5/8	14 2/8	13 1/8	8 2/8	14	16	Harbour Deep, NF	Drew E. Kline	Drew E. Kline	1998	12
326 7/8	35 1/8	37 7/8	32 6/8	5 3/8	5 3/8	15 7/8	15 4/8	10 1/8	9 3/8	17	15	Cat Arm River, NF	Steven R. Vande Giessen	Steven R. Vande Giessen	1997	13
326 7/8	37 2/8	37 4/8	32 1/8	6	7 2/8	16	13 3/8	14 4/8	10 7/8	17	20	Long Pond, NF	Lawrence J. Nolan	Lawrence J. Nolan	1999	13
325 6/8	40 2/8	38	27	5 3/8	5 4/8	16	14	10 2/8	12 4/8	19	17	Ten Mile Brook, NF	Bruce G. Miles	Bruce G. Miles	1999	15
324 7/8	40 5/8	41 3/8	30 6/8	5 6/8	5 5/8	14 2/8	13 3/8	10 4/8	8 4/8	17	16	Rocky Point, NF	Richard N. Gubler	Richard N. Gubler	2000	16
322	38 6/8	39 3/8	31 1/8	4 7/8	5	15	14 5/8	9 2/8	10 2/8	14	20	Gull Lake, NF	Michael J. Berenz	Michael J. Berenz	1999	17
321 2/8	44 4/8	41 7/8	35	6 4/8	6 3/8	14 4/8	16 5/8	9	11 5/8	12	16	Hare Bay, NF	William P. Bleckley	William P. Bleckley	1999	18
320 4/8	43 4/8	43 3/8	31 2/8	4 7/8	5	17 3/8	15 5/8	15 1/8	4 1/8	17	14	Gander River, NF	M.R. James	M.R. James	1999	19
319 4/8	39 4/8	39 1/8	23 7/8	4 7/8	4 6/8	14 3/8	13 6/8	9	8 2/8	18	17	Leander Lake, NF	James J. Dietz, Jr.	James J. Dietz, Jr.	1997	20
318 5/8	38 4/8	36 3/8	34 1/8	5 7/8	5 6/8	14 4/8	16 2/8	5 6/8	15	14	15	Portland Creek, NF	Picked Up	Gerard R. Beaulieu	1998	21
317 4/8	41 7/8	45	33 6/8	5 4/8	5 5/8	17 4/8	6/8	14 4/8	4/8	13	13	Eclipse Lake, NF	Matthew L. Wiskowski	Matthew L. Wiskowski	1998	22
316 7/8	30 4/8	32 4/8	32 2/8	5	5 4/8	14 3/8	14 6/8	11 5/8	12 5/8	20	16	Hinds Lake, NF	Daniel C. McNeill	Daniel C. McNeill	1998	23
316 4/8	35 5/8	35	26 6/8	5 3/8	5 1/8	18 6/8	18 7/8	14 6/8	7 1/8	15	16	Parson's Pond, NF	Frederick L. Gers, Jr.	Frederick L. Gers, Jr.	1999	24
312 1/8	35 5/8	35 5/8	29	5 4/8	5 2/8	15 3/8	15 4/8	11 7/8	13 5/8	18	17	Stag Lake, NF	James T. Kovac	James T. Kovac	1999	25
310	40 5/8	40 2/8	37	5 3/8	5 5/8	12 3/8	12	9	2 3/8	14	17	Hinds Lake, NF	David P. Weber	David P. Weber	1996	26
309 7/8	40 7/8	40	28 1/8	5 3/8	5 4/8	8 1/8	20 3/8	1/8	17 7/8	9	21	Adies Pond, NF	Dan J. Chaisson	Dan J. Chaisson	1999	27
309 5/8	35 4/8	38 5/8	28	5 6/8	5 6/8	12	13 4/8	8 1/8	10 4/8	18	13	Main River, NF	John V. D'Ambro, Jr.	John V. D'Ambro, Jr.	1998	28
308 4/8	35 7/8	36 2/8	31 6/8	5 3/8	5 5/8	15 3/8	14 7/8	11 2/8	13 4/8	12	15	Deer Pond, NF	George S. Walker III	George S. Walker III	1998	29
308 4/8	39	39 3/8	35	5 5/8	5 5/8	12	13 1/8	8 1/8	12 2/8	17	15	River of Ponds, NF	Roger B. Donahue, Jr.	Roger B. Donahue, Jr.	1999	29
308 3/8	40 2/8	42	29 6/8	5	5 1/8	13 3/8	14 6/8	5	10 2/8	15	16	Harbour Deep, NF	Mike Olmstead	Mike Olmstead	1996	31

WOODLAND CARIBOU

Rangifer tarandus caribou

Score	Length of Main Beam R	L	Inside Spread	Circumference at Smallest Place Between Brow and Bez Points R	L	Length of Brow Points R	L	Width of Brow Points R	L	Number of Points R	L	Locality	Hunter	Owner	Date Killed	Rank
308 3/8	39 3/8	39 7/8	38 6/8	5 2/8	5 3/8	1	15 2/8	1/8	11	11	15	Kitty's Brook, NF	H. Glen Dodd	H. Glen Dodd	1999	31
307 7/8	34 5/8	35	30 4/8	5 1/8	4 7/8	16	14 2/8	14 6/8	9 7/8	14	18	Crabbs River, NF	Robert D. Bostater	Robert D. Bostater	1995	33
307 6/8	39 2/8	39 3/8	30 4/8	5	5 2/8	16 7/8	14 6/8	13 6/8	10 5/8	17	17	Whites River, NF	Lawrence E. Kirby	Lawrence E. Kirby	1999	34
305 5/8	36 3/8	38	30	5 3/8	5 4/8	14 4/8	13 7/8	10	11	17	17	Cerf River, NF	Pat Genell	Pat Genell	1999	35
304 3/8	41 3/8	42 2/8	30 3/8	5 1/8	5 4/8	15	13	11 4/8	6	10	10	Hynes Cove, NF	David J. Sullivan, Jr.	David J. Sullivan, Jr.	1997	36
304 1/8	33	31 1/8	20 3/8	5 4/8	5 2/8	16 6/8	14 4/8	14 6/8	6 2/8	12	16	Island Pond, NF	John P. Polinski	John P. Polinski	2000	37
303 4/8	44 1/8	46 3/8	38 2/8	5 2/8	5 2/8	12 7/8	13 7/8	17	10 7/8	22	16	Parsons Pond, NF	Donald L. Strickler	Donald L. Strickler	1998	38
302 4/8	39 4/8	36	26 5/8	5 5/8	5 1/8	16 6/8	14 2/8	9 2/8	14 1/8	11	14	Rocky Ridge Pond, NF	Randal E. Daley	Randal E. Daley	1999	39
301	39 4/8	40 6/8	27	5 5/8	5	16 5/8	16 7/8	12 7/8	11 5/8	15	14	Long Range Mts., NF	Michael E. Wegner	Michael E. Wegner	1998	40
299 7/8	41 5/8	44 6/8	28 6/8	5	4 7/8	15 5/8	16 7/8	11 4/8	13 3/8	16	12	Deer Lake, NF	Kevin S. Peterson	Kevin S. Peterson	1994	41
299	38 3/8	39 3/8	34 7/8	5 7/8	6	15 2/8	13 4/8	12	7 3/8	16	13	Main Brook, NF	Picked Up	Gerard R. Beaulieu	1996	42
298 6/8	33 5/8	35 5/8	34 2/8	5 6/8	5 5/8	13	15 2/8	1/8	10 5/8	15	17	Koskaecodde Lake, NF	Joseph A. Strick	Joseph A. Strick	1999	43
298 4/8	39 4/8	37 5/8	33 3/8	4 7/8	4 7/8	17 4/8	19	13 1/8	9 2/8	18	14	Gander River, NF	John S. Griesinger	John S. Griesinger	1999	44
296 7/8	34 2/8	34 7/8	29 1/8	4 5/8	6	13	15	6 2/8	10	13	15	Loon Lake, NF	Lanny C. Fields	Lanny C. Fields	1999	45
295 6/8	37 6/8	37 5/8	29 6/8	5 1/8	5 1/8	15 5/8	15 7/8	13	13	18	17	Burnt Pond, NF	Richard C. Desjardins	Richard C. Desjardins	1999	46
295 3/8	37 5/8	40 5/8	22 6/8	4 4/8	4 5/8	16 3/8	15 6/8	12 4/8	8 6/8	16	15	North Lake, NF	Douglas S. Kennedy	Douglas S. Kennedy	1998	47
293 7/8	31 7/8	38 3/8	30 3/8	4 5/8	5	15	17 1/8	10 7/8	14 4/8	18	16	King George IV Lake, NF	Bryan W. Miller	Bryan W. Miller	1999	48
292 3/8	35 6/8	35 5/8	23 4/8	5 1/8	5	13 7/8	15 3/8	11 5/8	13 4/8	16	15	Parson's Pond, NF	Frederick L. Gers III	Frederick L. Gers III	1999	49
280 6/8	34 5/8	35 5/8	23	5 1/8	5 1/8	15 1/8	5 6/8	11	1/8	20	11	Aides Lake, NF	Michael Niemala	Michael Niemala	1999	50
280 4/8	31 5/8	30 2/8	22 1/8	5 2/8	6 1/8	13 3/8	14 2/8	13 3/8	12	16	18	Grey River, NF	William L. McKnew	William L. McKnew	1997	51
279 7/8	43	45 2/8	34 3/8	5 1/8	5	17 2/8	4 1/8	10 5/8	1 2/8	16	12	Cat Arm, NF	Hope J. Howes	Hope J. Howes	1999	52
279	33 7/8	31 7/8	22 5/8	5 7/8	5 1/8	14 2/8	14	10 1/8	13 2/8	20	21	Leslie Lake, NF	Samuel F. Fullerton, Jr.	Samuel F. Fullerton, Jr.	1998	53
275 7/8	36 5/8	35 2/8	37	5 6/8	5 6/8	12 1/8	13 1/8	8 4/8	11 4/8	15	13	Deer Pond, NF	John J. Rybinski	John J. Rybinski	1998	54
273 7/8	34 5/8	31 5/8	27 2/8	6 4/8	6	12 6/8	11 6/8	10 1/8	7 4/8	13	15	Middle Ridge, NF	Gerard R. Beaulieu	Gerard R. Beaulieu	1998	55
272 1/8	42 2/8	41 7/8	26 5/8	5 2/8	5 3/8	14 4/8	12 1/8	9	1/8	15	8	Cat Arm River, NF	Lawrence J. White	Lawrence J. White	1997	56
270 3/8	38 4/8	34 3/8	32 2/8	5 1/8	4 6/8	14	15	13 5/8	10	11	12	Koskaecodde Lake, NF	Randy L. Harbath	Randy L. Harbath	1997	57
270 3/8	35 4/8	35 4/8	27 6/8	4 6/8	4 6/8	16 6/8	15	8	11 7/8	14	12	Angus Lake, NF	David R. Baird	David R. Baird	1999	57
270 1/8	32 3/8	32 2/8	32	5 4/8	5 2/8	12 6/8	13 7/8	9 7/8	11 1/8	13	15	Mt. Peyton, NF	Edmund B. Wilson	Edmund B. Wilson	1998	59
269 3/8	30 1/8	31 3/8	23 1/8	5	4 7/8	12 4/8	12 5/8	10 1/8	11 4/8	14	14	Middle Ridge, NF	Jan M. Oden	Jan M. Oden	1999	60
267 7/8	33 2/8	36	26 3/8	5	5 4/8	16 6/8	15 3/8	10 7/8	13 4/8	13	17	King George IV Lake, NF	Charles F. Greenwald	Charles F. Greenwald	1999	61
267 5/8	42	40 2/8	46	5 1/8	5 1/8	15	15	2 1/8	11	7	10	Parsons Pond, NF	Donald L. Strickler	Donald L. Strickler	1999	62
375 3/8 *	42 1/8	43 3/8	37	6 5/8	5 7/8	17 1/8	15 5/8	15 2/8	13 5/8	16	15	Ten Mile Lake, NF	Picked Up	Baxter N. House	1999	

BARREN GROUND CARIBOU

Rangifer tarandus granti

Minimum Score 375

New World's Record 477

Barren ground caribou includes trophies from Alaska and northern Yukon Territory.

Score	Length of Main Beam R	L	Inside Spread	Circumference at Smallest Place Between Brow and Bez Points R	L	Length of Brow Points R	L	Width of Brow Points R	L	Number of Points R	L	Locality	Hunter	Owner	Date Killed	Rank
477	55 5/8	57 7/8	38 3/8	7 1/8	6 7/8	22 5/8	23 2/8	4 5/8	18 5/8	17	25	Iliamna Lake, AK	Daniel L. Dobbs	Daniel L. Dobbs	1999	1
438 7/8	51 3/8	50 6/8	47 3/8	6 7/8	7 2/8	23 4/8	6 1/8	16 6/8	1/8	19	15	Three Arm Bay, AK	Heber Simmons, Jr.	Heber Simmons, Jr.	2000	2
429	46 6/8	46 4/8	43 5/8	6 4/8	6 6/8	19 1/8	18	13 5/8	11 1/8	23	22	Mulchatna River, AK	Picked Up	Darryl Sanford	1999	3
419 1/8	49 6/8	48	42 7/8	5 7/8	5 7/8	15	15 1/8	5 7/8	11 6/8	18	22	Cinder Creek, AK	Al E. Neether	Al E. Neether	1972	4
418 6/8	50 6/8	52 7/8	28 1/8	5 4/8	5 4/8	18 6/8	20 3/8	18 4/8	11	20	17	Slate Creek, AK	John S. Wylie	John S. Wylie	1999	5
415 3/8	54 2/8	51 7/8	35 6/8	5 3/8	5 4/8	9 2/8	22 5/8	1/8	19 3/8	14	30	Portage Creek, AK	Harry P. Samarin	Harry P. Samarin	1998	6
414 6/8	47 6/8	48 2/8	33 2/8	5 5/8	5 4/8	19 5/8	20 1/8	12 4/8	2 4/8	17	16	Post River, AK	Shawn A. Lar	Shawn A. Lar	1998	7
414 2/8	47 1/8	49 1/8	39 6/8	5 7/8	6 2/8	20 1/8	18 6/8	13 3/8	10 4/8	19	18	Kvichak River, AK	Lee R. Nieman	Lee R. Nieman	1998	8
414 1/8	55 6/8	56	49 4/8	6	5 2/8	21 3/8	19 3/8	14 4/8	5 3/8	23	14	Indian Mt., AK	Jeffrey D. Lapp	Jeffrey D. Lapp	1998	9
412 3/8	56 4/8	57	48 5/8	6	6 4/8	4 5/8	18 6/8	1/8	15	14	20	Killey River, AK	Brett A. Aldridge	Brett A. Aldridge	1998	10
411 4/8	57 4/8	56 1/8	45 1/8	7 4/8	7 4/8	19 2/8	3 2/8	14 2/8	1/8	20	15	King Salmon River, AK	Gordon G. Chittick	Gordon G. Chittick	1994	11
410 7/8	55 4/8	54 3/8	42 4/8	7 2/8	6 5/8	1 6/8	22	1/8	17	15	23	Ugashik Lake, AK	Christian Heyden	Christian Heyden	1995	12
410 4/8	55	53 4/8	36 5/8	6 4/8	6 5/8	9 2/8	20	1/8	13	15	18	Caribou Pass, AK	David E. Krompacky	David E. Krompacky	1997	13
410	51 3/8	51 2/8	37 3/8	6 1/8	6 1/8	16 4/8	9 1/8	11 7/8	1/8	21	14	Mulchatna River, AK	Scott M. McDowell	Scott M. McDowell	1994	14
408 7/8	49 3/8	43 5/8	41 3/8	5 2/8	5 3/8	17 3/8	17 4/8	12	2 5/8	16	17	Hart River, YT	Gordon MacRae	Gordon MacRae	1999	15
407 7/8	55 4/8	56 1/8	48 5/8	5 6/8	5 3/8	16 3/8	18 1/8	4 4/8	16 1/8	16	21	Noatak River, AK	Christopher J. Sawyer	Christopher J. Sawyer	2000	16
405 6/8	44 2/8	50 3/8	43 3/8	5 4/8	5 2/8	13	15 3/8	8 5/8	11 1/8	20	18	King Salmon, AK	Brett D. Mattson	Brett D. Mattson	1994	17
405	51 7/8	52	30 4/8	6	6 1/8	17	14 4/8	9 5/8	8 5/8	22	16	Goodpastor River, AK	Allen E. Bird	Allen E. Bird	1997	18
404 5/8	52 5/8	53 2/8	36 5/8	4 7/8	5 2/8	18 3/8	17 3/8	15 7/8	12 1/8	23	20	Kobuck River, AK	Ron Herring	Ron Herring	2000	19
403 6/8	54 1/8	53 2/8	40	5 3/8	5 2/8	17 4/8	13 4/8	16 3/8	5 1/8	21	19	Omar River, AK	S. Preston Kelley	S. Preston Kelley	1997	20
403 1/8	46 5/8	49 4/8	34 4/8	8 3/8	7 1/8	15 4/8	12 6/8	14 1/8	7 6/8	17	24	Lake Clark, AK	Michael L. Brandt	Michael L. Brandt	1994	21
403 1/8	49 5/8	48 7/8	41 3/8	5 6/8	5 4/8	16 5/8	15 7/8	8 2/8	11	17	16	Tunkaleshna Creek, AK	Michael E. Craig	Michael E. Craig	1997	21
401 3/8	55 6/8	54 4/8	40 2/8	6 4/8	6 7/8	17 1/8	6	11 7/8	1/8	25	19	Lake Clark, AK	Donald L. Kolasinski	Donald L. Kolasinski	1998	23
401 1/8	51 4/8	51 7/8	37 4/8	7 2/8	6 2/8	22 7/8	21 4/8	12 4/8	16 6/8	17	17	Nushagak River, AK	John R. Thodos	John R. Thodos	1995	24
400 4/8	58 6/8	58 2/8	39 1/8	7 4/8	7 1/8	17 7/8	23	9 6/8	11 2/8	13	16	Koliganek, AK	Jeffrey T. Mardis	Jeffrey T. Mardis	1997	25
400 4/8	58	56 7/8	45 4/8	6 3/8	6 5/8	14 6/8	18 4/8	11 2/8	9	18	17	Purcell Mt., AK	Chris G. Sanford	Chris G. Sanford	1998	25
398 7/8	50 4/8	50 2/8	36 7/8	6 2/8	6 1/8	16 4/8	18	9 2/8	7 6/8	11	15	Tikchik Mts., AK	James T. McMahon	James T. McMahon	1999	27
398 5/8	53 2/8	52 2/8	29 4/8	5 6/8	5 3/8	16 4/8	14 2/8	13 2/8	8 5/8	22	18	King Salmon River, AK	James C. Lieber III	James C. Lieber III	1997	28
397 6/8	48 6/8	51	35 6/8	5 7/8	5 7/8	17 4/8	4 1/8	12 4/8	1/8	16	13	Reindeer Lake, AK	Derald A. Taggart	Derald A. Taggart	1998	29
396 1/8	54	51 4/8	40 3/8	7 4/8	8 7/8	19 2/8	1 5/8	16	1/8	21	16	Soldatna, AK	Timothy D. Evans	Timothy D. Evans	1997	30
395 2/8	53 6/8	51 1/8	47 5/8	5 2/8	5 1/8	15 4/8	19	6 1/8	13	13	17	Chichitnok River, AK	Douglas D. Closner	Douglas D. Closner	1997	31

BARREN GROUND CARIBOU

Rangifer tarandus granti

Score	Length of Main Beam R.	L.	Inside Spread	Circumference at Smallest Place Between Brow and Bez Points R.	L.	Length of Brow Points R.	L.	Width of Brow Points R.	L.	Number of Points R.	L.	Locality	Hunter	Owner	Date Killed	Rank
395	57 5/8	57 5/8	36 4/8	6 4/8	6 1/8	20 7/8	21 5/8	11 6/8	4 6/8	15	11	Stuyahok River, AK	Darryl L. McGraw	Darryl L. McGraw	1998	32
394	57	56 6/8	49 1/8	5 7/8	6 1/8	6	18 6/8	1/8	14	9	20	Mulchatna River, AK	Lonnie L. Ritchey	Lonnie L. Ritchey	1998	33
392 1/8	53 1/8	52 4/8	38 1/8	6 6/8	6 2/8	5 2/8	20 7/8	1/8	19	17	24	Kenai Mts., AK	James Standiford	James Standiford	1998	34
389 2/8	55 2/8	56 6/8	47	6 5/8	6 5/8	16	18 1/8	10 6/8	10 7/8	11	13	Mulchatna River, AK	Picked Up	Keith M. Nowell	1992	35
388 6/8	55 3/8	54 5/8	35 6/8	5 5/8	5 5/8	16 7/8	6 2/8	12 4/8	1/8	24	14	Iliamna Lake, AK	Carl W. Schmidt	Carl W. Schmidt	1998	36
388 5/8	52	50 7/8	36 2/8	5	5 3/8	22 5/8	19 6/8	3 6/8	15 2/8	16	15	Old Creek, AK	Bryce A. Luth	Bryce A. Luth	1997	37
388 4/8	51	54 3/8	38	6	5 6/8	2 5/8	19	1/8	15	12	17	Mulchatna River, AK	Stan A. Grebe	Stan A. Grebe	1998	38
388 3/8	44 7/8	47 3/8	37 3/8	6 1/8	6 4/8	16 7/8	17 6/8	12 7/8	11 4/8	18	18	Mulchatna River, AK	Ron J. Scribner	Ron J. Scribner	1998	39
384 1/8	52 2/8	50 6/8	36	5 3/8	5 5/8	14 7/8	14 6/8	10 5/8	10 7/8	23	17	Sagavanirktok River, AK	Dale G. Abbott	Dale G. Abbott	1998	40
383	53	51	33 2/8	7 5/8	7	21 3/8	6	15 4/8	1/8	19	15	Tikchick Lakes, AK	Loren M. Landerholm	Loren M. Landerholm	1996	41
382	50 6/8	52 6/8	37 4/8	8	8 2/8	14 2/8	14 7/8	6 4/8	4 7/8	15	17	Garden Cove, AK	Dan Bates	Dan Bates	1996	42
380 6/8	49 5/8	49 3/8	32 5/8	5 2/8	5 2/8	8 1/8	19 7/8	1/8	16 4/8	16	26	Omar River, AK	S. Preston Kelley	S. Preston Kelley	1996	43
380	57 3/8	57 4/8	34 1/8	6 4/8	6	18 2/8	15 4/8	5 4/8	11 3/8	17	19	Lake Clark, AK	Eric J. Josey	Eric J. Josey	2000	44
379 5/8	48 5/8	47	37 2/8	6 1/8	5 5/8	13 6/8	12 4/8	7 1/8	5 2/8	17	16	Mulchatna River, AK	Michael J. Spence	Michael J. Spence	1998	45
378 7/8	50 6/8	52 1/8	36 7/8	6 6/8	6 3/8	18 4/8	14 6/8	11 7/8	8 7/8	15	14	Nushagak River, AK	T.J. Lehnertz	T.J. Lehnertz	2000	46
377 5/8	54 4/8	56 1/8	39 7/8	6 4/8	6 4/8	22 7/8		17 7/8		16	10	Aniak, AK	George D. Holzhaus	George D. Holzhaus	1997	47
377 5/8	54 4/8	57	37 6/8	5	5	17 4/8	15 1/8	10 7/8	1/8	17	13	Squirrel River, AK	Tom Baker	Tom Baker	1999	47
377 4/8	52 6/8	51 7/8	34 2/8	5 6/8	5 7/8	17 6/8	15	9 6/8	5 2/8	16	13	Wide Bay, AK	Steven R. Bridge	Steven R. Bridge	1998	49
377 4/8	45 4/8	44 4/8	37	5 1/8	4 6/8	21 6/8	16 7/8	10 7/8	8 4/8	18	15	Iliamna Lake, AK	Eric D. Olson	Eric D. Olson	1998	49
377 3/8	47 3/8	49 5/8	28 5/8	5 2/8	5	3 4/8	20 1/8	1/8	17 2/8	13	19	Stony River, AK	Jerry L. Prescott	Jerry L. Prescott	1978	51
434 4/8	*53	54 2/8	49 1/8	6 4/8	6 4/8	16 3/8	13 7/8	9 7/8	5	21	18	Killey River, AK	Aaron Doshier	Aaron Doshier	1997	
427 7/8	*56 6/8	56 7/8	40 3/8	6 1/8	7 1/8	19 6/8	17 1/8	15 3/8	7	24	16	Kipchuk River, AK	Charles F. Craft	Charles F. Craft	1992	

* Final score subject to revision by additional verifying measurements.

CENTRAL CANADA BARREN GROUND CARIBOU

Minimum Score 345   *Rangifer tarandus groenlandicus*   World's Record 433 4/8

Central Canada barren ground caribou occur on Baffin Island and the mainland of N.W.T., with geographic boundaries of the Mackenzie River to the west; the north edge of the continent to the north (excluding any islands except Baffin Island); Hudson's Bay to the east; and the southern boundary of N.W.T. to the south. The boundary also includes the northwest corner of Manitoba north of the south limit of township 87 and west of the Little Churchill River, Churchill River, and Hudson Bay.

Score	Length of Main Beam R	L	Inside Spread	Circumference at Smallest Place Between Brow and Bez Points R	L	Length of Brow Points R	L	Width of Brow Points R	L	Number of Points R	L	Locality	Hunter	Owner	Date Killed	Rank
407	55 6/8	55	34 5/8	5 2/8	4 7/8	18 5/8	15 3/8	16 2/8	1/8	23	18	MacKay Lake, NT	Daniel J. Gartner	Daniel J. Gartner	1997	1
398 6/8	48 6/8	50 2/8	38 2/8	6 6/8	5 6/8	16 3/8	16 4/8	6 5/8	12 2/8	20	25	Little Marten Lake, NT	William J. Mills	William J. Mills	1998	2
391	51 1/8	51	43 1/8	5 7/8	5 6/8	19 5/8	20 6/8	15 4/8	8 4/8	14	15	Humpy Lake, NT	Dennis C. Campbell	Dennis C. Campbell	1996	3
388 5/8	54 1/8	53 4/8	35 2/8	4 5/8	4 5/8	18 1/8	17 7/8	13 4/8	13 1/8	17	18	Little Marten Lake, NT	Mike R. Coyle	Mike R. Coyle	1998	4
388 3/8	49 4/8	51 6/8	30 1/8	7	6 1/8	17 6/8	21 4/8	12 2/8	12 4/8	24	18	MacKay Lake, NT	John W. Scurfield	John W. Scurfield	1999	5
387 5/8	50 2/8	49	23 2/8	5 5/8	5 5/8	13 7/8	10 4/8	11 5/8	1/8	30	21	Whitewolf Lake, NT	M. Joseph Brough	M. Joseph Brough	1999	6
387 4/8	46 1/8	43 4/8	30 2/8	4 5/8	4 7/8	16 6/8	17 6/8	9 4/8	13	19	21	MacKay Lake, NT	Johnny Bliznak	Johnny Bliznak	1998	7
386 2/8	54 7/8	54 7/8	41 5/8	5 3/8	5 1/8	17 5/8	10 2/8	14 5/8	1/8	21	13	Little Marten Lake, NT	Ken G. Wilson	Ken G. Wilson	1998	8
385 5/8	52 7/8	51 3/8	36 7/8	6 7/8	6 3/8	16 3/8	15 2/8	10 4/8	9 5/8	13	22	Munroe Lake, MB	Thomas A. Koepke	Thomas A. Koepke	1997	9
384 7/8	51 7/8	49 5/8	21 3/8	4 7/8	4 4/8	21	18 1/8	19 3/8	6 2/8	30	20	MacKay Lake, NT	Picked Up	Carol A. Mauch	1993	10
383 5/8	54 2/8	54	39 1/8	5 5/8	5 1/8	18 4/8	16 4/8	12 2/8	17	17	15	Whitewolf Lake, NT	Chris E. Brough	Chris E. Brough	1999	11
383 4/8	51 5/8	51 7/8	34 6/8	5 7/8	5 1/8	21 6/8	16 2/8	16 7/8	7 6/8	16	14	Providence Lake, NT	James D. Nyce	James D. Nyce	1998	12
382 7/8	46 2/8	46 1/8	32 7/8	7 5/8	7 7/8	17	16 2/8	11 4/8	10 1/8	19	17	Desteffany Lake, NT	Kathleen N. Cook	Kathleen N. Cook	1999	13
382 6/8	42 1/8	41	32	5 3/8	5 3/8	15 2/8	14 1/8	11 4/8	8	26	23	Courageous Lake, NT	Ken Weber	Ken Weber	2000	14
381 2/8	50 6/8	47 3/8	31 4/8	6	5 4/8	17 3/8	16 4/8	15 4/8	11 7/8	21	20	Humpy Lake, NT	Seth R. Hootman	Lynn K. Richardson	1998	15
381 1/8	55	55 1/8	33	5 4/8	6 2/8	19	9 6/8	14 2/8	1/8	16	13	Little Marten Lake, NT	Brad S. Long	Brad S. Long	1996	16
381 1/8	50 3/8	51 5/8	31 1/8	5 5/8	5 4/8	15 2/8	20 4/8	9	6	23	14	MacKay Lake, NT	Tafford E. Oltz	Tafford E. Oltz	1997	16
381	54 6/8	54 4/8	38 1/8	5 4/8	5 5/8	21 7/8	12 4/8	17 7/8	1/8	18	12	Little Marten Lake, NT	Ken G. Wilson	Ken G. Wilson	1998	18
379 1/8	51 7/8	51 2/8	30 2/8	6 3/8	4 7/8	20	19 4/8	16	5 1/8	13	13	Jolly Lake, NT	Gordon L. MacKinnon	Gordon L. MacKinnon	1998	19
378 3/8	48	49 5/8	34 5/8	5 1/8	5 6/8	16 5/8	13 1/8	15 3/8	6 3/8	25	17	Courageous Lake, NT	Robert J. Clifton	Robert J. Clifton	1998	20
378 3/8	46 2/8	47 3/8	38	6 3/8	5 1/8	18 6/8	18 4/8	14 6/8	7 7/8	20	16	Wolf Lake, NT	Harry H. Sanford	Harry H. Sanford	1999	20
377 4/8	49 2/8	47 4/8	32 3/8	5 1/8	6 4/8	15 7/8	15 2/8	10 6/8	10 4/8	18	15	Whitewolf Lake, NT	Ray E. Stewart	Ray E. Stewart	1999	22
377 3/8	49 7/8	50 7/8	24 3/8	7	6 4/8	19 5/8	19	16 1/8	5 4/8	22	19	Desteffany Lake, NT	David W. Davison	David W. Davison	1998	23
376 3/8	45 7/8	47 5/8	31 6/8	4 3/8	4/8	4/8	15 7/8	1/8	11 5/8	17	19	Jolly Lake, NT	Frank Kacsinko	Frank Kacsinko	1997	24
375 2/8	52 2/8	52 7/8	34 6/8	5	5	13 4/8	15 5/8	6 7/8	11 4/8	14	14	Dymond Lake, MB	Al Kuntz	Al Kuntz	2000	25
373 7/8	62 1/8	61 4/8	36 1/8	6	7 2/8	13 7/8	16 2/8	9 1/8	7 6/8	15	12	MacKay Lake, NT	Ronald K. Serwa	Ronald K. Serwa	1999	26
372 7/8	47 1/8	46 7/8	36 1/8	5 2/8	6 2/8	13 7/8	14 1/8	11 5/8	9 7/8	21	18	Point Lake, NT	John Durand	John Durand	1997	27
372 5/8	59 4/8	60 3/8	34 6/8	5	5 2/8	16 2/8	15 2/8	7	10 3/8	10	15	Humpy Lake, NT	Calvin Conley	Calvin Conley	1998	28
371 6/8	51 3/8	50	36 4/8	4 7/8	5 1/8	15 1/8	16 5/8	8 6/8	9	17	18	Courageous Lake, NT	Ken Weber	Ken Weber	2000	29

CENTRAL CANADA BARREN GROUND CARIBOU

Rangifer tarandus groenlandicus

Score	Length of Main Beam R	L	Inside Spread	Circumference at Smallest Place Between Brow and Bez Points R	L	Length of Brow Points R	L	Width of Brow Points R	L	Number of Points R	L	Locality	Hunter	Owner	Date Killed	Rank
371 5/8	54 1/8	54 6/8	35 7/8	5 2/8	5 4/8	19 1/8	1 3/8	15 1/8	0 1/8	28	17	Humpy Lake, NT	David W. Baxter	David W. Baxter	1998	30
371 5/8	47 2/8	46 6/8	32 4/8	6 3/8	5 7/8	14 6/8	14 6/8	13 2/8	9 7/8	21	19	Jolly Lake, NT	Don LeCain	Don LeCain	1998	30
370 7/8	50 4/8	51	33 6/8	5 3/8	5 2/8	13 4/8	17 2/8	7 7/8	13 6/8	16	20	MacKay Lake, NT	James D. Powless	James D. Powless	1997	32
370 6/8	46 6/8	48 4/8	32 5/8	5 1/8	5 1/8	12 3/8	16 1/8	1 2/8	13 3/8	16	22	Courageous Lake, NT	Francis J. Kelsch	Francis J. Kelsch	2000	33
370 3/8	42	44 1/8	26 5/8	4 6/8	4 7/8	17	12 6/8	15	5	27	20	MacKay Lake, NT	Donald J. Malisani	Donald J. Malisani	1999	34
370 1/8	50 7/8	48 7/8	31 6/8	7 1/8	6	14 1/8	18 6/8	10		16	21	Courageous Lake, NT	Marion G. Macaluso	Marion G. Macaluso	1999	35
370	51 2/8	52 2/8	38 7/8	5	5 1/8		13 5/8		7 6/8	12	17	Nichols Lake, MB	Jeffrey W. Strain	Jeffrey W. Strain	1999	36
369 2/8	53 4/8	51 7/8	36 5/8	4 7/8	5 2/8	19 1/8	17 6/8	13 1/8	14 1/8	16	16	Whitewolf Lake, NT	David E. Combs	David E. Combs	1999	37
367 1/8	53 7/8	52 6/8	30	6 1/8	5 2/8	9 3/8	18 4/8	1/8	14 1/8	12	16	Commonwealth Lake, MB	Robert R. Theer, Jr.	Robert R. Theer, Jr.	1997	38
366 7/8	50 4/8	51 6/8	36 2/8	5 3/8	5 1/8	19 5/8	15 5/8	9 2/8	8 3/8	13	12	MacKay Lake, NT	K.D. Schwanky	K.D. Schwanky	1995	39
366 2/8	51 2/8	52 1/8	35 5/8	4 2/8	4 3/8	18 1/8	23 1/8	1 3/8	18 2/8	10	18	Courageous Lake, NT	Brad White	Brad White	1997	40
365	50 7/8	51 2/8	41	5 2/8	5 2/8	10 3/8	17 7/8	1/8	13 7/8	14	18	Providence Lake, NT	Linda A. Neifert	Linda A. Neifert	1998	41
364 4/8	49	50 5/8	29 2/8	4 7/8	4 5/8	18 2/8	17 7/8	12 1/8	15 4/8	16	19	Courageous Lake, NT	John E. Howard	John E. Howard	1998	42
363 7/8	46 3/8	46 6/8	33 2/8	4 6/8	4 6/8	15	13 4/8	7 4/8	5 1/8	22	19	Little Marten Lake, NT	Buck Taylor	Buck Taylor	1999	43
363 3/8	47 4/8	47 2/8	32 4/8	4 7/8	5	17 1/8	15 4/8	13 4/8	10 4/8	21	20	Jolly Lake, NT	Ronald D. Zelewski	Ronald D. Zelewski	1998	44
363 3/8	48	47	33 7/8	4 7/8	4 6/8	14 7/8	16 3/8	6 3/8	10 1/8	14	18	Nueltin Lake, MB	John W. Brand	John W. Brand	1999	44
362 7/8	47 6/8	48 7/8	31	7	6	13 4/8	14 1/8	11 7/8	12 3/8	14	25	MacKay Lake, NT	Vincent J. Strickler	Vincent J. Strickler	2000	46
362	51 6/8	53 2/8	35 7/8	5	5 2/8	11 2/8	20 3/8	1/8	15 1/8	14	22	Rocher Lake, NT	John C. Marsh	John C. Marsh	1998	47
360 6/8	52 2/8	51 2/8	40 2/8	4	4	19 6/8	2 1/8	15 4/8	1/8	19	12	MacKay Lake, NT	Johnny Bliznak	Johnny Bliznak	1998	48
360 3/8	52 7/8	52 2/8	39	5 4/8	4 7/8	15 4/8	14 5/8	11 2/8	1 6/8	14	12	Courageous Lake, NT	Robert J. Maslowski	Robert J. Maslowski	1996	49
360 3/8	45	43 4/8	27 7/8	5 4/8	5 3/8	16	2	14 2/8	6/8	21	13	Courageous Lake, NT	Ronald D. Zelewski	Ronald D. Zelewski	1998	49
360 1/8	48 4/8	48 1/8	27 3/8	7 1/8	5 6/8	15 2/8	14 7/8	6 3/8	10 6/8	20	22	Jolly Lake, NT	Jason C. Marsh	Jason C. Marsh	1998	51
359 6/8	53 5/8	54 5/8	44 6/8	5 4/8	5 5/8	17 1/8	13 7/8	11 2/8	4 4/8	16	11	Rocher Lake, NT	Scott R. Barefoot	Scott R. Barefoot	1997	52
359 3/8	53 1/8	54 5/8	27 6/8	4 6/8	4 7/8	16 4/8	16 1/8	10 7/8	4 3/8	13	15	MacKay Lake, NT	Harry G. Cooke, Jr.	Harry G. Cooke, Jr.	1997	53
359 2/8	49 5/8	47 7/8	32 4/8	4 6/8	4 6/8	2 3/8	14 7/8	1/8	11 7/8	16	26	Martin Lake, NT	Lee R. Skinner	Lee R. Skinner	1999	54
359 1/8	50 1/8	51 6/8	38 2/8	5 2/8	5 3/8	18 4/8	16	14	3 7/8	15	18	MacKay Lake, NT	Dale E. Harkins	Dale E. Harkins	1998	55
357 5/8	45 4/8	49 5/8	32 3/8	5 4/8	5 5/8	14 4/8	14 3/8	11 6/8	10 3/8	20	13	Tuktoyaktuk, NT	Randy D. Eastman	Randy D. Eastman	1997	56
356	55 1/8	55 2/8	39 4/8	5 7/8	6 3/8		19 2/8		14 4/8	14	18	Munroe Lake, MB	Timothy R. Reed	Timothy R. Reed	1998	57
355 5/8	54 5/8	53 1/8	39 3/8	6 2/8	5 7/8	18 4/8		16	14	14	15	Point Lake, NT	Duane George	Duane George	1999	58
354 1/8	54 3/8	50 1/8	34 2/8	4 6/8	5 1/8	17 4/8	18 3/8	10 7/8	5 7/8	20	12	Humpy Lake, NT	Raymond R. Rantala	Raymond R. Rantala	1998	59
353 1/8	53 2/8	57 2/8	42 2/8	4 2/8	4 3/8	17	20 4/8	1/8	19 1/8	13	17	Humpy Lake, NT	Kenneth M. Paullin	Kenneth M. Paullin	1999	60
349 2/8	42 5/8	44 2/8	22 6/8	4 4/8	4 3/8	17 7/8	11 6/8	15	1/8	23	14	Commonwealth Lake, MB	Michael H. Ye	Michael H. Ye	1997	61
348 4/8	48 3/8	46 2/8	35 6/8	5 1/8	5	14 2/8	17 2/8	2 1/8	10 3/8	15	16	Artillery Lake, NT	John Duggan	John Duggan	1999	62

346 6/8	54 2/8	55	42 1/8	4 5/8	4 6/8	8 7/8	14 4/8	1/8	11 3/8	9	14	MacKay Lake, NT	Stephen J. McCoy	1999	63
346	49 3/8	47 6/8	31 3/8	6	6 3/8	16 3/8	1 5/8	13 4/8	1/8	16	14	MacKay Lake, NT	Stephen J. McCoy	1999	64
417 5/8	*50 2/8	49 5/8	31 2/8	7	6 3/8	14 7/8	6 5/8	10	1/8	27	22	Pellatt Lake, NT	Aaron P. Hassler	1998	
406 2/8	*45 6/8	47	35 2/8	5 4/8	5 3/8	11 5/8	15	2 4/8	11 7/8	22	24	Artillery Lake, NT	Michael J. Siegler	1998	
395 2/8	*54 3/8	56 3/8	37 7/8	4 5/8	4 4/8	18 6/8	19 5/8	13 7/8	10 7/8	23	22	Commonwealth Lake, MB	Michael Reimer	1996	

* Final score subject to revision by additional verifying measurements.

QUEBEC-LABRADOR CARIBOU

Rangifer tarandus from Quebec and Labrador

Minimum Score 365

World's Record 474 6/8

Score	Length of Main Beam R	L	Inside Spread	Circumference at Smallest Place Between Brow and Bez Points R	L	Length of Brow Points R	L	Width of Brow Points R	L	Number of Points R	L	Locality	Hunter	Owner	Date Killed	Rank
416 7/8	48 7/8	48 5/8	38 4/8	6	5 4/8	14 5/8	18 4/8	11 4/8	16 4/8	23	24	Schefferville, QC	Picked Up	Michael L. Hoft	1997	1
415 7/8	59 4/8	55 6/8	44	5 1/8	5	16 1/8	17 4/8	10 2/8	14 2/8	20	22	Minto Lake Island, QC	Curt M. Coleman	Curt M. Coleman	1999	2
397 5/8	51 4/8	49 4/8	50 7/8	5 3/8	5 6/8	16 7/8	11 4/8	11 6/8	1/8	20	15	Lake Rigouville, QC	James M. Parker	James M. Parker	1998	3
396 5/8	47 7/8	50 4/8	46 3/8	5 4/8	5 4/8	16 4/8	16 2/8	13 4/8	5 2/8	20	12	Innuksuak River, QC	Michel Labbe	Michel Labbe	2000	4
393 6/8	50 4/8	48 2/8	52 5/8	5 6/8	5 5/8	3 4/8	15	1/8	11 5/8	16	22	Bourg Lake, QC	Fred F. Boyce	Fred F. Boyce	1997	5
393 1/8	51 3/8	50 2/8	53 2/8	5 1/8	5 1/8	1	16 2/8	1/8	9 5/8	17	22	Lake Ptarmigan, QC	Robert L. Sobolisky	Robert L. Sobolisky	1998	6
392 7/8	48 6/8	44 5/8	47 4/8	5 1/8	5 1/8	16 2/8	17 3/8	9 5/8	10 1/8	21	23	Manereuille Lake, QC	David MacDonald	David MacDonald	1999	7
391 3/8	44 4/8	44 2/8	45 6/8	7 1/8	6	16 7/8	17	12 4/8	11 4/8	16	22	Rose Lake, QC	Paul F. Frigault	Paul F. Frigault	1998	8
390 1/8	45 1/8	43 2/8	38 7/8	4 6/8	4 7/8	19 5/8	21 1/8	4 6/8	14 6/8	16	15	Lake Astree, QC	Peter W. Spear	Peter W. Spear	1994	9
389 6/8	53 3/8	54 6/8	44	5 5/8	5 6/8	11 1/8	22 4/8	1/8	20 6/8	15	20	Sardine Lake, QC	David L. Turner	David L. Turner	1997	10
389 3/8	57	56 7/8	51 5/8	5	4 7/8	19 3/8		15 7/8		25	17	Pons River, QC	Robert M. Johnston	Robert M. Johnston	1999	11
389 2/8	43	43	37 5/8	6 1/8	5 3/8	18	19 6/8	14 1/8	16 6/8	22	22	Dunphy Lake, QC	Clarence M. Pitsch	Clarence M. Pitsch	1998	12
386 7/8	56 2/8	52 4/8	50	4 6/8	4 4/8	19 6/8	21 5/8	17 1/8	15 7/8	16	15	Chapiteau Lake, QC	Matthew C. Ash	Matthew C. Ash	1999	13
386 6/8	55 2/8	54 4/8	43 7/8	5 6/8	5 7/8	17 5/8	19 5/8	11 5/8	11	15	15	Crossroads Lake, LB	Kenneth Mowerson, Jr.	Kenneth Mowerson, Jr.	1998	14
385 7/8	52 4/8	54 7/8	46 1/8	5 2/8	5 3/8	15 6/8	19 3/8	11 5/8	15 6/8	15	18	Minto Lake, QC	Anthony A. Moles	Anthony A. Moles	1999	15
385 4/8	52 2/8	51 2/8	36 2/8	5 1/8	4 7/8	15 1/8	18 3/8	6 6/8	10 2/8	16	14	Fort-Chimo, QC	James E. Carroll	James E. Carroll	1998	16
384 5/8	45 4/8	44 1/8	46 2/8	4 7/8	5	23 2/8	18 6/8	19 2/8	1/8	29	17	Charlieu Lake, QC	Ronald I. McDiarmid	Ronald I. McDiarmid	1998	17
382 3/8	47 1/8	46 6/8	42 1/8	4 7/8	5 2/8	18 2/8	19 1/8	13 4/8	14 7/8	17	23	Lake Fremin, QC	Jon D. Upton	Jon D. Upton	1997	18
378 4/8	49 7/8	49 1/8	49	5	5 1/8	21 1/8	6 1/8	13 7/8	1/8	21	15	May Lake, QC	D. Ross Sheridan	D. Ross Sheridan	1989	19
378 1/8	45 2/8	45	36	4 5/8	4 5/8	14 1/8	13 7/8	12 2/8	11 5/8	25	25	Little Cedar Lake, QC	David G. Baker	David G. Baker	1998	20
377 3/8	49 5/8	49 7/8	36 2/8	6 1/8	6 3/8	17 4/8	20 2/8	10 3/8	20 6/8	28	28	Minto Lake, QC	Charles F. Nopper	Charles F. Nopper	1997	21
377 3/8	47 4/8	45 3/8	43 6/8	5 5/8	5 5/8	3 2/8	16 5/8	1/8	10 1/8	19	27	Snow Lake, QC	John A. Irwin	John A. Irwin	1999	21
376 7/8	48 4/8	46 4/8	38 4/8	5 4/8	5 3/8	20 5/8	13 6/8	4 1/8	9 3/8	24	17	Chailly Lake, QC	John L. Guerra	John L. Guerra	2000	23
376 4/8	48 3/8	48 5/8	43 6/8	5 4/8	4 6/8	17 1/8	17 7/8	12 4/8	11 6/8	25	21	Pons River, QC	Richard A. Allen	Richard A. Allen	1999	24
376 1/8	46 7/8	46 5/8	50 4/8	5	5	17	18 6/8	13	13 4/8	21	20	Gordon Lake, QC	Karam Guergis	Karam Guergis	1999	25
375 6/8	49 4/8	46 2/8	48	4 7/8	5 1/8	15	13 2/8	7 4/8	7 4/8	12	18	Minto Lake, QC	Max Landers	Max Landers	1999	26
374 5/8	51 3/8	49	48	5 2/8	5 1/8	18 5/8	16 4/8	14	11 6/8	16	18	Dufreboy Lake, QC	John T. Ballantine	John T. Ballantine	1998	27
371 3/8	50 2/8	50 6/8	47 4/8	5 5/8	5 4/8	15 2/8	10 6/8	12 4/8	1/8	22	19	George River, QC	Robert K. Fosler, Jr	Robert K. Fosler, Jr	1978	28
371 1/8	51 3/8	50 4/8	52 4/8	5 7/8	5 2/8	16 1/8	18 3/8	11 3/8	7 3/8	20	13	Caniapiscau River, QC	Robert L. Evans	Robert L. Evans	1999	29
370 1/8	47 7/8	47 3/8	44 4/8	5	4 7/8	14 3/8	15 1/8	11 4/8	1/8	14	14	Mollette Lake, QC	Robert T. Dunn	Robert T. Dunn	2000	30
369 3/8	54 1/8	55 4/8	41 7/8	5 5/8	5 1/8	16 1/8	17	8 2/8	2 5/8	18	18	Pond River, QC	William Eyles	William Eyles	1991	31
367 6/8	48 7/8	46 1/8	44 4/8	4 5/8	4 6/8	14 4/8	17 1/8	4 7/8	12 7/8	20	19	Lake Nicholas, QC	Graham D. Gumley	Graham D. Gumley	1998	32
366 7/8	50 3/8	51 1/8	34 7/8	6 7/8	6 1/8	3 5/8	15 7/8	1/8	12 1/8	13	15	Fontisson Lake, QC	Leonard Sunram	Leonard Sunram	1998	32

													Locality	Hunter	Year	Rank
365 4/8	47 4/8	52	39 6/8	5 1/8	4 7/8	9 3/8	20	15 4/8	1/8	21	16		Leaf River, QC	William M. Slota	1999	34
365 3/8	47 4/8	48 1/8	44	4 7/8	4 6/8	12 4/8	14 4/8	3 7/8	12	21	23		Greenbush Lake, LB	Patricia D. Kerby	1999	35
407 1/8*	55 1/8	55 7/8	47 7/8	4 7/8	4 7/8	6/8	18 7/8	1/8	13	21	22		Dulhut Lake, QC	George J. West	1997	
394 4/8*	47 3/8	47 3/8	44 3/8	5 2/8	5 2/8	16	18 3/8	11 1/8	15 5/8	15	18		Ungava Bay, QC	Mark A. Brueggeman	1996	

* Final score subject to revision by additional verifying measurements.

PRONGHORN

Antilocapra americana americana and related subspecies

Minimum Score 80   World's Record 93 4/8

Score	Length of Horn R.	L.	Circumference of Base R.	L.	Circumference at Third Quarter R.	L.	Inside Spread	Tip to Tip Spread	Length of Prong R.	L.	Locality	Hunter	Owner	Date Killed	Rank
92 6/8	16 6/8	17 3/8	7 5/8	7 4/8	2 5/8	2 6/8	11 4/8	7	7 5/8	7 1/8	Harney Co., OR	Sam Barry	Sam Barry	2000	1
90 4/8	16 1/8	16 2/8	7 1/8	7 1/8	3 1/8	3 5/8	14 3/8	10	7 3/8	7 1/8	Washakie Co., WY	Alden L. Curtis	Alden L. Curtis	1998	2
90 4/8	18 4/8	18 4/8	7 7/8	7 7/8	3	3	10 3/8	5 4/8	5	4 7/8	Big Horn Co., WY	Michael P. Dellos	Michael P. Dellos	1998	2
90 2/8	17 4/8	17 3/8	6 4/8	6 4/8	2 7/8	2 6/8	10 3/8	6 7/8	7 2/8	7 1/8	Clark Co., ID	Randy Grover	Randy Grover	1997	4
90 2/8	17 3/8	17 2/8	6 7/8	6 7/8	2 6/8	2 4/8	12 1/8	9	7 2/8	7	Catron Co., NM	Robert N. Bushong	Robert N. Bushong	1998	4
90	18 4/8	19	6 6/8	6 6/8	3 1/8	3 1/8	11 2/8	2 6/8	5 1/8	5 1/8	Yavapai Co., AZ	Sam T. Aiton III	Sam T. Aiton III	1998	6
90	16 4/8	16 5/8	6 6/8	6 6/8	3 4/8	3 4/8	12 1/8	8 4/8	6 5/8	6 6/8	Socorro Co., NM	Len H. Guldman	Len H. Guldman	1999	6
89 6/8	16 4/8	16 2/8	7 3/8	7 3/8	3	3	9 7/8	4 4/8	6 5/8	6 7/8	Washoe Co., NV	Sam S. Jaksick, Jr.	Sam S. Jaksick, Jr.	2000	8
89 6/8	17 2/8	17 2/8	6 6/8	6 7/8	3 3/8	3 4/8	11	5 1/8	6	6	Yavapai Co., AZ	James M. Machac	James M. Machac	2000	8
89 4/8	17 1/8	17 1/8	7 1/8	7	2 6/8	2 7/8	14 4/8	11 2/8	6 1/8	6	Yavapai Co., AZ	Brian B. Bingham	Brian B. Bingham	1999	10
89 2/8	16 4/8	17	6 5/8	6 5/8	2 5/8	2 5/8	11 4/8	6 5/8	5 7/8	5 7/8	Moffat Co., CO	Glen E. Stinson	Glen E. Stinson	1997	11
89 2/8	18 4/8	18 3/8	7	6 7/8	3 1/8	3	15 3/8	12 1/8	5 4/8	5 3/8	Hudspeth Co., TX	Linda J. McBride	Linda J. McBride	2000	11
89 2/8	16 7/8	17 1/8	7	6 6/8	3 2/8	2 7/8	12	5 6/8	6 4/8	6 4/8	Coconino Co., AZ	Robert E. Petersen	Robert E. Petersen	2000	11
88 6/8	16 1/8	15 5/8	7 4/8	7 1/8	3 4/8	3 3/8	12	7 7/8	6 3/8	6 6/8	Yavapai Co., AZ	Jerry L. Van Cleve	Jerry L. Van Cleve	1998	14
88 4/8	16 7/8	16 4/8	7 5/8	7 4/8	2 7/8	3 2/8	12 3/8	8 5/8	5 5/8	5 2/8	Mora Co., NM	Thomas J. Shaw	Thomas J. Shaw	1999	15
88 4/8	15 3/8	15 4/8	7 3/8	7 3/8	3	3	10	6 1/8	7	6 6/8	Carbon Co., WY	Shawn M. Hullinger	Shawn M. Hullinger	2000	15
88 2/8	18	18 2/8	6 3/8	6 3/8	3	3	6 4/8	3 4/8	6 6/8	5 7/8	Yavapai Co., AZ	John Mullins	John Mullins	1997	17
88 2/8	18 6/8	18 1/8	6 2/8	6 2/8	3 2/8	2 7/8	8 2/8	2	6 5/8	6	Socorro Co., NM	Burgh K. Johnson	Burgh K. Johnson	1998	17
88	16	16 2/8	7 2/8	7 3/8	2 6/8	2 6/8	10 7/8	6 1/8	6 2/8	6	Cassia Co., ID	Douglas G. Freestone, Sr.	Douglas G. Freestone, Sr.	1998	19
88	15 3/8	15 1/8	6 6/8	6 6/8	3 4/8	3 3/8	8 2/8	5 4/8	6 6/8	6 5/8	Emery Co., UT	Burgh K. Johnson	Burgh K. Johnson	1998	19
88	16 3/8	16 4/8	7	7 2/8	3	3	8 7/8	4 1/8	6 7/8	7	Yavapai Co., AZ	Mark G. Mahaney	Mark G. Mahaney	1998	19
88	16 2/8	16 3/8	7	7	2 5/8	2 6/8	10 1/8	6 7/8	6 5/8	6 5/8	Harney Co., OR	Sherrie A. Rickman	Sherrie A. Rickman	1998	19
87 6/8	16 1/8	16 2/8	7	7	2 7/8	2 7/8	12 6/8	9 3/8	6 3/8	6 3/8	Natrona Co., WY	Robert R. Munro	Robert R. Munro	1998	23
87 6/8	16 6/8	16 7/8	7 1/8	7 1/8	3 3/8	3 3/8	10 7/8	6 1/8	5 2/8	4 7/8	Emery Co., UT	Burgh K. Johnson	Burgh K. Johnson	1999	23
87 6/8	14 3/8	14 5/8	7 4/8	7 4/8	3 2/8	3 2/8	9 6/8	6 2/8	6 5/8	6 6/8	Sweetwater Co., WY	Jason L. Ridgeway	Jason L. Ridgeway	2000	23
87 4/8	16 3/8	16 5/8	6 6/8	6 5/8	2 4/8	2 4/8	15 5/8	13 3/8	7	7	Moffat Co., CO	Preston J. Essex	Preston J. Essex	1997	26
87 4/8	17	17 2/8	7 2/8	7	3 2/8	3 3/8	9	3 6/8	4 7/8	4 6/8	Socorro Co., NM	Stephen C. LeBlanc	Stephen C. LeBlanc	1998	26
87 4/8	16 7/8	16 7/8	6 6/8	6 6/8	2 6/8	2 5/8	12 7/8	8 5/8	6 5/8	7 3/8	Harney Co., OR	Walt L. Kight	Walt L. Kight	1999	26
87 2/8	16 5/8	17	7 1/8	7 1/8	2 6/8	2 6/8	12 2/8	8 7/8	6 2/8	6 4/8	Hudspeth Co., TX	Lester P. Everetts	Lester P. Everetts	1998	29
87 2/8	16 2/8	17	7 1/8	7 1/8	3 1/8	3 1/8	15 6/8	14 2/8	5 7/8	5 6/8	Grant Co., NM	Bill Johnston	Bill Johnston	1998	29
87 2/8	15 2/8	15 3/8	6 7/8	6 7/8	3 4/8	3 5/8	12 5/8	11 2/8	6	6	Yavapai Co., AZ	David E. Evanow	David E. Evanow	1999	29
87 2/8	18 5/8	17 2/8	7 4/8	7 5/8	3 1/8	2 4/8	11 7/8	8 5/8	5 3/8	6	Grant Co., NM	Edwin C. Broun III	Edwin C. Broun III	2000	29
87	16 6/8	16 2/8	6 5/8	6 4/8	3	3	9	5	5 6/8	5 5/8	Socorro Co., NM	Mark D. Nuessle	Mark D. Nuessle	1997	33
87	18 1/8	18 4/8	6 4/8	6 4/8	2 5/8	2 5/8	14 5/8	8 6/8	5 5/8	5 4/8	Harney Co., OR	Scott J. Bernards	Scott J. Bernards	1998	33

Score												Locality	Hunter	Owner	Date	Rank
87	16 6/8	16 6/8	7 3/8	7 3/8	3	2 7/8	9 6/8	9 6/8	4 6/8	5 4/8	5 7/8	Carbon Co., WY	Larry S. Hicks	Larry S. Hicks	1999	33
86 6/8	15 4/8	15 4/8	7 3/8	7 3/8	3	3	9 6/8	9 6/8	5 1/8	6 1/8	5 5/8	Yavapai Co., AZ	James M. Machac	James M. Machac	1998	36
86 6/8	17 2/8	17 2/8	6 2/8	6 4/8	3	3 1/8	10 3/8	10 3/8	3 4/8	5 6/8	6 4/8	Yavapai Co., AZ	Kenneth F. Cook	Kenneth F. Cook	1999	36
86 6/8	17 2/8	17 2/8	6 6/8	6 7/8	2 4/8	2 6/8	8 7/8	8 7/8	2	7	6 1/8	Grand Co., UT	Chris H. Darnell	Chris H. Darnell	1999	36
86 6/8	16 2/8	16 4/8	6 6/8	6 5/8	2 5/8	2 5/8	8 5/8	8 5/8	4 7/8	6 5/8	6 1/8	Washoe Co., NV	Don E. Perrien	Don E. Perrien	1999	36
86 6/8	19 1/8	19	6 4/8	6 4/8	2 4/8	2 4/8	6 2/8	6 2/8	3 2/8	5 6/8	6 5/8	Washoe Co., NV	L. Victor Clark	L. Victor Clark	2000	36
86 6/8	16	16 4/8	6 4/8	6 4/8	3 2/8	3 1/8	14 7/8	14 7/8	10 4/8	6	4 3/8	Luna Co., NM	William H. Moyer	William H. Moyer	2000	36
86 6/8	17	16 7/8	7	7	2 7/8	3 1/8	9 4/8	9 4/8	4 4/8	5 7/8	6	Washoe Co., NV	Jennifer M. Piccinini	Jennifer M. Piccinini	2000	36
86 4/8	18 1/8	18 1/8	6 1/8	6 1/8	2 7/8	2 7/8	12 6/8	12 6/8	7 6/8	5 3/8	5 3/8	Catron Co., NM	David M. Asal	David M. Asal	1997	43
86 4/8	16 2/8	16 2/8	7	6 7/8	2 7/8	2 7/8	12 2/8	12 2/8	8 4/8	6 4/8	5 2/8	Coconino Co., AZ	Jim L. Yarbrough	Jim L. Yarbrough	1998	43
86 4/8	16 5/8	16 4/8	6 6/8	6 7/8	3	3 2/8	14	14	7 4/8	5 4/8	6 2/8	Coconino Co., AZ	Rosemary B. Hume	Rosemary B. Hume	1999	43
86 4/8	16 6/8	16 3/8	6 7/8	6 7/8	2 7/8	3	12	12	9 4/8	5 5/8	5 6/8	Sierra Co., NM	Jimmy J. Liautaud	Jimmy J. Liautaud	1999	43
86 2/8	17 4/8	17 1/8	6 4/8	6 4/8	3 1/8	3 1/8	10 3/8	10 3/8	5 5/8	5 5/8	5 5/8	Colfax Co., NM	William E. Pipes III	William E. Pipes III	1985	47
86 2/8	15 6/8	15 6/8	6 7/8	6 6/8	3 2/8	3 1/8	10 1/8	10 1/8	4 6/8	6 7/8	6 6/8	Emery Co., UT	Len H. Guldman	Len H. Guldman	1997	47
86 2/8	17 2/8	16 7/8	6 7/8	6 7/8	2 6/8	2 6/8	8 7/8	8 7/8	3 2/8	5 5/8	5 5/8	Malheur Co., OR	Terry M. Dittrich	Terry M. Dittrich	1998	47
86 2/8	15 7/8	16	7 2/8	7 1/8	2 4/8	2 3/8	11 5/8	11 5/8	8 4/8	7 1/8	6 4/8	Sweetwater Co., WY	Tyler A. Jack	Tyler A. Jack	1998	47
86	15 4/8	15 3/8	6 5/8	6 5/8	2 7/8	2 7/8	16 2/8	16 3/8	16 2/8	6 7/8	6 6/8	Cibola Co., NM	Bobby L. Beeman	Bobby L. Beeman	1997	51
85 6/8	16 2/8	16 2/8	7 2/8	7 2/8	2 4/8	2 3/8	13 4/8	13 4/8	10 5/8	6 1/8	6 4/8	Malheur Co., OR	Klaus D. Pagel	Klaus D. Pagel	1998	52
85 6/8	15 7/8	15 4/8	6 6/8	6 6/8	3 1/8	3 1/8	11 2/8	11 2/8	10 1/8	6 1/8	6 4/8	Yoakum Co., TX	William S. Pickett III	William S. Pickett III	1999	52
85 6/8	15 4/8	15 3/8	7 7/8	7 6/8	3	3	10 6/8	10 6/8	8 3/8	5	5 3/8	Carbon Co., WY	Robert E. Bergquist	Robert E. Bergquist	2000	52
85 4/8	16 1/8	16 2/8	6	6	3 1/8	3 1/8	14 6/8	14 6/8	14 1/8	6 5/8	6 3/8	Socorro Co., NM	Len H. Guldman	Len H. Guldman	1998	55
85 4/8	15 3/8	15 3/8	7 2/8	7 2/8	3	3	13 3/8	13 3/8	11	5 6/8	5 6/8	Colfax Co., NM	Robert D. Jones	Robert D. Jones	1998	55
85 4/8	17 2/8	17 2/8	6 6/8	6 5/8	3 2/8	3 2/8	15	15	13 7/8	4 4/8	5	Socorro Co., NM	Dale Hislop	Dale Hislop	1999	55
85 4/8	16 1/8	16 1/8	6 7/8	6 7/8	2 6/8	2 6/8	10 4/8	10 4/8	5 7/8	6 2/8	6 2/8	Lincoln Co., NM	Gary A. Lehnherr	Gary A. Lehnherr	1999	55
85 4/8	17 6/8	18	6 6/8	6 6/8	2 4/8	2 5/8	15 6/8	15 6/8	11 4/8	5 4/8	5 3/8	Colfax Co., NM	Donald E. Utecht	Donald E. Utecht	2000	55
85 2/8	17 5/8	18	6 3/8	6 6/8	2 7/8	2 6/8	10 2/8	10 2/8	5 7/8	5 5/8	5 5/8	Socorro Co., NM	E. Lance Whary	E. Lance Whary	1998	55
85 2/8	17 1/8	17	6 5/8	6 3/8	3	3	12 1/8	12 1/8	10 3/8	5 3/8	5 6/8	Catron Co., NM	Joseph S. Brannen	Joseph S. Brannen	1999	60
85 2/8	16 2/8	16	7 1/8	7 6/8	3 4/8	3 2/8	14 2/8	14 2/8	13	6	6	Socorro Co., NM	Edward J. Bordovsky, Jr.	Edward J. Bordovsky, Jr.	2000	60
85 2/8	15 5/8	14 5/8	6 6/8	6 5/8	3 2/8	3 2/8	10 2/8	10 2/8	10 6/8	4 5/8	5 1/8	Harney Co., OR	Jeffrey H. Edwards	Jeffrey H. Edwards	2000	60
85	15 5/8	15 6/8	7	6 6/8	2 7/8	3	9 5/8	9 5/8	9	5 1/8	4 6/8	Hudspeth Co., TX	Len H. Guldman	Len H. Guldman	1997	60
85	16 7/8	16 5/8	6 7/8	6 5/8	2 4/8	2 5/8	9	9	7 5/8	5 7/8	6 2/8	Carbon Co., WY	Tracey L. Arthur	Tracey L. Arthur	1999	64
85	16 5/8	16 4/8	7 1/8	7 1/8	3	3	14 6/8	14 6/8	10 4/8	4 5/8	5 1/8	Catron Co., NM	Mike J. Pilliken	Mike J. Pilliken	1999	64
85	16 1/8	16	6 3/8	6 3/8	2 4/8	2 4/8	13	13	7 5/8	3 3/8	4 6/8	Campbell Co., WY	Randall Russell	Randall Russell	1999	64
85	16 7/8	16 6/8	6 2/8	6 3/8	2 6/8	2 4/8	10 4/8	10 4/8	13	5 7/8	6 3/8	Socorro Co., NM	J. Bert Vargas	J. Bert Vargas	1999	64
85	16 2/8	16 1/8	7 1/8	7 1/8	3	3	13 1/8	13 1/8	10 4/8	5 5/8	5 7/8	Coconino Co., AZ	Robert E. Petersen	Robert E. Petersen	2000	64
85	16 3/8	16 3/8	6 3/8	6 3/8	2 5/8	3 3/8	15 2/8	15 2/8	12 2/8	6 1/8	5 5/8	Carbon Co., WY	Kenneth S. Sutter	Kenneth S. Sutter	2000	64
85	17	17 1/8	6 5/8	6 5/8	3	3 3/8	11 1/8	11 1/8	11 1/8	4 7/8	4 7/8	Otero Co., NM	William W. Shipton III	William W. Shipton III	1990	64
84 6/8	17 1/8	17 2/8	6 4/8	6	2 7/8	2 3/8	9 6/8	9 6/8	9 6/8	4 2/8	5 5/8	Navajo Co., AZ	Ronald D. Major	Ronald D. Major	1997	71
84 6/8	17 7/8	17 6/8	6	6	2 7/8	2 4/8	11 4/8	11 4/8	10 6/8	5 5/8	5 3/8	Catron Co., NM	Frank P. DeYoung	Frank P. DeYoung	1998	71
84 6/8	16	16	6 3/8	6 3/8	3 3/8	3 3/8	11	11	8 2/8	5 3/8	5	Apache Co., AZ	Denise S. Rhodes	Denise S. Rhodes	1998	71
84 6/8	16 2/8	16	7 1/8	6 2/8	2 3/8	2 4/8	8 2/8	8 2/8	8 2/8	5 4/8	5 4/8	Elko Co., NV	David G. Paullin	David G. Paullin	2000	71
84 4/8	15 6/8	16 1/8	7 1/8	7 1/8	2 5/8	2 5/8	12 4/8	12 4/8	3 2/8	6 6/8	6 3/8	Carbon Co., WY	Thomas McCulloch	Thomas McCulloch	1963	76
84 4/8	17 2/8	17 3/8	6 6/8	6 7/8	2 6/8	2 6/8	10	10	10	5 4/8	5 4/8	Carbon Co., WY	James P. Knudson	James P. Knudson	1992	76

PRONGHORN

Antilocapra americana and related subspecies

Score	Length of Horn R.	L.	Circumference of Base R.	L.	Circumference at Third Quarter R.	L.	Inside Spread	Tip to Tip Spread	Length of Prong R.	L.	Locality	Hunter	Owner	Date Killed	Rank
84 4/8	16 2/8	16 2/8	7 2/8	7	2 6/8	2 6/8	11 6/8	7 5/8	6	5 4/8	Moffat Co., CO	Patrick G. Diesing	Patrick G. Diesing	1997	76
84 4/8	16 6/8	16 7/8	6 4/8	6 4/8	2 6/8	2 5/8	10 4/8	6 1/8	5 4/8	5 7/8	Socorro Co., NM	Don W. Fullen	Don W. Fullen	1997	76
84 4/8	16 6/8	16 2/8	6 3/8	6 3/8	2 6/8	2 6/8	9 6/8	6 7/8	5 7/8	5 7/8	Catron Co., NM	D. Craig Heiner	D. Craig Heiner	1998	76
84 4/8	18 6/8	18 3/8	6	6	2 6/8	2 6/8	12 6/8	6 4/8	5 4/8	5 6/8	Catron Co., NM	R. Douglas Isbell	R. Douglas Isbell	1998	76
84 4/8	16 1/8	15 7/8	7 2/8	7 1/8	3	3	9	4 6/8	5 4/8	5 4/8	Colfax Co., NM	Michael B. Murphy	Michael B. Murphy	1999	76
84 4/8	16	16	6 5/8	6 5/8	2 6/8	2 5/8	7 7/8	2 3/8	5 7/8	5 4/8	Lewis & Clark Co., MT	John T. Mandell	John T. Mandell	2000	76
84 2/8	16	16	6 2/8	6 1/8	3	3 1/8	10 1/8	6	6 5/8	6 3/8	Yavapai Co., AZ	Vernon S. Stenseng	Vernon S. Stenseng	1996	84
84 2/8	15 6/8	15 5/8	6 3/8	6 3/8	3 3/8	3	12 3/8	7 7/8	4 7/8	4 6/8	Colfax Co., NM	Lydia Dick	Lydia Dick	1997	84
84 2/8	16	15 4/8	6 4/8	6 7/8	2 4/8	2 3/8	13 1/8	10 7/8	7 2/8	7	Sublette Co., WY	John L. Hutchins	John L. Hutchins	1997	84
84 2/8	15 7/8	16	7 2/8	7 1/8	2 7/8	2 7/8	12 3/8	8 3/8	5 2/8	5 7/8	Socorro Co., NM	Stephen C. LeBlanc	Stephen C. LeBlanc	1997	84
84 2/8	16	15 6/8	6 6/8	6 7/8	3	2 6/8	6 4/8	1 3/8	6 1/8	5 5/8	Yavapai Co., AZ	Steven L. Long	Steven L. Long	1997	84
84 2/8	16 1/8	16 1/8	6 5/8	6 4/8	3 4/8	3 3/8	8 3/8	2 6/8	5 6/8	5 4/8	Yavapai Co., AZ	David W. Miller, Jr.	David W. Miller, Jr.	1998	84
84 2/8	15 3/8	15 5/8	7 1/8	7 1/8	2 5/8	2 6/8	8 1/8	3	6 3/8	6	Moffat Co., CO	Kenneth M. Appelgren	Kenneth M. Appelgren	1999	84
84 2/8	16 2/8	16 3/8	6 2/8	6 2/8	2 6/8	2 7/8	10 3/8	5 1/8	5 7/8	5 7/8	Hudspeth Co., TX	Michael Cottrell	Michael Cottrell	1999	84
84 2/8	16 5/8	16 2/8	6 6/8	6 6/8	2 4/8	2 3/8	10 2/8	5 2/8	5 4/8	5 4/8	Lassen Co., CA	Donald F. Housen	Donald F. Housen	1999	84
84 2/8	16 4/8	16 4/8	6 4/8	6 6/8	2 5/8	2 4/8	7 4/8	2	6 4/8	6 4/8	Moffat Co., CO	Doug Palmer	Doug Palmer	1999	84
84 2/8	16 2/8	16 3/8	5 6/8	5 6/8	3 3/8	3 3/8	13 7/8	10 3/8	6 1/8	5 7/8	Rawlins Co., WY	Don E. Perrien	Don E. Perrien	1999	84
84 2/8	15 6/8	16 1/8	6 4/8	6 3/8	2 6/8	3 1/8	21	21	6	6 7/8	Colfax Co., NM	William N. Utecht	William N. Utecht	2000	84
84	17 2/8	16 6/8	7	6 6/8	2 4/8	2 4/8	13 1/8	9 7/8	5 3/8	5 3/8	Mora Co., NM	William E. Pipes III	William E. Pipes III	1977	96
84	16 7/8	16 7/8	7 1/8	7	2 4/8	2 4/8	10	5	4 7/8	4 7/8	Harney Co., OR	Mark A. Doner	Mark A. Doner	1992	96
84	16	16	6 7/8	6 6/8	2 6/8	2 7/8	9 3/8	4 1/8	5 6/8	5 5/8	Modoc Co., CA	Clyde E. Mandeville	Clyde E. Mandeville	1997	96
84	16 4/8	16 4/8	6 2/8	6 2/8	2 4/8	2 3/8	15 4/8	11 6/8	6 6/8	5 6/8	Modoc Co., CA	Trey Hickman	Trey Hickman	1998	96
84	16	15 6/8	6 4/8	6 4/8	3 2/8	3 1/8	12 1/8	8 4/8	5 7/8	5 6/8	Washoe Co., NV	Todd B. Jaksick	Todd B. Jaksick	1998	96
84	16 2/8	16 2/8	6 4/8	6 4/8	2 3/8	2 2/8	10	7 2/8	6 2/8	6	Elko Co., NV	Jack W. Peters	Jack W. Peters	1998	96
84	15 3/8	16 1/8	6 6/8	6 5/8	2 5/8	2 7/8	10	8	6 6/8	6 4/8	Washakie Co., WY	Scott J. Richins	Scott J. Richins	1998	96
84	16 4/8	16 4/8	6 3/8	6 2/8	3 1/8	3 1/8	14 3/8	11 4/8	5	4 6/8	Yavapai Co., AZ	Thomas R Devereaux	Thomas R Devereaux	1999	96
84	15 7/8	15 6/8	7 1/8	7 1/8	2 6/8	2 6/8	7 1/8	1 2/8	6 1/8	5 4/8	Mora Co., NM	Dennis J. Sites	Dennis J. Sites	1999	96
84	17 5/8	17 1/8	6 1/8	6 1/8	2 5/8	2 4/8	10 1/8	3 6/8	5 4/8	5 7/8	Rosebud Co., MT	Todd A. Wood	Todd A. Wood	1999	96
84	17	17 1/8	6 2/8	6 2/8	2 4/8	2 4/8	11 2/8	5 7/8	6 4/8	6 5/8	Lincoln Co., NM	Bob Nicholas	Bob Nicholas	2000	96
83 6/8	16 2/8	16 3/8	6 5/8	6 6/8	2 6/8	2 7/8	6 7/8	3 3/8	6 5/8	5 3/8	Lincoln Co., NM	G. Todd Ralstin	G. Todd Ralstin	1997	107
83 6/8	16 5/8	16 6/8	5 7/8	5 7/8	2 5/8	2 6/8	8 5/8	3	5 4/8	6 3/8	Sioux Co., NE	Moses Martinez	Moses Martinez	1998	107
83 6/8	15 4/8	15 7/8	7 4/8	7 4/8	2 4/8	2 5/8	18 4/8	15 5/8	5 3/8	5 4/8	Washakie Co., WY	Kevin P. Salzman	Kevin P. Salzman	1999	107
83 6/8	16 6/8	16 6/8	6 6/8	6 6/8	3	2 7/8	10 7/8	6 1/8	6	5 2/8	Socorro Co., NM	Ken A. Kuhn	Ken A. Kuhn	2000	107
83 6/8	15 6/8	15 6/8	7	6 6/8	2 6/8	2 5/8	10	4 3/8	5 5/8	5 7/8	Hudspeth Co., TX	Brandon D. McBride	Brandon D. McBride	2000	107

											Locality	Hunter	Owner	Date	Rank
83 6/8	16 1/8	16	6 4/8	6 5/8	3 1/8	2 7/8	7 4/8	3 4/8	6	5 6/8	Socorro Co., NM	Steve K. Scharf	Steve K. Scharf	2000	107
83 4/8	16 4/8	16	6 3/8	6 4/8	2 7/8	2 5/8	11 4/8	7 2/8	5 7/8	5 3/8	Hudspeth Co., TX	Harold W. Hahn	Harold W. Hahn	1997	113
83 4/8	15 5/8	15 5/8	7	6 6/8	2 6/8	2 6/8	9 1/8	3 6/8	6	6	Chaves Co., NM	Ben H. Ralston	Ben H. Ralston	1997	113
83 4/8	16 7/8	16 6/8	5 7/8	5 7/8	2 4/8	2 4/8	12 6/8	6 4/8	5 7/8	5 6/8	Catron Co., NM	Bill Bray	Bill Bray	1998	113
83 4/8	14 4/8	14 2/8	6 5/8	6 3/8	3 2/8	3	9 6/8	7	4 5/8	4 5/8	Grand Co., UT	Gordon W. Nelson	Gordon W. Nelson	1998	113
83 4/8	15 6/8	15 6/8	7	7	3	2 7/8	11 2/8	7 5/8	5 1/8	5 2/8	Navajo Co., AZ	Thad R. Tucci	Thad R. Tucci	1998	113
83 4/8	15 5/8	16 1/8	6 3/8	7	2 5/8	3	9 1/8	3 5/8	5 5/8	5 3/8	Lincoln Co., NM	Bob Nicholas	Bob Nicholas	1999	113
83 4/8	16 3/8	16 4/8	6 3/8	6 3/8	2 4/8	2 4/8	8 5/8	5 2/8	6	6 3/8	Carbon Co., WY	Rita K. Pettit	Rita K. Pettit	1999	113
83 4/8	16 1/8	16	6 7/8	6 6/8	3	3	13	9 5/8	5 1/8	4 7/8	Carbon Co., WY	Dale Hislop	Dale Hislop	2000	113
83 4/8	15 5/8	15 3/8	6 5/8	6 5/8	2 7/8	2 7/8	13 2/8	11 7/8	4 1/8	4 4/8	Garfield Co., MT	Daniel J. Roberts	Daniel J. Roberts	2000	113
83 2/8	18 4/8	18 7/8	6 2/8	6 1/8	2 6/8	2 6/8	8 6/8	2 7/8	4 4/8	4 3/8	Washoe Co., NV	Terry D. Scott	Terry D. Scott	1998	122
83 2/8	15 1/8	15 3/8	7 3/8	7 2/8	2 5/8	2 5/8	13 6/8	13 2/8	5 2/8	5	Jackson Co., CO	Stanley W. Bouse	Stanley W. Bouse	1999	122
83 2/8	15 3/8	15 4/8	6 3/8	6 2/8	3 3/8	3 3/8	11 6/8	8 5/8	6 6/8	6 2/8	Washoe Co., NV	John E. Christensen	John E. Christensen	1999	122
83 2/8	16 3/8	16 5/8	7	7 1/8	2 7/8	2 7/8	8 4/8	5 4/8	4 6/8	4 6/8	Albany Co., WY	Gail D. Fibranz	Gail D. Fibranz	1999	122
83 2/8	15 2/8	14 7/8	6 7/8	6 1/8	2 6/8	2 6/8	10 2/8	6 5/8	6	5 7/8	Carbon Co., WY	Tad W. Marshall	Tad W. Marshall	1999	122
83 2/8	17	17	6 2/8	7 1/8	2 6/8	2 6/8	10 4/8	4 7/8	4 6/8	4 6/8	Mora Co., NM	Daniel K. Sites	Daniel K. Sites	1999	122
83 2/8	16 6/8	16 6/8	6 5/8	6 2/8	2 7/8	2 7/8	8 3/8	2 2/8	5 5/8	5 3/8	Hudspeth Co., TX	Keith R. Eason	Keith R. Eason	2000	122
83 2/8	18 3/8	17 3/8	6 4/8	6 4/8	2 7/8	2 7/8	7 6/8	3 4/8	4 4/8	4 4/8	Hudspeth Co., TX	Steve Whiteaker	Steve Whiteaker	2000	122
83	15 7/8	15 7/8	6 7/8	7	2 3/8	3 1/8	12	4 2/8	5 6/8	6 4/8	Fremont Co., WY	Milo D. Smith	Marcia Darrow	1992	130
83	15 6/8	15 6/8	7	6 2/8	2 7/8	2 4/8	9 7/8	5	5 3/8	5 4/8	Mora Co., NM	William J. Smith	William J. Smith	1993	130
83	16 6/8	16 6/8	6 3/8	6 4/8	2 5/8	2 6/8	12 6/8	9 2/8	5 6/8	5 6/8	Fremont Co., WY	James W. Gibson	James W. Gibson	1995	130
83	15 4/8	15 6/8	6 6/8	7 1/8	3	2 6/8	13 6/8	11 1/8	6	6	Socorro Co., NM	Len H. Guldman	Len H. Guldman	1997	130
83	16 3/8	16 1/8	6 7/8	6 6/8	2 5/8	2 6/8	7 4/8	14 1/8	5 1/8	4 7/8	Washoe Co., NV	Carolyn L. Bertoldi	Carolyn L. Bertoldi	1998	130
83	16	15 7/8	6 6/8	7 2/8	2 4/8	2 7/8	11 1/8	8 7/8	5 3/8	5 3/8	Carbon Co., WY	Chuck Jaure	Chuck Jaure	1998	130
83	16 5/8	16 3/8	6 4/8	6 4/8	2 4/8	3 1/8	11 2/8	8 1/8	4 7/8	5	Carbon Co., NM	Don E. Perrien	Don E. Perrien	1998	130
83	17 2/8	17 3/8	6 3/8	6 3/8	2 6/8	2 4/8	11 2/8	5	5	4 4/8	Yavapai Co., AZ	Steven A. Bond	Steven A. Bond	1998	130
83	16 1/8	16	6 4/8	6 7/8	2 7/8	2 6/8	11	7 1/8	5 1/8	5 2/8	Socorro Co., NM	Michael T. Don	Michael T. Don	1999	130
83	16 5/8	16 3/8	6 7/8	6 7/8	3 1/8	2 6/8	12 2/8	6 5/8	6	5 3/8	Harney Co., OR	Ronald C. Garner	Ronald C. Garner	1999	130
83	16 1/8	15 6/8	6 7/8	7	2 4/8	3 2/8	11 2/8	6 3/8	5 1/8	5 4/8	Sweetwater Co., WY	Calvin E. Snyder	Calvin E. Snyder	1999	130
83	15 7/8	15 6/8	7	6 5/8	2 6/8	3	6 6/8	2 5/8	6 2/8	6	Sweetwater Co., WY	Vic R. Dana	Vic R. Dana	1999	130
83	17	17	6 5/8	7 1/8	2 6/8	2 5/8	10 4/8	6 4/8	4 3/8	4 5/8	Union Co., NM	Brad DeSaye	Brad DeSaye	2000	130
82 6/8	15 5/8	15 6/8	7 1/8	6 2/8	2 6/8	2 7/8	11	8	8	4 2/8	Elko Co., NV	Picked Up	T. Bottari & B. Anderson	1997	143
82 6/8	16 2/8	16	6 2/8	6 5/8	3 3/8	3 1/8	10 3/8	6 5/8	5 2/8	5 2/8	Yavapai Co., AZ	Paul I. Fritzinger	Paul I. Fritzinger	1998	143
82 6/8	16 2/8	17 1/8	6 6/8	6 6/8	2 5/8	2 4/8	8 3/8	4 4/8	4 7/8	4 4/8	Socorro Co., NM	David R. Harrow	David R. Harrow	1998	143
82 6/8	16 6/8	16 6/8	6 4/8	6 4/8	2 7/8	3	11 6/8	6 6/8	4 6/8	4 6/8	Lincoln Co., NM	Edward C. Joseph	Edward C. Joseph	1998	143
82 6/8	15 6/8	15 6/8	6 1/8	6 1/8	2 5/8	2 7/8	15 1/8	11 7/8	5 1/8	5 2/8	Grant Co., NM	Zeev Nederman	Zeev Nederman	1998	143
82 6/8	16 7/8	16 4/8	7 1/8	7	3	2 5/8	12 1/8	7	5 4/8	5 4/8	Custer Co., MT	Christopher D. Rarig	Christopher D. Rarig	1998	143
82 6/8	15 7/8	16	6 4/8	6 4/8	3 1/8	2 4/8	9 5/8	4 3/8	5 6/8	5 6/8	Socorro Co., NM	Clifford I. Bergman	Clifford I. Bergman	1999	143
82 6/8	17	16 5/8	6 3/8	6 3/8	2 5/8	2 5/8	7 4/8	1 2/8	4 7/8	5 2/8	Uintah Co., UT	Larry Gross	Larry Gross	1999	143
82 6/8	16 2/8	16 1/8	6 5/8	6 6/8	2 5/8	3	8 3/8	3 6/8	3 6/8	6	Socorro Co., NM	David A. Miller	David A. Miller	1999	143
82 6/8	15 3/8	15 1/8	6 6/8	6 7/8	2 5/8	3 1/8	10 2/8	6 7/8	5	5 2/8	Brown Co., NE	Rodney Olson	Rodney Olson	1999	143
82 6/8	15	15	7	7	2 7/8	2 5/8	8 4/8	5 4/8	5 5/8	5 5/8	Humboldt Co., NV	Kevin E. Robison	Kevin E. Robison	2000	143
82 6/8	15 6/8	15 4/8	7 3/8	7	2 7/8	2 7/8	11	6 2/8	5 5/8	5 5/8	Mora Co., NM	Bonnie B. Schaefer	Bonnie B. Schaefer	2000	143

PRONGHORN

Antilocapra americana americana and related subspecies

Score	Length of Horn R	L	Circumference of Base R	L	Circumference at Third Quarter R	L	Inside Spread	Tip to Tip Spread	Length of Prong R	L	Locality	Hunter	Owner	Date Killed	Rank
82 4/8	16 7/8	16 6/8	6	6	2 7/8	2 7/8	8 7/8	6 3/8	5 3/8	5 5/8	Navajo Co., AZ	Herman C. Meyer	Herman C. Meyer	1996	155
82 4/8	18	17 7/8	5 6/8	5 7/8	2 5/8	2 5/8	8 6/8	5 1/8	4 6/8	4 5/8	Albany Co., WY	Brian N. Beisher	Brian N. Beisher	1997	155
82 4/8	17 1/8	17	6 3/8	6 2/8	2 7/8	2 6/8	8 4/8	1 7/8	6 2/8	5 4/8	Hot Springs Co., WY	Arthur W. Andersen	Arthur W. Andersen	1998	155
82 4/8	15 5/8	15 2/8	7 2/8	7 3/8	2 5/8	2 4/8	9 7/8	5 2/8	5 3/8	5 7/8	Washington Co., CO	Timothy A. Baker	Timothy A. Baker	1998	155
82 4/8	15 6/8	15 4/8	6 7/8	6 6/8	2 4/8	2 5/8	8	3 4/8	6 2/8	6 2/8	Sweetwater Co., WY	Gilbert K. Davies	Gilbert K. Davies	1998	155
82 4/8	14 7/8	14 6/8	6 7/8	6 7/8	2 6/8	2 6/8	7 2/8	3 2/8	5	5 5/8	Campbell Co., WY	Richard E. LaCrone	Richard E. LaCrone	1998	155
82 4/8	16 2/8	16	6 4/8	6 2/8	3 1/8	2 6/8	13 2/8	7 5/8	5 5/8	5 4/8	Socorro Co., NM	Whitney M. Moore	Whitney M. Moore	1998	155
82 4/8	14 5/8	14 7/8	6 3/8	6 3/8	3 5/8	3 5/8	9	5 6/8	4 7/8	4 7/8	Coconino Co., AZ	Thomas J. Pawlacyk	Thomas J. Pawlacyk	1998	155
82 4/8	16 3/8	16 1/8	6 7/8	6 7/8	3	3	12 2/8	11 2/8	4 6/8	4 5/8	Fremont Co., WY	Wade A. Sikkink	Wade A. Sikkink	1998	155
82 4/8	17	17 1/8	6 2/8	6 3/8	2 5/8	2 5/8	15 6/8	12 7/8	5 3/8	5 7/8	Coconino Co., AZ	Jeffrey R. Stone	Jeffrey R. Stone	1998	155
82 4/8	16 2/8	16 5/8	6 7/8	7	2 4/8	2 6/8	10 5/8	7	5 2/8	5 3/8	Sweetwater Co., WY	Bradley A. Thoren	Bradley A. Thoren	1998	155
82 4/8	15 4/8	15 2/8	6 6/8	6 3/8	2 5/8	2 5/8	7 6/8	5 6/8	5 7/8	6 3/8	Weld Co., CO	Bob Chapman	Bob Chapman	1999	155
82 4/8	15 6/8	15 7/8	6 3/8	6 4/8	2 6/8	2 6/8	14 3/8	10 5/8	4 4/8	4 6/8	Grant Co., NM	Zeev Nederman	Zeev Nederman	1999	155
82 4/8	14 6/8	14 4/8	6 6/8	6 6/8	3	3 1/8	14 6/8	13	5 6/8	5 4/8	Harney Co., OR	Michael D. Tyrholm	Michael D. Tyrholm	1999	155
82 4/8	16 3/8	16 4/8	6 4/8	6 3/8	2 4/8	2 4/8	15	10 6/8	5	5	Socorro Co., NM	Turner R. Allen	Turner R. Allen	2000	155
82 4/8	16 3/8	16 5/8	6 7/8	6 7/8	2 5/8	2 6/8	7 7/8	1 2/8	4 7/8	5 1/8	Socorro Co., NM	J. Fred Ketcham	J. Fred Ketcham	2000	155
82 4/8	15 7/8	15 6/8	6 6/8	6 5/8	2 5/8	2 4/8	11 1/8	8	5 7/8	6 1/8	Fremont Co., WY	Picked Up	William J. Waller, Jr.	2000	155
82 2/8	17	17	6	6	2 5/8	2 5/8	9 2/8	6/8	5 4/8	6	Sweetwater Co., WY	Len H. Guldman	Len H. Guldman	1982	172
82 2/8	16	16	6 5/8	6 4/8	2 3/8	3	9 3/8	4 4/8	5 3/8	5 3/8	Mora Co., NM	Howard M. Barnett	Howard M. Barnett	1997	172
82 2/8	16	16 1/8	6 2/8	6 2/8	2 3/8	2 4/8	10 4/8	7 1/8	6 4/8	6 5/8	Beaverhead Co., MT	Kenneth A. Bujok	Kenneth A. Bujok	1997	172
82 2/8	15 4/8	15 1/8	6 5/8	6 5/8	3	3	18 5/8	17	5 6/8	5 6/8	Arapahoe Co., CO	Joseph P. Emily	Joseph P. Emily	1998	172
82 2/8	16 4/8	16 4/8	5 6/8	5 6/8	2 6/8	2 7/8	9 1/8	4 1/8	5 5/8	5 6/8	Socorro Co., NM	Peeler G. Lacey	Peeler G. Lacey	1998	172
82 2/8	15	14 4/8	6 4/8	6 3/8	2 5/8	2 3/8	8 6/8	4 2/8	6 3/8	6 4/8	Emery Co., UT	Rick M. Rasmussen	Rick M. Rasmussen	1998	172
82 2/8	16 3/8	16 4/8	6 1/8	6	2 5/8	2 6/8	13 5/8	9 1/8	5 7/8	5 3/8	Coconino Co., AZ	James R. Shaff	James R. Shaff	1998	172
82 2/8	16 3/8	16 2/8	7	7 2/8	2 6/8	2 6/8	10	4 3/8	4 3/8	4 3/8	Mora Co., NM	Justin Stewart	Justin Stewart	1998	172
82 2/8	16 2/8	16 2/8	6 4/8	6 4/8	2 4/8	2 5/8	9 2/8	4 5/8	5 7/8	5 7/8	Taos Co., NM	William R. Balsi, Jr.	William R. Balsi, Jr.	1999	172
82 2/8	15 6/8	15 5/8	7 3/8	7 2/8	2 4/8	2 4/8	12 2/8	8 5/8	4 6/8	5	Carbon Co., WY	Jeffrey J. Bode	Jeffrey J. Bode	1999	172
82 2/8	14 7/8	14 5/8	6 4/8	6 4/8	3 3/8	3 3/8	12 2/8	9 7/8	5 2/8	5	Socorro Co., NM	Mark T. Donovan	Mark T. Donovan	1999	172
82 2/8	16	15 6/8	6 7/8	6 7/8	2 3/8	2 3/8	13 1/8	10 2/8	6	5 3/8	Natrona Co., WY	Garrett Henry	Garrett Henry	1999	172
82 2/8	16 6/8	16 4/8	7	7	2 6/8	2 4/8	13	10	5 4/8	4 5/8	Carbon Co., WY	Michael D. Hirsch	Michael D. Hirsch	1999	172
82 2/8	15 2/8	14 7/8	7 5/8	7 5/8	2 6/8	2 6/8	10	7 2/8	5	5	Uinta Co., WY	Dolores M. Larson	Dolores M. Larson	1999	172
82 2/8	15 5/8	15 3/8	6 3/8	6 3/8	3	3	8 7/8	3 5/8	5 3/8	5 4/8	Fremont Co., WY	Michael D. Schauer	Michael D. Schauer	1999	172
82 2/8	16 2/8	16 1/8	6 5/8	6 6/8	2 5/8	2 4/8	12 4/8	9 1/8	5 7/8	5 5/8	Washakie Co., WY	Carol A. Schuette	Carol A. Schuette	1999	172
82 2/8	17 1/8	16	6 3/8	6 2/8	3 1/8	3 2/8	10	7 1/8	6 1/8	5 4/8	Socorro Co., NM	Ernie Davis	Ernie Davis	2000	172

Score										Locality	Owner	Hunter	Date	Rank
82 2/8	15	6 4/8	6 2/8	2 5/8	2 4/8	9 2/8	6 5/8	4 5/8	5 5/8	Modoc Co., CA	Ronald V. Giese	Ronald V. Giese	2000	172
82 2/8	15 6/8	6 6/8	6 7/8	2 4/8	2 5/8	13 6/8	5 5/8	10	5 5/8	S. Saskatchewan River, AB	John D. Gordon	John D. Gordon	2000	172
82 2/8	15 4/8	7	6 7/8	2 7/8	2 7/8	12	5 4/8	7 2/8	5 3/8	Cibola Co., NM	Russell E. Livingston II	Russell E. Livingston II	2000	172
82	15 6/8	6 7/8	7	2 3/8	2 3/8	10	6 1/8	7 3/8	5 7/8	Carbon Co., WY	William E. Pipes III	William E. Pipes III	1977	192
82	17	6 4/8	6 1/8	2 6/8	2 6/8	12 6/8	5	8 5/8	5	Guadalupe Co., NM	Kenneth J. Morga	Kenneth J. Morga	1989	192
82	16 4/8	6 3/8	6 3/8	2 6/8	3	10 2/8	5 4/8	9	5 2/8	Mora Co., NM	Robert I. Kelly	Robert I. Kelly	1997	192
82	16 2/8	6 1/8	6 4/8	3	3	8	6 2/8	2 4/8	5 7/8	Platte Co., WY	Rick L. Wiley	Rick L. Wiley	1997	192
82	16	7 1/8	7 1/8	2 5/8	2 4/8	12 2/8	5	9 1/8	4 7/8	Carbon Co., WY	Jon D. Crowley	Jon D. Crowley	1998	192
82	15 7/8	6 5/8	6 5/8	2 5/8	2 5/8	10 4/8	5 6/8	5 2/8	5 3/8	Carbon Co., WY	Jerry L. Hamel, Jr.	Jerry L. Hamel, Jr.	1998	192
82	16 2/8	6 7/8	6 7/8	3 1/8	3 1/8	15	5 3/8	11 6/8	5	Socorro Co., NM	William R. Hemphill	William R. Hemphill	1998	192
82	16 3/8	6 6/8	6 5/8	2 5/8	2 5/8	9 5/8	5 2/8	5 1/8	5	Socorro Co., NM	Alan W. Krause	Alan W. Krause	1998	192
82	15 5/8	6 4/8	6 4/8	2 2/8	2 2/8	8 2/8	6 4/8	5 5/8	6 4/8	Harney Co., OR	Dale R. Thornton	Dale R. Thornton	1998	192
82	16 5/8	6 4/8	6 4/8	2 7/8	2 6/8	13	5 2/8	8	5 2/8	Yavapai Co., AZ	Larry Adkins	Larry Adkins	1999	192
82	15 4/8	6 3/8	6 2/8	3 3/8	3 2/8	9 3/8	5	5 3/8	5	Yavapai Co., AZ	Lisa K. Beeman	Lisa K. Beeman	1999	192
82	15 5/8	6 3/8	6 3/8	2 6/8	2 6/8	12 1/8	5 1/8	8 6/8	5 6/8	Lomond, AB	Eric W. Dirks	Eric W. Dirks	1999	192
82	15 2/8	7 4/8	7 4/8	3 3/8	3	11 5/8	4 7/8	8 3/8	4 6/8	Cassia Co., ID	David R. Harrow	David R. Harrow	1999	192
82	16	6 5/8	6 3/8	2 6/8	2 7/8	7 3/8	5 6/8	2	5 5/8	Converse Co., WY	James E. Herren	James E. Herren	1999	192
82	16 3/8	6 3/8	6 3/8	3	3	11	5 4/8	6 1/8	5 1/8	Harney Co., OR	Earl E. Kessler	Earl E. Kessler	1999	192
82	17 4/8	6 1/8	6 1/8	2 6/8	2 7/8	11 4/8	3 7/8	7 6/8	4 5/8	Hudspeth Co., TX	Timothy L. Orton	Timothy L. Orton	1999	192
82	14	13 2/8	6 7/8	3	3	10	6 2/8	8 6/8	6 1/8	Washoe Co., NV	Harry B. Swanson	Harry B. Swanson	1999	192
82	16 3/8	6 2/8	6 4/8	2 5/8	2 5/8	10 1/8	5 4/8	5 6/8	5 3/8	Moffat Co., CO	George F. Bailey	George F. Bailey	2000	192
82	16	6 4/8	6 4/8	3	3	12	5 3/8	8 2/8	4 2/8	Washoe Co., NV	Warren T. Goodale	Warren T. Goodale	2000	192
82	15 3/8	7 1/8	7 2/8	3 2/8	3 2/8	11	4 2/8	7 7/8	5 1/8	Box Elder Co., UT	David R. Harrow	David R. Harrow	2000	192
82	17 5/8	6 3/8	6 3/8	2 4/8	2 4/8	9 3/8	5 1/8	5	5 5/8	Tide Lake, AB	Dale W. Heinz	Dale W. Heinz	2000	192
82	15 5/8	6 1/8	6 3/8	3 2/8	3	9 4/8	6 1/8	6 3/8	5 5/8	Hartley Co., TX	John K. Mikeman	John K. Mikeman	2000	192
81 6/8	16	6 3/8	6 2/8	2 5/8	2 4/8	11 1/8	5 2/8	5 2/8	5 4/8	Humboldt Co., NV	Dolores Harrison	Dolores Harrison	1998	214
81 6/8	15 2/8	7 2/8	7 2/8	2 4/8	2 4/8	15 7/8	5 4/8	14 6/8	5 3/8	Grant Co., NM	Gustavo Arredondo	Gustavo Arredondo	1999	214
81 6/8	15 6/8	6 4/8	6 4/8	2 5/8	2 5/8	11 7/8	6	8 4/8	5 6/8	Sweetwater Co., WY	Lance P. Burns	Lance P. Burns	2000	214
81 6/8	15 7/8	6 7/8	6 7/8	2 7/8	2 7/8	9 4/8	5 1/8	2 6/8	5 2/8	Mora Co., NM	Keith R. Eason	Keith R. Eason	2000	214
81 6/8	16	6 3/8	6 3/8	2 7/8	2 7/8	8 2/8	5 5/8	5 6/8	5 6/8	Sublette Co., WY	Kim Tanner	Kim Tanner	2000	214
81 4/8	16	6 2/8	6 1/8	3 1/8	3	9 7/8	4 2/8	5	4 2/8	Dallam Co., TX	Brad C. Hardin	Brad C. Hardin	1992	219
81 4/8	16 6/8	6 1/8	6 1/8	2 4/8	2 5/8	11 5/8	4 5/8	5 4/8	5	Washoe Co., NV	Philip C. Hanifan	Philip C. Hanifan	1997	219
81 4/8	17 3/8	6 4/8	6 4/8	3 1/8	3 2/8	8 3/8	4 6/8	4 5/8	4 7/8	Rio Blanco Co., CO	Rodney S. Cook	Rodney S. Cook	1998	219
81 4/8	15	6 5/8	6 5/8	2 6/8	2 6/8	9 4/8	5 2/8	4 7/8	5 2/8	Box Butte Co., NE	Raymond D. Freimuth	Raymond D. Freimuth	1998	219
81 4/8	16 2/8	6 5/8	6 5/8	2 7/8	2 7/8	5 5/8	5 4/8	4 7/8	5 4/8	Sweetwater Co., WY	Jerry W. Marchant	Jerry W. Marchant	1998	219
81 4/8	16 1/8	6 5/8	6 5/8	2 3/8	2 4/8	9 1/8	5 5/8	5 5/8	6	Rosebud Co., MT	Allen R. Ormesher	Allen R. Ormesher	2000	219
81 2/8	14	6 6/8	6 6/8	3 3/8	3 3/8	12	6	11 7/8	6	Carbon Co., UT	David E. Mason	David E. Mason	1997	225
81 2/8	15 6/8	6 6/8	6 6/8	2 4/8	2 3/8	10	5 6/8	7	5 5/8	Big Horn Co., WY	Brian P. Voss	Brian P. Voss	1998	225
81 2/8	15 1/8	6 5/8	6 5/8	2 7/8	2 5/8	10 1/8	5	7 5/8	5 4/8	Graham Co., AZ	Truman D. Collins	Truman D. Collins	1999	225
81 2/8	16 1/8	6 6/8	6 4/8	2 4/8	2 4/8	9 1/8	6	4	5 4/8	Socorro Co., NM	Jeffery K. Harrow	Jeffery K. Harrow	1999	225
81 2/8	15 7/8	6 6/8	6 6/8	2 6/8	2 6/8	7 6/8	5	6	5 2/8	Campbell Co., WY	Allen T. Vaile, Jr.	Allen T. Vaile, Jr.	1999	225
81 2/8	15	6 6/8	6 5/8	2 4/8	2 4/8	9 6/8	6 2/8	6	6 2/8	Lincoln Co., WY	Eric H. Boley	Eric H. Boley	2000	225
81	16 4/8	6 3/8	6 3/8	2 5/8	2 6/8	12 4/8	5 1/8	9 6/8	4 3/8	Stillwater Co., MT	Herbert R. Alvin	Herbert R. Alvin	1959	231

PRONGHORN

Antilocapra americana and related subspecies

Score	Length of Horn R.	L.	Circumference of Base R.	L.	Circumference at Third Quarter R.	L.	Inside Spread	Tip to Tip Spread	Length of Prong R.	L.	Locality	Hunter	Owner	Date Killed	Rank
81	15 5/8	15 4/8	6 1/8	6	2 4/8	2 3/8	9 4/8	6 6/8	7	7	Harney Co., OR	Rod Kelly	Rod Kelly	PR 1980	231
81	16 6/8	16 6/8	6 1/8	6 2/8	2 7/8	2 7/8	6 5/8	1 7/8	5 1/8	4 6/8	Coconino Co., AZ	John L. Bowden	John L. Bowden	1997	231
81	14 3/8	14 1/8	7	7	2 5/8	2 7/8	8 7/8	5	6 3/8	6	Fremont Co., WY	Trenna M. Sonnenschein	Trenna M. Sonnenschein	1999	231
81	15 3/8	15 3/8	7	6 5/8	2 5/8	2 6/8	9 5/8	7	5 4/8	5 1/8	Carbon Co., WY	Kurt D. Rued	Kurt D. Rued	2000	231
81	16	16	6 7/8	6 5/8	2 4/8	2 4/8	11 7/8	8 1/8	5 2/8	5 1/8	Rosebud Co., MT	Kurt D. Rued	Kurt D. Rued	2000	231
80 6/8	15 5/8	15 4/8	7	6 3/8	2 5/8	2 5/8	11 2/8	7 3/8	5 6/8	5 4/8	Laramie Co., WY	Kent A. George	Kent A. George	1994	237
80 6/8	15	14 5/8	5 7/8	5 6/8	3	3 1/8	9 2/8	5 2/8	6 4/8	6 4/8	Catron Co., NM	Ricardo Guardia	Ricardo Guardia	1996	237
80 6/8	16 1/8	16	6 1/8	6 2/8	2 5/8	2 5/8	11	9 1/8	5 7/8	5 7/8	Sweetwater Co., WY	Nicole Bowles	Nicole Bowles	1997	237
80 6/8	16 1/8	16 2/8	6 2/8	6 5/8	2 4/8	2 4/8	13 1/8	8 5/8	5	4 5/8	Lake Co., NM	Jerry D. Donovan	Jerry D. Donovan	1997	237
80 6/8	16 2/8	16 4/8	6	6	2 6/8	2 6/8	8	2	5 1/8	5	Rio Grande Co., CO	John R. Olson	John R. Olson	1997	237
80 6/8	15 4/8	15 3/8	6 2/8	6 2/8	3 2/8	3 2/8	7 7/8	3 3/8	5 3/8	4 7/8	Socorro Co., NM	Rusty Hall	Rusty Hall	1998	237
80 6/8	15 6/8	15 4/8	6 2/8	6 1/8	3 7/8	3 7/8	9 5/8	7 4/8	3 7/8	3 4/8	Colfax Co., NM	Robert H. Torstenson	Robert H. Torstenson	1998	237
80 6/8	15 4/8	15 2/8	6 6/8	6 4/8	2 5/8	2 5/8	10 5/8	6 4/8	5 4/8	5 3/8	Beaverhead Co., MT	Tara E. Helming	Tara E. Helming	1999	237
80 6/8	16 5/8	16 1/8	6 5/8	6 6/8	2 5/8	2 6/8	9 7/8	3 6/8	5 4/8	5 7/8	Socorro Co., NM	Alan J. Notvik	Alan J. Notvik	1999	237
80 6/8	15 1/8	15 3/8	7 1/8	6 7/8	2 4/8	2 4/8	12 2/8	7 7/8	5 4/8	5 4/8	Carbon Co., WY	James E. Schmid	James E. Schmid	1999	237
80 6/8	15 6/8	15 6/8	6 6/8	6 6/8	2 4/8	2 3/8	10	8 1/8	5 5/8	5	Fremont Co., WY	Elizabeth E. Berthod	Elizabeth E. Berthod	2000	237
80 6/8	13 6/8	13 5/8	6 6/8	6 6/8	3	3	11 4/8	9 2/8	5 3/8	5 3/8	Box Elder Co., UT	Jeffery K. Harrow	Jeffery K. Harrow	2000	237
80 6/8	15 4/8	15	6 5/8	6 5/8	3 1/8	2 6/8	13 2/8	9 4/8	5	5 3/8	Coconino Co., AZ	Keith E. Jones	Keith E. Jones	2000	237
80 4/8	16 1/8	16 4/8	6 7/8	6 7/8	2 6/8	2 5/8	21 1/8	19 6/8	5	4 4/8	Deschutes Co., OR	Edwin C. Shaver	Rod C. Shaver	1957	250
80 4/8	16 3/8	16	6 1/8	6 4/8	2 5/8	2 4/8	13 4/8	10 1/8	5 7/8	5 6/8	Deschutes Co., OR	Vera M. Riser	Vera M. Riser	1994	250
80 4/8	15 5/8	15 3/8	6 6/8	6 4/8	2 7/8	2 7/8	9 2/8	5 3/8	5	4 7/8	Sheridan Co., NE	David A. Feddern	David A. Feddern	1995	250
80 4/8	15 6/8	16	7	7	2 3/8	2 4/8	11 3/8	9	5 3/8	5	Sweetwater Co., WY	Eva Carrillo	Eva Carrillo	1997	250
80 4/8	14 6/8	14 6/8	6 2/8	6 2/8	3 1/8	3	7 7/8	2 7/8	5 6/8	5 6/8	Rio Blanco Co., CO	George J. Tidona	George J. Tidona	1998	250
80 4/8	15 3/8	15 2/8	7	7	2 6/8	2 6/8	13 2/8	10 4/8	4 3/8	4 7/8	Albany Co., WY	Jimmy L. Griswold	Jimmy L. Griswold	1999	250
80 4/8	15 1/8	16	6 7/8	6 7/8	2 4/8	2 6/8	9 4/8	4	5 5/8	5 5/8	Mora Co., NM	Wanda H. Bazemore	Wanda H. Bazemore	2000	250
80 4/8	16 2/8	16 1/8	6 3/8	6 4/8	2 7/8	2 7/8	10 2/8	6 6/8	5	5 2/8	Lake Co., OR	Bruce W. Hansen	Bruce W. Hansen	2000	250
80 2/8	16 1/8	16 2/8	5 5/8	5 5/8	2 6/8	2 6/8	14 2/8	10 6/8	6 4/8	6 2/8	Coconino Co., AZ	James L. Boyd	James L. Boyd	1998	258
80 2/8	14 7/8	14 7/8	6 3/8	6 3/8	3 2/8	3 1/8	10	6 5/8	5 5/8	5 5/8	Socorro Co., NM	Thomas D. Lund	Thomas D. Lund	1998	258
80 2/8	16 2/8	16 4/8	6 3/8	6 1/8	2 2/8	2 4/8	6 3/8	2 6/8	5 1/8	5 2/8	Ada Co., ID	Elizabeth T. Christiansen	Elizabeth T. Christiansen	1999	258
80 2/8	14 3/8	14 1/8	7 3/8	7 3/8	3	3 1/8	14	11 3/8	4 5/8	4 4/8	Box Elder Co., UT	Jeffery K. Harrow	Jeffery K. Harrow	1999	258
80 2/8	15 3/8	16 1/8	6 1/8	6	2 4/8	2 6/8	10 7/8	6 2/8	6 1/8	5 5/8	Socorro Co., NM	David R. Harrow	David R. Harrow	1999	258
80 2/8	15 6/8	16	6 4/8	6 5/8	2 7/8	2 7/8	8 3/8	5	4 7/8	4 3/8	Albany Co., WY	Mark W. Wade	Mark W. Wade	2000	258
80	15 7/8	16 2/8	7	6 6/8	2 4/8	2 4/8	9 6/8	3 1/8	5 1/8	5 1/8	Sweetwater Co., WY	Rick A. Roemke	Rick A. Roemke	1997	264
80	14	14	6 7/8	6 7/8	3 1/8	3 1/8	11 7/8	10 2/8	5 5/8	5 2/8	Coconino Co., AZ	Jacob L. Bowden	Jacob L. Bowden	1998	264

Score								Locality	Hunter	Owner	Date	Rank
80	$14^6/_8$	$14^3/_8$	$7^2/_8$	$7^4/_8$	$2^6/_8$	$2^4/_8$	$12^6/_8$	$10^7/_8$ 6 $5^2/_8$ — Natrona Co., WY	Bill B. Brauer	Bill B. Brauer	1998	264

Score	L	R	L	R	L	R				Locality	Hunter	Owner	Date	Rank
80	$14^6/_8$	$14^3/_8$	$7^2/_8$	$7^4/_8$	$2^6/_8$	$2^4/_8$	$12^6/_8$	$10^7/_8$	6	$5^2/_8$	Natrona Co., WY	Bill B. Brauer	Bill B. Brauer	1998	264
80	$16^6/_8$	$16^7/_8$	$6^3/_8$	$6^2/_8$	$2^4/_8$	$2^5/_8$	$11^6/_8$	$7^2/_8$	$5^7/_8$	5	Roosevelt Co., NM	James R. Catron	James R. Catron	1998	264
80	$14^4/_8$	$14^7/_8$	$6^6/_8$	$6^5/_8$	$2^3/_8$	$2^3/_8$	$13^5/_8$	$10^2/_8$	$6^3/_8$	$6^3/_8$	Uinta Co., WY	James A. Grivet, Jr.	James A. Grivet, Jr.	1998	264
80	$15^2/_8$	$15^3/_8$	$6^4/_8$	$6^2/_8$	$2^3/_8$	$2^3/_8$	$9^2/_8$	$4^4/_8$	$6^2/_8$	$6^2/_8$	Modoc Co., CA	Kyler N. Hamann	Kyler N. Hamann	1998	264
80	$16^1/_8$	$16^1/_8$	6	6	$2^4/_8$	$2^5/_8$	$9^7/_8$	$4^3/_8$	$5^3/_8$	$5^6/_8$	Navajo Co., AZ	Thomas M. Lowe	Thomas M. Lowe	1998	264
80	$14^7/_8$	$14^5/_8$	7	7	$2^6/_8$	$2^6/_8$	9	$8^1/_8$	$4^3/_8$	$4^1/_8$	Rich Co., UT	Wayne L. Richardson	Wayne L. Richardson	1998	264
80	16	$15^5/_8$	$6^2/_8$	$6^2/_8$	$2^4/_8$	$2^4/_8$	$9^4/_8$	$7^1/_8$	6	$5^4/_8$	Laramie Co., WY	Harold A. Weippert	Harold A. Weippert	1998	264
80	$16^2/_8$	$15^7/_8$	$6^3/_8$	$6^2/_8$	$2^5/_8$	$2^5/_8$	$12^3/_8$	$8^6/_8$	$4^6/_8$	$4^6/_8$	Torrence Co., NM	Joe M. Alford	Joe M. Alford	1999	264
80	$15^4/_8$	$15^2/_8$	$6^6/_8$	$6^5/_8$	$2^5/_8$	$2^5/_8$	$15^6/_8$	$14^4/_8$	$5^4/_8$	$4^4/_8$	Pershing Co., NV	Vernon E. Casci	Vernon E. Casci	1999	264
80	$15^4/_8$	$15^3/_8$	$6^6/_8$	$6^6/_8$	$2^5/_8$	$2^5/_8$	$10^3/_8$	$5^6/_8$	$4^6/_8$	$5^2/_8$	Hudspeth Co., TX	Linda J. McBride	Linda J. McBride	1999	264
80	$15^6/_8$	$15^7/_8$	$6^3/_8$	$6^5/_8$	$2^7/_8$	$2^6/_8$	$12^4/_8$	$10^2/_8$	$5^3/_8$	$4^3/_8$	Rosebud Co., MT	Duncan B. Gilchrist	Duncan B. Gilchrist	2000	264
$93^2/_8$*	$18^4/_8$	$18^4/_8$	$7^2/_8$	$7^2/_8$	$2^6/_8$	$2^6/_8$	$8^1/_8$	1	7	$6^7/_8$	Humboldt Co., NV	Todd B. Jaksick	Todd B. Jaksick	1999	
$92^6/_8$*	$16^5/_8$	$16^5/_8$	$7^6/_8$	$7^5/_8$	$3^2/_8$	$3^2/_8$	$9^1/_8$	$5^5/_8$	$7^2/_8$	$6^7/_8$	Socorro Co., NM	R. Steve Bass	R. Steve Bass	1999	
$91^2/_8$*	$17^7/_8$	$17^5/_8$	$6^6/_8$	$6^7/_8$	$3^3/_8$	$3^3/_8$	$8^3/_8$	$4^3/_8$	6	$5^7/_8$	Socorro Co., NM	R. Steve Bass	R. Steve Bass	1998	

* Final score subject to revision by additional verifying measurements.

BISON

Bison bison bison and *Bison bison athabascae*

Minimum Score 115

World's Record 136 4/8

Trophies from the lower 48 states are acceptable only for records, not awards, and only from states that recognize bison as wild and free-ranging and for which a hunting license and/or big game tag is required for hunting.

Score	Length of Horn R.	L.	Circumference of Base R.	L.	Circumference at Third Quarter R.	L.	Greatest Spread	Tip to Tip Spread	Locality	Hunter	Owner	Date Killed	Rank
125 6/8	20 1/8	20 4/8	14 6/8	14 5/8	6 4/8	6 3/8	30 4/8	21 2/8	Custer Co., SD	Robert B. Williams	Robert B. Williams	1999	1
124 6/8	19 2/8	20	15	15	6 2/8	6 2/8	31	26	Custer Co., SD	Donald A. Peterson	Donald A. Peterson	1998	2
124 6/8	18 1/8	18 1/8	14 7/8	13 3/8	7 3/8	7 4/8	29 6/8	24 2/8	Teton Co., WY	Heidi Anderson	Heidi Anderson	1999	2
124 2/8	18 4/8	18	15 2/8	15	6 7/8	6 7/8	30 6/8	25	Custer Co., SD	Richard C. Sturm	Richard C. Sturm	1999	4
124	20 6/8	20 2/8	13 6/8	13 6/8	6 6/8	7	31 4/8	23	Custer Co., SD	George Tulowetzke	George Tulowetzke	1997	5
123 4/8	19 1/8	19 4/8	15 4/8	15 5/8	5 4/8	5 3/8	31	25 4/8	Custer Co., SD	Jack L. Blachly	Jack L. Blachly	1997	6
122	17 4/8	18 2/8	14 7/8	14 6/8	7	7 5/8	31 1/8	26 2/8	Custer Co., SD	Kent Deligans	Kent Deligans	1999	7
121 6/8	19 5/8	18 5/8	14 6/8	14 7/8	5 7/8	5 7/8	31 2/8	24 2/8	Custer Co., SD	Horace Smith, Jr.	Horace Smith, Jr.	1999	8
120	16 2/8	16 2/8	15	15	7 2/8	7	30 6/8	28	Custer Co., SD	Robert D. Jones	Robert D. Jones	1997	9
120	16 7/8	16 4/8	15	14 7/8	7 1/8	7 4/8	26 7/8	20 4/8	Custer Co., SD	Gregory S. Oliver	Gregory S. Oliver	1998	9
119 6/8	20 2/8	19 2/8	14	13 6/8	6 2/8	6 7/8	32 2/8	25	Custer Co., SD	Bruce W. Anderson	Bruce W. Anderson	1998	11
119 4/8	18	18 6/8	14	14	6 2/8	6	26 7/8	15 4/8	Athabasca, NT	Picked Up	Tupper A. Blake	PR 1940	12
119 4/8	18 1/8	18	13 5/8	14 3/8	6 1/8	6	29 7/8	24 3/8	Custer Co., SD	Robert M. Anderson	Robert M. Anderson	1998	12
119	20 7/8	21 4/8	13 6/8	13 2/8	4 7/8	5 2/8	30 7/8	24 4/8	Pink Mt., BC	Wendy E. Olson	Wendy E. Olson	1998	14
117 2/8	17 5/8	18	14 5/8	14 6/8	5 6/8	5 6/8	29 1/8	23 4/8	Custer Co., SD	Louis J. Peterson	Louis J. Peterson	1998	15
117	18 1/8	18 6/8	13 7/8	13 5/8	6 3/8	7 1/8	31 2/8	25 1/8	Custer Co., SD	Richard H. Manly	Richard H. Manly	1998	16
117	18 5/8	18	13 5/8	13 4/8	6 3/8	6 5/8	30 6/8	23 5/8	Custer Co., SD	Duncan B. Gilchrist	Duncan B. Gilchrist	1999	16
116 6/8	17 6/8	18	14	14 1/8	5 2/8	5 4/8	27	20 4/8	Delta Junction, AK	Wallace J. Niles	Wallace J. Niles	1998	18
116 6/8	17 5/8	17 2/8	13 7/8	14	5 2/8	5	27 3/8	20 3/8	Sekulmun Lake, YT	Terry L. Fretz	Terry L. Fretz	2000	18
116 4/8	17 6/8	17 6/8	13 2/8	13 3/8	5 5/8	5 7/8	29 6/8	25	Park Co., MT	Picked Up	Glenn M. Smith	1990	20
116 4/8	17 2/8	17 3/8	13 6/8	13 4/8	6 6/8	6 6/8	30 4/8	25 3/8	Custer Co., SD	Ken G. Wilson	Ken G. Wilson	1998	20
116 2/8	17 4/8	17 5/8	13 4/8	14 1/8	6 7/8	6 1/8	30 3/8	24 2/8	Halfway River, BC	Mark J. Long	Mark J. Long	1998	22
116	20	19 3/8	13	12 5/8	5 5/8	5 4/8	27	19 1/8	Halfway River, BC	Picked Up	Gus Heather	PR 1998	23
115 6/8	17	17 2/8	14 1/8	14 2/8	5 5/8	5 4/8	26 4/8	21 1/8	Garfield Co., UT	Leo W. Mack, Jr.	Leo W. Mack, Jr.	1997	24
115 6/8	19 4/8	20 2/8	14	13 6/8	5	5 1/8	28 4/8	15	Sikanni Chief River, BC	Brian Nelson	Brian Nelson	1997	24
115 6/8	18 1/8	17 6/8	13 1/8	13 1/8	7 1/8	6 3/8	30	24 7/8	Custer Co., SD	James R. Weatherly	James R. Weatherly	1998	24
115 4/8	18 1/8	18 6/8	13 4/8	13	5 6/8	5 5/8	30 5/8	24 4/8	Park Co., MT	Picked Up	Glenn M. Smith	1998	27
115 4/8	17 5/8	18 4/8	13	13 2/8	6	5 7/8	27 6/8	20 3/8	Garfield Co., UT	Norman L. Reese	Norman L. Reese	1999	27
115 2/8	19 7/8	19 5/8	13 6/8	13 4/8	5	4 7/8	27 4/8	19 6/8	Garfield Co., UT	Rodney J. Davis	Rodney J. Davis	1997	29
115	16 4/8	17 4/8	13 5/8	13 4/8	6 2/8	6 6/8	28	26 3/8	Davis Co., UT	Rudell B. Willey	Rudell B. Willey	1998	30
115	18	18 2/8	13 2/8	13 2/8	5 7/8	6 1/8	30 6/8	26 6/8	Halfway River, BC	Brenda K. Bergen	Brenda K. Bergen	1999	30
129*	18 6/8	18 3/8	15 7/8	15 7/8	7 3/8	7 1/8	29 4/8	23 2/8	Custer Co., SD	Collins F. Kellogg, Sr.	Collins F. Kellogg, Sr.	2000	

$122^{2}/_{8}$	$*20^{6}/_{8}$	$19^{7}/_{8}$	$14^{2}/_{8}$	$14^{2}/_{8}$	$6^{2}/_{8}$	$6^{6}/_{8}$	28	$15^{7}/_{8}$	Pink Mt., BC	Norman L. Teng	Norman L. Teng	1997
$120^{2}/_{8}$	$*19^{7}/_{8}$	$19^{7}/_{8}$	$13^{4}/_{8}$	$13^{4}/_{8}$	$6^{4}/_{8}$	7	$30^{4}/_{8}$	$21^{7}/_{8}$	Halfway River, BC	Nadine B. Hall	Nadine B. Hall	1996

* Final score subject to revision by additional verifying measurements.

ROCKY MOUNTAIN GOAT

Oreamnos americanus americanus and related subspecies

Minimum Score 47 — New World's Record 56 6/8

Score	Length of Horn R	L	Circumference of Base R	L	Circumference at Third Quarter R	L	Greatest Spread	Tip to Tip Spread	Locality	Hunter	Owner	Date Killed	Rank
56 6/8	11 7/8	10 6/8	6 4/8	6 4/8	2 1/8	2 1/8	8 7/8	8 2/8	Bella Coola, BC	G. Wober & L Michalchuk	Gernot Wober	1999	1
54	12 3/8	11 7/8	6	6	1 6/8	1 6/8	9 2/8	7 6/8	Flathead Co., MT	Jason D. Beatty	Jason D. Beatty	1998	2
52 4/8	10 5/8	10 1/8	6	6	1 7/8	1 7/8	6 7/8	6 5/8	Kittitas Co., WA	James L. Hawk, Jr.	James L. Hawk, Jr.	1998	3
52 2/8	10 7/8	10 6/8	5 6/8	5 6/8	1 7/8	1 7/8	9 6/8	8 7/8	Telegraph Creek, BC	Paul L.C. Snider	Paul L.C. Snider	1998	4
52	11 2/8	10 7/8	5 4/8	5 4/8	1 6/8	1 6/8	8 3/8	7 7/8	Idaho Co., ID	Joseph A. Seagle	Jeff R. Seagle	1927	5
52	10 1/8	10 1/8	5 5/8	5 5/8	2	2	6 4/8	5 5/8	Kumealon Inlet, BC	Steven D. Einarson	Steven D. Einarson	1998	5
51 6/8	10 3/8	10 3/8	5 5/8	5 5/8	1 7/8	1 7/8	8	7 5/8	Chouteau Co., MT	Rhonda H. Tylinski	Rhonda H. Tylinski	1997	7
51 6/8	10	9 7/8	6	6	2	2	8 1/8	7 5/8	Kiniskan Lake, BC	Caroline R. Larsen	Caroline R. Larsen	1999	7
51 6/8	10 3/8	9 4/8	6 1/8	6 1/8	2 1/8	2	6 4/8	5 6/8	Skeena River, BC	James F. Sullivan	James F. Sullivan	1999	7
51 4/8	11 5/8	11 2/8	5 6/8	5 6/8	2	1 7/8	7 2/8	7 2/8	Castle Creek, BC	John Reinhart	John Reinhart	1976	10
51 4/8	10 2/8	10 3/8	5 5/8	5 6/8	1 7/8	1 7/8	8 1/8	8	Little Oliver Creek, BC	Rodney G. Chinn	Rodney G. Chinn	1993	10
51 4/8	10 3/8	10 4/8	5 7/8	6	1 7/8	1 7/8	8 5/8	8 2/8	Knik River, AK	Richard J. Jacob	Richard J. Jacob	1997	10
51 4/8	10 2/8	10 3/8	5 7/8	5 7/8	1 7/8	1 7/8	6 3/8	5 1/8	Gilltoyees Creek, BC	Gerald Volz	Gerald Volz	1997	10
51 2/8	10 4/8	10 4/8	5 4/8	5 4/8	1 7/8	1 7/8	7 5/8	7 4/8	Sand Lake, BC	William J. Kuehn	William J. Kuehn	1999	14
51 2/8	10 7/8	10 5/8	5 5/8	5 5/8	1 7/8	1 7/8	8 6/8	8 4/8	Inklin River, BC	John A. Morrison	John A. Morrison	1999	14
51	9 5/8	9 7/8	5 7/8	5 7/8	2	1 7/8	6 4/8	5 1/8	Tatla Lake, BC	James A. Kelley	James A. Kelley	1998	16
51	10 5/8	10 4/8	5 4/8	5 4/8	1 6/8	1 6/8	6 2/8	4 5/8	Cleveland Pen., AK	David K. Mueller	David K. Mueller	1998	16
51	10 3/8	10 2/8	5 6/8	5 6/8	2 1/8	2 1/8	7	6 2/8	Taku River, BC	Clifford D. Graham	Clifford D. Graham	1999	16
50 6/8	10 1/8	10 4/8	6	6 1/8	1 6/8	1 7/8	7 2/8	6 7/8	Syncline Hills, AB	Gilbert W. Davis	Gilbert W. Davis	1998	19
50 4/8	10 2/8	10 2/8	5 6/8	5 6/8	1 7/8	1 7/8	7 6/8	6 5/8	Sunset Creek, BC	William B. Deuink	William B. Deuink	1999	20
50 4/8	9 5/8	9 5/8	5 7/8	5 7/8	2	2	5 7/8	5 1/8	Quartz Creek, BC	Davin J. Jaatteenmaki	Davin J. Jaatteenmaki	1999	20
50 4/8	10	10	5 6/8	5 6/8	1 6/8	1 6/8	6 4/8	5 6/8	Brewer Creek, BC	Carlo Kathriner	Carlo Kathriner	1999	20
50 4/8	10	10 1/8	5 6/8	5 6/8	1 6/8	1 6/8	7 3/8	6 5/8	Judith Basin Co., MT	Norman A. Kingsland	Norman A. Kingsland	1999	20
50 4/8	9 7/8	10	5 6/8	5 6/8	1 6/8	1 6/8	6 7/8	6 5/8	Kittitas Co., WA	Garry G. Mathews	Garry G. Mathews	2000	20
50 2/8	10 3/8	10 4/8	5 6/8	5 6/8	1 6/8	1 6/8	6 2/8	6	Park Co., CO	Heath A. Hibbard	Heath A. Hibbard	1998	25
50 2/8	10 1/8	10 1/8	5 6/8	5 5/8	1 7/8	1 7/8	6	4 4/8	Bella Coola River, BC	Douglas N. Langkow	Douglas N. Langkow	1998	25
50 2/8	9 7/8	10	5 5/8	5 6/8	1 7/8	1 7/8	7 2/8	6 2/8	Little Oliver Creek, BC	Richard C. Berreth	Richard C. Berreth	1999	25
50 2/8	9 4/8	9 4/8	5 5/8	5 5/8	1 7/8	1 7/8	6 6/8	6 2/8	Gold River, BC	Wade Derby	Wade Derby	1999	25
50 2/8	10 4/8	10 4/8	5 4/8	5 4/8	1 6/8	1 6/8	6	5 2/8	Nakusp, BC	J. Henry Scown	J. Henry Scown	1999	25
50 2/8	9 5/8	9 4/8	5 6/8	5 6/8	2	2	6	5 2/8	Elko Co., NV	Rafael Betancourt, Jr.	Rafael Betancourt, Jr.	2000	25
50	10 1/8	10	5 4/8	5 4/8	2	2	6 5/8	5 5/8	British Columbia	John Oshea	Donnie J. Allen	1947	31
50	9 7/8	10 1/8	5 7/8	5 7/8	1 7/8	1 7/8	7 3/8	6 6/8	Lake Tatsamenie, BC	Philip W. Geisse	Philip W. Geisse	1996	31
50	10 2/8	10 2/8	5 5/8	5 5/8	1 6/8	1 6/8	7	6 5/8	Yakima Co., WA	Eric J. Horst	Eric J. Horst	1998	31
50	10 3/8	10 2/8	5 5/8	5 5/8	1 6/8	1 6/8	7 5/8	7 2/8	Sunset Creek, BC	Carl R. Kyser	Carl R. Kyser	1998	31
50	10 6/8	10 3/8	5 6/8	5 5/8	1 6/8	1 6/8	8 5/8	8 5/8	Tahltan River, BC	Daniel M. Mikutel	Daniel M. Mikutel	1998	31

50	9 7/8	9 6/8	5 7/8	5 6/8	1 6/8	1 6/8	7 5/8	7	Utah Co., UT	John J. Provost	John J. Provost	1999	31
50	10	9 6/8	6	6	2	2	7 5/8	7 6/8	Kaketsa Mt., BC	David J. Hucke	David J. Hucke	2000	31
50	9 6/8	9 6/8	5 5/8	5 5/8	1 7/8	1 7/8	6 6/8	6 2/8	Stikine River, BC	William J. Smith	William J. Smith	2000	31
49 6/8	9 7/8	9 7/8	5 3/8	5 4/8	1 6/8	1 6/8	6 7/8	6 2/8	Triumph Creek, BC	Gregory Powers	Gregory Powers	1999	39
49 6/8	9 6/8	9 6/8	5 4/8	5 4/8	2	2	8 4/8	8 4/8	Columbia Glacier, AK	Harold L. Donahue II	Harold L. Donahue II	2000	39
49 4/8	10 5/8	9 6/8	5 3/8	5 3/8	1 6/8	1 6/8	6 6/8	5 7/8	Missoula Co., MT	George Knapp	George Knapp	1958	41
49 4/8	9 6/8	9 7/8	5 6/8	5 6/8	1 7/8	1 7/8	7 2/8	6 2/8	Burrage Creek, BC	Mark W. Streissguth	Mark W. Streissguth	1998	41
49 2/8	10 3/8	10 2/8	5 4/8	5 5/8	1 6/8	1 6/8	6	5 2/8	Brewer Creek, BC	Jerry E. Jurena	Jerry E. Jurena	1997	43
49 2/8	9 4/8	9 7/8	5 7/8	5 6/8	1 7/8	1 7/8	7 4/8	7 1/8	Kodiak Island, AK	Paul A. Kuriscak	Paul A. Kuriscak	1997	43
49 2/8	10 2/8	9 4/8	5 3/8	5 3/8	1 7/8	1 7/8	5 4/8	4 6/8	Swan Lake, AK	Mark L. Chambers	Mark L. Chambers	1998	43
49 2/8	9 5/8	10 1/8	5 4/8	5 4/8	1 6/8	1 6/8	5 7/8	5 1/8	Lewis Co., WA	Larry E. Sides, Jr.	Larry E. Sides, Jr.	1999	43
49 2/8	10	9 5/8	5 6/8	5 6/8	1 6/8	1 6/8	7 5/8	7 3/8	Skeena Mts., BC	Patrick S. Stuart	Patrick S. Stuart	1999	43
49 2/8	10	9 4/8	5 6/8	5 4/8	2	2	7 4/8	6 7/8	Whatcom Co., WA	Randy E. Hess	Randy E. Hess	1995	43
49	9 2/8	9	5 7/8	5 6/8	1 6/8	1 6/8	6 5/8	6	Utah Co., UT	Bryan E. Nielsen	Bryan E. Nielsen	1997	48
49	9 7/8	9 7/8	5 6/8	5 5/8	1 6/8	1 6/8	6 5/8	5 6/8	Chouteau Co., MT	Rick L. Linquist	Rick L. Linquist	1998	48
49	9 7/8	9 6/8	5 4/8	5 3/8	1 6/8	1 6/8	7 7/8	7 5/8	Lincoln Co., WY	E. Jay Dawson	E. Jay Dawson	1999	48
49	9 2/8	9 4/8	5 6/8	5 6/8	2	2	6 1/8	5 5/8	Elko Co., NV	Douglas S. Neill	Douglas S. Neill	1999	48
48 6/8	9 5/8	9 4/8	5 5/8	5 4/8	1 6/8	1 6/8	7	6 2/8	Dease Lake, BC	John F. Abbott	John F. Abbott	1996	53
48 6/8	9 3/8	9 5/8	5 2/8	5 2/8	1 7/8	1 7/8	7 6/8	7 5/8	Elko Co., NV	Robert S. Lund	Robert S. Lund	1998	53
48 6/8	9 6/8	9 6/8	5 4/8	5 4/8	1 6/8	1 6/8	6 5/8	5 1/8	Elko Co., NV	John Crumb	John Crumb	1999	53
48 6/8	9 7/8	9 7/8	5 4/8	5 4/8	1 7/8	1 7/8	7 1/8	6 6/8	Babine Range, BC	Kelvin L. Finney	Kelvin L. Finney	1999	53
48 4/8	9 2/8	9 2/8	5 6/8	5 6/8	1 6/8	1 6/8	6 4/8	6	Mount Bonner, MT	Mitchell T. Hunt	Mitchell T. Hunt	1997	57
48 4/8	9 4/8	9	5 3/8	5 3/8	1 6/8	1 6/8	7 1/8	6 6/8	Salt Lake Co., UT	Daniel B. Sieminski	Daniel B. Sieminski	2000	57
48 2/8	10	10	5 3/8	5 3/8	1 6/8	1 6/8	6 1/8	5 6/8	Resurrection Bay, AK	Davin J. Jaatteenmaki	Davin J. Jaatteenmaki	1998	59
48 2/8	9 6/8	9 5/8	5 4/8	5 4/8	1 5/8	1 5/8	7 2/8	6 6/8	Quartz Creek, BC	Scott R. Byrne	Scott R. Byrne	2000	59
48 2/8	10 2/8	9 7/8	5 4/8	5 4/8	1 6/8	1 6/8	6 5/8	5 7/8	Ravalli Co., MT	Leonard Prescott III	Leonard Prescott III	2000	59
48	9 6/8	9 7/8	5 4/8	5 4/8	1 5/8	1 5/8	7 7/8	7 3/8	Gallatin Co., MT	Steve M. Heil	Steve M. Heil	1997	62
48	9 1/8	9 3/8	5 4/8	5 4/8	1 6/8	1 6/8	6 5/8	6	Toby Creek, BC	Claude A. Archuleta	Claude A. Archuleta	1998	62
48	9 2/8	9 2/8	5 6/8	5 5/8	1 6/8	1 6/8	6 2/8	5	Utah Co., UT	Kent Deligans	Kent Deligans	1999	62
47 6/8	9 4/8	9 4/8	5 4/8	5 4/8	1 6/8	1 6/8	7 6/8	7 2/8	Slope Glacier, AK	Stuart L. Aasgaard	Stuart L. Aasgaard	1992	65
47 6/8	9 3/8	9 4/8	5 4/8	5 4/8	1 7/8	1 7/8	6 2/8	5 3/8	Gallatin Co., MT	Harold D. Ramberg	Harold D. Ramberg	1997	65
47 6/8	9 5/8	9 5/8	5 3/8	5 3/8	1 5/8	1 5/8	7 4/8	7	Spatsizi Plateau, BC	W. David Howton	W. David Howton	1998	65
47 6/8	9	9	5 6/8	5 5/8	1 7/8	1 7/8	5	4 1/8	Tracy Arm, AK	Joseph D. Wiggs	Joseph D. Wiggs	1999	65
47 4/8	9 1/8	9 1/8	5 4/8	5 4/8	1 6/8	1 6/8	7 5/8	7 1/8	Okanogan Co., WA	Rodrick C. Cyr	Everett M. Brumaghim	1993	69
47 4/8	9 6/8	9 6/8	5 3/8	5 3/8	2	2	7 7/8	7 2/8	Chuck River, AK	Edward Jaatteenmaki	Edward Jaatteenmaki	1996	69
47 4/8	10	10	5 2/8	5 2/8	1 5/8	1 5/8	7	6 5/8	Quartz Creek, BC	Greg D. Gilbert	Greg D. Gilbert	1997	69
47 4/8	10 2/8	10 2/8	4 6/8	4 6/8	2	2	5	5	Chouteau Co., MT	Shaun P. Haseltine	Shaun P. Haseltine	1997	69
47 4/8	9 1/8	9 1/8	5 4/8	5 4/8	1 6/8	1 6/8	7 1/8	6 6/8	Peabody Mts., AK	John L. Hendrix	John L. Hendrix	1997	69
47 4/8	10 2/8	9 2/8	5 4/8	5 3/8	1 6/8	1 6/8	6 2/8	6	Fox River, AK	Joel M. Randrup	Joel M. Randrup	1997	69
47 4/8	9 3/8	9 3/8	5 3/8	5 3/8	1 7/8	1 7/8	7 5/8	7	LeConte Bay, AK	Charles A. LeKites	Charles A. LeKites	1999	69
47 4/8	8 7/8	9 2/8	5 2/8	5 2/8	1 7/8	1 7/8	6 7/8	6 6/8	Kenai Pen., AK	James A. Algerio	James A. Algerio	2000	69
47 4/8	9 7/8	9 7/8	5 3/8	5 3/8	1 6/8	1 5/8	9 1/8	8 7/8	Elko Co., NV	Raymond L. Howell, Sr.	Raymond L. Howell, Sr.	1998	69
47 2/8	9 4/8	9 7/8	5 2/8	5 3/8	1 7/8	1 7/8	7 2/8	6 1/8	Williston Lake, BC	Al Kuntz	Al Kuntz	1998	78

ROCKY MOUNTAIN GOAT

Oreamnos americanus americanus and related subspecies

Score	Length of Horn R.	L.	Circumference of Base R.	L.	Circumference at Third Quarter R.	L.	Greatest Spread	Tip to Tip Spread	Locality	Hunter	Owner	Date Killed	Rank
47 2/8	9 6/8	9 1/8	5 5/8	5 5/8	1 7/8	1 6/8	7 2/8	6 2/8	Jarvis Lake, BC	Jack R. Tindall	Jack R. Tindall	1999	78
47 2/8	9 1/8	9 2/8	5 2/8	5 3/8	1 6/8	1 6/8	6 3/8	6	Elko Co., NV	Stanley A. Marks	Stanley A. Marks	2000	78
47	9 6/8	9 6/8	5 3/8	5 4/8	1 5/8	1 6/8	6 4/8	6 4/8	Baker Co., OR	Jeffrey H. Millspaugh	Jeffrey H. Millspaugh	1998	81
47	9 4/8	9 4/8	5 3/8	5 3/8	1 6/8	1 6/8	7	6 4/8	Caribou Mts., BC	Mark B. Steffen	Mark B. Steffen	1998	81
47	9 4/8	9 4/8	5 3/8	5 3/8	1 6/8	1 5/8	7 3/8	7 2/8	King River, AK	James A. Wilken	James A. Wilken	1998	81
47	9 4/8	9 5/8	5 5/8	5 6/8	1 5/8	1 5/8	7 2/8	7	Park Co., MT	Richard J. Held	Richard J. Held	1999	81
47	9 7/8	9 7/8	5 1/8	5 2/8	1 4/8	1 4/8	7 2/8	6 4/8	Park Co., MT	Derry D. McLane	Derry D. McLane	2000	81
54*	11	11 1/8	6	6	1 7/8	1 7/8	8 2/8	8	Big Olive Creek, BC	John G. Jones	John G. Jones	1997	
52 6/8*	10 3/8	10 5/8	6	6	2	2	8 2/8	7 6/8	Shames River, BC	Rodney G. Chinn	Rodney G. Chinn	1997	

* Final score subject to revision by additional verifying measurements.

510

MUSKOX

Ovibos moschatus moschatus and certain related subspecies

Minimum Score 105   New World's Record 127

Score	Length of Horn R	L	Width of Boss R	L	Circumference at Third Quarter R	L	Greatest Spread	Tip to Tip Spread	Locality	Hunter	Owner	Date Killed	Rank
$126^{2}/_{8}$	$29^{2}/_{8}$	$29^{4}/_{8}$	$10^{5}/_{8}$	11	$5^{4}/_{8}$	$5^{5}/_{8}$	$27^{7}/_{8}$	$27^{4}/_{8}$	Kugaryuak River, NT	M.R. James	M.R. James	2000	1
125	$28^{6}/_{8}$	$28^{7}/_{8}$	$11^{1}/_{8}$	$11^{3}/_{8}$	$5^{6}/_{8}$	$5^{7}/_{8}$	$29^{1}/_{8}$	$27^{4}/_{8}$	Coppermine, NT	William L. Cox	William L. Cox	1998	2
$124^{4}/_{8}$	30	$29^{7}/_{8}$	$10^{2}/_{8}$	$10^{1}/_{8}$	$6^{2}/_{8}$	6	$29^{4}/_{8}$	29	Kugaryuak River, NT	Ronald G. McKnight	Ronald G. McKnight	2000	3
$123^{2}/_{8}$	27	$27^{2}/_{8}$	$10^{5}/_{8}$	$10^{4}/_{8}$	$6^{4}/_{8}$	$6^{6}/_{8}$	$25^{4}/_{8}$	24	Norman Wells, NT	Darcy Hernblad	Darcy Hernblad	1999	4
123	$29^{1}/_{8}$	$28^{7}/_{8}$	$10^{2}/_{8}$	$10^{3}/_{8}$	6	$5^{4}/_{8}$	$28^{2}/_{8}$	$27^{6}/_{8}$	Kent Pen., NT	Raymond L. Howell, Sr.	Raymond L. Howell, Sr.	2000	5
$122^{2}/_{8}$	29	$30^{3}/_{8}$	$10^{4}/_{8}$	$10^{1}/_{8}$	$5^{4}/_{8}$	$6^{2}/_{8}$	27	$25^{1}/_{8}$	Coppermine, NT	R. Stephen Irwin	R. Stephen Irwin	1995	6
$121^{6}/_{8}$	$26^{7}/_{8}$	$26^{4}/_{8}$	$10^{1}/_{8}$	$10^{5}/_{8}$	$6^{4}/_{8}$	$6^{2}/_{8}$	27	$26^{6}/_{8}$	Cambridge Bay, NT	Michael J. Drewnowski	Michael J. Drewnowski	1997	7
$120^{6}/_{8}$	$29^{5}/_{8}$	29	10	10	$5^{5}/_{8}$	$4^{7}/_{8}$	$26^{7}/_{8}$	$26^{2}/_{8}$	Paulatuk, NT	Derek A. Burdeny	Derek A. Burdeny	2000	8
120	$27^{2}/_{8}$	$26^{7}/_{8}$	$10^{3}/_{8}$	$10^{3}/_{8}$	$5^{6}/_{8}$	$5^{3}/_{8}$	$28^{3}/_{8}$	28	Kikerk Lake, NT	Charles A. LeKites	Charles A. LeKites	1999	9
$119^{4}/_{8}$	$28^{6}/_{8}$	29	$8^{6}/_{8}$	$8^{7}/_{8}$	$5^{7}/_{8}$	$5^{7}/_{8}$	$25^{2}/_{8}$	$23^{6}/_{8}$	Cambridge Bay, NT	Collins F. Kellogg, Sr.	Collins F. Kellogg, Sr.	1998	10
$119^{2}/_{8}$	$28^{4}/_{8}$	$28^{1}/_{8}$	$10^{2}/_{8}$	$10^{1}/_{8}$	$5^{2}/_{8}$	$5^{2}/_{8}$	$29^{1}/_{8}$	$26^{7}/_{8}$	Coppermine River, NT	John Zimmerman	John Zimmerman	1998	11
$118^{4}/_{8}$	$27^{4}/_{8}$	$27^{5}/_{8}$	$10^{6}/_{8}$	$10^{2}/_{8}$	$5^{7}/_{8}$	$5^{4}/_{8}$	$28^{6}/_{8}$	$28^{4}/_{8}$	Coppermine, NT	Glenn M. Smith	Glenn M. Smith	1998	12
$118^{2}/_{8}$	$28^{7}/_{8}$	$29^{7}/_{8}$	$10^{5}/_{8}$	$10^{6}/_{8}$	$5^{1}/_{8}$	$5^{6}/_{8}$	$27^{4}/_{8}$	$25^{6}/_{8}$	Coppermine, NT	Louis E. Dunyon	Louis E. Dunyon	1994	13
118	$27^{5}/_{8}$	$28^{4}/_{8}$	$10^{2}/_{8}$	$10^{4}/_{8}$	$5^{4}/_{8}$	$5^{2}/_{8}$	$30^{2}/_{8}$	$29^{2}/_{8}$	Coppermine River, NT	Robert M. Anderson	Robert M. Anderson	2000	14
$117^{4}/_{8}$	$28^{3}/_{8}$	29	$11^{2}/_{8}$	11	$4^{6}/_{8}$	$5^{3}/_{8}$	$27^{3}/_{8}$	$26^{3}/_{8}$	Coppermine, NT	Sean J. Lancaster	Sean J. Lancaster	1999	15
$117^{4}/_{8}$	$28^{2}/_{8}$	$28^{6}/_{8}$	$9^{4}/_{8}$	$9^{4}/_{8}$	$5^{4}/_{8}$	$5^{6}/_{8}$	$27^{6}/_{8}$	$26^{3}/_{8}$	Franklin Bay, NT	Bruce B. Faulkner	Bruce B. Faulkner	2000	15
$115^{6}/_{8}$	$26^{1}/_{8}$	$25^{2}/_{8}$	$10^{1}/_{8}$	10	$5^{1}/_{8}$	$5^{2}/_{8}$	$25^{4}/_{8}$	19	Paulatuk, NT	John F. Babler	John F. Babler	1999	17
$115^{6}/_{8}$	$29^{5}/_{8}$	$28^{4}/_{8}$	$9^{5}/_{8}$	$9^{6}/_{8}$	$4^{6}/_{8}$	$4^{4}/_{8}$	$26^{1}/_{8}$	$24^{3}/_{8}$	Smoking Hills, NT	Jack A. Michaelson	Jack A. Michaelson	1999	17
$115^{4}/_{8}$	$27^{7}/_{8}$	$26^{6}/_{8}$	$9^{4}/_{8}$	10	6	$5^{4}/_{8}$	$28^{2}/_{8}$	$27^{5}/_{8}$	Buchan Hills, NT	Craig S. Mortz	Craig S. Mortz	2000	19
115	27	$26^{4}/_{8}$	$9^{5}/_{8}$	$10^{1}/_{8}$	6	$5^{6}/_{8}$	$26^{4}/_{8}$	$27^{4}/_{8}$	Canoe Lake, NT	Ronald W. Wangerow	Ronald W. Wangerow	2000	20
$114^{6}/_{8}$	$27^{6}/_{8}$	$28^{6}/_{8}$	$9^{2}/_{8}$	$9^{3}/_{8}$	5	$5^{4}/_{8}$	$28^{6}/_{8}$	$27^{3}/_{8}$	Horton River, NT	Kevin Crowe	Kevin Crowe	1999	21
$113^{6}/_{8}$	$27^{1}/_{8}$	$26^{2}/_{8}$	$10^{2}/_{8}$	$10^{1}/_{8}$	$5^{5}/_{8}$	$5^{2}/_{8}$	$29^{4}/_{8}$	$28^{5}/_{8}$	Inulik Lake, NT	Heber Simmons, Jr.	Heber Simmons, Jr.	1998	22
$112^{6}/_{8}$	$26^{2}/_{8}$	26	$9^{3}/_{8}$	$9^{6}/_{8}$	$5^{2}/_{8}$	$5^{1}/_{8}$	$28^{6}/_{8}$	$28^{1}/_{8}$	Dease Strait, NT	Neil A. Briscoe, Jr.	Neil A. Briscoe, Jr.	1998	23
$112^{6}/_{8}$	$27^{2}/_{8}$	$28^{6}/_{8}$	$10^{4}/_{8}$	$10^{2}/_{8}$	$4^{2}/_{8}$	$4^{7}/_{8}$	31	30	Coronation Gulf, NT	William E. Wilson	William E. Wilson	1999	23
$112^{4}/_{8}$	$25^{7}/_{8}$	$26^{3}/_{8}$	$9^{2}/_{8}$	$9^{4}/_{8}$	5	$5^{2}/_{8}$	26	$25^{1}/_{8}$	Canoe Lake, NT	Randy Kaszeta	Randy Kaszeta	2000	25
$110^{4}/_{8}$	$27^{2}/_{8}$	$26^{4}/_{8}$	$9^{2}/_{8}$	$8^{2}/_{8}$	$5^{4}/_{8}$	$5^{4}/_{8}$	$28^{4}/_{8}$	$27^{6}/_{8}$	Rendez-vous Lake, NT	Joseph G. Zapotosky	Joseph G. Zapotosky	2000	26
$109^{2}/_{8}$	$26^{6}/_{8}$	$26^{6}/_{8}$	$8^{3}/_{8}$	$8^{4}/_{8}$	$5^{2}/_{8}$	$5^{1}/_{8}$	$30^{6}/_{8}$	30	Nunivak Island, AK	Wayne L. Evans	Wayne L. Evans	1999	27
$108^{6}/_{8}$	$26^{4}/_{8}$	$27^{7}/_{8}$	$9^{6}/_{8}$	$9^{4}/_{8}$	$4^{5}/_{8}$	$4^{7}/_{8}$	$25^{4}/_{8}$	$22^{2}/_{8}$	Rendez-vous Lake, NT	Chilton E. Miles, Jr.	Chilton E. Miles, Jr.	1997	28
108	26	26	$9^{2}/_{8}$	$9^{3}/_{8}$	5	$5^{2}/_{8}$	$25^{2}/_{8}$	25	Banks Island, NT	K-Tal G. Johnson	K-Tal G. Johnson	1997	29
$107^{6}/_{8}$	$26^{1}/_{8}$	$25^{6}/_{8}$	$8^{3}/_{8}$	$8^{2}/_{8}$	$5^{4}/_{8}$	$5^{4}/_{8}$	$27^{3}/_{8}$	$26^{6}/_{8}$	Ivishak River, AK	James L. Kedrowski	James L. Kedrowski	1999	30
$107^{4}/_{8}$	$26^{2}/_{8}$	$25^{5}/_{8}$	$8^{3}/_{8}$	$8^{4}/_{8}$	$5^{4}/_{8}$	$5^{1}/_{8}$	$27^{1}/_{8}$	$26^{7}/_{8}$	Nunivak Island, AK	Merle R. Frank	Merle R. Frank	1997	31
$107^{2}/_{8}$	$26^{2}/_{8}$	$26^{6}/_{8}$	9	$9^{1}/_{8}$	$4^{2}/_{8}$	$4^{6}/_{8}$	27	25	Victoria Island, NT	Johnnie R. Walters	Johnnie R. Walters	1999	32
$107^{2}/_{8}$	$25^{6}/_{8}$	$27^{3}/_{8}$	$9^{7}/_{8}$	$9^{6}/_{8}$	$4^{5}/_{8}$	$5^{4}/_{8}$	$26^{6}/_{8}$	$25^{4}/_{8}$	Bay Chimo, NT	Dyrk T. Eddie	Dyrk T. Eddie	1993	32
$107^{2}/_{8}$	26	$26^{4}/_{8}$	$8^{5}/_{8}$	$8^{2}/_{8}$	$4^{6}/_{8}$	$4^{7}/_{8}$	$27^{4}/_{8}$	$26^{2}/_{8}$	Paulatuk, NT	Mitchel C. Arnold	Mitchel C. Arnold	1998	32
$107^{2}/_{8}$	$25^{4}/_{8}$	$28^{2}/_{8}$	$9^{4}/_{8}$	$8^{5}/_{8}$	$3^{7}/_{8}$	$5^{2}/_{8}$	$29^{6}/_{8}$	$28^{4}/_{8}$	McDonald Lake, NT	W.G. Hawes	W.G. Hawes	2000	32

MUSKOX

Ovibos moschatus moschatus and certain related subspecies

Score	Length of Horn R.	L.	Width of Boss R.	L.	Circumference at Third Quarter R.	L.	Greatest Spread	Tip to Tip Spread	Locality	Hunter	Owner	Date Killed	Rank
107	25 1/8	24 6/8	7 7/8	8	5 3/8	5 2/8	27 6/8	25 4/8	Horton River, NT	Dwain Spray	Dwain Spray	1996	36
107	27 2/8	26 1/8	8 4/8	8 4/8	5 2/8	4 5/8	26 3/8	25 7/8	Nunivak Island, AK	David R. Lautner	David R. Lautner	1999	36
107	25 7/8	25 3/8	8 2/8	8 2/8	5	5 4/8	29 1/8	28 4/8	Granite Falls, NT	Pete Studwell	Pete Studwell	1999	36
106 6/8	24	24 4/8	12 4/8	12 4/8	4 1/8	4 7/8	22 6/8	20 7/8	Cambridge Bay, NT	William F. Kneer, Jr.	William F. Kneer, Jr.	1999	39
106	26 7/8	26 2/8	8 4/8	8 5/8	4 6/8	4 5/8	25 6/8	24 6/8	Cambridge Bay, NT	Collins F. Kellogg, Jr.	Collins F. Kellogg, Jr.	1998	40
105 6/8	24 3/8	26 2/8	10 1/8	9 7/8	4 6/8	5 5/8	26	24 1/8	Rendez-vous Lake, NT	David L. Hussey	David L. Hussey	1998	41
105 6/8	25 1/8	25 3/8	8 7/8	8 7/8	4 7/8	4 7/8	25 3/8	27 3/8	Nanwaksjiak Crater, AK	Robert R. Halpin	Robert R. Halpin	1999	41
105 6/8	24 3/8	25 4/8	8 6/8	8 5/8	5 3/8	5 3/8	26 3/8	24 2/8	Nunivak Island, AK	A. Timothy Toth	A. Timothy Toth	2000	41
105 2/8	25 6/8	28 2/8	9 7/8	9 5/8	3 7/8	5 2/8	26 5/8	26 2/8	Gjoa Haven, NT	Ken G. Wilson	Ken G. Wilson	1998	44
105	25 6/8	26 2/8	8 4/8	8 2/8	4 5/8	5	28 1/8	27 5/8	Mekoryuk, AK	Steven J. Bries	Steven J. Bries	1998	45
127 2/8*	29 2/8*	29 7/8	10 6/8	10 6/8	6	5 6/8	29 6/8	28 6/8	Kugluktuk, NT	Vicente S. Sanchez-Valdepenas	Vicente S. Sanchez-Valdepenas	1999	
125 2/8*	28 2/8*	28 1/8	10 3/8	10 3/8	6 2/8	6	29 4/8	28 2/8	Kugluktuk, NT	John Gehan	John Gehan	2000	
125 2/8*	28 7/8*	29 6/8	10 7/8	11	6	6 2/8	31	30 3/8	Omingmaktok, NT	Kent L. Prouty	Kent L. Prouty	2000	
125*	29 4/8	28 7/8	11 3/8	11 1/8	5 3/8	5 3/8	29 2/8	27 2/8	Kugluktuk, NT	James A. Cummings	James A. Cummings	2000	
122 4/8*	28 1/8*	28 4/8	11 5/8	11	5 6/8	6 1/8	28 4/8	27 6/8	Kugluktuk, NT	Jack L. Blachly	Jack L. Blachly	1999	

* Final score subject to revision by additional verifying measurements.

512

BIGHORN SHEEP

Ovis canadensis canadensis and certain related subspecies

Minimum Score 175 World's Record 208 1/8

Score	Length of Horn R	Length of Horn L	Circumference of Base R	Circumference of Base L	Circumference at Third Quarter R	Circumference at Third Quarter L	Greatest Spread	Tip to Tip Spread	Locality	Hunter	Owner	Date Killed	Rank
197 6/8	44 6/8	42	16	16 1/8	10 2/8	9 6/8	23 7/8	23	Sanders Co., MT	Steven M. Inabnit	Steven M. Inabnit	1995	1
195	41 6/8	40 2/8	16 3/8	16 3/8	10	10 4/8	24 2/8	17	Huerfano Co., CO	Donald W. Snyder	Donald W. Snyder	2000	2
194	37 6/8	38 4/8	17 1/8	17	10 6/8	10 3/8	23 5/8	22 3/8	Fergus Co., MT	Donald R. Hecht	Donald R. Hecht	1998	3
192 6/8	38 4/8	42 4/8	16 7/8	17	9	9 2/8	24 4/8	24 4/8	Wallowa Co., OR	Bryan C. Bailey	Bryan C. Bailey	1998	4
192 4/8	41 3/8	41 5/8	15 7/8	15 6/8	10 4/8	10	23	22 2/8	Granite Co., MT	James E. Ratcliffe	James E. Ratcliffe	1999	5
192 2/8	41	40 5/8	15 7/8	15 6/8	10 1/8	10 4/8	21 7/8	21 2/8	Fergus Co., MT	John Benes	John Benes	1997	6
192 1/8	36 6/8	37 5/8	16 2/8	16 2/8	12	11 5/8	26 4/8	24	Fergus Co., MT	George R. Harms	George R. Harms	1998	6
192 1/8	41 4/8	41 5/8	15 3/8	15 4/8	10 6/8	10 3/8	21 3/8	16 3/8	Luscar Mt., AB	William C. Cloyd	William C. Cloyd	2000	6
192	41 3/8	43 1/8	15 6/8	15 7/8	9 2/8	9 3/8	20 1/8	20 1/8	Granite Co., MT	Greg A. Stavish	Greg A. Stavish	1999	9
191	43 3/8	40 7/8	15	15 1/8	10 6/8	9 5/8	22 5/8	22 5/8	Cardinal River, AB	Eugene Kirk	Eugene Kirk	1997	10
190 6/8	43 4/8	40 2/8	16	16 2/8	9 3/8	8 2/8	23 7/8	24	Fergus Co., MT	David E. Buschena	David E. Buschena	1998	11
190 5/8	39 1/8	40 4/8	15 2/8	15 2/8	10 3/8	10	25	18 4/8	Missoula Co., MT	Picked Up	Lolo National Forest	1998	12
190 5/8	42 6/8	41 1/8	16 1/8	16 1/8	8 7/8	8 4/8	23	22 6/8	Granite Co., MT	Mark A. Donovan	Mark A. Donovan	1999	12
190 2/8	39 7/8	44 5/8	16 1/8	16 1/8	8 6/8	8 7/8	25 4/8	24 3/8	Sanders Co., MT	S. Douglas Shear	S. Douglas Shear	1999	14
190	41	40	14 6/8	14 6/8	11 2/8	11 5/8	24 3/8	20 4/8	Jackson Co., CO	Tracy C. Atkinson	Tracy C. Atkinson	1999	15
189 5/8	41 3/8	45 4/8	15 2/8	15 3/8	8 2/8	8 3/8	25 6/8	25 4/8	Fergus Co., MT	Edmund C. Bishop	Edmund C. Bishop	1999	16
188 6/8	41 4/8	40 4/8	15	15	9 7/8	10	19 6/8	17 2/8	Line Creek, BC	Jim Musil	Jim Musil	1998	17
188 2/8	38	39 4/8	15 7/8	15 6/8	10	10 1/8	21 3/8	19 4/8	Sanders Co., MT	Anders J. Brooker	Anders J. Brooker	1997	18
188 1/8	41 2/8	40 7/8	15 3/8	15 4/8	9 6/8	9 6/8	21 5/8	19 7/8	Cadomin, AB	Randy Hancock	Randy Hancock	1997	19
188	41 7/8	41 3/8	16	16 1/8	8 2/8	8 3/8	21 7/8	21 2/8	Leyland Mt., AB	Norman P. Harasym	Norman P. Harasym	1997	20
187 7/8	40 4/8	40 7/8	16 4/8	16 2/8	8 4/8	8 6/8	23 1/8	20	Missoula Co., MT	Richard P. Hughes	Richard P. Hughes	1998	21
187 3/8	41 4/8	40 7/8	15 7/8	16	8 3/8	8 4/8	22 7/8	21 6/8	Ravalli Co., MT	James A. Martin	James A. Martin	1997	22
187 2/8	38 5/8	37 5/8	16 3/8	16 3/8	9 4/8	9 6/8	20 4/8	18	Elk Valley, BC	Michael Podrasky	Michael Podrasky	1998	23
187 1/8	38 3/8	38	16 2/8	16 1/8	9 5/8	9 6/8	23 6/8	20 3/8	Huerfano Co., CO	Joshua S. Gunning	Joshua S. Gunning	1998	24
187	40 4/8	38 4/8	16 2/8	16 2/8	8 7/8	8 7/8	23 5/8	23 5/8	Sanders Co., MT	Steven M. Morgan	Steven M. Morgan	1999	25
187	40	40 2/8	14 7/8	14 6/8	10	10 2/8	20 3/8	17 2/8	Granite Co., MT	Nathan L. Mattioli	Nathan L. Mattioli	2000	25
186 5/8	39 3/8	38 4/8	16 3/8	16 3/8	9	9 3/8	21 4/8	21 4/8	Sanders Co., MT	G. Michael Martin	G. Michael Martin	1998	27
186 3/8	38	38 3/8	15 1/8	15 3/8	10 2/8	10 3/8	22 4/8	14 4/8	Luscar Mt., AB	Max Howard	Max Howard	1998	28
186 3/8	39 5/8	39 4/8	15 5/8	15 5/8	9 4/8	9 2/8	21 7/8	18 4/8	Blaine Co., MT	Martin K. Lyders	Martin K. Lyders	1998	28
186 3/8	37 6/8	36 5/8	16 5/8	16 1/8	10 5/8	10 4/8	19 3/8	17 4/8	Missoula Co., MT	Dale H. Truett	Dale H. Truett	1998	28
186 2/8	41 3/8	38 7/8	16 2/8	16 2/8	8 2/8	8 3/8	24 2/8	24	Deer Lodge Co., MT	Jennifer R. Jaap	Jennifer R. Jaap	1997	31
186	36 5/8	40 1/8	17 4/8	17 4/8	8 3/8	7 7/8	24 4/8	24 4/8	Granite Co., MT	Thomas J. Kubichek	Thomas J. Kubichek	1987	32
186	39 4/8	37 4/8	16 2/8	16	9 4/8	9 2/8	21 1/8	21 1/8	Fergus Co., MT	Kenneth R. Brandt, Jr.	Kenneth R. Brandt, Jr.	1998	32
185 7/8	40	41 5/8	14 7/8	14 7/8	9 5/8	10 1/8	21 1/8	17	Gregg River, AB	Thomas J. Pawlacyk	Thomas J. Pawlacyk	1997	34
185 5/8	39 2/8	39 7/8	15 3/8	15 3/8	9 5/8	9 4/8	21 5/8	21 4/8	Lewis & Clark Co., MT	Rick R. Rosekelly	Rick R. Rosekelly	1999	35

BIGHORN SHEEP

Ovis canadensis canadensis and certain related subspecies

Score	Length of Horn R	L	Circumference of Base R	L	Circumference at Third Quarter R	L	Greatest Spread	Tip to Tip Spread	Locality	Hunter	Owner	Date Killed	Rank
185 4/8	42	39	15 1/8	15 1/8	8 6/8	8 6/8	22 3/8	19	Highwood Range, AB	James Collings	James Collings	1998	36
185 4/8	40 1/8	39 7/8	15 7/8	15 7/8	8 3/8	8 4/8	23 1/8	22 2/8	Blaine Co., MT	Joseph A. Blades	Joseph A. Blades	1999	36
185 3/8	37 1/8	39 6/8	15 6/8	15 6/8	9	9 1/8	23	14 6/8	Rio Arriba Co., NM	Robert D. Mac Millan	Robert D. Mac Millan	1999	38
185 2/8	39 6/8	39 4/8	15	15	9 6/8	9 6/8	23 5/8	18 4/8	Teton Co., MT	Doug E. Larson	Doug E. Larson	1998	39
185 2/8	40	40 7/8	15 2/8	15	8 5/8	9	23 2/8	20 4/8	Cheviot Mt., AB	Leo D. Paquin	Leo D. Paquin	1999	40
184 7/8	40 2/8	40	15 3/8	15 4/8	8 3/8	8 3/8	26 6/8	26 2/8	Ravalli Co., MT	David G. Paullin	David G. Paullin	1999	41
184 6/8	38 6/8	39 1/8	16 1/8	16	8 6/8	8 7/8	26 2/8	25 2/8	Fergus Co., MT	Jason R. Cargill	Jason R. Cargill	1997	42
184 5/8	41 1/8	39 2/8	16	16	8 1/8	8 6/8	21	20 4/8	Missoula Co., MT	Lloyd D. Hanson	Lloyd D. Hanson	1999	42
184 5/8	41 1/8	44	14	13 6/8	9 4/8	9 5/8	22 2/8	19 2/8	Taos Co., NM	Perry D. Harper	Perry D. Harper	1999	42
184 4/8	37 7/8	38 1/8	16 1/8	16 2/8	8 3/8	8 7/8	21 1/8	19 1/8	Nez Perce Co., ID	Robert P. Ellingson III	Robert P. Ellingson III	1999	45
184 3/8	37 2/8	36 1/8	15 6/8	15 6/8	11	10 3/8	23 4/8	16 2/8	Baker Co., OR	Craig R. Droke	Craig R. Droke	2000	46
184 2/8	40 2/8	36 6/8	15 3/8	15 3/8	11 1/8	10 4/8	22 1/8	17 6/8	Mystery Lake, AB	David S. Stelter	David S. Stelter	1998	47
184 2/8	39 4/8	38 6/8	14 7/8	14 7/8	10	9 7/8	22 4/8	22	Granite Co., MT	Garry D. Seaman	Garry D. Seaman	2000	47
184 1/8	41	41 1/8	16 5/8	16 5/8	6 6/8	6 7/8	22	22	Lost Mt., BC	Paul R. D'Andrea	Paul R. D'Andrea	2000	49
184	40	38 4/8	15 3/8	15 3/8	9	9	20 1/8	17	Unknown	Unknown	Paul L.C. Snider	PR 1989	50
184	36 6/8	37 4/8	15 4/8	15 4/8	10 7/8	11	22 2/8	18 4/8	Sanders Co., MT	Robert Schultz	Robert Schultz	1994	50
184	38 6/8	37 4/8	15 7/8	15 5/8	9 2/8	9 4/8	23 7/8	21	Blaine Co., MT	Jim M. Forman	Jim M. Forman	1999	50
183 5/8	40	36 7/8	15 4/8	15 4/8	9	8 2/8	23 3/8	17 4/8	Pitkin Co., CO	D. Dean Spatz	D. Dean Spatz	1998	53
183 5/8	39 7/8	39 4/8	16 2/8	16	8 4/8	8 7/8	23 4/8	23	Granite Co., MT	Gary L. Zabel	Gary L. Zabel	1999	53
183 5/8	38	39 3/8	15 4/8	15 4/8	9	9 7/8	21 4/8	21 4/8	Fergus Co., MT	Marvin L. Dahl	Marvin L. Dahl	2000	53
183 4/8	38 7/8	38 3/8	15 7/8	16	8 3/8	8 4/8	22 7/8	19	Fergus Co., MT	Jeffrey M. Shouse	Jeffrey M. Shouse	1999	56
183 3/8	41 1/8	38 2/8	15 6/8	15 6/8	8 3/8	8 6/8	21 2/8	21 2/8	Lewis & Clark Co., MT	Scott A. Van Dyken	Scott A. Van Dyken	1997	57
183 3/8	40 7/8	39	16 2/8	16 2/8	7 5/8	7 5/8	23 4/8	22 6/8	Sanders Co., MT	Nanette M. Cox	Nanette M. Cox	1998	57
183 3/8	40	39 3/8	15 4/8	15 5/8	8 6/8	8 4/8	22 3/8	22 1/8	Granite Co., MT	Richard M. Bardwell	Richard M. Bardwell	2000	57
183	37 2/8	37 2/8	14 5/8	14 4/8	11 2/8	11 4/8	24	22 7/8	Timber Creek, AB	Picked Up	John E. Cassidy	1997	60
183	39	39 4/8	15 7/8	16	8 2/8	8 2/8	22 2/8	21 2/8	Granite Co., MT	Joseph M. Walsh	Joseph M. Walsh	1998	60
183	40 5/8	38 7/8	15 1/8	15 1/8	9 3/8	9 3/8	22 4/8	21 5/8	Granite Co., MT	Carole J. Beebe	Carole J. Beebe	1999	60
182 5/8	34 7/8	37 2/8	16 2/8	16 2/8	9 6/8	10 2/8	20 3/8	15 6/8	Galatea Creek, AB	Leo Ouellette	Leo Ouellette	1998	63
182 5/8	39 7/8	38 4/8	14 4/8	14 4/8	10	10 1/8	21	20 5/8	Mora Co., NM	Robert G. Ringer	Robert G. Ringer	2000	63
182 4/8	37 2/8	39 2/8	16 2/8	16 2/8	8 1/8	8 1/8	23 4/8	23 4/8	Blaine Co., MT	Daniel D. Doran	Daniel D. Doran	1997	65
182 4/8	39	41 2/8	15 2/8	14 7/8	8 7/8	9 3/8	23 5/8	15 5/8	Gregg River, AB	William C. Cloyd	William C. Cloyd	1998	65
182 4/8	39 7/8	40 1/8	14 5/8	14 6/8	9 3/8	9 2/8	21 6/8	21 4/8	Teton Co., MT	Josh B. Johns	Josh B. Johns	1998	65
182 2/8	40	40 6/8	15 7/8	15 7/8	7	7 3/8	20 4/8	20 4/8	Elbow River, AB	Glen R. Pickering	Glen R. Pickering	1998	68
182	39 6/8	41 2/8	14 4/8	14 3/8	9 6/8	10	22 6/8	21 2/8	Catron Co., NM	D. Scott Annala	D. Scott Annala	1997	69
182	36 1/8	37 1/8	15 4/8	15 4/8	10 6/8	10	20 1/8	14 2/8	Elk River, BC	Harry E. Seratt	Harry E. Seratt	1997	69

Score										Locality	Hunter	Owner	Date Killed	Rank
182	39 1/8	40 1/8	15 7/8	15 6/8	7 6/8	7 6/8	15 6/8	23 4/8	23 4/8	Sanders Co., MT	Bernard L. Robinson	Bernard L. Robinson	1998	69
181 7/8	43 4/8	44 3/8	14 7/8	15	6 1/8	5 6/8	15	22 4/8	17 1/8	Missoula Co., MT	Warren W. Dennis	Warren W. Dennis	1997	72
181 6/8	36 4/8	38 2/8	15 7/8	15 5/8	9	8 7/8	15 5/8	23 1/8	22 2/8	Blaine Co., MT	Dennis M. McCleary	Dennis M. McCleary	1997	73
181 6/8	37	37	15 6/8	15 5/8	8 6/8	8 7/8	15 5/8	23	21	Missoula Co., MT	James A. Hoiland	James A. Hoiland	1999	73
181 5/8	37 1/8	37 6/8	16 1/8	16 1/8	8 5/8	8 3/8	16 1/8	23 3/8	22 1/8	Blaine Co., MT	Clifford Wilber	Clifford Wilber	1999	75
181 4/8	38 4/8	39	15 6/8	15 5/8	8 5/8	8 2/8	15 5/8	20 6/8	19 6/8	Kootenay River, BC	Gerry Favreau	Gerry Favreau	1998	76
181 4/8	37 6/8	37 6/8	16 2/8	16 1/8	8 4/8	8 4/8	15 6/8	20	20	Granite Co., MT	Michael D. Swanson	Michael D. Swanson	1999	76
181 3/8	40 3/8	38 6/8	16	15 6/8	7 7/8	7 6/8	15	23 2/8	18 5/8	Teton Co., MT	Chad J. Bouma	Chad J. Bouma	1997	78
181 3/8	37 6/8	37 6/8	14 4/8	14 6/8	10 1/8	10 1/8	14 7/8	20	13 4/8	Panther River, AB	Earl Johnson	Earl Johnson	1998	78
181 3/8	38 1/8	38 1/8	14 6/8	14 6/8	9 5/8	9 1/8	15 5/8	23 2/8	11 3/8	Hinsdale Co., CO	Mary J. Johnson	Mary J. Johnson	2000	78
181 2/8	38 3/8	38 5/8	16 4/8	16 1/8	8	7 4/8	16	19 5/8	17 6/8	Calgary, AB	Max Howard	Max Howard	1990	81
181 2/8	38 2/8	38 6/8	15 4/8	15 4/8	9 3/8	9	15 5/8	21 3/8	19 6/8	Teton Co., MT	Joseph R. Balazs	Joseph R. Balazs	1996	81
181	37 4/8	38 6/8	15 1/8	15	9 2/8	9 6/8	15 3/8	20 5/8	20 2/8	Cadomin, AB	Steven A. Bowick	Steven A. Bowick	1999	83
181	36 6/8	38	15 2/8	15 3/8	9 5/8	9 4/8	14 6/8	21 3/8	19 4/8	Granite Co., MT	Robert W. Ehle	Robert W. Ehle	1999	83
180 7/8	38	38	15 3/8	15 2/8	8 1/8	8 1/8	15	23	13 4/8	Washout Creek, AB	Joseph P. Ambrose	Joseph P. Ambrose	1998	85
180 6/8	39 6/8	39 5/8	15 1/8	15 2/8	9 4/8	9 4/8	15 2/8	22 4/8	21	Sanders Co., MT	Picked Up	MT Dept. of Fish, Wildl., & Parks	1998	86
180 6/8	39	39	15 3/8	15 5/8	8	8 2/8	15 5/8	18 4/8	18	Mt. Solomon, AB	Dennis J. Tucker	Dennis J. Tucker	1998	86
180 4/8	36 2/8	36 2/8	15 7/8	16	10 1/8	9 6/8	16	21 7/8	18 4/8	Elko Co., NV	Picked Up	Shawn Espinosa	1996	88
180 4/8	34 4/8	34 7/8	16	16	10 1/8	10 1/8	16	22 4/8	16	Costilla Co., CO	John M. Gebbia	John M. Gebbia	1999	88
180 4/8	38	38	15 6/8	15 4/8	8 4/8	8 3/8	15 6/8	23 3/8	19 1/8	Columbia Co., WA	Graham G. Weiss	Graham G. Weiss	1999	88
180 3/8	38 5/8	38 3/8	15 5/8	15 5/8	8 5/8	8 4/8	15 5/8	23 2/8	20 3/8	Sanders Co., MT	Sara C. Reeder	Sara C. Reeder	1998	91
180 3/8	38 3/8	39 6/8	15 6/8	15 6/8	7 3/8	7 2/8	15 6/8	22 2/8	22 1/8	Fergus Co., MT	William R. Gibson, Jr.	William R. Gibson, Jr.	1999	91
180 3/8	39 5/8	38 5/8	14 6/8	14 6/8	9 2/8	9 2/8	14 6/8	22 7/8	19 6/8	Fremont Co., WY	John F. Babler	John F. Babler	2000	91
180 2/8	38 7/8	38 3/8	16	15 7/8	10 3/8	10 1/8	16	19 5/8	14 6/8	Mount Kidd, AB	Jay J. Fuller	Jay J. Fuller	2000	91
180 2/8	34 3/8	34 4/8	14 7/8	14 7/8	7 6/8	7 7/8	15	22 2/8	22 2/8	Blaine Co., MT	Roxana L. Laeupple	Roxana L. Laeupple	1997	95
180 2/8	41	40 4/8	15 5/8	15 5/8	7 7/8	8	15 5/8	23	19	Mt. Cornwall, AB	Fred Thomson	Fred Thomson	1997	95
180 2/8	37 7/8	39 5/8	16	16 1/8	9 1/8	8 6/8	16 1/8	21	20	Greenlee Co., AZ	Daniel J. Tout	Daniel J. Tout	1997	95
180 2/8	36 4/8	36	15 5/8	14 6/8	8 6/8	8	15 3/8	22 2/8	16 4/8	Taos Co., NM	George J. Elledge, Sr.	George J. Elledge, Sr.	2000	95
180 2/8	38	38 4/8	15 4/8	15 3/8	9 4/8	9 4/8	14 7/8	21 6/8	16 4/8	Condor Peak, AB	Flint J. Simpson	Flint J. Simpson	2000	95
180 1/8	38 2/8	37	15	15 2/8	9 3/8	9 1/8	15	22 1/8	18 3/8	Mineral Co., MT	Michael P. Hogan	Michael P. Hogan	1999	100
179 2/8	37 7/8	38	15 2/8	15 2/8	9	9 2/8	15 2/8	20 6/8	19 6/8	Taos Co., NM	Blaine M. Hadden	Blaine M. Hadden	1998	101
179 2/8	36 1/8	38 3/8	15 2/8	15 2/8	9	9 5/8	15	21 4/8	18	Ravalli Co., MT	Linda G. Kosnick	Linda G. Kosnick	1998	101
179 1/8	37 5/8	38 5/8	15 7/8	15	7 6/8	7 6/8	15 7/8	22 1/8	21 5/8	Granite Co., MT	John J. Wright	John J. Wright	1997	103
178 3/8	39 6/8	38 3/8	16	15 4/8	8 5/8	8 2/8	16	20 6/8	18 7/8	Granite Co., MT	Loretta Robinson	Loretta Robinson	1998	104
178 2/8	41	34 7/8	15 4/8	15 3/8	8 2/8	8 3/8	15 4/8	21	17 5/8	Sanders Co., MT	John F. Gossman	John F. Gossman	1998	105
177 7/8	37	38 4/8	15 3/8	15 4/8	9	9 7/8	14 7/8	23	17 1/8	Fremont Co., WY	Picked Up	Donald L. Marquiss	1998	106
177 5/8	35 7/8	37	15 4/8	15 4/8	7 5/8	7 6/8	15 4/8	25 4/8	24 5/8	Fremont Co., WY	William T. Jones	William T. Jones	1998	107
177 5/8	39 2/8	40 5/8	15 4/8	15	9 2/8	9 3/8	15	21 4/8	18 4/8	Wallowa Co., OR	Monte E. Davidson	Monte E. Davidson	2000	107
177 4/8	38 5/8	35 4/8	15 2/8	15 4/8	9 3/8	9 5/8	15 3/8	22	18 2/8	Forbidden Creek, AB	Stephanie Hull	Stephanie Hull	1998	109
177 4/8	36 4/8	36 2/8	15 3/8	15 1/8	9 5/8	9 5/8	15 4/8	23	22 6/8	Sanders Co., MT	Carol L. Hagedorn Clay	Carol L. Hagedorn Clay	1999	109
177 2/8	36 4/8	35 4/8	15 1/8	15 2/8	9 2/8	9 6/8	15 1/8	25 6/8	25	Lake Co., OR	Jesse A. McGee	Jesse A. McGee	1998	111
177 2/8	35 1/8	36 3/8	15 2/8	15 1/8	9 5/8	9 7/8	15 2/8	25	24 2/8	Harney Co., OR	Paul R. Guinther	Paul R. Guinther	1999	111

BIGHORN SHEEP

Ovis canadensis canadensis and certain related subspecies

Score	Length of Horn R.	L.	Circumference of Base R.	L.	Circumference at Third Quarter R.	L.	Greatest Spread	Tip to Tip Spread	Locality	Hunter	Owner	Date Killed	Rank
177 1/8	36 1/8	36	16 3/8	16 5/8	7 6/8	7 7/8	22 4/8	22 4/8	Gunnison Co., CO	Phillip C. Pierce	Phillip C. Pierce	1999	113
177 1/8	38 5/8	40	15 1/8	15	7 2/8	8 3/8	24 1/8	22 7/8	Fergus Co., MT	Gregory E. Kessler	Gregory E. Kessler	2000	113
176 4/8	38 3/8	36 1/8	15 2/8	15 3/8	8 2/8	8 3/8	18 4/8	16 2/8	Granite Co., MT	Daniel J. Harrison	Daniel J. Harrison	1999	115
176 3/8	36	35 7/8	15 3/8	15 3/8	8 7/8	8 6/8	20 5/8	15 2/8	Valley Co., ID	Steven S. Bruggeman	Steven S. Bruggeman	1997	116
176 1/8	35 5/8	37 4/8	14 4/8	14 4/8	9 6/8	9 6/8	20 2/8	16	Mt. Drummond, AB	Dallas Maloney	Dallas Maloney	1996	117
176	39 6/8	36 4/8	14 5/8	14 6/8	8 7/8	8 7/8	23	17 2/8	Ravalli Co., MT	Walter R. Sieler	Walter R. Sieler	1998	118
175 7/8	37 7/8	39 4/8	16	16 2/8	6 4/8	6 5/8	20 5/8	20 5/8	Blaine Co., MT	Ann E. Thomas	Ann E. Thomas	2000	119
175 6/8	37 4/8	36 6/8	15	14 6/8	9	8 6/8	20 1/8	14 1/8	Fremont Co., WY	Gayle M. Jacob	Gayle M. Jacob	1997	120
175 6/8	37 5/8	37 5/8	14 7/8	14 6/8	8 6/8	8 6/8	20 4/8	20	Lewis & Clark Co., MT	John R. O'Brien	John R. O'Brien	1997	120
175 6/8	34 7/8	35 7/8	14 7/8	14 7/8	9 6/8	10 3/8	21 2/8	17 2/8	Scalp Creek, AB	Chester Rudolf	Chester Rudolf	1997	120
175 5/8	36	38 1/8	14 5/8	14 5/8	8 7/8	8 6/8	19	19	Missoula Co., MT	Picked Up	MT Dept. of Fish, Wildl., & Parks	2000	123
175 1/8	36 6/8	36 7/8	14 7/8	15	9 2/8	8 7/8	21 2/8	18	Sanders Co., MT	Marvin Rehbein	Marvin Rehbein	1998	124
175	37 4/8	34 4/8	15 3/8	15 2/8	8 3/8	8 5/8	22 1/8	18 6/8	Fremont Co., CO	Robert C. Twohy	Robert C. Twohy	1999	125
204 4/8*	42 4/8	42 4/8	16 4/8	16 5/8	12 1/8	12	23 1/8	21 2/8	Cardinal River, AB	Picked Up	AB Govt. Natl. Resc. Ser.	1998	PR 1997
202*	41 6/8	41 4/8	16 4/8	16 4/8	11 1/8	10 6/8	23 6/8	17	Pennington Co., SD	Picked Up	SD Game, Fish, & Parks Dept.		
200 6/8*	40 7/8	40 7/8	16 6/8	17 1/8	11 3/8	11 3/8	25 3/8	20 7/8	Whitehorse Creek, AB	Todd K. Kirk	Todd K. Kirk	1998	
195 5/8*	42 6/8	43 1/8	16 2/8	16	10 3/8	10 6/8	22 5/8	22 4/8	Mystery Lake, AB	Ross D. Stelter	Ross D. Stelter	1998	
197 7/8*	41	39 7/8	16 4/8	16 5/8	10 6/8	11 5/8	22 2/8	15	Costilla Co., CO	West Ward	West Ward	1998	

* Final score subject to revision by additional verifying measurements.

DESERT SHEEP

Ovis canadensis nelsoni and certain related subspecies

Minimum Score 165 — World's Record 205 1/8

Score	Length of Horn R	L	Circumference of Base R	L	Circumference at Third Quarter R	L	Greatest Spread	Tip to Tip Spread	Locality	Hunter	Owner	Date Killed	Rank
188 4/8	41 2/8	38 4/8	15 7/8	16	9 4/8	10	21 2/8	16 4/8	Grant Co., NM	Picked Up	NM Dept. of Game & Fish	2000	1
178 6/8	35 6/8	36 2/8	15 7/8	16	8 6/8	9 2/8	25 2/8	22 6/8	Sonora, MX	George R. Harms	George R. Harms	2000	2
177 2/8	38 2/8	36 4/8	15 3/8	15 5/8	9	9 3/8	21 7/8	19	Sonora, MX	Anthony J. Conte	Anthony J. Conte	1999	3
176 6/8	38 6/8	37	15	15	9 1/8	9 1/8	21 1/8	16	Yuma Co., AZ	Steven E. Hopkins	Steven E. Hopkins	1998	4
176 1/8	38 2/8	38 3/8	14 5/8	14 6/8	8 4/8	8 6/8	21 3/8	20 7/8	Culberson Co., TX	Daniel F. Boone	Daniel F. Boone	1997	5
174 6/8	36 3/8	37 1/8	15 2/8	15 4/8	8 4/8	8 7/8	24	23	Brewster Co., TX	William W. Britain	William W. Britain	1997	6
174	35 6/8	35 7/8	15 2/8	15 4/8	8 3/8	8 1/8	23 5/8	23 2/8	Sonora, MX	Donald W. Jacklin	Donald W. Jacklin	2000	7
173 6/8	35 3/8	35 7/8	15 4/8	15 4/8	8 5/8	8 6/8	20 5/8	17 5/8	Sonora, MX	Ronald F. Mobley	Ronald F. Mobley	1998	8
173 5/8	36 3/8	35 4/8	15	14 7/8	8 7/8	8 5/8	19 5/8	18 6/8	Baja Calif., MX	Stephen B. Clark	Stephen B. Clark	1999	9
172 7/8	35 3/8	35 2/8	15 4/8	15 5/8	8 7/8	8 7/8	19 2/8	19 2/8	Baja Calif., MX	James G. Petersen	James G. Petersen	2000	10
172 5/8	37 4/8	36 5/8	14 2/8	14 3/8	8 5/8	8 5/8	20	17	Sonora, MX	C. Alan Still	C. Alan Still	2000	11
172 2/8	34 7/8	34 7/8	15 4/8	15 4/8	9 5/8	8 4/8	20 3/8	18 1/8	La Paz Co., AZ	John H. Gannaway	John H. Gannaway	1997	12
172 2/8	36	36	15 2/8	15 4/8	8 4/8	8 7/8	20 6/8	20 6/8	Pima Co., AZ	Wallace H. Duncan	Wallace H. Duncan	1998	12
171 6/8	35 6/8	34 4/8	15	15	9 4/8	9 5/8	22	22	San Bernardino Co., CA	Lee R. Anderson, Jr.	Lee R. Anderson, Jr.	1997	14
171 3/8	37 3/8	37 6/8	14 6/8	14 6/8	8	8 5/8	25 1/8	24	Lincoln Co., NV	Steven C. Hall	Steven C. Hall	1987	15
171 2/8	36 6/8	35 2/8	14 6/8	14 7/8	8 2/8	9	29 6/8	29 6/8	Mohave Co., AZ	Jayson K. Hatfield	Jayson K. Hatfield	1997	16
171 1/8	35 2/8	37 3/8	14	14 2/8	9 4/8	9 1/8	21 1/8	21	Baja Calif., MX	James Gay, Sr.	James B. Sisco III	1974	17
171 1/8	36 7/8	37	14 6/8	14 7/8	8	8 1/8	24 3/8	24	Clark Co., NV	Joel A. McMillin	Joel A. McMillin	1998	17
171 1/8	36 1/8	35 6/8	15 6/8	15 2/8	8 4/8	8 2/8	20 4/8	20 2/8	Baja Calif., MX	Thomas P. Wittmann	Thomas P. Wittmann	2000	17
170 6/8	34 4/8	37 4/8	14 7/8	14 7/8	8 4/8	8 2/8	22 4/8	21 2/8	Clark Co., NV	Timothy H. Humes	Timothy H. Humes	1999	20
170 4/8	38 5/8	38 5/8	14	14	7 6/8	7 6/8	22 6/8	22 6/8	Clark Co., NV	Gregory K. Goodin	Gregory K. Goodin	1997	21
170	33 4/8	33 6/8	15 6/8	15 6/8	8 4/8	8 5/8	18	18	Baja Calif., MX	Dennis C. Campbell	Dennis C. Campbell	1995	22
169 7/8	35 3/8	35 4/8	14 2/8	14 2/8	8 5/8	8 7/8	25 2/8	25 2/8	Mohave Co., AZ	Rita E. Steele	Rita E. Steele	1996	23
169 7/8	34 5/8	35 4/8	15 2/8	15	8 2/8	7 7/8	22 3/8	22 3/8	La Paz Co., AZ	Wilson W. Allen, Jr.	Wilson W. Allen, Jr.	1999	23
169 6/8	35	35	14 6/8	14 6/8	8 3/8	8 5/8	19	16 4/8	Sonora, MX	William R. Pritchard	William R. Pritchard	1999	25
169 5/8	34 2/8	34 3/8	14 6/8	14 5/8	9 1/8	8 7/8	22 3/8	21 6/8	Mohave Co., AZ	James E. Hicks	James E. Hicks	1998	26
169 5/8	35 5/8	35 2/8	14 5/8	14 5/8	8 4/8	8 4/8	23 1/8	22 3/8	Clark Co., NV	Jelindo A. Tiberti II	Jelindo A. Tiberti II	1999	26
169 2/8	35 5/8	34 5/8	15 3/8	15 2/8	7 7/8	8 2/8	20 2/8	18 4/8	Sonora, MX	Timothy K. Krause	Timothy K. Krause	1998	28
169	35 3/8	34 1/8	15 5/8	15 4/8	8	8	20 1/8	12 4/8	Sonora, MX	Marshall J. Collins	Marshall J. Collins	1999	29
169	34 3/8	34 1/8	15 1/8	15 1/8	8 4/8	8 6/8	23 3/8	22 6/8	Mohave Co., AZ	George F. Dennis, Jr.	George F. Dennis, Jr.	1999	29
168 7/8	34 1/8	34 7/8	15 1/8	15 1/8	8 2/8	8 6/8	20 6/8	17 2/8	Sonora, MX	Donald W. Snyder	Donald W. Snyder	1999	31
168 6/8	35 1/8	36 6/8	14 4/8	14 6/8	7 7/8	8	23 2/8	22 6/8	Clark Co., NV	Martha F. Dudley	Martha F. Dudley	1998	32
168 6/8	42 2/8	36 2/8	13	13	8	8	22 2/8	22 2/8	Mohave Co., AZ	Cerene J. Paul	Cerene J. Paul	1998	32
168 5/8	33	32 2/8	15 2/8	15 2/8	9 3/8	9 5/8	19 1/8	19 1/8	Sonora, MX	John M. Gebbia	John M. Gebbia	1998	34
168 2/8	34 5/8	34 6/8	16	16	8 2/8	8 2/8	30 4/8	30 1/8	Mohave Co., AZ	Stephen A. Miller	Stephen A. Miller	1997	35

DESERT SHEEP

Ovis canadensis nelsoni and certain related subspecies

Score	Length of Horn R.	L.	Circumference of Base R.	L.	Circumference at Third Quarter R.	L.	Greatest Spread	Tip to Tip Spread	Locality	Hunter	Owner	Date Killed	Rank
168 2/8	35	34 4/8	14 3/8	14 5/8	8 4/8	8 3/8	23 3/8	23 1/8	Mineral Co., NV	Brenda K. Stinson	Brenda K. Stinson	1997	35
168	33 6/8	36 2/8	13 5/8	13 5/8	9 4/8	9 6/8	21	20 2/8	Clark Co., NV	Gino J. Aramini	Gino J. Aramini	1998	37
167	34 5/8	35 5/8	14 4/8	14 5/8	8 4/8	8	20 3/8	16 1/8	Maricopa Co., AZ	Marleen K. Bynum	Marleen K. Bynum	1999	38
166 7/8	34 7/8	33 4/8	15 4/8	15 4/8	8 2/8	8 5/8	19 5/8	15 2/8	Sonora, MX	Charles C. Conte	Charles C. Conte	1999	39
165 6/8	35 7/8	37 3/8	15 3/8	15 3/8	7	6 5/8	24 4/8	23 7/8	Clark Co., NV	James A. Schneider	James A. Schneider	1999	40
165 5/8	34	34 1/8	14 4/8	14 3/8	9	8 7/8	24 2/8	23 4/8	Sonora, MX	Blaine E. Nimer	Blaine E. Nimer	1997	41
165	33 5/8	34 1/8	14 4/8	14 3/8	8 5/8	8 7/8	20 4/8	20 2/8	Sonora, MX	Robert M. Lee	Robert M. Lee	1998	42
182 2/8*	37 7/8*	37 1/8	16	16	9 1/8	9 2/8	24 1/8	23 5/8	San Bernardino Co., CA	John D. Bauder	John D. Bauder	1999	
181 5/8*	36 3/8*	36 4/8	16	15 7/8	9 6/8	9 6/8	22 1/8	21 5/8	Pima Co., AZ	Marshall G. Varner, Sr.	Marshall G. Varner, Sr.	1993	
181*	39 6/8	37 4/8	15 1/8	15 2/8	8 6/8	8 7/8	23 4/8	23 4/8	Churchill Co., NV	Dennis J. Sites	Dennis J. Sites	1999	
178 2/8*	39 4/8	41	15 1/8	15 4/8	7 6/8	8 2/8	21 6/8	21 3/8	Graham Co., AZ	Jason J. Gisi	Jason J. Gisi	1998	

* Final score subject to revision by additional verifying measurements.

DALL'S SHEEP

Ovis dalli dalli and *Ovis dalli kenaiensis*

Minimum Score 160 World's Record 189 6/8

Score	Length of Horn R.	L.	Circumference of Base R.	L.	Circumference at Third Quarter R.	L.	Greatest Spread	Tip to Tip Spread	Locality	Hunter	Owner	Date Killed	Rank
171 1/8	39 7/8	39 4/8	14 6/8	15	6	6	25	25	Godlin Lakes, NT	Paul Tadlock	Paul Tadlock	1980	1
171 1/8	38 4/8	40 1/8	14	14	7 6/8	7 5/8	21	20 1/8	Blackstone River, YT	Randy Pittman	Randy Pittman	1998	1
171	39	39	14 3/8	14 4/8	6 6/8	6 7/8	22 7/8	22 2/8	Chugach Mts., AK	James P. Driskell	James P. Driskell	1998	3
170 2/8	39 4/8	40	15	15	6 2/8	6 2/8	26	26	Alaska Range, AK	Jon A. Shiesl	Jon A. Shiesl	1988	4
169 7/8	41 2/8	35 3/8	14 4/8	14 5/8	6 6/8	7 1/8	21 3/8	20 6/8	Robertson River, AK	Vincent P. Greear	Vincent P. Greear	1997	5
169 2/8	41	40 6/8	13 6/8	13 6/8	7	7	25	25	Gerstle River, AK	Kenneth B. Ishmael	Kenneth B. Ishmael	1998	6
169 2/8	42 2/8	38 6/8	14 2/8	14 4/8	5 6/8	6 3/8	22 7/8	22 3/8	Ogilvie Mts., YT	Robert A. Shosted	Robert A. Shosted	1998	6
168 3/8	38 4/8	39 3/8	14 3/8	14 2/8	7	6 7/8	24	23 2/8	Aishihik Lake, YT	Marianne P. LeSage	Marianne P. LeSage	1999	8
167 3/8	39 5/8	37 6/8	14 4/8	14 5/8	6	6 1/8	20 2/8	20 2/8	The Mitre, AK	Lou Ann Bruner	Lou Ann Bruner	1996	9
167 2/8	38 2/8	38 6/8	14 4/8	14 2/8	6	6 1/8	24 3/8	24 3/8	Chugach Mts., AK	Ron Kotarski	Gina Kotarski	1998	10
166 6/8	40 7/8	40 7/8	13 4/8	13 4/8	6 5/8	6 2/8	25 7/8	25 7/8	Brooks Range, AK	Mike L. Billings	Mike L. Billings	2000	11
166 5/8	37 7/8	41 2/8	14 1/8	14 1/8	6 1/8	6 1/8	29	28 4/8	Mountain River, NT	Herb Klima	Herb Klima	1999	12
165 5/8	37 2/8	35 5/8	13 5/8	13 5/8	8 1/8	8 1/8	19 4/8	19	Castner Glacier, AK	Donny D. Bunselmeier	Donny D. Bunselmeier	2000	13
165 1/8	39 1/8	37 4/8	13 7/8	13 6/8	6 2/8	6 2/8	22 2/8	22	Chugach Mts., AK	Hubert R. Kennedy	Hubert R. Kennedy	1999	14
165 1/8	40 1/8	40 6/8	13 5/8	13 5/8	5 5/8	5 5/8	27 3/8	27 3/8	Timber Creek, AK	Edward J. Deichmeister	Edward J. Deichmeister	2000	14
165	39 5/8	38 7/8	14 3/8	14 1/8	5 3/8	5 4/8	25 6/8	25 6/8	Jo-Jo Lake, YT	Gerald S. Laurino	Gerald S. Laurino	1998	16
165	40 4/8	40 2/8	13 6/8	13 6/8	5 2/8	5 2/8	23 7/8	23 6/8	Ship Creek, AK	John R. Booher	John R. Booher	1999	16
164 6/8	38 4/8	40 4/8	14 2/8	14 4/8	5 1/8	5 5/8	23 7/8	23 3/8	Grayling Lake, AK	Jack R. Tindall	Jack R. Tindall	1998	18
164 5/8	36 5/8	36 2/8	14 1/8	13 6/8	6 6/8	6 6/8	26 2/8	24 6/8	Norman Wells, NT	Bryan B. Collier	Bryan B. Collier	1997	19
164 2/8	40	39 4/8	13 7/8	13 7/8	5 5/8	5 4/8	29 1/8	28 7/8	Ruby Range, YT	George G. Wasser	George D. Wasser	1967	20
164 1/8	40 1/8	41	13 6/8	13 7/8	5 5/8	5 4/8	30 2/8	30 2/8	Nisling Range, YT	John Tautin, Jr.	John Tautin, Jr.	1986	21
163 7/8	39 1/8	38 2/8	13 7/8	14	5 7/8	5 6/8	24 4/8	24 4/8	Mackenzie Mts., NT	Mike Harrison	Mike Harrison	1998	22
163 6/8	41	40 6/8	13 4/8	13 4/8	5 2/8	5 2/8	28 4/8	28 4/8	Mackenzie Mts., NT	Kevin D. Peterson	Kevin D. Peterson	1998	23
162 7/8	39 5/8	39 6/8	13 2/8	13 4/8	5 7/8	5 7/8	23 3/8	23 3/8	Pioneer Peak, AK	Wade M. Peterson	Wade M. Peterson	1996	24
162 3/8	40 4/8	40 5/8	13 1/8	13 4/8	5 7/8	5 7/8	25	24 6/8	Takhini River, YT	James R. Aubel	James R. Aubel	1997	25
162 3/8	36 2/8	36 7/8	13 5/8	13 7/8	6 7/8	6 4/8	24 3/8	24	Eklutna River, AK	John R. Linnell	John R. Linnell	2000	25
162 3/8	37 3/8	37 4/8	13 1/8	13 3/8	7	7	23	22 6/8	Aishihik Lake, YT	Axel Strakeljahn	Axel Strakeljahn	2000	25
161 5/8	36 3/8	37	13 5/8	13 6/8	7 4/8	7 2/8	24	24	Tazlina Glacier, AK	Robert Paige	David P. Moore	1961	28
161 4/8	39	39 2/8	13 2/8	13 2/8	6	6	25 4/8	25 4/8	Arctic Red River, NT	Harold J. Humes	Harold J. Humes	1998	29
161 3/8	37 6/8	38 1/8	14	14 1/8	5	5 2/8	21	20 6/8	Eklutna River, AK	Jerome L. Soukup	Jerome L. Soukup	2000	30
160 6/8	39 4/8	40	13 4/8	13 6/8	5 2/8	6 1/8	21 5/8	21 3/8	Eklutna River, AK	Dennis R. Linnell	Dennis R. Linnell	2000	31
160 4/8	40 4/8	38 6/8	12 1/8	12 1/8	6 4/8	6 7/8	26 6/8	26 6/8	Johnson Glacier, AK	Donald W. Bunselmeier	Donald W. Bunselmeier	1996	32
160 2/8	38 4/8	36 4/8	12 5/8	12 5/8	7 6/8	7 4/8	19	20 1/8	Mackenzie Mts., NT	Wes C. Talbert	Wes C. Talbert	2000	33
177*	41 6/8	41 4/8	15	15	6 7/8	7	23 6/8	23 3/8	Chugach Mts., AK	Richard Ballow	R. & C. Ballow	1997	
174 4/8* 42	43 2/8		14 2/8	14 2/8	6 2/8	6 3/8	23 7/8	23 5/8	Chugach Mts., AK	Curt D. Menard	Curt D. Menard	1998	

DALL'S SHEEP

Ovis dalli dalli and *Ovis dalli kenaiensis*

Score	Length of Horn R.	L.	Circumference of Base R.	L.	Circumference at Third Quarter R.	L.	Greatest Spread	Tip to Tip Spread	Locality	Hunter	Owner	Date Killed	Rank
174 1/8*	41 5/8	42	13 6/8	13 6/8	6 6/8	6 6/8	23	23	Ship Creek, AK	Dick A. Jacobs	Dick A. Jacobs	1999	
173*	42 6/8	40	15	14 7/8	5 6/8	6	24 3/8	22 3/8	Aishihik Lake, YT	Fred K. Koken	Fred K. Koken	1998	
171 3/8*	41 3/8	41 6/8	14 3/8	14 4/8	6	5 7/8	26 1/8	26 4/8	Takhini River, BC	Abe J.N. Dougan	Abe J.N. Dougan	1999	

* Final score subject to revision by additional verifying measurements.

STONE'S SHEEP

Ovis dalli stonei

Minimum Score 165

World's Record 196 6/8

Score	Length of Horn R.	L.	Circumference of Base R.	L.	Circumference at Third Quarter R.	L.	Greatest Spread	Tip to Tip Spread	Locality	Hunter	Owner	Date Killed	Rank
170 7/8	39 7/8	41	14	13 7/8	6 6/8	6 7/8	19 6/8	19 6/8	Toad River, BC	Rick G. Ferrara	Rick G. Ferrara	1998	1
170 5/8	40	41 1/8	14 6/8	14 6/8	5 5/8	6 1/8	25 6/8	25 4/8	Gathto Creek, BC	Steven J. LaFleur	Steven J. LaFleur	1999	2
170 5/8	39 3/8	40 2/8	14	14 1/8	7 5/8	8	23 2/8	22 2/8	McDonald Creek, BC	Joel D. Bedgood	Joel D. Bedgood	2000	2
170 4/8	42 3/8	42 3/8	14 2/8	14 2/8	5 7/8	5 5/8	22 6/8	21 3/8	Ice Lake, YT	Steven C. Rudd	Steven C. Rudd	1999	4
170 2/8	41	42 4/8	14 2/8	14 1/8	5 5/8	5 6/8	32 2/8	32 2/8	Pelly Mts., YT	Dennis L. Merrey	Dennis L. Merrey	1999	5
170 1/8	40 1/8	40 2/8	14	14	6	6 1/8	23 5/8	23 5/8	Toad River, BC	Timothy K. Krause	Timothy K. Krause	1997	6
168 6/8	40 6/8	39	14 4/8	14 6/8	6 4/8	6 2/8	21 5/8	21 4/8	Toad River, BC	Thomas P. Powers	Thomas P. Powers	1998	7
166 7/8	38 1/8	38 4/8	14	14	7 1/8	7 4/8	23	22 2/8	Muskwa River, BC	Greg Shuttleworth	Greg Shuttleworth	1998	8
165 6/8	40 6/8	39 6/8	13 6/8	13 6/8	5 7/8	5 7/8	25 7/8	25 5/8	West Toad River, BC	Chad Smith	Chad Smith	1998	9
165 2/8	36 4/8	39 6/8	13 7/8	13 6/8	6 6/8	6 6/8	24 4/8	24 2/8	Kechika River, BC	James D. Jurad	James D. Jurad	1999	10
165	41	33 2/8	14 2/8	14 2/8	7	6 6/8	20 6/8	20 6/8	Muskwa River, BC	Al Kuntz	Al Kuntz	2000	11
182 6/8*	43 5/8	43 7/8	15 5/8	15 2/8	6 4/8	6 3/8	24 6/8	24 6/8	Tuchodi Lakes, BC	Aldo Guglielmini	Aldo Guglielmini	1998	
172 7/8*	42 3/8	39 6/8	13 7/8	14	6 3/8	6 3/8	22 5/8	22 5/8	McDonald Creek, BC	Rod Parkin	Rod Parkin	1997	
172 7/8*	42 7/8	42 4/8	13 7/8	13 7/8	6 4/8	6 4/8	27 1/8	27 1/8	Coal Creek, YT	Dennis C. Campbell	Dennis C. Campbell	1998	
171 6/8*	40 5/8	42 7/8	14 5/8	14 5/8	5 5/8	5 5/8	23 2/8	23	Scoop Lake, BC	Craig A. Miller	Craig A. Miller	1998	

* Final score subject to revision by additional verifying measurements.

OFFICIAL SCORE CHARTS FOR NORTH AMERICAN BIG GAME TROPHIES

250 Station Drive
Missoula, MT 59801
(406) 542-1888

BOONE AND CROCKETT CLUB®

OFFICIAL SCORING SYSTEM FOR NORTH AMERICAN BIG GAME TROPHIES

BEAR

	MINIMUM SCORES	
	AWARDS	ALL-TIME
black bear	20	21
grizzly bear	23	24
Alaska brown bear	26	28
polar bear	27	27

KIND OF BEAR (check one)
☐ black bear
☒ grizzly
☐ Alaska brown bear
☐ polar

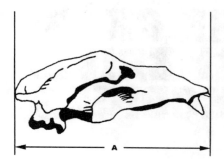

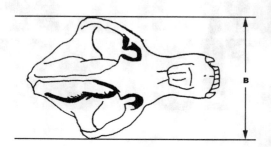

SEE OTHER SIDE FOR INSTRUCTIONS	MEASUREMENTS
A. Greatest Length Without Lower Jaw	16 11/16
B. Greatest Width	10 10/16
FINAL SCORE	27 5/16

Exact Locality Where Killed: Toklat River, Alaska

Date Killed: 9/14/99   Hunter: David F. Malzac

Owner: David F. Malzac   Telephone #:

Owner's Address:

Guide's Name and Address:

Remarks: (Mention Any Abnormalities or Unique Qualities)

I, _____ Robert A. Black _____ , certify that I have measured this trophy on ___ 05/05/2001 ___
    PRINT NAME   MM/DD/YYYYY

at _____ Bass Pro Shops   Springfield, Missouri _____
    STREET ADDRESS   CITY   STATE/PROVINCE

and that these measurements and data are, to the best of my knowledge and belief, made in accordance with the instructions given.

Witness: _____ Larry Streiff _____   Signature: _____ Robert A. Black _____   I.D. Number [ ][ ][ ][ ]
                                                    B&C OFFICIAL MEASURER

COPYRIGHT © 2000 BY BOONE AND CROCKETT CLUB®

INSTRUCTIONS FOR MEASURING BEAR

Measurements are taken with calipers or by using parallel perpendiculars, to the nearest **one-sixteenth** of an inch, without reduction of fractions. Official measurements cannot be taken until the skull has air dried for at least 60 days after the animal was killed. All adhering flesh, membrane and cartilage must be completely removed **before** official measurements are taken.

A. Greatest Length is measured between perpendiculars parallel to the long axis of the skull, without the lower jaw and excluding malformations.

B. Greatest Width is measured between perpendiculars at right angles to the long axis.

ENTRY AFFIDAVIT FOR ALL HUNTER-TAKEN TROPHIES

For the purpose of entry into the Boone and Crockett Club's® records, North American big game harvested by the use of the following methods or under the following conditions are ineligible:

I. Spotting or herding game from the air, followed by landing in its vicinity for the purpose of pursuit and shooting;
II. Herding or chasing with the aid of any motorized equipment;
III. Use of electronic communication devices, artificial lighting, or electronic light intensifying devices;
IV. Confined by artificial barriers, including escape-proof fenced enclosures;
V. Transplanted for the purpose of commercial shooting;
VI. By the use of traps or pharmaceuticals;
VII. While swimming, helpless in deep snow, or helpless in any other natural or artificial medium;
VIII. On another hunter's license;
IX. Not in full compliance with the game laws or regulations of the federal government or of any state, province, territory, or tribal council on reservations or tribal lands;

Please answer the following questions:

Were dogs used in conjunction with the pursuit and harvest of this animal?
☐ Yes   ☒ No

If the answer to the above question is yes, answer the following statements:

1. I was present on the hunt at the times the dogs were released to pursue this animal.
☐ True ☐ False

2. If electronic collars were attached to any of the dogs, receivers were not used to harvest this animal.
☐ True ☐ False

To the best of my knowledge the answers to the above statements are true. If the answer to either #1 or #2 above is false, please explain on a separate sheet.

I certify that the trophy scored on this chart was not taken in violation of the conditions listed above. In signing this statement, I understand that if the information provided on this entry is found to be misrepresented or fraudulent in any respect, it will not be accepted into the Awards Program and 1) all of my prior entries are subject to deletion from future editions of **Records of North American Big Game** 2) future entries may not be accepted.

FAIR CHASE, as defined by the Boone and Crockett Club®, is the ethical, sportsmanlike and lawful pursuit and taking of any free-ranging wild, native North American big game animal in a manner that does not give the hunter an improper advantage over such game animals.

The Boone and Crockett Club® may exclude the entry of any animal that it deems to have been taken in an unethical manner or under conditions deemed inappropriate by the Club.

Date:_____ Signature of Hunter:_____
(SIGNATURE MUST BE WITNESSED BY AN OFFICIAL MEASURER OR A NOTARY PUBLIC.)

Date:_____ Signature of Notary or Official Measurer:_____

250 Station Drive
Missoula, MT 59801
(406) 542-1888

BOONE AND CROCKETT CLUB®

OFFICIAL SCORING SYSTEM FOR NORTH AMERICAN BIG GAME TROPHIES

COUGAR AND JAGUAR

	MINIMUM SCORES		
	AWARDS	ALL-TIME	
cougar	14 - 8/16	15	
jaguar	14 - 8/16	14 - 8/16	

KIND OF CAT (check one)

☒ cougar

☐ jaguar

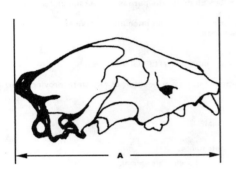

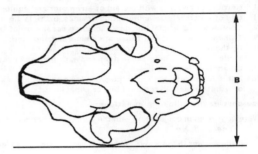

SEE OTHER SIDE FOR INSTRUCTIONS	MEASUREMENTS
A. Greatest Length Without Lower Jaw	9 5/16
B. Greatest Width	6 10/16
FINAL SCORE	15 15/16

Exact Locality Where Killed: Hinton, Alberta

Date Killed: 12/23/99   **Hunter:** Roy LePage

Owner: Roy LePage   **Telephone #:**

Owner's Address:

Guide's Name and Address:

Remarks: (Mention Any Abnormalities or Unique Qualities)

I, _____ Jack Reneau _____ , certify that I have measured this trophy on _____ 05/09/2001
                        PRINT NAME   MM/DD/YYYYY

at _____ Bass Pro Shops   Springfield, Missouri _____
    STREET ADDRESS   CITY   STATE/PROVINCE

and that these measurements and data are, to the best of my knowledge and belief, made in accordance with the instructions given.

Witness: ____ C. Randall Byers ____   **Signature:** ____ Jack Reneau ____   **I.D. Number**
                                                                    B&C OFFICIAL MEASURER

INSTRUCTIONS FOR MEASURING COUGAR AND JAGUAR

Measurements are taken with calipers or by using parallel perpendiculars, to the nearest **one-sixteenth** of an inch, without reduction of fractions. Official measurements cannot be taken until the skull has air dried for at least 60 days after the animal was killed. All adhering flesh, membrane and cartilage must be completely removed **before** official measurements are taken.

- **A. Greatest Length** is measured between perpendiculars parallel to the long axis of the skull, without the lower jaw and excluding malformations.
- **B. Greatest Width** is measured between perpendiculars at right angles to the long axis.

ENTRY AFFIDAVIT FOR ALL HUNTER-TAKEN TROPHIES

For the purpose of entry into the Boone and Crockett Club's® records, North American big game harvested by the use of the following methods or under the following conditions are ineligible:

- I. Spotting or herding game from the air, followed by landing in its vicinity for the purpose of pursuit and shooting;
- II. Herding or chasing with the aid of any motorized equipment;
- III. Use of electronic communication devices, artificial lighting, or electronic light intensifying devices;
- IV. Confined by artificial barriers, including escape-proof fenced enclosures;
- V. Transplanted for the purpose of commercial shooting;
- VI. By the use of traps or pharmaceuticals;
- VII. While swimming, helpless in deep snow, or helpless in any other natural or artificial medium;
- VIII. On another hunter's license;
- IX. Not in full compliance with the game laws or regulations of the federal government or of any state, province, territory, or tribal council on reservations or tribal lands;

Please answer the following questions:

Were dogs used in conjunction with the pursuit and harvest of this animal?
☒ **Yes**   ☐ **No**

If the answer to the above question is yes, answer the following statements:

1. I was present on the hunt at the times the dogs were released to pursue this animal.
   ☒ **True** ☐ **False**
2. If electronic collars were attached to any of the dogs, receivers were not used to harvest this animal.
   ☒ **True** ☐ **False**

To the best of my knowledge the answers to the above statements are true. If the answer to either #1 or #2 above is false, please explain on a separate sheet.

I certify that the trophy scored on this chart was not taken in violation of the conditions listed above. In signing this statement, I understand that if the information provided on this entry is found to be misrepresented or fraudulent in any respect, it will not be accepted into the Awards Program and 1) all of my prior entries are subject to deletion from future editions of **Records of North American Big Game** 2) future entries may not be accepted.

FAIR CHASE, as defined by the Boone and Crockett Club®, is the ethical, sportsmanlike and lawful pursuit and taking of any free-ranging wild, native North American big game animal in a manner that does not give the hunter an improper advantage over such game animals.

The Boone and Crockett Club® may exclude the entry of any animal that it deems to have been taken in an unethical manner or under conditions deemed inappropriate by the Club.

Date:_____ Signature of Hunter:_____

(SIGNATURE MUST BE WITNESSED BY AN OFFICIAL MEASURER OR A NOTARY PUBLIC.)

Date:_____ Signature of Notary or Official Measurer:_____

250 Station Drive
Missoula, MT 59801
(406) 542-1888

BOONE AND CROCKETT CLUB®
OFFICIAL SCORING SYSTEM FOR NORTH AMERICAN BIG GAME TROPHIES

WALRUS

	MINIMUM SCORES	
	AWARDS	ALL-TIME
Atlantic	95	95
Pacific	100	100

KIND OF WALRUS (check one)
- ☒ Atlantic
- ☐ Pacific

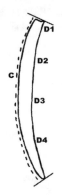

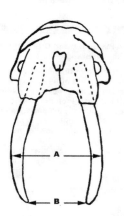

SEE OTHER SIDE FOR INSTRUCTIONS		COLUMN 1	COLUMN 2	COLUMN 3
A. Greatest Spread (If possible)	10 2/8	Right Tusk	Left Tusk	Difference
B. Tip to Tip Spread (If possible)	9 2/8			
C. Entire Length of Loose Tusk		22	22 2/8	2/8
D-1. Circumference of Base		6 5/8	6 7/8	2/8
D-2. Circumference at First Quarter		7 3/8	7 7/8	4/8
D-3. Circumference at Second Quarter		6 5/8	6 7/8	2/8
D-4. Circumference at Third Quarter		5 1/8	5 2/8	1/8
TOTALS		47 6/8	49 1/8	1 3/8

ADD	Column 1	47 6/8	Exact Locality Where Killed: Foxe Basin, NT
	Column 2	49 1/8	Date Killed: 08/16/1996 Hunter: Archie J. Nesbitt
	Subtotal	96 7/8	Owner: Archie J. Nesbitt Telephone #:
	SUBTRACT Column 3	1 3/8	Owner's Address:
FINAL SCORE		95 4/8	Guide's Name and Address:
			Remarks: (Mention Any Abnormalities or Unique Qualities)

I, _____ David R. Coupland _____ , certify that I have measured this trophy on _____ 12/12/1996 _____
        PRINT NAME   MM/DD/YYYYY

at _____ 2005 - 355 4th Avenue S.W., Calgary, Alberta _____
   STREET ADDRESS   CITY   STATE/PROVINCE

and that these measurements and data are, to the best of my knowledge and belief, made in accordance with the instructions given.

Witness: _____ Signature: _____ David R. Coupland _____ I.D. Number [ ][ ][ ][ ]
                                              B&C OFFICIAL MEASURER

COPYRIGHT © 2000 BY BOONE AND CROCKETT CLUB®

INSTRUCTIONS FOR MEASURING WALRUS

All measurements must be made with a 1/4-inch wide flexible steel tape to the nearest one-eighth of an inch. Enter fractional figures in eighths, without reduction. Tusks **should** be removed from mounted specimens for measuring. Official measurements cannot be taken until tusks have air dried for at least 60 days after the animal was killed.

   A. Greatest spread is measured between perpendiculars at a right angle to the center line of the skull.
   B. Tip to Tip Spread is measured between tips of tusks.
   C. Entire Length of Loose Tusk is measured over outer curve from a point in line with the greatest projecting edge of the base to a point in line with tip.
   D-1. Circumference of Base is measured at a right angle to axis of tusk. **Do not** follow irregular edge of tusk; the line of measurement must be entirely on tusk material.
   D-2-3-4. Divide length of longer tusk by four. Starting at base, mark **both** tusks at these quarters (even though the other tusk is shorter) and measure circumferences at these marks.

ENTRY AFFIDAVIT FOR ALL HUNTER-TAKEN TROPHIES

For the purpose of entry into the Boone and Crockett Club's® records, North American big game harvested by the use of the following methods or under the following conditions are ineligible:

   I. Spotting or herding game from the air, followed by landing in its vicinity for the purpose of pursuit and shooting;
   II. Herding or chasing with the aid of any motorized equipment;
   III. Use of electronic communication devices, artificial lighting, or electronic light intensifying devices;
   IV. Confined by artificial barriers, including escape-proof fenced enclosures;
   V. Transplanted for the purpose of commercial shooting;
   VI. By the use of traps or pharmaceuticals;
   VII. While swimming, helpless in deep snow, or helpless in any other natural or artificial medium;
   VIII. On another hunter's license;
   IX. Not in full compliance with the game laws or regulations of the federal government or of any state, province, territory, or tribal council on reservations or tribal lands;

I certify that the trophy scored on this chart was not taken in violation of the conditions listed above. In signing this statement, I understand that if the information provided on this entry is found to be misrepresented or fraudulent in any respect, it will not be accepted into the Awards Program and 1) all of my prior entries are subject to deletion from future editions of **Records of North American Big Game** 2) future entries may not be accepted.

FAIR CHASE, as defined by the Boone and Crockett Club®, is the ethical, sportsmanlike and lawful pursuit and taking of any free-ranging wild, native North American big game animal in a manner that does not give the hunter an improper advantage over such game animals.

The Boone and Crockett Club® may exclude the entry of any animal that it deems to have been taken in an unethical manner or under conditions deemed inappropriate by the Club.

Date:_____ Signature of Hunter:_____
                             (SIGNATURE MUST BE WITNESSED BY AN OFFICIAL MEASURER OR A NOTARY PUBLIC.)

Date:_____ Signature of Notary or Official Measurer:_____

Records of North American Big Game

250 Station Drive
Missoula, MT 59801
(406) 542-1888

BOONE AND CROCKETT CLUB®
OFFICIAL SCORING SYSTEM FOR NORTH AMERICAN BIG GAME TROPHIES

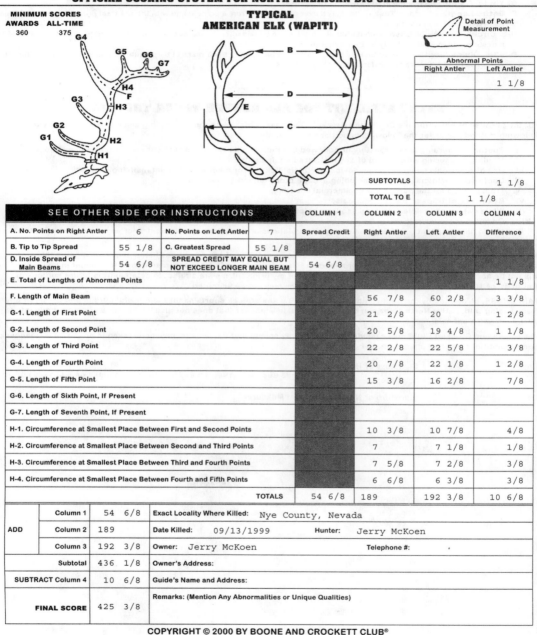

TYPICAL AMERICAN ELK (WAPITI)

MINIMUM SCORES
AWARDS 360
ALL-TIME 375

Detail of Point Measurement

Abnormal Points		
	Right Antler	Left Antler
		1 1/8
SUBTOTALS		1 1/8
TOTAL TO E	1 1/8	

SEE OTHER SIDE FOR INSTRUCTIONS			COLUMN 1	COLUMN 2	COLUMN 3	COLUMN 4
A. No. Points on Right Antler	6	No. Points on Left Antler	7	Spread Credit	Right Antler	Left Antler	Difference
B. Tip to Tip Spread	55 1/8	C. Greatest Spread	55 1/8				
D. Inside Spread of Main Beams	54 6/8	SPREAD CREDIT MAY EQUAL BUT NOT EXCEED LONGER MAIN BEAM		54 6/8			
E. Total of Lengths of Abnormal Points							1 1/8
F. Length of Main Beam					56 7/8	60 2/8	3 3/8
G-1. Length of First Point					21 2/8	20	1 2/8
G-2. Length of Second Point					20 5/8	19 4/8	1 1/8
G-3. Length of Third Point					22 2/8	22 5/8	3/8
G-4. Length of Fourth Point					20 7/8	22 1/8	1 2/8
G-5. Length of Fifth Point					15 3/8	16 2/8	7/8
G-6. Length of Sixth Point, If Present							
G-7. Length of Seventh Point, If Present							
H-1. Circumference at Smallest Place Between First and Second Points					10 3/8	10 7/8	4/8
H-2. Circumference at Smallest Place Between Second and Third Points					7	7 1/8	1/8
H-3. Circumference at Smallest Place Between Third and Fourth Points					7 5/8	7 2/8	3/8
H-4. Circumference at Smallest Place Between Fourth and Fifth Points					6 6/8	6 3/8	3/8
		TOTALS	54 6/8	189	192 3/8	10 6/8

	Column 1	54 6/8	Exact Locality Where Killed: Nye County, Nevada
ADD	Column 2	189	Date Killed: 09/13/1999 Hunter: Jerry McKoen
	Column 3	192 3/8	Owner: Jerry McKoen Telephone #:
	Subtotal	436 1/8	Owner's Address:
SUBTRACT Column 4		10 6/8	Guide's Name and Address:
FINAL SCORE		425 3/8	Remarks: (Mention Any Abnormalities or Unique Qualities)

COPYRIGHT © 2000 BY BOONE AND CROCKETT CLUB®

I, _____ Timothy H. Humes _____ , certify that I have measured this trophy on _____ 11/22/1999 _____
PRINT NAME   MM/DD/YYYYY

at _____ 1100 Valley Road, Reno, Nevada _____
STREET ADDRESS   CITY   STATE/PROVINCE

and that these measurements and data are, to the best of my knowledge and belief, made in accordance with the instructions given.

Witness: _____ San Juan Stiver _____   Signature: _____ Timothy H. Humes _____   I.D. Number
                                                          B&C OFFICIAL MEASURER

INSTRUCTIONS FOR MEASURING TYPICAL AMERICAN ELK (WAPITI)

All measurements must be made with a 1/4-inch wide flexible steel tape to the nearest one-eighth of an inch. (Note: A flexible steel cable can be used to measure points and main beams only.) Enter fractional figures in eighths, without reduction. Official measurements cannot be taken until the antlers have air dried for at least 60 days after the animal was killed.

A. **Number of Points on Each Antler:** To be counted a point, the projection must be at least one inch long, with length exceeding width at one inch or more of length. All points are measured from tip of point to nearest edge of beam as illustrated. Beam tip is counted as a point but not measured as a point.

B. **Tip to Tip Spread** is measured between tips of main beams.

C. **Greatest Spread** is measured between perpendiculars at a right angle to the center line of the skull at widest part, whether across main beams or points.

D. **Inside Spread of Main Beams** is measured at a right angle to the center line of the skull at widest point between main beams. Enter this measurement again as the Spread Credit if it is less than or equal to the length of the longer main beam; if greater, enter longer main beam length for Spread Credit.

E. **Total of Lengths of all Abnormal Points:** Abnormal Points are those non-typical in location (such as points originating from a point or from bottom or sides of main beam) or pattern (extra points, not generally paired). Measure in usual manner and record in appropriate blanks.

F. **Length of Main Beam** is measured from the center of the lowest outside edge of burr over the outer side to the most distant point of the main beam. The point of beginning is that point on the burr where the center line along the outer side of the beam intersects the burr, then following generally the line of the illustration.

G-1-2-3-4-5-6-7. **Length of Normal Points:** Normal points project from the top or front of the main beam in the general pattern illustrated. They are measured from nearest edge of main beam over outer curve to tip. Lay the tape along the outer curve of the beam so that the top edge of the tape coincides with the top edge of the beam on both sides of point to determine the baseline for point measurement. Record point length in appropriate blanks.

H-1-2-3-4. **Circumferences** are taken as detailed in illustration for each measurement.

ENTRY AFFIDAVIT FOR ALL HUNTER-TAKEN TROPHIES

For the purpose of entry into the Boone and Crockett Club's® records, North American big game harvested by the use of the following methods or under the following conditions are ineligible:

I.   Spotting or herding game from the air, followed by landing in its vicinity for the purpose of pursuit and shooting;
II. Herding or chasing with the aid of any motorized equipment;
III. Use of electronic communication devices, artificial lighting, or electronic light intensifying devices;
IV. Confined by artificial barriers, including escape-proof fenced enclosures;
V.   Transplanted for the purpose of commercial shooting;
VI. By the use of traps or pharmaceuticals;
VII. While swimming, helpless in deep snow, or helpless in any other natural or artificial medium;
VIII. On another hunter's license;
IX. Not in full compliance with the game laws or regulations of the federal government or of any state, province, territory, or tribal council on reservations or tribal lands;

I certify that the trophy scored on this chart was not taken in violation of the conditions listed above. In signing this statement, I understand that if the information provided on this entry is found to be misrepresented or fraudulent in any respect, it will not be accepted into the Awards Program and 1) all of my prior entries are subject to deletion from future editions of **Records of North American Big Game** 2) future entries may not be accepted.

FAIR CHASE, as defined by the Boone and Crockett Club®, is the ethical, sportsmanlike and lawful pursuit and taking of any free-ranging wild, native North American big game animal in a manner that does not give the hunter an improper advantage over such game animals.

The Boone and Crockett Club® may exclude the entry of any animal that it deems to have been taken in an unethical manner or under conditions deemed inappropriate by the Club.

Date: _____ Signature of Hunter: _____
                                  (SIGNATURE MUST BE WITNESSED BY AN OFFICIAL MEASURER OR A NOTARY PUBLIC.)

Date: _____ Signature of Notary or Official Measurer: _____

250 Station Drive
Missoula, MT 59801
(406) 542-1888

BOONE AND CROCKETT CLUB®
OFFICIAL SCORING SYSTEM FOR NORTH AMERICAN BIG GAME TROPHIES

NON-TYPICAL
AMERICAN ELK (WAPITI)

MINIMUM SCORES
AWARDS ALL-TIME
385   385

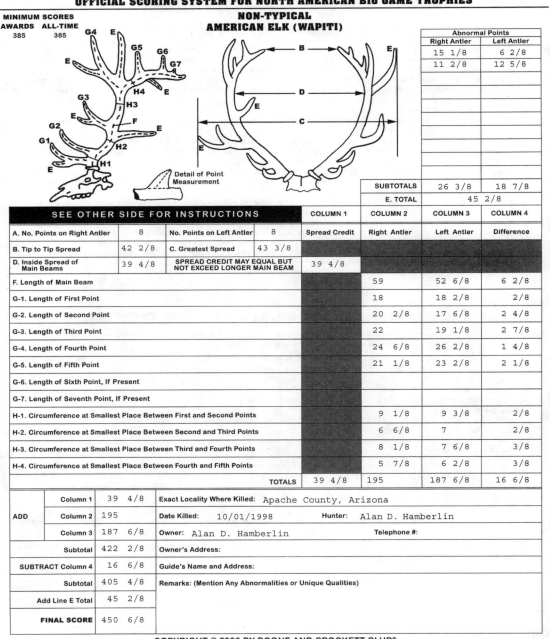

Detail of Point Measurement

Abnormal Points	
Right Antler	Left Antler
15 1/8	6 2/8
11 2/8	12 5/8
SUBTOTALS 26 3/8	18 7/8
E. TOTAL 45 2/8	

SEE OTHER SIDE FOR INSTRUCTIONS			COLUMN 1	COLUMN 2	COLUMN 3	COLUMN 4
			Spread Credit	Right Antler	Left Antler	Difference
A. No. Points on Right Antler	8	No. Points on Left Antler	8			
B. Tip to Tip Spread	42 2/8	C. Greatest Spread	43 3/8			
D. Inside Spread of Main Beams	39 4/8	SPREAD CREDIT MAY EQUAL BUT NOT EXCEED LONGER MAIN BEAM	39 4/8			
F. Length of Main Beam				59	52 6/8	6 2/8
G-1. Length of First Point				18	18 2/8	2/8
G-2. Length of Second Point				20 2/8	17 6/8	2 4/8
G-3. Length of Third Point				22	19 1/8	2 7/8
G-4. Length of Fourth Point				24 6/8	26 2/8	1 4/8
G-5. Length of Fifth Point				21 1/8	23 2/8	2 1/8
G-6. Length of Sixth Point, If Present						
G-7. Length of Seventh Point, If Present						
H-1. Circumference at Smallest Place Between First and Second Points				9 1/8	9 3/8	2/8
H-2. Circumference at Smallest Place Between Second and Third Points				6 6/8	7	2/8
H-3. Circumference at Smallest Place Between Third and Fourth Points				8 1/8	7 6/8	3/8
H-4. Circumference at Smallest Place Between Fourth and Fifth Points				5 7/8	6 2/8	3/8
TOTALS			39 4/8	195	187 6/8	16 6/8

ADD	Column 1	39 4/8	Exact Locality Where Killed: Apache County, Arizona
	Column 2	195	Date Killed: 10/01/1998 Hunter: Alan D. Hamberlin
	Column 3	187 6/8	Owner: Alan D. Hamberlin Telephone #:
	Subtotal	422 2/8	Owner's Address:
SUBTRACT Column 4		16 6/8	Guide's Name and Address:
	Subtotal	405 4/8	Remarks: (Mention Any Abnormalities or Unique Qualities)
Add Line E Total		45 2/8	
FINAL SCORE		450 6/8	

COPYRIGHT © 2000 BY BOONE AND CROCKETT CLUB®

I, _____ John L. Stein _____ , certify that I have measured this trophy on ___ 05/05/2001 ___

PRINT NAME   MM/DD/YYYYY

at _____ Bass Pro Shops   Springfield, Missouri _____

STREET ADDRESS   CITY   STATE/PROVINCE

and that these measurements and data are, to the best of my knowledge and belief, made in accordance with the instructions given.

Witness: ___ Paul D. Webster ___   Signature: ___ John L. Stein ___   I.D. Number | | | | |

B&C OFFICIAL MEASURER

INSTRUCTIONS FOR MEASURING NON-TYPICAL AMERICAN ELK (WAPITI)

All measurements must be made with a 1/4-inch wide flexible steel tape to the nearest one-eighth of an inch. (Note: A flexible steel cable can be used to measure points and main beams only.) Enter fractional figures in eighths, without reduction. Official measurements cannot be taken until the antlers have air dried for at least 60 days after the animal was killed.

A. Number of Points on Each Antler: To be counted a point, the projection must be at least one inch long, with length exceeding width at one inch or more of length. All points are measured from tip of point to nearest edge of beam as illustrated. Beam tip is counted as a point but not measured as a point.

B. Tip to Tip Spread is measured between tips of main beams.

C. Greatest Spread is measured between perpendiculars at a right angle to the center line of the skull at widest part, whether across main beams or points.

D. Inside Spread of Main Beams is measured at a right angle to the center line of the skull at widest point between main beams. Enter this measurement again as the Spread Credit **i**f it is less than or equal to the length of the longer main beam length; if greater, enter longer main beam length for Spread Credit.

E. Total of Lengths of all Abnormal Points: Abnormal Points are those non-typical in location (such as points originating from a point or from bottom or sides of main beam) or pattern (extra points, not generally paired). Measure in usual manner and record in appropriate blanks.

F. Length of Main Beam is measured from the center of the lowest outside edge of burr over the outer side to the most distant point of the main beam. The point of beginning is that point on the burr where the center line along the outer side of the beam intersects the burr, then following generally the line of the illustration.

G-1-2-3-4-5-6-7. Length of Normal Points: Normal points project from the top or front of the main beam in the general pattern illustrated. They are measured from nearest edge of main beam over outer curve to tip. Lay the tape along the outer curve of the beam so that the top edge of the tape coincides with the top edge of the beam on both sides of point to determine the baseline for point measurement. Record point length in appropriate blanks.

H-1-2-3-4. Circumferences are taken as detailed in illustration for each measurement.

ENTRY AFFIDAVIT FOR ALL HUNTER-TAKEN TROPHIES

For the purpose of entry into the Boone and Crockett Club's® records, North American big game harvested by the use of the following methods or under the following conditions are ineligible:

    I. Spotting or herding game from the air, followed by landing in its vicinity for the purpose of pursuit and shooting;

    II. Herding or chasing with the aid of any motorized equipment;

    III. Use of electronic communication devices, artificial lighting, or electronic light intensifying devices;

    IV. Confined by artificial barriers, including escape-proof fenced enclosures;

    V. Transplanted for the purpose of commercial shooting;

    VI. By the use of traps or pharmaceuticals;

    VII. While swimming, helpless in deep snow, or helpless in any other natural or artificial medium;

    VIII. On another hunter's license;

    IX. Not in full compliance with the game laws or regulations of the federal government or of any state, province, territory, or tribal council on reservations or tribal lands;

I certify that the trophy scored on this chart was not taken in violation of the conditions listed above. In signing this statement, I understand that if the information provided on this entry is found to be misrepresented or fraudulent in any respect, it will not be accepted into the Awards Program and 1) all of my prior entries are subject to deletion from future editions of **Records of North American Big Game** 2) future entries may not be accepted.

FAIR CHASE, as defined by the Boone and Crockett Club®, is the ethical, sportsmanlike and lawful pursuit and taking of any free-ranging wild, native North American big game animal in a manner that does not give the hunter an improper advantage over such game animals.

The Boone and Crockett Club® may exclude the entry of any animal that it deems to have been taken in an unethical manner or under conditions deemed inappropriate by the Club.

Date: _____ Signature of Hunter: _____

                                    (SIGNATURE MUST BE WITNESSED BY AN OFFICIAL MEASURER OR A NOTARY PUBLIC.)

Date: _____ Signature of Notary or Official Measurer: _____

Records of North American Big Game

250 Station Drive
Missoula, MT 59801
(406) 542-1888

BOONE AND CROCKETT CLUB®
OFFICIAL SCORING SYSTEM FOR NORTH AMERICAN BIG GAME TROPHIES
ROOSEVELT'S AND TULE ELK

MINIMUM SCORES

	AWARDS	ALL-TIME
Roosevelt's	275	290
Tule	270	285

KIND OF ELK (check one)
- ☐ Roosevelt's
- ☒ Tule

Subtotals

Crown Points

Right Antler	Left Antler
3 4/8	5 3/8
2 7/8	4 2/8
	5 7/8

I. Crown Points Total	21 7/8

Abnormal Points

Right Antler	Left Antler
1 2/8	

Detail of Point Measurement

TOTAL TO E	1 2/8

SEE OTHER SIDE FOR INSTRUCTIONS

				COLUMN 1	COLUMN 2	COLUMN 3	COLUMN 4
A. No. Points on Right Antler	9	No. Points on Left Antler	9	Spread Credit	Right Antler	Left Antler	Difference
B. Tip to Tip Spread	51 3/8	C. Greatest Spread	51 5/8				
D. Inside Spread of Main Beams	51 3/8	SPREAD CREDIT MAY EQUAL BUT NOT EXCEED LONGER MAIN BEAM		48 6/8			
E. Total of Lengths of Abnormal Points							1 2/8
F. Length of Main Beam					48 6/8	47 4/8	1 2/8
G-1. Length of First Point					15 1/8	14 6/8	3/8
G-2. Length of Second Point					16 4/8	12 5/8	3 7/8
G-3. Length of Third Point					11 5/8	9 5/8	2
G-4. Length of Fourth Point					17 1/8	17 1/8	
G-5. Length of Fifth Point					13 7/8	16	
G-6. Length of Sixth Point, If Present							
G-7. Length of Seventh Point, If Present							
H-1. Circumference at Smallest Place Between First and Second Points					7 1/8	6 4/8	5/8
H-2. Circumference at Smallest Place Between Second and Third Points					5 4/8	5 6/8	2/8
H-3. Circumference at Smallest Place Between Third and Fourth Points					6 2/8	7 2/8	1
H-4. Circumference at Smallest Place Between Fourth and Fifth Points					6	6 1/8	1/8
			TOTALS	48 6/8	147 7/8	143 2/8	10 6/8

ADD			
	Column 1	48 6/8	Exact Locality Where Killed: Solano County, California
	Column 2	147 7/8	Date Killed: 08/25/1990 Hunter: Quentin Hughes
	Column 3	143 2/8	Owner: Florence Sparks* Telephone #:
	Total of I	21 7/8	Owner's Address:
	Subtotal	361 6/8	Guide's Name and Address:
	SUBTRACT Column 4	10 6/8	Remarks: (Mention Any Abnormalities or Unique Qualities)
	FINAL SCORE	351	* Loaned to the B&C National Collection of Heads and Horns

COPYRIGHT © 2000 BY BOONE AND CROCKETT CLUB®

I, _____ Roger W. Atwood _____ , certify that I have measured this trophy on ___ 05/03/2001 ___

PRINT NAME

MM/DD/YYYYY

at _____ Bass Pro Shops   Springfield, Missouri _____

STREET ADDRESS   CITY   STATE/PROVINCE

and that these measurements and data are, to the best of my knowledge and belief, made in accordance with the instructions given.

Witness: _____ Robert A. Black _____ Signature: _____ Roger W. Atwood _____ I.D. Number

B&C OFFICIAL MEASURER

INSTRUCTIONS FOR MEASURING ROOSEVELT'S AND TULE ELK

All measurements must be made with a 1/4-inch wide flexible steel tape to the nearest one-eighth of an inch. (Note: A flexible steel cable can be used to measure points and main beams only.) Enter fractional figures in eighths, without reduction. Official measurements cannot be taken until the antlers have air dried for at least 60 days after the animal was killed.

- **A. Number of Points on Each Antler:** to be counted a point, the projection must be at least one inch long, with length exceeding width at one inch or more of length. All points are measured from tip of point to nearest edge of beam as illustrated. Beam tip is counted as a point but not measured as a point.
- **B. Tip to Tip Spread** is measured between tips of main beams.
- **C. Greatest Spread** is measured between perpendiculars at a right angle to the center line of the skull at widest part, whether across main beams or points.
- **D. Inside Spread of Main Beams** is measured at a right angle to the center line of the skull at widest point between main beams. Enter this measurement again as the Spread Credit if it is less than or equal to the length of the longer main beam; if greater, enter longer main beam length for Spread Credit.
- **E. Total of Lengths of all Abnormal Points:** Abnormal Points are those non-typical in location or pattern occurring below G-4. Measure in usual manner and record in appropriate blanks. **Note: do not confuse with Crown Points that may occur in the vicinity of G-4, G-5, G-6, etc.**
- **F. Length of Main Beam** is measured from the center of the lowest outside edge of burr over the outer side to the most distant point of the main beam. The point of beginning is that point on the burr where the center line along the outer side of the beam intersects the burr, then following generally the line of the illustration.
- **G-1-2-3-4-5-6-7. Length of Normal Points:** Normal points project from the top or front of the main beam in the general pattern illustrated. They are measured from nearest edge of main beam over outer curve to tip. Lay the tape along the outer curve of the beam so that the top edge of the tape coincides with the top edge of the beam on both sides of point to determine the baseline for point measurement. Record point length in appropriate blanks.
- **H-1-2-3-4. Circumferences** are taken as detailed in illustration for each measurement.
- **I. Crown Points:** From the well-defined Royal on out to end of beam, all points other than the normal points in their typical locations are Crown Points. This includes points occurring on the Royal, on other normal points, on Crown Points, and on the bottom and sides of main beam after the Royal. Measure and record in appropriate blanks provided and add to score below.

ENTRY AFFIDAVIT FOR ALL HUNTER-TAKEN TROPHIES

For the purpose of entry into the Boone and Crockett Club's® records, North American big game harvested by the use of the following methods or under the following conditions are ineligible:

- I.   Spotting or herding game from the air, followed by landing in its vicinity for the purpose of pursuit and shooting;
- II.   Herding or chasing with the aid of any motorized equipment;
- III. Use of electronic communication devices, artificial lighting, or electronic light intensifying devices;
- IV. Confined by artificial barriers, including escape-proof fenced enclosures;
- V.   Transplanted for the purpose of commercial shooting;
- VI. By the use of traps or pharmaceuticals;
- VII. While swimming, helpless in deep snow, or helpless in any other natural or artificial medium;
- VIII. On another hunter's license;
- IX. Not in full compliance with the game laws or regulations of the federal government or of any state, province, territory, or tribal council on reservations or tribal lands;

I certify that the trophy scored on this chart was not taken in violation of the conditions listed above. In signing this statement, I understand that if the information provided on this entry is found to be misrepresented or fraudulent in any respect, it will not be accepted into the Awards Program and 1) all of my prior entries are subject to deletion from future editions of **Records of North American Big Game** 2) future entries may not be accepted.

FAIR CHASE, as defined by the Boone and Crockett Club®, is the ethical, sportsmanlike and lawful pursuit and taking of any free-ranging wild, native North American big game animal in a manner that does not give the hunter an improper advantage over such game animals.

The Boone and Crockett Club® may exclude the entry of any animal that it deems to have been taken in an unethical manner or under conditions deemed inappropriate by the Club.

Date: _____ Signature of Hunter: _____

(SIGNATURE MUST BE WITNESSED BY AN OFFICIAL MEASURER OR A NOTARY PUBLIC.)

Date: _____ Signature of Notary or Official Measurer: _____

Records of
North American
Big Game

250 Station Drive
Missoula, MT 59801
(406) 542-1888

BOONE AND CROCKETT CLUB®
OFFICIAL SCORING SYSTEM FOR NORTH AMERICAN BIG GAME TROPHIES

TYPICAL
MULE DEER AND BLACKTAIL DEER

MINIMUM SCORES	AWARDS	ALL-TIME
mule deer	180	190
Columbia blacktail	125	135
Sitka blacktail	100	108

KIND OF DEER (check one)
- ☒ mule deer
- ☐ Columbia blacktail
- ☐ Sitka blacktail

Detail of Point
Measurement

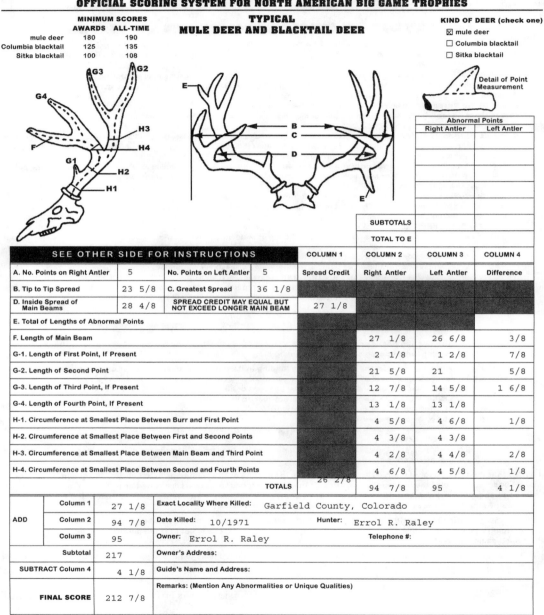

Abnormal Points	
Right Antler	Left Antler

SUBTOTALS	
TOTAL TO E	

SEE OTHER SIDE FOR INSTRUCTIONS			COLUMN 1	COLUMN 2	COLUMN 3	COLUMN 4
A. No. Points on Right Antler	5	No. Points on Left Antler	5	Spread Credit	Right Antler	Left Antler	Difference
B. Tip to Tip Spread	23 5/8	C. Greatest Spread	36 1/8				
D. Inside Spread of Main Beams	28 4/8	SPREAD CREDIT MAY EQUAL BUT NOT EXCEED LONGER MAIN BEAM	27 1/8				
E. Total of Lengths of Abnormal Points							
F. Length of Main Beam				27 1/8	26 6/8	3/8
G-1. Length of First Point, If Present				2 1/8	1 2/8	7/8
G-2. Length of Second Point				21 5/8	21	5/8
G-3. Length of Third Point, If Present				12 7/8	14 5/8	1 6/8
G-4. Length of Fourth Point, If Present				13 1/8	13 1/8	
H-1. Circumference at Smallest Place Between Burr and First Point				4 5/8	4 6/8	1/8
H-2. Circumference at Smallest Place Between First and Second Points				4 3/8	4 3/8	
H-3. Circumference at Smallest Place Between Main Beam and Third Point				4 2/8	4 4/8	2/8
H-4. Circumference at Smallest Place Between Second and Fourth Points				4 6/8	4 5/8	1/8
TOTALS			26 2/8	94 7/8	95	4 1/8

ADD	Column 1	27 1/8	Exact Locality Where Killed: Garfield County, Colorado
	Column 2	94 7/8	Date Killed: 10/1971 Hunter: Errol R. Raley
	Column 3	95	Owner: Errol R. Raley Telephone #:
Subtotal		217	Owner's Address:
SUBTRACT Column 4		4 1/8	Guide's Name and Address:
FINAL SCORE		212 7/8	Remarks: (Mention Any Abnormalities or Unique Qualities)

COPYRIGHT © 2000 BY BOONE AND CROCKETT CLUB®

I, _____ L. Victor Clark _____, certify that I have measured this trophy on _____ 05/02/2001 _____
PRINT NAME   MM/DD/YYYYY

at _____ Bass Pro Shops   Springfield, Missouri _____
STREET ADDRESS   CITY   STATE/PROVINCE

and that these measurements and data are, to the best of my knowledge and belief, made in accordance with the instructions given.

Witness: _____ Jack Graham _____   Signature: _____ L. Victor Clark _____   I.D. Number | | | | |
                                                          B&C OFFICIAL MEASURER

INSTRUCTIONS FOR MEASURING TYPICAL MULE AND BLACKTAIL DEER

All measurements must be made with a 1/4-inch wide flexible steel tape to the nearest one-eighth of an inch. (Note: A flexible steel cable can be used to measure points and main beams only.) Enter fractional figures in eighths, without reduction. Official measurements cannot be taken until the antlers have air dried for at least 60 days after the animal was killed.

- **A. Number of Points on Each Antler:** To be counted a point, the projection must be at least one inch long, with length exceeding width at one inch or more of length. All points are measured from tip of point to nearest edge of beam. Beam tip is counted as a point but not measured as a point.
- **B. Tip to Tip Spread** is measured between tips of main beams.
- **C. Greatest Spread** is measured between perpendiculars at a right angle to the center line of the skull at widest part, whether across main beams or points.
- **D. Inside Spread of Main Beams** is measured at a right angle to the center line of the skull at widest point between main beams. Enter this measurement again as the Spread Credit **if** it is less than or equal to the length of the longer main beam; if greater, enter longer main beam length for Spread Credit.
- **E. Total of Lengths of all Abnormal Points:** Abnormal Points are those non-typical in location such as points originating from a point (exception: G-3 originates from G-2 in perfectly normal fashion) or from bottom or sides of main beam, or any points beyond the normal pattern of five (including beam tip) per antler. Measure each abnormal point in usual manner and enter in appropriate blanks.
- **F. Length of Main Beam** is measured from the center of the lowest outside edge of burr over the outer side to the most distant point of the Main Beam. The point of beginning is that point on the burr where the center line along the outer side of the beam intersects the burr, then following generally the line of the illustration.
- **G-1-2-3-4. Length of Normal Points:** Normal points are the brow tines and the upper and lower forks as shown in the illustration. They are measured from nearest edge of main beam over outer curve to tip. Lay the tape along the outer curve of the beam so that the top edge of the tape coincides with the top edge of the beam on both sides of point to determine the baseline for point measurement. Record point lengths in appropriate blanks.
- **H-1-2-3-4. Circumferences** are taken as detailed in illustration for each measurement. If brow point is missing, take H-1 and H-2 at smallest place between burr and G-2. If G-3 is missing, take H-3 halfway between the base and tip of G-2. If G-4 is missing, take H-4 halfway between G-2 and tip of main beam.

ENTRY AFFIDAVIT FOR ALL HUNTER-TAKEN TROPHIES

For the purpose of entry into the Boone and Crockett Club's® records, North American big game harvested by the use of the following methods or under the following conditions are ineligible:

- I.   Spotting or herding game from the air, followed by landing in its vicinity for the purpose of pursuit and shooting;
- II.   Herding or chasing with the aid of any motorized equipment;
- III. Use of electronic communication devices, artificial lighting, or electronic light intensifying devices;
- IV.   Confined by artificial barriers, including escape-proof fenced enclosures;
- V.   Transplanted for the purpose of commercial shooting;
- VI.   By the use of traps or pharmaceuticals;
- VII. While swimming, helpless in deep snow, or helpless in any other natural or artificial medium;
- VIII. On another hunter's license;
- IX.   Not in full compliance with the game laws or regulations of the federal government or of any state, province, territory, or tribal council on reservations or tribal lands;

I certify that the trophy scored on this chart was not taken in violation of the conditions listed above. In signing this statement, I understand that if the information provided on this entry is found to be misrepresented or fraudulent in any respect, it will not be accepted into the Awards Program and 1) all of my prior entries are subject to deletion from future editions of **Records of North American Big Game** 2) future entries may not be accepted.

FAIR CHASE, as defined by the Boone and Crockett Club®, is the ethical, sportsmanlike and lawful pursuit and taking of any free-ranging wild, native North American big game animal in a manner that does not give the hunter an improper advantage over such game animals.

The Boone and Crockett Club® may exclude the entry of any animal that it deems to have been taken in an unethical manner or under conditions deemed inappropriate by the Club.

Date: _____ Signature of Hunter: _____
                                                (SIGNATURE MUST BE WITNESSED BY AN OFFICIAL MEASURER OR A NOTARY PUBLIC.)

Date: _____ Signature of Notary or Official Measurer: _____

Records of
North American
Big Game

250 Station Drive
Missoula, MT 59801
(406) 542-1888

BOONE AND CROCKETT CLUB®
OFFICIAL SCORING SYSTEM FOR NORTH AMERICAN BIG GAME TROPHIES

NON-TYPICAL MULE DEER

MINIMUM SCORES
AWARDS   ALL-TIME
215   230

Abnormal Points	
Right Antler	Left Antler
*	*

SUBTOTALS	38 6/8	42 7/8
E. TOTAL	81 5/8	

SEE OTHER SIDE FOR INSTRUCTIONS			COLUMN 1	COLUMN 2	COLUMN 3	COLUMN 4
			Spread Credit	Right Antler	Left Antler	Difference
A. No. Points on Right Antler	17	No. Points on Left Antler	12			
B. Tip to Tip Spread	22 2/8	C. Greatest Spread	29 6/8			
D. Inside Spread of Main Beams	22 5/8	SPREAD CREDIT MAY EQUAL BUT NOT EXCEED LONGER MAIN BEAM	22 5/8			
F. Length of Main Beam				27 6/8	26 7/8	7/8
G-1. Length of First Point, If Present				2 2/8	3 1/8	7/8
G-2. Length of Second Point				17 2/8	16 2/8	1
G-3. Length of Third Point, If Present				11 7/8	10	1 7/8
G-4. Length of Fourth Point, If Present				9 7/8	12 1/8	2 2/8
H-1. Circumference at Smallest Place Between Burr and First Point				4 7/8	5	1/8
H-2. Circumference at Smallest Place Between First and Second Points				4 4/8	4 4/8	
H-3. Circumference at Smallest Place Between Main Beam and Third Point				4	4	
H-4. Circumference at Smallest Place Between Second and Fourth Points				4 1/8	4 3/8	2/8
TOTALS			22 5/8	86 4/8	86 2/8	7 2/8

ADD	Column 1	22 5/8
	Column 2	86 4/8
	Column 3	86 2/8
Subtotal		195 3/8
SUBTRACT Column 4		7 2/8
Subtotal		188 1/8
ADD Line E Total		81 5/8
FINAL SCORE		269 6/8

Exact Locality Where Killed: Sherman County, Oregon

Date Killed: 10/09/1998   Hunter: James G. Peterson

Owner: James G. Peterson   Telephone #:

Owner's Address:

Guide's Name and Address:

Remarks: (Mention Any Abnormalities or Unique Qualities)

*Listed below are the subtotals for the abnormal points. Due to limited space the numerous point measurements could not be listed individually.

COPYRIGHT © 2000 BY BOONE AND CROCKETT CLUB®

I, _____ Roger W. Atwood _____ , certify that I have measured this trophy on ____ 05/03/2001 ____
            PRINT NAME   MM/DD/YYYYY

at _____ Bass Pro Shops   Springfield, Missouri _____
   STREET ADDRESS   CITY   STATE/PROVINCE

and that these measurements and data are, to the best of my knowledge and belief, made in accordance with the instructions given.

Witness: _____ Robert A. Black _____   Signature: _____ Roger W. Atwood _____   I.D. Number | | | | |
                                                                   B&C OFFICIAL MEASURER

INSTRUCTIONS FOR MEASURING NON-TYPICAL MULE DEER

All measurements must be made with a 1/4-inch wide flexible steel tape to the nearest one-eighth of an inch. (Note: A flexible steel cable can be used to measure points and main beams only.) Enter fractional figures in eighths, without reduction. Official measurements cannot be taken until the antlers have air dried for at least 60 days after the animal was killed.

A. **Number of Points on Each Antler:** To be counted a point, the projection must be at least one inch long, with length exceeding width at one inch or more of length. All points are measured from tip of point to nearest edge of beam as illustrated. Beam tip is counted as a point but not measured as a point.

B. **Tip to Tip Spread** is measured between tips of main beams.

C. **Greatest Spread** is measured between perpendiculars at a right angle to the center line of the skull at widest part, whether across main beams or points.

D. **Inside Spread of Main Beams** is measured at a right angle to the center line of the skull at widest point between main beams. Enter this measurement again as the Spread Credit if it is less than or equal to the length of the longer main beam; if greater, enter longer main beam length for Spread Credit.

E. **Total of Lengths of all Abnormal Points:** Abnormal Points are those non-typical in location such as points originating from a point (exception: G-3 originates from G-2 in perfectly normal fashion) or from bottom or sides of main beam, or any points beyond the normal pattern of five (including beam tip) per antler. Measure each abnormal point in usual manner and enter in appropriate blanks.

F. **Length of Main Beam** is measured from the center of the lowest outside edge of burr over the outer side to the most distant point of the main beam. The point of beginning is that point on the burr where the center line along the outer side of the beam intersects the burr, then following generally the line of the illustration.

G-1-2-3-4. **Length of Normal Points:** Normal points are the brow tines and the upper and lower forks as shown in the illustration. They are measured from nearest edge of main beam over outer curve to tip. Lay the tape along the outer curve of the beam so that the top edge of the tape coincides with the top edge of the beam on both sides of point to determine the baseline for point measurement. Record point lengths in appropriate blanks.

H-1-2-3-4. **Circumferences** are taken as detailed in illustration for each measurement. If brow point is missing, take H-1 and H-2 at smallest place between burr and G-2. If G-3 is missing, take H-3 halfway between the base and tip of G-2. If G-4 is missing, take H-4 halfway between G-2 and tip of main beam.

ENTRY AFFIDAVIT FOR ALL HUNTER-TAKEN TROPHIES

For the purpose of entry into the Boone and Crockett Club's® records, North American big game harvested by the use of the following methods or under the following conditions are ineligible:

   I.   Spotting or herding game from the air, followed by landing in its vicinity for the purpose of pursuit and shooting;

   II.   Herding or chasing with the aid of any motorized equipment;

   III.   Use of electronic communication devices, artificial lighting, or electronic light intensifying devices;

   IV.   Confined by artificial barriers, including escape-proof fenced enclosures;

   V.   Transplanted for the purpose of commercial shooting;

   VI.   By the use of traps or pharmaceuticals;

   VII.   While swimming, helpless in deep snow, or helpless in any other natural or artificial medium;

   VIII.   On another hunter's license;

   IX.   Not in full compliance with the game laws or regulations of the federal government or of any state, province, territory, or tribal council on reservations or tribal lands;

I certify that the trophy scored on this chart was not taken in violation of the conditions listed above. In signing this statement, I understand that if the information provided on this entry is found to be misrepresented or fraudulent in any respect, it will not be accepted into the Awards Program and 1) all of my prior entries are subject to deletion from future editions of **Records of North American Big Game** 2) future entries may not be accepted.

FAIR CHASE, as defined by the Boone and Crockett Club®, is the ethical, sportsmanlike and lawful pursuit and taking of any free-ranging wild, native North American big game animal in a manner that does not give the hunter an improper advantage over such game animals.

The Boone and Crockett Club® may exclude the entry of any animal that it deems to have been taken in an unethical manner or under conditions deemed inappropriate by the Club.

Date: _____ Signature of Hunter: _____
                                            (SIGNATURE MUST BE WITNESSED BY AN OFFICIAL MEASURER OR A NOTARY PUBLIC.)

Date: _____ Signature of Notary or Official Measurer: _____

Records of North American Big Game

BOONE AND CROCKETT CLUB®
OFFICIAL SCORING SYSTEM FOR NORTH AMERICAN BIG GAME TROPHIES

250 Station Drive
Missoula, MT 59801
(406) 542-1888

MINIMUM SCORES		
	AWARDS	ALL-TIME
whitetail	160	170
Coues'	100	110

TYPICAL
WHITETAIL AND COUES' DEER

KIND OF DEER (check one)
☒ whitetail
☐ Coues'

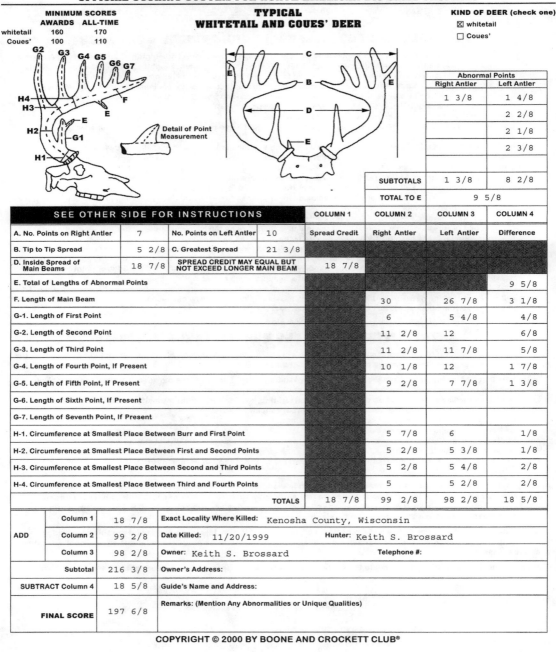

Detail of Point Measurement

	Abnormal Points	
	Right Antler	Left Antler
	1 3/8	1 4/8
		2 2/8
		2 1/8
		2 3/8
SUBTOTALS	1 3/8	8 2/8
TOTAL TO E	9 5/8	

SEE OTHER SIDE FOR INSTRUCTIONS				COLUMN 1	COLUMN 2	COLUMN 3	COLUMN 4
				Spread Credit	Right Antler	Left Antler	Difference
A. No. Points on Right Antler	7	No. Points on Left Antler	10				
B. Tip to Tip Spread	5 2/8	C. Greatest Spread	21 3/8				
D. Inside Spread of Main Beams	18 7/8	SPREAD CREDIT MAY EQUAL BUT NOT EXCEED LONGER MAIN BEAM	18 7/8				
E. Total of Lengths of Abnormal Points							9 5/8
F. Length of Main Beam					30	26 7/8	3 1/8
G-1. Length of First Point					6	5 4/8	4/8
G-2. Length of Second Point					11 2/8	12	6/8
G-3. Length of Third Point					11 2/8	11 7/8	5/8
G-4. Length of Fourth Point, If Present					10 1/8	12	1 7/8
G-5. Length of Fifth Point, If Present					9 2/8	7 7/8	1 3/8
G-6. Length of Sixth Point, If Present							
G-7. Length of Seventh Point, If Present							
H-1. Circumference at Smallest Place Between Burr and First Point					5 7/8	6	1/8
H-2. Circumference at Smallest Place Between First and Second Points					5 2/8	5 3/8	1/8
H-3. Circumference at Smallest Place Between Second and Third Points					5 2/8	5 4/8	2/8
H-4. Circumference at Smallest Place Between Third and Fourth Points					5	5 2/8	2/8
			TOTALS	18 7/8	99 2/8	98 2/8	18 5/8

ADD	Column 1	18 7/8	Exact Locality Where Killed: Kenosha County, Wisconsin
	Column 2	99 2/8	Date Killed: 11/20/1999 Hunter: Keith S. Brossard
	Column 3	98 2/8	Owner: Keith S. Brossard Telephone #:
	Subtotal	216 3/8	Owner's Address:
SUBTRACT Column 4		18 5/8	Guide's Name and Address:
FINAL SCORE		197 6/8	Remarks: (Mention Any Abnormalities or Unique Qualities)

COPYRIGHT © 2000 BY BOONE AND CROCKETT CLUB®

I, _____ Brian Tessmann _____, certify that I have measured this trophy on ____01/26/2000____

PRINT NAME

MM/DD/YYYYY

at _____ 2215 Matterhorn CT., Lake Geneva, Wisconsin _____

STREET ADDRESS   CITY   STATE/PROVINCE

and that these measurements and data are, to the best of my knowledge and belief, made in accordance with the instructions given.

Witness: ____Stanley R. Godfrey____   Signature: _____Brian Tessmann_____   I.D. Number

B&C OFFICIAL MEASURER

INSTRUCTIONS FOR MEASURING TYPICAL WHITETAIL AND COUES' DEER

All measurements must be made with a 1/4-inch wide flexible steel tape to the nearest one-eighth of an inch. (Note: A flexible steel cable can be used to measure points and main beams only.) Enter fractional figures in eighths, without reduction. Official measurements cannot be taken until the antlers have air dried for at least 60 days after the animal was killed.

A. Number of Points on Each Antler: To be counted a point, the projection must be at least one inch long, with the length exceeding width at one inch or more of length. All points are measured from tip of point to nearest edge of beam as illustrated. Beam tip is counted as a point but not measured as a point.

B. Tip to Tip Spread is measured between tips of main beams.

C. Greatest Spread is measured between perpendiculars at a right angle to the center line of the skull at widest part, whether across main beams or points.

D. Inside Spread of Main Beams is measured at a right angle to the center line of the skull at widest point between main beams. Enter this measurement again as the Spread Credit if it is less than or equal to the length of the longer main beam; if greater, enter longer main beam length for Spread Credit.

E. Total of Lengths of all Abnormal Points: Abnormal Points are those non-typical in location (such as points originating from a point or from bottom or sides of main beam) or extra points beyond the normal pattern of points. Measure in usual manner and enter in appropriate blanks.

F. Length of Main Beam is measured from the center of the lowest outside edge of burr over the outer side to the most distant point of the main beam. The point of beginning is that point on the burr where the center line along the outer side of the beam intersects the burr, then following generally the line of the illustration.

G-1-2-3-4-5-6-7. Length of Normal Points: Normal points project from the top of the main beam. They are measured from nearest edge of main beam over outer curve to tip. Lay the tape along the outer curve of the beam so that the top edge of the tape coincides with the top edge of the beam on both sides of the point to determine the baseline for point measurements. Record point lengths in appropriate blanks.

H-1-2-3-4. Circumferences are taken as detailed in illustration for each measurement. If brow point is missing, take H-1 and H-2 at smallest place between burr and G-2. If G-4 is missing, take H-4 halfway between G-3 and tip of main beam.

ENTRY AFFIDAVIT FOR ALL HUNTER-TAKEN TROPHIES

For the purpose of entry into the Boone and Crockett Club's® records, North American big game harvested by the use of the following methods or under the following conditions are ineligible:

   I. Spotting or herding game from the air, followed by landing in its vicinity for the purpose of pursuit and shooting;
   II. Herding or chasing with the aid of any motorized equipment;
   III. Use of electronic communication devices, artificial lighting, or electronic light intensifying devices;
   IV. Confined by artificial barriers, including escape-proof fenced enclosures;
   V. Transplanted for the purpose of commercial shooting;
   VI. By the use of traps or pharmaceuticals;
   VII. While swimming, helpless in deep snow, or helpless in any other natural or artificial medium;
   VIII. On another hunter's license;
   IX. Not in full compliance with the game laws or regulations of the federal government or of any state, province, territory, or tribal council on reservations or tribal lands;

I certify that the trophy scored on this chart was not taken in violation of the conditions listed above. In signing this statement, I understand that if the information provided on this entry is found to be misrepresented or fraudulent in any respect, it will not be accepted into the Awards Program and 1) all of my prior entries are subject to deletion from future editions of **Records of North American Big Game** 2) future entries may not be accepted.

FAIR CHASE, as defined by the Boone and Crockett Club®, is the ethical, sportsmanlike and lawful pursuit and taking of any free-ranging wild, native North American big game animal in a manner that does not give the hunter an improper advantage over such game animals.

The Boone and Crockett Club® may exclude the entry of any animal that it deems to have been taken in an unethical manner or under conditions deemed inappropriate by the Club.

Date: _____ Signature of Hunter: _____

(SIGNATURE MUST BE WITNESSED BY AN OFFICIAL MEASURER OR A NOTARY PUBLIC.)

Date: _____ Signature of Notary or Official Measurer: _____

250 Station Drive
Missoula, MT 59801
(406) 542-1888

BOONE AND CROCKETT CLUB®
OFFICIAL SCORING SYSTEM FOR NORTH AMERICAN BIG GAME TROPHIES

NON-TYPICAL
WHITETAIL AND COUES' DEER

MINIMUM SCORES		
	AWARDS	ALL-TIME
whitetail	185	195
Coues'	105	120

KIND OF DEER (check one)
☐ whitetail
☒ Coues'

Abnormal Points	
Right Antler	Left Antler
4 7/8	5 1/8
3 4/8	7 4/8
7 3/8	3 4/8
9 6/8	10

	Right Antler	Left Antler
SUBTOTALS	25 4/8	26 1/8
E. TOTAL	51 5/8	

G2 G3 G4 G5 G6 E F H4 H3 G1 H2 H1

Detail of Point Measurement

B C D

SEE OTHER SIDE FOR INSTRUCTIONS		COLUMN 1	COLUMN 2	COLUMN 3	COLUMN 4
A. No. Points on Right Antler	8	No. Points on Left Antler	8	Spread Credit	Right Antler	Left Antler	Difference
B. Tip to Tip Spread	18 1/8	C. Greatest Spread	20 3/8				
D. Inside Spread of Main Beams	18 2/8	SPREAD CREDIT MAY EQUAL BUT NOT EXCEED LONGER MAIN BEAM		17 6/8			
F. Length of Main Beam					17 6/8	16 5/8	1 1/8
G-1. Length of First Point					4 4/8	4 3/8	1/8
G-2. Length of Second Point					13 2/8	13 6/8	4/8
G-3. Length of Third Point					11	8	3
G-4. Length of Fourth Point, If Present							
G-5. Length of Fifth Point, If Present							
G-6. Length of Sixth Point, If Present							
G-7. Length of Seventh Point, If Present							
H-1. Circumference at Smallest Place Between Burr and First Point					4 5/8	4 6/8	1/8
H-2. Circumference at Smallest Place Between First and Second Points					4 1/8	4 3/8	2/8
H-3. Circumference at Smallest Place Between Second and Third Points					4 6/8	4 5/8	1/8
H-4. Circumference at Smallest Place Between Third and Fourth Points					2 6/8	3 1/8	3/8
		TOTALS		17 6/8	62 6/8	59 5/8	5 5/8

ADD	Column 1	17 6/8	Exact Locality Where Killed: Hidalgo County, New Mexico
	Column 2	62 6/8	Date Killed: 11/1941 Hunter: Peter M. Chase
	Column 3	59 5/8	Owner: W.B. Darnell Telephone #:
	Subtotal	140 1/8	Owner's Address:
SUBTRACT Column 4		5 5/8	Guide's Name and Address:
	Subtotal	134 4/8	Remarks: (Mention Any Abnormalities or Unique Qualities)
ADD Line E Total		51 5/8	
FINAL SCORE		186 1/8	

I, _____L. Victor Clark_____, certify that I have measured this trophy on ___05/02/2001___
　　　　　　PRINT NAME　　　　　　　　　　　　　　　　　　　　　　　　　　　　　　　　　　MM/DD/YYYYY

at _____Bass Pro Shops　　Springfield, Missouri_____
　　STREET ADDRESS　　　　　　　　　　　　　　　　　　　　　　　　　　CITY　　　　　　　　　　　STATE/PROVINCE

and that these measurements and data are, to the best of my knowledge and belief, made in accordance with the instructions given.

Witness: ___Jack Graham___　　　　　Signature: ___L. Victor Clark___　　I.D. Number | | | | |
　　　　　　　　　　　　　　　　　　　　　　　　　　　　B&C OFFICIAL MEASURER

INSTRUCTIONS FOR MEASURING NON-TYPICAL WHITETAIL AND COUES' DEER

All measurements must be made with a 1/4-inch wide flexible steel tape to the nearest one-eighth of an inch. (Note: A flexible steel cable can be used to measure points and main beams only.) Enter fractional figures in eighths, without reduction. Official measurements cannot be taken until the antlers have air dried for at least 60 days after the animal was killed.

A. **Number of Points on Each Antler:** To be counted a point, the projection must be at least one inch long, with the length exceeding width at one inch or more of length. All points are measured from tip of point to nearest edge of beam as illustrated. Beam tip is counted as a point but not measured as a point.

B. **Tip to Tip Spread** is measured between tips of main beams.

C. **Greatest Spread** is measured between perpendiculars at a right angle to the center line of the skull at widest part, whether across main beams or points.

D. **Inside Spread of Main Beams** is measured at a right angle to the center line of the skull at widest point between main beams. Enter this measurement again as the Spread Credit if it is less than or equal to the length of the longer main beam; if greater, enter longer main beam length for Spread Credit.

E. **Total of Lengths of all Abnormal Points:** Abnormal Points are those non-typical in location (such as points originating from a point or from bottom or sides of main beam) or extra points beyond the normal pattern of points. Measure in usual manner and enter in appropriate blanks.

F. **Length of Main Beam** is measured from the center of the lowest outside edge of burr over the outer side to the most distant point of the main beam. The point of beginning is that point on the burr where the center line along the outer side of the beam intersects the burr, then following generally the line of the illustration.

G-1-2-3-4-5-6-7. **Length of Normal Points:** Normal points project from the top of the main beam. They are measured from nearest edge of main beam over outer curve to tip. Lay the tape along the outer curve of the beam so that the top edge of the tape coincides with the top edge of the beam on both sides of the point to determine the baseline for point measurement. Record point lengths in appropriate blanks.

H-1-2-3-4. **Circumferences** are taken as detailed in illustration for each measurement. If brow point is missing, take H-1 and H-2 at smallest place between burr and G-2. If G-4 is missing, take H-4 halfway between G-3 and tip of main beam.

ENTRY AFFIDAVIT FOR ALL HUNTER-TAKEN TROPHIES

For the purpose of entry into the Boone and Crockett Club's® records, North American big game harvested by the use of the following methods or under the following conditions are ineligible:

I. Spotting or herding game from the air, followed by landing in its vicinity for the purpose of pursuit and shooting;
II. Herding or chasing with the aid of any motorized equipment;
III. Use of electronic communication devices, artificial lighting, or electronic light intensifying devices;
IV. Confined by artificial barriers, including escape-proof fenced enclosures;
V. Transplanted for the purpose of commercial shooting;
VI. By the use of traps or pharmaceuticals;
VII. While swimming, helpless in deep snow, or helpless in any other natural or artificial medium;
VIII. On another hunter's license;
IX. Not in full compliance with the game laws or regulations of the federal government or of any state, province, territory, or tribal council on reservations or tribal lands;

I certify that the trophy scored on this chart was not taken in violation of the conditions listed above. In signing this statement, I understand that if the information provided on this entry is found to be misrepresented or fraudulent in any respect, it will not be accepted into the Awards Program and 1) all of my prior entries are subject to deletion from future editions of **Records of North American Big Game** 2) future entries may not be accepted.

FAIR CHASE, as defined by the Boone and Crockett Club®, is the ethical, sportsmanlike and lawful pursuit and taking of any free-ranging wild, native North American big game animal in a manner that does not give the hunter an improper advantage over such game animals.

The Boone and Crockett Club® may exclude the entry of any animal that it deems to have been taken in an unethical manner or under conditions deemed inappropriate by the Club.

Date: _____ Signature of Hunter: _____
　　　　　　　　　　　　　　　　　　　　　(SIGNATURE MUST BE WITNESSED BY AN OFFICIAL MEASURER OR A NOTARY PUBLIC.)

Date: _____ Signature of Notary or Official Measurer: _____

Records of North American Big Game

BOONE AND CROCKETT CLUB®
OFFICIAL SCORING SYSTEM FOR NORTH AMERICAN BIG GAME TROPHIES

250 Station Drive
Missoula, MT 59801
(406) 542-1888

MOOSE

MINIMUM SCORES

	AWARDS	ALL-TIME
Canada	185	195
Alaska-Yukon	210	224
Wyoming	140	155

KIND OF MOOSE (check one)

☐ Canada
☒ Alaska-Yukon
☐ Wyoming

Detail of Point Measurement

	Abnormal Points	
	Right Antler	Left Antler
NUMBER OF POINTS		1
TOTAL TO B.	1	

SEE OTHER SIDE FOR INSTRUCTIONS	COLUMN 1	COLUMN 2	COLUMN 3	COLUMN 4
A. Greatest Spread	78 2/8	Right Antler	Left Antler	Difference
B. Number of Abnormal Points on Both Antlers				1
C. Number of Normal Points		16	15	1
D. Width of Palm		17 3/8	18 2/8	7/8
E. Length of Palm Including Brow Palm		49 6/8	50 5/8	7/8
F. Circumference of Beam at Smallest Place		7 5/8	7 6/8	1/8
TOTALS	78 2/8	90 6/8	91 5/8	3 7/8

ADD	Column 1	78 2/8
	Column 2	90 6/8
	Column 3	91 5/8
	Subtotal	260 5/8
SUBTRACT Column 4		3 7/8
FINAL SCORE		256 6/8

Exact Locality Where Killed: Beluga River, Alaska
Date Killed: 11/16/1997   Hunter: William G. Nelson
Owner: William G. Nelson   Telephone #:
Owner's Address:
Guide's Name and Address:
Remarks: (Mention Any Abnormalities or Unique Qualities)

I, _____ John L. Stein _____ , certify that I have measured this trophy on ___ 05/03/2001 ___
PRINT NAME   MM/DD/YYYYY

at _____ Bass Pro Shops   Springfield, Missouri _____
STREET ADDRESS   CITY   STATE/PROVINCE

and that these measurements and data are, to the best of my knowledge and belief, made in accordance with the instructions given.

Witness: _____ Ronald L. Sherer _____   Signature: _____ John L. Stein _____   I.D. Number [ ][ ][ ][ ]
                                                         B&C OFFICIAL MEASURER

COPYRIGHT © 2000 BY BOONE AND CROCKETT CLUB®

BOONE AND CROCKETT CLUB'S

INSTRUCTIONS FOR MEASURING MOOSE

Measurements must be made with a 1/4-inch wide flexible steel tape to the nearest one-eighth of an inch. Enter fractional figures in eighths, without reduction. Official measurements cannot be taken until antlers have air dried for at least 60 days after animal was killed.

- **A. Greatest Spread** is measured between perpendiculars in a straight line at a right angle to the center line of the skull.
- **B. Number of Abnormal Points on Both Antlers:** Abnormal points are those projections originating from normal points or from the upper or lower palm surface, or from the inner edge of palm (see illustration). Abnormal points must be at least one inch long, with length exceeding width at one inch or more of length.
- **C. Number of Normal Points:** Normal points originate from the outer edge of palm. To be counted a point, a projection must be at least one inch long, with the length exceeding width at one inch or more of length. Be sure to verify whether or not each projection qualifies as a point.
- **D. Width of Palm** is taken in contact with the under surface of palm, at a right angle to the inner edge of palm. The line of measurement should begin and end at the midpoint of the palm edge, which gives credit for the desirable character of palm thickness.
- **E. Length of Palm** including Brow Palm is taken in contact with the surface along the underside of the palm, **parallel** to the inner edge, from dips between points at the top to dips between points (if present) at the bottom. If a bay is present, measure across the open bay if the proper line of measurement, parallel to **inner edge**, follows this path. The line of measurement should begin and end at the midpoint of the palm edge, which gives credit for the desirable character of palm thickness.
- **F. Circumference** of Beam at Smallest Place is taken as illustrated.

ENTRY AFFIDAVIT FOR ALL HUNTER-TAKEN TROPHIES

For the purpose of entry into the Boone and Crockett Club's® records, North American big game harvested by the use of the following methods or under the following conditions are ineligible:

- I. Spotting or herding game from the air, followed by landing in its vicinity for the purpose of pursuit and shooting;
- II. Herding or chasing with the aid of any motorized equipment;
- III. Use of electronic communication devices, artificial lighting, or electronic light intensifying devices;
- IV. Confined by artificial barriers, including escape-proof fenced enclosures;
- V. Transplanted for the purpose of commercial shooting;
- VI. By the use of traps or pharmaceuticals;
- VII. While swimming, helpless in deep snow, or helpless in any other natural or artificial medium;
- VIII. On another hunter's license;
- IX. Not in full compliance with the game laws or regulations of the federal government or of any state, province, territory, or tribal council on reservations or tribal lands;

I certify that the trophy scored on this chart was not taken in violation of the conditions listed above. In signing this statement, I understand that if the information provided on this entry is found to be misrepresented or fraudulent in any respect, it will not be accepted into the Awards Program and 1) all of my prior entries are subject to deletion from future editions of **Records of North American Big Game** 2) future entries may not be accepted.

FAIR CHASE, as defined by the Boone and Crockett Club®, is the ethical, sportsmanlike and lawful pursuit and taking of any free-ranging wild, native North American big game animal in a manner that does not give the hunter an improper advantage over such game animals.

The Boone and Crockett Club® may exclude the entry of any animal that it deems to have been taken in an unethical manner or under conditions deemed inappropriate by the Club.

Date:_____ Signature of Hunter:_____

(SIGNATURE MUST BE WITNESSED BY AN OFFICIAL MEASURER OR A NOTARY PUBLIC.)

Date:_____ Signature of Notary or Official Measurer:_____

250 Station Drive
Missoula, MT 59801
(406) 542-1888

BOONE AND CROCKETT CLUB®
OFFICIAL SCORING SYSTEM FOR NORTH AMERICAN BIG GAME TROPHIES

CARIBOU

MINIMUM SCORES		
	AWARDS	ALL-TIME
mountain	360	390
woodland	265	295
barren ground	375	400
Central Canada		
barren ground	345	360
Quebec-Labrador	365	375

KIND OF CARIBOU (check one)
- ☒ mountain
- ☐ woodland
- ☐ barren ground
- ☐ Central Canada
  barren ground
- ☐ Quebec-Labrador

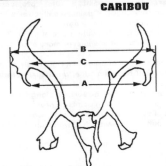

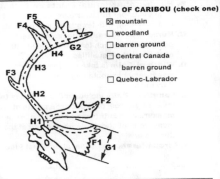

Detail of Point
Measurement

SEE OTHER SIDE FOR INSTRUCTIONS			COLUMN 1	COLUMN 2	COLUMN 3	COLUMN 4
A. Tip to Tip Spread		35 5/8	Spread Credit	Right Antler	Left Antler	Difference
B. Greatest Spread		48 5/8				
C. Inside Spread of Main Beams	45 6/8	SPREAD CREDIT MAY EQUAL BUT NOT EXCEED LONGER MAIN BEAM	45 6/8			
D. Number of Points on Each Antler Excluding Brows				16	19	3
Number of Points on Each Brow				7	2	
E. Length of Main Beam				48 2/8	49 5/8	1 3/8
F-1. Length of Brow Palm or First Point				20	17 1/8	
F-2. Length of Bez or Second Point				25 2/8	27 3/8	2 1/8
F-3. Length of Rear Point, If Present				5 6/8	4 6/8	1
F-4. Length of Second Longest Top Point				18 1/8	18 6/8	5/8
F-5. Length of Longest Top Point				25 2/8	24 2/8	1
G-1. Width of Brow Palm				13 1/8	4	
G-2. Width of Top Palm				5 4/8	6 6/8	1 2/8
H-1. Circumference at Smallest Place Between Brow and Bez Point				6 3/8	6 5/8	2/8
H-2. Circumference at Smallest Place Between Bez and Rear Point				6 4/8	6 1/8	3/8
H-3. Circumference at Smallest Place Between Rear Point and First Top Point				6 7/8	7	1/8
H-4. Circumference at Smallest Place Between Two Longest Top Palm Points				10 4/8	11 4/8	1
		TOTALS	45 6/8	214 4/8	204 7/8	12 4/8

ADD	Column 1	45 6/8	Exact Locality Where Killed:	Prospector Mt., Yukon Territory
	Column 2	214 4/8	Date Killed: 8/17/1998	Hunter: C. Candler Hunt
	Column 3	204 7/8	Owner: C. Candler Hunt	Telephone #:
	Subtotal	465 1/8	Owner's Address:	
	SUBTRACT Column 4	12 1/8	Guide's Name and Address:	
	FINAL SCORE	453	Remarks: (Mention Any Abnormalities or Unique Qualities)	

COPYRIGHT © 2000 BY BOONE AND CROCKETT CLUB®

I, _____ Jack Graham _____, certify that I have measured this trophy on ____ 05/04/2001 ____
PRINT NAME   MM/DD/YYYYY

at _____ Bass Pro Shops   Springfield, Missouri _____
STREET ADDRESS   CITY   STATE/PROVINCE

and that these measurements and data are, to the best of my knowledge and belief, made in accordance with the instructions given.

Witness: ___ Albert C. England ___   Signature: ___ Jack Graham ___   I.D. Number [ ][ ][ ][ ]
                                                    B&C OFFICIAL MEASURER

INSTRUCTIONS FOR MEASURING CARIBOU

All measurements must be made with a 1/4-inch wide flexible steel tape to the nearest one-eighth of an inch. (Note: A flexible steel cable can be used to measure points and main beams only.) Enter fractional figures in eighths, without reduction. Official measurements cannot be taken until the antlers have air dried for at least 60 days after the animal was killed.

A. Tip to Tip Spread is measured between tips of main beams.

B. Greatest Spread is measured between perpendiculars at a right angle to the center line of the skull at widest part, whether across main beams or points.

C. Inside Spread of Main Beams is measured at a right angle to the center line of the skull at widest point between main beams. Enter this measurement again as the Spread Credit if it is less than or equal to the length of the longer main beam; if greater, enter longer main beam length for Spread Credit.

D. Number of Points on Each Antler: To be counted a point, a projection must be at least one-half inch long, with length exceeding width at one-half inch or more of length. Beam tip is counted as a point but not measured as a point. There are no "abnormal" points in caribou.

E. Length of Main Beam is measured from the center of the lowest outside edge of burr over the outer side to the most distant point of the main beam. The point of beginning is that point on the burr where the center line along the outer side of the beam intersects the burr, then following generally the line of the illustration.

F-1-2-3. Length of Points are measured from nearest edge of beam over outer curve to tip. Lay the tape along the outer curve of the beam so that the top edge of the tape coincides with the top edge of the beam on both sides of point to determine the baseline for point measurement. Record point lengths in appropriate blanks.

F-4-5. Length of Points are measured from the tip of the point to the top of the beam, then at a right angle to the bottom edge of beam. The Second Longest Top Point **cannot** be a point branch of the Longest Top Point.

G-1. Width of Brow is measured in a straight line from top edge to lower edge, as illustrated, with measurement line at a right angle to main axis of brow.

G-2. Width of Top Palm is measured from midpoint of lower edge of main beam to midpoint of a dip between points, at widest part of palm. The line of measurement begins and ends at midpoints of palm edges, which gives credit for palm thickness.

H-1-2-3-4. Circumferences are taken as illustrated for measurements. If brow point is missing, take H-1 at smallest point between burr and bez point. If rear point is missing, take H-2 and H-3 measurements at smallest place between bez and first top point. Do not depress the tape into any dips of the palm or main beam.

ENTRY AFFIDAVIT FOR ALL HUNTER-TAKEN TROPHIES

For the purpose of entry into the Boone and Crockett Club's® records, North American big game harvested by the use of the following methods or under the following conditions are ineligible:

I. Spotting or herding game from the air, followed by landing in its vicinity for the purpose of pursuit and shooting;
II. Herding or chasing with the aid of any motorized equipment;
III. Use of electronic communication devices, artificial lighting, or electronic light intensifying devices;
IV. Confined by artificial barriers, including escape-proof fenced enclosures;
V. Transplanted for the purpose of commercial shooting;
VI. By the use of traps or pharmaceuticals;
VII. While swimming, helpless in deep snow, or helpless in any other natural or artificial medium;
VIII. On another hunter's license;
IX. Not in full compliance with the game laws or regulations of the federal government or of any state, province, territory, or tribal council on reservations or tribal lands;

I certify that the trophy scored on this chart was not taken in violation of the conditions listed above. In signing this statement, I understand that if the information provided on this entry is found to be misrepresented or fraudulent in any respect, it will not be accepted into the Awards Program and 1) all of my prior entries are subject to deletion from future editions of **Records of North American Big Game** 2) future entries may not be accepted.

FAIR CHASE, as defined by the Boone and Crockett Club®, is the ethical, sportsmanlike and lawful pursuit and taking of any free-ranging wild, native North American big game animal in a manner that does not give the hunter an improper advantage over such game animals.

The Boone and Crockett Club® may exclude the entry of any animal that it deems to have been taken in an unethical manner or under conditions deemed inappropriate by the Club.

Date: _____   Signature of Hunter: _____
                                        (SIGNATURE MUST BE WITNESSED BY AN OFFICIAL MEASURER OR A NOTARY PUBLIC.)

Date: _____   Signature of Notary or Official Measurer: _____

250 Station Drive
Missoula, MT 59801
(406) 542-1888

BOONE AND CROCKETT CLUB®

OFFICIAL SCORING SYSTEM FOR NORTH AMERICAN BIG GAME TROPHIES

PRONGHORN

MINIMUM SCORES

AWARDS	ALL-TIME
80	82

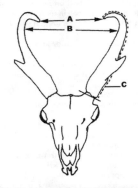

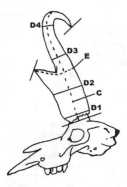

SEE OTHER SIDE FOR INSTRUCTIONS		COLUMN 1	COLUMN 2	COLUMN 3
A. Tip to Tip Spread	7	Right Horn	Left Horn	Difference
B. Inside Spread of Main Beams	11 4/8			
C. Length of Horn		16 6/8	17 3/8	5/8
D-1. Circumference of Base		7 5/8	7 4/8	1/8
D-2. Circumference at First Quarter		8 2/8	8 2/8	
D-3. Circumference at Second Quarter		4 1/8	4 2/8	1/8
D-4. Circumference at Third Quarter		2 5/8	2 6/8	1/8
E. Length of Prong		7 5/8	7 1/8	4/8
TOTALS		47	47 2/8	1 4/8

ADD	Column 1	47	Exact Locality Where Killed: Harney County, Oregon
	Column 2	47 2/8	Date Killed: 08/24/2000 Hunter: Sam Barry
	Subtotal	94 2/8	Owner: Sam Barry Telephone #:
SUBTRACT Column 3		1 4/8	Owner's Address:
FINAL SCORE		92 6/8	Guide's Name and Address:
			Remarks: (Mention Any Abnormalities or Unique Qualities)

I, _____ L. Victor Clark _____ , certify that I have measured this trophy on _____ 05/02/2001
PRINT NAME   MM/DD/YYYYY

at _____ Bass Pro Shops   Springfield, Missouri _____
STREET ADDRESS   CITY   STATE/PROVINCE

and that these measurements and data are, to the best of my knowledge and belief, made in accordance with the instructions given.

Witness: _____ Jack Graham _____   Signature: _____ L. Victor Clark _____   I.D. Number
B&C OFFICIAL MEASURER

COPYRIGHT © 2000 BY BOONE AND CROCKETT CLUB®

INSTRUCTIONS FOR MEASURING PRONGHORN

All measurements must be made with a 1/4-inch wide flexible steel tape to the nearest one-eighth of an inch. Enter fractional figures in eighths, without reduction. Official measurements cannot be taken until horns have air dried for at least 60 days after the animal was killed.

A. Tip to Tip Spread is measured between tips of horns.

B. Inside Spread of Main Beams is measured at a right angle to the center line of the skull, at widest point between main beams.

C. Length of Horn is measured on the outside curve on the general line illustrated. The line taken will vary with different heads, depending on the direction of their curvature. Measure along the center of the outer curve from tip of horn to a point in line with the lowest edge of the base, using a straight edge to establish the line end.

D-1. Circumference of Base is measured at a right angle to axis of horn. **Do not** follow irregular edge of horn; the line of measurement must be entirely on horn material.

D-2-3-4. Divide measurement C of longer horn by four. Starting at base, mark **both** horns at these quarters (even though the other horn is shorter) and measure circumferences at these marks. If the prong interferes with D-2, move the measurement down to just below the swelling of the prong. If D-3 falls in the swelling of the prong, move the measurement up to just above the prong.

E. Length of Prong: Measure from the tip of the prong **along the upper edge** of the outer side to the horn; then continue around the horn to a point at the rear of the horn where a straight edge across the back of both horns touches the horn, with the latter part being at a right angle to the long axis of horn.

ENTRY AFFIDAVIT FOR ALL HUNTER-TAKEN TROPHIES

For the purpose of entry into the Boone and Crockett Club's® records, North American big game harvested by the use of the following methods or under the following conditions are ineligible:

  I. Spotting or herding game from the air, followed by landing in its vicinity for the purpose of pursuit and shooting;
  II. Herding or chasing with the aid of any motorized equipment;
  III. Use of electronic communication devices, artificial lighting, or electronic light intensifying devices;
  IV. Confined by artificial barriers, including escape-proof fenced enclosures;
  V. Transplanted for the purpose of commercial shooting;
  VI. By the use of traps or pharmaceuticals;
  VII. While swimming, helpless in deep snow, or helpless in any other natural or artificial medium;
  VIII. On another hunter's license;
  IX. Not in full compliance with the game laws or regulations of the federal government or of any state, province, territory, or tribal council on reservations or tribal lands;

I certify that the trophy scored on this chart was not taken in violation of the conditions listed above. In signing this statement, I understand that if the information provided on this entry is found to be misrepresented or fraudulent in any respect, it will not be accepted into the Awards Program and 1) all of my prior entries are subject to deletion from future editions of **Records of North American Big Game** 2) future entries may not be accepted.

FAIR CHASE, as defined by the Boone and Crockett Club®, is the ethical, sportsmanlike and lawful pursuit and taking of any free-ranging wild, native North American big game animal in a manner that does not give the hunter an improper advantage over such game animals.

The Boone and Crockett Club® may exclude the entry of any animal that it deems to have been taken in an unethical manner or under conditions deemed inappropriate by the Club.

Date:_____ Signature of Hunter:_____

(SIGNATURE MUST BE WITNESSED BY AN OFFICIAL MEASURER OR A NOTARY PUBLIC.)

Date:_____ Signature of Notary or Official Measurer:_____

250 Station Drive
Missoula, MT 59801
(406) 542-1888

BOONE AND CROCKETT CLUB®
OFFICIAL SCORING SYSTEM FOR NORTH AMERICAN BIG GAME TROPHIES

BISON

MINIMUM SCORES
AWARDS   ALL-TIME
115   115

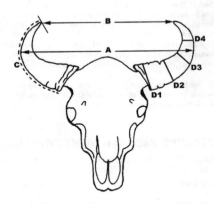

SEE OTHER SIDE FOR INSTRUCTIONS		COLUMN 1	COLUMN 2	COLUMN 3
A. Greatest Spread	29 4/8	Right Horn	Left Horn	Difference
B. Tip to Tip Spread	23 2/8			
C. Length of Horn		18 6/8	18 3/8	3/8
D-1. Circumference of Base		15 7/8	15 7/8	
D-2. Circumference at First Quarter		12 5/8	12 4/8	1/8
D-3. Circumference at Second Quarter		10 5/8	10 6/8	1/8
D-4. Circumference at Third Quarter		7 1/8	7 3/8	2/8
TOTALS		65	64 7/8	7/8

ADD	Column 1	65	Exact Locality Where Killed: Custer County, South Dakota
	Column 2	64 7/8	Date Killed: 01/06/2000 Hunter: Collins F. Kellogg, Sr.
	Subtotal	129 7/8	Owner: Collins F. Kellogg, Sr. Telephone #:
SUBTRACT Column 3		7/8	Owner's Address:
FINAL SCORE		129	Guide's Name and Address:
			Remarks: (Mention Any Abnormalities or Unique Qualities)

I, _____ Robert Estes _____ , certify that I have measured this trophy on ___ 03/21/2000 ___
      PRINT NAME   MM/DD/YYYYY

at ___ 90 Maxwell Road, Caledonia, New York ___
   STREET ADDRESS   CITY   STATE/PROVINCE

and that these measurements and data are, to the best of my knowledge and belief, made in accordance with the instructions given.

Witness: ___ Sally Estes ___   Signature: ___ Robert Estes ___   I.D. Number ☐ ☐ ☐ ☐
                                            B&C OFFICIAL MEASURER

COPYRIGHT © 2000 BY BOONE AND CROCKETT CLUB®

INSTRUCTIONS FOR MEASURING BISON

All measurements must be made with a 1/4-inch wide flexible steel tape to the nearest one-eighth of an inch. Wherever it is necessary to change direction of measurement, mark a control point and swing tape at this point. Enter fractional figures in eighths, without reduction. Official measurements cannot be taken until horns have air dried for at least 60 days after the animal was killed.

    A. Greatest Spread is measured between perpendiculars at a right angle to the center line of the skull.

    B. Tip to Tip Spread is measured between tips of horns.

    C. Length of Horn is measured from the lowest point on underside over outer curve to a point in line with the tip. Use a straight edge, perpendicular to horn axis, to end the measurement, if necessary.

    D-1. Circumference of Base is measured at right angle to axis of horn. **Do not** follow the irregular edge of horn; the line of measurement must be entirely on horn material.

    D-2-3-4. Divide measurement C of **longer** horn by four. Starting at base, mark **both** horns at these quarters (even though the other horn is shorter) and measure the circumferences at these marks, with measurements taken at right angles to horn axis.

ENTRY AFFIDAVIT FOR ALL HUNTER-TAKEN TROPHIES

For the purpose of entry into the Boone and Crockett Club's® records, North American big game harvested by the use of the following methods or under the following conditions are ineligible:

    I. Spotting or herding game from the air, followed by landing in its vicinity for the purpose of pursuit and shooting;

    II. Herding or chasing with the aid of any motorized equipment;

    III. Use of electronic communication devices, artificial lighting, or electronic light intensifying devices;

    IV. Confined by artificial barriers, including escape-proof fenced enclosures;

    V. Transplanted for the purpose of commercial shooting;

    VI. By the use of traps or pharmaceuticals;

    VII. While swimming, helpless in deep snow, or helpless in any other natural or artificial medium;

    VIII. On another hunter's license;

    IX. Not in full compliance with the game laws or regulations of the federal government or of any state, province, territory, or tribal council on reservations or tribal lands;

I certify that the trophy scored on this chart was not taken in violation of the conditions listed above. In signing this statement, I understand that if the information provided on this entry is found to be misrepresented or fraudulent in any respect, it will not be accepted into the Awards Program and 1) all of my prior entries are subject to deletion from future editions of **Records of North American Big Game** 2) future entries may not be accepted.

FAIR CHASE, as defined by the Boone and Crockett Club®, is the ethical, sportsmanlike and lawful pursuit and taking of any free-ranging wild, native North American big game animal in a manner that does not give the hunter an improper advantage over such game animals.

The Boone and Crockett Club® may exclude the entry of any animal that it deems to have been taken in an unethical manner or under conditions deemed inappropriate by the Club.

Date:_____ Signature of Hunter:_____

                                            (SIGNATURE MUST BE WITNESSED BY AN OFFICIAL MEASURER OR A NOTARY PUBLIC.)

Date:_____ Signature of Notary or Official Measurer:_____

250 Station Drive
Missoula, MT 59801
(406) 542-1888

BOONE AND CROCKETT CLUB®
OFFICIAL SCORING SYSTEM FOR NORTH AMERICAN BIG GAME TROPHIES

ROCKY MOUNTAIN GOAT

MINIMUM SCORES
AWARDS ALL-TIME
47   50

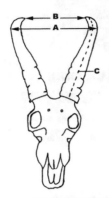
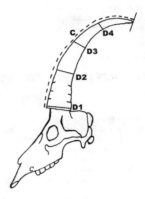

SEE OTHER SIDE FOR INSTRUCTIONS		COLUMN 1	COLUMN 2	COLUMN 3
A. Greatest Spread	8 7/8	Right Horn	Left Horn	Difference
B. Tip to Tip Spread	8 2/8			
C. Length of Horn		11 7/8	10 6/8	1 1/8
D-1. Circumference of Base		6 4/8	6 4/8	
D-2. Circumference at First Quarter		5 2/8	5 2/8	
D-3. Circumference at Second Quarter		3 6/8	3 6/8	
D-4. Circumference at Third Quarter		2 1/8	2 1/8	
TOTALS		29 4/8	28 3/8	1 1/8

ADD	Column 1	29 4/8	Exact Locality Where Killed: Bella Coola, British Columbia
	Column 2	28 3/8	Date Killed: 09/12/1999 Hunter: G. Wober and L. Michalchuk
Subtotal		57 7/8	Owner: Gernot Wober Telephone #:
SUBTRACT Column 3		1 1/8	Owner's Address:
FINAL SCORE		56 6/8	Guide's Name and Address:
			Remarks: (Mention Any Abnormalities or Unique Qualities)

I, _____ Ronald L. Sherer _____ , certify that I have measured this trophy on ___ 05/02/2001 ___
PRINT NAME

at _____ Bass Pro Shops Springfield, Missouri _____

and that these measurements and data are, to the best of my knowledge and belief, made in accordance with the instructions given.

Witness: Albert C. England   Signature: Ronald L. Sherer   I.D. Number: ____
B&C OFFICIAL MEASURER

COPYRIGHT © 2000 BY BOONE AND CROCKETT CLUB®

INSTRUCTIONS FOR MEASURING ROCKY MOUNTAIN GOAT

All measurements must be made with a 1/4-inch wide flexible steel tape to the nearest one-eighth of an inch. Wherever it is necessary to change direction of measurement, mark a control point and swing tape at this point. Enter fractional figures in eighths, without reduction. Official measurements cannot be taken until horns have air dried for at least 60 days after the animal was killed.

    A. Greatest Spread is measured between perpendiculars at a right angle to the center line of the skull.

    B. Tip to Tip spread is measured between tips of the horns.

    C. Length of Horn is measured from the lowest point in front over outer curve to a point in line with tip.

    D-1. Circumference of Base is measured at a right angle to axis of horn. **Do not** follow irregular edge of horn; the line of measurement must be entirely on horn material.

    D-2-3-4. Divide measurement C of longer horn by four. Starting at base, mark **both** horns at these quarters (even though the other horn is shorter) and measure circumferences at these marks, with measurements taken at right angles to horn axis.

ENTRY AFFIDAVIT FOR ALL HUNTER-TAKEN TROPHIES

For the purpose of entry into the Boone and Crockett Club's® records, North American big game harvested by the use of the following methods or under the following conditions are ineligible:

    I.   Spotting or herding game from the air, followed by landing in its vicinity for the purpose of pursuit and shooting;

    II. Herding or chasing with the aid of any motorized equipment;

    III. Use of electronic communication devices, artificial lighting, or electronic light intensifying devices;

    IV. Confined by artificial barriers, including escape-proof fenced enclosures;

    V. Transplanted for the purpose of commercial shooting;

    VI. By the use of traps or pharmaceuticals;

    VII. While swimming, helpless in deep snow, or helpless in any other natural or artificial medium;

    VIII. On another hunter's license;

    IX. Not in full compliance with the game laws or regulations of the federal government or of any state, province, territory, or tribal council on reservations or tribal lands;

I certify that the trophy scored on this chart was not taken in violation of the conditions listed above. In signing this statement, I understand that if the information provided on this entry is found to be misrepresented or fraudulent in any respect, it will not be accepted into the Awards Program and 1) all of my prior entries are subject to deletion from future editions of **Records of North American Big Game** 2) future entries may not be accepted.

FAIR CHASE, as defined by the Boone and Crockett Club®, is the ethical, sportsmanlike and lawful pursuit and taking of any free-ranging wild, native North American big game animal in a manner that does not give the hunter an improper advantage over such game animals.

The Boone and Crockett Club® may exclude the entry of any animal that it deems to have been taken in an unethical manner or under conditions deemed inappropriate by the Club.

Date:_____ Signature of Hunter:_____

                                 (SIGNATURE MUST BE WITNESSED BY AN OFFICIAL MEASURER OR A NOTARY PUBLIC.)

Date:_____ Signature of Notary or Official Measurer:_____

250 Station Drive
Missoula, MT 59801
(406) 542-1888

BOONE AND CROCKETT CLUB®
OFFICIAL SCORING SYSTEM FOR NORTH AMERICAN BIG GAME TROPHIES

MUSKOX

MINIMUM SCORES
AWARDS ALL-TIME
105   105

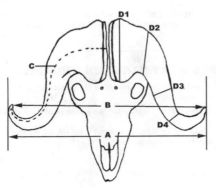

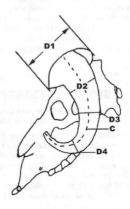

SEE OTHER SIDE FOR INSTRUCTIONS		COLUMN 1	COLUMN 2	COLUMN 3
A. Greatest Spread	27 7/8	Right Horn	Left Horn	Difference
B. Tip to Tip Spread	27 4/8			
C. Length of Horn		29 2/8	29 4/8	2/8
D-1. Width of Boss		10 5/8	11	3/8
D-2. Width at First Quarter		7 1/8	7 3/8	2/8
D-3. Circumference at Second Quarter		10 5/8	10 5/8	
D-4. Circumference at Third Quarter		5 4/8	5 5/8	1/8
TOTALS		63 1/8	64 1/8	1

ADD	Column 1	63 1/8	Exact Locality Where Killed: Kugaryguak, Northwest Territories
	Column 2	64 1/8	Date Killed: 03/30/2000 Hunter: M.R. James
	Subtotal	127 2/8	Owner: M.R. James Telephone #:
	SUBTRACT Column 3	1	Owner's Address:
			Guide's Name and Address:
FINAL SCORE		126 2/8	Remarks: (Mention Any Abnormalities or Unique Qualities)

I, _____John M. Vore_____ , certify that I have measured this trophy on ___08/24/2000___
PRINT NAME   MM/DD/YYYYY

at ____490 Meridian, Kalispell, Montana____
STREET ADDRESS   CITY   STATE/PROVINCE

and that these measurements and data are, to the best of my knowledge and belief, made in accordance with the instructions given.

Witness: _____   Signature: ___John M. Vore___   I.D. Number [ ][ ][ ]
                                          B&C OFFICIAL MEASURER

COPYRIGHT © 2000 BY BOONE AND CROCKETT CLUB®

INSTRUCTIONS FOR MEASURING MUSKOX

All measurements must be made with a 1/4-inch wide flexible steel tape and adjustable calipers to the nearest one-eighth of an inch. Enter fractional figures in eighths, without reduction. Official measurements cannot be taken until horns have air dried for at least 60 days after the animal was killed.

A. Greatest Spread is measured between perpendiculars at a right angle to the center line of the skull.

B. Tip to Tip Spread is measured between tips of horns.

C. Length of Horn is measured along center of upper horn surface, staying within curve of horn as illustrated, to a point in line with tip. Attempt to free the connective tissue between the horns at the center of the boss to determine the lowest point of horn material on each side. Hook the tape under the lowest point of the horn and measure the length of horn, with the measurement line maintained in the center of the upper surface of horn following the converging lines to the horn tip.

D-1. Width of Boss is measured with calipers at greatest width of the boss, with measurement line forming a right angle with horn axis. It is often helpful to measure D-1 before C, marking the midpoint of the boss as the correct path of C.

D-2-3-4. Divide measurement C of longer horn by four. Starting at base, mark **both** horns at these quarters (even though the other horn is shorter). Then, using calipers, measure width of boss at D-2, making sure the measurement is at a right angle to horn axis and in line with the D-2 mark. Circumferences are then measured at D-3 and D-4, with measurements being taken at right angles to horn axis.

ENTRY AFFIDAVIT FOR ALL HUNTER-TAKEN TROPHIES

For the purpose of entry into the Boone and Crockett Club's® records, North American big game harvested by the use of the following methods or under the following conditions are ineligible:

    I.   Spotting or herding game from the air, followed by landing in its vicinity for the purpose of pursuit and shooting;

    II. Herding or chasing with the aid of any motorized equipment;

    III. Use of electronic communication devices, artificial lighting, or electronic light intensifying devices;

    IV. Confined by artificial barriers, including escape-proof fenced enclosures;

    V. Transplanted for the purpose of commercial shooting;

    VI. By the use of traps or pharmaceuticals;

    VII. While swimming, helpless in deep snow, or helpless in any other natural or artificial medium;

    VIII. On another hunter's license;

    IX. Not in full compliance with the game laws or regulations of the federal government or of any state, province, territory, or tribal council on reservations or tribal lands;

I certify that the trophy scored on this chart was not taken in violation of the conditions listed above. In signing this statement, I understand that if the information provided on this entry is found to be misrepresented or fraudulent in any respect, it will not be accepted into the Awards Program and 1) all of my prior entries are subject to deletion from future editions of **Records of North American Big Game** 2) future entries may not be accepted.

FAIR CHASE, as defined by the Boone and Crockett Club®, is the ethical, sportsmanlike and lawful pursuit and taking of any free-ranging wild, native North American big game animal in a manner that does not give the hunter an improper advantage over such game animals.

The Boone and Crockett Club® may exclude the entry of any animal that it deems to have been taken in an unethical manner or under conditions deemed inappropriate by the Club.

Date: _____ Signature of Hunter: _____

                                      (SIGNATURE MUST BE WITNESSED BY AN OFFICIAL MEASURER OR A NOTARY PUBLIC.)

Date: _____ Signature of Notary or Official Measurer: _____

250 Station Drive
Missoula, MT 59801
(406) 542-1888

BOONE AND CROCKETT CLUB®
OFFICIAL SCORING SYSTEM FOR NORTH AMERICAN BIG GAME TROPHIES

SHEEP

MINIMUM SCORES

	AWARDS	ALL-TIME
bighorn	175	180
desert	165	168
Dall's	160	170
Stone's	165	170

KIND OF SHEEP (check one)

- ☐ bighorn
- ☒ desert
- ☐ Dall's
- ☐ Stone's

PLUG NUMBER

_____

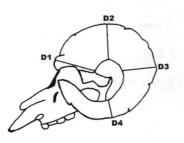

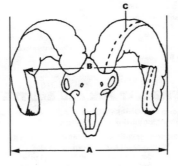

Measure to a
Point in Line
With Horn Tip

SEE OTHER SIDE FOR INSTRUCTIONS		COLUMN 1	COLUMN 2	COLUMN 3
A. Greatest Spread (Is Often Tip to Tip Spread)	25 2/8	Right Horn	Left Horn	Difference
B. Tip to Tip Spread	22 6/8			
C. Length of Horn		35 6/8	36 2/8	
D-1. Circumference of Base		15 7/8	16	1/8
D-2. Circumference at First Quarter		15 5/8	15 4/8	1/8
D-3. Circumference at Second Quarter		13 2/8	13 4/8	2/8
D-4. Circumference at Third Quarter		8 6/8	9 2/8	4/8
	TOTALS	89 2/8	90 4/8	1

ADD	Column 1	89 2/8
	Column 2	90 4/8
Subtotal		179 6/8
SUBTRACT Column 3		1
FINAL SCORE		178 6/8

Exact Locality Where Killed: Sonora, Mexico

Date Killed: 03/23/2000   **Hunter:** George R. Harms

Owner: George R. Harms   **Telephone #:**

Owner's Address:

Guide's Name and Address:

Remarks: (Mention Any Abnormalities or Unique Qualities)

I, _____ Frederick J. King _____ , certify that I have measured this trophy on ____ 07/07/2000 ____
           PRINT NAME   MM/DD/YYYYY

at _____ Cape Horn Taxidermy, Whitehall, Montana _____
    STREET ADDRESS   CITY   STATE/PROVINCE

and that these measurements and data are, to the best of my knowledge and belief, made in accordance with the instructions given.

Witness: Jennifer King   **Signature:** Frederick J. King   **I.D. Number**

                                                           B&C OFFICIAL MEASURER

INSTRUCTIONS FOR MEASURING SHEEP

All measurements must be made with a 1/4-inch wide flexible steel tape to the nearest one-eighth of an inch. Enter fractional figures in eighths, without reduction. Official measurements cannot be taken until horns have air dried for at least 60 days after the animal was killed.

- **A. Greatest Spread** is measured between perpendiculars at a right angle to the center line of the skull.
- **B. Tip to Tip Spread** is measured between tips of horns.
- **C. Length of Horn** is measured from the lowest point in front on outer curve to a point in line with tip. **Do not** press tape into depressions. The low point of the outer curve of the horn is considered to be the low point of the frontal portion of the horn, situated above and slightly medial to the eye socket (not the outside edge). Use a straight edge, perpendicular to horn axis, to end measurement on "broomed" horns.
- **D-1. Circumference of Base** is measured at a right angle to axis of horn. **Do not** follow irregular edge of horn; the line of measurement must be entirely on horn material.
- **D-2-3-4. Divide measurement C** of longer horn by four. Starting at base, mark **both** horns at these quarters (even though the other horn is shorter) and measure circumferences at these marks, with measurements taken at right angles to horn axis.

ENTRY AFFIDAVIT FOR ALL HUNTER-TAKEN TROPHIES

For the purpose of entry into the Boone and Crockett Club's® records, North American big game harvested by the use of the following methods or under the following conditions are ineligible:

   I. Spotting or herding game from the air, followed by landing in its vicinity for the purpose of pursuit and shooting;
  II. Herding or chasing with the aid of any motorized equipment;
 III. Use of electronic communication devices, artificial lighting, or electronic light intensifying devices;
  IV. Confined by artificial barriers, including escape-proof fenced enclosures;
   V. Transplanted for the purpose of commercial shooting;
  VI. By the use of traps or pharmaceuticals;
 VII. While swimming, helpless in deep snow, or helpless in any other natural or artificial medium;
VIII. On another hunter's license;
  IX. Not in full compliance with the game laws or regulations of the federal government or of any state, province, territory, or tribal council on reservations or tribal lands;

I certify that the trophy scored on this chart was not taken in violation of the conditions listed above. In signing this statement, I understand that if the information provided on this entry is found to be misrepresented or fraudulent in any respect, it will not be accepted into the Awards Program and 1) all of my prior entries are subject to deletion from future editions of **Records of North American Big Game** 2) future entries may not be accepted.

FAIR CHASE, as defined by the Boone and Crockett Club®, is the ethical, sportsmanlike and lawful pursuit and taking of any free-ranging wild, native North American big game animal in a manner that does not give the hunter an improper advantage over such game animals.

The Boone and Crockett Club® may exclude the entry of any animal that it deems to have been taken in an unethical manner or under conditions deemed inappropriate by the Club.

Date:_____ Signature of Hunter:_____

(SIGNATURE MUST BE WITNESSED BY AN OFFICIAL MEASURER OR A NOTARY PUBLIC.)

Date:_____ Signature of Notary or Official Measurer:_____

Acknowledgements for:
Boone and Crockett Club's
24th Big Game Awards, 1998-2000

Data compiled with the able assistance of:
C. Randall Byers - Chair, Boone and Crockett Club's Records Committee
Jack Reneau - Director of Big Game Records, Boone and Crockett Club
Chris Tonkinson - Assistant to Director of Big Game Records, Boone and Crockett Club
Sandra Poston - Office Manager, Boone and Crockett Club
Mary Armour - Support Specialist, Boone and Crockett Club
Brian J. Browning - Controller, Boone and Crockett Club

86 Award stories gathered and edited by:
Keith Balfourd - Jackman Creek Creative

Book, dust jacket and cover designed by:
Julie T. Houk - Director of Publications, Boone and Crockett Club

American elk artwork on dust jacket by:
Ken Carlson — *Moving Into Timber*

Copy editing by:
George A. Bettas - Executive Director, Boone and Crockett Club
Jack Reneau - Director of Big Game Records, Boone and Crockett Club
Sydney Rimpau

Printed and bound hardcover trade editions by:
R.R. Donnelley & Sons Company
Crawfordsville, Indiana

Limited Editions binding by:
Campbell-Logan Bindery
Minneapolis, Minnesota

Sketch by Ken Carlson